7.00

THE CRUSADES

Also by Zoé Oldenbourg

The Crusades

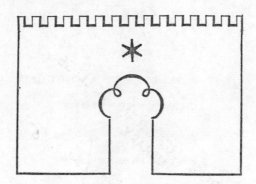

ZOÉ OLDENBOURG

TRANSLATED FROM THE FRENCH BY

ANNE CARTER

PANTHEON BOOKS

A DIVISION OF RANDOM HOUSE

NEW YORK

Originally published in French as
Les Croisades © 1965, by Éditions Gallimard.

DESIGN BY VINCENT TORRE

Preface

This book is not intended to be a complete history of the Crusades. It deals only with what are generally known as the three first Crusades and with the history of the kingdom of Jerusalem up to the time of its conquest by Saladin.

I have considered the story of these three first Crusades and of the Frankish states of Syria chiefly from the point of view of the political situation in the Near East in the twelfth century. Given the breadth of the subject, the manner in which I have dealt with the whole phenomenon of the Crusades, with the relations between the Latin West and Byzantium and Islam, and with the attempt, unique of its kind, to graft a European state onto an Oriental environment, is inevitably sketchy and incomplete. What I, in the wake of a great many eminent historians with whom I do not aspire to comparison, have tried to do is to study the human aspect of this long, complex, and yet in spite of everything, glorious adventure.

Whatever one means by the word, there is no doubt that the early Crusades gave rise to a particular concept of glory which belongs specifically to the Latin West and which consequently contributed more than a little to the formation of that European civilization which, in our own time, has finally come to mean civilization itself.

The First Crusade was not a popular migration or a war of conquest undertaken by an ambitious monarch, nor was it a search for new colonies and trade routes, though all these elements were present in the Crusades to a comparatively minor degree. It remains an adventure without parallel in history because it was a real war which does not appear to have been provoked by any of the normal causes of war. It cannot be compared to the lightning expansion of Islam in the seventh century in which a poor and warlike people, fired by the example of a great leader who was also the initiator of a new religious movement, set out to conquer the world. The Crusading phenomenon was infinitely more modest in its scope and objectives, but it possessed the one remarkable feature that for once a holy war was conducted in an apparently disinterested spirit, without real necessity and not inspired by any single great leader or prophet. Looking at the bare facts of the case, the First Crusade was an extravagant adventure which by sheer luck—and perhaps just because it was so extravagant—did not end in disaster but finally succeeded beyond all expectation.

The sole object, motive, and justification of this adventure—which in time grew vast enough to involve more or less deeply the conscience of the whole of Catholic Christendom—was the mirage of the Holy City, Jerusalem. It is Jerusalem alone which still gives this long succession of sufferings, atrocities, wars, feudal squabbles, and frequently disastrous military enterprises a glory which even the centuries have not dimmed. And yet at the end of the eleventh century, when Christianity had endured for a thousand years and the Moslems dominated Syria for four hundred, there was no need for the men of France, Flanders, and Provence to go out and fight for Jerusalem.

It is necessary to take a brief look at the situation in that part of the world which was not Europe as we know it today but which, from the time of Alexander and the Roman conquests, can be regarded as the cradle of our civilization. Geographically, it was made up of present-day Europe, North Africa, Egypt, Asia Minor, Syria, Mesopotamia, and Persia.

Latin Catholic Christendom was far from being the dominant force in the vast territorial area at that time under the control of the Biblical religions of Christianity, Judaism, its rejected ancestor, and Islam. It laid no claims to ascendancy over the wealthier, more powerful, and more civilized world of the Byzantine and Moslem East, a world from which it had been to a great extent cut off by the great invasions.

By the seventh century, the Eastern Roman Empire, the great civilized and civilizing power of Christendom, had already lost touch with its possessions in Africa and Asia (where it retained only its provinces in Asia Minor), but Byzantium still dominated the eastern Mediterranean and maintained its influence, and the influence of the Greek Orthodox Church, over the Balkan peoples, the nomadic invaders who had settled in those provinces, and the Slavonic tribes of the great Eastern plains. Latin Christianity was still gaining ground in the North and West through the conversion of the Nordic races, which followed the spread of Christianity to England and Ireland in the first centuries of our era. Greek and Latin Christianity, which until 1054 were one Church, together represented the orthodox Christian faith as defined by the Council of Nicaea; but a number of heretical Christian sects still flourished, especially in the East, and in the lands which had been overrun by Islam in particular. To all appearances the two great Churches of Rome and Constantinople were divided only by hierarchical and administrative disputes, but in practice political divergences and the difference of liturgical language were already turning them into two rival Churches.

The Byzantine Church, richer, more civilized, and more deeply attached to tradition, seemed to be the stronger of the two, but it was weakened both by its effective dependence on the secular power and by a constant struggle against the heresies which, in the East, were as ancient as the Church itself.

From the eighth century onward, Western Catholicism, having defeated the Arian religions and steadily eliminated Teutonic paganism, found few new heresies to contend with, and owing obedience only to the pontiff in Rome, it enjoyed a considerable measure of independence.

The two Churches had not yet come into open conflict, but both were playing a tricky political game. The Catholic Church had the advantage of not being officially dependent on any one monarch "anointed by the Lord" and hence of being able to manipulate affairs by relying for support on first one secular power and then another. This gave it a moral independence which, however precarious to begin with, became increasingly real.

The ninth to eleventh centuries saw the emergence of two fresh forces in the Christian and Moslem worlds which, after centuries of periodical invasions, upset the balance still further. In the West, there were the marauding bands of Scandinavian pirates, so numerous and so ferocious that their raids were a disaster comparable to the barbarian invasions. However, in the lands where they settled, the Norsemen became assimilated without great difficulty and adapted themselves very quickly to the local customs and religion. Meanwhile in the East, by about the end of the tenth century, other poor and warlike races were beginning their expansion westward. These were the Turks and Turkomans, who were of Mongol origin. While the West was able to absorb and assimilate the Norse invaders comparatively quickly, the Turks, though converts to Islam, made a habit of treating the countries they occupied as conquered territory and installing themselves as the superior race. Persia, Mesopotamia, and Syria endured their military overlordship only with the utmost reluctance. By the end of the eleventh century, the Turks had occupied practically the whole of Asia Minor—which had formerly belonged to Byzantium—and were becoming a serious threat to both Byzantium and Egypt.

The Byzantine Empire was therefore caught as if in a vise between the Turks, who had penetrated almost as far as the Bosporus, and the Normans from France, who after conquering Sicily and southern Italy were already turning their attention to the Balkans and to Constantinople.

While the Roman Church was engaged in waging a bitter struggle for physical and moral independence with the German Holy Roman Empire, in the course of which the popes found themselves driven out of Rome and replaced by antipopes appointed by the Emperor, the Normans were busy driving the Arabs out of Sicily, conquering England from the Saxons, and (although they did not form themselves into a single united state) emerging as one of the driving forces of Europe. They were the popes' allies against the Moslems and also, by definition, the enemies of the Greeks.

Even for those Christians who adhered to the Latin Church, the Byzantine Empire—and Constantinople in particular—remained one of the great centers of Christianity, and it still enjoyed immense prestige. The Empire's enemies in the West were the Normans, whose thirst for plunder and conquest was notorious, and also, from time to time, the mercantile republics of the Italian coast, for whom Byzantium was a commercial rival. It was not only the Greeks themselves who viewed the progress of the Turks with alarm; the danger which threatened Constantinople was felt as a threat by the whole of Christendom.

When the Byzantine Emperor Alexius Comnenus wrote to Pope Urban II in 1095 asking for aid against the Turks, this was an appeal by one Christian leader to another with a view to joint action for the defense of Christendom, and it was as such that Pope Urban quite naturally took it. The safety of the Greek Empire was in fact a matter of great urgency, and one which deserved to attract all right-minded Christian soldiers.

In practice, however worth while that task, it can be seen that the results and even the objects of the wars we know as the Crusades were quite different. The armies which gathered in response to Pope Urban's appeal were not concerned with the safety of the Empire but with conquest on their own account. As it happened, the land to be conquered was Jerusalem.

Contents

Illustrations

Between pages 298 and 299

Maps

THE CRUSADES

CHAPTER

I

Medieval Man

At the risk of seeming to labor facts which are already all too familiar, I believe it will be as well to remind ourselves briefly of the conditions of life in Western Europe during the period immediately preceding the Crusades. We shall find events becoming much closer and more understandable if we try to detach ourselves from our own time and take a good look at the differences between life as it is for us and as it was for our ancestors.

In fact, the seventeenth-century historians who depicted King Clovis in a wig like Louis XIV's may not have been so far wrong. Wig or no wig, the Frankish King was much nearer to them, and they judged him as man to man. We, on the other hand, tend to lay exaggerated stress on different attitudes of mind and in so doing set up an almost insuperable barrier between ourselves and the people of past centuries. Because we regard the Middle Ages as a period psychologically very different from our own, we tend to lay too much to the account of the so-called "spirit of the age." It is true that we are unaware of a great many of the facts which, even across the impassable mountain range of the past, might show us the explanation of many of the "errors" which in those days passed for truths. All the same, we are not dealing with prehistory, and there is no lack of documentary evidence. We have only to study this to realize that mankind, in any time or place, remains very much the same; the things that change are living conditions, modes of expression, and the nature and degree of people's intellectual experience.

The information we have shows that Western man in the eleventh and twelfth centuries possessed an intelligence and sensibility very similar to our own. A man like Godfrey of Bouillon is easier for us to understand than a twentieth-century Hindu or Tibetan, and Moslems in medieval times were already the brothers of Moslems today. We are dealing with the comparatively recent past, and this is why it is important to remember the things that undoubtedly do separate us from those centuries.

Conditions of Life

The first essential fact to be borne in mind is the simple and obvious one that at this period man was still the measure of all things. Machines were still at a very rudimentary stage. The great motive power was the horse or, more generally, the pack animal. Everything, from the most massive fortress to the finest fabric, had to be made by the living strength of human hands and human arms. Even books were copied out by hand and were each the work of one skilled and patient worker. Man was therefore infinitely closer to physical reality than we can be now. Tools and raw materials had a value and immediacy not easy for us to understand. This direct contact with matter whose laws he knew only empirically made man simultaneously more superstitious than we are today and more skillful and enterprising.

In the eleventh century life in the West, and in the countries of Western Europe in particular, was very hard compared with today, but even so it was much less harsh than in certain parts of South America and the Far East in the twentieth century. Western Europe was comparatively sparsely populated, but it was not so in proportion to the acreage of cultivable land. More than half the land was covered by forests, and hunting and clearing new ground were still tasks of the utmost importance, while wolves, deer, and wild boars were a constant threat to fields, flocks, and men.

The fields were plowed by hand, sown one year in every two or three, and the rest of the time allowed to lie fallow and unfertilized. The yield per acre was only half what it would be today, and produce was not enough to feed the population. Nearly all the peasants were serfs, who were compelled to give up half their harvest to their masters, while what remained was not enough to last them the year. Moreover, the population was increasing appreciably faster than the amount of arable land.

The countries of Western Europe were almost exclusively agricultural, although there were great commercial centers such as the big river and sea ports. Cities like Marseilles, Paris, Troyes, London, Cologne, Toulouse, Barcelona, Lyons, Milan, Genoa, Venice, and many others were all in varying degrees cosmopolitan meeting places for merchants of all nations, but especially those from the East, because the East was still the source of most manufactured goods. Local industries, though numerous, had barely advanced beyond the stage of handicrafts. Basic necessities were manufactured at home: peasants spun wool and wove linen, and every city had its textile-weaving houses, as well as smithies, potteries, tinsmiths, saddlers, and so forth; major centers of the textile industry were already established along the Rhine valley and in northern France. Transport, except for merchants' caravans, was disorganized and manufactured articles very expensive. The poor, and the rich too, did without things we should regard as necessary to the most elementary comfort, things which had been in common use in ancient Rome and were still so in the East in medieval times.

Beds were a luxury and even quite wealthy nobles frequently slept on straw on the ground. Tableware was scarce and several people might eat their soup out of the same wooden bowl, using slices of stale bread for plates. When it was time to eat, wooden planks were set up on trestles for use as tables. The principal article of furniture was the coffer. This was a very necessary item because it had a lock: clothes and valuables could be kept in it and it could also be used as both a seat and a bed. Princes and great lords had carved wooden chairs for ceremonial occasions, but if necessary they could be equally at home sitting on a mat or a bale of straw on the ground.

The rich—the nobility, that is—lived in stone-built castles and measured their wealth by the thickness of their walls and the strength of their outer fortifications. Peasants built themselves huts of mud and wattle and though these burned down from time to time, they could be rebuilt almost at once without their owner suffering any great loss in the catastrophe beyond a few clay pots and blankets of skins. But if the village's reserve stocks of grain were burned, it meant starvation, and to prevent this the sacks were frequently buried underground. Townsmen's houses were still built largely of wood rather than stone, and in the densely packed alleys inside city walls, fire was an ever-present menace.

There were no sewers nor any system of drainage for surplus water, and a spell of wet weather turned castle courtyards and the streets of towns and villages into quagmires. The quantities of dung produced by the large numbers of animals meant that even in the cities and the houses of great lords there was a prevailing smell of ordure, smoke, and damp. Under the tables at great feasts the beggars and dogs fought for the generous scraps of meat and bones flung to them by the guests.

Nevertheless, we must not take too seriously this lack of hygiene and comfort and the promiscuity which resulted from it. All things considered, the smell of stables is not a great deal more unpleasant than the reek of gasoline fumes, and people from the eleventh century would probably find our own lives hard to bear. When water had to be fetched from a well or spring, fires lit and tended, and the only light came from candles which were precious and expensive or resin torches which provided as much smoke as light, these things were valued at their true worth. People who traveled on foot were rewarded by learning about the country through which they passed. Men were enriched as well as enslaved by having to struggle for the basic necessities of life, and in those days manual dexterity and the spirit of initiative and invention were comparatively more widespread than they are today. Everything had to be made by hand, and even for the very modest demands of the time, the number of master craftsmen—carpenters, smiths, metalworkers, tinsmiths, sculptors in wood or stone, weavers, potters, saddlers, seamstresses, lacemakers, engravers, shoemakers, and others—was proportionately much greater than in our own day.

Shortage of adequate tools encouraged greater adaptability. Writing was a luxury and so people developed good memories. A man had no intellectual baggage beyond what he could carry in his head, which does not mean that this was necessarily meager. The average man was able to tell his direction by the stars and the movement of the sun, had a sure hand and eye, was wise in the lore of plants, and carried in his head an accurate calendar according to which the seasons progressed from one feast or saint's day to the next, with weather forecasts for each day. For theoretical knowledge, he relied on old men, travelers' tales, professional storytellers, and the sermons of the parish priest, and in practical matters on the painfully acquired experience of his job.

The Land

Man depended on the land to a far greater extent than today, and the land was at once harsher and kinder to him. Fertilizers and irrigation methods were rudimentary, harvests were poor, livestock more difficult to feed, periodically decimated by epidemics, and comparatively speaking more numerous. Horses, donkeys, mules, and oxen did the work of trains, cars, and machines, and provided raw materials as well as motive power. Cement for building was manufactured from a basis of bull's blood, and in time of war the flayed skins of hundreds of bulls served men for protection under fire. The creatures' hides, intestines, sinews, and horns were in daily domestic use and were among the most necessary raw materials. Sheep were everywhere, providing wool for clothes. Fields of flax and hemp lay alongside the fields of wheat and barley, and the peasants spun and wove, and bleached the linen and woolen stuffs in their own meadows. The fabric was hard to make but it was very strong, and one dress might last an entire lifetime. In the absence of soap, people washed with ashes, and that only rarely. As far as the poor were concerned, minstrels claim that they never washed at all, except in the rain. The poor, like the happy man in the fable, had no shirts and the rich did not always wear them either. Children up to the age of six or seven ran about stark naked when the weather was not too cold, and adults' clothes were simple and roughly made, though they preserved a rigorous decency.

For lighting there was tallow, wood dipped in resin, oil, and wax, but people rose and went to bed with the sun rather than waste their store of illumination. The fields and meadows provided mattresses and floor coverings as well as bread and fodder; people slept on palliasses and strewed their floors of wood or beaten earth with straw. Poultry was plentiful and supplied the rich with feathers for covers and cushions, and the horns of slaughtered animals were used for cups and drinking horns.

With the multiplication of the human race and the gradual disappearance of the great forests, varieties of wild animals are vanishing so fast today that we are being compelled to restock what is left of our forests artificially, and it is hard for us to imagine the abundance of game that existed eight or even four hundred years ago: forests, scrub, and heathland seething with earths and nests, woods filled with the clamor of birdsong every morning, and the sky black with clouds of migrating birds in spring and autumn. Herds of deer browsed in the clearings and would even come into the fields around the village. Wild boars ravaged the harvests, to say nothing of the damage done by hares and rabbits, and foxes and wolves preyed constantly on the poultry and cattle. Man bitterly defended the soil he had conquered against the depredations of wild beasts.

Medieval man's passion for the chase had undoubtedly very little in common with the kind of enthusiasm people feel for it in the twentieth century. Hunting was not a luxury or a pastime; it was a serious job of work, though one that contained elements of sport, war, and holiday, and its object was usually the daily nourishment of the hunter and his family. Pigs and poultry apart, domestic animals were rarely kept for meat, but the nobles, who were great meat eaters, brought back hecatombs of partridge, gamecock, hare, and deer from their raids on the forest. Slaughtered bear, stags, and wild boar were carried home in triumph, and on the eve of any great feast small birds such as thrushes, quails, and ortolans were killed in their hundreds, to be tipped out of the gamebag in sticky, bleeding heaps on kitchen floors. Castles reeked with the smell of blood and freshly tanned hides, and the aroma of roasting meat mingled with the odors of dogs, hawks, and men. Meat, even when dried in the sun or smoked in the great chimneys, did not keep well and supplies had to be frequently replenished. There was never enough of the salt and pepper which were indispensable for preserving perishable foodstuffs and also for making them more palatable.

Trees were felled in countless numbers to provide wood for fuel and building. The poor made do with twigs and brushwood, but the rich consumed hundreds of trees in constructing palisades, bridges, and fortifications for their castles, which were periodically destroyed by fire. Wherever they happened to be, they would use the wood they found on the spot to build siege engines, drawbridges, barrels, grandstands, boats, gibbets, ladders, and a host of other things. Wood at that time was the most basic raw material, and it still seemed a gift as freely given as the air men breathed and was squandered with total disregard. At this stage, men were still having to struggle against the encroaching trees, clearing and deforesting to make cultivable land. Even so, there was all too little available because men had to work too hard to wrest a living from the existing fields and vineyards to undertake the immense labor of clearing the woods. In the eleventh century, man had not yet tamed his land and he regarded it as an apparently inexhaustible source of wealth which he had to conquer by the unceasing sweat of his brow.

Though agriculture had fallen into a state of decadence and was inferior to that of the Gallo-Roman era, progress was nevertheless being made in domesticating the land. Wealthy landowners possessed lakes stocked with fish, vines were cultivated almost everywhere, and the breeding of sheep and pigs was more widespread than it is today. Every village had its beehives, and oleaginous plants such as sunflowers and colza were widely grown, while in the South there was the very ancient cultivation of the olive. Local trade, based as much on barter as on silver or copper money, was highly developed, but more organized commerce, such as the trade in spices and in articles manufactured abroad, remained the monopoly of the big cities and had little impact on the bulk of the population, who were too poor to have access to commodities which transport difficulties and customs duties made ten times more costly than they were in their country of origin. A fur wrap was easier to come by than a silk dress, and pepper fetched fantastic prices.

The standard of living common among European princes would have seemed poor and rustic to the nobles of Byzantium, Egypt, and Persia, had they shown any desire to visit such backward regions. As it was, apart from sending the occasional ambassador, these Eastern lords seem to have ignored the names and sometimes even the very existence of these peoples. In the West, on the other hand, far from disregarding the existence of the East, people cherished fabulous and highly colored visions of the lands from which came silks, spices, carpets, and gold—visions made up of a mixture of wonder and envy.

However, the eleventh century saw the beginnings of industrial development in the major European cities. Although the manufacture of articles in iron, leather, and wood was already established in the larger towns, this had still not advanced beyond the stage of individual craftsmanship; but the textile industry, especially in northern France, Flanders, and south Germany, was beginning to assume large enough proportions to have a sensible effect on the social economy of these regions. Textile factories needed a great many workers. They attracted impoverished peasants to the towns, and in the absence of any statutes regulating relations between workers and employers, the former rapidly became a distinct class, underprivileged, harshly exploited, and threatened with starvation whenever there was a slump or unemployment. They formed an urban proletariat a great deal more helpless and depressed than the serfs who were attached to the land. At the end of the eleventh century, these underprivileged workers were still only a small minority out of the great mass of the people, a turbulent and somewhat anarchic minority which had not thought of seizing by force the rights which a hierarchical society withheld from it.

Europe in the eleventh century had already forged for itself a social structure rich in customs and traditions and possessed a civilization of its own which was, for all its diversity, remarkably coherent. The Christian West, however apparently anarchic, was already a whole, and conscious of a very profound inner unity.

Society in the Middle Ages

THE PEOPLE

Bound to the soil as farmer, shepherd, and hunter, the medieval peasant, like peasants the world over, lived to the rhythm of the seasons, knowing exactly how much sun, rain, snow, and wind was needed to make his yearly crops flourish or die. His life depended on it, because in the absence of adequate transport famine was frequent and cruel. The peasant spent almost as much of his energies on religious practices (inherited from his pagan ancestors) as he did on his daily toil. Processions, exorcisms, feasts, penitential ceremonies, and pageants representing the lives of the saints or symbolizing a favor requested (such as rain or sun) were all carried out with the solemnity due to such mysteries, and a pride in celebrating local rites better than one's neighbor. But we can only guess at this wealth of spontaneous creativity in the life of peasants in this distant age from scattered references in the songs of the troubadours or the work of much later poets (fourteenth or fifteenth century), because the powerful, educated classes never considered these manifestations of popular life worthy of record.

Medieval society—and society before the Crusades in particular —was divided into clearly defined classes, each living its own life. The urban middle class was already numerous, but ill-organized and still dominated by the nobility, who held practically all the privileges, such as the administration of justice and the right to make war and levy taxes in cash or in kind. In contrast to the serfs, the nobility was the class of free men.

THE CHURCH

Theoretically the Church was extremely powerful. In fact it was so only to the extent that the bishops and abbots were sufficiently rich and well armed to put up a resistance to the secular nobility. It formed to some extent a state within a state. It had its own laws, recruited its members from the nobility and the common people, and acted as an intermediary and a moderating and civilizing influence.

The strong religious and cultural tradition which it alone possessed and which it had succeeded in guarding throughout centuries of poverty and anarchy made it a class profoundly different from both the nobility and the common people. By the eleventh century the Cluniac reforms had proved their vitality and spiritual force, and the Church was rapidly regaining the prestige it had lost through feudal wars, the struggle against the German Empire, and the decline of the papacy. It represented the one undisputed moral force, and since the conversion of the West to Christianity had been virtually complete for two centuries, the mere fact that society could not do without religion gave immense power to the Church.

The language of the Church was Latin, although even in Latin countries this was a language no longer understood by the people. It is a fact that even within the Church itself there were a great many illiterate clerics, but this was merely one of the numerous abuses against which popes and bishops were fighting an energetic battle. Mass could be celebrated only in Latin, and the Bible, the Gospels, and the writings of the Fathers of the Church read only in Latin, and this meant that in principle the clerk was a man able to speak Latin. This gave the Roman Church the advantage of being a supranational organization and contributed greatly to its internal unity, but it also served to make it aware of being a class apart, which in fact it was. The privileges enjoyed by the Church, privileges generally recognized and respected by the rich as well as the poor, meant that it played an enormously important part in society. Help for the needy, the sick, and those in misfortune, though still inadequate and irregular, was a task left to the Church, which performed this service according to its means and the charitable inclinations of its bishops. Monasteries had their hospitals and guesthouses, bishops organized collections and provided for the entertainment of poor pilgrims, and private charity was administered in church porches in the name of God. The Church ran the only schools, and to all intents churchmen were the only educated class. They acted as secretaries, advisers, scribes, and accountants to princes and barons. Engineers, architects, doctors, lawyers, diplomats, and jurists were all clerics. The monks transcribed books and kept registers, and it was in religious houses that the form of artistic inspiration took shape which led ultimately to the flowering of Romanesque art, while the arts of the goldsmith, of painting and illumination, released from the straightforward imitation of Byzantine models, were already at their height. Intellectual pursuits, such as theology and philosophy, which still had very little to do with everyday life, also helped to make the Church a respected power. Even so, it was by no means invariably successful in imposing its wishes, or in exercising a real influence on the nobles who were the actual ruling class.

THE NOBILITY

Throughout the Middle Ages, and especially at the time of the Crusades, the nobility was the ruling class and the only class to wield real and undisputed power: the power of arms. As we shall see, the Crusading movement contributed a great deal to the rise of another power on the political scene, one which, if not exactly pacific, possessed other weapons than those of warfare. This was the power of trade and the merchant middle classes. But in the second half of the eleventh century, commercial interests, although active, were still not sufficiently important to play a major part in political events. The nobles kept the lion's share for themselves.

These nobles were, for the most part, of Frankish or Germanic origin. Four centuries after the Germanic peoples first appeared in Gaul, Spain, and northern Italy, the descendants of the invaders still formed the aristocracy of the conquered lands. The mingling of the various races took place quite smoothly but very slowly, since the Germanic peoples had not arrived as conquering armies but in nomadic tribes, bringing their wives and children with them. The barbarians were gradually assimilated, but they remained the dominant race and the word "Frank" became synonymous with "free," which the non-Franks, in theory, were not. Over the centuries, the descendants of the Franks, Visigoths, Burgundians, and the rest lost all memory of their former religions and languages, but they still formed a kind of military aristocracy; and although the idea of national differences had disappeared and the great Frankish families were actually more anxious to trace Roman ancestry for themselves than to boast of their barbarian origin, the European nobles remained in blood, and still more in mind, more Germanic than Latin. They had inherited the proud, unstable temperament of the old nomadic German conquerors and, in particular, their cult of honor, which was linked to a strong sense of military solidarity. Their history as a ruling race gave them a strong caste pride, and even when latinized and converted to Christianity they remained, in spite of everything, very little affected by outside influences.

The Norse invasions of the ninth and tenth centuries represented a peril which had a galvanizing effect on this Frankish nobility. The Northmen, who settled on the coast on either side of the English Channel, were a powerful stimulant to the warlike nobles. The Northman very soon ceased to be an enemy and was accepted as a relative in blood and spirit, and before long a complicated system of intermarriage had injected Scandinavian blood into most of the great families of Western Europe.

This Scandinavian element—which by the eleventh century was already thoroughly assimilated—coupled with the still more ancient Germanic one, was clearly not so important that we have to regard European nobility as a kind of ruling class of foreign origin. Racial memory is short, especially among illiterate peoples, and it is language and religion rather than racial stock which define a nation. Even the most purebred Franks were incontestably Latins, while their neighbors across the Rhine had remained Teutons, but they were Latins with a short past and therefore with a comparatively meager intellectual and emotional background.

Nevertheless, theirs was a strong society, overflowing with vitality and strong in other ways than the mere possession of military strength. It was strong because it was fully conscious of its own worth, and had its own ethic and its own tried and tested concept of life.

The Feudal System

The feudal system was already an ancient institution. It had grown and developed gradually according to the needs of the time until by the eleventh century it had become the only imaginable social system, and was so generally recognized throughout Western Europe that men conceived even their relations to God in terms of feudal laws. These laws bound man to man by a personal and, in principle, indissoluble tie, and they were based much more on the idea of the individual than on more abstract concepts of state, justice, or the public good.

In fact, the feudal system recognized two basic values: man and land. In these exclusively agricultural countries, land ultimately meant wealth. "No lord without land and no land without its lord." Beginning as a system of reciprocal contracts between a sovereign and the subject to whom he entrusted the administration of certain lands, by the tenth century feudalism had come to be almost entirely based on the laws of heredity. The fief which the suzerain granted to his vassal became, in effect, the inalienable property of the latter's family. In the case of a province or a very large domain, this fief might be further divided into smaller and likewise hereditary fiefs held by the vassal's vassals. The great baron who was nominal lord of all the lands held by his vassals and his vassals' vassals could actually enjoy only those lands which formed his personal inheritance, and might often have vassals who were richer and more powerful than himself.

A vassal's obligations to his overlord were not extensive. They were confined to: (1) Military service. This was generally a fixed number of days in any year (usually forty). In the case of liege service, the period was for the duration of the war the overlord was engaged in, but as we shall see, there were good reasons why such wars could not be allowed to drag on indefinitely at the whim of the suzerain. (2) Financial assistance on certain clearly defined occasions. These included wars, the knighting of the lord's eldest son, the marriage of his eldest daughter, and the payment of ransom should the lord be taken prisoner. (3) Attendance at councils, parliaments, and possibly court sessions. In other words, the vassal was obliged to be present two or three times a year at a general reunion of all his suzerain's vassals, to assist him in dealing with matters of general concern such as wars or building operations, to administer justice, or merely to increase the overlord's prestige at banquets and state occasions. (4) Offering his suzerain hospitality should he happen to pass through the vassal's domain.

Beyond these four obligations the vassal was, for all practical purposes, independent. Indeed, since the suzerain was bound to defend his vassals in the event of injury or attack, the feudal system seems to have been designed for the express purpose of providing the nobles with the maximum freedom combined with the maximum security possible in these conditions.

When he could grant no more fiefs without leaving himself completely landless, the prince or great baron possessed only a symbolic authority, dependent on the goodwill of his principal vassals, who in their turn had not always the means to make their own vassals obey them. In practice, power was so effectively divided that the feudal system should be regarded as organized anarchy rather than as a social order. The multiplication of fiefs led inevitably to administrative complications. Only the lords of the great provinces had the right to coin money, but even their subsidiary vassals possessed the right to administer high justice (that involving the death penalty). Furthermore, since the same lord might have a hereditary title to a number of fiefs held from different overlords, circumstances could arise in which he found himself fighting for one suzerain against another. Only a leader who was gifted with an exceptionally power-ful personality could boast of being able to rule effectively, and in fact, no prince was able to take a decision of any importance without his vassals' consent. The fact that their interests rarely coincided made it difficult to arrive at any decision at all.

But if there was anarchy, at least it was indisputably "organized." The oath of allegiance was no mere formality. It was taken very seriously—and this in spite of exceptions so numerous that they can-not even be said to prove the rule. On the lowest level, that binding the small *vavasseur* (the vassal of a vassal) to his immediate over-lord, it was nearly always regarded as a sacred obligation, as was perfectly natural. The bond generally becomes increasingly lax as one travels up the social scale, and it is quite clear that the king of France, as suzerain of the count of Toulouse, the duke of Guyenne, and the king of England, no longer received from them anything but the most nominal homage. On the level of provinces, dioceses, and cantons, loyalty to an overlord was frequently bound up with clan solidarity, and the most faithful vassals were obviously those united to their overlords by ties of propinquity, kinship, or friend-ship, and especially those whom the overlord had knighted with his own hand. But the oath of allegiance or investiture was above all else a mystical and symbolical act whose force was universally ac-knowledged.

Although in practice this system of contracts for mutual assistance led to situations of inextricable complexity, the principle on which it was based was simple enough and had in fact resulted in the for-mation of a remarkably homogeneous society with a strong sense of caste solidarity, a kind of international brotherhood so real that later centuries were to regard it as an actual order of chivalry.

The concept of chivalry did not exactly coincide with the idea of nobility, or with the profession of arms. In present-day terms, it cor-responds more accurately to the idea of the officer class, but the title applied equally to a commander in chief and to the youngest sub-altern. It was simultaneously a title, a rank, and a virtue, and to say that a man was "a good knight" was the highest possible praise. Young or old, rich or poor, a model of virtue or a sink of iniquity, a soldier of noble birth was judged first and foremost on his qualities as a knight. In the eleventh century the concept of chivalry certainly involved no moral values beyond courage in battle, although knights were expected to refrain from too violently infringing current no-tions of morality. But they were not the only people of whom this was demanded, and in the event it was the knighthood which could most easily override them.

However, the obligations imposed by the profession of arms were many, complex, and strictly honored, and constituted a moral code which had all the force of law. There was no written manual laying down the qualities of the perfect knight—and even if there had been, not many knights were able to read—but there was an unwritten law which was universally recognized. This was something like a professional qualification, and concerned the use of arms and all the technical knowledge expected of a knight. With so little in the way of mechanical tools, a knight needed quick wits and considerable ingenuity as well as an ability to turn his hand to a variety of tasks: he must be able in case of need to direct the building of siege engines; to become, at a moment's notice, engineer, architect, general (even if only on a small scale), doctor (or sick nurse, at least), or veterinarian; and also must possess some rudimentary knowledge of ballistics, mechanics, and even accounting, all of which were necessary to the profession of soldiering.

Loyalty to his suzerain and the duty of protecting the soldiers under his command figured largely among a knight's obligations. The concept of military discipline as such did not exist, except in the most elementary form, so that the knight's personal initiative counted for a good deal. Intelligence was one of the knightly virtues, especially the kind of practical intelligence which consists in the ability to adapt readily to unexpected situations and turn them to the best advantage.

Evidently a good knight was not an ignoramus, but he lived in an age and environment when the average man thought no more of reading or writing than most people today think of learning to ride or fence: these were luxury occupations, expensive and without much practical application in everyday life. The learned clerk's academic knowledge was valued according to its usefulness, and in war it was not vital.

Feudal nobility was, by definition, almost exclusively military. The nobles were soldiers by profession and vocation, and though it is not easy to see how a relatively numerous ruling class could be one with the life of the country and yet solely taken up with fighting, they were so well trained and educated for war that in the end they had no other aim in life. The time of the great invasions was past. Even the struggles against the Moors in Spain and the Slavonic and Lithuanian pagans in the north of Germany had become merely spasmodic local outbreaks. The Norman advance had ceased to be a menace to the West, and there was no longer a powerful aggressor to be driven back or new lands to conquer. The West was discovering its own internal balance. This was, admittedly, precarious. There were bitter struggles between pope and emperor for the domination of Italy, uprisings among the great feudal lords in Germany and the great vassals of the French crown, the quarrels of Saxons and Normans in England, and the Christians' fight against the Moors in Spain, but none of this could prevent Europe from becoming gradually what it still is: a collection of peoples belonging to one civilization, the product of Western feudalism and of the Catholic religion. The feudal system was the life and soul of this new civilization, but feudal society was essentially warlike, and the West no longer offered sufficient scope for military aggression.

Might Is Right

Socially the feudal lord was an oppressor. Nevertheless the people had their rights, and peasants would not compromise over the raising of the dues they paid to their overlord or the amount of time they devoted to his service. Once a custom had become established, the people would tolerate no infringement. Social relations were based on a system of joint contracts, in general respected by both parties. But for the bulk of the people, for the small farmers, nearly all of whom were serfs, the terms of this contract were singularly harsh. The lord was supposed to protect the peasants and this, within the limits of his means, he did because it was in his interest to do so, but he also exploited them severely. Not content with taking his share of their produce, which might be a half or more according to the region, and exacting his days of free labor, he also retained a monopoly over such essential items as the mill, wine press, and bread ovens and made the peasant pay for the right to use them.

The rights of the people were paltry compared with those of the nobility, but they existed, and the notion of law existed, and this in itself was a good deal. The spirit of revolt also existed naturally enough in every peasant, although it rarely took the form of action because the punishments for rebellion were terrible.

The Christian Church proclaimed that all men were equal, at least in the sight of God. Pictures of the Last Judgment showed kings and bishops among the first ranks of the damned. But it was understood that the poor must wait for the end of the world and the life hereafter before they could contemplate any such reversal of values. On earth, it was the rich who ruled. If things are still very much the same today, it is only fair to point out that in the Middle Ages this state of affairs was accepted with cynical realism. Moreover, community of religion on the one hand and low economic and cultural standards on the other made the gulf between rich and poor, comparatively speaking, smaller than it is in our own times.

The noble, like the peasant, ate with his fingers, frequently slept on straw, shivered with cold or stifled in smoke-filled rooms in winter, tramped through the mud, and bathed in lakes and rivers. Like the peasant he studied the sky, because he too depended on the fields for his livelihood, and hunted himself the venison he ate. For lack of spacious halls and splendid palaces, even the greatest lords entertained their guests in "flowery meadows" and voluntarily camped out in the open air, taking with them wherever they went what little they possessed in the way of carpets, plate, chests of clothes, and caskets of jewels. They were not above sitting on the grass and weaving themselves crowns of field flowers, or decorating their tents, banqueting halls, and lists with garlands of foliage.

A nobleman's chief wealth was in his lands and therefore in the peasants who worked them. The peasants were serfs, that is to say they were attached to the land. Over and above what they owed to their lord, they paid a tithe, or tax, to the Church of a tenth of all their income. Forests and rivers were reserved, almost exclusively, for the lord's hunting and fishing; common land on which the peasants could graze their cattle was not extensive, and they had to pay for the right to pasture their animals on the lord's meadows. The same was true of wood, a basic necessity for heating as well as for making tools.

Small landowners were entitled to dispense low justice, for crimes involving penalties of corporal punishment, fines, or imprisonment. High justice, dealing with crimes punishable by mutilation or death, was the prerogative of the wealthy lord, the suzerain of vast domains. For the common people, such crimes were numerous: a man could be hanged for stealing a horse, an ox, or a sum of money, especially if the person from whom he stole them happened to be of noble birth; and the lords were tempted to extend their rights of high justice to such derelictions as poaching. Saint Louis, in the thirteenth century, punished with imprisonment a lord who was guilty of hanging three young men accused of poaching. Though the good King was simply punishing a most illegal abuse of power, this action of justice was considered courageous and aroused admiration.

Those of the common people who had to come into direct contact with their lord, such as his servants, were completely at his mercy and he was free to beat them or abuse them with no risk of interference from the law. At most he incurred the disapproval of the Church, which at one time found itself obliged to issue a formal reminder to noblewomen that it was a sin to beat their servants to death.

Punishable offenses, even among the nobility, were as a rule those committed by inferiors against those above them, although here the chances of an abuse of power were limited by the custom decreeing that a free man—a noble, clerk, or merchant—could be judged only by his peers.

In fact, the nobles were often above the law, and for one very good reason: the force of arms. Even a small landowner, if he possessed a well-fortified castle, could either fail to turn up at his trial or declare himself dissatisfied with the verdict; and once he was behind his own walls, there was every chance that the law would tire of pursuing him, especially since, in the absence of an official police force, it was up to the plaintiff to prosecute the miscreant. Strong power was needed to enforce the law, and at that time a man like Hugh of Puiset could barricade himself in his castle a few miles outside Paris and defy even the king himself.

The nobles lived by a code which may be described as legalized vendetta. Any man, if he had good cause, had the right to seek justice on his own account. Murderers were regularly hunted down by the families of their victims and quarrels settled by the sword, in duels—both official and unofficial—ambushes, and clan warfare. A man who assaulted his personal enemy or the enemy of a member of his family was acting in legitimate self-defense, while an outraged husband had power of life and death over his adulterous wife and her lover, and so on. But in this, as in all else, might was right, and if the offender was much more powerful than his victim, then the latter had small chance of retribution.

This meant that the lord in possession of a castle and soldiers was able to do more or less as he liked, provided he did not attack anyone stronger than himself. In actual fact, robber barons were only a small minority and public opinion was strongly against brigandage; but the feudal lord, who loved his independence above all things, believed in the cult of strength as the only guarantee of his own freedom.

Consequently, even lords who lived very modestly, owning scarcely any linen or tableware, might spend the greater part of their income on military equipment such as weapons and horses, and build themselves homes with walls as thick as they possibly could be. Castles dating from the eleventh century frequently have walls more than six feet thick. It was during the eleventh century also that the outer walls and fortifications surrounding the castles began to be built of stone, replacing the palisades of wooden stakes which had previously been common. Moats were dug and people built watchtowers on castle keeps and at crossroads on their domains. Armor, the basic elements of which had been tried and trusted for centuries, became tougher and stronger, and although the coat of chain mail was still unknown in the West, the *broigne,* a short-sleeved leather tunic covering the whole body down to the knees, was completely overlaid with metal rings or plaques set into the leather, making it proof against swords and lances. Horses were big, strong, and thickset, suitable for carrying heavy equipment, but they were also swift and given a long and arduous training for battle. The trial of strength was to show that the European warrior of the time was superior to the Moslem and Byzantine as much in the quality of his weapons as in his military virtues. But although better organized for war, he seems to have had fewer and fewer reasons for fighting and to have wasted his energies on petty local quarrels. This was particularly true in France, where the Church was continually protesting in vain against the state of affairs. The evidence of popes and bishops indicates that the belligerence of Western barons was becoming a real national disaster. The knights emerged from these wars comparatively unscathed, but the common soldiers, the archers and infantry who were less well armed, were slaughtered in great numbers. Even when no actual loss of life was involved, the fighting caused great suffering to the peasants, since burning the enemy's fields and carrying off his cattle was an accepted part of military tactics. This resulted in a paradoxical situation in which the nobility who were supposed to protect the land were making a substantial contribution to its ruin, while a great part of the country's wealth was employed in providing the nobles with the materials they needed for their wars. Things went on in this way for some hundreds of years, and the feudal wars ended only with the end of the feudal system itself. Nevertheless, as we shall see, the Crusades provided a powerful remedy for this ill.

Feudal Customs

WOMEN IN THE MIDDLE AGES

The customs of this warlike nobility were rude: not, as has sometimes been alleged, dissolute, but simply rather primitive. In this, as in other things, the doctrine of might is right had all the force of law. Here men had all the rights and women, even in law, had virtually none. They were lifelong minors. A noble lady's virtue and absolute marital fidelity were forced upon her on pain of a violent death, while men, who were supposed to be naturally polygamous, could permit themselves more or less complete sexual freedom. They were, however, expected to refrain from dishonoring the wives and daughters of other nobles, but this was out of respect for other people's property.

A man who was rich enough to maintain concubines need take little notice of his wife's protests or the Church's condemnation. Far from blushing for his bastards, he could be proud of them as valuable additions to his *mesnie,* and they enjoyed very much the same privileges among their father's followers as his legitimate children, although they were excluded from rights of inheritance. (This was a reasonable law, since disputes over inheritance were all too common even among legitimate offspring.)

The noble lord not only possessed a *droit du seigneur* over the baseborn women on his estate, but he also—if he were rich and influential—clung to his ancient privilege of being able to repudiate his wife. Divorce was quite common in feudal society, although expressly forbidden by the Church. Whether it liked it or not, the Church was compelled to bow to the will of the great, and had therefore agreed to a compromise which permitted the dissolution of individual marriages while maintaining intact the principle of indissolubility. There was no official divorce proceeding, but it was comparatively easy to obtain an annulment—nearly always on grounds of consanguinity of the parties concerned. It did not strike anyone as odd that a man should suddenly become aware, after years of marriage, that his wife was his cousin four times removed. Consanguinity could even be invoked in the case of a couple who shared the same godfather, of a man married to his godfather's daughter, and similar instances. Since the separated couple were both permitted to remarry (in this, at least, the repudiated wife enjoyed the same advantages as her husband) and often did so more than once, and each might have children by two or even three marriages, family relations rapidly became so complicated that it could be genuinely difficult to determine the degree of kinship between a husband and wife.

The Church, too, would sometimes revenge itself by making harsh use of its right of forcibly separating (excommunication being still a fearsome weapon) a husband and wife who had one great-grandfather, or great-great-grandfather, in common.

More often than not, women of noble birth were married off for reasons of interest and convenience: to unite two families or provide a pledge of friendship between enemies who had become reconciled. A knight would offer his daughter, sister, or even his mother to any *seigneur* with whom he wished to conclude an alliance. Widows were given by their suzerains to any man able to defend their lands, heiresses to a vassal who deserved a reward. It was an unsentimental age, and a girl might even demand and obtain the hand of the man who had killed her father. One example of this is to be found in the romance of the Cid. It was "a man for a man," and because they were basically noncombatants, women, even those of noble birth, belonged to a secondary class of humanity.

The "spinning songs," which are all that remain to show us what feminine feelings must have been like in the period of the first Crusades, show us a worship of men almost comparable to that of certain "heartthrobs" of our own day. They were composed for and perhaps by women, and they show man as the master, the thing most desired. Nevertheless, girls of noble blood were brought up in relative freedom, side by side with their brothers. They were great horsewomen, they hunted and were occasionally expert in minor sports such as javelin throwing, and they naturally tended to adopt masculine values as their own, since these were acknowledged from the first to be superior. A woman of noble birth, if she possessed any character at all, took for herself the rights which the law denied her; but in general her authority extended only over other women, the estates in the master's absence, defending it in time of war and per-to find the wife or mother of a *seigneur* governing his castle and baseborn, and the lesser nobility. All the same, it was not infrequent sonally commanding the garrison.

Some went still further: the Norman Robert Guiscard's wife, Sigelgaita, herself led her men into battle, dressed in armor and using a sword and lance like a man. The Byzantine Anna Comnena describes this woman as a kind of monster, hateful to her sex, but

European knights regarded the energetic matron as a heroine. The female warrior, like the warrior monk, though a shocking phenomenon to Eastern Christians, inspired the admiration of feudal society in the West, for whom military courage represented the highest moral value. Even so, Amazons like Sigelgaita remained glorious exceptions, just as now that women are no longer debarred from masculine activities, we come across few with ambitions to be boxers, champion cyclists, or football players.

Life on a medieval manor was hard and comparatively poor, and it is not surprising if its women had not yet developed the arts of pleasing or adornment, or indeed any specifically feminine activity beyond the age-old one of running a household. They remained a kind of second-rate man, rough and uncouth themselves, and with little time to spare for making a world of their own. One reason for this was the lack of prejudice in feudal society regarding any systematic segregation of the sexes. This did not exist in anything like the degree common in ancient or Oriental societies. There were no harems or women's quarters; European nobles had inherited Nordic traditions and did not expect their wives to shun masculine company. Women ate—and drank—with men, spoke up boldly in their presence, and conversed freely with strangers. It was perfectly proper for the daughter of the house to pour wine for a guest her father wished to honor, and sometimes even to assist him in his bath. In the story of Tristan and Yseult, there is a scene in which Yseult is attending the young knight as he sits in his bath, and recognizing him for Morholt's murderer, she rushes at him with a sword in the intention of killing him. Twelfth-century readers would have seen nothing shocking in this: to them, both the young girl's action and the curious situation which prompted it would have been perfectly natural.

The feminine ideal of the period was not entirely that of a virago laying about her with fists and steel. It would be truer to say that there was not really an ideal at all. Society, based exclusively on masculine values, had lost interest in women to the extent of neglecting to build up the mesh of conventions, prohibitions, and intellectual and moral prejudices which, in more civilized societies from China to Greece, had turned women into creatures radically different from men. The Church was certainly intent on filling this gap, but it was resolutely antifeminist. Deeply respected as a loyal and courageous associate, though treated as a subordinate because of her physical weakness, woman in feudal society tended to be rather masculine because she spontaneously adopted men's ways of thinking and acting. A time was coming when this unconscious masculinity of character, combined with a desire on the part of Western man to create his own image of woman, would give rise to that curious phenomenon known to us by the somewhat colorless name of "courtly love."

So-called courtly love was born of the love of war. It was a simultaneous sublimation of the duel, of feudal homage, the soldier's voluntary sacrifice, and the whole warrior mystique made up of a mingled desire for victory, total submission, and death. All that was needed to complete it was the impulse of the Crusades, adding a final touch of sublimity to the idea of war and bathing even the most worldly ambitions in the glow of sacred love. But it also demanded that woman, this at once proud and humiliated counterpart of man, should be ready to assume the dominant role which no previous civilization had granted her.

MEDIEVAL MAN

The average expectation of life was between thirty and thirty-five years. It was to remain so in Europe for centuries to come, and it is about the same in many underdeveloped countries today. For all times and places, the reasons are fundamentally the same: undernourishment, lack of hygiene, insufficient medical knowledge.

Infant mortality was terrible. Three-quarters of all children in every class of society died in infancy, generally below the age of one. This was such a universally acknowledged fact that families were resigned to it in advance. The birth rate was high, and women married young and were perpetually pregnant. Out of ten, fifteen, or twenty children, a sufficient number survived, and the population was growing rapidly, too rapidly for the countries' resources. Undernourishment was the inevitable result.

Children who succeeded in weathering their first two or three years were usually strong and resistant to polluted water, tainted meat, bread made of bran and chaff, drafts, damp, heat, vermin, and wounds. But the day-to-day scourges of famine, dysentery, tetanus, and puerperal fever overcame even the strongest, and to these were added periodic epidemics of typhus, cholera, smallpox, and—more rarely—plague.

Men's helplessness in the fight against these scourges is hard for a present-day European to understand. In fact, their only defense against epidemics was a terrified and superstitious trust in the divine mercy to be obtained by prayer and sacrifice, and a panic fear which drove parents to abandon their children and people to wall up their friends while still alive. Those who had the courage to bring help to the stricken were regarded as heroes and sometimes as madmen, and were themselves treated as plague carriers. We know that lepers were cruelly ostracized, although they were feared more on account of the horror of their condition than because of any real risk of contagion.

Medicine was crude and brutal. Apart from the frequent and indiscriminate use of bleeding and purgatives—still resorted to in the time of Molière—it relied largely on empirical methods whose value varied with the worth of the individual doctor. A doctor could kill as easily as cure, according to the condition of the invalid. The concept of antisepsis did not exist, except in the form of disinfection by cauterization. Wounds were dressed with boiling oil, often causing an infection which the original injury would not have produced. Even a superficial wound or an untended abscess could lead to septicemia or gangrene. Cases of acute appendicitis, perforated ulcers, and even heart attacks were often put down to poisoning, and people searched for—and found—the possible culprit. Cases of genuine poisoning also occurred, since it was easier to kill than to cure.

In the absence of an organized police force, murder for motives of revenge or gain was easier to commit than it is today. Moreover laws were harsh, especially for common folk, and prescribed the death penalty for crimes which in our own day would mean a prison sentence of between two and five years. Transport was inefficient, and bad harvests in any particular district might well mean famine. Death by starvation was not uncommon.

On the whole, then, human beings died younger and—especially in battle, on journeys, and in times of plague or famine—at such an appalling rate that it brought about a certain hardening in the survivors toward other people's sufferings. Even in our own day, Western observers are amazed at the indifference with which people in India will sometimes stand by and watch expressionlessly while beggars and children die of starvation in the open street. Europeans seem to have been more emotional, even in the Middle Ages, perhaps because they were less wretched. But suffering generally brings hardness of heart rather than compassion, and medieval man was more accustomed to suffering than we are. This does not mean that he was necessarily less sensitive, but that his sensitivity extended in other directions. We should think it strange today to see experienced soldiers bursting into tears, tearing their hair, and scratching their cheeks at the news of the death of a comrade, and grown men are no longer moved to tears in the presence of a religious shrine.

There is a common assumption—based on the works of seventeenth- and eighteenth-century authors who, like Molière, saw graybeards in men of forty—that our ancestors aged unnaturally fast and that youth of body and mind is in some way proportional to the average length of life. However, this does not appear to have been the case, although women who married very young and often had eight or ten children by the time they were thirty naturally tended to age quickly. Contemporary evidence shows that men who did not die in their prime aged no more quickly than people do today: Bohemond was still strikingly handsome when he was past forty, and Andronicus Comnenus had the reputation of an irresistible seducer at the age of forty-seven. Abelard was over forty when he first met Héloïse, and considered himself to be in the prime of life. Raymond of Saint-Gilles, at sixty, displayed a physical energy in his military operations that many younger men might have envied, and the Empress Zoë was still lovely at seventy, although she was not vain and took little care of her appearance. Military service was obligatory for knights up to the age of sixty, and this was more or less the limit assigned to physical youth, although men of sixty and over were admittedly few and far between.

Men did not age more quickly, but they matured earlier. They were brought up more harshly. Although their maternal and paternal feelings are not in question, people in the Middle Ages did not indulge in the cult of childhood. From the age of five or six a child was not only dressed like a miniature adult, but was also treated as a virtual adult. Rich and poor alike were trained the hard way for their position in life and treated as inferiors, however dearly loved. Children were held to be fully responsible for themselves from the moment their physical development allowed them to compete with adults. It was not unusual to find youths of sixteen or seventeen exercising the privileges of their high birth to command troops and govern estates, and displaying a maturity of character which would seem astonishing today. (Contemporaries of King Baldwin IV marveled, not at his youth, but at his courage in the face of illness, and yet at the time of his victory at Montgisard the leper King was not quite seventeen years old.)

Physically, medieval man was not very different from people in the twentieth century. On the average he was shorter and probably more robust, and there was a greater difference in ethnic type between the noble and the common man. Beyond this, there are in existence a number of sculptures sufficiently realistic to suggest that the type of European man has changed very little over the centuries. As today, Germans and Scandinavians were taller and fairer than Celts and Latins, and both, to judge from contemporary evidence, were struck by the diminutive size of Eastern peoples, and of the Greeks in particular. Physically, we can picture the man of this period as very like ourselves, although he was more likely to suffer from blindness, pockmarks, and other aftereffects of infectious diseases. But what idea should we form of his mental make-up and inner world?

Spiritual Life

THE PEOPLE

Few documents tell us anything about the thoughts and feelings of the people in Europe at this period when the vast majority of the population were unable to read or write. The writing class stood, after all, somewhat apart from the secular life of the people, and even when this was not the case, they were writing in a foreign language and based their judgments on criteria which were alien to the spirit of the people as a whole. The more highly educated churchmen belonged to a supranational aristocracy, and although differences existed on philosophical and theological matters within the Church of Rome, they did not rupture the intellectual unity brought about by the use of the same language and reference to the same authorities, not to mention the unity of faith, doctrine, and liturgy. Right up to the end of the eleventh century, churchmen were, with very rare exceptions, the only people able to write, and their evidence as historians or chroniclers dealing with secular affairs tells us the facts certainly, but they are facts passed through the somewhat standardized prism of ecclesiastical intellectual discipline.

This does not mean that the Church completely dominated social life in the Middle Ages, or that it imposed its own way of thinking on all classes of society, or even that the Church possessed a monopoly of intellectual or moral values. What the Church omitted to report has been buried in oblivion, and there are whole centuries which we know only through its generally honest and perspicacious but limited testimony. All that has survived of popular poetry is a few legends on religious subjects—even these are still semipagan—written down at a later date, and a few warrior epics. We know that in the seventh century Saint Eligius was still waging a bitter struggle against paganism in the countryside. The peasants showed a fierce attachment to their traditional rites and the celebration of traditional festivals, and regarded Christianity as a religion imposed on them by force. Everywhere the ancient pagan rites, probably still dating from pre-Roman times, survived with an official, and often only superficial, veneer of Christianity. By the eleventh century, however, hardly any conscious vestiges of paganism remained.

Religious legends, whether of Eastern origin like the majority of the stories of the Golden Legend, or local tales confined more or less to a single province or even village, conformed, with individual variations, to much the same laws that are found in all folklore and legend the world over. They feature dragons, monsters, redeemer heroes avenging martyred innocence, mystical and symbolical quests, miracles of amazing simplicity, and—a more specifically Christian theme—the eternal fight against the devil, consisting above all in victory over carnal temptation. In all these tales, whether originating in Europe, or in the East long before the Great Schism, there is the same erotic obsession which may surprise us today by its violence. These legends were collected and retold by monks, and ultimately the whole of Western civilization bore the mark of an utterly monastic horror of the sins of the flesh, although secular society in the Middle Ages was never tormented in the slightest by anxieties of this kind. The purely popular tradition seems to have been influenced very little by Christianity, and the saints and heroes figuring in peasant folklore are essentially not very different from the characters of popular pre-Christian and Hindu mythology.

Can we truly claim that our ancestors' intellectual life was so restricted? Often nothing remains to help us piece together the fragments of these stories, whether stirring or edifying, fantastic or humdrum, but a single stained-glass window of a much later date (say fourteenth or fifteenth century). The legends were told in the long night watches, by travelers on journeys, feeding the imagination of the listeners, some of whom might then take up the role of storyteller. We have no means of telling what beauty, mystery, and spiritual wealth were contained in the story of a local saint; but we do know that man is an imaginative animal, and if people found in these stories the intellectual nourishment they needed, this can have been no better or worse than that diffused today by the collective myths of press and cinema. But the comparative difficulty of communication, and the very real isolation in which the peasant lived, meant that fables and superstitious beliefs of this kind had a much greater diversity than would be the case today, and the same timeless tale might be retold in a different way in every village and province across a whole continent for hundreds of years.

Men had an individuality which has been lost today, and however similar to their ancestors in the fifth century and their descendants of the seventeenth, they also retained a distinctive character which made it impossible to confuse a man from Auvergne with one from Limousin, or a native of Artois with an inhabitant of Picardy. Different saints were worshipped and different local customs observed from one town to the next, and people showed a strong tendency to support their own particular Virgin and run down the one from the next village.

Nevertheless, there was a unity of religion, although the one faith which had replaced all others was itself developing an increasingly familiar and localized character. But people could not worship local saints alone, and so the more important ones, such as the Virgin and the Apostles, were transplanted in one way or another from the East where they belonged and brought nearer home, either through relics or by miraculous apparitions. The body of Saint James very early made the voyage across the Mediterranean to lie interred at Compostela, while Mary Magdalene, Martha, and Lazarus were popularly supposed to have come to end their days in Provence. In this way their presence became more real. People were able to go and worship at their shrines and it was even possible, by violence or pious theft, to bring one's native land the benefit of a saint's presence. Acting on this theory, a monk from Vézelay stole the body of Saint Mary Magdalene from its resting place in the convent at Les Saintes-Maries-de-la-Mer in the Camargue.

The Virgin, since she had left no corpse for veneration, was in the habit of making frequent appearances and giving unequivocal directions about the sites where she wished her churches to be built. She also appeared in the form of miraculous statues, like the Virgins of Chartres and Le Puy, dug up with the help of providence. Popular faith in the West grew up on this gradual, passionate appropriation of the tangible relics of divinity and so made up for the undoubted advantages possessed by the East in this respect.

It is an unarguable fact that this cult of saints and relics had its roots in the kind of paganism, or more accurately fetishism, which man cannot generally discard without discarding faith itself. It is also true that this passionate love of all the physical manifestations of sanctity was at the same time a way of apprehending the idea of the communion of saints. It is perhaps more generous to credit the

virgin martyr Apollonia with the gift of curing toothache than to
refuse to venerate her at all on the grounds that she is not God.

There is no need to point out that the cult of saints and the
veneration of relics, far from being peculiar to the Latin West, were
fundamentally of Eastern origin. But over the centuries Latin Christianity gradually broke away from the East, not for doctrinal reasons
but as a result of differences of language and difficulties of communication, and it is this division, due to external causes, which in the
somewhat backward and provincial West produced a kind of partic-
ularism, a growing fondness for the physical manifestations of
divinity, and an increasingly keen desire to draw nearer to the object
of worship and to possess it. Western piety was, and still is, infinitely
less transcendental than Eastern. It was more familiar, more materialistic, closer to the human nature of Christ than to his divine
personality. On neither side was this a matter of deviation or heresy.
Even in the manifestations of popular piety there was already a
real difference of conception: a difference so great that the Orientals
never succeeded in understanding the outbreak of pious feeling which
in the West led to the rush to Jerusalem. They felt no less fervently
about the Holy Places, but their fervor was less active because more
inward and directed more toward mysticism and theological speculation.

All popular culture had an essentially religious background. Every
aspect of life was imbued to some extent with Christianity: Christian
ritual, pagan rites which had become Christianized, traditions, and
cosmology; and the Christian faith was by now so firmly established as
to be no longer a monopoly of priests and monks, who could sometimes find themselves severely judged by the people. The common
man in the Middle Ages was a Christian in the same way as a
twentieth-century man is an Englishman or a Frenchman, a worker,
a peasant, or a city dweller. In Russian, for example, the word
"peasant" means literally "Christian," and the distinction existing
between the two ideas in the present-day language is a later development. This etymological synthesis corresponds to an attitude that
was more or less general in the Middle Ages. Men thought of themselves first and foremost as religious beings, members of a community of the faithful. The notion of humanity came only afterwards.

Man was entirely dependent on God, a God who could dispense
rain or drouth, peace or war according to His will. God controlled
epidemics, fires, and all human ills, individual and collective, and was
master of men's fate after death. He was a sovereign not to be lightly
offended. The laws of current morality may have been observed to the

extent which everyday social life demanded, but prescriptions of a purely religious order, such as fasts, the veneration of sacred objects, attendance at church, and so forth, were generally much more strictly observed by adherents to every religion. When the Turkish general Mawdud was mortally wounded, he refused to take the medicine which might have saved him rather than break the fast of Ramadan, an act of virtue which earned him more admiration than any purely human display of heroism or charity.*

Men lived in a mental climate radically different from our own. Nowadays religion is no longer expected to hold a monopoly of truth on every plane: science has deprived it of its element of absolute necessity. In the Middle Ages, scientific knowledge was restricted to purely technical and utilitarian matters and no one would have considered basing his concept of the world on the method of building a machine. What we today would call scientific knowledge was thought to have been entirely revealed in the Scriptures, and there had been no discoveries to make men question the accuracy of these revelations. It would not be fair to accuse our forebears of being unduly naive or gullible because they accepted unquestioningly tales of miracles and facts in general which seem to us in direct contradiction to the laws of physics. These laws simply did not exist for them, or only on empirical evidence, to be treated with caution.

It was experience which told them that the earth did not move and was bigger than the sun, and that the sun moved around the earth. The converse is by no means obvious to us, and we believe it is true with about as much reason as people in the Middle Ages had for believing in miracles. Assuming that a miracle can be defined as a phenomenon which cannot be explained by natural laws, then ignorance may make natural phenomena appear miraculous and leave a very large margin of interpretation for observable facts: the appearance of a comet becomes a sign sent from God, hallucinations look like supernatural visions, and any everyday occurrence such as a storm or a shower of rain happening at a particular moment may be interpreted as a direct manifestation of divine power, while the same may be true of a sudden death or unexpected recovery. Miracles were frequent, something that could be readily expected and hoped for. Men lived in a universe created by their own imaginations. About the real world they knew practically nothing. Saints, demons, and angels occupied very much the same position in the mind of an

* See below, page 234.

average man of the time as subjects like the atom, medicine, psychoanalysis, or romantic love do in ours.

It is doubtful whether the average man was a Christian in the sense that we understand the word today, or even as the primitive Church would have understood it. Popular religion, as we have seen, was —as it still tends to be—largely pagan, while the doctrine of the Trinity and the veneration of images encouraged Jews as well as Moslems to regard Christians as idolaters and polytheists. Medieval man was a Christian simply insofar as he was devoted to the person of Christ, and of Christ who was acknowledged to be God. On this point the Church had succeeded in banishing all doubts. All literature of popular origin bears witness to a universal and unquestioning acceptance of the divine nature of Jesus Christ. It was God who was born at Bethlehem: the one God who created the universe.

The people did not read the Gospels, and priests rarely explained these to them. Their faith was fed as much by apocryphal stories and later traditions as by the facts related in canonical works, although most people were familiar with the life of Jesus, the Old Testament, and the lives of the saints. In this they were aided by the religious festivals which involved them all year round in continuous re-enactions of the mysteries of the Nativity, Passion, and Resurrection, each stage of Christ's life on earth, and those of the Apostles, the Virgin, and the most venerated saints. The piety of the common people was in general keener and closer to primitive Christianity than that of the upper classes, and even at times than that of the clergy.

THE NOBILITY

The nobility was undoubtedly pious, but as we have seen, it also possessed values of its own which were to some extent independent of religion but were none the less singularly powerful.

Some authorities have suggested that Christianity in the tenth and eleventh centuries underwent a process of "Germanization" or, as Waas prefers to call it, "feudalization." Both these terms are fair enough. Even in Latin-speaking countries like France and Spain, the ruling class was exclusively a warrior caste whose ideals were Germanic in inspiration. The wave of Norman invasions had brought a race of overlords of Scandinavian origin to Mediterranean countries such as Sicily and southern Italy which had previously been under Byzantine or Arabic influence. From the eighth century onward, northern Italy had been settled by Teutonic colonists. These soon became assimilated and latinized, but their conversion to Christianity was still comparatively recent, dating from the time of Charlemagne.

England, which had been Christian since very early times, had undergone a succession of conquests by the Saxons and Normans, both of whom were comparatively fresh to Christianity. Scandinavia as a whole remained pagan until the tenth century and parts of it were still so in the eleventh, as were the lands along the Baltic coast. Germany, where Christianity was firmly established, was still open to more or less conscious pagan influences because of its community of language with its northern neighbors. The same was true of Bohemia, where memories of pagan times were still sufficiently vivid to form the basis of the national epic. (Eastern Europe derived both culture and religion directly from Byzantium. The various races here were also recent converts, one reason being that the great plains to the southeast were constantly being invaded by nomadic tribes of Mongol origin. These tribes were pagans, who were sometimes easily converted from their traditional shamanism but whose Christianity was no more than skin deep.)

Feudal society was therefore the result of the Germanic invasions of the fourth and fifth centuries, strengthened periodically from the ninth century onward by influxes from Scandinavia. Many of its attitudes originated in the old Germanic pagan religion which had dominated the so-called barbarian lands for nearly a thousand years. Its history and origins are not easy to trace, but what little information we can glean from Roman historians shows that in the first century B.C. and the first century of our own era the majority of the Germanic peoples belonged to this religion and that it was modified very little over the centuries.

The descendants of Clovis's warriors had forgotten the very names of their ancient gods just as they had forgotten the language of their forebears. It was different for those who retained their original language, but even there memories of paganism were more vivid among the common people than among the upper classes, who had been consciously won over as a whole to the Church of Rome. But this essentially warrior class still retained values from its old religion which, even when unacknowledged or called by another name, gave to feudal piety a distinctly pagan character which was all the stronger in that it was unconscious.

German paganism was a somewhat primitive religion of Indo-Iranian origin and was clearly not in any way concerned with the worship of idols. The Germanic tribes were no more idolatrous than medieval Christians were. They were polytheists, and the gods they worshipped were symbolized by the forces of nature but were in no way identified with them. They were strongly individual gods, neither perfect nor omnipotent, and they were moreover doomed—in some more or less distant future—to exterminate one another and so disappear, making way for the triumph of sovereign justice.

It was a pessimistic religion. The great chief of all the gods, Odin or Wotan, the seer and god of war, was blind in one eye; Tyr, another war god, had only one hand. The only perfect being, Balder, son of Odin, he who was all beauty, wisdom, and goodness, possessed the curious distinction of never being able to bring anything he undertook to completion. Furthermore, his death was brought about by the machinations of the demon Loki and he remained forever the prisoner of Loki's daughter, Hel, whose name is still perpetuated in the Germanic languages as *Hölle* or *hell*.

It can be seen that there were certain elements in this religion which might facilitate a transference to Christianity: in particular the mysterious figure of Balder, the idea of the final destruction of the gods, and the song of Odin "hanged from a tree," "himself immolated by himself" (here the text possibly shows a remote Christian influence, but it also suggests the initiation rites of shamanism). In its evocation of a suffering god, voluntarily sacrificed, this has an almost Christian sound. The Church naturally made no attempt to exploit these resemblances. On the contrary, it solidly and determinedly consigned the whole of pagan mythology to hell, avoiding all compromise and all danger of syncretism—anything, in fact, which might have turned the physical person of Christ into a mythological figure to be merged with other legendary divinities.

When the Germans were converted they made a clean sweep of everything they had previously worshipped and bravely faced the thunder of the gods they abandoned. Since their pagan religion was polytheist, they may at first merely have renounced the lesser gods in favor of a more powerful one. But the descendants of those worshippers of Odin still had the love of a warrior god in their blood, a god of warriors whose ultimate symbol was war. Those who died in battle, struck by Odin's lance, were certain of paradise; and sick men dying in their beds would give themselves a ritual wound in the side before they died, so that they might enter the delights of Valhalla. Moreover Odin was an aristocratic god, and the bliss imagined by this warrior aristocracy reflected their earthly aspirations. The souls of the brave never felt pain any more and they measured their strength in endless combat, interrupted only by feasts at which they got drunk on the elixir of the gods, until the day of the final cataclysm. It is not difficult to imagine, on reading the battle stories of the twelfth century, that this paradise would probably have suited the majority of Christian knights down to the ground.

The paradise which Christ and the Catholic Church promised them was very different, yet in spite of this, from the first centuries of Christianity the Germans were easily won over by missionary preaching. Their chiefs were voluntary converts and compelled their armies to accept baptism also. But whether spontaneous or enforced, the conversion of the German barbarians was a lasting one, and the ancient gods were swiftly forgotten, while Christianity in the West found itself affected much more by the warlike qualities of the Germans than it had been by those of Constantine's successors in the East.

The old pagan religion was a religion of caste, and it was a powerful caste pride which drove the Viking nobles to claim for themselves the special protection of the god of battles and his home of the brave after death. This pride survived, in a latent form, through centuries of feudal Christianity. No ruling class spontaneously abandons such undeniable advantages, and the most the Church's teaching could do was reduce it to an unconscious level. It could not prevent the nobles from creating their own idea of religion within the framework of Christianity.

A Mystique of War (Medieval Epics)

Waas, in his distinguished work on the Crusades, has demonstrated that the Church was not directly responsible for this particular form of Christian piety. The Cluniac reforms encouraged more than one knight to renounce the profession of arms in order to live according to the tenets of religion. In the eleventh century, a knight who remained in the world but had been converted to the Cluniac movement might boast of never having used his sword, a rare achievement for the period and unquestionable proof of the sincerity of his conversion. Cases of this kind were quoted by the Church as examples, and admired by pious men. Fifty years later, such a knight would have been the object of more astonishment than admiration.

Even among the first Crusaders there were men inspired by a Christian ideal which owed nothing to the Crusading spirit. Walter Sans-Avoir, who died fighting under the walls of Nicaea, was apparently one such: a layman won over by the preaching of the Gospels who gave all his goods to the poor and dedicated his life to charitable works. (Walter's behavior, as one of the leaders of the so-called People's Crusade, is a sufficient indication that he was a man who had taken the cross not with any warlike intentions but simply in order to serve as a guide and protector to pilgrims.) The same spirit was partly responsible for the creation of the military orders. The Templars and Hospitalers were originally monks first and soldiers afterward.

A basically military society, long severed from the few traditions of pagan culture which its ancestors had possessed, and living in a land where the Church was the only seat of intellectual and moral culture, was becoming gradually imbued with a faith which was essentially foreign to it. The permanent hostility between clerics and knights (which persisted throughout the Middle Ages) is a sufficient indication of the extent to which the military aristocracy of the land was ill-adapted to a religion which, nevertheless, it had professed for centuries. The Church may have been too powerful and too independent for laymen's liking, but ultimately the barons' constant attacks on ecclesiastical power showed clearly enough that the Church had, as it were, only half converted the feudal classes. There is no example of such a systematic antagonism in either Byzantium or Islam.

Secular society, conscious of its strength and jealous of its moral independence, was creating its own values and "Christianizing" values which in themselves had nothing to do with Christianity. The common people, in their own way, had done precisely the same. Just as, in the first centuries of the Christian era, the old Gallic and Roman sanctuaries had been converted into chapels and occasional local saints had inherited the actual names of pagan divinities, so the knighthood adapted itself to Christianity by bending the Christian religion to fit its own moral ideals. The Christian faith possessed no warrior divinities as such, but it was not long before the Christian pantheon acquired, through the cult of saints, a number of figures who could readily be identified with the earlier warrior gods. Moreover, one had only to go back beyond the New Testament to Biblical antiquity to find ample justification for the right to make war.

Christian warriors were ready to take the term "God of battles," applied to Jehovah, at its face value and to turn themselves into Israelites whenever the enemy they faced could be considered an enemy of their faith. Saint Michael, as the leader of the heavenly host, naturally became transformed into a warrior divinity, and all saints who had been soldiers in their earthly lives were regarded by soldiers east and west alike as peculiarly their own. Chief among these martyr saints were Saint George, Saint Theodore, Saint Maurice, Saint

Mercury, and Saint John (all of whom came originally from the East), but the one who was loved and prayed to above all the rest was Saint George, the slayer of the dragon. It was not the martyr's constancy which aroused men's admiration, but the warrior's courage, and this Christian soldier had become so thoroughly transformed into a soldier of Christ that, far from peacefully enjoying heavenly bliss, he was supposed to be constantly returning to earth to take part in battles that were anything but spiritual or symbolic.

The idea that warrior saints could intervene in earthly battles was not specifically a Western one. There is a very ancient tradition attributing the death of Julian the Apostate to a wound dealt him by the lance of the martyr Saint Mercury, and legends of this kind, circulating from East to West, undoubtedly appealed to the popular imagination everywhere. It was the custom of Byzantine emperors to go into battle brandishing a sword in one hand and clutching an icon of the Virgin to their breast with the other. It was the Virgin who got the credit for routing the opposing armies and bringing about the sudden death of the enemy leaders. In Europe, the warlike temper of feudal society made the warrior saint and archangel the objects of special devotion, to such an extent that it is not easy to see what distinguishes them from minor deities.

Chivalry was not originally an institution, still less a specifically Christian one. A natural desire for order and organization had led feudal warriors to form what was, theoretically at least, a kind of military fraternity, bound by the same already existing rules, obeying the same moral code and subject to the same prohibitions, and this society, no longer primitive but not yet wholly civilized, developed, if not an ideal, at least a conscious picture of its own vocation. A knight in the eleventh century was not simply a soldier who happened to be more or less rich and powerful.

When a young man was to be made a knight, he underwent a form of initiation ceremony. The ceremony itself was rudimentary, since at this stage it did not have a religious character, but a certain mystical importance attached to it which was a survival from forgotten Celtic and Teutonic traditions. In dubbing the new candidate, his sponsor conferred upon him the chivalric virtues which he himself was assumed to possess in the highest degree, while the years of apprenticeship which the youth had served also corresponded to a lengthy preparation for the dignity of knighthood. Chivalry did not become connected with religion, or at least place itself under religious patronage, until the middle of the eleventh century. The

Church was naturally more than willing to extend its influence over a military caste which in practice did without it wherever possible. Priests and prelates began to play a part in the ceremony of making a knight, demanding, in return for the blessings they pronounced, a promise to respect the Church's possessions, to fight its enemies, and—it goes without saying—to observe the precepts of religion.

There can be no doubt that the Cluniac reforms had a real influence on all levels of the population and that this influence was felt in the very spirit of chivalry. But in the majority of cases, the faith of these Christian warriors was still extraordinarily primitive. There is a striking example of this in *Ralph of Cambrai,* a *chanson de geste* dating, in its written form, from the twelfth century. Ralph, who has just burned down a convent with all the nuns inside, asks his servants for a dish of meat. His knights are horrified. "Today is Good Friday," they tell him. "Would you then *slay our souls?*" Not wishing to offend God, Ralph reluctantly forgoes his meat. Genuine piety was combined with the crudest superstition; people imagined that gifts to the Church and acts of a purely ritual kind were a surer way of appeasing God's wrath than a true repentance.

Chivalric morality bore the mark of a stoic pride that was not without beauty but that owed little to the morality of the Church. It is only from the *chansons de geste* that we can derive some idea of the mental and spiritual life of this illiterate but not barbaric society, and even these were not written down until a later date, none dating from as far back as the eleventh century.

The *chansons de geste* are obsessed with the constant, almost mystical exaltation of strength, courage, and vital energy. They are full of prodigious deeds of valor, adversaries vanquished by the dozen, descriptions of horses, armor, and weapons, and a cruelty that is both grim and joyous. Brains are dashed out, bowels ripped open, hands lopped off, teeth smashed, and knights cleft from chin to chine, and more often than not this orgy of blood and violence comes to its logical conclusion in the violent death of the hero. The *chanson de geste* is not like a Western: its inspiration does not lie in the desire to see virtue triumphant but in the desire for death. The hero may be virtuous, like Roland or Oliver, or he may be wicked, like Ralph; all that is necessary is that he should be strong and brave. He is generally killed—often, like King Reynald, bleeding to death after countless wounds, "clutching his guts in his hands." His shattered brains run down his face, but he is incredibly tough and even this does not finish him off. Another hero, Bègue, is stupidly murdered by gamekeepers who mistake him for a poacher, and Ralph is killed in a duel in fair revenge. The survivors lament the dead and the fighting begins all over again, blood calling for blood.

Those heroes who have time to be aware that they are dying all turn to God in their last moments. Roland is the last survivor of the massacre and no priest is present at his death. Young Vivian dies in the arms of his uncle William and confesses his few sins to him. The heroes proclaim their guilt, pray on their swords, the hilts of which are encrusted with relics, sometimes swallow the sacred Host which they carry in a bag around their necks, and then commend themselves to God with all the fervor of dying men. Their humble, violent faith does not need the assistance of the Church and its priests. They die, as they have lived, the servants of the highest of all virtues, courage.

Men like these could never have brought themselves to believe that this was not the virtue most prized by God. Their love of physical strength and physical courage was also a kind of religion, a conscious, burning faith which sometimes clashed with the other. The priest was often an object of contempt as a man who refused to fight and therefore, by a simple but logical train of thought, a coward. The cloister was the obvious refuge for boys who were weak or timid, just as it was for unmarriageable girls. But it is only fair to point out that long before the foundation of the military orders, Western nobility had also furnished the Church with more than one fighting monk and more than one warrior prelate.

The spiritual life of these French knights, as it emerges from the medieval epics, seems to have been somewhat poverty-stricken. Its poverty was not emotional but lay in a lack of ideals and traditions. It was not steeped in a legendary, pre-Christian past, such as that revealed in the Norse sagas, the Teutonic epics, and even the Breton romances. The *chanson de geste* has neither the symbolism nor the power of enchantment found in popular mythology. Frankish chivalry had no known ancestry, and its evocation of the mystery of times past goes no further back than the age of Charlemagne. The French warrior epic is staunchly human and already contains elements of the historical chronicle and the romance. Despite a fondness for marvels which is largely superficial, it is basically realistic and there is much to be gained from a closer look at the image of man it reveals.

The one essential element of the poem is the hero's strength, a strength which is united to remarkable energy and courage. Since the hero's weapons are an integral part of his personality, these are also of exceptional caliber. His two most important possessions are his horse and his sword, especially the sword, whose fame is inseparable from that of its owner, but all the warrior's arms and equipment enjoy to some extent the same prestige. The knight's concern to make his battle gear as fine as possible is due to the fact that his weapons are an object of love for their own sake.

No fewer than twenty lines of *The Song of Roland* are devoted to describing the accouterments of a Moslem knight who appears only once and is promptly dealt a mortal blow, while the description of Aude the beautiful takes precisely three words: "a lovely lady." To a modern reader this might seem an unsatisfactory manner of writing, but at the time the *chanson* was written down a fine helmet or a well-made coat of mail was literally more precious and more worth dreaming of and scheming for than a pretty woman. When Roland is dying he does not spare a single thought for Aude the beautiful, but he speaks to his sword Durandal as though to a lover, and his audience found this perfectly natural. ("Softly he began to lament: 'Ah, Durandal, how white and lovely you are! How many relics in your golden hilt . . .'")

Here faith and war are united in the same feeling of love. Durandal is sacred, and not simply on account of the relics. It is the pure, sharp-edged blade which is the real object of love, and not the golden hilt. It is the blade that will be broken before it is allowed to fall into enemy hands, and the blade that can miraculously split the living rock. The relics protect it, add their virtue to it, and finally complete its sacred character.

Now this is a deadly weapon, stained countless times with human blood, but this does not pollute it. On the contrary, little credit would attach to a sword which had never killed anyone. The relics are there not only to protect the hero's life but to make his weapon more murderous. No Christian nation was altogether free of this contradiction, but it seems to have been Western knights, and the French in particular, who carried it to its extreme. In the eleventh century, the love of war and the love of God showed a tendency to become increasingly confused. It was as though chivalry, once it was morally strong, organized, and conscious of its own worth, had tried to set up its own vision of the world, and consequently its own religion, in opposition to that of a Church which was pacifist on principle. It is worth noting that it was not in Germany, where Christianity was younger and pre-Christian traditions stronger, nor in Spain, where the Moslem had long been a neighbor, part enemy and party ally, but in France itself where the idea of the holy war was to find the strongest support. French chivalry was not the most belligerent, but it was the most tormented by the need to find a moral justification for its passion for war.

The *chanson de geste,* which bears witness to this state of mind, was not created with a moral purpose. Its heroes are constantly fighting because the public for which they were created was interested in little else. The *chansons* include tales of family feuds, of just and unjust conquests and feudal wars, but the favorite subject, which crops up repeatedly, is the story of Charlemagne, the legendary hero already half identified with the heroes of antiquity. Charlemagne is always portrayed as an old man with a hoary beard, which he was not in fact. He is an unconsciously mythological figure, the incarnation of forgotten warrior divinities, or even of Jehovah the God of Battles himself.

What Charlemagne was fighting for was to conquer as much land as possible, and he conquered it from the pagans. The pagans, in this case, were not Saxons or Lombards but the Moslems of Spain and the south of France. The same theme recurs in the cycle of poems about William of Orange. The Moslems were so far and away the only imaginable pagans that in the poem William's wife, the Scandinavian pagan Witburgis (or Guibourc), becomes Orable, a Saracen princess carried off and baptized by William. It is around these mythical Saracens, who are the regular adversaries of Charlemagne and his knights, that the French warrior imagination turns. In fact these Moslems were almost entirely imaginary, and although a few genuine recollections of wars and travels in Spain do find their way into the descriptions of pagan "knights," these are only very superficial observations. Indeed, according to French poets the Saracens were the most primitive kind of pagans and worshipped idols which they looked on as actual gods. Mohammed himself was merely one of their idols. In everything else they behaved very much like French knights.

Consequently, the enemy was not a priori an object of hatred. He was not even properly known, except in imagination. The Saracen, strong, brave, and fierce and always vanquished in the end, was the ideal adversary of the medieval warrior's imagination, replacing the adversary who was only too real, the everyday enemy: the neighboring duke, count, or even bishop one happened to be fighting at the time. To be truly heroic, the hero must have a clear conscience; he must be fighting to defend his country and his faith. But in France there was no longer any real threat to the safety of what the French already regarded as their native land, and still less to their faith: therefore they had to go back to the time of

Charlemagne. France at this time was divided into provinces more or less independent of one another, but she already possessed her dream of national greatness, and this was now projected into the past in fantasies about the great Emperor with his vast empire and spectacular wars of conquest. Roland and the twelve peers were not fighting and dying for the Christians of Spain but for the honor of *la douce France*. Listeners to the *chansons de geste* did not have to go back to Charlemagne to imagine the splendors and miseries of war, but what made the exploits of epic heroes noble and moving was the fact that their adversaries were pagans.

Transformed, not without a struggle, into a Christian epic, the warlike legends lived on as a kind of subconscious yearning in the hearts of the people. Urban II's appeal certainly touched some deep spring in the minds of all those soldiers who, overnight, discovered in themselves a vocation as soldiers of God.

Long before the Crusades, popes had been appealing to the religious feelings of any who placed themselves and their arms at the service of the Church, either to defend it directly or to fight the infidel. The Church never lacked pious mercenaries to claim the promised spiritual rewards. Even so, Urban II's action had consequences which that pope was very far from foreseeing. Urban was an aristocrat from Champagne, born into the same feudal society which looked on war as the supreme honor and goal of a man's life. He remembered his ancestral traditions, perhaps even with some nostalgia. He aimed at exploiting the warlike temper of the French nobility for the greater good of Christendom. He was an eloquent speaker, with a talent for touching his hearers' emotions and appealing simultaneously to their generosity and their pity, to their national pride, their love of war, their piety, and even their cupidity and their fear of eternal punishment. Altogether his speeches, as reported by the chroniclers, are adroit and inspired, and nothing could have been more natural than for the Pope in a public address (and he had not come to France only to ask for help for the Holy Land) to summon the faithful to a pious work.

Urban was certainly not departing from the traditional preaching of every pope before and after him, in energetically scourging the fratricidal wars indulged in by laymen: the ears of the nobility had long been hardened to sermons of this kind. The majority of the audience on this memorable occasion had long been aware of the misfortune of the Holy Land and the difficulties attending pilgrimages there, and Urban was telling them nothing new when he announced that the Turks were threatening the Eastern Roman Empire.

What he did was to point out extremely cleverly both the trouble and the remedy, and show that these wicked wars could be replaced with another war which was holy and approved by God. Urban may not have known it, but the whole future of Western political thought was contained in this sermon: the use of unemployed and undisciplined military forces toward a common goal, generally acknowledged to be just, and the proclamation of a divine mission imposed on the Christians of the West.

Urban II had long been familiar with the problems of international politics. He was well informed about the progress of the Turks in Asia Minor, the troubles facing Byzantium, the intrigues of the Vizier of Cairo, and the rivalries among the Seljuk princes, and he saw the possible intervention of a Western military force as a way of reuniting the Greek and Latin Christians in an undertaking which would be in their mutual interest since it offered a hope of breaking the power of Turkey, which appeared to be already on the decline.

As for his audience, their reactions prove that they saw his appeal, first and foremost, as a mystical adventure: the deliverance of Jerusalem. It was the idea of Jerusalem and the Holy Land which spread like a patch of oil from this first sermon to catch the imagination of the crowds. Nobles and common people responded to it with the same enthusiasm. The military expedition proposed by the Pope came at exactly the right moment to answer a real, though hitherto unexpressed, need.

Jerusalem

In discussing the First Crusade, it is important to distinguish between the "People's Crusade" and that of the barons. These, though parallel and simultaneous, were in fact two quite separate movements. It is not always easy to trace the demarcation line between the two. The nobility and the poorer folk were united in the pursuit of a common ideal and vied with and influenced each other, and this was certainly the first time in the history of the Latin and Catholic West that all classes of society had been drawn to the support of an enterprise of common interest. Even if it did not cause the mass departure of the common people, the Crusade was, from the very moment it was preached, undoubtedly a popular movement.

The nobility quite naturally regarded it as a military undertaking and the people as a pilgrimage. Both translated a completely new kind of undertaking into the terms most familiar to them, and both believed firmly in the greatness of their mission and the divine protection granted to any man who took the cross.

As we have seen, feudal aristocracy, and the nobility of France in particular, had long been moving toward a reappraisal of its intellectual and moral values, or rather to a consecration of these values by religion. People were finding it increasingly necessary to see the Christian faith endorse and even exalt the things that formed the structure of feudal society. This was a moral and not a political need.

Urban II had struck home. At last Christian knights understood that their condition and occupation were not contrary to religion but constituted the most glorious means of winning paradise. This was something they had long believed in their inmost hearts, but the Church had never before solemnly pronounced it through the mouth of a pope. Private wars inspired by greed and personal enmity were wicked and sinful; war itself, pure, disinterested war, could be holy.

Now they were offered a war to be waged against the enemies of Christians for the defense of brothers in the faith, but as we shall see, the humanitarian considerations were not those which the Crusaders placed first, although they too had their importance. The Christians being persecuted in Spain and Sicily aroused no demonstrations of public enthusiasm and those in the East still less. The One who was oppressed, the One it was their duty to defend, was Christ himself: Jesus Christ was suffering humiliation in the very scenes of his earthly life: Jerusalem, the Holy Sepulcher, Bethlehem —all places which for Christians had a legendary and mystical significance, and possessed the strange and unique virtue of being at once places which really existed on earth and symbols on which the love and meditation of the faithful had been concentrated for centuries.

The attraction of Jerusalem for Christians was never as strong as that of Mecca for the Moslems: pilgrimage formed no part of religious obligations properly speaking, but it had been extremely popular even before Constantine's day, and had long been a habit. A large part of the population of every Christian country traveled the roads to this or that shrine, and pilgrim routes developed into great commercial arteries. To people in the West, Jerusalem was a distant place of pilgrimage where few could go. In fact Jerusalem remained, before all else, a symbol. The Jerusalem of the Psalms, the celestial Jerusalem of the Apocalypse, lived in the hearts of the faithful. An eleventh-century clerk, describing the various shrines of Palestine for pilgrims (*Itineraria Hierosolymitana*), found himself obliged to warn his readers, to save them disappointment, that the city of Jerusalem was not exceptionally large and wealthy. It was just a town like any other. They already knew this. In fact it was not the land itself which inspired the Crusaders in their vocation and made the crowds cry out, "God wills it!" If there was an element of collective hysteria behind the phenomenon of the Crusade, it was provoked by an involuntary confusion between the elements of time and eternity, between the earthly and the heavenly Jerusalem. The Crusader took up the Cross of Christ at the same time as he took up the cross of consecrated fabric, and he set out to conquer heaven as well as Palestine. Men hastened to the rescue of Jesus Christ as though Jesus Christ were still on the point of being betrayed by Judas and crucified by Pontius Pilate.

Such a state of exaltation could clearly not be sustained for years on end; but constantly fanned and revived by sermons, it enabled those who volunteered for the First Crusade to overcome the most appalling odds and finally to attain their desired goal—the purely terrestrial goal at least, the liberation of Jerusalem.

It must not be forgotten that the barons and knights who pledged themselves to exchange their impious wars for a holy one were not invited to win paradise cheap. They needed more than a pure and upright heart in order to deserve the promised reward: they had also to incur expenses which could easily prove ruinous and which in many cases did actually ruin them, and to expose themselves to countless dangers and fatigues. The Pope certainly promised them a number of guarantees of a material kind and the chance of winning rich spoils, and a great many adventurers were tempted to join the movement out of self-interest. But even for adventurers of this kind, the effort demanded was out of all proportion to the likelihood of making a fortune out of the infidel.

The Crusading armies did not take the road until a year after the Council of Clermont. The military leaders and their knights needed time to equip and organize their armies, because the projected expedition was no ordinary war. Men like Raymond of Saint-Gilles and Godfrey of Bouillon did not take the cross in a careless burst of enthusiasm, and indeed the former may have been contemplating something of the sort even before Urban II's call to arms. He had taken part in an earlier Crusade in Spain, and the idea of a fight against the Turks had already been suggested by other popes (notably Gregory VII). Godfrey of Lorraine and his brother Baldwin had very quickly realized the practical advantages to be gained from a campaign in the East, and the same was true of Robert,

Duke of Normandy, and of the Count of Flanders. All these feudal lords were men of mature judgment and meant to serve God as they would serve their temporal lords, reasonably, calculating the chances of success and aiming at tangible results. There can be no doubt whatever of their sincerity, nor of their desire to accomplish a work which was both glorious in itself and in the interests of their religion. The leaders of the Crusade were not acting out of personal ambition. Godfrey of Bouillon ruined himself and mortgaged his estates in order to equip his army. Raymond of Toulouse swore an oath to die in the Holy Land, no mean sacrifice for an aging man full of honors who was lord of one of the wealthiest provinces in Europe. We shall see later that neither Robert of Normandy nor Robert of Flanders ever raised any claim to the land conquered by the Crusaders. The benefit these barons looked for was above all a spiritual or, possibly, a political one. The term "politics" did not exist in the sense that we understand it today. The public good, good in itself, and the glory of God were terms very nearly synonymous, and the Crusader chiefs were not fanatics eager for heroism and martyrdom, nor adventurers greedy for conquest, but professional soldiers with the ideas and policies proper to their time and environment.

Once these great lords had done so, hundreds of less important *seigneurs* hastened to answer the call. For them it meant willingness to abandon their lands for an indefinite period and risk a large part of their fortune in the process. Many knights were compelled to sell or pledge their lands and castles hastily, on ruinous terms. The volunteers had to bear their own traveling costs, so that they had to take considerable sums of money with them to pay for food and other expenses on the journey, quite apart from the cost of weapons, armor, horses, and equipment. Everything had to be carefully prepared and calculated. All these preparations took nearly a year because the knights had little ready money and had to spend weeks and even months in bargaining, arranging loans, settling their affairs, and seeing to the running of their domains while they were away, as well as getting together equipment, horses, cattle, and means of transport. They were a sedentary people but still partly nomadic in their day-to-day lives, and they flung themselves eagerly into preparations for years of vagabond existence, fraught with dangers and difficulties.

A glance at the traveling arrangements for the four armies which made up the First Crusade makes it clear that the leaders of these armies were excellent organizers. They had to travel for months through territory that was often poor and hostile, leading an army which included, in addition to the professional troops, a considerable mob of undisciplined and irresponsible hotheads, and they succeeded in bringing this great host all the way to Constantinople fit, healthy, and in good order with a minimum of trouble and delay.

All the chroniclers agree that throughout the campaign, which was to last for nearly four years, the morale of these troops was exceptionally high. At the outset, few of the soldiers or even of their leaders had foreseen the obstacles which this enormous volunteer army would have to overcome, but in general the men stood firm, and the foot soldiers even gave their commanders an occasional lesson in initiative.

Each soldier shared the absolute conviction that in taking the cross he was enlisting directly in the service of God Himself. The cross of red fabric sewn on his garments—a brilliantly effective idea—became for each man who wore it a tangible sign that he belonged to God and was under divine protection, and this gave it a mystical, even a magical significance. The Crusaders set out under this or that baron, but their actual leader was God Himself, and the barons were His temporal lieutenants. The Crusader chiefs, and especially the official leader of the Crusade, Adhemar of Monteil, Bishop of Le Puy and papal legate, were respected by the bulk of the army, although the only really great leader of men in the First Crusade was "Little Peter," the frail little old man riding on a small donkey. The outstanding personality among the leaders was Bohemond of Taranto and his popularity among the troops was immense. Godfrey inspired the keenest admiration, as much for his physical strength as for his very real virtues. But it was not they the men followed, nor the legate, highly esteemed though he was, nor even the Pope, whose name quickly dropped into the background as far as the general public was concerned since he was not leading the army in person.

The army was led by Jesus Christ himself.

The facts are remarkable enough in themselves. Here were not one but several armies gathered together, but not, as one might expect, to follow a great conqueror or outstanding leader, nor in response to the more or less conscious need for expansion or a suddenly awakened national pride. All these elements were present in the First Crusade, but they were of only secondary importance. The prime motive was a genuine desire to serve God, and the average Crusader really believed that he was marching under God's orders. The famous cry of "God wills it!" was more than simply a catchphrase.

It is a fact that the warlike nobility was constantly at odds with the Church. The knights had their own values and ideals which were quite different from those of the Church. But here, for once, the Church was speaking to them in language which reconciled their conscience as Christians with their deepest aspirations. The result was a singular transmutation of values, for if the best of the Crusaders spontaneously devoted their aggressive instincts to God's service, a great many more made their faith an excuse for their natural belligerence and gave themselves up without scruples to their passion for war once they had decided that it was sacred and in accordance with God's wishes.

Whatever the reasons, once Jesus Christ was proclaimed and acknowledged as the God of Battles he was a source of boundless confidence and unlimited devotion. This was a God for whom men were willing to fight and die, a God worthy of their service.

Christ's Army

The image of Christ as the warrior king was not a later invention due to pagan influence. Its source lay in the most ancient and venerable traditions: in the Messiah of the Jews. The Jewish Apocalypse, the Apocalypse as it appears in the Christian Apocrypha, and most important of all, the Revelations of Saint John the Divine, a canonical work with commentaries by theologians of all Christian sects, show God's ultimate triumph over evil and the victorious Messiah holding all nations under his sway.

Whatever the interpretations of Christian exegetes, behind the idea of a holy war and the destruction of evil by the sword lay the image of a terrible avenging Messiah, riding at the head of the cohorts of the just and trampling his enemies beneath his horse's hoofs. The Church had existed for a thousand years and no longer lived in daily expectation of the end of the world, but even so there were so many passages in the Gospels referring to the ultimate cataclysm—passages made all the more menacing and disturbing by their very vagueness—that sincere Christians could hardly help taking them literally. As early as the time of Origen, the Church was attempting to play down people's anticipation of Armageddon by projecting it simultaneously into the distant past—Christ's Crucifixion and Resurrection—and also into a far-off, indeterminate future. But even this proclamation of an end of the world to be preceded by catastrophes of every description, wars and natural disasters, combined with the detailed though symbolic descriptions of the Apocalypse, could be interpreted in such a variety of ways that for many Christians the end of the world was a living, day-to-day reality, and the thought was always in their minds: "Suppose it were tomorrow?" Those who were acquainted directly or indirectly with the revelations of the Apocalypse were apt to interpret the "signs of the times" and see Antichrist (or one of his immediate precursors) in every bad ruler or every powerful enemy of Christianity.

It is true that the Apocalypse does not prophesy an earthly war, but something more on the lines of a cosmic disaster in which the forces of the Holy Spirit will triumph over evil when it has reached the last excesses of horror. Man plays only a minor part in this fearful confrontation. The ultimate victory belongs to Christ himself and his celestial hosts. But this warrior Christ, commanding the legions of the angels, was a mixture of the Jehovah, God of Battles, of Hebrew religion and the pagan warrior gods.

This was a God made more terrible and interesting by the fact that he was also the sacrificial lamb, the victim of the Crucifixion. The invincible warrior and the eternal martyr God, inspiring pity of the most uplifting kind, were one and the same. (This is not an attempt to explain or argue with the dogma and its interpretations, but simply to underline the purely emotional power of religious beliefs.) In the Christian religion all men's pity for a pure and innocent victim and all their admiration for a terrible conquering God were concentrated on a single Being, and the consequences of this apparent paradox (which, from any but a purely religious standpoint, it is) are extremely far-reaching, and are among the ideas which have transformed the souls of nations and the destiny of civilizations.

The horror of the Crucifixion was partially avoided by Eastern Christians, who—even the most orthodox—always remained implicitly Monophysite, but it had been fully adopted by Western Christianity. Even as early as the eleventh century, the Christ of Latin Christianity was first and foremost God made man, and although this attitude did not become fully apparent until the thirteenth century, this was because the West before the Crusades was not yet culturally free from a more or less thoroughly assimilated Byzantine influence. The success of the Crusades was largely due to a sincere passion for the land where Christ lived on earth; for the traces of Christ's passing on earth still left in the Holy Land, for the Holy Sepulcher, for Golgotha, and for Bethlehem. Nothing comparable occurred in the Christian countries of the East, although piety there was no less fervent and Christian inspiration no less authentic. Europe at that time was poor, greedy, and provincial, and it possessed a faith which corresponded to its ideals. For the landowning society of Europe, Christ was the Child born at Bethlehem. The restoration of his birthright and wreaking vengeance on his persecutors were matters of absolute necessity.

Godfrey of Bouillon, Raymond of Saint-Gilles, Robert of Flanders, and Robert of Normandy do not seem to have seriously believed that by conquering the Holy Land they would be hastening Christ's second coming and the Day of Judgment—although we cannot be sure about this. They were soldiers and too closely in touch with immediate reality to believe that their personal actions could have any such repercussions. After all, they were simply fighting the Turks. God was certainly on their side, but they relied principally on swords and lances and war machines. Their subsequent behavior proves that they did not regard this war as a priori different from any other war.

We have less evidence about the state of mind of lesser knights and professional soldiers who took the cross either out of piety or from loyalty to their overlords. But it seems probable that in general their hopes and objectives were very much the same as their leaders'. Feudal society at that time was monolithic; the average knight was a man who valued courage, strength, and the glory of combat above everything else.

It was quite different with the bulk of the common soldiers. Most professional soldiers were simply mercenaries, fighting to earn a living, but the majority of the Crusaders were gripped by the fever of the holy war. This was especially true of the ordinary volunteers who took the cross without being professional soldiers. The number of these volunteers in the barons' armies which made up the bulk of the troops was relatively small, but among the troops which set out in 1096 under the leadership of Peter the Hermit and his imitators they were legion. These were the so-called "People's Crusades." Tens of thousands (possibly over a hundred thousand people) in several bands set out from northern and central France and southern Germany. They met various fates, but none of them ever reached Jerusalem.

René Grousset has labeled this phenomenon—the mass exodus of civilians unprepared for war—the "demagogy of the Crusade." It is a harsh term and the blame falls naturally on those who initiated an enterprise so fated for disaster, and on Peter the Hermit in particular. I shall have more to say about this strange individual later on, but for all his faults, he was a remarkable man. He was unquestionably sincere and there seem to be no grounds for accusing him of demagogy.

The crowds which followed Peter the Hermit were full of the enthusiasm inspired by Pope Urban II's appeal, and it is hard to say whether Peter actually led them or whether he himself was carried away by the exaltation of his disciples. The chroniclers[1] tell us that the Pope's address at Clermont was known all over France by the next day, a fact which makes the invention of the telegraph sound somewhat superfluous. The great news of the declaration of a holy war to free Jerusalem was, we can only imagine, so much in tune with popular aspirations—in France and southern Germany, at least —that it was like a spark setting fire to a parched field. Were people really expecting it? Had vague rumors already preceded Urban's journey to France? Undoubtedly the ground had been prepared by propaganda for which the Pope could not have been responsible. Peter the Hermit himself, although we have no proof of this, must have undertaken a journey to Jerusalem: he was certainly aware of the difficulties of a pilgrimage and prized very highly the spiritual benefits accruing to visitors to the Holy Places. But ultimately, the idea of attacking the Turks, who were reputed in the West to be the finest soldiers in the world, with troops composed of civilians with no experience of battle, women, and children seems so bizarre that it is hard to blame it on Peter the Hermit or one of his associates.

The peasants set out in their thousands, taking their families with them. The volunteers included out-of-work laborers from the neighborhood of towns supported by the textile industry and hosts of impoverished peasants from regions which had been ravaged by the famine of the previous year, to say nothing of the beggars and vagabonds who took the cross to find food and company. Men of substance such as burghers or knights sold their goods and set out to help and protect "God's poor." These mass departures may be put down to famine and unemployment, which were an almost constant plague in those regions affected by Peter's preaching. People fled from their poverty in the hope of finding better things elsewhere, encouraged by the fact that the Pope, in his address, had alluded to the fertile lands and pleasant climate which would fall to the share of the Christians once the Turks were driven out. Also to be taken into account is the spirit of adventure which is always lively in young people, although contemporary evidence suggests the army of the poor was not made up principally of young, strong men. There were also a great many women, children, and old people.

It was not the hope of conquering the Turks by their own strength which drove this makeshift army to face the hardships of a long journey. The idea which set this voluntary band of vagabonds on the road was even more absurd: they really do seem to have believed that the last days were approaching and that God was summoning them to Jerusalem in order to be there to witness His ultimate triumph. God, if it pleased Him to do so, would annihilate the Saracens and grant His poor the victory He denied to the rich and strong, while those who fell in the campaign would instantly be admitted to paradise.

The people's army, made up of wretches who had nothing more to lose, fanatics resolved to risk everything, voluntary martyrs, marauders, repentant sinners and adventurers of all descriptions, and even of secular saints motivated by simple charity, marched under the banner of miracles, putting their whole trust in the God whose emblem they wore sewn on their garments. The heavenly and earthly Jerusalem were so thoroughly confused in their minds that they apparently understood the Pope's appeal to mean that paradise could be seized on earth by main force.

The inspiration of the movement was undoubtedly largely mystical, and it is hard to say how much it was based on a spirit of revolution and social anarchy. These strange revolutionaries, proudly casting their challenge to the rich barons, who were too slow in taking the road, were committing suicide with an unawareness which not even their simple natures can account for. Their leaders, Peter the Hermit, Walter Sans-Avoir, and Walter of Teck, were certainly neither simple nor ignorant, but they too may have hoped for some kind of providential intervention by God in favor of His poor. We know that Peter had urged his followers to make the journey, and it is clear that his real object was pilgrimage rather than war; and it was undoubtedly a venture grand and heroic enough in itself to earn those who engaged in it a pardon from God.

Just how far this crowd of pilgrims was haunted by hopes of an eschatological order is hard to say. Certainly they were animated by a very different spirit from that which drove the barons and knights to the Holy Land. Feelings of this kind recurred throughout the Middle Ages, and from the eleventh century onward in particular, whenever there was a great plague or any new or unexpected movement of opinion. They are not expressly mentioned by the chroniclers who describe Peter the Hermit's Crusade, but it should be added that these chroniclers were educated churchmen and somewhat unfamiliar with the beliefs and aspirations of the lower orders. The adventure was doomed to failure, but contemporaries were astonished by the

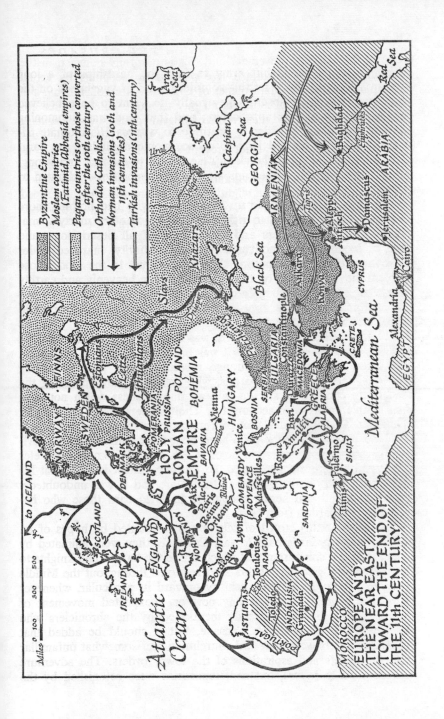

EUROPE AND
THE NEAR EAST
TOWARD THE END OF
THE 11th CENTURY

Legend:
- Byzantine Empire
- Moslem countries (Fatimid, Abbasid empires)
- Pagan countries or those converted after the 10th century
- Orthodox Catholics
- Norman invasions (10th and 11th centuries)
- Turkish invasions (11th century)

Miles 0 100 300 500

to ICELAND

Atlantic Ocean

IRELAND
SCOTLAND
ENGLAND
NORWAY
SWEDEN
FINNS
DENMARK
Scotians
Letts
Lithuanians
Slavs
Khazars
Ural
Volga
POLAND
POMERANIA
PRUSSIA
HOLY ROMAN EMPIRE
BOHEMIA
NORMANDY
Paris
Aix-la-Ch.
Reims
Orleans
Rhine
BAVARIA
Vienna
Danube
HUNGARY
POITOU
Bordeaux
Lyons
Toulouse
Provence
Marseilles
LOMBARDY
Venice
BOSNIA
SERBIA
CROATIA
Drava
Sava
Dnieper
Dniester
ARAGON
Ebro
SARDINIA
Rome
Amalfi
Bari
CALABRIA
SICILY
Palermo
Tunis
BULGARIA
Durazzo
MACEDONIA
GREECE
CRETE
Constantinople
Black Sea
GEORGIA
ARMENIA
Caspian Sea
Aral Sea
Ankara
Iconia
CYPRUS
Antioch
Aleppo
Damascus
Jerusalem
ARABIA
Baghdad
Euphrates
Tigris
Red Sea
Cairo
Alexandria
EGYPT
Mediterranean Sea
MOROCCO
ANDALUSIA
Granada
Toledo
Cordova
PORTUGAL
ASTURIAS
Bougie

scope of this popular movement and this is naturally reflected in the attention given it by historians. We possess no accounts by actual participants. Albert of Aix, Fulcher of Chartres, Anna Comnena, and most of all Raymond of Aguilers all pay tribute to the religious enthusiasm which animated the crowds of pilgrims, but they also remark on their poverty and lack of organization. We know that the sufferings of these first Crusaders did not prevent Peter the Hermit from continuing his role of preacher and inspiration to the masses. Later on, the poor formed a not inconsiderable element in the barons' armies.

The knighthood and to a slightly lesser extent the Church reaped the moral and material benefits of the Crusades, but it was the poor people who paid most dearly for the honor of serving God.

CHAPTER

II

The Latin West and Byzantium

The Crusades, the people's as well as the knights', were expeditions undertaken by Christians with the object of driving the Moslems out of the Holy Land. Yet the Moslems had occupied the Holy Places for over four hundred years and this was the first time that Christian nations had decided that it was an intolerable scandal.

One of the principal political reasons underlying the First Crusade was the rise in the East of a new power which, for almost a century, had been constantly moving westward, imposing its dominion on the old Abbasid Persian empire, taking possession of Syria and Mesopotamia, and advancing into Asia Minor, where it was pressing the Byzantine Empire increasingly hard. A new race of conquerors whose power was to endure for eight hundred years had made its entry into history. In the second half of the eleventh century, its progress became such a threat that it was beginning to cause anxiety even in the West. The existence of Arabic Islam had been an accepted fact for so long that it seemed legitimate. The newcomers, the Turks, were reputed to be as barbarous as they were invincible, and by disturbing a balance of power which had been established for centuries they were emerging as a real danger to Christianity.

Actually the Turks were still a long way from Rome, and were not yet a threat to Western Christendom except insofar as raids and warfare interfered with trade and added to the difficulties of pilgrimage. The Christians who were directly threatened by the Turks were those in the East, and of them, not so much the Christian subjects of the Arab empire as the inhabitants of Byzantine provinces conquered by the Turks during the eleventh century and the Byzantine Empire itself. On the eve of the Crusades, one Turkish prince of the Seljuk family had actually established his capital at Nicaea, almost overlooking the Bosporus. There was no immediate threat to the Holy Places, since the Turks were at least as favorable to Christians as the Arabs, but Constantinople seemed in imminent danger of a Turkish attack.

The Byzantine Empire was the largest and most ancient of all Christian states. Even in the eleventh century it was still a center of cultural and economic enlightenment, and its influence on the West was considerable. The capture of Constantinople by the Turks would at that time have been felt, not only in the East but throughout Europe as well, as the most frightful disaster which could befall Christendom. Urban II at the Council of Clermont had reminded his audience that it was the great Christian empire of the East which was in danger and that by coming to the aid of the Greek Emperor they would be defending the common heritage of all Christians. A short while before, this very Emperor had sent a message to the Pope, an appeal for aid, calling on him in the name of the common interests of Christianity.[1] To drive back the Turks and reconquer the Christian provinces of Asia Minor were the first objectives presented to the Crusaders. We know that Urban II had greater plans in mind, but in all these the enemy in view was the Turk. The moment chosen for the attack was all the better in that Turkish power seemed to be on the point of cracking as a result of internal rivalries in the heart of an empire which was still not altogether secure. In theory, the chief benefit from this pious expedition would go to Byzantium, Christianity's bastion against Islam.

For a long time the actual power of Byzantium had not matched up to its reputation and ambitions. It had once ruled the whole of the Near East, from Libya and Egypt to the Caucasus and the Persian frontiers, as well as the Balkans, Greece, the east and south of Italy, and Sicily. By the end of the eleventh century, the Empire was reduced to the Balkan peninsula in Europe, the islands of Cyprus and Crete in the Mediterranean, and Asia Minor. Even of Asia Minor, three-quarters had already been lost and only the coast was still in Byzantine hands. All the same, the Empire was by far the most powerful of the Christian nations.

At about the same time as the Turks were setting out to conquer the Eastern empires, another no less enterprising race of nomadic warriors was busy spreading terror, with equal vigor but somewhat less method, along the Mediterranean coasts of Europe. The Normans were a Scandinavian people, converted to Christianity, who had made themselves masters of northeastern France in the tenth century. In the early years of the eleventh century they had set out to conquer the Arab and Byzantine possessions in the Mediterranean. As a result, the Byzantine Empire found itself caught between two fires: forced to repel the Turks in the east and the Normans in the west. Both were formidable fighters, while the Empire, whose frontiers on land and sea were dangerously extended in relation to its total area, was constantly short of soldiers.

This threatened Christian empire was the Crusaders' chief natural ally. Constantinople became the rallying point for the volunteer armies, and the Emperor was to be their helper, guide, and arbitrator. Nevertheless Byzantium was destined to play a secondary if not an actually equivocal part in this great venture of Christian reconquest. It is important to realize from the outset what exactly was the relationship between the two Christian powers, because unconsciously at first and later consciously, the Crusades were a clash between the two Christian rivals quite as much as they were a war against Islam.

Byzantium

The sufferings of the Christian peoples of the East under Turkish oppression and the sufferings of Latin pilgrims were themes which Urban II and his followers exploited at length in their sermons. With the second of these their hearers were already familiar. As for the Eastern Christians, the crowds who listened to the Pope undoubtedly regarded them as brothers in the faith, but brothers whose existence had little reality for them. (The first time Peter the Hermit's followers came across Christians in Asia Minor, they mistook them for Turks and slaughtered them savagely.) The Christians of Asia Minor were completely unknown. As for the other Eastern Christians, the Byzantine Greeks, Europeans could not be unaware of their existence, but in general they had a very vague picture of them in which respect and admiration were beginning to give way to scornful contempt, a contempt due partly to feelings of inferiority and partly to disappointment at the Greeks' recent defeats in Turkey.

From 1054 onward, the schism between the Greek and Latin

Churches had been considered an accomplished fact, and the two Churches regarded one another as schismatics, though without altogether giving up hope of a reconciliation. The Roman Catholic West was becoming increasingly settled in the belief that its own tradition was the only authentic Christian one. This was more the result of ignorance and indifference than of deep doctrinal divergences. The same was true of the Greek Church.

But the fact remains that in the eyes of the Moslem East (which was at that time infinitely richer, more powerful, and more civilized than the Latin West) Byzantium—or "Rome," as it called itself and as the Moslems called it—was still in the eleventh century the greatest Christian power. (Admittedly there was the Norman peril to counterbalance the Greek threat to Islam in the Mediterranean.) This second Rome had, it is true, suffered plenty of reverses in the course of the century. It had been considerably weakened by internal revolutions and by constant attacks from warlike neighbors on its frontiers, but it was still a great empire. Its fleet controlled the eastern Mediterranean, and the threat of a great imperial army was still capable of intimidating the Seljuk rulers.

Alexius Comnenus's appeal to Urban II was not the sole cause of the Crusades, but it was one excuse for them. The Byzantine Emperor undoubtedly hoped that the Pope's intervention would enable him to obtain reinforcements for his army. He was short of soldiers and he had turned to Urban, pointing out the difficulties of his position with regard to the continuing Turkish advance into the Byzantine provinces of Anatolia, and had asked the sovereign pontiff to use his moral influence to encourage volunteers to enlist in the imperial armies. It was a reasonable request. There was no shortage of unemployed soldiers in the West and the Emperor was prepared to pay well.

As we have seen, the plan conceived and executed by Urban II had little to do with Alexius Comnenus's request. The last thing potential Crusaders were asked to do was to enter the service of the Greek Emperor. The question is: What part did the Pope expect the Emperor to play and how did his audience understand it?

We know that the success of his preaching of the holy war was so far beyond Urban's expectations that the Greeks decided in terror that they were faced with a popular migration rather than an army of volunteers. But in considering the probable consequences of his great project, the Pope thought that he was, to some extent at least, acting in accordance with the Emperor's wishes. He believed that by inaugurating a period of collaboration between the two Churches in the service of Christianity he was working toward the reunification of the Greek and Latin Churches. He might well have hoped that the *basileus,* grateful for the aid against the Turks and impressed by the spectacle of Western military power, would no longer haggle over officially recognizing the primacy of the Holy See.

Alexius was undoubtedly prepared to be accommodating, although, it is true, the prelates of the Greek Church were a great deal more intransigent than himself. He realized that the Pope was not an ally to be scorned, and he was in desperate need of allies. At the time of the call to the Crusade, Alexius Comnenus had occupied the imperial throne for fifteen years. By means of stratagems, diplomacy, and bold and dangerous financial measures, this able monarch, despite incessant wars abroad, had managed to save the "Roman" Empire from the disaster into which ten years of civil war had almost led it. But for nearly a hundred years Byzantium had been a prey to slow disintegration from within, and now, cut off from a large part of its possessions by Turkish and Norman inroads, it was finally compelled to face up to problems of an extent inconceivable to the Pope, well informed though he was.

In actual fact, in his concern to help the Emperor and so acquire a claim on his gratitude, the Pope failed to see that as far as Alexius Comnenus was concerned it was a case of "God protect me from my friends." Not only was the *basileus* being given ten times more than he asked for (which was irritating enough in itself), he was being given the precise opposite of what he wanted. He had been seeking reinforcements for his own army and he found his territory being invaded by an independent army which had not the faintest intention of placing itself at his disposal.

On their side, the volunteers who had responded to Urban II's appeal had every reason to believe that the Eastern Emperor was only waiting for their arrival in order to hurl himself at the Turks and drive them out of the Christian provinces they had overrun. At the very least they thought that if the Emperor lacked men or his men lacked courage, he could only rejoice to see other Christians taking it upon themselves to recover the Holy Places in his stead.

Unfortunately this Christian solidarity was a myth, or more accurately, it was the kind of lofty principle which exists only as a reproach to other people. Christians in Europe had been squabbling ceaselessly among themselves for centuries, kingdom against kingdom and one province against another, while the majority of petty lords were continually at war with their neighbors or even with their own families. The Church itself had been compelled to subordinate the interests of Christendom to more pressing considerations of policy. At the time of the Turkish occupation of Antioch, one of the oldest and greatest Christian cities in the Near East, the Pope found himself in alliance with the Normans, who, although Christians, were solely concerned with turning the troubles of Byzantium to their own profit by robbing the Empire of its western possessions. Thus, indirectly, the Pope had become the ally of the Turks against Byzantium. The Pope (Gregory VII) had his excuses: he needed the support of the Normans in the war he was waging against the German Emperor; he had been driven out of Rome by the imperial armies; wandering about Italy menaced by the German antipope, he could not afford to be nice in his choice of allies, and the interests of the Church of Rome came before a hypothetical loyalty to a Christian but schismatic empire. Alexius Comnenus, on his side, when threatened in his own capital by Robert Guiscard's Norman troops, did not hesitate to appeal to the Turks with a request for mercenaries for his army. In addition, through force of circumstances, he found himself the ally of the German Emperor against the Normans—and hence against the Pope.

Thus, on at least one point, Urban II was gravely mistaken: the Crusade he preached, far from clearing the way for a reconciliation between the Churches, could only give rise to numerous occasions for conflict, disagreement, and mutual irritation. As we shall see, this atmosphere of suspicion grew from the first moment the Crusaders came in contact with Byzantium. The Pope was a realist, but overgenerous, and he overestimated the generosity of the allies on whom he was forcing a co-operation for which neither side felt itself ready.

Alexius Comnenus

Alexius Comnenus, not altogether unreasonably, considered the fight against the Turks to be his own personal affair. He meant to conduct it in his own way and for that he needed only two things: peace on his western borders and a powerful army. On the Norman front, the danger had been provisionally removed. (To this end Alexius had established good relations with the Pope and sacrificed his alliance with the German Emperor.) But the Byzantine provinces in the Balkans were constantly being harried by the Petchenegs and for more than a hundred years there had been no possibility of a peaceful alliance with these fierce nomadic peoples, who were occasionally joined by other kindred tribes.

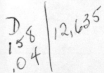

The eleventh century had seen the meteoric rise followed by a rapid disintegration of Turkish power in the Middle East. At the time of the summons to the Crusades, twenty-four years after the disaster of Manzikert had rung the knell of Greek domination in Asia Minor, the descendants of the great Malik Shah were still disputing his heritage. Byzantium was no longer faced by a single great Turkish power, but by several rival princes who were still only precariously established in a recently conquered country. By a policy of division, intrigue, and constantly changing alliances, Alexius Comnenus was hoping gradually to weaken his adversaries by inciting them against one another so that he would be able to deal with them more easily afterwards.

The *basileus* belonged to a family which came originally from Asia Minor. He regarded Anatolia, Cilicia, Cappadocia, and the province of Antioch as morally and geographically Greek, and was prepared to sacrifice a good deal in his eagerness to return these provinces to the Empire. Had the Crusading armies been willing to pledge themselves to serve him loyally and obediently, he would gladly have taken them all into his pay despite the heavy financial burden on his country. He would have been equally ready to exploit the idea of a holy war to further his own conquests, just as his predecessor Heraclius had done in the seventh century.

But Alexius saw no reason to fight the Turks simply because they were infidels (he had suffered too much from Christians to share any prejudice of this kind), and he was not particularly interested in liberating the Holy Sepulcher, which he regarded as a dangerous and uncertain enterprise, however praiseworthy. To Alexius, the appearance of a powerful Western army in Asia Minor was a two-edged weapon: such an army might possibly be able to keep the Turks in check, but it could also bring about a reconciliation between the warring brothers and force the Moslem princes to unite in the face of a common danger. Now the Emperor knew better than the Crusaders that the only way to beat the various Seljuk kingdoms which had been set up in the Middle East in the previous hundred years or so was to tackle them individually, one at a time, constantly attacking one while maintaining friendly relations with the others.

One important fact which must not be lost sight of is that the lands into which the Crusading armies were advancing had not been in Turkish hands for very long and the bulk of the population was composed of Greek or Armenian Christians. Relations between the Armenians and Byzantium were strained, but this was very far from being the case with the populations of Anatolia and Cappadocia, while even in Cilicia and at Antioch, Orthodox Greeks were in the majority. Since he regarded them as his own subjects, the Emperor was not anxious to expose them to the tender mercies of a foreign army.

Nevertheless, the oath of allegiance he demanded seemed to the leaders of the Crusade to be merely a piece of insufferably humiliating pretentiousness. Why should this have been so?

Very early on in his *Historia,* William of Tyre informs us that at the time of the First Crusade the throne of Constantinople was occupied by a "false and disloyal Greek" (*vir subdolus*) named Alexius Comnenus. The Archbishop of Tyre was writing eighty years afterward and viewed matters in the light of later events, but in fact "Byzantine perfidy" was a political byword of the time, not only in the twelfth but already at the end of the eleventh century. The chroniclers from whom William of Tyre took his information were eyewitnesses of the First Crusade, and they are almost unanimous in their execration of the Greeks and their condemnation of Alexius Comnenus's behavior.

On Alexius' withdrawal from the siege of Antioch, William of Tyre has this curious comment to make: "Even so this thing [the retreat] was the work of God: for if this emperor, coming with his great army of fresh troops, had raised the siege and beaten the Turks, Our Lord would not have been so well honored."[2] In fact this expresses the feelings of most Western Christians. Christians though they were, the Greeks were apparently not thought worthy to take part in the task of liberating the Holy Places (or even in that of liberating of their own territories): God had rejected their aid because He wished to conquer by the forces of Latin Christianity alone! Never before had the schism dividing the two Churches been proclaimed with such tranquil pride.

The Crusaders marched across Byzantine territory, installed themselves on the outskirts of the imperial capital, and demanded help to go and make war in provinces which, until they were lost only twenty years before, had belonged to Byzantium for centuries. At the same time they proclaimed an attitude of total independence with regard to the Greeks, apparently forgetting that the whole campaign concerned Byzantium at least as much as it did themselves. However, if they objected—not entirely unjustifiably—to entering the Emperor's service, the Emperor was certainly in no mood to serve them, and it was for this that the Crusaders, in their enthusiasm for the cause of Jerusalem, could never forgive him.

It is true that Byzantium had done something to deserve the scorn poured on her by her Western allies. She had shown herself incapable of holding on to her provinces in Asia Minor, and the defeat of Romanus Diogenes at Manzikert in 1071 had revealed how powerless were the imperial armies in the face of a Turkish invasion. In the years that followed this battle—one of the most terrible disasters in the whole history of Byzantium—a succession of rebellious generals attempted to seize power by appealing to the Turks for aid against their own countrymen, trading or pledging whole cities and provinces in return for military help, and so irreparably consolidating Turkish dominion over Asia Minor. Things like this were calculated to arouse indignation in the West. (Although it should not be forgotten that the Norman mercenary Roussel of Bailleul, a Christian and a Catholic, had played a somewhat equivocal part in the disaster of Manzikert and had done his utmost to weaken Byzantium by trying to carve out a realm for himself in Anatolia.) The political errors committed by Byzantium and the evident blindness of the court at Constantinople in the face of the Turkish menace after 1071 encouraged the West in the belief that the Greeks were a degenerate people, lacking either courage or vigor. Alexius Comnenus, in all fairness, did not exactly deserve this stigma. He had not waited for the Crusaders before embarking on the reconquest of the territories which had been overrun by the Turks. In 1092 he had retaken Cyzicus and successfully recovered Phocaea, Clazomenae, and the islands of Lesbos, Chios, and Rhodes. By extremely clever political maneuvering, he was setting his adversaries at one another's throats and so preparing the ground for an offensive of his own, and he would undoubtedly have done more if he had not been so hard pressed by the Normans and the Petchenegs in the west.

Alexius was an army general who had become emperor through a series of palace intrigues, thanks to the popularity he enjoyed among the troops. By nature he was a diplomat rather than a man of action, but he was also a professional soldier, accustomed from his earliest youth to campaigns against the Turks, and had spent half his life in camps and battlefields. He may not have been as warlike as the Crusaders could have wished, but neither could they accuse him of cowardice.

Twenty years later, when the Emperor was old and dying, and had to fight to maintain the rights of his son John against the intrigues of his wife and daughter, he gave secret orders for John to go and receive the oath of allegiance from the army. Seeing herself outwitted, the Empress Irene flung these bitter words in the dying man's face when he was already beyond speech: "All your life you have been able to do nothing but plot and you will not give it up, even on your deathbed!" (Though the plot in question was a perfectly legitimate one, designed to protect the rights of the natural heir to the Empire.) Alexius was a man of many wiles; these could be kind as well as cruel, innocent as well as perfidious. He was a Greek, a worthy successor to Ulysses, and he considered cunning a noble weapon. The Crusaders were sufficiently perceptive to discern this trait in his character, but they were mistaken in supposing that because he was so crafty his designs on them were necessarily sinister. It is certainly true that the Emperor was not inclined to run any great risks for their sake, and that he was hoping to use them to further his own interests and policies, but there is nothing in his behavior to suggest that he was actually double-crossing them.

The Western barons, brought up in the feudal tradition to believe in at least a nominal respect for a sworn oath, in dynastic succession, and in the mutual obligations of vassal and suzerain, found it irritating to be treated with courteous condescension by a man who was after all nothing more than a rebel general and "usurper" who, fifteen years earlier, had taken the capital by storm and ousted Nicephorus Boteniates from the throne with the help of the very troops which the Emperor had placed under his command. This was undeniably true, just as it was also true that to gain his ends Alexius had secretly won the favors of the Empress; but as a nephew of one of the Emperor's predecessors, Alexius believed that he possessed as good a claim to the throne as Boteniates, another army officer who had risen to power by force of arms. The Empress, however, had formerly been the wife of the previous Emperor, Michael, who had been dethroned by Boteniates. She had been forcibly married to the man who had overthrown her husband. The reason she did not become empress for the third time was that after his coup, Alexius needed the support of the Ducas family, of which his young wife Irene, who was also related to the former Emperor, was a member. The rivalries among the great Greek families, the clan feuds, alliances made and broken by the fluctuations of palace intrigue, and revolutions in which the Church took a hand by supporting first one and then another candidate to the throne: all this was in good Byzantine tradition and the majesty of the purple covered all. To people from the West it merely seemed like further proof of corruption and decadence.

The Emperor was smiling and affable, but always majestic and surrounded by a solemn splendor which the Latins thought excessive. To them it seemed as if he were constantly trying to make them feel his superiority, and although they may have been dazzled by Byzantine luxury, they were determined not to be taken in by it. No one should take them for savages, to be disarmed by an insolent display of gold and precious stones. Neither Alexius' personal charm nor the lavish presents which the Emperor distributed generously among his new allies succeeded in winning the Crusaders over to the Byzantine cause.

The "Barbarians"

The only Byzantine historian to have left even a cursory account of the Crusaders' stay in Constantinople is Alexius' daughter, Anna Comnena. An event of some magnitude when viewed from a distance of nine hundred years, it did not strike Greek contemporaries as worthy of special attention. It was a phenomenon which might well have astonished them had they not been too busy with their own wars and their own political problems to recognize its historical significance, and at the time it caused them no small amount of trouble and anxiety, although admittedly this was nothing new.

Anna Comnena herself, generally a mine of information and circumstantial detail, passes over this episode in her father's story in a brief and summary fashion which proves how little interest her society felt in the "barbarians," or "Celts" as she calls them. They swarmed through the Empire and Constantinople itself like a cloud of locusts, doing some damage, though the *basileus* skillfully kept this to a minimum, and then passed on toward their real objective: the conquest of the Holy Places. The only Crusader in whom Anna shows any real interest is the Norman Bohemond, and in her eyes he was not a Crusader; the man who appears in the *Alexiad* is the stubborn and intractable enemy of the Greek Empire.

Anna's explanation of the origin of the Crusades is highly vague and imaginative, and presented like a folk tale, in a style which seems astonishing from the pen of a serious historian. One day, she says, a certain monk whose name was Peter (evidently Peter the Hermit) decided to travel to Jerusalem. Put off by the dangers and difficulties of the journey, and realizing that it was less perilous to travel in a large company under the protection of armed men, he returned to his own country and went about preaching sermons to his compatriots, urging them to set out for Jerusalem. (Anna Comnena was not alone in crediting Peter the Hermit with initiating the movement, but she appears completely oblivious of the Pope's part in the affair.) This

Peter, simply because he was afraid to travel alone, had been so successful in exploiting the piety and credulity of the "Celts" and other Frenchmen, who were notoriously a naive and superstitious race (the Byzantine princess had a poor opinion of the intellectual level of the Latin peoples), and so successfully worked on their spirits that huge crowds assembled to follow him to Jerusalem. A great horde of people, priests, soldiers, and civilians, with women and children and old men and a whole host of pilgrims, all set out for Constantinople.

Anna was thirteen years old in 1096 and she saw Peter the Hermit, Godfrey of Bouillon, Bohemond, the Count of Toulouse, the Count of Flanders, and Hugh of Vermandois with their armies pass by in successive waves. Then, four years later, came the troops from Lombardy, Aquitaine, Poitiers, Germany, and elsewhere. Her memory of them is a little confused; the events are so distant and the people so uninteresting to her. "With the best will in the world," she says, "I had rather not give the names of their leaders. The words will not come to me, partly because I am incapable of pronouncing these barbarous sounds, and partly because I shrink from their numbers. What is the good of attempting to rehearse the names of so many people when the mere sight of them was unspeakably boring to people at the time?"[3]

Anna is not an impartial witness, and as an old woman she gives us a revealing glimpse of remembered girlhood resentments. She speaks more than once of the tiresome length of those official visits when the Franks came to unfold their plans to the *basileus*. It may seem odd to us to realize, through the legendary halo with which time has invested these events, that the mere sight of the Crusader heroes could strike anyone as boring. Godfrey of Bouillon, Robert of Flanders, and the Count of Toulouse would certainly have been surprised to learn what the young Greek princess thought of them.

Anna Comnena informs us that this man Peter succeeded in arousing a great popular movement in his own country and in Germany, resulting in a mass onslaught on Jerusalem. With a characteristic tendency to exaggerate, the princess describes the arrival of countless hosts in exactly the same terms as she might have described any large-scale migration of a nomadic people. This in itself is an indication that the appearance of Peter the Hermit's bands made a vivid impression on the imagination of contemporaries, and the thing that struck them particularly was the poverty of the crowd of pilgrims and the presence of large numbers of women and children among them. Actually, by the time this first Crusade, made up of poor people, reached Constantinople, it numbered no more than twenty to thirty thousand persons—a figure which was only a thirtieth of the total population of the city.

These first "Crusaders" were followed, five months later, and all through the spring of 1097, by other troops of armed men and civilians. There were so many of them—even Bohemond's, the smallest, numbered several thousand men—that in the long run the arrival of these successive waves of Latin pilgrims must have seemed like some monstrous and unprecedented invasion.

Anna, who was a rationalist and something of a cynic, simply could not believe that the Latin barons were really motivated solely by the desire to free the Holy Sepulcher from Moslem domination. She observes that many of the poor pilgrims were animated by a sincere piety, and this does her credit because some of these poor people behaved little better than brigands in the suburbs of Constantinople. However, the Greeks generally speaking regarded them indulgently, making due allowance for human weakness and the inevitable disorders resulting from an undertaking of this kind. The piety of Peter the Hermit's followers was so evident and their passion for the Holy Places so touching that people forgave them their excesses and their lack of common sense. Alexius graciously consented to grant Peter a personal interview, treated him courteously, and did his best to help "God's poor" in their undertaking. To Anna they were merely simple, pious souls being exploited by ambitious adventurers whose objectives had nothing to do with the service of God. This was also her verdict on the armies of the Crusader princes: the common soldiers and poor people with the army, she said, were sincere. As for the others . . .

These others included Godfrey of Bouillon, Duke of Lower Lorraine, and his brother Baldwin, Hugh of Vermandois, brother to the King of France, Robert, Count of Flanders, Robert, Duke of Normandy, and lastly two outstanding personalities, Raymond of Saint-Gilles, Count of Toulouse, and Bohemond of Taranto. Anna states categorically that not one of these barons (with the exception of the Count of Toulouse) was either pious or sincere; they thought of nothing but enriching themselves at the expense of the *Roman* Empire and possibly even of seizing Constantinople itself.

(It must be admitted that the initial meetings between Alexius Comnenus and Godfrey of Bouillon do much to explain her opinion, however mistaken it may have been. The two men were immediately at loggerheads. Alexius Comnenus may have been wrong in brusquely demanding an oath of homage from the Duke of Lower Lorraine, who was already the German Emperor's vassal. But in the end, for both men, what was involved was a matter of principle and prestige. Alexius, as the victor, showed a readiness to forgive which is less a proof of his own generosity than of the poor esteem in which he held the Latin barons. Certainly Godfrey, for his part, never forgave.)

As far as the Greeks were concerned, the leaders of the Crusade were dangerous men, motivated solely by greed and ambition. Their piety could hardly be taken seriously when Duke Godfrey had not scrupled to lead his troops in an attack on Constantinople on Holy Thursday, of all days, when all the city's inhabitants, soldiers included, were at their prayers and had no reason to expect such treachery on the part of fellow Christians. (It was true that Alexius had chosen that particular day to cut off the supplies of food to the Crusaders, but although the Emperor may have been prepared for some retort to his unchristian behavior, neither he nor any of his subjects had ever envisaged the possibility of taking up arms on a Holy Thursday.) Appalled by such sacrilege, the Greeks could no longer regard their guests as anything but savages, creatures of primitive sensibilities whose reactions were liable to be as crude as they were unpredictable.

Notwithstanding, once the Duke of Lower Lorraine had been reduced to accepting his terms and swearing the oath which for three months he had obstinately refused, the Emperor loaded his new vassal with gifts and handed out gold and silver, rich garments and costly fabrics, horses and mules with a generosity that to the proud Godfrey was almost humiliating. Godfrey needed the money and he accepted the presents and the payments made to his army, but without enthusiasm or gratitude—as later events were to prove. Neither Alexius nor his advisers nor—many years later—Anna Comnena could ever understand why the foreigners were so disloyal and why they felt so little sympathy for the *Romans* when the Emperor had been so good to them and (apart from a few small misunderstandings for which their own stubbornness was entirely responsible) so polite. Yet the answer is there, in the writings of Anna Comnena herself. It is possible, at a pinch, to feel sympathy for one's enemies, but not for people who are "unspeakably bored" at the mere sight of one.

These people, Anna complains, no doubt echoing the opinions expressed by her father and his entourage, have their eyes always on the main chance. Their greed is incredible. They ask for and accept money and then refuse to perform the task for which they have been paid. You can heap favors on them only to find their arrogance and ingratitude redoubled. They break their oaths with shameful ease; they are frivolous, inconsistent, superstitious, and unreliable. This is the kind of thing a European today might say about some "underdeveloped" people, and in comparison with Byzantium this, economically at least, is exactly what the Franks were. But even setting aside grudges of a more general nature, the exotic characters of the Crusading leaders had not the honor to awaken any curiosity in the lively and intelligent daughter of the imperial purple. Anna, usually so observant and capable of drawing the most vivid and psychologically fascinating portraits of her compatriots, does not pause to wonder about the personalities of men like Godfrey or Baldwin or Robert of Flanders, and her praise of the Count of Toulouse is limited to a few conventional lines. (She tells us, among other things, that the *basileus* valued Isangeles—Saint-Gilles —for "the superiority of his mind, the uprightness of his heart, and the purity of his life" and also for his "care for truth." This eulogy is clearly dictated by political considerations, since Raymond was later to become an ally of Byzantium.)

Hugh of Vermandois provided the princess with an excuse for exercising her satirical wit. As brother to the ruler of a small, poor, and backward country (France) a very long way away, he thought himself such a grand personage that he took the trouble to send a letter to Constantinople announcing his arrival and asking the *basileus* to make ready to welcome him with the honor due to his rank! Unlikely as it seems, Anna quotes him as saying, "I am the *basileus* of the *basileis* . . ." but perhaps she is embroidering a little for the pleasure of having some fun at the barbarians' expense.

Godfrey, especially, appears to have struck the court of Constantinople with his conceited behavior: "The man was very rich and very proud of his nobility . . ." This is not saying a great deal, but it is something all the same. The Greeks could afford to look down on the barbarian lords, but the pride of this Walloon prince, descended from Charlemagne, must have impressed them and they were willing to grant him a kind of crude majesty. Beyond this, our historian has very little comment to make about the personalities of the various Frankish leaders. She does mention, in passing, one rather comic incident when a knight seated himself on the imperial throne, an incident which gives us a revealing glimpse of the character of Baldwin of Boulogne, although Anna herself does not appear to attach much importance to it.

Admittedly, the daughter of Alexius Comnenus devotes more than one page, indeed more than one chapter, to Bohemond, and goes so far as to paint a picture of his physical appearance which is both detailed and flattering. Perhaps because in the eyes of the young princess the Norman's powerful personality put the features of all the other "Celts" in the shade, or simply because Bohemond interested her by reason of the part he played in the history of Byzantium, Anna is never tired of dwelling on the man's intelligence, cunning, perfidy, cruelty, and superhuman energy. He was one of the greatest leaders of the Crusades, although he hardly deserves to be called a Crusader at all.

The Greco-Latin Alliance

When the "Celts" arrived before Constantinople and encamped on the outskirts of the city, the *basileus* busied himself with inexhaustible patience in securing food for their armies, smoothing over any disturbance which might be provoked by the presence of so many foreign soldiers in the vicinity, and organizing the transport of the bulk of the troops, horses, and cattle by boat across the Bosporus together with all their equipment. While this lengthy emigration of men-at-arms and pilgrims was being completed, Alexius entertained the leaders in his own palaces, gave banquets in their honor, and conferred with them on the subject of plans for a future campaign against the Turks.

Godfrey of Bouillon reached Constantinople at the end of December 1096, and by May 1097 the Crusading army was complete. It was made up of four great armies: the men of Lorraine under Godfrey of Bouillon; the Normans from Italy under Bohemond; the Provençal contingent under Raymond of Saint-Gilles and the papal legate Adhemar of Monteil; and the French and the vassals of the King of France under the Duke of Normandy and the Counts of Flanders and Blois. Godfrey arrived three months in advance of the others. Bohemond did not reach Constantinople until after Easter (April 5), Raymond of Saint-Gilles toward the end of April, and the French in early May.

It was an impressive army—the greatest assembly of Western military forces which had ever been seen—and the Greeks, who were continually short of soldiers, had every reason to regard it with apprehension. It took all Alexius Comnenus's powers of diplomacy and every available means of intimidation to prevent these armies from joining forces under the walls of Constantinople itself. The army of Lorraine crossed the Bosporus on the very day that Bohemond arrived with his Normans. In the end, however, reasonably good relations were established once more. The Crusader chiefs were loaded with gifts, treated as friends and "sons," and allowed to enter and admire the beauties of the capital and venerate the relics kept in the sanctuaries of the great city. The Emperor's fears of a threat to Byzantium seemed to have been removed, and instead of virtual enemies, Alexius Comnenus now had better than allies; he had vassals, and even mercenaries. An impressive, well-equipped army was ready to set out to reconquer Asia Minor on behalf of the Empire. Matters had turned out very well for the Emperor, after all. It was true he was digging recklessly into his coffers, and the whole affair had proved very expensive, but if at the price he could drive the Turks out of Anatolia he would be in no position to regret the sacrifices he had made.

From the moment the Emperor accepted their homage, he gave the Crusaders no cause for complaint. He treated them so generously that the Count of Blois—one of the last to arrive—wrote enthusiastically to his wife: "Truly, I tell you, there is no other such man living under heaven today!" As we shall see, Stephen of Blois was an impressionable character, easy to please but also prone to fits of depression, but even so his feelings must have been shared by a great many barons. Not for nothing does Anna Comnena make such a point of stressing the greed with which the Latin barbarians grabbed at all the treasures offered them: their wonder and delight must have been only too obvious. Among the principal leaders only Raymond of Saint-Gilles, a more mature and cultivated man than his companions, seems to have been genuinely impressed by the Emperor's personality, and this sympathy was apparently mutual. We know that despite the Count's intransigent attitude (he was the only one not to swear fealty to the Emperor), the two men had long talks in private, each trying to warn the other against putting any trust in Bohemond—and each preaching to the converted. They agreed on other subjects too, for Anna assures us that her father held the old Count's lofty character in the highest esteem.

All was now agreement and both sides could consider themselves satisfied. Alexius Comnenus, anxious not to lose such an excellent opportunity of crushing the Turkish power, was preparing to set out on the campaign in person, and was equipping his army, half of which was to go with the Crusaders under the command of the Greek general Taticius, while the other half harassed the Turks in the coastal provinces. Thus Urban's vow was accomplished, and

Greeks and Latins took the cross together and were joined in a common offensive against Islam.

This was how it looked. The facts were somewhat different: the Greeks were trying to use the Latins in order to reconquer their own lost provinces, while the Latins thought the Greeks had a duty to help them in the much more important task of recovering the Holy Places. In an otherwise perfectly sound alliance there was no real confidence because each of the partners was convinced that the other was fundamentally untrustworthy. William of Tyre, basing his assertion on contemporary writings, later accused Alexius of plotting to betray the Crusaders at the very moment when he was distributing to them lavish amounts of his own gold and precious stones and war horses. As for the "Celts," their contempt for a sworn oath was notorious. According to his daughter, the *basileus* had no illusions about these people because he was too well acquainted with the nature of their race.

As far as the Crusaders were concerned, the Greeks were a soft, effeminate, and useless people, devoted to luxury and—the ultimate sin—bad soldiers. The Greeks certainly did not find the Latins guilty of these faults, but they would have been very surprised to realize that the Greeks considered them weathercocks, weaklings, and mischievous and treacherous people. It seems odd to us today to discover that the worst fault the formidable Anna Comnena can blame on the Crusaders, the defect which seems to have irritated, astonished, and appalled her beyond all others, was their excessive garrulity. According to her, the Crusaders were a race of the most impossible windbags, ready to launch into endless and irrelevant digressions at the smallest excuse, without even the common decency of glancing at the hourglass to check the flow of their eloquence, and literally boring their audiences to death with their pointless verbosity and their passion for futile argument. (She does not seem to have been exaggerating in her description of one particular session at which the Emperor, who was forced to remain standing to greet his Latin guests, contracted a serious malady in his feet as a result of the protracted audiences which went on until well into the night, while his exhausted courtiers, almost fainting with weariness, leaned on the walls and took turns to leave the audience chamber and rest in the next room.)

The Latin Crusaders were clearly not under the impression that they were talking nonsense, and it is even possible they might have been able to teach the Greeks a thing or two had the latter only taken the trouble to listen.

Byzantium and Byzantinism

As we have seen, Greeks and Latins were both equally ready with their accusations of treachery, and with about the same amount of justification on either side, but since the writing of history after the fall of Byzantium was largely in Latin hands, it is the Greeks who have gone down to posterity as forever perfidious, although with the passing of time they too have found some notable defenders. Moreover, it is a curious fact that on one level, and especially where Byzantium is concerned, we have really progressed very little since 1097. People in the twentieth century may not share the Crusaders' enthusiasm and religious exaltation, but they have inherited their prejudices. If the word "Byzantine" has become in some contexts a term of abuse, this may be because of a misunderstanding between Godfrey of Bouillon and Alexius Comnenus, or—likelier still—because Bohemond had dreams of conquering Constantinople. Whatever the real faults of Byzantium, she was judged and ultimately condemned by the West on a basis of imaginary emotional grievances.

The Greeks, so intolerant of the endless speeches made by these fanatical advocates of the holy war, probably never understood what all this talk was about. It certainly never occurred to them that it was these people's way of life which would triumph in the end.

The Crusaders accused the Greeks of being "soft," of disliking war as a profession. Reading Anna Comnena and other Greek historians of the period, one can scarcely believe this. Byzantium had plenty of warmongers, every bit as fierce and hotheaded as Baldwin or Bohemond. True, they were fewer than in the West, and many Greek nobles preferred the delights of literature or theological argument, or simply of social life, to those of battle. The Western nobles, for whom war was the only profession, were so little able to understand this that they heartily despised these "effeminate" nobles. They thought that if these people did not make war, it must be for the obvious reason that they were cowards. (It could be said that, at a time when their country badly needed soldiers, these patricians might have done better to devote themselves to the profession of arms, as their government was continually urging them to do, but theirs was not a society which considered an interest in things other than war in the least shameful, and this is not in itself a sign of degeneracy.)

Byzantium, always at war and under constant threat of attack, was suffering from a shortage of native Greek soldiers, largely because of the shortsighted policies of Basil II's successors, who had seen fit to cut down the honors and privileges enjoyed by the army for fear of a military *coup d'état*. This was an administrative measure rather than a failure in the Greek nobility and people, but the fact remained that by the eleventh century the powerful Byzantine army was largely made up of foreign mercenaries and even some of its commanders were of foreign origin. Some of the mercenaries, the Turks, Petchenegs, and Normans, were a mixed blessing to the Empire, since they were recruited from the very peoples with whom the Greeks were at war.

It is not surprising that the Crusaders were shocked at this state of affairs. The Latin princes also made use of mercenaries, but the better part of their armies was made up of vassals who had sworn an oath to serve them loyally, and although this system had its own drawbacks, at least no one could accuse the French nobility of shirking a fight.

This exclusive, even excessive, exaltation of physical valor was something the Byzantines could never understand. The people of Western Europe believed implicitly that a man's worth was, first and foremost, measured by his prowess in battle. To the Greeks, courage was certainly an estimable virtue, but it was one which could be readily found in any mercenary—they were too much accustomed to purchasing heroism for money. The *basileus* and the principal Greek nobles were expected to be good soldiers, but they would not have been pleased to be thought no more than that: their position required that they should also be theologians, men of letters, and even poets, lawyers, and musicians, as well as being familiar with all the refinements of court etiquette and able to compete with bishops in philosophical debate. The ideal of the seventeenth-century "worthy" would have seemed to them crude and superficial. The Greeks were the heirs of the oldest European civilization and they did not do things by halves. (This may have been no more than an ideal, and Byzantine high society was not entirely made up of men capable of assimilating such a vast culture, but it is still true to say that it was a genuinely cultivated society in the modern sense of the word.)

In the West, however, people could not yet begin to conceive the idea of such a standard of education. Even that of the churchmen seemed limited and fragmentary by comparison, while the great nobles were practically illiterate. The result was the accusation of

"Byzantinism" leveled at the Greeks, since people always tend to despise values they do not understand. In the same way, the Latins could not help looking like barbarians in the eyes of the Greeks.

In Byzantium not only the aristocracy but the people too had reached a cultural level to be met with at that time only in the great Moslem cities such as Baghdad or Cairo. The citizens of Constantinople were famous for their love of theological argument. Masons, water carriers, and market traders argued about matters of dogma with all the enthusiasm their present-day equivalents would bring to a political discussion, and they must have possessed a well-developed critical faculty and a good deal of intellectual curiosity. Intellectual curiosity may be a disintegrating factor, but at the same time it is also an undoubted asset. It was possible for a European prelate—even one sufficiently eminent to be sent as an envoy to Constantinople for discussions on various doctrinal differences*—to be unaware that the word *filioque* was a later addition which did not appear in the Nicene Creed. This may have shocked the Greeks, but the Latins do not appear to have been particularly disturbed about it; and yet Cardinal Humbert's ignorance was one of the causes of the official split between the two Churches.

The difference in language was also a considerable obstacle to mutual understanding between the two civilizations. The Crusaders were completely indifferent to the intellectual merits of the Greeks. What struck them more than anything else was the fact that the Greeks hardly ever fought and allowed strangers to do their fighting for them. The Greeks were rich, or were supposed to be, and there was a strong element of envy in the hostility they aroused. They were able to purchase human blood and human lives with their money, and in return demanded the kind of loyalty which a man owed only to his country and his natural lords. The Greeks thought that anything could be bought, while the Crusaders had just given striking proof of their contempt for money by selling their possessions and setting out from their own lands for the honor of serving God. They could not forgive Alexius Comnenus for treating the Crusade like a business deal.

The Greeks did not despise courage or the profession of arms. Their system of fortifications, their battle fleet, their artillery and war machines were all ahead of their time. The Empire was constantly at war, on land and sea. In the eleventh century these wars

* Cardinal Humbert of Silva Candida, head of the papal delegation to Constantinople in 1054, accused the Greeks of *removing* the *filioque* from the Nicene Creed.

were chiefly defensive and frequently turned out badly. Although the writings of historians of the period do not exactly throb with martial feeling, they do reveal a deep and passionate interest in anything concerned with war. Even a woman like Anna Comnena becomes for the moment an engineer or a general as she describes in detail the working of a crossbow, the disposition of a fortress, or the conduct of a naval engagement, and she can describe a general or a siege engine with exactly the same degree of clinical detachment. There is no doubt that, in addition to their other talents, the Greeks were good soldiers. They had a long experience of war to draw on and they were still a vigorous people with a capacity for aggression of which Alexius' son, John Comnenus, was to give living proof.

What they did lack was what might be called a sense of the poetry of war. They might be glad to win a battle, but they greatly preferred to avoid one by adroit negotiations. In their eyes diplomatic victory was a real victory, and they could regard a peace purchased with money as honorable and even glorious, because it was more pleasing to God. Even in our own time the war myth is still powerful enough to make successes gained by bloodshed seem somehow more impressive, and in 1097 the Crusaders were inflamed with the desire to spill their own blood as well as that of the Turks. However, when we remember the fearful casualties suffered by the foot soldiers and common people on these Crusades, while their leaders were nearly always ransomed and escaped scot free from the fiercest battles, then the relative "cowardice" of the Greek generals seems to have its noble side.

Not that there is any reason to think the Greeks possessed a greater share of human kindness than the Latin barbarians. In provinces where the population was largely Christian but non-Greek, they made themselves hated by their severity, and the citizens of Constantinople were capable of a cruelty which horrified Western observers, while the rapaciousness of the nobles and officials of the Empire made the condition of peasants and small farmers worse than it was in Europe. There were a number of customs of Eastern origin, including the current practice of voluntary or enforced castration, at which the Latins were rightly shocked, and the openly despotic Byzantine system of government might well strike a feudal people as barbaric. But there was in the old imperial civilization, still powerful even in its decline, a certain humanitarian tradition of which no trace was to be found in the West.

Theoretically at least, and even this is saying a good deal, the Byzantines had a genuine respect for human life. Putting out a man's eyes is admittedly a horrible punishment, and the victim sometimes died as a result, but we must not forget that in Byzantium it had practically replaced the death penalty altogether.* In the tenth century, the Greeks under Basil II were virtually guilty of racial murder in exterminating the Bulgarians, but although the Emperor Basil may have been proud to be called "the Bulgar-slayer" (Bulgaroctonus) none of his eleventh-century successors ever distinguished themselves by exploits of this kind, and it is hard to imagine a man like Alexius Comnenus coveting such a bloodthirsty title.

There is one curious anecdote, set down in some detail by Anna Comnena, which is highly illustrative both of the character of Alexius himself and of a certain aspect of Byzantine morality. In 1074 Alexius Comnenus, as a young general fighting the Turks in Anatolia, also found himself confronting the rebellious Norman mercenary, Roussel of Bailleul. Roussel, a remarkably enterprising commander, had seized control of a number of Greek fortresses and captured Alexius' elder brother, Isaac Comnenus, and the general John Ducas. In terror the Emperor Michael VII had appealed to the Turks for help and by clever negotiation with the Turkish prince Tutush, Alexius Comnenus finally succeeded in laying hands on the redoubtable Norman in exchange for the promise of a huge sum of money which he did not even possess. Alexius had his prisoner shut up in the castle of Amasea. The inhabitants sympathized with Roussel, and the Greeks, who had only a very small force at their disposal, had reason to fear that the people would seize their captive from them. Alexius therefore resorted to a trick, one of the first of those for which he was to become famous. It was an extravagant piece of deception. He summoned the executioner and with the people looking on, made a pretense of putting out Roussel's eyes. The prisoner, who had been forewarned, played his part to perfection, and since a blinded man was a finished man, all ideas of a rising in his favor were at an end. However, a cousin of Alexius, whose name was Dokeianos, believing like everyone else that the Norman had been well and truly blinded, went to his cousin and reproached him bitterly, saying that he had no right to treat "such a hero" so cruelly, even though this heroism had chiefly been displayed at Greek

* Blinding was a penalty frequently inflicted on deposed emperors and in law was the equivalent of death. Romanus Diogenes is known to have died as a result. In medieval Russia, on the other hand, a state in many ways resembling Byzantium, there is a case of a Muscovite prince, Basil II, being returned to power after having his eyes put out, and actually proving himself an extremely able ruler.

expense. The young general smilingly led his cousin to the prisoner's tent, savoring in advance the pleasant surprise in store for Dokeianos. There he showed him Roussel, whose eyes were intact and "as bright as stars," and the two cousins rejoiced together. Their joy can hardly be said to be interested, since it is unlikely that the Greek government considered making any further use of the Norman's somewhat troublesome services. Nevertheless Anna assures us that the Emperor Michael and all his court rejoiced greatly when they learned that Roussel had not in fact lost his eyes.

The deep, irreconcilable difference between the traditions of Rome and Byzantium lay in the attitude of both to *murder,* or to war. This was something which emerged from the Crusades and it was more than a detail, more than just a matter of emphasis. Both were Christian, and both made war as a matter of course, celebrated their triumphs, prayed to God to grant them victory, and charged into battle carrying crosses and banners bearing the images of the saints. But for the Greeks no war, however "holy," could ever be anything but a sin, something concerning men alone. It was a venial and even a necessary sin, but a sin all the same, and sufficiently serious for a soldier of any kind, however just the war in which he was fighting, to be excluded from participating in the sacraments for at least some time as a penance. Bloodshed of any kind—even when the blood belonged to God's enemies—could on no account be looked on as virtuous. Like the good thief on Calvary, the most that any hero who fell fighting the Turks could hope for was a pardon *in extremis,* if he had the time to confess.

In theory things were exactly the same in the West: Christian doctrine was explicit on such matters. However, from the middle of the eleventh century onward the popes had begun granting special indulgences to soldiers who were going to fight the Moors in Spain or placing themselves directly in the service of the Church, so that murder, under its noble name of war, had long enjoyed a strong prejudice in its favor. The secular ruling class was a military class and consequently its intellectual and ethical values were military values, a state of affairs against which the Church struggled in vain. Despite constant threats of excommunication, God's truce and God's peace were observed only by a small minority of knights, and understandably the Church could not condemn those who were fighting to defend her. She could only encourage the Spanish Christians in their efforts to win back their lands from the Moslems. Although the Emperor, the temporal head of the Byzantine Church, was also the head of the army, the Church herself, while granting her blessing to those waging a "just" war, remained on one side, faithful in principle to her horror of all bloodshed. The Greeks would have been appalled to see their archbishop mounted on a battle charger, a helmet on his head and a sword in his hand, but we know the Latins, at least the knights, were by no means dismayed by such a sight.

The fundamental difference lay in the coexistence in the Western mind of two quite separate ideals, the warrior and the Christian. Byzantium never seems to have been affected by any such ambivalence: it was too blatantly paradoxical for the logical Greek mind to accept.

CHAPTER

III

The First Crusade

(1 0 9 6 – 1 0 9 9)

Peter the Hermit's Expedition

Credit for the original idea of the Crusade, in the form in which it was finally undertaken, belongs without doubt to Urban II. After Urban, the person chiefly responsible was probably Raymond of Saint-Gilles. The Pope made a special point of consulting him before launching his appeal at the Council of Clermont, and the Count took such a prompt and active part in the propaganda and preparations for the holy war that it seems very likely that he too may have had the idea in his mind for some time.

Popular opinion, however, very quickly took over and produced its own version of the facts, relegating the Pope, and more justifiably, the Count of Toulouse, to the background. According to this version of the story, which was sufficiently widespread to be quoted by contemporary chroniclers, the real instigator of the Crusade was Peter the Hermit, to whom Jesus Christ appeared in a dream, giving him a letter addressed to the Pope. Peter went to Rome to see the Pope, tell him about the vision, and show him the miraculous letter, which was quite real. Using Peter as his intermediary, Christ commanded Urban II to preach a holy war for the deliverance of Jerusalem.

Now it is an established fact that Peter did not go to Rome in the years preceding the Council and that he had never met the Pope.

As for the letter, he did in fact speak of it, and even showed it to his hearers, actually claiming that it had been given into his hands by Jesus Christ, all of which suggests that the legend must have been of his own creation. Whatever the truth of this, Peter the Hermit's fame rapidly eclipsed that of all others who were involved in promoting the Crusade, a fact which is the more surprising because the man addressed himself largely to the poor and had no direct contact either with the Church or with the Crusader barons.

He has been judged in a great variety of ways, particularly by historians in the nineteenth and twentieth centuries. He has been called a demagogue, a visionary, and even a saint. The fact is that, apart from one temporary lapse at the siege of Antioch, he consistently inspired the greatest respect in all those who met him, and no one ever questioned his saintliness. He was, in all eyes, a *man of God*. Peter was regarded as one of the spiritual leaders of the Crusade, and the barons sent him as ambassador to the Moslems, who were equally impressed by his reputation for holiness. At Constantinople, the Emperor received him with every mark of respect, and listened to what he had to say with more deference than he showed to the great barons. His moral prestige was immense, and the least that can be deduced from this is that he possessed an exceptionally powerful personality.

He was one of those men who have the power to fascinate literally everyone with whom they come into contact, and he had a gift of eloquence which made those who heard him feel they were listening to an angel from heaven. Small, thin, shabbily dressed, and always seen riding on the little donkey which soon became part of his legend, Peter was one of those wandering preachers whom the common people revered more than they did bishops and abbots. The people followed these "holy men," with their apostolic appearance and way of life, with a fervor that was all too often disappointed by the attitude of the official clergy. They existed on the fringes of the ecclesiastical hierarchy, and wherever they went they were sure of drawing large crowds. Many were charlatans, exhibitionists, or madmen, but they also included more or less openly declared heretics whose numbers increased steadily throughout the thirteenth and fourteenth centuries, despite merciless persecution by the Church. Some founded sects which had their short-lived hour of glory but were soon dispersed, while others belonged to more widespread heretical movements such as that which swept the south of France. Certainly the majority were treated with suspicion by the Church, which regarded them as troublemakers even when the doctrines they preached were not actually heterodox. (Notwithstanding, it is to this deep undercurrent of popular religious feeling and the holy men, genuine or otherwise, which it produced that we owe the foundation of the Franciscan Order, which itself only narrowly escaped condemnation by Rome.)

Of all these lay apostles and inspired preachers, Peter the Hermit was, and still is, the most famous, because of the part he played in the First Crusade. This does not mean to say that his popularity was based on his preaching of the holy war. On the contrary, it was the Crusade which owed a great deal of its popularity to "little Peter's" support. Peter was in fact well known as a preacher throughout northern and northwestern France, and at the time of the preaching of the Crusade he had already been traveling about the Ile de France, Normandy, Champagne, and Picardy for some years, followed by crowds of the faithful who, following his example, had chosen the wandering life of the apostles. Peter was the leader of a community. His disciples gave their goods to the poor and led an ascetic life, devoting themselves to charitable works and preaching the Gospels.

Wherever Peter made his appearance with his little donkey, crowds would gather to listen to him. He preached repentance and charity, and he preached to such good effect that he filled his hearers with genuine devotion. Those fortunate enough to snatch a hair from his donkey would treasure it as a holy relic. He was said to be the son of a Norman knight, and although he was neither priest nor monk, he maintained strict obedience to the Church and no one ever accused him of saying anything with a taint of heresy. Moreover, his preaching was on a popular level; it was not concerned with subtleties of dogma but was directed chiefly at a program of moral reforms. Many wealthy and aristocratic believers, converted by Peter's preaching, gave him all or part of their possessions, and the community, which possessed a substantial fortune, was devoted to works of charity. Albert of Aix informs us, in particular, that one of Peter's greatest preoccupations was providing dowries for reformed prostitutes in order to enable them to lead respectable lives.

Adored by the people and respected by the great, Peter the Hermit was already, in 1095, a leader of crowds. Whether or not we are to believe that he would have exploited the idea of a holy war in order to increase his own popularity, it is certainly a fact that he attempted to dispute with the Pope the credit for an enterprise which had appealed to the popular imagination from the outset—although this does not mean that he was not himself an enthusiastic supporter of the idea.

With his disciples, he traveled through the French provinces, picking up the money needed for the journey and taking with him all who wanted to take the cross and whom the barons, as sensible, practical men, did not want—including some whose parish priests had forbidden them to join him. Peter appealed to the nobles and wealthy citizens, and even to the Jews, for help in his pious undertaking and his movement quickly swelled to considerable proportions. Some gave him money from motives of piety, and others—the Jews—because they were afraid. In Rouen, Peter even obtained a letter from the chief rabbi of the city to the Jews of Mainz, urging them to show charity to God's poor. (This last touch seems to show that Peter had not abandoned his evangelical work when he undertook the Crusade, and was able to remain on good terms even with the Jews. Allegations that, in Normandy, the preaching of the Crusade gave rise to demonstrations of anti-Semitism appear to be unfounded; if this had been so, Peter's letter of introduction would have been unlikely to win the good graces of the Jews of Mainz.)

Theoretically these civilian Crusaders were merely simple pilgrims determined to brave every danger for love of the Holy Land, but they were accompanied by a strong escort of soldiers, the majority of whom were disciples of Peter the Hermit. Other bands of civilian pilgrims, similar to Peter's, were also gathering, at first in France and later in Germany. One of these, led by Walter Sans-Avoir (the surname is obviously one adopted voluntarily as a sign of humility), actually set out in advance of Peter the Hermit and his band. All witnesses are unanimous in praising Walter's courage and bearing, and he was clearly neither a fanatic nor a common adventurer. He may not always have succeeded in avoiding clashes with the inhabitants of countries through which he passed, or in re-establishing order after the inevitable brawls which broke out in his camp, but it does not seem as though he, any more than Peter, can be blamed for the disturbances which occurred in Constantinople or held responsible for the ultimate disaster.

Nevertheless, these popular armies very rapidly acquired an unsavory reputation: bloody conflicts broke out in Hungary and later outside Belgrade. At Semlin in Hungary there must have been a pitched battle, since there are reports of four thousand Hungarian dead (Albert of Aix), while the governor of Belgrade had to evacuate the city, fearing for the safety of the inhabitants. Order was finally restored by means of exhortations from Peter and threats from Byzantine officials, and at last, after four months on the road, the company arrived at Constantinople.

Peter had not restricted his preaching to the French provinces where he was already well known; in his zeal he even went so far as to preach the expedition to Jerusalem in the countries he and his followers had to pass through on the way to Palestine. Wherever he appeared at the head of his pilgrims, who were like a great tribe of nomads, singing psalms and carrying the banners of the cross, he would call the local population together in a field and preach the good news of the great departure of the poor and the sinners to Jerusalem. Even in Germany, where the people could not understand what he said, he made a deep impression, for there too he preached with great success. In Germany, as in France, there were already many people preaching the Crusade; but whereas in France the great majority of volunteers had joined the followers of Peter the Hermit, forming a body of impressive size even if not very formidable from a military point of view, in Germany a number of pious expeditions set out at short intervals. Their strength was much less; most numbered only a few thousand men and certainly none reached twenty thousand. (It is not known how many pilgrims followed Peter the Hermit and his companions. At the time it left Germany their company, which was the largest of all, must have contained at least forty or fifty thousand people, for wherever they passed, they gave the impression of an unnumbered horde, like a whole people on the march.)

The leaders of the German People's Crusades included some honorable men like Walter of Tübingen and Walter of Teck, but they were not "men of God" and officially acknowledged as such. There were other leaders, too, who were acting in anything but a Christian spirit.

Emich (or Emico) of Leisingen was a robber baron, notorious for a life of pillage. One fine day Emich got word of the preaching of the Crusade, and afire with holy zeal in the cause of Jesus Christ, he promptly went one better than Peter the Hermit. Peter claimed to have a letter from Christ; Emich claimed that he had received the stigmata and bore the Cross of Christ miraculously imprinted on his flesh. He had a real talent for swaying a crowd, but a pilgrimage was the last thing he had in mind. Emich believed himself destined by God to become emperor of Jerusalem. Such was the fascination he exercised over people's minds that long after his death his memory lived on in his native province and there were constant rumors that he had been miraculously brought back to life again. Emich was not a pilgrim or a professional soldier and he thought of his Crusade as a pirate raid: his one idea was to hurl his troops, armed with pikes and staves, on the nearest and most defenseless of "God's enemies": the Jews of Germany. His bands earned themselves a sordid reputation by massacring the Jews, who were in fact the only infidels they ever encountered.

While Emich of Leisingen was busy slaughtering the Jews of Speyer, Mainz, Cologne, Trier, and Worms, despite opposition from the bishops and lords of the towns concerned, another captain, Volkmar, was letting his soldiers loose on the Jewish community in Prague. The real object of this pogrom was plunder and religious hatred was merely an excuse, but this hatred, once aroused, was easily fed. Men's zeal for Jerusalem revived their fervor for Christ's Passion and hatred for the people responsible. Several thousand German Jews perished in this way, victims of the greed and fanaticism of these marauding bands.

Beginning by wreaking violence on the Jews, these ill-organized troops, made up largely of ruffians, beggars, and fugitives from justice, did not stop there but soon started attacking the Christian populations of the countries they passed through. In Hungary they clashed with the armies of the king, Coloman, who wiped out the dangerous Crusaders as he would have exterminated wild beasts. Emich of Leisingen escaped, almost alone, thanks to the swiftness of his horse. His followers, including women and children, had numbered seven or eight thousand.

The "poor" from northern France did not suffer the tragic fate of the German Crusaders (or not while still in Europe, at least). It took them several months to pass through Germany, Bohemia, Hungary, and the Balkans, and their numbers put appalling difficulties in the way of their journey. Even with money it was almost impossible to find food for such numbers, especially in regions where the country was already poor. Shortage of supplies and transport difficulties resulted in merchandise being sold to them at exorbitant prices, which led inevitably to clashes with the local population. The journey, on foot through mountainous country, was very hard and many of the half-starved pilgrims died of exhaustion on the way. The numbers of Peter the Hermit's "poor" were further diminished by the countless accidents bound to occur when any large and ill-equipped body of people took the road: many were drowned at river crossings, were killed in falls, or died of sunstroke or disease. Yet even so, to judge from the stupefying effect their appearance produced on the Greeks, some tens of thousands of them seem to have finally reached Constantinople. "A countless people . . . more numerous than the sands of the sea . . ."[1] Anna Comnena makes it sound as though the

Greeks believed that all the Western barbarians had suddenly taken the road en masse and had emptied every province of its inhabitants.

The poor from the southern part of France had wisely attached themselves to the armies of the Count of Toulouse, who made it a point of honor to take them under his protection. The result of this was to make things more difficult for his own troops as far as provisions and relations with local populations were concerned, but at least the poor were always surrounded by an adequate armed escort and shared the lot of the army throughout the campaign.

From the moment they came in sight of Constantinople, Peter the Hermit's Crusaders had only one desire: to obtain boats from the Emperor and cross the Bosporus, in order to continue their march toward Jerusalem. They had joined forces with the troops of Walter Sans-Avoir, the Count of Tübingen, and Walter of Teck, and felt strong enough to brave any dangers. They did not know—and even their leaders cannot have been fully aware—what a long, hard road still lay ahead, and how terrible was the threat presented by the nomadic Turkish armies.

Alexius Comnenus received Peter the Hermit in his palace, treated him with great respect, but advised him to wait for the arrival of better-armed troops. This was disinterested advice indeed, since the obligation to feed such a quantity of useless mouths represented a considerable drain on the imperial treasury, while the rabble's presence in the outskirts of the capital was anything but reassuring. The poor, impatient to be on the road once more and annoyed that the "Greek king" seemed anxious to prevent their fulfilling their vow, gave way to an excitement which their leaders could no longer keep in check. Before long, bands of so-called "Crusaders" were to be found burning and pillaging the villages around Constantinople, not even respecting the churches, and from this they went on to attack the outskirts of the city itself. Alexius was worried, and finally his patience gave out and he agreed to supply them with boats. He did, however, advise the unruly pilgrims to keep close to the shore, in the area which was under the control of the Empire, and promised to keep them supplied with food until the arrival of the Crusader barons.

But as far as "God's poor"—or a great many of them—were concerned, they were already in "infidel" territory from the moment they set foot in Asia Minor. As we have seen, this vast army was an incongruous mixture of genuine pilgrims, worthy people whose simple piety made a deep impression on the Greeks, with a fair number of dangerous fanatics who were closer in spirit to Emich of Leisingen than to Peter the Hermit—and probably also a good many common malefactors whose conversion was, to say the least, sketchy. It is only too probable that these constituted the most dynamic element in this strange army.

A party of armed men, led by a certain Reynald, left the camp and began ravaging the countryside. They stormed a fortified village inhabited by Greek peasants, and mistaking the Christian villagers for Saracens, the "Crusaders" butchered them all with unheard-of refinements of cruelty (according to Anna Comnena, who describes children being spitted and roasted alive). One particularly enterprising party took it into their heads to advance into enemy territory and attack the Turks—the real ones this time—and actually succeeded in carrying off one success and capturing the castle of Xerigordon, before the Turks fell upon them and slaughtered them to a man.

Terrified at the thought of losing control of his army, Peter the Hermit went to Constantinople in the hope of persuading the Emperor to provide effective military protection for his followers. His untimely departure turned an army which was already sufficiently disoriented and confused into a leaderless rabble. Refusing to listen to the few experienced knights among them, the bulk of the pilgrims set out to recapture the city of Nicaea from the Turks. The Sultan Kilij Arslan had been warned of the arrival of a considerable body of Latin Christians, and his troops were already advancing on Nicaea. They fell upon the host of pilgrims, only a quarter of whom, if not less, were men able to fight. The result was a fearful massacre. Out of the thirty or forty thousand present, barely two or three thousand survived, and most of those were stragglers who had never reached the field of battle. Walter Sans-Avoir was killed, and so were Walter of Teck and the Count of Tübingen. On this occasion, the Turks do not seem to have wasted any time, as they usually did, in sorting out and sparing able-bodied men and young women for slaves. All the historians, Raymond of Aguilers and Albert of Aix as well as Anna Comnena, describe it as a straightforward massacre.

The so-called "People's Crusade" was over, and Peter the Hermit could only wait, with his handful of survivors, for the arrival of the barons. He joined the main army, where he continued in his role, preaching and stirring the crowds. His prestige, though shaken, remained as great as ever, if not among the barons themselves, at least among the ordinary soldiers of the army. The unfortunate pilgrims were declared to have been martyrs and their souls were said to be accompanying and protecting the army of Christ from on high. In more practical terms the involuntary sacrifice of these early Crusaders was useful to the barons' army. Kilij Arslan and his emirs, who were supremely ignorant as to the causes of the mystical folly which had driven the poor to their cruel fate, imagined that they had been fighting the real Frankish army and concluded that the Western barbarians were not adversaries to be feared. While the powerful army of the united Latin barons continued its march into Asia Minor, the Seljuk princes went on indulging in their family feuds, with no thought of guarding against attack from such a negligible enemy. This mistake accounted for a great deal in the Crusaders' first—decisive—victories.

The Barons

The army or armies of the Latin barons were, for the period, very considerable. Taken individually, each one was large enough to decide the fate of a country on the field of battle. Historians of the time are generally so vague when it comes to estimating the effective strength of an army that it is difficult to put forward even an approximate figure.* It is, however, established that the ranks of the Crusading armies taken as a whole must have included several thousand knights. Raymond of Saint-Gilles, Godfrey of Bouillon, and Robert of Normandy each commanded about a thousand knights, the Count of Blois and the Count of Flanders had several hundred, while Bohemond, whose army of seven or eight thousand men was said to be small, probably had fewer than five hundred knights under his command. A knight implied a fighting unit of five or six picked soldiers in addition to the knight himself. Besides the knights, these armies included archers, technicians of all grades from engineers to the common soldiers who worked the siege engines, and a vast personnel of servants and auxiliaries who were all professional soldiers. Then there were the common soldiers, the foot men, armed with short lances, clubs, and daggers; these soldiers also had their servants, who did not fight but were usefully employed in the thousand and one tasks to be done about the camp and during a siege.†

* Anna Comnena estimates Godfrey's army alone at 12,000 knights and 70,000 foot. Fulcher of Chartres puts the total number of Crusaders at 600,000, Ekkehard at 300,000, and Raymond of Aguilers at 100,000. A comparison of the figures given by the various historians for the battles of the Crusades suggests that at the beginning of the campaign the combined strength of these armies may have amounted to between 6,000 and 7,000 knights and 60,000 foot.

† The number of noncombatants is impossible to estimate, although it is unlikely that it amounted to more than a quarter or a third of the army's total strength.

There were four armies in all: the men of Lorraine, the Provençaux, the French, Flemings, and French Normans, and the Normans from Sicily. Alexius Comnenus, experienced soldier though he was and accustomed from his youth to fighting the Normans and rebel Greek generals as well as the Turks, was horrified by their size. Anna Comnena states (though probably with some exaggeration) that all the imperial armies put together would not have compared with a single one of the "Celtic" armies. Not only Constantinople but no other country in the known world had ever beheld such a gathering of armed men. Consequently the Greeks were terrified, and believed that the Latins could take possession of Constantinople and the whole Empire whenever they liked. But there was no real armed clash, and Alexius had reason to congratulate himself on his shrewd diplomacy, while all the Crusaders really wanted was to gain the Emperor's help in their campaign against the Turks.

They were well prepared: they knew that the Turks were formidable adversaries and did not imagine they could conquer them merely with the help of divine intervention. They knew too that the Turks in Asia Minor had the country firmly under control, that they held all the fortified places and controlled the roads. Being securely established in the country, they were more numerous than the largest army from outside could ever be, and all supplies of food and drinking water in the country were in their hands. The Crusaders were perfectly well aware of the risks run by a great army in a hostile foreign land. Moreover their adversaries were conquerors, a dominant, military race which held the country by force of arms and was therefore constantly on the alert.

On the other hand, the Crusaders also knew even before they set out, and better still since their encounter with Alexius Comnenus, that the Turks were not a single, united power. The heritage of Malik Shah had fallen into the hands of a number of heirs who were quarreling among themselves, and the moment for the attempt to crush Turkish power was well chosen. They knew too that the road to Jerusalem passed through Nicaea, Anatolia, Antioch, and Syria, and that for them, as for the Byzantines, the immediate task was to fight the Turks in Asia Minor and re-establish Greek power along the route to the Holy Places.

Consequently the first objective of the Crusading army (whose ranks now included a Greek contingent under the command of Taticius) was naturally the city of Nicaea, a great fortress situated almost directly across the Bosporus. The venerable city, which had a long Christian past, was a place of vital importance to the safety of

Constantinople. Nicaea had fallen into Seljuk hands sixteen years earlier and was now the capital of the present ruler of Anatolia, the Sultan Kilij Arslan, son of Suleiman, a prince distantly related to the sons of Malik Shah. At the time the Crusading armies disembarked, the Sultan was fighting in the mountains of Armenia against another Turkish ruler, Malik Ghazi Gümüshtekin, a Danishmend emir who had long been disputing the mastery of the northern part of Asia Minor, from the Black Sea to the Caspian, with the Seljuks. When Kilij Arslan finally realized that the Christian army might present a real danger to his capital he hastily sent reinforcements, but it was too late. The Crusaders had already invested the city and easily beat off the Turkish troops. After a six weeks' siege, the garrison of Nicaea and the Sultana, Kilij Arslan's wife, negotiated the surrender of the city.

During the siege, a harsh one because the city was large and well defended, Crusaders and Greeks worked in close collaboration, outdoing one another in keenness and technical proficiency. The Latins had far more men, but their fleet and superior war machines enabled the Greeks to play a far from negligible part in the operation. However, the siege of Nicaea gave both Greeks and Turks an opportunity to realize that these Christian barbarians, who until then had been little feared because little was known of them, were a first-class military force.

The capture of Nicaea was the Crusading army's first great victory, but it also resulted in a noticeable cooling of relations between the Greeks and the Latins. The garrison of the besieged city had in fact considered it wiser to negotiate with Taticius and, through him, with the Emperor, all unknown to the Crusaders. The Turks regarded the "King of Roum" as the leader of Christendom and since he was, moreover, their neighbor it seemed natural to address themselves to him rather than to the barbarian chiefs who were his allies. Neither Alexius nor Taticius thought fit to inform the Crusaders, who were preparing a general assault and planning to take the city by storm, that negotiations were in progress. On the morning of June 19, just as the Crusaders were about to hurl themselves at the city walls with their rams and scaling ladders, they suddenly saw the imperial standards floating from the towers: Nicaea once again belonged to Byzantium, and there was nothing for it but to return to their tents.

It is understandable that a surprise of this kind should have annoyed them. Nevertheless, their leaders were correct enough not to show their discontent too obviously, and Alexius Comnenus hastily demonstrated his gratitude to them by fresh largesse. There was great bitterness among the rest of the army. The soldiers considered their courage had earned them the right to rich booty, and this was exactly what the Emperor and his lieutenants had been anxious to avoid.

Nicaea was a Greek city which for sixteen years had been under foreign domination. Alexius was chiefly concerned to liberate it, and he would no doubt have preferred to leave it to the Turks rather than see it delivered up to the perils of an assault. Even so, the most elementary courtesy dictated that the leaders of the Crusade should at least have been consulted or informed of the negotiations. Their behavior after the capture of the city shows that they would have been perfectly capable of appreciating the *basileus*'s reasons.

In the face of considerable displeasure on the part of the army, which was already beginning to murmur about Greek "treachery," the barons (with the exception of Bohemond's nephew Tancred) renewed their oaths of allegiance to the Emperor. Alexius, on his side, promised to assemble all his armies and join them before long on the road to Syria. Both parties regarded the enterprise as something to be undertaken together: while the Latins were engaged in the interior, the Emperor and his armies were to advance along the Black Sea coast, recapturing the Greek provinces of Mysia, Ionia, and Lydia from the Turks. This being the case, the Greeks can scarcely be accused of sitting with their arms folded allowing others to act in their place. But as invariably happens on these occasions, those who did the fighting tended to see nothing beyond their own exploits and their own difficulties. All the Latin historians agree in asserting that the Emperor first cheated the Crusaders out of the rewards of an initial victory and then knowingly sent them off to be massacred by the Turks.

It is true that Alexius had not given up his policy of divide and rule, which consisted in establishing good relations with first one Turkish prince and then another, while simultaneously rousing their mutual hatred by treacherous advice. By a strange irony of fate, at the very moment when the Crusaders, with Greek help, were capturing Nicaea from Kilij Arslan, Alexius Comnenus was doing his best to humor the young Sultan, who he then thought was much less to be feared than the emir of Smyrna and the Danishmend emirs. Whether out of policy or common courtesy, he entertained the Sultana who had been captured at Nicaea with the greatest honors, loaded her with presents, and sent her back to her husband without exacting a ransom. This chivalrous gesture was extremely unpopular with the Crusader knights, who still, if the truth be told, had a great deal to learn about good manners.

Dorylaeum

When Kilij Arslan learned that his capital had fallen he finally realized that matters were becoming serious. Five days after leaving
Nicaea, the Crusading armies suffered a surprise attack from a formidable Turkish army commanded by the Sultan himself, who had
hastily gathered together all the forces at his disposal in Anatolia and
appealed for help to his erstwhile enemy, Ghazi ibn Danishmend.
The two premier Turkish princes of Asia Minor aimed at delivering
one crushing blow that would utterly annihilate the new enemy whose
strength they had hitherto underestimated.

Without being able to quote exact figures, Latin accounts of the
battle, obviously derived from the memories of eyewitnesses, reveal
the terror of the Christians as they confronted the multitudes of enemy soldiers, "Turks, Arabs, Saracens," who assailed them on that
day. "All the highlands and the hills and valleys and all the plains
within and without were entirely covered with this race."[2]

This time the Crusaders were not only much weaker numerically,
but they had also been careless enough to separate into two bodies
following different routes in order to simplify the problem of supplies.
They were not expecting such a swift attack. On July 1, 1097, the
Turks fell upon the weaker half of the army, which was under Bohemond's command. Bohemond was not a man to lose his head and
since his only hope was to hold out until the arrival of the other army,
he swiftly laid plans for his defense. Just when the Turks, having first
softened up their adversaries by a relentless hail of arrows, were
going in to the attack, the troops of Lorraine, France, and Provence
fell upon them from behind and surrounded them on all sides. Here
the French knights' superior horses and armor carried the day over
their more numerous but more lightly armed opponents. By a clever
tactical maneuver a much smaller force had succeeded in encircling
and taking the Turkish troops in the rear and spreading panic in their
ranks.

The defeat of Kilij Arslan and Ghazi was complete. Their soldiers
broke ranks and fled, with the Sultan himself in their train, abandoning his camp and everything in it, including his royal treasure which
he took with him on all his campaigns.

When the two adversaries came face to face, there was, as we have
seen, a fundamental difference in their equipment and method of
warfare. On this occasion both sides were surprised and disconcerted

by the unfamiliar tactics. The account by the author of the *Anonymi Gesta Francorum* vividly describes the terror which seized the Frankish warriors at the sight of the hordes of light cavalry charging forward in serried ranks, emptying their quivers and falling back to give way to fresh waves of mounted archers. He describes arrows and javelins falling as thick as hail, the savage, piercing shrieks of the enemy, and the diabolical swiftness of their cavalry, constantly darting in to the attack and then away again.

The battle ended in a complete rout for the Turks. For them, too, the new enemy was unfamiliar: the huge horses and armor which made each man a kind of moving fortress. Frankish armor, although not yet as bulky as it became in the twelfth and thirteenth centuries, was already a veritable carapace of iron and leather, rendering the knight invulnerable to arrows and often to sword cuts, as indeed he had to be, since the work he had to do is done today by tanks and armored cars. These iron men with their heavy weapons must have seemed to the Turkish soldiers like so many monsters out of hell. What was perhaps still more important, they fought with the desperate energy of men intoxicated by danger. They knew they had to win. The very number of their assailants told them that defeat would be massacre, or at best, safety in flight for the few who possessed good horses.

The Franks had earned their victory, and it was followed by great rejoicings on account of the vast spoils taken from Kilij Arslan's camp. Coming as it did less than two weeks after the capture of Nicaea, the battle of Dorylaeum was one of those decisive events which can alter the destiny of a whole people. A myth had been created—the myth of an invincible Frankish army; this first encounter acquired something of a symbolic value.

The Christians interpreted it as a manifest proof of divine favor. The Turks explained their defeat by the irresistible, inhuman fury of the Latin barbarians. At all events, it had been a formidable encounter. With the defeat of the two greatest Turkish rulers in Asia Minor, the Crusaders' cause was half won: the Moslem princes, who had established themselves as conquerors in lands as yet only superficially subdued, were disconcerted by the sudden unexpected attack, while the local populations, the majority of whom were Christian, held up their heads again and prepared to join the allies providence had sent them from the West. The Turks considered themselves anything but beaten, and the Crusading army went on its way to meet yet more fearful odds. But the moral effect of their initial triumph lasted long enough to give the Crusaders a certain advantage over their opponents.

It was Dorylaeum, even more than the Pope's sermons, which finally set the seal on their role as God's army. Thanking God for their victory and gratefully acknowledging Him as their leader, they moved onward through the burning, devastated countryside, beset with ambushes, in the joyous confidence that their sufferings were for God and that they were guided and protected by Him.

We can form a very clear idea of what the army suffered in this crossing of Asia Minor, for those who lived through it did not quickly forget. Their chief enemies were hunger and thirst. As the Turks withdrew, they turned a land already ravaged by incessant warfare into a desert. The horses and pack animals vital to an army on the march perished in their hundreds, and the people, especially the women, of whom there were still a great many with the army, died of exhaustion or sunstroke.

Taticius, who knew the country, decided to lead the army through Phrygia. He had not anticipated finding the entire region utterly laid waste and the wells filled in or poisoned, while at this season of the year the watercourses were all dry. The Crusaders immediately accused the Greek general of trying to destroy them by making them follow such a bad route, although he could have had no possible interest in doing so, since he and his own body of men shared with the Crusaders all the discomforts of the journey. The sufferings of the poor people with the army were terrible. We do not know exactly how many of them died in the course of this forced march, which even historians writing long after the event describe with horror as a foretaste of hell. The terrific heat and urgent need to press on as fast as possible for fear of being surprised by marauding bands of Turkish nomads meant that the rich suffered almost as much as the poor, although their resistance was probably greater. However, this cannot have been true of the women, for William of Tyre informs us that every woman who was with child on that crossing of the Lycaonian desert, noble ladies and poor peasants alike, was brought to bed before her time, "a pitiful sight to see."[3]

The march through the ancient Byzantine provinces of Asia Minor took four months. The Crusaders set out from Nicaea on June 26 and the first detachments of the army reached the outskirts of Antioch on October 20. The great cosmopolitan city of Antioch was the key to Syria and the Palestine littoral. Its defenses were formidable, but the Crusaders had to capture the city at all costs if they were to pursue their march on Palestine. As far as the Greeks were concerned it was also the main object of the expedition, because it had been one of the principal cities of the Byzantine Empire.

When they arrived before Antioch, the Crusaders had already got over the first flush of victory. They had gained a certain amount of experience of the country, of their adversaries and their indigenous allies, and had settled down resolutely to a war which they knew would be long and hard. Also they had learned to live together, the Normans and the men from Lorraine, "Frenchman" and Provençal, Breton and Fleming, and at this stage a spirit of co-operation seems to have reigned among the leaders as well as the common soldiers. The army had had an opportunity of measuring the prowess of their commanders in action, and these were still working as a team, united by the necessity of a communal effort.

The only foreigner in this Christian army was Taticius, with his contingent of Greek mercenaries. The distinguished Greek had not succeeded in inspiring much confidence in his allies, who more and more tended to avoid him and regard him as a traitor and a spy. There is no reason to think that his loyalty was suspect, although he probably aroused the Crusaders' suspicions by his haughty and distant behavior. As the war against the infidel progressed, the Crusaders appear to have directed all their bitterness and exasperation increasingly toward the Greeks rather than the Turks. There was a very good reason for this. Up to the time they reached Antioch, all the Crusaders' heroism and suffering throughout the agonizing four months of the campaign had benefitted no one but the Greeks. All the cities and lands they had captured belonged of right to the *basileus,* and as they installed Byzantine governors or vassals of Byzantium in the citadels of Caesarea, Placentia, Marash, Artah, and other places abandoned by the Turks, the Crusaders bore with understandable though unspoken impatience the role of mercenaries which Alexius Comnenus seemed anxious to impose on them.

This thankless role weighed so heavily on them that two of the less prominent leaders of the Crusading army had made up their minds, even before reaching Antioch, to leave their companions and go off and wage war on their own account. Bohemond's nephew Tancred and Godfrey of Bouillon's younger brother Baldwin left the army on the fourteenth of September and struck out into the mountains of Cilicia, a route which took them away from Syria but also from the provinces to be reconquered for the benefit of Byzantium. The Crusaders were beginning to realize that the Greeks were still the rightful masters of the territory which had been overrun by the Turks. The Turks were only in temporary possession, an occupying army largely

confined to local military garrisons. For the moment, therefore, the
war was going through a phase of singularly little interest, either
moral or material. It had already proved terribly expensive, and the
ones who reaped the benefit of these sacrifices inherited the accumu-
lated bitterness of months. The army was exceptionally patient and
enduring, but it was undoubtedly more dominated by passion and
prejudice than a regular professional army would have been.

By Antioch, the die was already cast: while remaining faithful in
principle to their oath to the Emperor, the Crusaders privately considered they had amply acquitted themselves of their debt.

Antioch was a vast and splendid city and nothing in the West could
remotely compare with it for size and wealth. It was magnificently
fortified and equipped with all the latest developments of Byzantine
military techniques. The outer walls were over six miles long, and
with its four hundred towers, its citadel towering well over six hundred feet above the lower quarters of the town, and its mountainous
hinterland, it was very nearly impregnable. The only way to take it
seemed to be by relying on the panic effects of surprise and terror.
This at least was the opinion of Raymond of Saint-Gilles, an old and
experienced soldier who also possessed a natural talent for strategy.
His calculation was sound, although it was regarded as foolhardy by
the other leaders.

The strongest opposition to the plan put forward by the Count of
Toulouse came from Bohemond of Taranto, and he succeeded in winning over the majority of the council of barons to his point of view.
Bohemond was a man more renowned for his excessive boldness than
for his prudence. Events were to show that Bohemond, a less straightforward character than the old Count, had his eye on something else
besides the capture of one stronghold, and the opportunity of carrying Antioch by surprise was lost. It had been a good opportunity because the mere sight of the formidable Frankish army outside his
walls was enough to bring the governor of the city, the Turkoman
emir Yaghi-Siyan, to the point of surrender.

However, Antioch was a position of such importance that, from
the Emperor's point of view, its recovery alone would have made the
Crusade worth while. The quick capture of the city would automatically have resulted in Antioch and the entire province being handed
back to the Greeks. No one at that time would have dreamed of disputing the rights of Byzantium. Whatever the secret feelings of the
other leaders, Bohemond had undoubtedly tried to prevent this happening at all costs, preferring to expose the army to the perils of a
difficult siege rather than abandon Antioch to the Greeks.

So, instead of the overwhelming onslaught which stood a good chance of success, the Crusading army found itself condemned to a singularly difficult siege, with very little prospect of success. Only a series of lucky chances and the pilgrim soldiers' almost superhuman endurance saved the Crusade from total annihilation.

The Leaders

The Crusading army was actually led by a council of barons presided over by the papal legate Adhemar of Monteil, Bishop of Le Puy. Officially, all the great barons respected the legate's authority as nominal head of the Crusade, but in practice each had his own reasons for claiming precedence over the rest, and not one of them had sworn unconditional obedience to the legate. The one who showed him the most deference was the Count of Toulouse. Adhemar's family were the Count's vassals and the two men were old friends. But the Count was not the type to take a back seat: he meant to play the part of temporal leader of the Crusade, and he was prepared to use the Bishop of Le Puy's authority in order to undermine that of the other barons. Godfrey of Bouillon, a disciplined but ambitious soldier, was careful not to dispute the Bishop's decisions because he wanted to keep in with the Church party. The third great leader of the Crusade, Bohemond of Taranto, was also ambitious, thoroughly unscrupulous, and too naturally independent to take orders from anyone, but now he was deeply committed to the Crusade and he had no intention of clashing with Adhemar while the prelate was as popular with the knights as he was with the common soldiers.

The legate, who came of a noble family, had once been a knight himself. He was like Bishop Turpin in *The Song of Roland,* riding his charger into battle against the Turks at the head of his men. At Dorylaeum, he was even partly responsible for a strategic maneuver which had a decisive effect on the course of the battle, but in general he merely led the soldiers and did not smite the Turks himself. He was an eminently respectable man, who led an exemplary life. He had sound judgment and undeniable moral authority. While he presided over the army council, he seems to have succeeded in creating —on the surface at least—a climate of understanding among the temporal leaders. Moreover, he allowed no one to forget that this was a *holy* war.

Raymond of Saint-Gilles, Count of Toulouse, had been the first to take the cross. He had already been a Crusader in Spain, and flattered himself that he had given the Pope valuable advice before the Council of Clermont, and he believed so ardently in the cause of Jerusalem that he is known to have sworn an oath to die in the Holy Land. He had pledged his entire personal fortune, left his county in charge of his son Bertrand, and equipped a much larger army than those of his colleagues and rivals. He even carried piety to the length of assuming responsibility for the poor and the civilian pilgrims who wished to travel with his army. He was the richest and most powerful of all the Crusaders, as well as the oldest (being well over fifty) and the most experienced in the profession of arms. He was also the most refined, more subtle than his companions. His wealth and his rank were enough in themselves to assure him the superiority of a man who had engaged in the holy war for pure love of Jesus Christ, with no ulterior motive. He was ambitious, but in a dilettante fashion, dazzled more by dreams of personal glory than by an appetite for conquest.

He was impulsive and unstable, more stubborn than strong-willed, but whatever his defects of character no one has questioned his virtues as a man, his irreproachable private life, his sincere piety and faith to his given word. (On this point, Anna Comnena makes a curious observation which shows the somewhat naive idea which the cultivated princess had of the rude "Celtic" barbarians. When the Holy Lance was discovered, she says, the relic was entrusted to "Isangeles" because he was "purer than the rest." It is not easy to imagine Godfrey, the Count of Flanders, or Bohemond paying such official tribute to the "purity" of one of their rivals.)

Raymond had an instinct for a fine phrase and a theatrical gesture —as we shall see later. Being a man of imagination rather than action, he flung himself (and there can be no doubt of his sincerity) more wholeheartedly than the other barons into the part of a Crusader. He alone among the great barons steadfastly refused to swear fealty to Alexius Comnenus, declaring proudly that he had placed himself in God's service and would serve no other lord than Jesus Christ. It was he, too, who promised his homage on condition that the *basileus* would march in person at the head of the Crusading army, thus reminding the Emperor of Byzantium of his historic role as champion in the fight against Islam. Alexius declined the offer, saying that he could not undertake an expedition into Asia on account of his wars in the Balkans. (Anna Comnena claims that her father, knowing their forces were greatly superior to his own, was simply afraid of the Crusaders' uncertain temper.) Consequently Raymond of Saint-Gilles remained inflexible and never swore the oath demanded of him. Yet he alone among the leaders of the Crusade was admitted to intimate terms with the *basileus,* held long conversations with him, and succeeded in arousing an esteem which the Emperor never granted to any of the others.

We know that Raymond was neither a clever diplomat nor an obstinate idealist. He was not a man of great ambition or a fanatic, and in him military vigor was allied to the somewhat whimsical temperament of a great lord who can please himself in his actions. Despite all his undoubted advantages, he never succeeded in making the other barons take him altogether seriously.

Godfrey of Bouillon, Duke of Lower Lorraine, was the son of the Count of Boulogne. With the passing of time, his fame has grown to such proportions that the renown of the other leaders of the Crusade pales beside it. A number of contemporary historians, René Grousset in particular, have cast doubt on his personal merits and have gone so far as to suggest that Godfrey, though a worthy man, was personally dull and altogether mediocre. This opinion was not shared by his contemporaries. Anna Comnena is a witness that, even before legend took hold of the *Advocatus Sancti Sepulchri,* Godfrey of Lorraine had fired the popular imagination by his proud bearing and his energy and military valor.

In 1095 Godfrey was about thirty-five years old, handsome, or at least endowed with great personal charm, and built according to the canons of beauty laid down in the *chansons de geste:* he was very tall, "broad-shouldered and narrow-hipped," with a physical strength that was proverbial, and—not the least of his assets—capable in moments of crisis of inspiring an entire army by his simple, direct eloquence. But in spite of his accomplishments, he had not managed to acquire a great reputation in his own country. A descendant of Charlemagne through his father, Eustace II, Count of Boulogne, and of Norman stock on the side of his mother, Ida of Brabant (Lower Lorraine), Godfrey was certainly nobly born, but compared with the Count of Toulouse his status was not impressive. He was only the Count of Boulogne's second son and the paternal inheritance went to the eldest, Eustace. Even so, as a nephew, through his mother, of the Duke of Lower Lorraine, Godfrey finally inherited the duchy from his uncle, but this did not happen until he was twenty-eight. He had to wait a long time for his inheritance because, although the duchy was rightfully his, the Emperor Henry IV had disposed of it in favor of his own son Conrad. Consequently Godfrey spent his youth as a poor younger son, anything but resigned to the loss of his great fortune. Once he was Duke of Lower Lorraine, and as such a vassal of the Emperor of Germany, Godfrey took little interest in his duchy, to judge by the ease with which he abandoned it. As an administrator he seems to have been mediocre and somewhat harsh: he has been accused of despoiling the abbeys on his domains, and after taking the cross at the Council of Clermont, he was rumored to be contemplating an onslaught on the Jews of his province as a means of "avenging" Jesus Christ. This so alarmed the Jews that they hastened to appease him by gifts of money, which he accepted. In fact all he had done was to profit from the insecurity of the Jewish community, but they must have known him well enough to be aware that he was capable of putting his threat into execution.

So far there is nothing to indicate that Godfrey was a religious fanatic, but neither have we any reason to believe that his decision to serve God was not sincere. It is a fact that he settled the affairs of his duchy, pledged all his personal possessions to the abbeys of Brabant, and, being unmarried and childless, left his native land with the definite intention of settling in the East. This was also the intention of Godfrey's brother Baldwin, who was neither a count nor a duke and therefore stood only to gain by the change. Younger sons of great families had a deep craving for land which in general they had little chance to satisfy.

Baldwin, a year or two younger than Godfrey, was not one of the principal leaders of the Crusade but acted as his brother's second in command. He took with him his wife, Godvere of Tosni, and his young children. This was not a wise move, but there were countless knights who did the same, thinking that their fortune would enable them to spare their families the fatigues and dangers of the journey. The wives who accompanied their husbands in this way, whether for reasons of piety or conjugal affection, were merely falling in with a long-established custom, since feudal lords habitually went to war, fought battles, and laid siege to towns with their families installed in the finest tent in the camp. All the same, Baldwin's decision leaves room to suppose that he was very fond of his young wife, and he undoubtedly set out with the firm intention of winning a fief for himself and never returning to Europe. He was much less interested in the holy war than in the prospect of becoming the lord of vast lands in the East.

We shall have more to say about Baldwin, but at this point, in the early stages of the Crusade, the younger son, who from the moment of his arrival in Syria broke away from Christ's army to launch out on his own account, was only an apprentice in his chosen profession. Like his brother, he was a courageous soldier, but lacking the same handsome appearance and engaging manners, he was apt to suffer in comparison with Godfrey. Baldwin was almost a giant in height ("Like Saul he stood a head taller than all other men"[4]), a broad, impressive figure with a stern face and rigid bearing, not the kind of man to inspire enthusiasm or great personal devotion, and better able to command obedience than love. As a child he was intended for holy orders, and as the son of a great baron his education had been calculated to fit him for a high position in the Church. William of Tyre tells us that he was a canon of Reims, Cambrai, and Liège, but that having no vocation, he early abandoned the clerical state for the profession of arms. The years spent in the cloisters had left their mark on him and much later, in middle age, he looked, with his cloak wrapped around him, "more like a bishop than a knight."[5] Notwithstanding, a knight he was to his fingertips. As a fighter he was bold, fierce, indefatigable, but this was not all: he had a quick, eager, intelligent, and extremely agile mind. Although possessed of a devouring ambition, he was something more than merely ambitious; he had the makings of a politician and a statesman. But he started from very small beginnings and encountered the kind of strange and sordid adventures only faced by men determined to stop at nothing, before his promise was finally fulfilled.

In the first year of the Crusade, the man who in the eyes of his contemporaries seemed to dominate all the rest was the Norman Bohemond of Taranto. For a long time he was regarded by the army as the great hero of the holy war, and inspired an excessive and fanatical devotion. Yet his driving ambition was not the recovery of the Holy Sepulcher.

Bohemond, the eldest son of Robert Guiscard, was warring in Italy when he happened to hear from sailors' gossip the great news, which had long been common knowledge in France, that a holy war was in preparation with the ultimate object of Jerusalem and the point of assembly was Constantinople. Surprised at first, and then interested, Bohemond decided that he too would take the cross. He was already forty and nearly all his life had been spent in fighting, first at his father's side and later on his own against successive Byzantine emperors and their generals for mastery of the Mediterranean. Robert Guiscard was a high-flying soldier of fortune who, starting from nothing, had conquered Sicily and southern Italy, and was already at the gates of Constantinople when he fell victim to a plague that was ravaging his army. Bohemond meant to carry on his father's work, and his great ambition was to destroy the power of the Greeks and found a Norman empire in the Mediterranean. His brother and his uncle had their kingdoms in Italy and Sicily, while Bohemond, who was actually the eldest son, although his mother was less nobly born than Guiscard's second wife, Sigelgaita, possessed little land of his own. He had partially conquered Lombardy and recruited an army there, but he aimed higher than this. His real goal was Constantinople.

This ambition was not in itself so very extraordinary: the Norman and Scandinavian pirate chiefs, known for their boldness and rapacity, had long cast greedy eyes on the imperial city. Bohemond, a French Norman, was descended from Rollo's warriors who had settled on the Channel coasts, and though his mother tongue was French he was in temperament and tradition still a Viking. But this latinized and Christianized Viking lacked the simplicity of his ancestors who had once ranged the coasts of the southern lands as far as they could reach, ravaging and laying waste the country and taking home rich shiploads of plunder to the greater glory of their clan. Centuries of easy, ruthless conquest had made them one of the great scourges of Christendom, and even when they had more or less settled down in France, England, Italy, and Sicily, they still had this yearning for the wide open spaces in their blood. They waged a fierce struggle against the Greeks and Arabs for control of the Mediterranean. In this they were motivated not by religious intolerance but simply by the lust for conquest. Their temper was in general too proud to permit them to feign a religious ardor they did not feel, but becoming, largely in spite of themselves, the champions of Catholic Christendom, they exploited the moral advantages to be gained from the role. In Italy they were the pope's allies, but in Asia Minor they just as readily allied themselves with the Turks.

The other European barons had dreams of carving out principalities for themselves in the East at the expense of God's enemies. Bohemond was different. His boundless ambition was nourished by a passionate and abiding hatred of Byzantium. Twenty years of warfare had allowed this hatred to ripen in him until it became a veritable obsession. As a man he was rough, obstinate, and ferocious, like a great beast of prey, endowed with the sharp, practical intelligence often found in people dominated by a single idea.

Anna Comnena tells us that he was remarkably beautiful: tall and fair, with his curly hair cut short and his chin clean-shaven (the other Franks were long-haired and heavily bearded), he answered exactly, she says, to the canons of beauty laid down by Polycletes, but his smile was disturbing and there was something frightening in the gaze of his blue eyes. He exerted a real fascination, and there is no doubt of his command over his men, who sensed in him a leader who was utterly sure of himself to the end and capable of using any means to make himself obeyed. In the *Anonymi* he is always referred to as "the wise Bohemond." His was the wisdom of Ulysses; he was wily and cunning, never at a loss, and an experienced and audacious soldier. Before the walls of Antioch his courage and invention were put to the test and he proved himself to the full. The bulk of the army looked to him instinctively as the leader of the Crusade. Yet of all the great barons, he was the poorest in men, money, and —as Anna Comnena scornfully points out—nobility.

His personal troop comprised at the very most seven or eight thousand men. Anna Comnena says he was compelled to recruit old men, boys, and peasants hardly able to bear arms and send them into battle after the most perfunctory training. He was perpetually short of money because whatever his campaigns brought him in he immediately spent on making war on an even bigger scale. But for all this, Alexius Comnenus feared him to such an extent that he was ready to come to blows with Godfrey of Bouillon and extract an oath of fealty from him by main force, rather than let the army of Lorraine join up with Bohemond's outside the walls of Constantinople.

The old enemy of Byzantium appeared at the *basileus*'s court in the guise of an ally and made no bones about taking the oath at which the other barons jibbed. He made a great show of friendliness to the Empire, and followed this up by a request that he be appointed Grand Domestic of the East, that is, commander in chief of all the armies. Alexius politely refused. Bohemond continued to proclaim his goodwill toward the Emperor but was rumored to be so afraid of being poisoned that he would touch none of the dishes set before him at table. Hoping to mollify him with gifts, Alexius presented him with enough gold and silver and precious things to fill a whole room, but although Bohemond accepted them, it did not lull his suspicions. Considering the actual relations between the two men, this distrust seems scarcely surprising.

Bohemond is an important figure in the Crusade, but although he contributed greatly to ensuring the military triumph of the Crusaders and to consolidating their position in Syria, he himself was only a temporary Crusader. His real dreams and ambitions were not concerned with Jerusalem, but were both vaster and more down to earth. What he was doing had already been attempted, on a smaller scale, by another Norman, Roussel of Bailleul, but he was to learn to his cost that the Byzantine Empire was too big for him to swallow.

In the long run, the barons whose aim was simply the conquest of Jerusalem were the more realistic.

Antioch

The siege of Antioch lasted seven and a half months, from October 20, 1097, to June 3, 1098. Then the Crusaders in their turn were besieged in Antioch for three weeks, and in the end the army did not resume its march on Jerusalem until January 1099.

Strange as it seems, throughout this memorable siege and the long halt on the road to the Holy Land, the enthusiasm of the troops did not flag. Far from disintegrating under its heavy losses, the army set out once again with redoubled ardor in pursuit of its original goal. A complete *chanson de geste* was composed in honor of the epic story of Antioch. Briefly, in the various stages of the siege and capture of the city the Crusaders, knights, soldiers, and simple pilgrims alike, learned to appreciate the dangers they faced. They learned to know one another and also, to some extent, to know the enemy, and those who had the strength, or the courage, to endure to the end were able to embark once more on the conquest of the Holy Land, hardened, resolute, and ready to bear all things for the love of Jesus Christ.

It is already clear that this siege was a fantastic undertaking, since however large the Crusading army, it was impossible to blockade the city completely. Not only was Antioch amply provided with food and water; it could also be constantly supplied with fresh food, weapons, and soldiers from outside. The Crusading armies encamped outside the principal gates of the city and in positions commanding all the bridges, but they could not patrol the mountainous district behind the citadel. The Crusaders built wooden forts and siege towers, but the city was so formidable that all attempts at bombardment or encirclement were equally ineffective. Moreover, after commandeering all the provisions to be found in the district—and the countryside was rich—the besieging army squandered them very imprudently. Local peasants brought food to the camp, but they had to travel long distances and prices were high. Inadequate supplies brought the besiegers to near-starvation at the end of two months.

The winter, always severe in these mountainous regions, was a particularly harsh one and the Crusaders, who had been led to expect a milder climate than at home, found themselves bitterly disappointed. Icy, torrential rain turned their camps into huge quagmires.

Their tents and shelters were a totally inadequate protection and for weeks on end the common soldiers and the poor pilgrims who accompanied the army lived literally up to their necks in water, never able to dry their clothes, "which rotted on their backs."[6] Undernourished as they were, the mortality rate during these winter months was appalling, and each day brought dozens of new corpses to be buried.

Yaghi-Siyan, on the other hand, once he had recovered from his initial panic, set about organizing the defense of the city. The lord of Antioch sent for fresh soldiers, turned out all useless mouths who, being Christians, then became so many useless mouths in the Crusaders' camp, and appealed for help to his overlords, Kerbogha, the *atabeg,* or governor, of Mosul, and Duqaq, ruler of Damascus. Luckily for the Crusaders, Yaghi-Siyan had not long before rejected his allegiance to his natural overlord, Ridwan, King of Aleppo, and ranged himself instead on the side of Ridwan's brother and rival Duqaq. Consequently, the King of Aleppo, whose lands ran close to the besieged city (being less than 60 miles away, while Mosul was 400 miles from Antioch as the crow flies, and Damascus 250), did nothing to help his vassal. Yaghi-Siyan dispatched his two sons, one to Mosul and the other to Damascus, and they finally obtained promises of substantial reinforcements from the two Turkish princes. Antioch was no longer in danger of being taken by storm and it was becoming increasingly clear that the siege would end in disaster for the besieging army.

Shortage of supplies forced the barons to send out detachments to scour the countryside for food. The Turks had a firm hold on the country and the Crusaders dared not venture far afield except in battalions of several hundred armed men, and as fever and epidemics raged in the camp, the want of able-bodied men made itself felt increasingly. A large section of the army, under Bohemond and Robert of Flanders, set off along the Orontes in the direction of the sea, pillaging the rich countryside and the coastal plain, but it was surprised by the Turks of Syria and returned to Antioch after a battle in which it sustained serious losses and was forced to abandon all its plunder. The army's morale was at its lowest.

This was the moment Bohemond chose to rid himself of Taticius, who had long been regarded with suspicion by the Latins and now became the scapegoat of the army. The Frankish knights were growing restive: they naturally tended to consider themselves the victims of treachery and this could come only from the Emperor of Byzantium and his representative, Taticius. This resentment never found vent in

open conflict, but Anna Comnena (who can only have got her information from Taticius himself) asserts that Bohemond went to the
Greek general in secret and warned him against the other barons
who, he said, driven to desperation by their lack of success, were
blaming it on the *basileus* and preparing to avenge Alexius' betrayal
on the person of his lieutenant. Accordingly Taticius, still acting on
Bohemond's advice, stole away from the camp by night, taking with
him his detachment of Greek soldiers, whereupon Bohemond lost no
time in loudly proclaiming the Greek a traitor and earning him the
unanimous condemnation of the whole Crusading army.

In fact, Taticius' company had not been a large one and counted
for very little in the general course of operations, but the Byzantine
general's departure provoked the barons to understandable annoyance since they interpreted it as a hostile move against them on the
part of the Emperor, and dejected as they were, they saw themselves
betrayed on all sides and delivered up by Byzantium to the Turks.
The chroniclers' accounts suggest that their anger was mingled with a
secret relief: they had long detested the Greeks and were glad to have
their perfidy unmasked, and well satisfied to have their own hands
free for the future. There are some grounds now for thinking that
Taticius departed of his own accord, whether because he was frightened by the attitude of the Latins or simply tired of the siege, and
that he made Bohemond responsible for his departure in order to
justify himself in the eyes of the Emperor. Bohemond certainly
never boasted of his ruse, and we can only take Taticius at his word,
but his story fits in admirably with what we know of Bohemond's
character.

The siege dragged on for months in the worst possible conditions,
and the Crusaders had no alternative but to sit and wait for the
arrival of a Turkish army superior to their own, or strike camp and
risk an inglorious withdrawal to the ports on the Mediterranean
coast, with every likelihood of their army deserting or being massacred on the way. Besides, they had no intention of abandoning the
siege, and here Bohemond displayed such energy that the other
barons, whether they liked it or not, came to look on him as their
leader, or at least as the most influential member of their council. It
will be seen that the Norman had excellent reasons for appearing
more ardent than the rest. Not for nothing did he have before his
eyes, from morning to night, the spectacle of the great city with its
four hundred towers, its palaces and gardens, and its formidable
citadel perched high above the town.

Exhausted, sick, and depressed, the Franks still had sufficient energy to repel attacks by Turkish armies attempting to relieve Antioch. Gradually, obtaining supplies from the sea through the port of St. Symeon, the Crusaders were able to accomplish the almost complete encirclement of the city. Every time Yaghi-Siyan's garrison made a sortie they were driven back, but now the Turks had picked troops inside the city and each sortie was a ferocious battle. On the sixth of March the besieged are reported to have lost fifteen hundred men, including twelve emirs, but their courage did not fail. They knew that the governor of Mosul, Kerbogha, was advancing on Antioch at the head of his army, on the orders of the Sultan Barkiyarok. Kerbogha was a formidable and hitherto unvanquished warrior.

The Crusaders knew it too, but at last they had an unexpected piece of good luck—luck from which Bohemond reaped the benefit. This was quite rightly so because he had acquired the reputation in both camps, the besieged as well as the besiegers, for being the "wisest" and most powerful of the Crusaders. Consequently it was to him that a messenger came from the beleaguered city with an offer to let the Franks into Antioch by treachery. (The man in question was the officer in charge of one of the principal towers in the outer wall, known as the Tower of the Two Sisters, a man named Firouz. Firouz was a renegade Christian of Armenian descent. He had not forgotten his origins and his sympathies were naturally with the Christians.) Bohemond took care not to share the good news with his colleagues, but hinted that he knew a way of entering the city. He suggested that by mutual consent possession of the city should be given to the man who, by force or cunning, succeeded in taking it. Guessing something of what was afoot, the other barons at first refused, but then, faced with the news of Kerbogha's approach, they promised the Norman everything he asked. (The only one to make no promises was Raymond of Saint-Gilles, but his opposition was overridden.)

Bohemond made contact with Firouz and on the night of June 2–3 succeeded in scaling the tower, which immediately surrendered to him, and opening the gates to the rest of the army, and the Crusaders poured into the city. Taken by surprise, the garrison had no time to act: the indigenous population went over to the Franks, and the Turks who were inside the city only escaped massacre by taking refuge in the citadel. A great many failed to reach it and were slaughtered. When Yaghi-Siyan saw the Crusaders' banners floating from the walls, he leaped on his horse and galloped, almost alone, out of the city.

Thanks to the treachery of one of its defenders, Antioch was in

the hands of the Christians. The next day local peasants brought the
victors the head of Yaghi-Siyan, who had been killed by Armenian
woodcutters outside the city. The citadel was still holding out, commanded by Yaghi-Siyan's son, Shams ad-Daula. The Crusaders had
no time to do more than get inside the city and barricade themselves
in. The day after the capture of Antioch, Kerbogha's army was already at the gates. If he had arrived two days earlier he could have
taken the Crusaders in the rear and wiped them out; caught between
the besieged garrison and the governor of Mosul's forces, they would
not have stood a chance.

(In fact the Crusaders owed their safety to another Frankish chief
of whom little had been heard for some time, as well as to Bohemond.
Instead of marching directly on Antioch, Kerbogha had wasted three
weeks unsuccessfully laying siege to the town of Edessa, which was
held at that time by Baldwin of Boulogne.)

From the besiegers the Franks had become the besieged, and far
from celebrating their victory they found themselves in a more critical
situation than ever. Inside the captured city, provisions were running
short and the army was decimated, weak, and at the end of its endurance, while Kerbogha and his emirs were launching constant
attacks from without. The triumph of June 3 had been merely a
respite and it looked as though the Crusaders had only got into the
city to be the more easily slaughtered. In those weeks of June they
reached such a low ebb that the soldiers, weak with hunger, refused
to leave their billets. There were mass desertions, and in their panic the
deserters were spreading the rumor that Antioch had already fallen
to Kerbogha. It was at this moment that Peter the Hermit attempted
to flee. He was brought back and sharply reprimanded by Bohemond,
but in spite of this, his prestige does not seem to have suffered, for
not long afterward he was sent as an ambassador to Kerbogha.
More serious was the defection of one of the great French barons,
Stephen of Blois, who escaped with all his men. Another who departed
was William of Grant-Mesnil. These two lords, fleeing as though
Kerbogha were hard on their heels, took the road back through Asia
Minor and sought refuge with Alexius Comnenus.

The Emperor had finally kept his promise to join the Crusade, and
after reconquering the Mediterranean coastal provinces, was advancing on Antioch with the whole of his army, intending to force Kerbogha to raise the siege. Both the Turks and the Crusaders knew
this. But now something occurred which proved providential for one
side and nearly disastrous for the other. The cause was purely the
desperate shame of men trying to justify their own cowardice, but

the consequences were serious. Stephen of Blois assured the Emperor that the Crusade was finished and that by then Kerbogha had certainly annihilated the entire Christian army and must already be advancing victoriously to meet the *basileus*. He insisted that it would be both useless and dangerous to continue the march on Antioch and that it would be better to fall back on a safer position. Horrified, Alexius decided to listen to councils of prudence and withdraw his army, despite the entreaties of Bohemond's brother Guy, who was serving under his command. To make him take such a decision, the fugitives must have painted the situation in exceedingly somber colors, quite unrelated to the facts; but even so, the Emperor might have done better to seek further information before giving up the proposed campaign.

Chroniclers of the Crusade, although Latins and hostile to Byzantium, are compelled to admit that the part played by Stephen of Blois in this affair was crucial, and that but for him the Emperor would never have halted his advance.[7] But the Crusaders shut up in Antioch were unaware of this fact. All they knew was that while they waited for the *basileus* as a savior, ready to forgive him all his past offenses, he had suddenly withdrawn his forces for no ascertainable reason and abandoned them to their fate when he was actually within a few days' march of Antioch. There was despair in the Frankish camp and great joy in the camp of Kerbogha and the Turks.

At that moment it seemed as though only a miracle could save God's army, now so demoralized and broken that the soldiers were refusing to obey their commanders and were no longer strong enough even to man the walls adequately. In these terrible days, Bohemond was able to prove himself one of those men worth, as they say, an army in themselves. He defended the city bought so dearly, which he already looked on as his own, with savage energy. The other leaders no longer even considered disputing his command: he organized the defense of the ramparts and gates and seemed to be everywhere at once, seeing to everything that needed doing. At night he patrolled the city by torchlight, ferreting out spies and deserters and personally escorting back to their quarters any he caught in the act of flight. During an attack by Kerbogha on June 12 some of the soldiers were so demoralized that they refused to leave their houses in answer to the call. Bohemond had the lower quarters of the town set on fire and smoked them out of their earths like animals, so that the soldiers had no alternative but to hurry to the ramparts and the assault was beaten off.

The Holy Lance

Even so, the Crusading army was saved by a miracle. All the historians are unanimous on this point, even when they disagree in their interpretation of the facts. The person responsible for the "miracle" was someone so unworthy of attention that non-Latin historians could not even identify him. "A cunning monk," says Ibn al-Athir; "the Bishop Peter" says Anna Comnena (confusing the man in question with Peter the Hermit or with the Bishop of Le Puy). In fact he was neither a bishop nor a monk, nor even a common soldier: he was the servant of an ordinary citizen, a common man from Provence who made one of the civilian pilgrims who had followed the Count of Toulouse's army.

His name was Peter Bartholomew, and besides being a man of low birth, he had an unsavory reputation among his comrades as a debauchee and a ne'er-do-well.* Nevertheless, this anything but saintly Crusader was several times visited by dreams in which he saw sometimes Saint Andrew and sometimes Christ himself. He was so obsessed by these dreams that in the end he told his superiors and finally the Count of Toulouse himself about them. Christ and Saint Andrew commanded Peter Bartholomew to tell the Crusaders that their wicked lives and debauches with pagan women had brought on them the divine anger. This revelation contained nothing remarkable in itself, but there was more to follow: God, in His mercy, was ready to forgive His soldiers their sins and sent them a clear sign of His forgiveness. He revealed to them that the Holy Lance which had pierced the Savior's side lay buried under the pavement of one of the churches in Antioch.

Now there was a duly authenticated version of the Holy Lance reposing in Constantinople, where the leaders of the Crusade had been able to adore it along with the other relics of the Passion, so when Adhemar of Monteil was told of Peter Bartholomew's visions he did not take the "revelation" seriously. However, in their weak and overexcited condition, the soldiers and pilgrims were constantly producing phenomena which could be taken for messages from on high: a number of other Crusaders, a highly respectable priest among them, heard voices and even saw visions which had some connection with the precious relic buried somewhere in the city. In the end the

---

* He had, however, received some education. Although at first he pretended to be unable to read, it was later discovered that this was in fact untrue.

army chiefs, led by Raymond of Saint-Gilles, decided to get to the bottom of the matter. The papal legate remained obstinately skeptical, but at length he authorized Peter Bartholomew, accompanied by priests from the Count of Toulouse's following, to excavate under the Church of Saint Peter.

After a long and at first fruitless search, a piece of rusty iron which might or might not have been the Holy Lance was actually discovered under the pavement of the ancient church. When Peter Bartholomew emerged from the hole in the ground clutching the spearhead in his arms, all doubts were forgotten and everyone present, beginning with Raymond of Aguilers, chaplain to the Count of Toulouse (and author of the chronicle), fell upon the poor relic, still caked with earth, and smothered it with tears and kisses. The news spread like wildfire through the camp and the whole city, and the joy of the army was so great that it was more than the Bishop of Le Puy's life was worth not to admit that the relic was genuine. Moreover the secular leaders of the Crusade had already realized the advantage to be drawn from this providential event. With the exception of Raymond of Saint-Gilles, the barons do not seem to have had a genuine belief in the Lance's authenticity, but they thought it politic to appear to believe in it rather than disappoint their soldiers.

The discovery of this dubious relic probably aroused more enthusiasm among the rank and file of the Crusaders than the invention of a new nuclear device or the launching of a satellite to the moon would cause in our own day. It is to an event of this kind that we must look for a parallel if we are to understand the sudden transformation which took place in the army in Antioch. Men who had been utterly exhausted and demoralized were transformed into resolute soldiers, ready to face an enemy superior in numbers and with fresh troops. Even Moslem historians, who are generally rather ill-informed as to what was going on in the Frankish camp, attributed the Crusaders' victory at Antioch to the intervention of the Holy Lance, although they were convinced that the whole thing was a fraud designed to raise the morale of the army. It seems impossible that the mere discovery of a piece of rusty iron could suddenly restore strength and courage to thousands of men when only the day before, setting their houses on fire had been scarcely enough to drag them from their beds. It was proclaimed throughout the city that the Holy Lance was a sign sent expressly by God, a certain gauge of victory, and so indeed it seemed. In a desperate situation, commanders are always ready with promises of victory and claims that heaven is on their side, but rarely are their efforts crowned with such spectacular results.

The Holy Lance may not have been an interplanetary rocket, but in the minds of these simple people it was much more than that because it was the actual spear which had pierced the flesh of Jesus Christ himself. It was primarily an object of love, of an almost hysterical adoration, for it must not be forgotten that the common soldiers were in a state of weakness which left them equally prone to depression and to wild exultation. It was also the object of veneration and pride, the more so in that it was to one of themselves, one of the "poor," that the honor had fallen of discovering the marvelous relic so long hidden from men's eyes. Lastly it was an object endowed with supernatural powers, capable of routing the pagans by its mere presence. Fasting was ordered in the camp for several days, accompanied by prayers and public penance. Once again, the army remembered its call to martyrdom and the joy of serving God.

The high command, led by Bohemond, took over both the relic (which was entrusted to the care of Raymond of Saint-Gilles since it was the Provençal contingent which had been responsible for its discovery) and the visionary. Peter Bartholomew's revelations were henceforth dictated by saints exceedingly well informed on the military necessities of the time and extremely well disposed toward Bohemond. The Franks decided to make a mass sortie, leaving only a small garrison to defend the city, and fight the besieging army in the open country. It seemed a desperate enterprise, but organized by experienced commanders, skilled in every kind of military strategy, the attempt succeeded beyond all expectation. Against the advice of his emirs, Kerbogha rashly allowed the entire Crusading army to leave the city and group itself into battle formation, instead of attacking the various detachments as they emerged onto the drawbridge. He thought his adversaries were so weakened that he chose to let them all out, intending to wipe them out in a single battle, rather than risk an extension of the siege. Moreover his own camp was split by serious disagreements and half his emirs refused to intervene in time. The Turkish army, surrounded and driven back to the river, finally broke before the Crusaders' attack. At last, seeing his allies had deserted him, Kerbogha also took to his heels, abandoning his camp with all the riches it contained.

The Crusading army wasted no time plundering the camp. Acting on the instructions given by Peter Bartholomew, they pursued the enemy to the plain of the Orontes, scattering and cutting down the fugitives. The Turkish commander returned to Mosul in a desperate plight, his army almost annihilated, and disgraced forever in the eyes of all Islam. Nothing, it seemed, could stand against the savage men of iron who had come from the North. Antioch was the turning point of the Crusade. The atabeg of Mosul's defeat, coming after Nicaea and Dorylaeum, spread terror in the path of the "Franks." Only a little while before, they had been completely unheard of; now they emerged as the world's most formidable warriors.

The victory had immense repercussions, but instead of pushing home their advantage the Crusaders dallied for a further six months in Antioch. The soldiers, it is true, were in need of a rest. Now there was no one to threaten them: they were undisputed masters of Antioch and all the surrounding countryside, and such castles as were still in Turkish hands were capitulating for lack of soldiers to defend them. The Turkish garrisons, hated by the local inhabitants, were leaving the country, and the Crusaders, welcomed everywhere as liberators, took over their strongholds and installed their own garrisons. Meanwhile, their leaders wrangled over possession of Antioch.

The war had been going on for fifteen months and the Crusade was beginning to seem a practical proposition, on a much larger scale and perhaps more difficult and complex than those responsible for it had ever foreseen. It was a fact that in spite of constant numerical inferiority God's army had defeated the Turkish armies several times over, when no one in the East had previously been able to resist them. So great was the Turks' reputation that the Christians, with a nice blend of modesty and pride, attributed their success to the divine favor. Moreover, however courageous the soldiers and however resourceful their leaders, it was the morale of the army as a whole which enabled the Crusaders to hold out. Kerbogha was conquered as much by the Holy Lance and the humble Peter Bartholomew as by Bohemond or Godfrey.

First Contacts Between the Franks and the Natives

The Franks penetrated the East like a foreign body, or like some hitherto unknown virus against which no natural defense as yet existed. In the beginning, they disturbed the balance of power in a way which acted in their favor.

At first the Crusade disconcerted its adversaries in the same way that it had disconcerted its potential allies, the Greeks. But Islam was not entirely unaware of the existence of the Franks, whom they called by the name of their most numerous representatives, the *Firenj*

(French). In the course of their conflict with Byzantium in Asia Minor, the Turks had had frequent encounters with the Norman, Scandinavian, German, English, and French mercenaries, who made up the elite corps of the *basileus*'s armies, and these had long been known as formidable, intrepid, and ferocious warriors. The Arab kingdoms of the Mediterranean were even better acquainted with the fiercely belligerent Normans. In Spain, too, the Christian warriors, Norman and French as well as Spanish, were renowned as worthy adversaries.

Islam as a whole had little idea of the real reasons for the Crusade (their chroniclers blamed it on the machinations of the Norman Roger of Sicily) and was surprised by the size of the Crusading army and its internal cohesion, which long familiarity with Western mercenaries had not led them to expect.

The Turks, who were the Crusaders' first and principal adversaries, were the first to build them a reputation as incomparable warriors; indeed, after suffering such spectacular defeats at their hands, they could scarcely do otherwise. But the author of the *Anonymi Gesta Francorum* probably exaggerates in asserting that the Turks reciprocated the feelings of esteem which the Franks genuinely felt for the Turks. In fact, they came to regard the Crusaders more as a horde of barbarians, wild beasts clad in iron, whose very courage did not seem astonishing because it came from an innate and diabolical insensitivity.

Yet it cannot be said that the Franks, at the beginning of the Crusade, were remarkable for their ferocity: certainly they were no more cruel than the Turks themselves. So far, with the exception of the excesses committed by Peter the Hermit's unfortunate "Crusaders," they could not be accused of anything more than the brutalities inevitable with any army in a foreign land. But after the siege of Antioch there was a change in the army's behavior, principally because of the difficulties of obtaining supplies. For months troops of armed men ravaged the countryside around the Orontes, pushing their raids further and further afield. When they fell on a town with a Moslem population, they slaughtered the men and took the women into slavery. The Franks were an army at bay, isolated in a country that was strange if not invariably hostile, and they were beginning to fall back on the weapon most usual in such circumstances: terror. William of Tyre shows in the clearest possible way that this policy of terrorizing both the enemy and the local inhabitants was deliberate and attributes the original idea to Bohemond. With the object of striking terror into the hearts of any spies inside the camp, the Norman commander had a certain number of prisoners killed and their heads roasted on spits, encouraging the rumor that the Frankish barons fed on human flesh.[8] The spies—and anyone else who had reason to fear being taken for one—deserted the camp the same day and went about telling everyone that "these people [the Franks] . . . were harder than rock and iron and their cruelty surpassed that of the bear and the lion" (who at least refrain from roasting their victims before they devour them). This curious method of intimidation impressed not only the Turks but also the local population, and in showing open amusement at Bohemond's stratagem the Archbishop of Tyre seems to have forgotten that a reputation for cannibalism might be considered undesirable by men claiming to be soldiers of Christ.

However, the kind of stupid pride in passing for men of the most unbridled ferocity which drove the Franks to the sort of distasteful stratagem practiced by Bohemond does in fact make only rare appearances in the accounts of the historians. It becomes clear that not all the Franks were "swords of God," loosed against the enemies of their faith: far from it. But their reputation for extreme cruelty, partially deserved and carefully fostered by the Turks, stuck to them.

After the fall of Antioch, the whole of Syria was plunged into a state of terror and dismay. The defeat of the atabeg of Mosul, the general in chief of the Persian sultanate, convinced the kings of Aleppo and Damascus—and still more the petty princes of the Syrian coast—that no resistance was possible, and had they been bold —and strong—enough to continue the campaign the Crusaders could easily have conquered the whole of Palestine in that one summer of 1098.

All the same the Turks, who were the Crusaders' principal adversaries, were not affected in their vital interests by this war. The Seljuk princes who had divided the empire of the great conqueror Malik Shah between them ruled from the great cities of Iran and Mesopotamia; their capitals were Ispahan, Baghdad, and Mosul, and closer to Syria, Aleppo and Damascus. Asia Minor was a country only recently subdued and still liable to reconquest by the Greeks. The Turkish rulers' inadequacy in face of the Crusaders' attack on Antioch has been amply demonstrated, but to these princes the great city, more Greek than Moslem, was merely wealth to be exploited and its loss does not appear to have upset them very much. They were too busy quarreling over the possession of lands, much more important in their eyes, which had long been under Moslem domination, and regarded wars against the Christians, whether Latin or Greek, merely as inevitable frontier skirmishes. Reading the Turkish and Arab chroniclers who deal with the events of this period, it is clear that their real interests were centered wholly on the quarrels between the various sultanates of the Near East and Egypt, the policies of the various sultans, viziers, and caliphs, religious dissensions, dynastic rivalries, and feudal squabbles. The "Franks" were simply temporary invaders, an objectionable nuisance but of little real significance.

But for Cilicia and to an even greater extent for Syria, the Crusade was an event of major importance. On the coast of Asia Minor, the effect of the Crusade was, as we have seen, the reconquest of these provinces by the Greeks. Bithynia and the provinces of Smyrna and Ephesus came once more under the rule of the Byzantine Emperor and it is possible, although not entirely certain, that without the Crusaders' help this reconquest might not have taken place. In those provinces which bore the chief brunt of the holy war, Cilicia, the province of Antioch, western Syria, and of course Palestine, the populations were largely made up of Christians, although the actual proportions varied. They included Armenians, who were especially numerous in Cilicia; Syrians, autochthonous Christians who, despite numerous conversions to Islam, still after four hundred years of Moslem rule formed the basis of the rural population; and finally, the Greeks. All these countries, and Palestine in particular, also had strong Jewish communities. In southern Syria and Palestine the Moslems accounted for almost half the population, but these were Syrians or Arabs and for the most part hostile to the Turks.

The Crusaders had begun by conquering countries the majority of whose populations were Christian, recently overrun by the Turks. Nearly everywhere they were welcomed as liberators. Before the siege of Antioch, we find the Turkish garrison of "Maressa" (Marata) fleeing at the approach of the Crusaders for fear of reprisals by the native population, and at Artah (Artesia) the Armenian citizens massacred all the Turks inside the city even before the Crusaders arrived, and then flung open the gates to welcome them with great rejoicing. Wherever the Frankish army successfully carried enemy strongholds, it owed some of this success to the support of local Christians. To them, the Crusaders appeared as saviors, fellow Christians who had come from the ends of the earth to drive out the Turks; and in spite of countless reasons for mutual dissatisfaction, some at least among the Christians of these provinces—the

Armenians—were to remain on friendly terms with the Franks for a very long time.

The Greeks had many reasons for distrusting the Latins, mostly stemming from the climate of misunderstanding which had been established between the Crusaders and the Byzantine government from their first encounters. The Syrians, who made up the greater part of the rural population, suffered, like the common people of every land, from any kind of war and were unlikely to be well disposed toward any foreign soldiers, whether they were Christians or not. Moreover, all these peoples, Armenians as well as Greeks and Syrians, soon discovered that their brothers in the faith were masters quite as harsh as the Turks.

The Syrians and Armenians had at least one excellent reason for welcoming the Crusaders: these Christian liberators were not Greeks. The Crusaders came from distant lands and they had little interest in theology: for them, any man who worshipped the Cross was a Christian. Even their priests and bishops never thought of asking the people they liberated to explain their views on the nature of Jesus Christ. The Christians of the Syriac or Jacobite rite were Monophysites, while the Armenians adhered to the Gregorian rite, but with a wisdom born largely of indifference the Crusaders did not condemn as heretics people whose language and customs were in any case too remote for them to be able to judge them. As we shall see, the Latin clergy later adopted a less tolerant attitude, but even then it was actually remarkably broad-minded when compared to the attitude of the Byzantine clergy.

The Greeks were cordially detested by the people who had for centuries submitted to their dominion. In the provinces of Asia Minor and northern Syria, a suspicious and heavy-handed policy of oppression had lost the Greeks the sympathies of the Armenian population, who were jealous of their independence, while the Christians of the Jacobite rite loathed the "Chalcedonian" tyranny so bitterly that they rejoiced openly at the Turkish victories and hailed the Seljuk Malik Shah as a liberator. The Latins could have no conception of the violence of the religious and national feelings dividing the various Christian communities of the East, because they had known nothing like it in their own countries.

The Christian population of Antioch, which was made up of Greeks, Armenians, and Syrians, although there the Greek element predominated, had been very harshly oppressed by the Turks, who, from motives of prudence rather than religious intolerance, had forbidden Christians to carry arms or attend public meetings. (They had good reason for this. It was the treachery of an officer of Armenian origin which enabled the Crusaders to capture the city.) When the Crusading army laid siege to Antioch, Yaghi-Siyan, partly to rid himself of useless mouths and even more for fear of a rising inside the town, drove out a large number of the Christians to seek shelter with the Crusaders or scatter over the countryside. Those Christians who remained in Antioch, and the clergy in particular, suffered greatly from Turkish hostility during the siege. At one point, the Patriarch of Antioch, John IV, was fastened to the battlements in a place particularly exposed to the Crusaders' fire. Such a spectacle could only fill the Latin Christians with indignation, and in fact, after the capture of the city the prelate, one of the foremost dignitaries of the Christian Church, was treated with the utmost respect. The Crusaders restored the reverend old man to his functions, and it did not occur to the Bishop of Le Puy to dispute his rank or treat him as a "schismatic."

Finding the churches of Antioch profaned, the frescoes and mosaics covered with whitewash and images of the saints broken, the Crusaders were overcome with brotherly feelings for these Christians so different from themselves. They set to work, in a spirit of pious sadness, to repair what the Turks had sacked, reconstructing statues and icons piece by piece, cleaning the walls, and washing down pavements and altars so that the churches could be restored to religious use. In this the Latin and Greek clergy fraternized unreservedly, the sufferings endured by both sides making them forget their grounds for disagreement. But this state of affairs could not last.

To begin with, the Latins regarded themselves—and were to go on regarding themselves increasingly—as the lawful lords of Antioch, while the Greeks, from the Patriarch down, could recognize no other authority than the *basileus*. Secondly, the gulf dividing the two civilizations was already too deep and the ordinary people, whether pilgrims or soldiers, could not bring themselves to believe that these dark-skinned men who dressed in Oriental style and spoke in incomprehensible languages were real Christians, and found it hard to distinguish them from Moslems. During the siege, the camp had been invaded by hundreds of merchants and deserters, many of whom were actually spies. The local peasants, although Christian, were not always willing to sell their produce to the Crusaders, or made them pay exorbitant prices, while the Crusaders had no scruples about taking what they wanted by force when they could not obtain it on other terms.

After the fall of Antioch, the Crusaders (helped by the native

Christians) massacred all Turks they could find inside the city. They felt no remorse because they believed that a massacre of this kind was pleasing to God. The wives and daughters of the slaughtered Moslems fell to the share of the victors. A similar fate befell any Christian women who had been left without protection, and the poorest were tempted to sell themselves to the soldiers to get food. If the chroniclers are to be believed, there were a great many native women in the Crusaders' camp, and the "revelations" of Peter Bartholomew endorse this. Rumor attributed the army's misfortunes to the wicked commerce of God's soldiers with "pagan" women. The stigma was due not so much to the actual debauchery as to the impure contact with foreign women, racial prejudice becoming confused with religious intolerance. In addition, the Crusaders, having used their privilege as victorious soldiers to take possession of the finest houses in the city, were not always scrupulous about returning these houses to their lawful owners, even if they were Christians. In short, from the time of Antioch onward relations between the Latins and the Orientals started to become those—never very cordial—of occupiers and occupied.

Baldwin

If the barons intended to establish themselves firmly in the Holy Land, they had to have a policy based, in principle, on collaboration between the indigenous Christians and the Crusading army. This was their intention, even if only in order to keep the Holy Sepulcher under Christian control. Only one of them, however, was trying consciously from the outset to pursue a policy of collaboration with the natives, and even he went about it in such a way that he very nearly destroyed the goodwill of his potential allies forever.

At first sight, Baldwin of Boulogne was no different from any other of the countless younger sons of great families whose only fortune was a princely education (according to the standards of the time), good weapons, and an indomitable pride. In Europe a man without lands had scant hope of ever becoming rich and powerful. Wealth was reckoned in fields and woods and castles, and lands were all in the hands of hereditary owners. The feudal system consisted of an arrangement of mutual contracts so thoroughly worked out that it was difficult for even the boldest adventurers to take another man's lands. "No land without a lord, no lord without lands" was the rule. One had to travel a long way to find lands without a lord.

Baldwin, blessed with two brothers older than himself, had, as we have seen, at first been intended by his parents for the Church. He gave up this career when very young, and married. The main thing he seems to have grasped from Urban II's speech was the promise of lands to be conquered from God's enemies. He knew the story of Roussel of Bailleul, and it is worth while remembering that Roussel had successfully won the sympathies of the local population and by this means had very nearly eluded the Greeks. The three brothers of Boulogne had all taken the cross. Godfrey, the second, was actually one of the leaders, because he had equipped a substantial army and had virtually renounced his duchy of Lower Lorraine. The eldest, Eustace, Count of Boulogne, had not been prepared to make such great sacrifices and intended ultimately to return to his own country. As for Baldwin, he had been entrusted by Godfrey with command of half his troops, and when the army reached Constantinople it was he who, acting on his brother's orders, sacked the suburbs of the Greek capital. The three brothers got on very well together and there were no rivalries or jealousies between them.

One day when Alexius Comnenus was giving a solemn reception in Constantinople in honor of the Latin barons, one of the knights (Anna Comnena does not tell us his name) went and seated himself on the imperial throne. The Greeks, although scandalized, were too polite to make the enormity of his behavior clear to the barbarian. "Count Baldwin," says Anna, took the uncouth individual by the hand and forced him to rise, explaining that such behavior was improper because it was contrary to the customs of the country in which he found himself. Baldwin was no flatterer and was certainly not afraid of Alexius Comnenus's anger, but he did possess a certain natural gentility and must have been more deeply shocked than the other barons by his compatriot's tasteless action.

Not long afterward, before the walls of Nicaea, Baldwin became friendly with a man named Bagrat (Pakrad), the "Pancras" of the Latin chroniclers, an Armenian noble serving under Taticius. This shows that from the outset, Godfrey of Bouillon's brother had made a point of joining the cosmopolitan society formed by the Byzantine army of the time. In the army, Europeans of every nationality rubbed shoulders with Greeks, Armenians, Petchenegs, and even Turks, and this must already have given many Norman, English, and Scandinavian knights some basic idea of this Oriental world so different from their own. Baldwin, who had never served abroad before, took the first opportunity to learn to know the East, and the Armenian Bagrat must have realized very quickly that this Frank was the kind of man who makes his home wherever he can make his fortune.

It was probably on the advice of his Armenian friend that Baldwin left the Crusading army at Marash with a body of five hundred knights and two thousand foot, leaving his wife and children in the care of his brothers. While the rest of the army continued its journey south, the force led by Baldwin ventured into the mountains of Cilicia, where the Armenian element was predominant, although even then many strongholds were occupied by the Turks.

In planning his conquest of Cilicia in concert with Bagrat, Baldwin had not reckoned on meeting a rival, someone who, as another Crusader baron, should logically speaking have been his ally. This was Bohemond's nephew Tancred. The young Norman had no direct agreement with the Armenian chiefs but he was certainly familiar with the local situation, through Norman mercenaries with the Byzantine army. (His uncle Guy was serving in the Emperor's army.) Consequently the two men left the main body of the army in the same place and almost at the same time, with the same idea in mind, although there was no arrangement between them.

Tancred was a boy of unusually independent temperament and had already given Bohemond some trouble during his negotiations with Alexius Comnenus. He had very nearly come to blows with the Emperor's kinsman Michael Paleologus, and proclaimed to all comers that he had never sworn any loyalty to the Greeks and meant to make war on his own account. He was not a rich man and his company numbered no more than a hundred knights and a few hundred foot soldiers, but what he lacked in soldiers he undoubtedly made up for in boldness and talent for warfare.

With his little troop, Tancred laid siege to the city of Tarsus in Cilicia, which, although occupied by a Turkish garrison, was inhabited almost exclusively by Armenians. The young Norman succeeded in opening negotiations with them, and since the Turks feared a rising of the local population, he was actually on the point of taking the city when Baldwin appeared before the walls with his five hundred knights. The terrified garrison took flight. The city of Tarsus became Christian once more and the grateful local population immediately flew Tancred's banners from every tower. To their surprise they discovered that the Latin brothers, who all appeared so alike, could not bear the sight of one another's flags, even if they were marked with the sign of the cross. Baldwin followed Tancred into Tarsus and, in a blind rage, tore down the Norman's banners and gave orders for him and his men to be sent packing as soon as possible. Bowing before his rival's superior forces, Tancred left the city he had captured and laid siege to another one, Adana. Baldwin installed himself as master of Tarsus and held court to all the local notables.

On the evening of the same day, a troop of about three hundred Normans, the second half of Tancred's contingent, arrived at Tarsus. They found the gates closed. Despite all their entreaties, Baldwin refused to let them in and they were forced to camp out in the open fields, where during the night they were surprised by a detachment of Turks and slaughtered to the last man.[9]

Baldwin was still only in his apprenticeship: later he would avoid such mistakes. But for the present his behavior toward Tancred's men provoked such indignation among his companions that he had difficulty in controlling a mutiny of his own men. He got out of it as best he could with the feeble excuse that he had promised the notables of the city of Tarsus to let in no soldiers but those serving under his own command. This technique of appealing to the feelings of the local population was something the Frankish knights never understood.

The incident of the three hundred slaughtered Normans was held against Baldwin of Boulogne by the other Crusaders for a long time, but in any case he was not particularly anxious to rejoin them. There was a fresh encounter with Tancred outside Mamistra, where the two barons fought each other under the astonished eyes of the infidels, then on October 15, 1097, Baldwin went down toward Marash where the great army was at that time encamped. His wife was dying and his brother Godfrey gravely ill after a hunting accident in which he had been wounded by a bear. Baldwin arrived just in time to say farewell to his wife. His children were already dead. Despite his mourning and his brother's illness, he stayed only two days with his family, and it seems likely that the other barons had heard of what had passed at Tarsus and gave him to understand that his presence was not wanted. He set off again, in a direction in which he would be certain not to meet Tancred.

This was the beginning of Baldwin of Boulogne's real career as the Latin conqueror of the East. This time, still guided by his friend Bagrat, he made for the city of Edessa, an ancient and powerful city, with the object not of dislodging the Turks but of installing himself as the ally of the ruling prince, the Armenian Thoros. From the moment of his arrival in the province of Edessa his exploits marked him out as a worthy captain, and this region, for the most part held by petty Armenian princelings sorely pressed by the Turks, struck him as a field of action ideally suited to his plans. The first of these was to "help" the Eastern Christians, and here the wisest course was still to ally himself with those Christians who were in a fit condition to fight the Turks. Secondly, given the few forces at his disposal, Baldwin could not attempt to conquer a country of any size without the co-operation of the inhabitants. The Armenians represented a real force in the province of Edessa, and Baldwin aimed to make himself master, not of a stronghold captured from the Turks, but of a Christian city.

Bagrat himself was a brother of Kogh Vasil (Basil the Thief), the daring captain who had taken the fortresses of Kaisun and Raban from the Turks, and he had led Baldwin into these Armeno-Syrian provinces in the hope of completing the conquest of the region by the Armenians who, throughout the eleventh century, had been migrating there in great strength and numbers and dominating the autochthonous Syrian population by force of arms. The Prince of Edessa, Thoros, son of Hethoum, had maintained his position despite the conquest of the greater part of the country by the Turks. He was an able and energetic man who had succeeded in safeguarding his city's independence and reigned there, not as hereditary sovereign, but as *curopalates,* an official of Byzantium. This was a purely nominal title since Byzantium was in no position to protect or subdue such distant provinces.

Unfortunately, the Armenian princes of the country, if they hoped to make a career in the Byzantine army, were obliged to adopt the Greek Orthodox religion, with the result that they found themselves morally cut off from their own people and to a still greater extent from the local population, which belonged to the Jacobite rite. Thoros was no exception to this rule. Religious feelings among the Eastern Christians overrode national sentiments and in their eyes an Armenian who belonged to the Greek religion was a Greek, whether he was a champion of national independence or not. Consequently, Baldwin's arrival in Edessa unleashed passions which he himself was perhaps incapable of foreseeing.

When, using Bagrat as his intermediary, Thoros invited the Latin adventurer into his city, he was simply hoping to enlist the services of a *condottiero* who could protect him against Turkish attacks. On realizing this, Baldwin became violently angry and promptly started preparing to leave. Thoros, whose advanced age prevented him from commanding his troops in person, was already too dependent on this unexpected auxiliary to let him go, and it was agreed between the two men that Thoros, who had no children of his own, should adopt Baldwin, designate him his heir, and share his power with him. The adoption ceremony was held publicly in the throne room of the palace at Edessa. (Baldwin, naked to the waist, was obliged to insert himself between Thoros's shirt and his person, and the old man then clasped him to his breast and kissed him.)

Once he had become the old Armenian's son, Baldwin lost no time in ridding himself of the adoptive father who was already in his way: Thoros perished a few days later in a riot which Baldwin had, admittedly, done nothing to engineer but to which he was a party. Although Latin historians seem anxious to exonerate the Crusader baron from responsibility in this affair, the Armenian historian Matthew of Edessa openly accuses Baldwin of having dabbled in the plot hatched by the old ruler's enemies.[10] Albert of Aix himself suggests that Baldwin had been let into the secret of the plot but had refused to take part, the inference being that he did not carry cynicism to the point of giving his open support (which would also have made him lose face in front of his own knights), but that he let his tacit agreement be understood. At that time he was installed in the fortress with his men and could easily have suppressed the proposed rising if he had so wished.

Once they were sure of the foreign Christian's backing, Thoros's vassals took advantage of the opportunity of getting rid of a "Greek" and roused the populace against him. Thoros, in terror, begged Baldwin to allow him to retire with his wife to Melitene. Baldwin gave him a solemn promise on the holiest relics in the city, but he proved so little able to implement it that the unfortunate old man and his wife were lynched by the crowd at their own palace gates. Baldwin became, by right and in fact, lord of the city of Edessa, and he wasted no time in making his new subjects sorry for their ungrateful conduct toward Thoros.

He was not a man to spare anyone or anything. Suspecting, perhaps wrongly, that his "friend" Bagrat had been in secret communication with his brother Kogh Vasil, he had Bagrat put to the torture, deprived of his possessions, and flung into prison. When the emir Balduk, lord of Samosata, who was now the new Count of Edessa's vassal, attempted to conquer the town of Saruj on his own account, he was accused of treason and beheaded. The Armenian nobles of Edessa who were plotting to overthrow their new lord were punished in the Byzantine fashion by mutilation—having their eyes put out and their feet, hands, or noses cut off. From the moment of his installation in Edessa, Baldwin flung off the mask. He no longer hid his contempt for the natives, openly favored his fellow Franks, and installed them in all the highest offices. More than anything else he needed Frankish soldiers, and to attract the greatest possible number of Crusaders to his side he offered generous largesse at the expense of the local populace. After the long, disappointing siege of Antioch, Edessa offered houses, money, horses, lands, and a less perilous war.

The Count of Edessa was not interested in conquering the Holy Sepulcher and devoted himself entirely, with indomitable energy, to founding a kingdom of his own in the East. As a matter of policy as well as self-interest, he had asked for the hand of the daughter of one of the wealthiest Armenian lords of the region, Taphnuz (Thatoul?), but here he made a bad bargain, for his father-in-law was terrified by his son-in-law's savage methods and fled into the mountains, taking with him the better part of the dowry, while Baldwin himself had little time or thought to devote to his young Armenian bride.

Baldwin had realized from the outset that he could never really count on any but his own men, on the knights who were his closest followers or were actually related to him, and at a pinch, on such Crusading lords as he could win over by gifts. It has been amply demonstrated that he did not possess a talent for getting on with people, and unlike his brother Godfrey and Bohemond, he did not enjoy the unconditional devotion of his troops. He could make himself respected and feared, and his courage and the swiftness of his decisions compelled the admiration of friends and enemies alike. But he had few friends.

His reign as Count of Edessa was marked by a policy of systematic spoliation of the native population for the benefit of the Frankish knights, and Baldwin's service attracted neither the most honest nor the most disinterested of God's soldiers. With a fine impartiality Albert of Aix and after him William of Tyre both denounce the scandalous behavior of the Crusaders in settling in Christian cities where they had been welcomed as friends and proceeding to an unscrupulous exploitation of the nobles and citizens of the country, seizing their houses and goods from them by force and subjecting them to outrages of all kinds. The first year of Baldwin's rule in Edessa saw the formation of a Frankish "aristocracy," haughty, brutal, and disdainful and determined to treat the Armenians, like the Syrians, as an inferior race. Their contempt had no justification in a superior level of civilization or in religious intolerance. What was the reason? It is a fact that the Franks were better soldiers, as they themselves had realized with some astonishment, and drunk with success, they certainly had a tendency to consider themselves a superior race. Religious feeling had little to do with this consciousness of superiority. They were perfectly prepared to respect the faith of the local Christians and did not accuse them of heresy, but they did blame them for their lack of military strength. This, at least where the Armenians were concerned, was somewhat unfair, because they were remarkably courageous soldiers. But the Armenians were well aware of the complexities of their country's politics and they were capable, if circumstances demanded, of making alliances with the Greeks, the Arabs, or even the Turks in the hope of safeguarding the precarious independence of their principalities.

In 1098, Baldwin had forged no strong ties of friendship with them and understood very little of the expedients demanded by local politics. He was a practical man and always devoted himself entirely to the most urgent task at hand. Within a few months he had succeeded in crushing the whole province of Edessa beneath his iron fist and giving the principal strongholds as fiefs to his knights. From a landless younger son he had become, in one year, a great lord, the overlord of considerable fiefs, and at the head of his Frankish and Armenian troops he was progressively eliminating the Turks from the land he had made his own. When, on his way to Antioch with his great army, Kerbogha attempted to win back Edessa from its new lord, Baldwin put up a vigorous resistance. The Turkish generalissimo wasted three weeks outside Edessa and then lifted the siege. As we have already seen, Baldwin had unwittingly saved the Crusading army from disaster. Kerbogha reached Antioch only to learn that the city had fallen.

The Quarrel over Antioch

After the fall of Antioch and the defeat of Kerbogha, Baldwin thought less than ever of leaving Edessa: he had the interests of his county so much at heart that he had succeeded in persuading his brother Godfrey to come to his aid in driving out the Turks from the valley of the Upper Euphrates. For his trouble Godfrey received the strongholds of Tel-Basheir and Ruwandan (Ravendel) from his younger brother. Baldwin was a good brother, but Godfrey had greater ambitions and did not stay long at Edessa.

However, even at Antioch, which had been thoroughly subdued by the main Crusading army, the other barons were also apparently forgetting that their real objective was the conquest of Jerusalem. At least one of their number, and not the least important, had firmly made up his mind not to continue the pilgrimage: Bohemond regarded the city of Antioch as rightfully his, and the only way to keep it was to stay there.

Raymond of Saint-Gilles had never promised Bohemond to leave him in possession of this city, because he coveted it for himself and was actually in possession of one of the principal towers. Seeing that he would never succeed in dislodging Bohemond with his own forces, he suddenly and in the most unexpected fashion made himself the most zealous champion of the Emperor of Byzantium's rights. The city, he said, was part of the Empire, of that there was no possible doubt, and the Crusaders were under a moral obligation to hand it back to Alexius Comnenus's ambassadors. Although this pro-Byzantine attitude on the part of the great baron who had previously refused to the bitter end to swear fealty to the Emperor might be suspect, these arguments did not lack weight and the other barons —with the exception of Bohemond—all agreed to send Hugh of Vermandois, the King of France's brother, to Constantinople, charged with offering the possession of Antioch to the Comnenus in return for a promise of a Byzantine Crusade in the near future. The army was so weakened and its effective strength so diminished that the commanders were resigned to this bargain, and in any case they had no intention of confining their conquests to the valley of the Orontes.

Antioch had therefore been directly offered to Alexius Comnenus, although it is true that there were conditions. Busy with other tasks, the *basileus* neglected to reply and Bohemond carried the day. Seeing the Norman's fierce obstinacy and remembering the promise they had made on the eve of the city's capture, all the leaders of the Crusade (with the exception of Raymond of Saint-Gilles) were ready to let him extricate himself from the business with Alexius Comnenus and the rights of the Empire on his own.

The summer passed and then the autumn, and still they awaited a reply from the Emperor which did not come. The army, demoralized by months of enforced inaction and decimated by epidemics, was becoming restless and showing its discontent more and more obviously. On the first of August, 1098, the man who was, in name and in fact, the leader of the Crusade, Adhemar of Monteil, Bishop of Le Puy, died. This was a severe blow for the army. The Crusade no longer had an official leader, and no real leader either since none of the barons was able to assume the role. Even those who did not want it for themselves were not prepared to submit to the orders of one of their peers.

There was one man, however, who fiercely coveted the title of leader of the Crusade: Raymond of Saint-Gilles, Count of Toulouse. He even went so far as to assemble the barons and offer to keep them all in his pay, and indeed he was the only one whose wealth was not yet exhausted. The plan came to nothing. The Count's aim was to get Bohemond away from Antioch by leading him off to conquer Palestine. In return Bohemond demanded that certain quarters of the city, which Raymond still held, should be given back into his hands, and to this the Count would not agree at any price.

November, the date fixed for the resumption of the campaign, was long past. The conference of the barons had taken place at the beginning of January and still nothing was decided. The leaders were haggling and arguing among themselves more than ever. In fact, those responsible for this state of affairs were Bohemond and the Count of Toulouse, but neither Godfrey of Bouillon, the Duke of Normandy, nor Robert of Flanders seems to have been in any hurry to pack his bags, probably largely because they were not best pleased at the prospect of marching under Raymond's command, and none of them could decently claim the title which the old Count appeared to be assuming as his by right.

After the legate's death, Raymond regarded himself as the natural choice for the role of secular leader of the holy war. His age, reputation, and wealth gave him incontestable rights, and he had an additional advantage which, if the truth be told, had nothing to do with his personal qualities but which, in the eyes of the soldiers, weighed heavier than fortune and rank: the Holy Lance, whose discovery had helped them to defeat Kerbogha, was in his possession. He believed with stubborn sincerity in the authenticity of the relic. Perhaps he would not have believed in it in the same way if the Holy Lance had been in the possession of Bohemond or Godfrey. Seeing this, the visionary Peter Bartholomew chose this moment to revenge himself for the skepticism of the defunct Bishop of Le Puy by claiming to have had dreams in which Adhemar of Monteil, surrounded by the flames of purgatory, confessed his sin: the crime of having failed to believe in the Holy Lance. Not only the clergy but all the Crusaders who had respected the legate were shocked by these revelations—but although half the clergy failed to believe in him, in the Provençal camp Peter Bartholomew was regarded as a holy man.

With the possible exception of the knights, the remainder of the army, the common soldiers and pilgrims, saw the conquest of the

Holy Sepulcher and the pilgrimage to Jerusalem as the sole object of the war. The only thing that kept them going, lost and bewildered in this strange land where heat, rain, sickness, famine, and the interminable months of kicking their heels in the same place were steadily wearing out their nervous resistance, was the lure of an adventure at once heroic and mystical which had been promised them, was still promised, and which they believed was theirs by right. In the end, the common people grew so tired of watching the barons wrangling over possession of the places they had conquered that on January 5, 1099, at Maarat an-Numan, a castle near Antioch, their impatience broke out into genuine rebellion. The nature of this rising was quite specific, and it forced the barons to remember the existence of the poor and simple.

The soldiers and pilgrims made up their minds to deprive their leaders of every pretext for quarreling by destroying the cities and castles which were the object of the disputes, beginning with the city of Maarat where they happened to be at the time. Rousing themselves from their enforced lethargy, they set to with a fine display of energy, pulling down the fortifications and setting fire to the residential quarters. Refusing to listen either to their own commanders or to the Bishop (Peter of Narbonne), they proclaimed that they had not come to the East to conquer cities but to serve God, and that they were capable of forcing the barons to do the same.[11] They made their point. On January 13 the army, or most of what remained of it, left Antioch. The Count of Toulouse marched at the head of the army, barefoot, dressed in sackcloth like a simple pilgrim and carrying a cross in his hands.

By this spectacular gesture, which almost certainly sprang from a spirit of demagogy as much as from sincere piety, Raymond of Saint-Gilles earned a degree of popularity with the poor which all his efforts had not been able to win him from the knights and barons. The common people did in fact merit some consideration for their feelings. Weakened, undisciplined, decimated by war and disease, Christ's soldiers were still a real force and the outcome of the war rested ultimately on these "poor." They were unstable, hotheaded, weary, and tenacious, as eager for martyrdom as for plunder, greedy for miracles and pagan blood. These poor, who never hoped for riches, placed their wealth in the acquisition of spiritual benefits of which they had a vague, magnificent, and somewhat materialistic idea.

The Crusade—the Crusade properly speaking—was saved, partly by the revolt of the foot soldiers at Maarat and partly by the ambition of Raymond of Saint-Gilles. The Count of Toulouse left his most powerful rivals, Godfrey of Bouillon, Robert of Flanders, and of course Bohemond, in Antioch. Taking with him the Holy Lance (and Peter Bartholomew), he led his army straight to Jerusalem. Three years after setting out, four years after the preaching of the Crusade, Christ's army was at last about to enter the Holy Land.

The March on Jerusalem

To tell the truth, the army had melted away on the road and now comprised no more than a thousand knights and five thousand men-at-arms. In addition there were the pilgrims, who were either ill-armed or not armed at all, women and children and priests and monks. With Raymond of Saint-Gilles were Robert of Normandy, Tancred, and later on, somewhat despite themselves, Godfrey of Bouillon and Robert of Flanders who rejoined the army in the Holy Land, while from the West, fleets sent from Genoa and Pisa in response to the preaching of the papal emissaries reached the Syrian coast bringing fresh supplies and an appreciable number of technicians and fighting men. But the Frankish army, desperately reduced in numbers, could not ultimately expect the Jerusalem campaign to be no more than a military exercise. The road was long and hard, local enemies numerous though ill-organized, and at any moment the Crusaders could expect the arrival of a powerful army either from the east or from Egypt.

The paralyzing effect produced by the battle of Dorylaeum and the subsequent capture of Antioch lasted a remarkably long time. It did not occur to the Moslem princes of Syria to offer any resistance to the Northern barbarians, and they asked nothing better than to see them pass through their lands with as little damage as possible. The emirs of Shaizar bought off the Crusaders with a tribute and even offered to provide them with guides whose task would be to lead them through the valley of Sarout. The lords of Tripoli, the Banū Ammar, were also hoping to escape the Frankish peril by money, but tempted by the extreme wealth of the city and the surrounding countryside, Raymond of Saint-Gilles made up his mind to conquer Tripoli, took Tortosa, a tributary of the Banū Ammar, by main force, and laid siege to Arqa. With characteristic obstinacy, he devoted himself heart and soul to a siege which was entirely unnecessary to the conduct of the holy war. Had it depended on himself alone, he would undoubtedly have stayed there until the town fell and pursued his plan of conquest by laying siege to Tripoli itself.

At this point Godfrey of Bouillon, leaving his brother as governor of Edessa and letting Bohemond install himself firmly in Antioch, was also planning to carve out a principality for himself in the Levant. He began by laying siege to Jabala (or Gibel), another fief of the lords of Tripoli. Unfortunately for him, the cadi of Tripoli, hoping to dislodge the Crusaders, sent spies to tell them that a powerful force led by the Caliph of Baghdad in person was advancing to crush the Frankish army. Far from striking camp, Raymond of Saint-Gilles hastily sent messengers to Godfrey and to Robert of Flanders, asking them to come to his assistance. Godfrey generously abandoned the siege of Jabala and came to join Raymond at Arqa with all his troops, only to learn that the news was untrue. His reaction to the news was intense annoyance, and some of his followers even suspected that the Count of Toulouse had invented the story of intervention by the "pope of the Turks" in order to prevent him, Godfrey, from taking possession of Jabala. As a result, relations between the two commanders were extremely strained from the first day. Now it was Godfrey who became the champion of the holy war and insisted on the necessity of marching on Jerusalem. Raymond, however, wanted to capture Arqa at all costs, and by a strange coincidence, Peter Bartholomew's visions informed the Crusaders that God commanded them to continue the siege.

More and more, to the leaders of the Crusade, the will of God was becoming, if not merely a pretext, at least a somewhat ambiguous fact, and one which altered according to the desires and interests of first one and then another. In Godfrey's camp and in that of Robert of Flanders, men were beginning to say openly that Peter Bartholomew was merely an imposter and that the Holy Lance was no more than a bit of old iron which he himself had buried under the Church of Saint Peter in Antioch. Raymond of Saint-Gilles, who like most of the men from Provence felt for the Holy Lance an ardor that almost amounted to a kind of local patriotism, rejected these rumors indignantly. In this situation, the Crusaders from North and South sat outside the walls of a Moslem town to which they were supposed to be laying siege and engaged in passionate debates about the authenticity of the famous relic. The most passionate and the most indignant of them all was Peter Bartholomew himself, who, whatever the authenticity of his visions, defended *his* Holy Lance with an ardor which was irrefutably genuine.

The affair ended in tragedy. The Duke of Normandy's chaplain,

Arnulf Malecorne (of whom there will be more to say at a later stage), demanded that Bartholomew be made to submit to an ordeal by fire. To prove the lance genuine, he must clasp it in his arms and hurl himself into a fire, or better still, run the gauntlet of two lines of burning fagots. Peter Bartholomew accepted without hesitation and died, twelve days later, in appalling agonies. This immediately discredited the Holy Lance to some extent.[12] Nonetheless, Raymond of Saint-Gilles continued to venerate the fragment of iron, encased in gold and precious stones, carrying it everywhere with him closely guarded by priests. But Godfrey of Bouillon had his way: the army was no longer anxious to waste time at Arqa and was ready to march on Jerusalem. Miserably, the Count of Toulouse resigned himself to raising the siege. What increased his wretchedness was the fact that this time it was Godfrey of Bouillon who had made himself the champion both of the popular will and of the holy war.

It was May when they set out (May 13, 1099). On April 10 the leaders of the Crusade had received a letter from Alexius Comnenus. The Emperor asked them to wait outside Tripoli until Saint John's Day, by which date he hoped to join them in person at the head of his army, bringing siege engines. Then, all together, they could resume their march on Jerusalem. Raymond of Saint-Gilles, who was chiefly anxious not to abandon a province in which he had already had considerable successes, and thinking it more prudent to be sure of the help of the Greek army, once again made common cause with the *basileus*. But his allies were already so prejudiced against the Greeks that they preferred to conquer by themselves, however great the dangers involved, rather than accept the authority of Byzantium. Moreover, Alexius' offer seemed to them somewhat vague, and the men of the army were demanding a resumption of the march on the Holy City, now only 250 miles away. Once more the plan for a Greco-Latin Crusade to reconquer the Holy Places went astray. The blame lay partly on Alexius Comnenus for his dilatoriness and partly on the Northern barons and their stubborn distrust of the Greeks. It must be admitted that Raymond of Saint-Gilles showed more political sense than his companions in the matter. If a genuine agreement between the two great forces of Christianity could have been reached, then the Crusade would have emerged as a much more important undertaking than the Crusader barons ever realized.

Consequently Alexius Comnenus's offer was rejected by the majority, partly because the leaders knew that a collaboration with Byzantium would be first and foremost to the advantage of Raymond of Saint-Gilles, who was the principal advocate of this collaboration.

They signed a treaty with the cadi of Tripoli, who furnished them with abundant supplies of money, horses, and provisions and gave them guides to lead the army through the passes of the Lebanese littoral. The Syrian Moslems were actually disposed to help the Western Christians in their attempts at conquest. With their independence threatened simultaneously by the Turks and by Egypt, they did not regard the appearance of a third force, capable of neutralizing their powerful neighbors, with too much disfavor.

While the Crusaders were besieging and capturing Antioch, the Vizier of Cairo, al-Afdal, had taken advantage of the rivalries among the Turkish princes and the difficulties the Franks were causing them to march on Jerusalem and capture it from the Sultan of Persia's lieutenant, the emir Soqman.* Al-Afdal was an Armenian convert to Islam and asked nothing better than to reach an agreement with the Crusaders. He was congratulating himself on their conquests, which were weakening the power of the Seljuks. Seeing that they had decided to install themselves in the north of Syria, he sent ambassadors to them proposing an alliance by which the Franks were to keep the lands they had already won and leave southern Palestine and Jerusalem to Egypt. Naturally such an arrangement did not suit the Crusaders at all, since their object was nothing less than possession of the Holy Places. The promise that small, unarmed groups would be allowed to make peaceful pilgrimages to Jerusalem could not tempt them in the least. The barons answered the Vizier's proposals with an outright declaration of war.

Egypt was a considerable military power and, for anyone aiming at possession of Jerusalem, the first adversary to be feared. The Crusaders were so well aware of this that at one time they considered marching directly on Cairo and conquering Egypt in order to make themselves masters of Palestine. Considering the small forces at their disposal this was a bold plan, and moreover Jerusalem was very close now and it seemed better to begin there.

On June 7, 1099, the Crusading army appeared in full force before the walls of Jerusalem.

On the dry, barren plateau of Judaea in high summer, the army, already worn out by months on the road, suffered cruelly from heat and thirst. The Holy Land which for so long had haunted the dreams of great and small alike turned out in fact to be a disappointing

---

* This was a bitter blow for the Crusaders, who hitherto had been able to count on Egyptian neutrality. It is a fact which explains their reluctance to march on Jerusalem.

enough place, and there were many who were amazed that the Lord should have chosen such a country for the scene of His Incarnation. But whatever it was like, it was unquestionably the actual land where Jesus Christ had lived. Hundreds of places of pilgrimage bore witness to the fact, with churches and chapels where for centuries pious, humble people had cheerfully venerated relics ranging from the well authenticated to the most fantastic, including a fragment of Noah's Ark, the coffin of Saint George, the house of the Virgin, and the forge where the nails for the Passion had been made. The names of even the smallest villages could be found in the Bible. No Christian, even the most cynical adventurer, could fail to be affected by all this, and the barons and knights who visited the Church of the Nativity in Bethlehem could scarcely believe their eyes when they were told that the object they were being shown was really the cradle in which the infant Jesus had lain. The native population, most of whom were Christians (the majority of the Moslems having fled at the Crusaders' approach), welcomed the soldiers of Christ with tears of joy and organized banquets and processions in their honor. In the camp there was a spirit of mounting exaltation and joy which made men forget their weariness and the dangers that lay ahead.

When at last the army came in sight of the towers and domes of Jerusalem, there was a veritable explosion of delirious excitement. Knights and soldiers fell on their knees, uttering cries of joy, and burst into floods of tears.

Chroniclers who witnessed this first encounter, the joy of at last beholding Jerusalem which was the culmination of so many hopes and prayers and dreams, give us some idea what it was like, though even this must still be a long way from the reality. The city, set among olive- and cypress-covered hills, was surrounded by a twisting belt of ramparts flanked by towers. With its great gardens, white-painted houses, domes, and minarets it was a beautiful place, but infinitely more modest than Constantinople or even Antioch. The pilgrims in their imagination may have confused it with the heavenly Jerusalem, but even so, they knew that the splendor of this Jerusalem was entirely spiritual, and in the words of William of Tyre, there was not a man among them so hardhearted that he could hold back his tears.

This wave of passion and mystical enthusiasm which swept with such sudden violence over a whole army was a unique phenomenon. Only the name of Jerusalem can explain it, and it was something which never occurred again. It was the first time such a vast crowd of pilgrims from the West had come to the Holy City, and they had endured years of suffering sustained by the hope of reaching Jerusalem.

We have already seen that among the poor and the common people drawn by the preachers were plenty of fanatics who believed that they had only to enter a Jerusalem liberated from the pagan to see a new heaven and a new earth. They believed that the angels were fighting on the side of the Christians, and that the poor and just would reign peacefully in a Jerusalem which had been purified forever and flowed with riches of all kinds. It is not easy to assess the exact nature of these dreams or to what extent the will to conquer was consciously mingled with the desire for martyrdom, but it is certain that the pilgrims and the bulk of the army envisaged something very different from the simple capture of a particularly venerable city. The whole adventure had a mystical rather than a warlike quality about it, and it was infinitely more important to them to touch the ground trodden by the Savior's feet than to cover themselves with glory. Certainly a greater degree of disinterested selflessness was to be found in that war at that particular moment than in any other war before or since. Now more than ever the army believed it was fighting for Christ. Its object was to defend Christ, to avenge Christ, and to win Christ, and Christ seemed to them as much present as if he had been reincarnated in fact. Simply to be in the very country, in the very place where the Passion of Jesus Christ had taken place was, to some extent, to relive the mystery of the Incarnation. Whatever may be said of the future conduct of this army of God, it would be unjust to underestimate the grandeur of this experience and the sincerity of those who lived through it.

The Crusaders had not come to Jerusalem merely to pray and to worship. They were there to fight and to snatch the city from the infidel. Whatever their relations with these infidels, Turks or Arabs, had been over the previous two years (and as we have seen, they had not always been bad), once outside Jerusalem the entire nature of the war suddenly changed. The Moslem became, or became once more, the diabolical enemy of God in the full meaning of the word, because by his presence he was profaning and polluting the place which, to the Christians, was the Holy of Holies. They had known the truth for a long time but now it suddenly dawned on God's soldiers in all its force. They could see it before their eyes in the churches which had been turned into mosques and the Egyptian banners floating from the towers. The Moslems, who could never have borne even the idea of infidels inside Mecca, were making a mistake when they let the fanaticism of the Christians surprise them.

To keep up the morale of the army the priests were continually preaching sermons to remind the soldiers of the insults which the Moslems were inflicting not only on the local Christians—a minor detail—but on the person of Christ himself and on the most sacred shrines, crosses, and relics. The Moslems were in fact guilty of many fewer and less serious acts of sacrilege than the Christians imagined, but the mere fact of such a holy place being in the hands of a "pagan" faith was an intolerable scandal in itself (although Christianity had managed to tolerate it perfectly well for over four centuries), and it was particularly so to this horde of pilgrims who for years had been obsessed by the idea of Jerusalem.

Jerusalem

The siege continued for one month and ten days. The torrid June heat in those parts, and the shortage of water due to the fact that the wells had all been poisoned or filled in by the enemy and nothing remained but the pool of Siloam, which could not supply enough water for a whole army, all helped to make it an extremely painful one. The city was fairly well defended. The Egyptian governor, Iftikhar ad-Daula, had had plenty of time to take steps to ensure that the besiegers had no means of obtaining supplies on the spot: the walls of Jerusalem were stout and the garrison composed of picked Arab and Sudanese troops. For fear of treachery, the majority of Christians in Jerusalem had been driven out of the city, making so many fewer useless mouths.

The assault launched on June 13 was unsuccessful: the Crusading army was ill-equipped and weak from thirst. For all their holy zeal and longing for martyrdom, the men were powerless against well-defended walls. Fulcher of Chartres asserts that the attack failed simply for lack of ladders. The assailants were forced to withdraw, leaving numerous dead on the field, and prepare for a siege which their lack of engines promised to make a difficult one. To find wood to build machines they had to comb the countryside for miles. With the help of a Genoese squadron which had successfully captured the port of Jaffa, the Crusaders did manage to build some mangonels and movable towers. Two big wooden "castles" were equipped, one by Godfrey of Bouillon, the other by Raymond of Saint-Gilles, and Tancred's Normans later constructed a third.

While the barons, with the help of the Genoese engineers and carpenters and their own teams of technicians, were building the battle engines and completing the encirclement of the city, the army waited for the final assault in a state of exaltation rendered still more intense by heat and thirst. Just as at Antioch, their suffering and physical exhaustion became a source of strength in themselves, giving rise to visions, outbreaks of mass hysteria, a longing for purification, and a belief in miracles. In spite of the bloody failure of his own Crusade, Peter the Hermit still retained a certain ascendancy over the crowd, and led countless disciples down to the river Jordan where, carrying palms in their hands and singing hymns, the pilgrims washed away their sins in the waters of the river in which Jesus had been baptized. A clerk named Peter Desiderius saw an apparition of the defunct Bishop of Le Puy, the legate Adhemar, below the walls of Jerusalem. The Bishop had been admitted to the number of the Blessed, but he had returned to direct his army and on his instructions, interpreted by Peter Desiderius, a solemn procession was organized. This was on July 8, a month after the beginning of the siege. Everyone, clergy, barons, knights, archers, foot soldiers, and civilians, marched around the walls of the Holy City singing psalms, and although the walls of Jerusalem did not tumble down like those of Jericho, in the minds of the people, at least, this solemn investment of the beleaguered city was certainly a decisive step toward victory. This was how the Christians saw it as they walked barefoot, singing and praying, to the Mount of Olives, with memories of the Passion, love for the Holy City, and hatred of the pagans fused into a single fervent outburst of emotion.

From the summit of the walls, Iftikhar ad-Daula's garrison contemplated this demonstration of piety with misplaced cynicism. They were rough soldiers, recruited among the nomads of the Arabian desert and the warrior tribes of the Sudan, and they did not understand that in these religious songs, these tears, and these prayers chanted aloud lay the real strength of their adversaries, nor that the crosses held high in the air could well prove more dangerous than swords. Iftikhar's soldiers, simple, ignorant Moslems, raised answering crosses on the walls, pillaged from the churches of Jerusalem. To annoy the enemy they abused them, spat on them, and subjected them, in the words of William of Tyre, "to still greater shames, and outrages of which it is not decent to speak."[13] Soldiers of every age and nation have always been given to such crude and stupid behavior, but to the devout pilgrims who were at that moment climbing the Mount of Olives, it must have seemed a living proof of the perversity of Satan, and the men who insulted Jesus Christ in this way in his own city, devils incarnate. In the words of William of Tyre: "their hearts swelled with desire *to avenge this shame done to Jesus Christ."*

Five days later the general assault was launched. This was a full-scale attack including a massive bombardment of the walls and gates. After two days' fierce fighting in which the defenders hurled down fire to repel the attackers, Godfrey of Bouillon's men succeeded in making their way into the city by means of a footbridge slung from the movable tower to the outer wall at Bab al-Sahira, close to Herod's Gate. Godfrey and his elder brother, Count Eustace, were among the first Crusaders to set foot on the walls of Jerusalem.

This happened at about midday on July 15 and from that moment on the capture of the city was no more than a matter of hours. The Walloon and Brabançon troops commanded by the two brothers of Boulogne occupied the whole of the northern wall and penetrated into the interior of the city, driving the defenders before them through the town to fall back on the mosque of al-Aqsa (Solomon's Temple). Taking refuge in the great mosque, the soldiers of the garrison held out there all day long, and when the Flemings finally broke into the temple there was such slaughter there that (according to the *Anonymi*) "our men were wading in blood up to their ankles."[14] Very soon the bulk of the Crusading army was inside the walls, including the Count of Flanders and the Duke of Normandy, Tancred, Godfrey's cousin Baldwin of Le Bourg, Gaston of Béarn, and Gerard of Roussillon. At this point a terrible battle broke out inside the city. The Egyptian garrison was large, and faced with adversaries whose numbers were ten times greater, was determined to make them pay dearly for their victory, while the victors themselves were determined to give no quarter.

To the south of the city, in the direction of the citadel, the resistance was more long drawn out. This was where Raymond of Saint-Gilles was attacking with his tower and his Provençal troops. There was still bitter fighting on the ramparts when the groups of terrified men fleeing through the city toward the citadel spread panic among the defenders of the Sion Gate. Now it was the turn of the Provençaux to gain a foothold in the city. The resistance was at an end and Jerusalem was in the hands of the Crusaders. The governor, Iftikhar ad-Daula, with a small party of the garrison, had managed to barricade himself inside the citadel and from there, surrounded by the men of Provence, he surrendered to the Count of Toulouse in return for a promise that his own and his men's lives should be spared. This promise was kept. It was the only one. If other similar promises had been given that day the commanders had no means of enforcing them, and there is no doubt that Iftikhar ad-Daula owed his life to the thickness of the walls of his citadel quite as much as to the honor of Raymond of Saint-Gilles.

The Great Massacre

The massacre perpetrated by the Crusaders in Jerusalem has long been reckoned among the greatest crimes of history. There is no lack of psychological explanations for it, and all historians, those who favor the Crusade and those who do not, rightly blame the state of almost morbid excitement which gripped a rabble made fanatical by the preaching of the holy war. It does not seem as though blame can be attached to the leaders on this score. They had nothing to gain from a massacre, and would no doubt have preferred good ransoms to such a drastic revenge for the shame put upon Jesus Christ. Tancred is known to have promised their lives to several hundred Arab soldiers who had taken refuge on the roof of the al-Aqsa mosque, and he did not conceal his fury when he learned that the prisoners protected by his banner had been slaughtered. He had in fact been powerless to ensure their protection.

During the days of July 15 and 16 the "soldiers of Christ" were masters of the Holy City. They scoured streets and alleys, gardens and courtyards, breaking down doors of houses and mosques and killing, killing all who fell in their path, no longer the soldiers, who had been killed first, but civilians, men, women, children, and old people.

The Jews, or as many of them as the building would hold, were shut up in the synagogue, which was then set on fire. The entire Jewish community of Jerusalem perished in the flames. Ibn al-Athir also records that the Crusaders' rage was particularly directed against imams and ulemas, that they profaned mosques and destroyed Moslem holy books. What is certain is that these manifestations of fanaticism were only one aspect of the murderous rage which took hold of the army on that day, because it is a fact that women and children were massacred without mercy.

Some eminent historians have attempted to "excuse" this monstrous act by recalling that, a century earlier, Moslems and Jews in the same city had turned against the Christians and put to death the Patriarch of Jerusalem. The pilgrims and the soldiers were probably not unaware of this, but it would be assuming a great deal to credit them with a desire to avenge local Christians who had been

dead for over a hundred years, especially since they were largely un-
concerned about the fate of contemporary Syrians, Armenians, and
Greeks. If there was any avenging to be done—and the desire was
certainly very strong—the person to be avenged was Jesus Christ.

Possibly responsibility for the disaster—for disaster it was—rests
with the ecclesiastical and lay preachers for arousing in the men not
only a laudable zeal for their faith but also hatred of the enemies of
that faith. The preaching of the clergy (beginning with Urban II's
celebrated sermon) had certainly excited the indignation of those
who volunteered for the Crusade by descriptions of the sufferings of
the Holy Land, but it is questionable whether this indignation, consciously inflamed by the priests, could still be so strong after two
years of war.

A great deal can be explained by the name of Jerusalem alone
and also by the blasphemous behavior of the soldiers of the garrison
on July 8. The mere sight of such sacrilege might well have been
enough to arouse in more than one Crusader the desire to destroy
everything that had to do with the Moslems. The men saw the capture
of Jerusalem as the ultimate goal of their pilgrimage and the fulfillment of all the promises which had been made to them. They sincerely believed that they were taking part in a great act of divine
justice and saw themselves transformed into destroying angels falling
on the children of the devil.

It would be unfair to lay all responsibility for the massacre on the
"poor," or on the vagrants, vagabonds, thieves, and repentant
murderers of whom there were certainly plenty among the civilians
and even in the regular army. All the same, it does seem probable
that in their state of excitement the troublemakers infected the rest,
and that in the fever of storming the city the more reasonable elements lost their heads at the sight of blood. Thousands of women
and children were butchered. Exactly how many we shall never know,
because the figures given by the medieval chroniclers are vague and
certainly exaggerated. Ibn al-Athir (and Abu'l Feda) mention
seventy thousand killed in the mosque of al-Aqsa alone (according
to other versions this includes the sector of the city surrounding the
mosque). But it is a known fact that there were fewer than seventy
thousand inhabitants in the whole city at the time of the siege. If we
subtract the number driven out before the siege began, there can
not have been more than fifty thousand in July 1099, not including
the garrison, which probably numbered some two to three thousand
men. Even so, a number of the people are known to have succeeded
in escaping and making their way out of the city, as there was a

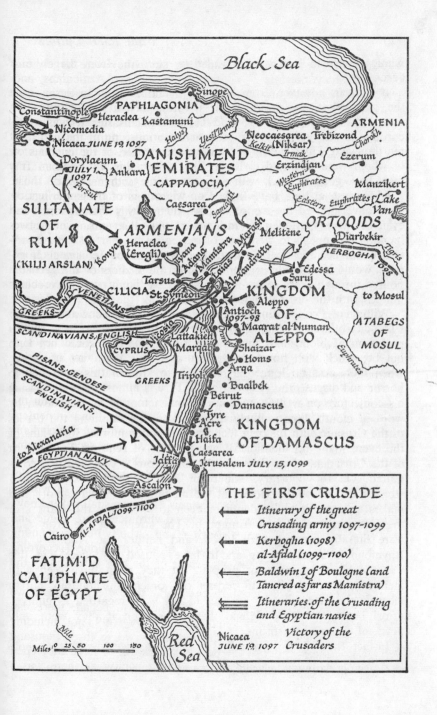

THE FIRST CRUSADE.

← Itinerary of the great
   Crusading army 1097-1099

⇠ Kerbogha (1098)
   al-Afdal (1099-1100)

← Baldwin I of Boulogne (and
   Tancred as far as Mamistra)

⇚ Itineraries of the Crusading
   and Egyptian navies

Nicaea   Victory of the
JUNE 19, 1097 Crusaders

whole suburb in Damascus founded by survivors from the siege of Jerusalem.

It is clear, however, from both Latin and Moslem historians that the population was more or less completely exterminated. This means that between July 15 and 16, 1099, the Crusaders who, according to the estimates of modern historians, numbered at most ten thousand, killed nearly forty thousand people, the great majority of whom were unarmed civilians. To achieve this the regular army must have gone to work with as much ardor as the "pilgrims." The knights must, at best, have looked on without interfering; the leaders must have allowed the troops to have their way without protest and even the priests evinced no indignation. At all events, eyewitnesses mention no appeals to clemency or reason on the part of the authorities, either ecclesiastical or secular, probably because any such appeals would have made no impression on the maddened horde which poured through every sector of the Holy City like a pack of ferocious hounds with the lust for blood upon them.

William of Tyre, writing ninety years afterward, describes the scene: "The city offered a spectacle of such a slaughter of enemies, such a profusion of bloodshed, that the victors themselves could not help but be struck with horror and disgust."[15] But that was afterward, when there was no longer anyone left to kill. In this reference to horror and disgust, the Archbishop of Tyre is almost certainly basing his conjecture on written evidence or on memories handed down by word of mouth. It is unlikely that he is merely crediting the heroes of the Crusade with his own feelings. But contemporary historians of the event make no mention of any feelings of remorse on the part of the Crusaders when they saw the monstrous deeds they had committed. On the contrary, Albert of Aix (himself a churchman) stresses the joy of the victors at the magnitude of their victory and makes no attempt to condemn or even to exonerate the authors of the massacre.* *God* had triumphed. The streets of the Holy City were literally running with blood, and neither the *Anonymi* nor Raymond of Aguilers appears to have paused to reflect that this was the blood of innocent people. Yet they must have seen with their own eyes the piled-up corpses of women and children, not to mention the men, who by an age-old law were regarded as guilty a priori because able to defend themselves even if they were only peaceful citizens or artisans.

In fact, the only word of regret or blame connected with the whole

* Albert of Aix was admittedly not an eyewitness and never set foot in Syria.

affair is the anger of Tancred, and this is simply the anger of a soldier who, having promised other soldiers their lives, has to suffer the indignity of having his word broken for him, and also the anger of a man who finds himself deprived of the opportunity of collecting a considerable ransom. Raymond of Saint-Gilles did succeed in protecting his captives—the governor of the city with a number of his officers and a contingent of mamelukes and Arabs—and in escorting them safe and sound as far as Ascalon. Evidently Iftikhar was not ungrateful, and if Raymond accepted a ransom there was nothing in this contrary to the rules of war. But because he had been the only one who took prisoners, he was immediately accused of treachery by the Crusaders from the North. Albert of Aix voices their opinion that the Count of Toulouse must have been bought off by the Moslems. How else were they to explain his clemency toward Christ's enemies? In actual fact Raymond had saved only a handful of soldiers from the massacre, but in the eyes of an army that was already drunk with blood and a religious frenzy amounting to madness, even this was unforgivable.

On the evening of that terrible July 15, while the massacre was still raging in the city, the barons went all together to the Church of the Holy Sepulcher. Once the city had been taken they considered their job was done and had stopped thinking of killing anyone. Robert of Flanders, Robert of Normandy, Tancred, Godfrey of Bouillon, and Raymond of Saint-Gilles, accompanied by their knights, chaplains, and servants, were already moving into the conquered city with the calm adaptability which makes a soldier feel at home anywhere. Wounded, bleeding, drenched with sweat and broken with fatigue after a battle of unprecedented ferocity, they swiftly installed themselves in the fine city houses, deserted now for a very good reason, then hastily washed and changed their clothes, not of course to rest, but to go to the Holy Sepulcher and give thanks to God and to Jesus Christ.

They went, says William of Tyre, "barefoot, with sighs and tears, through the holy places of the city where Jesus Christ Our Savior lived in the flesh. Devoutly they kissed the places where his feet had trod."[16] They were welcomed by the Christian clergy, who had remained in the city sheltering in churches and monasteries, and were led in procession to the Church of the Holy Sepulcher. William of Tyre again, on the basis of earlier witnesses, gives a deeply moving description of the religious fervor of these barons on reaching the end of their pilgrimage. They shed tears "of joy and pity" as they prostrated themselves before the Holy Sepulcher. "To each one it seemed as though he saw the body of Jesus Christ still lying there, all dead. . . . They felt as if they had entered into Paradise."[17] Can we doubt the sincerity (one might almost say the purity) of the deep surge of love which suddenly took hold of these very mediocre Christians? Perhaps the Holy Sepulcher, the Holiest of Holies, could accomplish even that miracle.

Two hundred yards outside the Holy Sepulcher, men were still murdering others blindly and savagely, wading in blood and trampling on corpses, on thousands upon thousands of corpses belonging to people whose skins, it was true, were somewhat darker than their own and who did not dress like Christians. Drawing inspiration from the words of the Psalmist, soldiers may have been taking little children by the feet and dashing their heads against the stones because they were the "little children of Babylon." But the knights and barons were praying and weeping for joy as they received the blessings of Greek and Syriac priests, among the candles and the smell of incense. At the gates of paradise.

Jerusalem was delivered. More accurately, it had simply changed masters once again. The massacre of the population of Jerusalem filled the entire Moslem world with horror. As soon as the news of the Crusaders' victory spread throughout Christendom, the hearts of the faithful everywhere in the West overflowed with joy. Urban II, the man who had promoted and been largely responsible for the Crusade, did not live to hear the great news. He died on July 29, before the letter announcing the capture of Jerusalem could reach him.

CHAPTER

IV

The Pioneers of Frankish Syria

(1 0 9 9 – 1 1 0 2)

The Holy Land

Jerusalem was a city almost two thousand years old, the capital of Judaea and the holy city of the Hebrews since the time of the prophets. It was a holy city to Christians and Moslems alike, though in the Moslem hierarchy it came third, after Mecca and Medina. In the course of its long history it had suffered so many ups and downs, fallen victim to so many conquerors that it was only owing to its character as a holy place that it had remained a great city. Ruined, devastated, and depopulated, it always grew up again, thanks to a constant influx of pilgrims of all three faiths.

Set in the midst of poor and barren country, of little strategic or commercial importance, Jerusalem was not a great thoroughfare and politically had always been treated by its successive conquerors as a place of secondary importance. Its character as a great religious center, on the other hand, was so well established that after the Jews and the Christians, the Arab conquerors took it over in their turn and for centuries the caliphs of Baghdad tried to make it a rival to Mecca. By the Moslems it was aptly called al-Quds—the Holy.

The fall of Jerusalem was therefore an undisputed victory for Christianity over Islam, a victory that was symbolic rather than purely military. But the two great Moslem empires of Baghdad and Cairo, divided by irreconcilable political and military enmity, had long been used to regard Palestine as a frontier zone, a sphere of influence on the borders of their two states, to be conquered now by one and now by the other. It was at best an uncertain asset. At least half the population were Christians, and the cities of the coast and along the valley of the Jordan were held by petty Arab princes, jealous of their own independence. In short, for Persia and for Egypt the loss of Jerusalem by Islam was a defeat on a religious plane, an unprecedented affront, but not a real disaster.

At all events, the Seljuk of Persia, the Sultan Barkiyarok, evinced no desire for a counter-Crusade. After all, the Christians had conquered the city from the Egyptians, who had taken possession of it in the preceding year. The Vizier of Cairo, who was more directly concerned, showed more initiative, but as we shall see, he gave up at the first sign of opposition, leaving Palestine and Syria to their fate.

In fact, the Holy Land which the Crusaders dreamed of conquering for Jesus Christ and for themselves had for so long been a land delivered up to the tender mercies of various conquerors that it possessed no national identity nor any kind of unity, political or religious. It could fairly be said that it had no existence at all as a *nation*. As we have seen, the emirs of Tripoli and Jabala were already prepared to accept the Frankish princes as neighbors, and the Christian population was greeting them as liberators.

Something the Moslems of Palestine had not anticipated, and which their experience of the Greeks had given them no reason to expect, was the extreme religious intolerance of the Christians from the West.

The Moslems had never attempted to convert the people of the lands they conquered by force. The object of the holy war waged by the first followers of Mohammed had been to extend the dominion and raise the prestige of the chosen people—the Arabs—and naturally to announce the light of the Koran to the whole world. But the Arab conquerors had nothing to gain from the mass conversion of the infidels since these were subject to a tax from which believers were exempt, and in the conquered countries this tax constituted one of the state's principal sources of revenue. As time passed, however, throughout North Africa, Syria, Palestine, and Spain conversions to Islam became increasingly numerous and finally led to a noticeable decrease in the number of infidels liable to the tax. By the eleventh century, almost the whole of North Africa, the greater part of the population of Egypt, nearly half that of Syria, and almost a quarter of all Spaniards were Moslems. Millions of Christians went over to Islam, from motives of self-interest as well as a genuine admiration for the religion of the conquerors, and also as a result of proselytizing by missionaries who cared little for fiscal considerations.

While not subjected to active persecution, the Christians (like the Jews) were regarded as second-class citizens. Moslem governments did not encourage Christian communities to expand and forbade the building of new churches. Although in principle no career except that of high-ranking military office was barred to them, and both Christians and Jews did occasionally rise to the highest positions, things were always easier for anyone who had been converted to Islam than they were for an infidel. As a result, the indigenous population, especially in Palestine, which had been wholly Christian or Jewish at the time of the Arab conquest, was by the eleventh century half made up of Moslems.

The Jews, who were not as a rule receptive to conversion, formed less than a tenth of the total population. Ever since their expulsion from Palestine after the capture of Jerusalem by Titus, the massacres which followed their revolt under Hadrian, and the persecutions of which they were the victims under the Christian emperors and later under the first Arab conquerors, the Jews, who were the autochthonous inhabitants of Palestine, had left the land of their fathers and fled either to the West or to Persia or North Africa. Only a few remained in Judaea and on the coast. Although there were still a few Samaritan communities living in the uplands of Judaea, actual Jewish villages were few.* The bulk of the Jewish population had settled in the towns and was chiefly engaged in the trades of dyeing and glassmaking, both of which were important industries at the time and of which they had a monopoly. The Jews, like the Christians, were forbidden to carry arms. They were a fiercely energetic people, whose aggressive qualities not even twelve centuries of oppression had been able to destroy, but successive conquerors had systematically deprived them of all outlets for satisfying their warlike instincts except by occasional massacres in some foreign war. Despite the savage persecution they had suffered from the original followers of the Prophet, they still preferred the Moslems to the Christians, and in areas where Christians were numerous the Moslems took care to win the support of the Jews. The most vigorous resistance to the Crusaders came from cities such as Haifa, where the civilian population was predominantly Jewish.

* Mohammed had exterminated almost the whole of the Jewish peasantry of southern Palestine.

There were many Christians, descendants of the Samaritans, Aramaeans, and Jews who had become converted in the first centuries after Christ. They had as much right to be called an autochthonous people as the Jews, and like them had been severely repressed by the Romans and later by the Greco-Roman Empire of Byzantium. Despite the fact that they were Christians, and Christians of very long standing, most of them had suffered even more than the Jews from the religious intolerance of their masters because they belonged to the Syriac or Jacobite rite and were therefore Monophysites. A minority of them coming originally from Syria and Palestine belonged to the Greek Orthodox rite, and these Christians were contemptuously referred to by their Jacobite compatriots as "Melkites" (those who belonged to the religion of the king—*malka*). In addition, there were also a certain number of genuine Greeks in the Holy Land, members of the clergy serving the churches, monks and nuns in the numerous religious houses of Jerusalem and the other holy cities, merchants, artists and craftsmen, scholars, lawyers, and so forth. Lastly, and in Jerusalem in particular, a religious colony of the Latin rite had been established since the time of Charlemagne. These had their own convent, a hospital or hospice for pilgrims, and were permitted to visit the shrines and celebrate mass in the churches. Although after the schism of 1054 the two Churches were officially divided, in these Eastern provinces under Moslem domination Latins and Greeks continued to regard themselves as members of the same Church. (It must not be forgotten that the Greeks, who were extremely punctilious in matters of dogma, considered the Latins, for all their "errors," orthodox Christians, very far removed from the multiple heresies of the Syrians and Armenians.)

Jerusalem had its own Greek Orthodox patriarchate which was officially recognized by the Church of Rome. At that time all hope of a reconciliation between the two Churches had not yet been abandoned and many believers regarded the schism merely as a temporary inconvenience. Christians of the Latin rite, although there were not many of them in the Holy Land, shared the lot of the other Christians and found themselves, through force of circumstances, under the protection of a local patriarch who was a subject of Byzantium.

The Syrians, as we have seen, loathed the Greeks and had no wish to see the Holy Land under Byzantine control. In practice, since they had never known any form of national independence, they had not had a great deal to complain of in the Arabs, who at least allowed them to practice their religion in peace. They were a great deal more unhappy under Turkish rule, less as a result of intolerance than because of the wars which had ravaged the country for a quarter of a century. In these wars between Moslems, the Christians suffered from both sides, and whenever the Turks were suspicious of the local Moslem population and favored the Christians, this earned them the hostility of the Arabs.

It would therefore be true to say that Christians in Palestine suffered from the anarchy reigning in their country as a result of the wars indulged in by their Moslem rulers, princes, and governors in much the same way as the people in Europe suffered from feudal quarrels, with the additional fact that religious differences between the ruling class and the civilian population aggravated the latter's feelings of resentment and bitterness to an even greater extent.

Moslems were numerous in the countryside, where they made up about half of the peasantry, and were equally so in the cities, with the result that they naturally felt themselves in the stronger position and treated their non-Moslem fellow citizens with condescension or even disdain. In towns and strongholds it was the Moslems (Arabs for the most part) who constituted the military and administrative aristocracy, and also made up a large part of the bourgeois and merchant classes. For centuries, therefore, the civilization of the country had been essentially Moslem or at any rate Arabic. Even the Jacobite Christians had largely forgotten their own language and usually spoke Arabic.

Moslem civilization was not, properly speaking, Arabic. From earliest times it had been subject to Persian and Byzantine influences. It was, however, firmly established, refined, and profoundly religious, and was undoubtedly greatly superior to Western civilization of the time, to judge at least by modern criteria of determining a people's degree of civilization. In comparison with the emirs of Tripoli, Shaizar, Tyre, or Beirut, the Crusader barons were boors, just as they were when compared to Alexius Comnenus's courtiers. If they had remained insensible to the charms of Greek civilization, they were to find it harder still to appreciate that of the Arabs. As in Byzantium, it was the wealth of the Orientals more than their intellectual and moral refinement which made the deepest impression on them.

It is worth remarking, however, that this ruling class, the culture-loving aristocracy which cared for literature, art, philosophy, and mystical contemplation, was comparatively small. The middle classes were on the whole remarkably cultivated, thanks to the many schools and universities, and urban standards of living were very high. But the common people in general lived in greater poverty than anything to be found in rural districts in Europe. Moslem or not, the peasant and unskilled laborer were exploited the more harshly because the needs for luxury and technical perfection among the high society were greater. Public and private charity, as in Christian countries, was encouraged by religion and generally practiced, but laborers were often treated with less consideration than pack animals. In fact, the peasant had so little share in the wealth and civilization of Moslem society that a change of masters made very little difference to him.

The Crusaders had arrived in Palestine with the firm intention of staying there, keeping possession of the Holy Sepulcher, and conquering lands for themselves. They were not destroying an established order; they were not depriving a land of its independence or its inhabitants of their country. As the latest in a long succession of conquerors, they brought the miseries of war to a land which had already seen much of them and occupied a place to which they had just as much right as the armies of Egypt or Baghdad. True, they were foreigners, come from a long way off, but they were Christians in an age when men were divided more by religious differences than by nationality. The land they came to had a long Christian past and a population which was certainly half Christian.

The idea of a Christian kingdom of Syria, prolonging or restoring Byzantine rule in the Near East, was not incongruous in itself, and whatever mistakes the Crusaders made, their war cannot be considered an arbitrary undertaking for motives of conquest and pillage. It rested fundamentally on lawful claims. The land to which the Crusaders carried their swords and their thirst for salvation had been already so terribly torn and divided that their appearance might well have proved, as the native Christians hoped, a force for order. In the event, the massacre of Jerusalem had already seriously compromised this hope.

The Advocate of the Holy Sepulcher

The day after the capture of Jerusalem, the leaders of the Crusade were compelled to realize that they were not yet at the gates of paradise. The Holy City, the ground trodden by the feet of Jesus Christ, was soiled with dried blood and piled high with corpses crawling with flies and visibly decomposing in the July heat. The houses were given up to plunder, fire, and sack. The soldiers and the poor pilgrims who were perhaps hoping to behold a new heaven and a new earth, and enter in their lifetime into the ultimate triumph of Jesus Christ, now saw that nothing had changed. They were still alone in the center of a dry and burning landscape, an easy prey to any fresh Moslem army.

It was urgently necessary to establish a plan of campaign. The barons held a great meeting to which, as was proper, representatives of the clergy were also invited, to consider the matter. The object of the whole campaign had been the conquest of Jerusalem. Now that Jerusalem had been captured, the next thing was to keep it, and this meant laying down the basis of a military and administrative organization which would allow the Christians to maintain themselves there.

There was clearly no question of handing the place back to Byzantium. Alexius Comnenus himself had never asked for it, for the excellent reason that he was incapable of guaranteeing the defense of a city so far from his own frontiers. In theory, the first Christian lord of Jerusalem ought to have been its patriarch, an office which in the Holy City had hitherto always been filled by a candidate officially installed from Constantinople. By a providential piece of luck for the Crusaders, the prelate who had occupied the seat, the Patriarch Symeon, had recently died in Cyprus, whither he had fled two years previously, and no other prelate had yet been elected to fill his place. Since Jerusalem had after all been liberated by the Catholics, this was the moment to elect a patriarch of the Latin rite. In this way, the Holy Places, under the legal government of their patriarch, would belong automatically to the Holy See, which provided for their defense and sent out fresh armies of Crusaders.

When this proposal was put forward by the clergy, the barons regarded it "as madness." However much they might agree that things spiritual took precedence over things temporal, in the circumstances the first thing to be done was to choose a military governor who, with the consent of all, would be given the Holy City in fief and keep it, the better to defend it. In other words, the immediate matter in hand was to nominate a *king* of Jerusalem. The majesty of the Holy City demanded that it should be the capital of a kingdom.

The final choice of barons and clergy fell on Godfrey, Duke of Lower Lorraine. This came as no surprise to anyone since only two of the great barons present could lay claim to the title. These were Godfrey of Bouillon and Raymond of Saint-Gilles. The Count of Flanders and the Duke of Normandy were not in the least anxious to end their days in the Holy Land. The Count of Toulouse was apparently—though for what reason we do not know—not regarded as a candidate who could command a unanimous vote, and he himself was so well aware of this that he refused the royal title when the delegates first offered it to him, as they naturally did. Indeed, considering his age and reputation they could hardly have done otherwise. This leads to the conclusion that the offer was merely a courtesy one, and that Raymond understood it as such. Even so, it was the custom in matters of the kind to begin by refusing and yield only to lengthy persuasion, and it is quite possible that the Count of Toulouse's refusal may have been accepted somewhat too readily. The difficulties of the task were certainly not of a kind to deter an old warrior like Raymond, and he had made no secret of the fact that he coveted the title of King of Jerusalem more than any other. He was obviously the most acceptable candidate from all points of view, and he was also the one with the best chance of establishing a policy of collaboration with Byzantium, a collaboration which—at first sight—appeared to be necessary if a lasting Christian settlement was to be made in the East. If, in that July of 1099, the vote of the barons and clergy had fallen on Raymond of Saint-Gilles, the Crusade might perhaps have led in the end to a combined Greco-Latin campaign to win back the Near East—the thing Pope Urban had been hoping for.

This was exactly what the Northern barons did not want, and the members of the clergy who were with the army were equally concerned to avoid it because any collaboration with the Emperor would involve, first and foremost, the enthronement of a Greek patriarch in Jerusalem. It is conceivable that Raymond of Saint-Gilles's defeat was due to a fear that the Greeks would interfere in the Crusaders' affairs. To set out to build a Latin kingdom in the East with an isolated few thousand men in a land which had belonged to Islam for centuries, and to attempt to do so without the help of the one great Christian power in the East, was a piece of folly worthy of Frankish arrogance. But it is a fact that at that moment the Crusaders preferred to risk everything on a single throw rather than be compelled to fall back on the inevitably self-interested assistance of the Greeks. But Raymond's character undoubtedly did him more harm than his political ideas. He was a man who possessed an abundance of admirable qualities: he was intelligent, honest, brave, devout, he possessed great military experience and great nobility in speech and action; but there is no doubt that he did not possess the qualities of a leader.

Consequently Godfrey was elected, after a purely formal preliminary inquiry into his character, which emerged as so perfect that nothing could be said against him except that he was excessively devout. He remained, said his chaplains, so long at prayer in the churches that he often allowed mealtimes to go by and thus condemned his entire household to eat cold or overcooked food: a diplomatic accusation if ever there was one. The clergy who were attached to the service of the Duke of Lower Lorraine had nothing to gain from complaining of their lord's other faults and these faults, whatever they may have been, have been passed over in silence by all contemporary historians. Godfrey became a legendary character at a very early date.

It was necessary to create this legend of an ideal leader of the Crusade, worthy to take his place beside Roland and Oliver in the Christian pantheon, partly in order to raise the morale of the great mass of the Crusaders, and partly to add to the prestige of the Crusade as a whole. Not one historian has dared to criticize the Duke of Lower Lorraine, and the picture of the man which has come down to posterity is somewhat hazy—so much so indeed that some modern historians, as we have seen, have concluded from it that the famous Knight of the Swan was a placid, mediocre, and apathetic character.

His behavior, as revealed by actual events, suggests on the other hand a character both strong and supple: calculating, ambitious, and excessively jealous of its authority. We have already seen that his feelings about the Holy Sepulcher were by no means fanatical, and both at Antioch and before Jabala he had wasted time holding back his men simply in order to conquer lands on his own account. The part he played during the siege of Jerusalem gives some grounds for placing a good deal of the responsibility for the great massacre on Godfrey and his Brabançons and Ardennais, if in the heat of the assault there was any question of responsibility at all. The chroniclers emphasize the fact that the *Duke* was burning with desire to avenge the affronts put upon Jesus Christ "in the blood of the infidel." Godfrey's was a soldier's faith, and not so very different from that of the humblest of his soldiers.

Ambitious he certainly was, to an inordinate degree, but he also had the kind of modesty which was one of the most highly prized virtues of feudal society. Men praised him for refusing the title of King, but he was probably only bowing to the general feeling when he declared that he did not wish to wear "a golden crown in the place where Jesus Christ had worn a crown of thorns." This apparent modesty was dictated equally by a desire to please the clerical party.

On the day when, after a resistance which may or may not have been sincere, he finally accepted the title, not of King, but of "Advocate of the Holy Sepulcher," he made it clear that he had no intention of being content with a pretense of power. The Count of Toulouse still held the citadel of Jerusalem, the Tower of David. Godfrey demanded the return of the citadel into his hands, and went so far as to threaten to resign, "for how could he be the lord of this land when another had a force inside the city superior to his own?" Raymond, characteristically, refused to listen. He had taken the Tower and he had a right to keep it. Faced with Godfrey's threats, he agreed to return the citadel provisionally to the Bishop of Albara (one of his own Provençal clergy whom he had had nominated bishop of a conquered city) and a few days later the Bishop handed over the Tower of David to Godfrey. Raymond left the city in a rage, with all his followers, announcing that he intended to return to his own land. In the event, however, he contented himself with making a pilgrimage to the river Jordan.

Godfrey was triumphant. Moreover, he was intelligent enough to realize that he would never get on with the Count of Toulouse and that the kingdom of Jerusalem—if there was any chance of such a kingdom being created—would be built without Raymond and in spite of him. The Count's great fault was that he did not know how to rule or how to submit.

The Crusaders could not expect the Fatimid Caliph of Cairo to resign himself to the loss of Jerusalem and to sit back and watch while they settled in Syria and Judaea. Egypt was extremely slow to move, but her fleet, the size of her armies, and her technical development made her a formidable military power. The capture of Jerusalem had produced such a wave of feeling in every Moslem capital that the Vizier al-Afdal, although not a very zealous Moslem (it will be remembered that he was of Armenian origin), decided to strike a firm blow. Less than three weeks after the fall of the Holy City, a powerful Egyptian army, led by the Vizier in person, was encamped beneath the walls of Ascalon, some forty miles from Jerusalem.

Godfrey hastily summoned all his companions and allies. Despite some initial reluctance they joined him as soon as they realized the extent of the danger. Then he advanced to meet the Egyptian army. His forces at that time numbered twelve hundred knights and nearly nine thousand foot. The Fatimid army was considerably larger. The Crusaders launched a surprise attack, and according to Ibn al-Athir, al-Afdal's warriors could not even put on their armor and mount their horses because "the Franks did not give them time."[1] Creating panic in the Egyptian camp by simultaneous attacks on both flanks and in the center, the Crusaders routed the enemy army with such speed that the Vizier and a number of his emirs had barely time to take refuge inside Ascalon (whence he later made his way back to Egypt by sea). Some of the soldiers were driven back into the sea by the Provençal contingent and drowned, while others took refuge in a sycamore wood and were burned to death by the Franks' setting fire to the trees. In a few hours the Crusaders had completely annihilated the Egyptian army and won enormous quantities of booty from al-Afdal's camp. Once again events had confirmed the legend of Frankish invincibility.

The city of Ascalon now struck the victors as a desirable prize and they promptly laid siege to it, counting on the effects of terror to help them. Remembering the fate of those inside Jerusalem, the people of Ascalon were already prepared to surrender. They did however make one condition, which came as something of a blow to the pride of the Advocate of the Holy Sepulcher: knowing that in Jerusalem, Raymond of Saint-Gilles had been the only one to guarantee the lives of his prisoners, they refused to yield themselves to any but Raymond of Saint-Gilles. Raymond gladly sent them his banner as soon as possible. Instead of reflecting that the stronghold was still better off in the hands of the Count of Toulouse than in those of the infidels, Godfrey intimated to Raymond that Ascalon belonged to the kingdom of Jerusalem and consequently to the Advocate of the Holy Sepulcher. The Count struck camp in a rage and led his army away, thus breaking off the negotiations. He went further, and actually sent the people of Ascalon a message bidding them stand firm, and telling them that Godfrey had insufficient troops at his disposal to take the city. Robert of Flanders and Robert of Normandy, annoyed by the Duke of Lower Lorraine's pretensions, also withdrew, and to this quarrel Ascalon owed the distinction of not falling into Frankish hands for another fifty-three years.

Much the same thing happened outside Arsuf. Raymond was negotiating for the surrender of the city when Godfrey arrived and forbade him to take possession of the stronghold on his own account. Raymond withdrew, after urging the people of the town to hold out. Apparently unable to perceive the ridiculous side of the situation, Godfrey considered, in all seriousness, setting his troops on those of the Count of Toulouse. The holy war was developing into a feudal squabble. Not without difficulty the two irascible barons were finally reconciled, and in the end Arsuf surrendered and carried Godfrey's banners while Raymond, angry but not discouraged, withdrew into northern Syria in the hope of carving out a kingdom for himself away from his rival's sphere of influence.

In principle, this left Godfrey firmly established as king, or at least as governor of Jerusalem in the name of the Church and of Christendom; but so great was the spirit of independence and competition which reigned among the Latin barons that the man chosen by the whole army to be the leader of the Crusade soon found himself a ruler without vassals. Robert of Flanders and Robert of Normandy, considering their pilgrimage at an end, were making ready to return to France, while the Count of Toulouse had lost interest in Jerusalem and its uncrowned king. Out of all the barons, the only one Godfrey managed to keep at his side was Tancred, of whose humility the chroniclers make a special virtue, claiming that "out of love for Christendom" he had deigned to offer submission to the Duke of Lower Lorraine and become his vassal. The truth may be that, far from being the complaisant and easygoing person presented to us by modern historians, or the pure paladin of the faith described in the legends, Godfrey was an impossibly conceited individual, eaten up with pride and self-importance.

Although Godfrey's pride is unquestionable, there are more grounds for supposing that the attitude of the other barons can be explained by their own pride as great lords, not at all accustomed to bowing before anyone. This is clear enough from the lines Radulph of Caen and Tudebod dedicate to Tancred (see above): for a Norman prince of quite modest lineage, the fact of "serving" anyone, even a duke of the Empire, even the Advocate of the Holy Sepulcher, was a shame only to be explained by great devotion to the cause of Jesus Christ. A count of Flanders could scarcely become the vassal in the Holy Land of a man he would never have dreamed of serving in his own country, without demeaning himself. Feudal lords could not be expected to forget in three years the code of honor by which they had lived all their lives and which they had inherited from their ancestors. But in the circumstances, Godfrey was behaving sensibly rather than otherwise in demanding from his colleagues the obedience due his rank as leader of the Crusade.

He can have had few illusions. He had been offered a glorious title, so glorious that he had not even dared to accept it, and yet the very men who had elected him were already disputing the rights bestowed on him by his rank. It was useless to count on Raymond of Saint-Gilles, who had led his army off to the north when all the Holy Land still remained to be conquered. As for the Count of Flanders and the Duke of Normandy, they were taking ship for Europe with their knights and foot soldiers: as far as they were concerned the Crusade was over. They were returning home victorious, and the least of their soldiers would be haloed to the end of his days with the glory of a liberator of the Holy City.

Meanwhile, the Advocate of the Holy Sepulcher was left with the task of guarding Jerusalem and only a few hundred knights to do it with, and some additional support from Tancred, who had only agreed to serve him because he had too few men of his own to try and make any conquests on his own account. The other two great leaders of the Crusade, Bohemond and Baldwin, were busy subduing their respective provinces of Antioch and Edessa. Godfrey apparently regarded the territorial ambitions of these two barons as natural and legitimate, since he made no attempt to distract them from their tasks. He merely asked the Count of Flanders and Robert of Normandy to send him some reinforcements, and to explain to people in the West just how precarious his situation really was. He was also counting heavily on the support of the Church and on a new propaganda campaign launched by Urban II's successor. It was not for nothing that he was doing all he could to ingratiate himself with the prelates who were already settled in Jerusalem.

Within a few months of the fall of Jerusalem, Godfrey and Tancred had subdued the strongholds of Galilee, and by the end of 1099, they held Bethlehem, Hebron, Ramleh, Lydda, Jaffa, Nablus, Haifa, Beisan, Tiberias, and Nazareth, a good half of the cities of the Holy Land properly speaking. Abandoned by their overlord, the garrisons of these castles lost their nerve and surrendered fairly easily (always excepting Haifa, where, as we have seen, it was the Jewish civilian population which largely undertook its defense).

Terror of the Franks and the reputation for barbarity which the Franks enjoyed in the country had made the Crusaders' task easier. In fact, the Frankish forces (according to William of Tyre) amounted to no more than "three hundred mounted men and two thousand foot." The rural districts of Judaea were mostly peopled by Moslems, the majority of whom had emigrated either to Egypt or to Damascus for fear of meeting the same fate as the inhabitants of Jerusalem. It was the same in the cities, whence the Moslem citizens, who were the wealthiest and most active, had fled en masse, as also had the Jewish communities. The inevitable result was that the country was impoverished and disorganized. The Christian kingdom of Jerusalem got off to a bad start, and it was only by extraordinary luck that it did not occur to any Moslem army to take advantage of the situation. If he had wanted to, al-Afdal could easily have recaptured

Jerusalem at that moment, because he cannot have been unaware that the Crusaders had left it in a body. (Albert of Aix estimates the number of people who set sail for the West during the autumn of 1099 at twenty thousand, and even allowing for exaggeration in this figure, it is certain that the army which had triumphed at Ascalon no longer existed and that the three hundred knights remaining in Judaea, scattered among the garrisons of occupied cities, could by no means be looked on as a formidable force.)

Neither al-Afdal nor the King of Damascus nor the Sultan of Persia would lift a sword in the defense of the Moslems of Palestine. Songs about the sufferings of Jerusalem were now being sung in every Moslem court in the East, since at that time songs and verses took the place of newspapers and propaganda talks. The Caliphs of Cairo and Baghdad had put on mourning and welcomed the fugitives from Palestine with honor, but the fugitives' appeals to Moslem solidarity were useless. The only people who actually fought the Crusaders were the garrisons of cities which were in immediate danger and the nomadic Bedouin tribes who, if the truth be told, were more interested in plunder than in anything else. More often than not, local emirs preferred to come to an agreement with the new masters of Palestine.

In the absence of an army, Godfrey could count on the help of the Genoese and Pisan squadrons, which arrived in large enough numbers to protect the ports of the Syrian coast. Since Jaffa had fallen into the hands of the Crusaders and Arsuf had been captured in December 1099, the ports of Ascalon, Caesarea, and Acre had concluded treaties with Godfrey. To prevent the ruin of their trade, they had purchased peace at the price of an annual tribute of five thousand bezants, as well as other gifts in kind, such as horses and provisions. At a time when the Crusade might have been thought on the point of failure, it was losing, willy-nilly, its character of a holy war, and the King of Jerusalem was becoming simply another feudal prince, concluding commercial treaties with his Moslem neighbors and negotiating agreements for the security of roads and seaways.

Although dictated by circumstances, this sudden transformation of the Crusaders' attitude was nonetheless to a great extent the work of Godfrey of Bouillon, who seems to have been as accommodating in his treatment of the emirs of Palestine as he was the reverse toward his companions in the Crusade. Once he had thoroughly made up his mind to play his part as defender of the Holy Sepulcher to the end, he was realist enough to succeed admirably in bowing to local conditions, entering into no rash undertakings, attacking only where he was sure of victory, making treaties without ever departing from his role as victor, and receiving the homage of his Arab vassals and tributes from the emirs with impassive dignity. Far from burning with a holy hatred for the infidel, he was trying (without forgetting to make war on them when he could) to win their sympathies, being well aware that he was condemned to live as their neighbor for the rest of his days.

There is a well-known anecdote, quoted by William of Tyre, concerning an interview between Godfrey and some Arab sheiks during the siege of Arsuf. The Arabs came to bring presents to the great chief of the Franks, and they were amazed to find him sitting on the bare earth in his tent, resting on a bale of straw, without any armed guard around him. Seeing their astonishment, Godfrey told them, through an interpreter, that no man need be ashamed to sit on the ground since all men returned to the earth after death and became earth themselves. From this, says William of Tyre, the Arabs concluded that "this man well deserved to be the lord of that land, for he was without pride and knew the poverty of his nature."[2] In fact, Godfrey was always chronically short of money and could not afford to buy fine clothes and silken carpets, for which, in any case, he cared little. He was a confirmed bachelor of very simple habits, brought up in camps and a soldier to his fingertips, one of those ascetic professional soldiers of a type very common in Europe at that period.

Godfrey's reign in Jerusalem (if one can call a life of expedients, wars, and skirmishes in a country less than half subdued a reign) was to last for only a year. He died on July 18, 1100, a year almost to the day after the fall of Jerusalem. At his death the departure of all his rivals had made the Crusader baron who had once had such a struggle to make his colleagues obey him the officially acknowledged master of the new Christian province of Jerusalem, respected as such by friends and enemies alike. Tiring of the squabbles of the clergy, Godfrey had allowed them to resolve the question of the primacy of Church and State over his head: he needed pontifical aid too desperately to quarrel with his clergy. He even went so far as to promise to resign from his position in favor of the Patriarch when the position of the new kingdom should become sufficiently strengthened. According to William of Tyre, who undoubtedly bases his statement on well-attested sources, the Duke of Lower Lorraine did actually make a will in favor of the Church, bequeathing the Holy City and the Tower of David to the Patriarch of Jerusalem. Was it piety or policy which led him to do so? Godfrey was still young, only forty-one, and it is possible that he allowed this testament to be extracted from him by an ambitious prelate, simply as a temporary pledge of friendship. The date of the will is not known and it is hard to say how far the Advocate of the Holy Sepulcher was sincere in thus returning the kingdom to the hands of the Church. It is a fact that Godfrey relied very heavily on the support of the Church.

The Church

Immediately after the capture of Jerusalem, the Crusading clergy had, as we have seen, attempted to make the barons agree to the supremacy of the patriarchate over the secular power by asserting that the Holy City could only belong to the Holy See and ought to become part of the pontifical domains.

If Adhemar of Monteil had been still alive, this solution would probably have been adopted. But after his death there was no prelate in the army capable of uniting the barons' votes or even those of a majority of the clergy. The reason the leaders of the Crusade rejected the clerical proposal with some asperity was because at that time they had a grudge against the Pope. Once he had by his exhortations and promises launched the volunteers for the Crusade on an enterprise as risky as it was onerous, Urban II had gradually lost interest in his project. In particular, after the death of Adhemar of Monteil he had failed to respond to a request by the leaders of the Crusade that he should come in person to lead it, or at least send them a new legate. It is a fact that he encouraged the maritime republics of Italy to work for the cause of Jesus Christ by supplying the Crusaders with war materials, provisions, and soldiers, and it has already been seen that Genoese sailors played a large part in military operations at the siege of Jerusalem. But God's army, which after the capture of Jerusalem numbered only a quarter (at the most) of the soldiers who had crossed the Bosporus in 1097, was greatly in need of reinforcements. It was relying on a new propaganda campaign and complaining of the sovereign pontiff's feebleness. Their complaints were, in fact, unfair because Urban was ill and died less than a fortnight after the capture of Jerusalem.

His successor, Paschal II, took some time to familiarize himself with the difficulties of his new position. Meanwhile the representatives of the clergy who were with the Crusade were left to themselves.

The least that can be said is that they had no idea of the greatness of their task.

The main idea of these clerics—the most influential of whom was Arnulf, Bishop of Marturano—was to keep Jerusalem and the Holy Land under the control of the Church of Rome at all costs. For this, in all fairness, they can hardly be blamed. However, their plan threatened the rights of the Greek Patriarch, and hitherto no pope had attempted to dispute the rights of patriarchs of the Eastern Churches. In spite of the schism, relations between the two Churches were still cordial. Moreover Symeon, the Greek Patriarch of Jerusalem, had written letters of encouragement to the Crusaders and sent them large quantities of food and money from Cyprus as gifts from the Cypriot population. While he was alive it would have been awkward to consider replacing him by a Latin patriarch. After his death it was logical to wait for the decision of the Eastern clergy, and of the Emperor and the Pope. A matter of this gravity demanded the participation of all the interested ecclesiastical parties.

The city, holy as it was, was still polluted by Moslem blood and at the mercy of the soldiers. Inside it the Latin bishops and clergy were behaving exactly like people entering an empty house and taking possession of it and everything in it heedless of the rights of the lawful owners. The creation of the Latin patriarchate of Jerusalem was decided upon in a real spirit of plunder, and just as the barons took over the towers and palaces of aristocratic Moslems who had fled or been killed, so the clergy hastened to despoil of their rights the very Eastern Christians they had come to liberate. The Greeks and Syrians who had welcomed them with tears of joy were spontaneously included by the victors among the conquered population whose presence was barely to be tolerated.

William of Tyre gives the "clerks with the army" the following speech: "We beg and require you [the barons] in the name of Our Lord, not to undertake to elect a king until we shall have elected a patriarch in this city."[8] The barons, who were unversed in matters of ecclesiastical procedure, may not have found this language at all surprising. And yet the mere fact of allowing a handful of abbots and bishops, without a mandate from the Pope, from any other bishops, or from the local community, to decide in this way on the spur of the moment that one of their number was to be patriarch of a city like Jerusalem, this fact alone reveals how little interest the barons took in the affairs of the Church and reveals also the unconscious contempt of the clergy for the Church of such a remote province, even if its capital were Jerusalem.

There was no lack of precedents. During the Antioch campaign we already find the great barons installing clergy from among their own followers in the conquered cities and giving them the title of bishops. In this country a comparatively obscure priest could become a bishop in the same way that a landless younger son might become a count or castellan. The man the Bishop of Marturano was seeking to place on the patriarchal throne of the holiest of cities was the personification of the spirit of adventure which guided the clergy, intoxicated by the triumph of God's army. Arnulf of Rohes, known as Arnulf Malecorne, the Duke of Normandy's chaplain, was anything but a holy man.

When Raymond of Saint-Gilles was laying siege to the city of Arqa, Arnulf's cruel challenge had led to the death of the unfortunate Peter Bartholomew and been responsible for discrediting the Holy Lance. He was not lacking in either intelligence or energy and possessed a real talent for oratory; his sermons during the siege of Jerusalem had done a great deal to raise the morale of the army. But he was ambitious and intriguing and his private life was so scandalous that the soldiers made up songs about his amorous exploits. This notorious evil-liver was the man who, although he had never even been invested with episcopal dignities, nevertheless succeeded in getting himself elected patriarch. He owed his election to the efforts of the Bishop of Marturano and to the influence of Robert of Normandy, who had great affection for his chaplain.

The hastily appointed "Patriarch" took advantage of his new position to deprive the Greek and Syriac ecclesiastics of their property, and when, justly incensed at such treatment, they refused to reveal to their new Patriarch where they had hidden the piece of the True Cross which they kept at Jerusalem, Arnulf had them thrown into prison and threatened with torture. The True Cross was handed over to the Latins. But ever afterward Frankish dominion in the East was regarded by the native Christians as a foreign occupation, scarcely less loathsome than that of the Moslems.

The Greek clergy, in particular, conceived a profound grudge against the Latins. In this way the hazards of a war of conquest deepened still further the growing gulf between the two rival forms of Christianity. The rapacity and insolence of a man like Arnulf Malecorne was merely a practical demonstration of the more or less conscious scorn which the Latins as a whole felt for the Eastern Church, as for all Eastern Christendom.

As "Patriarch," Arnulf Malecorne was hardly the man to override Godfrey's authority, and this was undoubtedly the reason why he

put up with such a shady character for six months. But at the end of
1099, in December, important guests came to the new kingdom of
Jerusalem, men who, although they had not taken part in the conquest of the Holy City, nevertheless meant to make it clear that
they too had an interest in it and were demanding their share of the
glory, the profits, and even the responsibilities. Baldwin, Count of
Edessa, and Bohemond, Prince of Antioch, feeling themselves sufficiently secure in their new possessions, had come to Jerusalem to
worship at the Holy Places. Their men, too, had a right to the spiritual benefits which only a visit to Jerusalem could bestow.

They arrived in force with a great cortege of knights and foot
soldiers, as well as a contingent of Pisans who had joined them after
disembarking at Lattakieh (Laodicea). (According to Fulcher of
Chartres their troops at that moment comprised some twenty-five
thousand men, and this suggests that the reality must have been at
least several thousand.) Godfrey, Tancred, and their companions
welcomed the new arrivals with understandable delight. They prostrated themselves before all the shrines of Jerusalem, took part in
the processions and other Christmas festivities, and received their
share of the homage and acclaim which the city's population was
generously ready to bestow on the great Christian leaders. Then,
their religious duties, and more important, those of their soldiers,
satisfied, after ten days devoted to pious rejoicings and councils of
state, Baldwin and Bohemond went back to their respective provinces. They left in Jerusalem someone they had brought with them—
someone whom Godfrey could well have done without.

The troop of Pisan Crusaders was led by the first lord of the city
of Pisa, the Archbishop Daimbert in person, a domineering old man
with a long experience of the holy war in Spain, where he had held
the post of pontifical legate. Daimbert was an educated man, an
able and keen politician, and he came from Italy armed with his
battle fleet and his Pisans, who were devoted to him body and soul,
and armed also with his title of Archbishop and possibly even a mandate from the Pope. He also brought considerable wealth, which un-
kind tongues accused him of having purloined illegally from the
coffers of the Church during his stay in Castile. In fact, this eminent
prelate was rumored to be unpleasantly greedy. But Daimbert was
still greedier for honors and power than he was for money and he
employed the treasure he had amassed to bribe Bohemond, Baldwin, and even Godfrey himself.

He arrived in the Holy Land full of zeal for the cause of the Holy
Sepulcher. Albert of Aix describes how the old man had barely

landed on the Syrian coast before he hurried up to the Crusaders who had come to meet him, hugging them in his arms and wetting their cheeks with his tears, forcing on Bohemond's Normans and the Provençal contingent belonging to Raymond of Saint-Gilles a temporary and highly unsought-for reconciliation. (In fact the Archbishop, who was a Pisan first and a Christian second, had begun by laying siege with his fleet of twenty ships to the Byzantine city of Lattakieh, where there were also Provençal troops. When he failed to take it, he feigned indignation against Bohemond for making him believe that the Greeks were allies of the Moslems.)

Then Daimbert had set off for Jerusalem with Bohemond and Baldwin, and this gave him time to win over the two barons, who were not particularly interested in the welfare of the Church, to his point of view. He had no sooner arrived in the Holy City than he hastily busied himself proving that Arnulf Malecorne's election to the patriarchal seat was contrary to canon law. He called an assembly of all the Latin clergy of Jerusalem and had Arnulf deposed (although he left him the archdeaconry, with all the financial advantages which the impromptu Patriarch had so far enjoyed). Daimbert's next step was naturally to get himself elected patriarch in Arnulf's place.

To support his claims, the Archbishop had his Pisans and his fleet, which was a vital source of supply to the Crusade. Contemporary chroniclers also insist that it was Bohemond who forced Godfrey to accept the new Patriarch.[4] Furthermore, the Advocate of the Holy Sepulcher was so short of men and money that he was ready to agree to anything. We know from Albert of Aix that he himself accepted splendid presents from Daimbert.

But the old Italian exacted a high price for his gifts. The day after his election he made Godfrey and Bohemond his vassals and invested them, in the name of the Church, with the lands they had conquered by force of arms. Furthermore, the two barons had to come and "humbly request" him on their knees to grant them this favor. The Archbishop intended to leave nothing to chance. He intended to make it clear that Jerusalem and all the lands conquered by the Crusaders in the East belonged to the Church and the patriarchate of Jerusalem, and hence to Daimbert himself.

It almost looks as though Daimbert, an active and more than ordinarily warlike prelate, reckoned himself in military matters something of a general. In a land where the Latins held only a few castles and these garrisoned only by skeleton forces, he was behaving like another pope in a second Rome miraculously rid of her temporal enemies. He was already announcing that the patriarchate of Jerusalem was the first in Christendom, and doing all he could to oust Godfrey from his position. In the end the Advocate of the Holy Sepulcher, finding this ambitious and intractable old man more difficult to deal with than the Arabs or the Bedouin had ever been, finally promised, as we have seen, to give up Jerusalem to Daimbert when he had conquered another city of equal importance such as Cairo or Damascus for himself. This promise did not commit him to very much: Godfrey was not in any position to dream of conquests on such a scale, unless in the very distant future. It was the help provided by the Pisan fleet more than his much vaunted piety that forced Godfrey to humor the old man's pride. We have no means of knowing what would have been his attitude in the long run, or the ultimate consequences of his policy. Worn out as he was by four years of incessant warfare, yet he cannot have expected to die so soon. In June 1100 he fell sick (it was thought of the plague) at Jaffa, and he returned to Jerusalem where he died three weeks later, on July 18. In accordance with Godfrey's agreement with Daimbert, Jerusalem passed into the hands of the Church. The Archbishop of Pisa could consider himself the master after God of the province of Judaea.

In fact, the power of the Church in these foreign lands where even soldiers could only maintain a foothold at spear's point could be nothing more than a fiction. Daimbert, in his senile dream of a theocratic kingdom, seems to have been confusing Jerusalem with his own good city of Pisa. He demanded in vain that supreme power and the possession of the citadel should be given into his hands: the companions of the late Advocate of the Holy Sepulcher, Godfrey's cousin Warner of Gray, Geldemar Carpenel, and the other Flemish and Walloon barons, as well as Robert, the new Archbishop of Ramleh, and of course Arnulf Malecorne, formed a strong enough party to resist the Patriarch. They held the Tower of David and declared that they would recognize as their leader only a brother or relative of their former master. That the revolt of Godfrey's companions was not strictly lawful even William of Tyre, who disapproved of Daimbert's policies, cannot deny. However, it was in accordance with feudal custom, and the countless disputes between the leaders of the Crusade had at least amply demonstrated one thing: the only kind of unity and solidarity which could exist among the Latins was that created by the most direct feudal bonds and an extremely narrow local patriotism.

Godfrey, Bohemond, Raymond of Saint-Gilles, and the rest, after fighting side by side for years, remained rivals and enemies; but the pirate Guynemer of Boulogne, when he learned that Baldwin, the son of his natural overlord the Count of Boulogne, was fighting in Cilicia, promptly hurried to offer Baldwin his services. In the East just as in the West, a feudal lord could count only on his own countrymen and was truly served only by men whose parents had known his parents.

Consequently, Godfrey's companions and vassals turned naturally toward Baldwin: for the men who had served under Godfrey, it would have appeared contrary to honor and good sense to acknowledge another lord. As we have seen, Baldwin was not personally very popular, but if he had been the devil incarnate, to those Flemish and Walloon knights he would have been, first and foremost, one of their own people.

Once again a conflict of ambitions was breaking out in the course of this holy war in which the Crusaders—or their leaders at least —seem to have been constantly determined to give the lie to the proverb that there is strength in unity. They believed themselves so strong that they were squabbling exactly as though they were still at home in their native land. Daimbert, seeing himself in the role of a new Gregory VII persecuted by a new Henry IV, was furiously denouncing the acts of the late Godfrey and even more those of his vassals, and of Warner of Gray in particular. In his view, these men were unlawfully withholding Jerusalem and the Tower of David from him "to the ruin of the Church and the oppression of Christianity." This, according to William of Tyre, is how he wrote to Bohemond.[5] Not possessing sufficient forces himself to throw these turbulent knights out of the city (the same knights who, a year earlier, had conquered Jerusalem amid fire and slaughter), Daimbert summoned the Norman Prince of Antioch to do his duty as a Christian by forbidding Baldwin to enter the Holy Land and, if necessary, declaring war on him. The Archbishop wrote that Bohemond was the son of Robert Guiscard, who had formerly defended the papacy against the German Emperor, and that he had a duty to follow his father's example. The Patriarch appears to have dismissed as unworthy of his attention such practical details as the existence of powerful Moslem kingdoms only a few days' march from Jerusalem.

He had one vassal of some standing in the person of the late Godfrey's one major vassal, Tancred. Tancred had absolutely no reason to wish for the coming of Baldwin, who had been his sworn enemy ever since their quarrel over Tarsus. He was therefore quite ready to assist his uncle should he decide to defend the rights of the Church.

The first Latin patriarch of Jerusalem had been a priest who was a byword throughout the army for his dissolute life, and the second was trying to start a war between the first two great Catholic barons who had had time to establish their dominion in Syria. After such beginnings, the Latin patriarchate was never to win the place it should have had as a universally acknowledged ecclesiastical authority, a symbol of the majesty of the Church. There were to be a number of reputable prelates among the Latin patriarchs of Syria, but the equivocal circumstances in which the patriarchates had been created left them at the mercy of political intrigues and the ups and downs of the temporal powers.

The King of Jerusalem

At the time when Jerusalem was left without a master, or with no official master beyond an aged patriarch hardly capable of understanding the political and military situation of the country, there were already two Latin principalities in the East—principalities ruled over by Latin barons, at least. These were Baldwin's county of Edessa and the "princedom" of Antioch, governed by Bohemond. Along the coast, a third Latin province was, still hesitantly, beginning to emerge through the efforts of Raymond of Saint-Gilles, who had returned after many disappointments to his original idea of taking possession of the province of Tripoli.

All told, several thousand knights had already settled in the Near East and intended to stay there, and this represented a considerable military force. The only drawback was that the provinces of Edessa and Antioch were hundreds of miles north of Jerusalem and cut off from it by country which, with the exception of one or two castles along the coast near Tripoli, was almost entirely in Moslem hands.

Although the petty Arab princes of Syria preferred to avoid open conflict with the Franks, this was not the case with the kingdoms on the other side of the Jordan. Aleppo and Damascus and, further east, Mosul were held by a vigorous and warlike Turkish aristocracy, who had already recovered from the shock of the fall of Antioch. It was a simple matter for Warner of Gray and his friends to nominate Baldwin of Boulogne to the throne of Jerusalem, just as appealing to Bohemond's Christian feelings seemed simple to the Patriarch Daimbert. But Baldwin and Bohemond still had to reach Jerusalem before they could accomplish what was expected of them. Daimbert's letter to Bohemond never reached its destination and we shall never know if the Norman prince, who was already fully occupied in fighting the Greeks and the Turks simultaneously, would ever have committed the folly of quarreling with Baldwin. The letter was intercepted by Provençal troops near Tripoli and taken to Raymond of Saint-Gilles, who took good care to see that it never reached his old enemy. Bohemond was engaged in fighting the Danishmend Turks in the Taurus Mountains near Melitene, and had been taken prisoner at about that time. Despite one attempt at rescue on the part of Baldwin, who very loyally came to the Norman's aid when he learned of the affair, Bohemond, chained hand and foot, was taken northward into what had formerly been Armenian territory and was now in fief to the house of Danishmend. His captor, Ghazi Gümüshtekin ibn Danishmend, was not going to let such a fine prize go easily. He imprisoned his captive in a tower of his capital of Niksar (Neocaesarea), a city buried in the Taurus Mountains where no Christian army would dare venture.

So ended the "Crusade" of Bohemond of Taranto, Prince of Antioch. He emerged from captivity three years later, but events in the East at that time were moving with such speed that when the Norman commander returned he was no longer welcome and was compelled to take his ambitions and his energy elsewhere.

As for Baldwin, he certainly received the message from his brother's vassals. He learned of Godfrey's death and of his own elevation to the rank of king of Jerusalem at the same time. His chaplain, Fulcher of Chartres, who knew him well, describes him for us in a phrase which has become famous, as "somewhat afflicted by his brother's death, but more glad at his inheritance." But this inheritance was by no means a sinecure, or even one that was easy to take up. Leaving his county of Edessa in the hands of a cousin, Baldwin of Le Bourg (or of Bourcq), Baldwin took the road to Jerusalem at the head of a small, hand-picked body of knights.

His county of Edessa had already cost him too much effort for him to think of sacrificing it, even in exchange for the kingdom of Jerusalem. He left strong garrisons in the city itself and in the surrounding castles, commanded by vassals determined to defend their fiefs, and Baldwin of Le Bourg was to prove as capable a master of Edessa as his cousin had been. The new candidate for the throne of Jerusalem took with him his personal suite, the young Armenian princess he had married, and as many men as he needed to stand some chance of crossing the country without being captured or killed. The danger was great. Baldwin knew this so well that first he hastened to reassure the Normans in Antioch (in great distress on account of the recent capture of their commander), and then the Greeks and Provençaux installed in Lattakieh. We know that both of these received him very well and that at Lattakieh he also met the papal legate Maurice of Porto, who had arrived with a fleet from Genoa. Godfrey's brother had already realized the need for a good understanding between Christians, whether they were Norman, Walloon, or Provençal, and it is a significant fact that from the moment he left Edessa he established himself, apparently almost unconsciously, as the champion of solidarity among the Crusaders.

The title of King of Jerusalem which fell so unexpectedly on his head, and which indeed was still not properly his, was already giving him a calm confidence which brought him the respect of his former rivals. In order to reach Jerusalem he had to cross enemy country. This was so dangerous that he chose to put his wife on a ship at Lattakieh and send her by sea to Jaffa, while barely half his knights dared follow him across country. "Let any who are afraid turn back!" he said. Crossing Palestine at that time appeared such a foolhardy undertaking that even this challenge did not prevent a good many knights from deserting. Very fortunately for Baldwin, the powerful Emir of Tripoli was not burning with vengeful hatred against the infidel and had no idea of blaming Godfrey's brother for the horrors of the massacre at Jerusalem. On the contrary, he welcomed the Frankish leader with gifts and protestations of friendship and told him that Duqaq, King of Damascus, was preparing to attack him somewhere between Tripoli and Beirut. (In fact, as we shall see, Ibn Ammar was at that time on extremely bad terms with Duqaq and not ill-pleased to see a buffer state, even a Christian one, set up between his own province and Damascus.) Warned of the trap laid for him by the Damascenes, Baldwin extricated himself as well as he could. He had to traverse a narrow ledge with "enemy ships to seaward, beetling cliffs on the other hand, and the whole Turkish army in front." Another man might have waited for a more propitious moment to pass, or gone by another route, but Baldwin was in a hurry: he had to reach Jerusalem before the Patriarch could take possession of the city. He pressed forward, feigned a hurried retreat, and then, having lured the Turks into following him, he and his handful of knights and foot soldiers (there were only 160 knights) suddenly turned and, by throwing the enemy army into confusion, managed to cut themselves a path along the ledge. Duqaq was compelled to flee and the road was clear. The King of Damascus did not dare make another attempt. Once again the Turks realized that the fury and cunning of these people was beyond all their expectations.

Baldwin arrived at Jerusalem in triumph. He was welcomed by the Christian population and by the Frankish chivalry with a boundless enthusiasm which forced the Patriarch Daimbert to hold his peace. The Franks saluted him as Godfrey's brother; the native Christians, as a valiant warrior able to protect them. At that moment, whatever the causes of friction between the Latins and the Eastern Christians, the latter were entirely won over to the Crusaders' cause. After the slaughter of Moslems in Jerusalem, the Christian civilians knew that they would share the same fate if the Franks were ever defeated.

Baldwin was well aware that his military talents were his greatest asset, and he began by organizing raids in the neighborhood of Jerusalem against the Arabs and the nomadic Bedouin who were attacking the villages of Judaea. These expeditions, from which he returned laden with booty and the spoils of fallen enemies, were his propaganda campaigns, if he still needed any. Fearing his rival's revenge, the Patriarch had immediately retired to the Church of Mount Sion, and he was willing to make peace. Rather than lose the patriarchal seat at which the former "Patriarch" Arnulf Malecorne was already casting covetous eyes, Daimbert with his own hands crowned the man who only the day before he had been calling a traitor and persecutor of the Church.

On Christmas Day 1100, for the first time since the days of Herod, there was a king in Jerusalem. The golden crown which the conquerors of the Holy City had been unwilling to wear "in the place where Jesus Christ had worn a crown of thorns" was placed on the head of the Count of Boulogne's third son, the landless younger son who had become Count of Edessa. His first claim to the honor lay in his family connection with Godfrey, the Advocate of the Holy Sepulcher who had established himself so firmly in the course of his short reign that his natural heir seemed to be the only man whose rights were incontestable. Whatever his arguments, the Patriarch had on his side only a handful of clerics and Tancred. Baldwin, for his part, had no hesitation in demanding the crown and a solemn coronation in the Church of the Nativity in Bethlehem. He was not a man to receive visitors sitting on the ground leaning on a bale of hay. He meant to make the most of the title which his brother could not, or would not, take. He was a king almost without an army and very nearly without lands, an impromptu king unwillingly accepted by the Patriarch, a mercenary with a dubious past, but a man so fiercely certain of his rights and even of his duties that what began as an adventure was to become truly a reign. Moreover, Jerusalem was not just any city, and its name alone gave this precarious kingdom artificially implanted on foreign soil a reality which made it something more than a mere adventure.

Baldwin, now Baldwin I, King of Jerusalem, possessed an army very little superior to that which his brother had had at his disposal. He had brought some of his own vassals with him, but on the other hand he had lost the support of Tancred. Not forgetting his clashes with Baldwin in Cilicia, and fearing the new King's vengeance, Tancred refused outright to acknowledge him. He even refused to meet him except on the banks of the river Nahr al-Aiya, and on condition that he and Baldwin kept the waters of the river between them. At last, summoned to Antioch to take over the regency of the city in place of his uncle who was still a prisoner, the young Norman was able to leave the city without appearing to be running away. Baldwin was relieved of a somewhat awkward vassal, but also of his valuable soldiers.

The new King of Jerusalem therefore found himself in a curiously critical situation, with only a few hundred knights to defend the Holy Places whose possession was so important to Christianity. To the north were the Kings of Damascus and Aleppo, in the south lay the Egyptian caliphate, to the east, across the Jordan, were the Arab and Bedouin tribes, and in the west was a coastline partially held by Arab emirs who were more or less dependent on Egypt, and the sea, controlled by the Egyptian fleet. Baldwin was a realist as well as a fierce warrior, and he immediately set about enlarging his possessions, since the best way of keeping Jerusalem was still to control the surrounding territory. A mere list of the campaigns which this man led in the course of eighteen years makes amazing reading. Hardened as these twelfth-century warriors were to a life of battle, this kind of persistent fighting day after day, in one sector after another, in all the agonizing discomfort imposed by medieval armor and methods of warfare, compels us to bow before the man and his like as before forces of nature. Baldwin was nearly forty when he was crowned king, yet it was not age or exhaustion which overcame him as he approached his sixtieth year, but the effects of a terrible wound which even then he survived long enough to continue the fight. To the Moslems of Syria, Baldwin (Bardawil) became so much *the* Frank, the Frankish king above all others, that the chronicler Ibn al-Athir, writing a century afterward, was convinced that all the "Frankish lands" at that time were ruled by one Bardawil.

Baldwin began his reign by organizing raids against the desert Arabs of the Jordan. He attacked and plundered caravans, intending, if he could not enlarge his army, which was still very small, at least to improve his financial position and the resources of his cavalry. War horses were the sinews of an army and a shortage of horses was almost as serious as a shortage of men. Once he had spread terror among the nomads east of Jerusalem, the new King set about conquering the coastal towns, still with his three hundred knights and the same number of foot soldiers. In this, he had the help of the Italian fleets from Genoa and Pisa, who were still eager to supplant the Egyptian fleet and compete with Byzantium in these waters. With the help of the Genoese, Baldwin was able to take first Arsuf and later Caesarea, where he permitted a terrible massacre. This was not the result of religious fanaticism but was done with the deliberate intention of terrorizing the defenders of other coastal cities.

After two years of somewhat surprising inaction, the Grand Vizier al-Afdal once again made up his mind to deal with the Christians. He dispatched a powerful army under the command of the emir Saad ed-Daula al-Qawasi, but the least that can be said of it is that it was extremely slow to strike. Instead of attacking, the army encamped for several months near Ascalon (the most powerful Egyptian fortress along the coast) and did not march on Jerusalem until September 1101. Baldwin went to meet the enemy with his 260 knights and challenged him at Ramleh. He divided his small army into four companies, which were to attack in successive waves. The first two, led by the bravest knights of his Walloon contingent, were cut to pieces, and only a handful of men succeeded in escaping and making their way back to Jaffa. Then, when the Egyptian army thought victory was theirs and were pursuing the fleeing Franks, Baldwin himself led the second half of his troops in such a furious charge that he created a panic in the enemy lines and the Egyptian army retreated in disorder. Baldwin took possession of the camp and the booty. At the very moment when he was believed in Jaffa and in Jerusalem to have been killed, and his wife was already sending a desperate appeal for help to Tancred in Antioch, he appeared, bloody and laden with the spoils of the enemy, outside the walls of Jaffa. Beside him was the Bishop of Ramleh, Gerard, bearing aloft the True Cross.

From this time on, the True Cross, which had been present at the battle and given strength to the soldiers as they fought, was carried in every major engagement and its fame was almost as great among the Moslems as among the Christians.

The victory of Ramleh saved the Frankish kingdom. Baldwin

emerged covered with glory, but he left nearly half his knights on the field. It was not long before his army received fresh reinforcements. Men of great nobility and renown who came to serve under his command included William IX of Poitiers, Duke of Aquitaine, Hugh VI of Lusignan, the Emperor of Germany's constable Conrad, Geoffrey, Count of Vendôme, the Duke of Burgundy's son Stephen, and finally, Stephen, Count of Blois, the wealthiest man in France and the same who had earlier fled so shamefully from Antioch.

The reason why all these great lords were gathered together, ready to place themselves in the King of Jerusalem's service, is in fact a somewhat melancholy one, of which there will be more to say. They had come as pilgrims, accompanied by such a small following that Baldwin gained little from their presence beyond the honor (which at that particular moment meant very little to him) of including in his small army a dozen men nobler and wealthier than himself. They were refugees from the greatest disaster in the history of the Crusades, and they owed the privilege of being able to pray at Jerusalem to the swiftness of their battle chargers. But if they can be accused of cowardice on that occasion, Baldwin soon showed them that they had lost nothing by waiting.

In 1102, a fresh Egyptian army appeared on the coast of Palestine and advanced on Ramleh, the very place where Baldwin had won his victory of the previous year. The King of Jerusalem, unaware of the enemy's numbers, advanced to meet the Egyptians with a small force. With him went some of the new arrivals: Hugh of Lusignan, Stephen of Blois, the constable Conrad, Stephen of Burgundy, and Geoffrey of Vendôme. In his haste to join battle, Baldwin had neglected to obtain proper information. Now he found himself facing the whole of the great army which had arrived from Egypt, under the command of al-Afdal's son.

This rash action was typical of Baldwin's headlong bravery. He was a man who could be accused of many faults, but not of hating the Moslems, but he was so far possessed by his passion for fighting that he was inclined to fall upon the enemy with the fury of a wounded beast. He was, says William of Tyre, "swift and hasty." This time he was committing suicide. Unfortunately the only one of his companions who had ventured to council prudence was Stephen of Blois, a man who for five years had been branded throughout Christendom as the worst of cowards. Baldwin made it clear to him that he had no right to raise his voice. The little band of two hundred knights found themselves suddenly face to face with an army of twenty thousand men, and they had no alternative but to be killed and force their enemies to buy their victory as dearly as they could. They were utterly defeated. A few knights did succeed in escaping to Jaffa, while Baldwin, with all of his company who remained, withdrew to the castle of Ramleh, which was so ill-defended that he could not hope to hold out for more than twenty-four hours. According to Ibn al-Athir, there were seven or eight hundred men, foot soldiers for the most part, since no more than a hundred of them were knights. Ibn al-Athir says that three hundred men were taken prisoner. Certainly all the knights were killed, Stephen of Blois among them. Baldwin escaped during the night—alone.

The three squires who accompanied him in his flight lost their lives, and he himself was saved only by the swiftness of his horse, his famous Gazelle. For two days he roamed the country alone in the desolate mountains, hunted by Egyptian scouts. The victorious Egyptians galloped up and down before Jaffa, where the Queen was at that time together with a fairly large body of pilgrims and Crusader knights, brandishing severed heads on their lances, among them the head of a Flemish knight, Gerbod of Winthinc, who was as like the King as his twin brother.

That day the kingdom of Jerusalem had lost the greater part of its knighthood, in addition to the great barons mentioned above. One of these, the constable Conrad, fought so well that the Moslems granted him his life. As for Stephen of Blois, William of Tyre later dedicated this curious epitaph to him: "It was *a great joy* to hear that he died so honorably. . . . It appears that Our Lord had forgiven him [for his past cowardice] since He so appreciated his service that He permitted him to die serving Him."[6] Undoubtedly, taking into account the spiritual benefits which Christ's soldiers expected to obtain from their pilgrimage, the battle of Ramleh (1102) ought to have filled heaven with glorious martyrs. One advantage at least of this Eastern war was its habit of turning into a holy war when things were going badly. Baldwin was well aware of this.

When, three days after the disaster, he reappeared in Jaffa with nothing but his life, the confidence he inspired was so great that no one dared blame him for the loss of his army. A fortnight later, with the help of newly landed pilgrims from France, England, and Germany, the King built up a new army, launched an attack, and routed the Fatimid army, which fled back in the direction of Ascalon. Once again the chroniclers describe camps deserted by the enemy and vast quantities of booty. Once again the Egyptians were discouraged and gave up trying to dislodge the Franks from the coast of Judaea.

Baldwin was able to continue his dogged, methodical conquest of the coast.

In 1104 he captured Acre; in 1105 he drove off another Egyptian army (once again at Ramleh); in 1110 he took Beirut and then Sidon, using the prestige of the holy war for the purpose of his own war of conquest and enrolling powerful contingents of passing pilgrims under his banners. Under constant threat of Moslem reconquest the kingdom of Jerusalem and the Frankish principalities of the north (Antioch, Edessa, and later Tripoli) learned increasingly to make use of their role as defenders of Christ, while adapting themselves more and more to local conditions.

The Crusade of 1101

The capture of Jerusalem aroused an understandable enthusiasm for the Crusade among people in Europe. France, in particular, rejoiced because the principal part in the conquest of the Holy City had been played by Frenchmen. In Germany, as in the Scandinavian countries, the news that the French Crusaders had covered themselves with glory made the knighthood, princes, and bishops eager to follow suit. In Italy, where the maritime republics were more influential than the knighthood as such, enthusiasm for the Crusade was largely connected with the ambition to conquer fresh trading markets, while those provinces which were under Norman rule were afire with admiration for the exploits of Bohemond.

The new Pope, Paschal II, realized the advantages to the Christian cause of the conquest of the Holy Land and encouraged fresh propaganda campaigns on behalf of the Crusade. The victory won by the Crusaders seemed a manifest sign of divine favor; but even so, they were few in number and surrounded by powerful enemies, while most of the pilgrims who set out on the great voyage were dead or had returned to Europe. Jerusalem was becoming the collective property of every Christian in Europe, an infinitely precious possession placed in trust to their own nation, which it was their duty to defend.

The second wave of enthusiasm for the Crusade did not equal the first. Once conquered, Jerusalem no longer had the appeal of Jerusalem in bondage, unknown and virtually inaccessible, to be reached only by the elect. The great dream which had sustained the crowds who rose in answer to Peter the Hermit's call, the hope of a Last Judgment, of some mystical regeneration of the land in blood, suffering, and celestial light, was a dream which never came true, unless it was for the tens of thousands of poor folk whose dry bones, heaped in mounds "higher than hills," lay whitening in the sun on the road to Nicaea. These and many others were martyrs, shining now in heaven like so many new stars, for the poor are tenacious of hope, and for a long time people in the West who had nothing more to lose on earth had been priding themselves on a poverty blessed by Jesus Christ himself.

There were deserters, men who had escaped from one hell after another—on the road to Constantinople, in the deserts of Anatolia, at the siege of Antioch, or among the arid mountains of Judaea—and these survived to tell how much suffering must be endured as the price of the great pilgrimage. Their accounts made many volunteers think twice. On the Pope's orders, even before the departure of the First Crusade, bishops had been denouncing the cowardice of those who, once they had taken the cross, failed to implement their vows. Deserters were judged still more severely. We know that when the Count of Blois returned home after his inglorious departure from Antioch, he endured so many humiliations and suffered so much from the reproaches of his wife Adela, a daughter of William the Conqueror, that much against his will he was compelled to set out again on another Crusade. Less illustrious deserters were treated no better by their friends and neighbors. Crusaders who were too slow in making up their minds and never left home became objects of scorn once the news of the capture of Jerusalem brought the memory of the Crusade forcibly back to people's minds.

In short, after the surge of enthusiasm aroused by the great news, the Latin West experienced a fresh wave of Crusading fever. This time the French, who had already gained their share of vicarious glory through the Crusaders of 1097, were not in the majority.

A great army composed largely of Lombards left Italy in September 1100. Its leaders were Albert, Count of Biandrate, Anselm of Buis, Archbishop of Milan, Guibert, Count of Parma, and Hugh of Montebello. This army was partly made up of civilian pilgrims, poor people who were hoping to win lands conquered from the Arabs, since it was already known that colonists were needed for the Holy Land. The presence of these civilians made the army more vulnerable, but even so it was an impressive force comprising, noncombatants included, some tens of thousands of men.

The French army, on the other hand, was chiefly made up of extremely well equipped fighting men. Not only Stephen of Blois who, in his anxiety to reinstate himself, had not spared his money, but also the Duke of Burgundy's son Stephen, the Bishop of Soissons, and

Conrad, constable of the Empire, took with them picked bodies of knights and infantry.

These two armies were the first to set out. They were followed, in February 1101, by an army belonging to William II, Count of Nevers. He had fifteen thousand men, all professional soldiers, under his command, forming a compact and well-disciplined army. This time the leaders were determined not to repeat the mistakes of the First Crusade. There was also a fourth army, an extremely large one, estimated at sixty thousand persons including a great many civilian pilgrims, which was led by William IX, Duke of Aquitaine, by Welf IV, Duke of Bavaria, and by the Margravine Ida of Austria, mother of Duke Leopold of Austria.

These four armies, taken all together, constituted a more formidable force than the armies of 1097. But they never succeeded in joining up and all four crossed the Bosporus separately: the first—the Lombards—in April 1101; the second—the French barons—a few days later. These two then continued their march together. The Count of Nevers's army passed through Constantinople in May or early June, and the army of the Dukes of Aquitaine and Bavaria a little later. This time, Alexius Comnenus appears to have been chiefly anxious to get the new Crusaders across into Asia Minor, giving them no time to effect a junction outside Constantinople.

Admittedly he welcomed them kindly (in spite of some trouble caused by civilians from the Lombard army), lavished gifts and good advice on them, gave them ships, and behaved altogether in an irreproachable manner, but there was no longer any question of Alexius' linking the fate of the Empire with these volunteers for the holy war, who in any case asked nothing more of him than the right of way. There is no doubt that he was afraid of them, and although he hoped they would conquer the Turks and reach Jerusalem, he was not in any mood to run great risks to help them. Something further calculated to discourage him from helping them was the fact that the Lombard army was utterly devoted to Bohemond and made no secret of it, and Bohemond, although for some time a prisoner of the Turks, was the Emperor's *bête noire*. All the same, there can be no doubt that at that moment the Emperor's feelings of Christian solidarity were livelier than those of the Crusaders, and it was these which, although they had been seriously shaken by legitimate grievances as well as instinctive antipathy, drove him to assist Christians who were on their way to fight the Turks. He even gave the Franco-German army an escort of five hundred picked troops. It is true that these were turcopoles (Turkish mercenaries), but he also gave them as

commander in chief Raymond of Saint-Gilles, who happened at that
time to be in Constantinople and had become a great friend of the
basileus.

The Lombard and Franco-German armies, under the leadership of
Raymond of Saint-Gilles (a very badly chosen leader since both
French and Lombards alike regarded him as a foreigner), took the
same road as that followed by the first Crusaders five years earlier.
The two armies together totaled an impressive number of troops:
Albert of Aix gives the figure as 200,000, and although this is unlikely and the total was certainly not even as many as 100,000, yet
even so it was one of the greatest assemblies of troops ever seen up
to that time. Numbers of this kind were a two-edged weapon in themselves, especially since a good quarter of them were civilians—women
and children, old men and clergy.

This disparate army, united under the sign of the cross, had to
choose an itinerary and establish a plan of campaign, and here a fact
intervened, so odd in itself as to be reminiscent of Pascal's comment about Cleopatra's nose: the reason that this Crusade ended as
it did was largely the fault of Bohemond's excessive popularity with
the Lombards. If the Norman had been a less able public-relations
man on his own behalf and if he had not succeeded, through his
friends and troubadours, in making himself out to be the greatest
champion of Christianity against Islam, the fate of the Latin East
might have been altogether different. What happened was that the
Lombards (who made up over half the army), led by their general
Albert of Biandrate, took it into their heads to cross over into Asia
Minor and push on as far as Neocaesarea, in the mountains near the
Black Sea coast, with the object of freeing Bohemond (who, it will be
remembered, was still held prisoner by Ghazi Gümüshtekin ibn
Danishmend).

This proposal was an outright challenge to Raymond of Saint-Gilles,
the Greeks, and the constable Conrad's Germans, all of whom were
known to be more or less antagonistic to Bohemond. In any case, the
whole undertaking was the purest folly. The Counts of Blois and
Toulouse and the Greek general Tsitas tried in vain to recall their
allies to their real object, the defense of the Holy Land, pointing out
the rashness of venturing in high summer into country entirely controlled by the Turks, and moreover, a desert, when by following the
road taken by the armies of the First Crusade they would be crossing
land partly reconquered by the Greeks and would have a good chance
of reaching Antioch and Syria without losses.

Finding the Lombards obdurate, they would certainly have done better to leave them to their fate, but this they dared not do, probably thinking their own army too weak in numbers to tackle any Turkish forces they might encounter on the way and also knowing that the Lombards, with their thousands of noncombatants, would all too easily fall victims to the Turks. When the mass of the Lombards (the civilians among them being more ardent in their desire to release Bohemond than the soldiers) threatened to break out into open rebellion, the leaders resigned themselves to taking the road through Galatia and Cappadocia in the direction of Ankara and if need be fighting the Turks in Asia Minor (who were not a direct threat to the Holy Sepulcher).

Diverted from its real objective by the irrational enthusiasm of a crowd of pilgrims and the mirage of Bohemond's great name, the great army set out into hostile territory, moving further and further away from the lands under Greek control. Initially they did quite well, because the Byzantines held the coast and the western half of the peninsula and kept them regularly supplied with provisions. In June 1101, the Crusading army took the city of Ankara, which belonged to the Sultan Kilij Arslan. The city was given back to Byzantium. But this time, the Turks of Asia Minor had learned by experience and they were not going to allow the new Frankish army to beat them again. They made preparations to defend themselves, and this was made easier by the fact that the country through which the army was now passing was practically a desert.

The province of Ankara was the fief of the Seljuk Kilij Arslan ibn Suleiman, while the north of the peninsula belonged to the Danishmend emir Ghazi Gümüshtekin. The Danishmends, rivals of the Seljuks of Asia Minor, joined forces with Kilij Arslan, and the new Crusading army was opposed by all the Turkish forces of the peninsula. In these recently conquered regions the Turks were still seminomadic warriors, able to move their armies with disconcerting speed, with an absolute knowledge of the country. They were also more numerous than all the Western Crusaders put together could ever be, and with vivid memories of the defeats of Dorylaeum and Antioch, they took the new danger very seriously.

Harried by the enemy, the soldiers dying of hunger and thirst, the army seemed lost. Its only hope of safety still lay in trying to reach the Black Sea, with its Greek-owned ports. Once again, against the advice of their leaders, the Lombards, although they had failed lamentably to stand firm under a Turkish charge, succeeded in carrying their original idea of pushing eastward to Ghazi Gümüshtekin's capital, the accursed city where Bohemond languished in chains. Their god was no longer Jesus Christ but their Norman chief, and it was to Bohemond that they looked for their salvation. In fact, if the man who inspired such unreasoning devotion had actually been at the head of the army at that moment, he might have been able to save it by the sheer ability to act quickly and make himself obeyed. It was a leader, a real leader, that the unfortunate pilgrims were seeking by that blind instinct which was leading them ever further into the desert mountains, baked by the sun and swarming with Turkish horsemen. But their leader was far away over the trackless wastes, deep in some subterranean dungeon, loaded with chains, nursing his impotent rage and almost certainly unaware of the advancing army several hundred miles away, an army ravaged by hunger but still coming on, with thousands of men and women who even now put their trust in him. The strange thing is that the leaders, who were experienced soldiers, should have believed it possible for the army, in its present condition, to beat on his own ground an enemy it had already proved itself unable to withstand. Seeing the Franks penetrating deeper into his province and threatening his capital, Ghazi Gümüshtekin summoned to his assistance the Seljuk Ridwan, King of Aleppo, the very man who had formerly refused to come to the aid of his vassal and neighbor Yaghi-Siyan, lord of Antioch.

The terror inspired by the Franks was beginning to have its effect. This time Ridwan did not hesitate. He hurriedly left Aleppo, which was divided from the Danishmend emirate as the crow flies by six hundred miles of mountainous country, and led his army to join those of his former enemies, Ghazi and Kilij Arslan. Somewhere between Amasea and Mersivan (apparently), the united Turkish forces came upon the Crusaders and prepared to fight a decisive battle.

Although the Crusaders had lost the greater part of their infantry (or in any case many more foot soldiers than knights) in ambushes and skirmishes, as well as from hunger and disease, they were still able to offer fierce resistance. Conrad had lost seven hundred of his Germans, and Albert of Biandrate three or four hundred of his Lombards, but the French force was more or less intact, and even at the lowest estimate it seems likely that at that time the Franco-Lombard army numbered between two and three thousand knights. The army is known to have been a large one, and the French and German contingents were made up chiefly of professional soldiers. The Provençal company led by Raymond of Saint-Gilles was small. To judge by the ease with which they were able to impose their own wishes on the rest, the Lombard knights, who in the course of the campaign had already acquired a somewhat unsavory reputation, must have been roughly equal in numbers to the French.

It was a powerful army, but like all Frankish armies, the only way it could really use its strength was in a full-scale cavalry charge. Knowing this from experience, the enemy took care not to give them a chance to attack, but concentrated on wearing them down by constant volleys of arrows and javelins. According to Albert of Aix, who is in fact inclined to put all the blame for the disaster on them and takes every opportunity of criticizing them, the Lombards were the first to break. The battle lasted all day, and the Frankish knights were continually on the defensive. They had no chance to re-form and take the initiative. Toward evening, Raymond of Saint-Gilles, finding himself deserted by his Byzantine mercenaries (turcopoles), had no alternative but to withdraw and take refuge with a few of his Provençal soldiers on an isolated rock where, but for the assistance of Stephen of Blois and Conrad, he would have been surrounded by the Turks.

The end of the battle did not seem to be in sight: there could be no question of an attack; the Frankish army was steadily retreating toward its camp, with great losses of men and horses. In the night, the Count of Toulouse, the official leader of the army, struck camp and fled toward the sea with his Provençaux.

When the other barons learned of Raymond's flight, they too fled under cover of darkness. It is not known how many escaped, but the chroniclers state that those who escaped from this battle and took ship at Sinope for Constantinople were few. The army had ceased to exist. All that remained of the armies of the Count of Blois, the Count of Burgundy, the constable Conrad, the Bishop of Soissons, the Count of Biandrate, and the Count of Parma was a mere handful of knights, a few hundred at the very most, including their squires and servants. How many knights had been killed on the preceding day neither Albert of Aix nor any other historian can say.

What is known is who remained alive on the field of battle the next morning when the army realized that it no longer had any leaders: the thousands of ordinary soldiers, clerics, and monks, and all the women and children. The Turkish army had only to fall on the helpless, panic-stricken rabble and mow them down. This was the signal for a desperate flight by such knights as still remained in the camp and any of the foot soldiers who could trust their legs. The Turkish horsemen who were not fully occupied with the massacre on the field set off across the valley in pursuit of the refugees, and few escaped.

Nearly all the men were killed. The women—the young ones, at least—and children were rounded up like cattle. Thirty or forty thousand people were killed or enslaved on that day, and the Turkish markets and harems were swollen by the addition of several thousand Christian slaves. Even so, some three thousand men did succeed in escaping through the mountain passes to the sea and reassembled at Sinope, from which port they were later put on board Greek ships.

As for their leaders, they reached Constantinople safe and sound less than a fortnight after the battle, throwing all the blame for the disaster on the Lombards. They were not exactly proud of their behavior, but Christendom would have gained nothing if they too had stayed to be slaughtered. Alexius Comnenus reproached Raymond of Saint-Gilles bitterly for abandoning his army and the poor pilgrims, because he believed that but for the flight of their general the Crusading army might not have been utterly annihilated. This is not certain and it is possible that Raymond, on the spot, had been a better judge of the situation; but however that may be, his conduct during this campaign does him little credit. This is not to impugn his personal courage, for he fought well, but on the one occasion when he was finally in command of a great army, things could scarcely have gone worse had the army been without a leader altogether.

This time the disaster was complete and irremediable. What had been wiped out was not simply a band of undisciplined pilgrims but a great army. It is true that the large numbers of civilians had been a severe handicap to the army and may even have been the cause of the Crusade's deviation and consequently of the disaster itself; but the Turks now knew that the Franks were not invincible and that they had only to unite against them and launch a determined attack. Anna Comnena had these cruel words to say: "Among other characteristics, the Celtic race is independent and not willing to ask advice; they make no use of military discipline nor of the art of strategy, but when they have to fight and wage war, anger howls in their hearts and they are irresistible. . . . If, on the other hand, their enemies continually lay ambushes for them based on experience in military matters and attack them according to the rules of the art of war, they pass from the utmost bravery to its opposite extreme."[7] In fact the Franks, although they did not learn their strategy from books, were as expert in the art of warfare as the Greeks and Turks, but their armies, just like those of other races, had their good and bad generals.

The significant fact is that the Latins (not the Count of Toulouse or his companions in misfortune, but most people in the West whose opinion has been followed by historians) were quick to throw the responsibility for this terrible defeat on the one man who was in no way to blame. Alexius Comnenus was accused of having, "like the scorpion who does not attack face to face but with his tail" (William of Tyre), sent the Crusaders deliberately into desert country under Turkish domination, hoping that they would be massacred. (However, Albert of Aix, while at one moment he expounds the Emperor's odious conduct in detail, also tells us that Alexius rescued the remnants of the army which had fled to Sinope, and—here the chronicler forgets his prejudice in order to put the Count of Toulouse in a bad light—that he severely censured Raymond of Saint-Gilles for his flight. These contradictory assertions do not prevent our historian from believing firmly in the "treachery" of the Greeks.) Nevertheless, Alexius was quite prepared to go on helping the Crusaders, on condition that he himself did not become too involved. All the leaders who passed through Constantinople were welcomed kindly by him and appear to have regarded him as a kind of father figure or protector who could be asked to provide help, money, or advice and from whom a great deal more was expected than he could possibly give. There were bitter complaints of his lack of enthusiasm and the bitterest reproaches were heaped on him—behind his back— if he failed to perform impossibilities to get his allies out of trouble. The prestige of Byzantium was still great and the unconscious respect it inspired deeper than the Latins themselves realized; their attitude had in it a strong element of unrequited love.

Force of circumstances had made those who escaped from the Crusade dependent on Alexius Comnenus, but even so, they had no reason to bear a grudge against the Emperor. He comforted them, re-equipped them, and put them on his own ships bound for Syria so that they could join King Baldwin and at least make their pilgrimage to Jerusalem. Meanwhile, the army belonging to the Count of Nevers, with its fifteen thousand fighting men, was advancing along the road to Anatolia with the intention of moving down to Antioch and from there to Syria.

After passing through Ankara and deciding not to join the Lombards and Raymond of Saint-Gilles, William II of Nevers had, in fact, traveled southward in a semicircle and was advancing on Kilij Arslan's capital of Konya (Iconium). Just as he was approaching the city, he was met by the entire army of Ghazi and Kilij Arslan, and the Turks, still drunk with triumph at their recent comparatively easy victory over the Franco-Lombard army, fell upon the Niver-

nais with such fury that, after resisting valiantly in a succession of
battles, Count William's fine army was finally surrounded near
Heraclea and slaughtered almost to a man. William of Nevers escaped, almost alone, with a few of his knights. He reached Antioch
in rags, like a beggar, having been robbed and deserted on the way
by his infidel guides. (In spite of this he survived for another forty-
six years.)

The third army, which was much larger than that of the Count of
Nevers although it too included a considerable number of civilians,
had passed through Constantinople a short time earlier and followed
the route taken by the First Crusade. Its leaders, as we have seen,
were William IX, Duke of Aquitaine (who was to acquire more fame
as a troubadour than as a Crusader), Welf IV, Duke of Bavaria,
and the Margravine Ida of Austria. The Turks had destroyed everything in the path of the enemy—not a particularly difficult feat in
a country which was already almost entirely desert. It was high
summer (June, July, and August) and in the intolerable heat the
army was broken by hunger and thirst long before its defeat by the
Turks. In no condition to fight, it fell an easy prey to the archers of
Kilij Arslan and Ghazi Gümüshtekin. On September 5, 1101, the
Crusaders of Aquitaine and Bavaria were surrounded near the river
Eregli, where they had been hoping to quench their thirst, and
nearly all slaughtered on the spot. The two Dukes, William and
Welf, escaped with difficulty only by throwing away their armor.
William fled quite alone except for his squire. The Margravine, be-
ing only a woman, was less fortunate. She remained on the field of
battle and no one ever knew what became of her. She had been one
of the most famous beauties of her time.

In the space of a month, the Turkish princes of Asia Minor, the
Seljuk Kilij Arslan and the Danishmend Ghazi, with the help of the
King of Aleppo, had wiped out three (or more accurately four)
great Frankish armies: had annihilated them so utterly and completely that even the Latin chroniclers mention only a few who
escaped. These were probably more numerous than they appear, for
the historians are chiefly concerned with the leaders; but even among
the knights, it is doubtful whether one-tenth survived, and the foot
soldiers (to say nothing of the civilians) perished almost to a man.
For the Turks of Anatolia it was a splendid victory and one which
was made even more dazzling by the prestige of the victors of Antioch and Jerusalem. If Greece and the West had ever succeeded in
believing for one moment that Turkish military power was on the

wane, the Crusade of 1101 cruelly disillusioned them. The Crusaders' initial victories had been a lucky chance, due largely to the effects of surprise.

The immediate result of the crushing defeat suffered by this second Crusade, a defeat so swift and in appearance so ridiculously easy, was to discourage volunteers from setting out for the Holy Land in any numbers for dozens of years to come. Contemporary historians agree in passing over this inglorious adventure in silence, as far as possible. All the same, the considerable loss of human life involved was not in itself a disaster for the nations who had sent out these armies of volunteers. There were too many impoverished knights and professional and amateur soldiers. The Latin West at the end of the eleventh century had more soldiers than it needed, and plenty of those who took the cross did so because they could not find a living in their own lands. The mass of poor people (for although there were wealthy civilian pilgrims, these were still few) had most of them left their countries because they had nothing to lose. Life in the West was so harsh and the resources of the soil still so slender that even mass departures of tens of thousands of poor people still left too many useless mouths at home. Those lords who had, at great expense, fitted out their armies and lost nine-tenths of them, suffered considerable material loss (not to mention the loss of face), but as we shall see, neither William of Aquitaine nor William of Nevers nor Welf of Bavaria suffered greatly when they returned to their own lands from the consequences of their disastrous odyssey. The death of Stephen of Blois did not result in ruin for his family (they learned of his death "with great joy"). This campaign, which made so many widows and orphans in the West, was no more than an accident which did not profoundly affect the basis of feudal society.

In the East, on the other hand, for the little Latin principalities which were beginning to grow up in Syria, the annihilation of this Crusade was an irreparable disaster. In fact, it meant the failure of the Western attempt to establish a real Christian power in the Levant. If by any chance they had succeeded in reaching the Holy Land, the four armies which had been destroyed, by their military strength and by sheer numbers, might well have made possible the creation of a state strong enough to pave the way for immigration on a still greater scale and to fight their divided adversaries one after another. This hope was never realized. When Baldwin, Tancred, and their companions saw the great barons, to whose arrival with reinforcements of men and equipment they had been looking

forward so impatiently, appear one after the other in such a sorry
condition, all they could do was comfort the unfortunates by allowing them to make their pilgrimage to the Holy Places. Then, by a
crowning irony of fate, some of those who had escaped were led
pointlessly to their deaths by Baldwin himself.

The pioneers of the First Crusade, the present lords of the Latin
provinces in the Levant, such as Baldwin, King of Jerusalem, Tancred, regent of Antioch, and Baldwin of Le Bourg, Count of Edessa,
seem to have managed to bear up under the misfortune the more
easily because the armies which had been wiped out were not made
up of their own countrymen. Far from giving way to despair, they
continued their policy of systematic, semidefensive warfare, making
the best use they could of the slender forces at their disposal to
maintain themselves in a country where they no longer numbered
more than a few thousands.

As far as the West was concerned the *Crusade,* as such, was over
and there is no knowing what would have happened if al-Afdal's
armies had succeeded in recapturing Jerusalem at that moment. All
the efforts of the Pope and the bishops would probably never have
been sufficient to bring about a third mass rising of Christendom.
There were still the scattered survivors of the horrors perpetrated
during the massacres of Amasea and Eregli, and their stories were
enough to make even the boldest lose heart. The time for fanatical
enthusiasm was past. The cry of "God wills it" had lost its meaning
when it was perfectly obvious that God had clearly not willed this
Crusade.

Meanwhile Jerusalem was still in Christian hands, and Latin and
Catholic hands at that, and the Pope was determined not to let this
be forgotten. In the years that followed, the Crusaders clinging to
Syrian soil regularly received modest but none the less important reinforcements by sea. These reinforcements were purely military,
"pilgrim" soldiers who came to pay their debt of armed service at
the Holy Sepulcher, as well as less disinterested reinforcements in
the shape of the merchant fleets which were of necessity fighting
units at the same time. It is fair to say that the second phase of the
Crusaders' establishment in the East was, to a great extent, the work
of squadrons from Pisa and Genoa and later on from Venice.

This commercial maritime aspect of the history of Frankish Syria
was by no means the least important, but it was chiefly a matter of
trade and economic exchanges which had already been in operation
for hundreds if not thousands of years on the great silk and spice

routes. There will be more to say of it at a later date. If the interests
of the Crusade and the political and religious upheavals it caused
coincided with the interests of the great international power represented by commerce in the Middle Ages, it is only fair to say that this
power was already of the kind which turns everything ruthlessly to
its own profit. The Crusades were good for trade, each was useful to
the other, but it cannot be said that trade had any deep or decisive
influence on the course of events.

The kingdom of Jerusalem, the principality of Antioch (princeless
for the moment, since Bohemond was still in captivity), and the
county of Edessa were embarking on their difficult yet glorious career of wars and skirmishes very similar to feudal wars in Europe,
with the difference that the other side were usually, though not invariably, infidels. A fourth tiny Frankish state was coming into being
on the coast of the Lebanon where, after countless failures, Raymond of Saint-Gilles was setting out to conquer the province of
Tripoli on his own account.

After being taken prisoner by Tancred and being forced to swear
to him that he would lay no further claim to Antioch or to any city
dependent on that province, the old baron had returned to the country which four years earlier Godfrey of Bouillon had compelled him
to leave in order to march on Jerusalem. As the ally of Alexius
Comnenus and unpopular with the other Crusaders on this account,
Raymond had disappointed the Emperor by his conduct in Asia Minor
and could no longer aspire to the role of leader of the Crusade, or
arbiter between the Greeks and Latins. He had given up all idea of
returning to his own country, and to those who counseled him to end
his days in the "delights" of his native land he replied, according to
William of Tyre, "like a good Christian, that his Lord and Master
Jesus Christ, when he was put upon the cross for his sake and for
that of other sinners, would not come down from his cross, but remained there until death. . . . He desired to do the same, and he
would not set down his cross until his soul was parted from his
body."[8] Raymond's cross may have been the fight against the infidel, but it also meant the conquest of a rich, fertile province with
a mild climate and fine fortified cities full of gardens and palaces.
Not even God could repay the services of a count of Toulouse with
anything less.

Although Raymond never had the satisfaction of taking Tripoli, he
nevertheless spent the last years of his life, with tireless patience and
courage and exemplary energy, in conquering, city by city, the neighborhood of the powerful maritime citadel. (The city itself was ac-

tually captured by his successors four years after his death.) Much more competent in small matters than in large-scale projects, he was a stubborn man who settled in the Lebanon with the firm intention of turning it into a Provençal kingdom. When he was over sixty, he was still busy organizing and directing the siege of various castles, and after taking possession of Tortosa and Jebail, he built a strong castle directly facing Tripoli, to which the Moslems gave the name of Qalat Sanjil (Saint-Gilles), after its founder. There he lived, concentrating on making life increasingly hard for the people of Tripoli. Ibn Ammar had a poor reward for his policy of goodwill toward the Franks. On two occasions he had made the coastal passage easy for them and his gifts and advice had made it possible for them to settle in Judaea and Galilee. By the time he attempted to appeal to his neighbors and then to his distant overlord, the Caliph of Egypt, when his own forces were no longer adequate to halt the progress of the Provençal army, it was already too late. Tripoli fell into Frankish hands in 1109.

Thanks to Raymond of Saint-Gilles, a Frankish state was to grow up to form a territorial link between the kingdom of Jerusalem and the Frankish states of northern Syria. From this point of view, it may be said that ultimately the Count of Toulouse rendered an appreciable service to the cause of Latin Christianity in the East.

CHAPTER

V

The Formation of the Frankish States of Syria

(1 1 0 2 – 1 1 1 2)

Islam

The gradual settlement in Syria and Palestine of Christians from the West, after their sensational irruption onto the military and political chessboard of the Levant, caused increasing anxiety to the Moslem states as the insolence of the newcomers began to affect them more or less directly. They were not as yet unduly worried, and with the exception of the three ill-fated attempts by al-Afdal, and of course, those made by Kerbogha, the only princes who fought against the intruders were those whose own lands were attacked. Possibly the great victories of 1101 gave the Moslems the idea that the Franks, few and isolated, were now adversaries who could be crushed at any time and who might meanwhile be useful as a weapon. The Moslem princes were much too preoccupied with squabbling among themselves to take the call to a holy war at all seriously, however necessary they might consider it in theory.

From a distance Islam appeared to Westerners as a united force, uniform at least in its "miscreance." The Moslems indeed had much the same idea about Christians, and did not differentiate between Franks and *Roumis,* or Byzantines. In fact Islam had been rent for two hundred years by religious and political schisms. The two great religious traditions which clashed in the heart of Islam were Sunna, or Sunnism, which represented official orthodoxy, on the one hand, and Shiism, the breakaway sect, on the other. The Shiites went back to the descendants of Ali, the husband of the Prophet's daughter Fatima, and were a reformist party who rejected the oral and written tradition (the Sunna) and recognized no authority but the Koran. The Shiite, or Fatimid, caliphate of Egypt stood in opposition to the orthodox caliphate of Baghdad; but while Egypt was the principal home of Shiism, the sect also had numerous supporters in all Moslem countries, especially in Persia and Mesopotamia, where at one point (in 1058) the Shiites actually seized power, and also in Syria.

In the tenth century the Abbasid caliphate of Baghdad, harassed and weakened by the Greeks to the west, fell under the semiofficial dominion of the Buyid emirs, Shiites from Iran, and lapsed into decadence. The eleventh century saw a rapid rise, followed by an apparent but only temporary decline, in Turkish power.

The Turks were a seminomadic Central Asian people of Mongol origin, gifted with a prodigious energy, and their sudden advance in successive waves is not unlike that of the Normans in the West. They were Moslems, fairly recently converted, and Sunna Moslems. Their Moslem faith, although genuine, was still superficial, and Moslems of earlier traditions regarded them as barbarians, which in fact they were. Their armies, like those of the Huns—their distant relatives— and of the ancient Teutonic races, took with them in their train their women and children and all their movable goods including the tents which served them as houses. As their conquests spread, so they moved their vast herds of cattle in search of pasture. Their numbers and their adventurous spirit made these rudely equipped nomads a force to be reckoned with. Beginning at the end of the tenth century, their expansion in the Near East resulted, by the eleventh, in the foundation of a vast Turkish empire.

Originally drawn from their steppes by the Abbasid caliphs and their provincial governors, who saw these poor nomadic warriors as potentially excellent mercenaries, the Turkish chieftains soon grew tired of being kept in a state of vassalage and raised themselves by sheer force of arms from mercenaries to arbiters between the rival princes, and then to their more or less acknowledged masters.

Successive Turkish conquerors, such as the Ghaznavids and later the Seljuks, drove the Byzantines from Asia Minor almost altogether and established control over the Moslem kingdoms of Mesopotamia, Iran, Iraq, and Persia, where they became a kind of military aristocracy with all real power in their hands. The caliphs, whose power

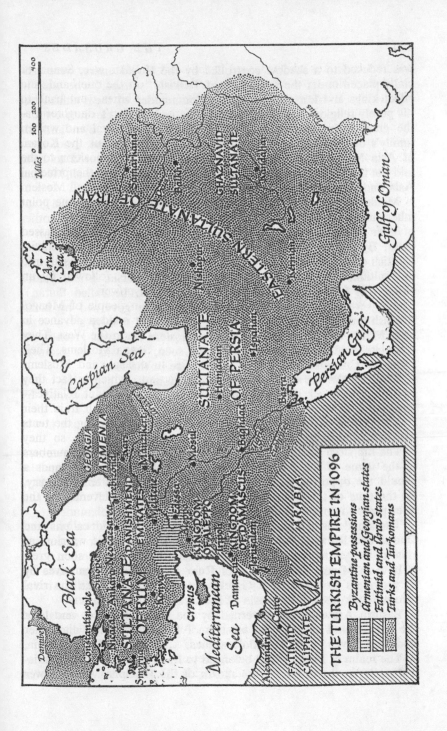

THE TURKISH EMPIRE IN 1096

Byzantine possessions
Armenian and Georgian states
Fatimid and Arab states
Turks and Turkomans

was reduced to a shadow controlled by the Buyid emirs, were officially placed under the protection of Turkish "sultans," who were in
effect kings and left nothing to the Commander of the Faithful but
his purely religious functions. Toward the end of the eleventh century
the great Seljuk Sultan Malik Shah held under his own and his
family's dominion Persia, Mesopotamia, Syria, Palestine, Iraq, most
of Asia Minor, and Armenia, and at one point appeared to have
laid the foundations of a great Turkish empire by uniting all Moslem
Asia under the hand of the same dynasty.

Malik Shah died in 1092 and his brother and sons divided the great
inheritance between them. They were too busy robbing one another
of their respective shares to extend their dominion over new provinces. Byzantium and Egypt could breathe again: the vast Seljuk
Turkish empire was finished. In its place were a number of kingdoms,
or "sultanates" (although only the Seljuk of Persia, Malik Shah's
eldest son Barkiyarok, was actually entitled to be called Sultan).
These were still formidable because they were governed by harsh
Turkish military discipline, but so utterly divided that by a few years
after Malik Shah's death the whole of Moslem Asia was given up to
complete feudal anarchy. As we have seen, this was the moment
when the Crusaders made their appearance in the East.

Thus, by the end of the eleventh century and the beginning of the
twelfth, nearly all the Moslem states of Asia were governed by
Turks.

The throne of Persia was occupied by Barkiyarok, whose power
also extended to Baghdad, the seat of the Caliph.

The kingdom of Mosul, a vassal province of Persia, was governed
in the name of the Sultan by lieutenants who were quite capable,
should the opportunity arise, of overriding their master's authority.
At the time of the Crusade, Mosul was governed by Kerbogha and
later passed into the hands of Barkiyarok's brother Mohammed.

The kingdoms of Damascus and Aleppo were held by two brothers,
Duqaq and Ridwan, the sons of Tutush, an uncle and long-standing
rival of the young Sultan. The two brothers hated one another.

In Asia Minor, the sultanate of Rum (Byzantium) was made up
of provinces won from the Greeks, and governed by Kilij Arslan,
also a Seljuk but a fifth cousin of Barkiyarok.

Eastern Armenia was governed by the Ortoqid emirs, vassals of
the Seljuks and at one time masters of Palestine, from which they
had been driven out by al-Afdal's armies.

The realm of Eastern Iran belonged to Barkiyarok's brother Sanjar.

Finally, in the north, on the shores of the Black Sea and in what had formerly been Cappadocia, the ruling family were Danishmend emirs, members of a Turkoman tribe never completely subdued by the Seljuks, with whom they disputed lands in Asia Minor and Armenia.

All these Turkish or Turkoman princes, although they belonged to the same nationality, and were for the most part members of the same family, all belonging to the Sunnite sect, hated and were jealous of one another. They were incorrigible fighters (with the notable exception of Barkiyarok), and spent their time making wars to seize towns and provinces from one another and concluding short-lived alliances among themselves or with any neighbor who could be useful to them. Altogether, the great Turkish feudal aristocracy, although still in control of the armed forces, only constituted a real military power on the rare occasions when a number of these princes decided to unite for purposes of common action.

Elsewhere, along the Syrian littoral, the great coastal cities were held by Arab emirs who were theoretically vassals of Egypt but were in practice quite independent. There were the Banū Ammar of Tripoli, the Banū Munqidh of Shaizar, and in the Orontes valley, the Banū Mula'ib of the emirate of Homs. Lastly, in the southwest of Asia Minor (between the valley of the Upper Euphrates and Anatolia) were the perilous and uncertain domains of the Armenian princes. These, though constantly harried by the Turks, were sufficiently forceful to maintain themselves in their possessions: Gabriel at Melitene, Thatoul at Marash, Kogh Vasil at Raban, the Roupenian dynasty at Vakha, and the sons of Hethoum at Lampron.

From 1097 onward a Latin county began to develop at Edessa, where Baldwin had replaced the Armenian Thoros, and after 1098 the Norman Bohemond reigned in Antioch whence the Crusaders had driven out the Turkoman Yaghi-Siyan. Then, in 1099, Jerusalem had no sooner fallen out of Turkish and into Egyptian hands than it became the capital of a small Frankish kingdom.

This, in a nutshell, was the political situation in the Near East at the beginning of the twelfth century. A complex situation if ever there was one, but with nothing in it to astonish the Crusaders, to whom feudal squabbles, disputes between vassals and suzerains, broken alliances, vendettas, and clan warfare were all perfectly familiar. In these matters, Moslems were not so very different from Christians, except that in Syria and in Palestine the situation was still further aggravated—and doubly so—by religious factors.

Most important, naturally, was the clash between Christians and Moslems—and also between Christians and Jews and between Jews and Moslems, but the Jews were only a small minority—which created a perpetual source of friction, especially in time of war, and the country was continually at war. Second, as we have seen, was the irreconcilable hostility between the various Christian sects, and to the Syriacs, Greeks, and Armenians were now added the Latin Christians. Lastly, and this was for a long time a determining factor in events in Syria, the religious hatred dividing Sunnites (represented by the Abbasid caliphate of Baghdad) and Shiites (represented by the Fatimid caliphate of Cairo) had in the twelfth century begun to assume a particularly grave aspect and one whose consequences were to have a profound influence on the policies of the various Moslem princes.

The Shiites, or Ismailians, formed a powerful current of mysticism and philosophy whose adepts, in spite of persecution, would not abandon their missionary activities in lands under Sunnite control. They had numerous followers in Iran as well as in Syria and Baghdad, among the Arabs and Persians but not among the Turks, who, having been converted once and for all to the Sunnite tradition, took no further interest in theological speculation but held the Shiite heresy in proper abhorrence.

As foreign conquerors and barbarians the Turks (although they adapted themselves very quickly to Moslem civilization) were never very popular with the Arab and Syrian populations, despite the prestige they had earned by their victories over the Christians. Among many Arabs who belonged to the older tradition, hostility toward the Turks became confused with a leaning toward Shiism. Although in Baghdad the Turks appeared as the champions of orthodoxy (and moreover, as we shall see, the caliphs did occasionally break free of their heavy yoke), in the Syrian provinces which were vassals of Egypt the progress of the Seljuk conquerors inspired a fear only made the more vivid by the fact that the Turks, as hard and fast Sunnites, threatened the material and spiritual independence of populations who, whether openly or in secret, favored Shiism.

Shiites (or at least active members of the dissident sect) were numerous in Syria and in Persia, and they formed a highly organized secret brotherhood for the simultaneous pursuit of religious and political aims. Naturally enough, they were Egyptian agents, but they had their own organization, their own leaders, and their own policy, taking orders from no one but engaged in an intense activity the object of which was to ensure the triumph of their religious beliefs by all means. They were not like the Sufis, mystics and philosophers who converted by the example of their ascetic lives; the most notorious of them, the Ismailians, were a minority group existing within Shiism itself, a sect more powerful because of the zeal of their followers than their numbers. These men indulged quite openly in terrorist activities carried out in the name of religion. That their name Hashishyun (Assassins) ultimately passed into everyday language was due to the amazing number of their exploits and to the fact that murder (perpetrated by order, as a sacred duty) was the thing for which they existed and the source of all their power. It is by no means certain that fear of the Assassins did not exert an influence on the policies of Arab and even Turkish princes, and on many occasions this influence made itself felt in the total elimination—by means of the ritual dagger—of certain powerful individuals. It was therefore quite real, and just as real was the state of insecurity which these dangerous agitators succeeded in creating in a society already sufficiently demoralized by the Turkish and Frankish threats.

Just as, in their distrust of one another, the Greeks and Latins had sometimes to resort to the aid of Islam, so the Arabs and Turks, and especially the former, frequently found it preferable to have Christians as neighbors rather than their brothers in religion. Acting on this assumption, Ibn Ammar had believed that by good treaties and gifts of money he could create allies for himself against the Seljuks of Damascus. Then, when he found himself gradually being stripped of his lands and cooped up in his capital of Tripoli by the Italian fleets at sea and the army of "Sanjil" by land, he pleaded in vain with his distant suzerain, al-Afdal, to undertake a holy war, and later went in person to the Turk Toghtekin, regent of Damascus, to appeal to Moslem solidarity. This solidarity, for which he had had so little regard in times gone by, had no more effect in determining the behavior of al-Afdal or Toghtekin, and the latter only decided to occupy Tripoli in order to try and take the city for himself, although it finally fell into Provençal hands none the less.

The Franks in the East

UNEASY BEGINNINGS

The intrusion of the Crusaders into a land under Moslem domination did, however, bring a considerable threat to the Kings of Damascus and Aleppo and to the Fatimid caliphate of Egypt. The first two were threatened by the Frankish principalities in the north and the last by the kingdom of Jerusalem.

In 1100 both Edessa and Antioch had lost the two strong men who had originally taken possession of them: Baldwin of Boulogne and Bohemond. Baldwin had been replaced by his cousin Baldwin of Le Bourg, and Bohemond, after an interregnum lasting several months, by his nephew Tancred. Both these revealed themselves to be men of action, intrepid warriors and energetic generals; both ruled over provinces with largely Christian populations and this made their task a good deal easier, Baldwin of Le Bourg's in particular, for he had been compelled, whether he liked it or not, to embrace the cause of the Armenian military aristocracy and to conclude alliances with the Armenian princes of the neighboring provinces such as Melitene, Raban, and Vakha. At this time the Armenians had only recently migrated to this part of the country, but it had already earned the name of Lesser Armenia. They were a fairly considerable force and, despite the fall of Melitene (captured by Gümüshtekin in 1103), were clinging more and more fiercely to these provinces where, with the help of the Franks, they hoped to remain. The Frankish county of Edessa was originally intended to become a Franco-Armenian province, and despite the severity of the two Baldwins, a political alliance and reciprocal concessions were imposed on the Franks by the needs of the moment. As time went by, the third Frankish count of Edessa was to acquire a real and well-deserved popularity with the Armenians.

The Armenians themselves were only a minority, although admittedly a numerically important one and more so by reason of the military functions they exercised, from which the Syrians were to all intents excluded. But this minority was itself split by religious quarrels between "Greeks" (Orthodox), who were few in number but held most of the important posts, and Armenians of the Gregorian rite. The Syriac population was almost as hostile to the Armenians as to the Turks themselves. Their attitude to the Franks, foreign Christians and therefore neutral, was one of reserve and suspicion, and despite Frankish efforts to conciliate these unfriendly Christians, they remained an unreliable element from whom treachery was continually to be feared. The Franks were not easy masters, and even had they wished to be, they would have found it difficult because they were constantly at war and war is hard on the poor. It was easier to get on with the Armenians.

A year after the Normans installed themselves in the province, Bohemond had driven the Greek Patriarch, John IV, out of Antioch, together with most of the higher Greek clergy. Considering his policy of hostility to Byzantium, this was a natural enough move, but it was hardly likely that the Greeks would regard it as such. The insult to the Patriarch of Antioch was one of Alexius Comnenus's major grievances against the Normans. The old prelate, who was respected by Latins and Greeks alike, had been solemnly reinstated on his patriarchal throne by the Crusaders, and no one at the time of the capture of Antioch had thought of disputing his rights. William of Tyre explains, not without some trace of embarrassment, that the venerable man left Antioch "of his own free will, without any violence having been done him," simply because the Latins did not understand Greek and he "was not getting very much income": odd reasons for a prelate who, in the days of the Turks, had courageously faced martyrdom rather than leave his church and his congregation. Even if the Latins did not understand Greek, there were still enough Greeks in the city to justify the Patriarch's keep. Greeks and Orthodox Syrians were always a great deal more common in Antioch than Franks.

All this makes it hard to believe that John IV left his post of his own free will, unless it was his intention to solicit the Emperor's help against the Latin invaders. At all events, he never renounced his title and was not deposed by anyone. After his death, the Greek Church continued regularly to consecrate patriarchs of Antioch, who remained in Constantinople but were regarded as the legal heads of the Orthodox community in Antioch. Bohemond, however, following the precedent set by Jerusalem, encouraged the Latin clergy with his army to elect a new patriarch from among themselves, and Bernard of Valence, a man who had formerly been chaplain to Adhemar of Monteil and since elected Bishop of Artah, was nominated Patriarch of Antioch. His authority extended over seven archbishoprics and seven bishoprics.* Antioch was one of the oldest cities in Christendom and its patriarchate had formerly been third in importance after Rome and Constantinople. After centuries of Moslem occupation and in spite of being several times reconquered by Byzantium, these bishoprics and archbishoprics no longer boasted Christian communities to justify their titles: most of them no longer possessed even titular bishops, and this explains the ease with which the Latin bishoprics were initially created and handed out to those of the clergy accompanying the Crusading army who were favored by the secular leaders.

Bohemond—and while Bohemond was in captivity, Tancred—be-

---

* The archbishoprics of Karikos, Tarsus, Mamistra, Cyrrhus, Hierapolis, Edessa, and Apamea, and the bishoprics of Albara, Laodicea, Gabala, Valania, Antaradus, Tripoli, and Byblos.

gan by oppressing the Greek element, which was the more powerful
in Antioch because it possessed indisputable rights to the Byzantine
city. The Latins were still few and they needed the support of the
other Christians. In Antioch minor posts in the administration were
filled by Armenians, while the Syrians were excluded from all participation in public affairs, but both were better treated than the
Greeks and retained their own bishops and places of worship. Apart
from this, the Norman government was a crude military dictatorship.
Indeed, the perpetual state of war in which the country found itself
made it impossible for it to be anything else. It has already been
said that Bohemond had been taken prisoner by the Danishmends in
August 1100. The capture of this man, as formidable as he was
feared, may well have saved the Turkish kingdom of Aleppo, a
neighbor of Antioch. Bohemond was at that time the most able of
the Frankish leaders, and equally famous among the Moslems and
his own countrymen. It was obvious that he did not mean to confine
his ambitions to the one province of Antioch alone. But once removed from the theater of military operations he was, if not forgotten (as we have seen, in Lombardy he was remembered only too
well), at least eclipsed by others who were free to go on fighting.
Even in his dungeon in Niksar he still represented a cause of hope
for some and a danger to others. Ghazi Gümüshtekin found he had
a time bomb on his hands. He could have let the Frank die in prison,
but he was not sufficiently treacherous or sufficiently indifferent to
money for that. Bohemond was too valuable a property.

Then what appeared to be an admirable opportunity to obtain a
good ransom for his dangerous captive presented itself to Ghazi. In
1103, Alexius Comnenus offered the Danishmend 260,000 bezants in
return for having Bohemond delivered into his hands. Moreover, the
basileus could be relied on not to let the Norman show his face in
Asia Minor or in Syria again. Unfortunately the Sultan of Rum, Kilij
Arslan, was demanding half the promised ransom for himself. Highly
indignant that the Sultan should lay claim to *his* prisoner, Ghazi finally
came to an agreement with Bohemond himself. Bohemond promised
to pay half the 260,000 bezants and, in addition, to help his jailer
(now his liberator) fight Kilij Arslan, Byzantium, and all his other
enemies. As a result of this curious arrangement, which Alexius Comnenus had unwittingly instigated, the Norman left his prison after
three years in captivity, to the great fury of the Greeks and the
equally great fury of Kilij Arslan, who promptly declared war on
Ghazi and denounced him as a traitor to Islam.

Embittered and hardened—if that were possible—by his three years in prison, and burning with hatred against the Greeks who had so very nearly gained possession of his person, Bohemond returned to Antioch, scraped together the enormous sum of his ransom as best he could with the help of Baldwin of Edessa, the Christians of Antioch, and his Lombard subjects, and took his place in the city once again, after somewhat unceremoniously ousting Tancred not only from his title of regent but also from the territories he had conquered in the previous two years. Bohemond's nephew felt this bitterly, but despite everything his uncle's personal prestige was still so great that he dared not protest.

Had Bohemond been a fanatical supporter of the holy war, he might perhaps, even with his reduced strength and even after the terrible carnage of 1101, have succeeded in taking Aleppo, whose ruler, Ridwan, abandoned by his overlords, was unable to defend it on his own. At that time the whole region of Aleppo was controlled by the Franks of Edessa and Antioch, whose raids penetrated into the suburbs of the capital itself. It would have been more logical, in the interests of the Holy Sepulcher, first to consolidate the Christian position in Palestine, but Jerusalem was not and never had been Bohemond's objective, any more than it seems to have been Tancred's or Baldwin of Le Bourg's. Bohemond, whose besetting sin appears to have been overweening ambition, attacked neither the immediate neighbor, who would have been relatively easy to conquer, nor the more distant enemies who were directly threatening the Holy Sepulcher. Instead he was determined to push on further east, toward Baghdad and Mosul.

Taking advantage of the war at present raging between the Seljuk sultans, the sons of Malik Shah, the Franks of Antioch and Edessa moved with their little army, estimated by Albert of Aix at three thousand knights and seven thousand foot, against the castle of Harran on the river Balikh, a tributary of the Upper Euphrates. Harran, situated some thirty miles south of Edessa, was already under the jurisdiction of the emirs of Mosul. Furthermore the appearance of the Franks on the left bank of the Balikh constituted a threat to the Ortoqid emirs, who were immediate neighbors of the principality of Edessa. Already used to local conditions, the Crusaders had chosen as their moment to attack Harran a time when the city was in a turmoil after a revolt of the army and in the hands of a new and inexperienced ruler who was not yet in full command. Unfortunately, although the Frankish leaders did not, like the Turks, go so far as to cut one another's throats, they could not agree even in anticipation over the division of the spoils. While Bohemond and Baldwin of Le Bourg were still arguing over who should be first to set his banners on the walls when the city surrendered, they were surprised by a large Turkish army. The atabeg (governor) of Mosul, Jekermish, and the Ortoqid emir Soqman had called a halt to their private war and were advancing on Harran at the head of their cavalry.

At the first encounter the Turks pretended to flee, and by good luck managed to cut the Frankish army in half, throwing it into utter confusion and inflicting a crushing defeat. The Normans, who at first had stood firm, managed to save themselves by flight; most of the army of Edessa was slaughtered and the survivors, among whom were Baldwin of Le Bourg and his cousin and principal lieutenant Joscelin of Courtenay, taken prisoner. This was a magnificent prize for the Turks: the two leaders, Soqman and Jekermish, very nearly came to blows over the person of Baldwin of Le Bourg, and this proved the end of their brief alliance. (Baldwin had been taken prisoner by Soqman, and Jekermish carried him off from the Ortoqid emir's own tent, an insult which his ally never forgave.)

After this disaster, the two Normans could only withdraw with all speed, the uncle to his city of Antioch and his nephew to Edessa where he became, through force of circumstances, the regent. Edessa, the first to be attacked, underwent a severe siege, and it was here that the Franks were able to appreciate the usefulness of their alliance with the Armenians. For lack of Frankish knights, it was the Armenians who defended Edessa so energetically that, in a sortie led by Tancred, the defenders succeeded in putting the army of Jekermish to flight.

The Frankish drive toward Baghdad and Mosul was well and truly finished and only avoided becoming a complete catastrophe as a result of the incurable misunderstandings reigning between the Turkish leaders. But even so, after the defeat at Harran, not only did the Turks renew their pressure on the province of Antioch but the native Christians, weary of Frankish arrogance, also began to wonder seriously whether Turkish rule was not preferable. First Artah and then Albistan were surrendered to the Turks by the Armenians, "in loathing," says Michael the Syrian, "of the tyranny of the Franks." The Armenian Matthew of Edessa congratulates the inhabitants of Albistan on their revolt against the Frankish garrison: " 'Go back to your own country,' they told the Frankish leader. At these words the Franks hurled themselves on the inhabitants, but these were victorious and slew them all so that not a single one escaped. . . . The Lord recorded what the people of Albistan had done as an act of justice."[1]

Although the Turks were clearly too busy with their own quarrels to take advantage of the decline of the Frankish power in Syria,

Alexius Comnenus was careful not to let slip this opportunity of regaining the initiative. With the help of the Greek populations of the cities of Cilicia, he reconquered the cities of Tarsus, Adana, and Mamistra and then, with the help of his fleet, recaptured Lattakieh, which had been conquered by Tancred two years earlier.

Clearly the position of the two Frankish principalities of northern Syria was not at that time particularly healthy. Their already skeleton armies had lost a good quarter of their knighthood, and what was worse, their two most able leaders, Baldwin of Le Bourg and Joscelin of Courtenay. Nevertheless Bohemond's and Tancred's feudal egoism was still stronger than any sense of Christian or Frankish solidarity. They actually had one splendid opportunity to liberate Baldwin of Le Bourg when Tancred, in his sortie against Jekermish's army during the siege of Edessa, captured a great Turkish lady, a lady of such high nobility that Jekermish had offered either to release Baldwin or to pay fifteen thousand bezants in return for her release. When Baldwin, King of Jerusalem, heard of the negotiations, he begged the two Normans to accept the offer (not, of course, that of the fifteen thousand bezants, but of his cousin's release). But neither the Turkish lady nor Baldwin was set free: Tancred preferred to leave the Count of Edessa in prison and keep the province and its revenues for himself. Edessa was a great and busy commercial center. Baldwin of Le Bourg, one of the greatest captains in Frankish Syria, was to remain a prisoner for over four years. When he did regain his freedom it was in spite of Tancred's wishes—and his first act, once freed, was to make war on Tancred.

BOHEMOND

Bohemond was not the man to bear adversity with patience. Finding his province of Antioch reduced to half its size, invaded by the Turks in the east and Byzantium in the west, sick of a war which for him—no more than for Tancred or many others—had never been particularly "holy," Bohemond finally decided that this life of constant skirmishing with the Turkish princes (a life to which the Franks in the East seemed fated forever) was either unworthy of him or simply too monotonous, and made up his mind to leave the East and find a wider sphere for his activities. He installed as regent of the province of Antioch the very Tancred whom, two years previously, he had deprived of the title, and said he was going to seek help in the West.

He made a solemn speech in the basilica of Saint Peter in Antioch: "The storm raised against us is such that, without the help of Providence, our work is finished unless we do something. . . . We are a mere handful of men [*pauci*], ever decreasing in numbers. We need reinforcements."² In actual fact, this was a polite way of giving up. Bohemond had other dreams beyond the precarious and constantly threatened title of Prince of Antioch. To begin with, when he hoped to become the leader of a vast Crusading army, he may have anticipated the conquest of fabulous Eastern kingdoms, gaining possession of Baghdad or at least of Damascus, but he now realized that the Crusade, whether it was a holy war or not, was a very small-scale undertaking. Of the tens of thousands of Crusaders (maybe hundreds of thousands, counting all those who had taken the cross since 1096), only a few thousand were still left in the East. Even a general of genius—which Bohemond believed himself to be and may perhaps have been—could not attempt vast conquests with so few troops, and there was little hope of attracting strong armies of volunteers again to lands which already had all too wretched a reputation.

It is possible that Bohemond genuinely hoped to do this, but his actions show that he soon gave up any idea of preaching a third Crusade for the defense of the Holy Sepulcher. In any case, the Holy Sepulcher itself still seemed to be quite adequately defended by Baldwin, whose splendid title of King of Jerusalem no one thought of contesting. It was really no concern of Bohemond's to work for Baldwin of Boulogne.

Defeated, harried on two fronts after suffering three years of harsh captivity, and the semilawful possessor of a city conquered by the efforts of the great army of 1097, Bohemond had nothing in particular to be proud of. His achievements were not brilliant, even if his personal courage was not to blame for this. Nevertheless he arrived back in Europe in triumph, and went the rounds of the courts of Italy and France. (Anna Comnena's story that Bohemond, fearing the anger of the *basileus,* pretended to be dead and made the journey in a coffin, must be rejected as having no historical foundation.) The fact remains that by the luxury with which he surrounded himself and the glow of fierce energy emanating from his person, as well as by clever speeches, he was able to give an impression in Europe that he really was the first champion of the holy war, the principal author of its greatest victories, and the man who had struggled and fought and suffered more than any other for the cause of Jesus Christ.

Even so he was compelled to present himself as a hero in misfortune. It was well known that he had suffered defeats, but there was no reason to accuse him of lacking courage. Nor indeed could this accusation be leveled at any of the other Crusaders, or at the

Pope and the princes of the West who had done their best to send help to the Holy Land. Bohemond came from the East to tell the Latin peoples his own version of the truth: that the real responsibility for all the failures and all the sufferings of the Crusaders lay with Byzantium. He finally came out into the open and allowed his hatred of Byzantium free rein. It was a hatred inherited from his father, the old hatred of the Normans for the Greeks, made up of fierce envy and scorn for a "decadent" civilization. His ambition now (or rather his dream, for though a man of action he was first and foremost a great dreamer) was to place the imperial crown on his own head.

Bohemond received a warm welcome from the King of France, Philip I. He was an Italian Norman, but he spoke French and was popular in France, where the Crusade was already regarded as a national undertaking. He was feted appropriately and obtained from the King, for Tancred and himself, the hands of two daughters of France (one of them a natural daughter, it is true). Bohemond married the Princess Constance at Chartres, while the younger, Cecilia, child of Philip's adulterous marriage with Bertrada of Montfort, was sent to Antioch. The King gave his two daughters to the Normans richly dowered, but he did not give them any soldiers: after the defeats of 1101, even the French preferred to admire the Crusaders from a distance.

The unfortunate hero of the holy war found himself forced to be content with diplomatic victories while he waited for better things. He stayed for some time at Rome with Pope Paschal II, and gained the pontiff's complete confidence. Urban II, as a Frenchman, had enjoyed a large following in France. Paschal was an Italian, and Bohemond was basing his hopes on papal propaganda in Italy. But, satisfying his personal grievances and showing a great instinct for demagogy, Bohemond directed his propaganda campaigns not against Ghazi, Kilij Arslan, Ridwan, al-Afdal, and the other powerful Turkish or Arab figures whose names were little known in the West. As we have seen, in his eyes the major responsibility for the failure of the Crusaders lay with Byzantium; the Turks had been merely the instrument of the Greeks, and the real enemy of Christendom—of Latin Christendom, that is—was none other than Alexius Comnenus. Revelations of this kind were bound to appeal immensely to the maritime republics of Italy, since Byzantium was their chief rival.

By means of crude or subtle defamation and statements which were often not easy to verify (or for which no one was particularly interested in checking his authority), Bohemond succeeded in drawing so black a picture of the behavior of the *basileus* and the Greeks in general that the horrified Pope was actually considering preaching a Crusade against Byzantium. There is reason to believe that the attitude of the Latin chroniclers of the Crusade (all of whose works date from later than 1105) was largely influenced by Bohemond's stories. He was looked on as a hero and what he said was naturally believed. With the almost fanatical obstinacy of men capable of deep hatred, he used every means in his power to spread the calumnies which he may have genuinely believed were true.

Not all the Norman's grievances against Byzantium were unfounded. Alexius Comnenus's policies were "devious and changeable," anything but altruistic, and aimed first and foremost at safeguarding the interests of the *Roman* Empire. He tended to regard other Christian peoples—at best—merely as auxiliaries, allies of an irreparably inferior kind, and deserving of sympathy only insofar as they served the Empire faithfully and acknowledged its superiority. Alexius' indignation at the insolence, egotism, and greed of the Franks was not always justified: his attitude toward his allies was not always perfect, even at times when he had almost nothing to reproach them with. When he realized that Bohemond was really trying to keep Antioch for himself, he treated the Christian barbarian exactly as if he had been a pagan, and did not hesitate to conclude alliances with the Turks of Egypt against the Normans. Bohemond, on his side, would have had no hesitation in summoning the Turks to his assistance against Byzantium if the Turks would have had him as an ally. As the declared enemy of the Greeks he would have had his work cut out to denounce the Greeks for perfidy to him: before the Crusade such "perfidy" would have astonished or offended no one. What did matter was that, strong in his title as a Crusader, he was succeeding in making his own enemies the enemies of Christendom.

It is a fact that Bohemond's holy war, or rather his revenge on Byzantium, ended in lamentable failure. Despite all his efforts, he did not succeed in creating a sufficiently powerful current of opinion in the West to justify a Crusade. Constantinople was not the Holy Sepulcher, and in the last resort hatred is a weaker stimulant than love. In this case not even genuine hatred was involved as yet, and besides, the Crusading fervor had been extinguished in the West for a long time to come.

With his Normans and his Lombards, Bohemond embarked on the siege of the Albanian city of Durazzo, intending to attack Byzantium from the west. But he was not of sufficient stature to fight against the imperial armies alone, and he suffered the most humiliating defeat. He was forced to pledge himself to serve the *basileus* faithfully, to restore Antioch to its Greek overlords, to return to the Empire all the other places he had conquered, and finally, after making an entire and complete submission to the wishes of Alexius Comnenus, there was nothing left for him but to return to Italy. There, a broken man, his reputation gone, already mortally wounded by his defeat, he dragged out a now useless life for a further three years (one year according to Anna Comnena, four according to William of Tyre). The very uncertainty of chroniclers as to the date of his death shows that it passed, at the time, almost unnoticed. He left an infant son by his marriage to Constance of France named, after himself, Bohemond.

Such was the end of the man who had made Byzantium and the Turks tremble, a man whose natural gifts seemed to promise him a great destiny and who was, in reality, great. He was like a giant; everything in him, qualities and failings alike, seemed larger than life. The admiration of his enemies is probably the best proof of his valor. His popularity with the Crusading armies is another. And yet historians record few acts of goodness, piety, and loyalty performed by this fearsome man, and none of the characteristics by which greatness of spirit is usually judged. Single-minded, obstinate, indifferent to anything that could not serve his personal ambition, devoted to the cult of his own greatness, he possessed the blatant cunning of simple folk who cannot see the difference between intelligence and cheating. He was cruel, as an animal is cruel, out of indifference to the sufferings of others; his bravery and capacity for endurance were exceptional, but were the result of excessive passion rather than stoicism. He was a great man, drunk with the thirst for action, who never found a task worthy of his stature, but he may have had in him the stuff of which empire builders are made.

Perhaps he lacked the minimum of disinterestedness and cold reason needed to accomplish great designs and was, ultimately, nothing more than an adventurer on a vast scale. His dream of the destruction of Byzantium was fantastic not only because the Greek Empire was still, at that time, a great power, but because the dream itself was without substance, was no more than the fancy of a barbarian. A hundred years later the Venetian Enrico Dandolo conceived the same dream, but more forcefully, and events having had time to ripen, he made it a reality.

Meanwhile, Bohemond's work was not destroyed by his surrender at Durazzo. In spite of all the promises made by Bohemond, the principality of Antioch, which he had founded in the teeth of Byzantium, remained a Frankish possession. Tancred had made no promises and had no intention of implementing anyone else's. In this way a source of constant friction between Greeks and Latins was created, and with time these conflicts grew bitterer still. At the time of Bohemond's defeat, Antioch had been in Norman hands for ten years. Twenty-two years before that it had still been a city belonging to the Greek Empire. But if Alexius Comnenus believed that the Frankish occupation was merely an unfortunate episode and a step toward the reconquest of the city by the Greeks, he was mistaken. Annoyed by Tancred's haughty refusal, he conceived a violent hatred of the "barbarian" and all his allies, the effects of which were to be felt in the Byzantine attitude toward the Frankish states for many years to come.

Tancred, who was a good deal younger than his uncle and a less impressive figure altogether, was in fact the principal beneficiary of Bohemond's work. He was a good knight, capable and decisive, and perfectly fitted for his job. As regent and later after Bohemond's death as Prince of Antioch, he recaptured Artah from the Turks and Lattakieh from the Byzantines, conquered Apamea, and forced the King of Aleppo and the neighboring emirs of Shaizar to accept an alliance which almost amounted to a protectorate. Gradually, from one battle to the next, from defeat to victory, he consolidated his principality so effectively that within a few years the province of Antioch was incontestably a Frankish state and recognized as such, a feudal state like the other neighboring states but governed by a Christian emir. (It was not for nothing that Tancred, with the remarkable adaptability of the Normans, wore a turban and Oriental costume on solemn occasions, and styled himself, on the coins stamped with his image, the "great Emir Tankridos.")

Antioch became a Frankish province. Its nearness to the province of Edessa, which also belonged to the Franks and which leaned in turn on the Armenian principalities to the northwest, placed the Christian states founded on Eastern frontiers which had formerly belonged to Islam in a perilous but still fairly hopeful situation. Even so, it is obvious that if Bohemond, instead of taking the province for himself, had restored it to Alexius Comnenus, retained the Greek Patriarch, and been himself content to remain under the title of Curopalates, the situation of Christian Syria, Frankish or otherwise, would have been infinitely better. Antioch would have found in the Emperor a natural and loyal protector, instead of which she numbered him as one more and not the least of her enemies.

The conclusion is that Bohemond, far from serving the Crusade, at least in the sense meant by Urban II of the reconquest of the Holy Land for the benefit of Christianity, had done it dangerous harm by irreparably alienating the help of Byzantium, and whatever may be said, this help could only have been in the interests of Christendom. Whatever the faults of the Greeks, it is certain that throughout the twelfth century their attitude toward the Latins of the East was determined by the question of Antioch, and in this question right was on their side.

The other aspect of Bohemond's work, his efforts to poison relations between Latin Christendom and Byzantium, is less spectacular, since it is difficult to estimate how far Bohemond's attitude corresponded to a state of mind already fairly widespread in the West. The Norman's influence, however, appears to have been in proportion to his energy and still more to his hatred. He had given a name and a moral justification to feelings which may have been latent and unexpressed, and he had succeeded, if not in creating, at least in organizing and nourishing a real current of opinion. Once admitted, the idea of "Greek perfidy" was like a slick of oil, growing steadily until it became a basic assumption, generally acknowledged, which it occurred to no one to doubt.

In 1105, the Pope was seriously able to consider a Crusade—a holy war—against Christians, and the very Christians whom Urban II had presented in the past as the bulwark of Christianity against Islam. For such a thing to be possible, and this thanks to Bohemond's tales, it is clear that the gulf between the two Churches (which half a century earlier had been theoretically still one) could not have become much broader. After such a precedent it does not seem easy to accuse Alexius Comnenus and his successors of "treachery" to Christendom when they showed hostility to the Franks of Syria. They at least had never contemplated a holy war against Rome. As Christians—and Christians directly threatened by Islam—it was they who might legitimately accuse their Latin brothers of stabbing them in the back.

It is only fair to remember that when Paschal II was better informed, he partly retracted his charges against the Greeks and the scandal of a fratricidal Crusade was avoided. Bohemond was not strong enough to impose his own opinions on the West in their entirety, but a shadow of his own grandeur imparted itself to what he said even when it was a complete fabrication. The trial of strength between him and Alexius Comnenus was not over. The *basileus* thought he had won when he crushed and humiliated his enemy, but the Norman's real power was not in his armies, nor in his military genius.

Frankish Syria

We have mingled our blood with tears plenteously so that there is no longer room for those who would rival us [in lamentation].

Flowing tears are melancholy weapons for a man when sharp swords have kindled the fire of war!

What eye can close its lids in sleep, indifferent to events which would wake all sleepers?

Your brothers in Syria have nowhere to rest save their horses' backs or the bellies of the vultures.

The Roumis cover them with ignominy, and you, you let your gown trail softly, like someone who has nothing to fear.

How much blood has been shed! How many beauteous maidens have nothing but their hands with which to hide their charms.

Will the chieftains of Arabia sit down under such an insult? Will the warriors of Persia submit to such debasement?

Would to God that if they will not fight for zeal of religion, they would show themselves jealous of the honor of their women![3]

These verses come from a poem recited by the poet al-Modhafer at the court of Baghdad after the sack of Jerusalem. When they learned of the sufferings of Jerusalem the Holy, the people of Baghdad wept (according to Abu'l Feda) "until they broke the fast" (of Ramadan) by swallowing their own tears. But as we have seen, in spite of this explosion of grief which broke out in all the capitals of Islam, neither Arabs, Persians, nor Turks launched a holy war. Public opinion responded to the tragic accents of al-Modhafer's poem only with tears; and Oriental poets were equally in the habit of dedicating songs made up of imprecations and calls to battle to political and religious struggles among Moslems.

"Roumis" from strange, distant lands had come to spread terror in Syria. These Roumis were intrepid warriors, terrible ironclad men, mounted on ironclad horses, armed with lances of monstrous size. They were monstrous themselves, and infinitely more barbarous than the Greek Christians, who were already loathsome enough. They were primitive idolaters, inflamed with an incomprehensible zeal for the cross and for holy images. The Moslems of Syria had long been accustomed to the Christian enthusiasm for the Holy Places and relics, but they had never seen them display such a fervor of adoration; nor were they accustomed to seeing Christians so lightheartedly sacking mosques. The Greeks, more cautious even in their wars with the Moslems, showed a certain respect for their religion out of consideration for the Orthodox Christians living under the rule of Islam.

Five years after the fall of Nicaea, the Crusaders' first victory, these Roumis, who were henceforth known as Franks, were so firmly settled in Jerusalem and on the coast that three successive armies sent by the Vizier of Egypt could not dislodge them. This was an excellent excuse for the Sunnites to accuse the Fatimid court of inefficiency and lukewarmness. But al-Afdal had at least brought three armies, while the Crusaders' immediate neighbors had not stirred. The crushing defeat of the second Crusade in Anatolia had been the work of the Turks of Asia Minor. In northern Syria, the Franks ruled over populations the majority of whom were Christians, and could not hope to push their conquests much further for lack of troops. On the coast of Palestine they were becoming a real threat, thanks to their sea power and the fleets sent them several times a year by their brothers in the West. This was a matter of particular concern to Egypt, the only great maritime power of Eastern Islam.

The Moslem villages of Judaea and Galilee were deserted through no wish of the Franks, who found it very tiresome having no one to cultivate their lands. Some of the Moslem peasants had left the country in terror with their flocks and movables after the capture of Jerusalem. Those who remained continued to till their fields and gather their harvests as before, paying their tribute in kind to the local *seigneur*. Nothing had changed except the fact that the *seigneur* no longer venerated the Prophet, and prayed in a Christian church instead of in a mosque.

There were no more Moslems in Jerusalem. Since they had formed the majority of the population, the Holy City was now dangerously underpopulated. There were not enough Frankish Christians, says William of Tyre, "to fill a street." Local Christians were more numerous, but they were mostly poor folk or clergy.

In the cities captured by the Crusaders during the years which followed, the Moslems were spared (except in Caesarea, where the civilian population was massacred), but the wealthy among them, at least, preferred to move. They were replaced by Italian colonists and local Christians, but everywhere part of the Moslem population remained, submitting with resignation to the infidel yoke.

Insensibly—despite a constant state of war to which the country was by now only too well accustomed—the Frankish invaders were accepted by the conquered lands as an inevitable, probably temporary, evil, and certainly less terrible than had at first been believed.

Before 1101, the Crusaders who had settled in the Levant had been able to hope that a considerable number of Western Christians, encouraged by the news of the capture of Jerusalem, would come to the Holy Land and stay there to found a real Latin kingdom to be the guardian of the Holy Sepulcher. This hope had now been abandoned. No more crowds of pilgrims dared risk the overland journey to the Holy Land, and this pilgrim route, already dangerous before the Crusades, had now become quite impossible. Pilgrimage by sea was expensive and equally dangerous: the Mediterranean was infested by pirates of all nationalities, and Arab and Egyptian pirates in particular made a point of pursuing Christian ships. Pilgrims coming to Jerusalem by sea were now more numerous than before the Crusades, and in these years the majority of them were soldiers, Crusaders, either Italian or Scandinavian, but few of them showed any desire to exchange their native lands for another.

Frankish colonization—if it can be described as colonization—developed in the cities by means of trade and craftsmanship. Later on a Frankish peasantry also grew up, in the territory of the kingdom of Jerusalem properly speaking, and these colonists were mostly French. In the cities, the first "bourgeois" of Latin origin were Italian merchants, because the republics were establishing markets in the majority of conquered cities. The Pisans and the Genoese had their own streets in all trading cities, but there were never very many of them and they led their own characteristically Italian lives, keeping to their respective quarters and mingling with few of the other communities, Latin or native.

It was the same with the Moslems, Jews, and Christians—Jacobite, Greek, or Armenian—who made up distinct and quite separate communities in each city, living on good or bad terms with their neighbors as the case might be, but strangers to one another, divided by religious barriers more surely than by the most rigorous legal control, and submitting passively to the military dictatorship of the Franks.

In the Latin kingdom of the East, including the three Latin states of the north, Edessa, Antioch, and Tripoli, the Franks as such were really no more than a handful of soldiers with the job of governing and defending the country.

The historian Fulcher of Chartres, who was an eyewitness of the First Crusade, wrote this famous passage in about 1125, which has been widely quoted by all historians of the Crusades:

Westerners, we have become Orientals. The Italian and the Frenchman of yesterday have been transplanted and become men of Galilee or Palestine. Men from Reims or Chartres are transformed into Tyrians or citizens of Antioch. We have already forgotten the land of our birth; who now remembers it? Men no longer speak of it. Here one now has his house and servants with as much assurance as though it were by immemorial right of inheritance in the land. Another has already taken to wife, not a countrywoman of his own, but a Syrian or Armenian woman, sometimes even a baptized Saracen, and then lives with a whole new family. We use the various languages of the country turn and turn about; the native as well as the colonist has become polyglot, and trust brings the most widely separated races together. The Word of the Scriptures has come true, "and the lion shall eat straw like the bullock" (Isaiah 65: 25). The colonist has now become almost a native, and the immigrant is one with the inhabitants. Every day relatives and friends from the West come to join us. They do not hesitate to leave everything they have behind them. Indeed, by the grace of God, he who was poor attains riches here. He who had no more than a few deniers finds himself here in possession of a fortune. He who owned not so much as one village finds himself, by God's grace, the lord of a city. Why should we go back to the West, when the East is so kindly to us?[4]

The truth of Fulcher of Chartres's assertions has often been questioned, and this passage does actually seem to have been written for purposes of propaganda and the respectable cleric chiefly motivated by the desire to attract new colonists to the East. In spite of his claim that "relatives and friends" were constantly arriving from Europe to join the Franks in Palestine, even twenty years after the capture of Jerusalem the population of Latin origin was still a deplorable minority. It has been demonstrated that the Frankish princes were always short of soldiers, and even now those most ready to emigrate were still volunteers for the holy war. Whatever Fulcher of Chartres may say, Italian colonists did not fit easily into their new country, nor were they really accepted by Frankish society, which was military, aristocratic, and French.

Apart from the knights—the majority of whom were of French, Provençal, or Norman origin—the Frankish colony naturally included that class of soldier, noble or commoner, who formed to some extent an integral part of the military unit represented by the knight: squires, pages, sergeants, servants, and all the personnel who tended the machines, maintained equipment, and were concerned with organizing camp life, in addition to the infantry itself. But the casualty rate was much higher among foot soldiers and auxiliaries than among the knights, and their numbers dropped in the course of the war more quickly than they could grow through the arrival of pilgrims from the West.

Although this is not easy to establish, since no historian of the period took any interest in the matter, it is more than probable that a fairly large number of the poor people from the First Crusade, and even a few survivors from the Crusade of 1101, having nowhere else to go, did settle permanently in the Holy Land. These adventurous pilgrims must have very quickly become assimilated into the local population and lost their "Frankish" characteristics and often their mother tongue, practicing the humble trades within their reach or ending their days as beggars at the gates of the Holy Sepulcher. The bulk of the Frankish colony was made up of soldiers, active or retired, members of their families who had come East at their request, their civilian servants, and craftsmen attached to the army or to the noble families. We must also, of course, include the clergy: chaplains, scribes, secretaries, and so forth, and the numerous personnel, half clergy, half servants, attached to the service of the barons and to the numerous more or less unreal bishoprics created by the Crusaders.

The evidence of Fulcher of Chartres is eloquent enough in itself: "He who was poor, attains riches. . . . He who owned not so much as one village finds himself . . . the lord of a city." There were not so many cities available in Palestine and in Syria, especially in 1125, that their number could satisfy the greed of all the needy knights in Europe. But the great barons needed to conquer more and more castles, partly to defend their own territory and partly to guarantee the service of their men. A knight who received a small castle captured from the Moslems in fief from the King of Jerusalem would stay there, in command of what was generally a small garrison, levying revenues on the surrounding lands, holding his domain as best he could, and constantly exposed to the risk of seeing his handful of soldiers massacred either by the Turks or by the local inhabitants. However precarious his situation, he did find himself promoted from a state of poverty and dependence to the rank of castellan. Among the greatest, Baldwin of Boulogne, and after him Baldwin of Le Bourg and Joscelin of Courtenay—to take examples from the counts of Edessa alone—rose to fortunes which were indeed something to make the small feudal lords of their homeland dream. Because nepotism was the keystone of feudal society, the first to obtain fiefs were naturally the relatives, cousins or nephews, of the great barons, and after them their oldest and most faithful friends. Little by little, an aristocratic Walloon and Flemish society grew up in Judaea and Galilee and in Edessa, a Norman aristocracy in the region of Antioch, and a Provençal aristocracy in Tripoli. These were small, homogeneous feudal societies, completely devoted to their respective lords, numerically weak but strong in the prestige of their Frankish valor, and strong too in their pride as "soldiers of God."

"He who had no more than a few deniers finds himself here in possession of a fortune" (*possident bizantios numeros*). The way those who had only a few deniers could suddenly become so rich was first by plunder. The capture of cities such as Caesarea, Tripoli, Arsuf, Jabala, and the rest, to say nothing of those occupied earlier, like Edessa, Antioch, and Jerusalem, where vast amounts of property were left ownerless, enriched those soldiers who managed to find themselves in the right place at the right time, in the space of a few hours. It did not occur to anyone to regard this wealth as stolen. The rules of war in every country allowed the rights of plunder. According to contemporary witnesses, the wealth of the camps abandoned by the enemy in flight was fabulous. The lucky soldier or pilgrim might even acquire a house, and be able to choose, in the markets of the great cities, where despite the war commerce remained active (Jerusalem alone being the exception in this), objects which in Europe only princes could afford to buy.

Was Fulcher of Chartres merely thinking of the wealth to be gained by plunder? His text appears to suggest that the Westerner in the East had a relatively peaceful life among a friendly population, and he is clearly thinking of the other method of getting rich easily: marrying a wealthy local girl. By force of arms the Franks had won themselves a natural right to a choice of the finest dowries, and frequently the Syrian or Armenian was only too glad to ensure the protection of a Frankish son-in-law by giving away his daughter. The difference of language and customs made it all the easier for even the most hardened old soldier to pass himself off as a respectable nobleman.

Thus, by the spoils of war, by marriage, or simply by speculating on the fears they inspired, a good many poor Franks were able to provide themselves with "house and servants with as much assurance as though it were by immemorial right of inheritance." (Baldwin's companions in Edessa are known to have behaved like robbers, confiscating the houses of their Armenian allies without scruple.) They maintained their assurance by force of arms. What the local inhabitants thought of this is clear from Syrian and Armenian historians, and even from Albert of Aix, though Fulcher of Chartres passes over it in silence, merely stating that perfect understanding reigned between the Franks and the natives, and that the Franks became polyglot and were happy to live in the midst of an Oriental family.

What seems certain is that the average Frank, the man with slender means, and the poor Frenchman in particular, adapted very easily to

his new life and generally showed greater flexibility and curiosity
about Oriental ways and the Oriental mentality than the Orientals did
about the Franks. The Franks cannot be accused of keeping themselves to themselves out of pride as conquerors, nor of having striven
to impose their own customs on the native populations. It is true that
they had small means of doing so, but neither had they any wish to,
and this was equally true of the leaders and of the lower orders. Only
the clergy, in their zeal for the Roman faith, adopted a relatively oppressive attitude toward Christian heretics. The ordinary soldiers were
content to use their weapons to keep the people down, and not to
interfere with the local way of life.

This does not mean that the Crusaders admitted equality of rights
between themselves and the Syrians from the outset. The Syrians
always remained a conquered race. The Franks were so convinced
of their own superiority that it never occurs to any of the Latin
historians of the period to cast doubts on it.

William of Tyre records a well-known story concerning Baldwin
of Le Bourg, the cousin of Baldwin of Boulogne. When he became
Count of Edessa he asked for and obtained the hand of Morphia,
the daughter of the Armenian prince Gabriel, who was governor of
Melitene. This was a marriage of convenience, the only kind indulged in by the feudal barons, but it was also a happy marriage and
Baldwin is known to have been a model husband. Morphia brought
him a handsome dowry and her father was reputed to be immensely
rich. Shortly after his marriage the new Count of Edessa, pressed for
money as always, thought up a plan to extract money from his
father-in-law. He went to visit him with his knights, whom he had
first informed of what he planned. The knights burst into the room
where the father and his son-in-law were conversing amiably (in
pidgin Armenian, we may wonder?), loudly demanding their un-
paid wages. Baldwin, like a man at his wits' end, feigned embarrassment and terror. He said that he had no money, and that he had
promised his men that if their wages were not paid up by this day
he would sacrifice, of all things, his beard—in other words, he would
have his chin shaved.

Gabriel was horrified because, as William of Tyre complacently
explains, Orientals regarded their beards as an essential part of their
dignity. Westerners were also proud of their beards, but less fanatically so. Gabriel, says our chronicler, "began crossing himself, a
hundred times over, and then asked how he [his son-in-law] could
have agreed to such a thing and risked losing his honor as a man in
this way: for if he lost his beard, he might just as well permit him-

self to be castrated."[5] Finally, rather than submit to the humiliation of having a clean-shaven son-in-law, the Armenian offered to pay the large sum Baldwin needed. William of Tyre quite clearly finds this story amusing, and sees nothing unpleasant in an abuse of confidence based on the assumption that Gabriel must be unfamiliar with Frankish customs.

The man who played the part of Gerontius to the Crusader leader and his knights in this episode was not in any way a figure of fun. He was a formidable leader, a gallant fighter, and an Armenian patriot who had long defended his province against the Turks. He was a man of such fiery temper that he had in the past killed the Syriac Bishop Jacob with his own hands because the old man had dared to utter defeatist sentiments during the siege of Melitene. The story is told by Michael the Syrian: "He was on horseback, surrounded by his foot soldiers. Then the venerable old man began to entreat him [on behalf of some Syrians condemned to death]: 'Have mercy, O Prince, there is killing outside [the city], let there not be killing within!' Gabriel, who had already pondered killing the Bishop, answered, 'And you, would you then deliver the city up to the Turks?' Angrily he ordered one of his lancers, saying, 'Strike!' When the man dared not strike, he himself seized the sword and struck the saint on the head and killed him."[6] Between this cruel scene and that described by William of Tyre there is a great gulf: the gulf of scornful incomprehension which prevented the Franks from ever seriously considering the interests, passions, and troubles of these native Christians, although as Christ's soldiers they made use of them with a clear conscience.

It goes without saying that for their part, these Eastern Christians judged the Franks in very much the same way, sympathizing with them just so far as the new masters of the country served their interests. If Armenian or Syrian chroniclers appear to pay more attention to the Franks than the Franks accorded to their Christian subjects, this is because the Franks at that time were the masters. Even Michael the Syrian and Matthew of Edessa dwell only on the personalities of the leaders and their relations with the Christian communities.

We know that Baldwin I, the former Count of Edessa, had been execrated by Syrians and Armenians alike. To them he was nothing more than a brutal and greedy tyrant. Baldwin of Le Bourg did manage to attract a certain amount of genuine sympathy, since his marriage to Gabriel's daughter and the situation in Edessa compelled him to collaborate with the Armenian element (although he appears to have done so reluctantly and not altogether honestly). The great Armenian historian, Matthew of Edessa, praises him: "He was one of the most illustrious Franks, a noble and valiant warrior, the purity of his life was exemplary, he was the enemy of sin, full of gentleness and modesty . . . he was besides very orthodox, and very firm in conduct and character." But even in the midst of this panegyric, Matthew does not omit to mention the prince's extreme cupidity: "These qualities were tarnished by an ingenious lust to possess himself of the property of others, by an insatiable love of money and a want of generosity."7 The allusion to the ingenuity of his greed suggests that Gabriel may not have been taken in by his son-in-law's schemes for very long and that Baldwin had played the same kind of trick on other Armenians.

The thirst for money is the sin which foreign historians are most unanimous in attributing to the Franks: the coffers of the princes and castellans of Frankish Syria were like bottomless wells. They robbed or exploited on a grand scale those natives who possessed some fortune, amassed enormous spoils of war, plundered caravans, levied tributes, sold concessions to the mercantile republics, and still found themselves constantly in the most frightful financial difficulties. It is true that the best part of their income was swallowed up by wars, but it is also true that a glimpse of a life in the Orient that was the height of comfort and opulence compared to life in the West had done a great deal to increase the natural greed of barons who came as conquerors and were the more tempted to seize everything they could lay their hands on because they had arrived with nothing.

It is only fair to say that in their position the Turks would have behaved in exactly the same way, and that the local Christians generally—though not invariably—preferred to be ruled by Christians. As we shall see, the result of Latin influence in Cilicia was that the Armenian Church ultimately drew so close to the Catholic as to officially recognize the authority of the Pope (1198). In spite of, or perhaps because of, differences in language and ritual, the Latin barons were naturally tolerant toward other Christian communities. Fortunately, the leaders of the Crusade were soldiers first and foremost, indifferent to questions of dogma because they were ignorant of the subject. They did a good deal to make possible a *modus vivendi* between Orthodox Greeks, Armenians (Gregorians), and Syrians (Jacobites) that was precarious but real. They made real efforts to live at peace with one another, acting on common sense and practical considerations and not on religious prejudice. This alone was enough to make their government more bearable than that of the Byzantines. We find Jacobite Syrians appealing to the justice of Frankish princes to settle their differences. Baldwin of Le Bourg in particular tried, as a good suzerain, to reconcile the Jacobite bishop of his city of Edessa with his patriarch who had excommunicated him, and when the Prince of Antioch acted as arbiter between Syrian and Latin clergy he did on occasion decide in favor of the former. Obviously all the services and favors done by Latin princes to the representatives of the various sects were not done for nothing, but it occurred to no one to complain of this: it was simply the custom. But no Syrian would have been able to purchase the help of a prelate or official of Byzantium in this way.

We shall have more to say of the character of Frankish administration in the East. It was predominantly empirical and for this very reason it was the best possible system in the circumstances. The Franks had not colonized the land they held under their military guardianship. What they had done was to take over—and even this not completely—the place of those they had killed or driven out, and between campaigns they were beginning to adapt themselves to their new life.

The Orient which Fulcher of Chartres describes as such a pleasant place for Occidentals had very little in common with the picture of the "Promised Land" described in the Bible and was not exactly calculated to attract new settlers. At the beginning of the twelfth century, the coasts of Palestine, Syria, and the Lebanon were still partly in Moslem hands. It was this coastal strip with its mild climate and fertile soil which had excited the greed of the Crusaders from the outset, and they were trying, very methodically, to make themselves masters of it. At about the time when Fulcher of Chartres was penning his optimistic lines, the Moslems held Ascalon and Gaza on the coast, while going northward Jaffa, Arsuf, and Caesarea were in the hands of the Franks, as was Acre, conquered in 1104, and Sidon, captured in 1110; between these two cities, the great maritime center of Tyre was still Moslem. Beirut, Jebail, Tripoli (captured in 1109), and Lattakieh were under Latin dominion. With the fall of Tyre in 1124 and Ascalon in 1153, the Latins made themselves masters of the whole of the coastal region. On the other hand, the interior of the country was cut up to the end into Frankish and Moslem possessions, and this led to a perpetual state of war.

The kingdom of Jerusalem extended over Judaea, Samaria, and Galilee, countries much more remarkable for their historical and religious past than for any geographical advantages. Mostly poor, barren mountains, with a few fertile pockets such as the regions of Nablus and Tiberias, their yield was small and they had little to tempt peasants from Europe. In the principality of Antioch, the coast and environs of the city were fertile and amply provided with water, but the inland of the country was mountainous and fairly poor. Edessa, in the mountains, included the fertile regions near the plain of the Euphrates, but the immediate surroundings of the city were poor. Moreover, all these lands, whether rich or poor, were at the mercy of constant incursions by the Turks and the hazards of war in general.

Nevertheless there was some attempt at Frankish colonization during the twelfth century, and it is known that eighty years after the fall of Jerusalem the actual Frankish population had risen to twenty or thirty thousand people, not including several thousand half-caste Franks resulting from mixed marriages. However unreliable these figures, they make it quite clear that Frankish Syria was a Latin state existing in the East, with its own personality and history, and even at this stage its own traditions, and that the life of the state constituted an attempt, never since repeated, at collaboration and interpenetration between East and West. There will be time for a closer study of the life of this curious state, which nevertheless had a right to exist, in a later chapter. Now we must return to the history of the formation and political evolution of the Latin state.

The Kingdom of Jerusalem

That the consequence of the glorious dramatic adventure of the First Crusade was the establishment of a real Latin kingdom in the East was largely due to the man who was the first king of this kingdom, Baldwin of Boulogne, Count of Edessa, the somewhat impromptu sovereign who arrived in Jerusalem with a handful of knights to dispute his brother's succession with an ambitious patriarch and succeeded so well in putting forward his apparently slender claim that he gave the immediate impression of being a hereditary monarch and the descendant of twenty kings. The very name of his kingdom added a note of majesty to his position from the outset which made him, the younger son of a minor vassal of the King of France, the equal of the first kings in Christendom. Who among them could boast that the title he bore had once been borne by David and by Solomon?

As King of Jerusalem he became the very symbol of the triumph of Cross over Crescent. He was the Lord's anointed in the holiest place on earth. It mattered little that the holy oil had been poured on his head by the hand of a prelate who only the day before had been denouncing him as a usurper: a sacrament is a sacrament and a coronation a coronation. A patriarch of the Roman Church had placed the royal crown on the head of the Count of Edessa, and Baldwin was certainly not the last to believe in the mystical value of this act.

This "golden crown" worn "in the place where Jesus Christ had worn a crown of thorns" was more than simply a powerful weapon against the Patriarch Daimbert. It was also an asset of the highest order in Baldwin's relations with the other Crusaders and especially with his great vassals and the heads of the other Frankish principalities, and also to his position with the East and with the Pope himself. In its way, it too was a crown of thorns. As he fled alone in the night on the back of his horse Gazelle, after leading the best of his chivalry to their deaths at the defeat of Ramleh in 1102, Baldwin learned to his cost what it meant to be King of Jerusalem. No one blamed him for escaping rather than selling his life dearly like the rest. He could never have sold it dear enough, because already the very existence of the kingdom depended on it.

Later on, in his palace in Jerusalem (formerly the Mosque of al-Aqsa, the Temple of Solomon), he was seen receiving visitors in a burnous of cloth of gold, with his golden crown set above a turban also of cloth of gold, permitting his visitors and subjects (those who were not of noble blood) to prostrate themselves before him as people prostrated themselves before the emperors of Byzantium and the sultans. With his giant stature, long black beard, aquiline nose, and majestic, almost episcopal bearing, he must have been an extremely impressive monarch. Moslems who saw him no longer marveled as Godfrey's Arab visitors had done: the Frankish sultan was not so very different from the kings of Islam.

In his dealings with Daimbert, Baldwin succeeded in his own way in imposing the supremacy of the royal power over that of the Church. It was common knowledge that the Patriarch was his sworn enemy, but Daimbert was also rich. His greed and lack of scruple in money matters were proverbial. When Baldwin demanded money for his army, the Patriarch pretended that all he had was two hundred silver marks. One fine evening, the King burst into the patriarchal palace where Daimbert was giving a banquet for the papal legate Maurice of Porto, and delivered a tirade against the two prelates as eloquent as anything produced by the anticlerical writers of the period, accusing them of spending money intended for the service of Christendom on their own pleasures. To the Patriarch's angry retort that those who served the Church lived on the Church's funds and did not have to account to anyone, the King replied, "If that is the case, then my soldiers are the first who should live by the Church because it is they who serve her best defending her every day against the Saracen! And I do not simply desire alms from the clergy to pay my troops. I want the money from the shrines and all the gold of the Holy Sepulcher, and I shall take it to equip my army, for the Saracens are here!"[8] When Daimbert persisted in withholding the money, and what is more, later carried his avarice to the length of embezzling a sum of a thousand bezants sent by Prince Roger of Apulia to be used in the Holy Land, Baldwin had him stripped of his title and expelled from the kingdom and confiscated all his treasure for himself. What is significant in the King's attitude is the constant insistence that as the first defender of the Holy Places it is his right to be the first obeyed. The prerogatives he seems to wish to arrogate to himself are almost those of a priest-king, a king who is the head of the Church, as the Byzantine emperors were. If he was to impose his authority he could not afford to have lesser ambitions.

In fact the former Archbishop of Pisa was soon reinstated, thanks to the support of Tancred, whose hostility toward Baldwin made him only too happy to see an enemy of the King installed in Jerusalem. After his defeat at Ramleh the King urgently needed the help of the knights of Antioch, and Tancred bargained for Daimbert's restoration. Baldwin agreed, and then summoned a synod at which the old Patriarch was accused of the worst misdeeds (most of the accusations were well founded), declared guilty, and officially deposed. After brief reigns by two venerable but not particularly forceful patriarchs (the first appointment was revoked by the Pope on Daimbert's complaint and the second incumbent died of old age), the original Latin patriarch of Jerusalem, the able if not unduly respectable Arnulf Malecorne, got back the position he had coveted for twelve years. This time he was finally given a regular and canonical election. For a long time he had been a useful counselor to the King, with his fertile brain and readiness to do anything. The patriarchate of Jerusalem was in good hands.

Toward the end of 1104, Bohemond set sail for the West, never to return to the Holy Land. He left the regency of Antioch to Tancred. Edessa had lost all her Walloon and Flemish chivalry at the defeat at Harran and her Count, Baldwin of Le Bourg, was a prisoner of the Turks. For lack of an alternative the county temporarily accepted Norman rule and Tancred installed his brother-in-law, the Norman Richard of Salerno, better known under the name of Richard of the Principate. Tancred, as we know, was in no hurry to procure Baldwin of Le Bourg's liberty or that of his cousin Joscelin of Courtenay. The two Normans controlled all the Frankish possessions in northern Syria, but their dual regency was no sinecure. In the space of four years Tancred recaptured Artah and Kafartab, Lattakieh and Mamistra, and conquered Apamea. This extended his dominion from the coast (at Lattakieh) all the way to the frontiers of the King of Aleppo and the emirs of Shaizar. By constant incursions into the territory of first one and then the other, he succeeded in protecting his own lands, but the struggle waged back and forth across the country was no longer a matter of a holy war but a vital and so to speak automatic necessity.

For the knights of Outremer there was no other conceivable life but this constant riding from end to end of the province, with skirmishes and raids, hastily laying siege to cities where at any moment the besieger might become the besieged. Tancred was not dreaming of vast empires, but he was in a position to make himself a great emir comparable to his Moslem neighbors. All the same, while the Normans were gaining a reputation in the eyes of the Moslems, they were making themselves hated by their own subjects. In Edessa, Richard of the Principate's extortionate demands were making the Armenians look back with regret to Baldwin of Le Bourg and his more moderate exactions.

The Count of Toulouse, Raymond of Saint-Gilles, died on February 28, 1105. The old paladin ended his days in the fortress of Qalat Sanjil (Mount Pilgrim) that he had had built facing the city of Tripoli, which he had dreamed for years of taking and making the capital of his Eastern states. The splendid city advanced like a great ship to meet the sea, with its dozens of domes and minarets, its miles of white walls, its luxuriant gardens and groves of olive and cypress. It was this city which Raymond had chosen in his dying days for his last dream in the East, and he could contemplate it as he lay dying, so near and yet still inaccessible. He left his rights to it as an inheritance to his descendants.

By his wife, Elvira of Castile, he had one son, a year-old baby born in that very Castle Pilgrim. This child, Alfonso-Jordan, inherited the county of Toulouse. A deputation of nobles from Provence came to seek the Countess and the little prince, asking for his return to be their suzerain. Raymond's place in the Lebanon was taken by his closest relative in those parts at that time, William-Jordan, son of the Count of Cerdagne, a grandson of one of Raymond's maternal aunts.

Thus, by the beginning of 1105, the two greatest leaders of the First Crusade—Bohemond and Raymond of Saint-Gilles—had vanished from the scene, a fact which did much to consolidate Baldwin I's authority with the Franks of Syria. Godfrey of Bouillon's younger brother was now something of a veteran and however insecure his throne, his title of King gave him a moral advantage over William-Jordan and even over Tancred which certainly neither Bohemond nor the Count of Toulouse could have reckoned on. There could no longer be any question of a community of interests among the Frankish states in the East. There were only occasional alliances, grudgingly accepted and broken as soon as they were no longer considered absolutely necessary.

The Provençaux continued to make progress in the Lebanon, strengthening the blockade of Tripoli and taking more fortresses in the vicinity. They had no intention of asking the King of Jerusalem for help which might ultimately give him some rights over their conquests. Tancred, William-Jordan, and Baldwin were all fighting on their own account, but in the eyes of the Moslems they were all incorporated under the name of Franks, and in the eyes of the Western world, under that of soldiers of Christ. Consequently it was from outside that, little by little, a certain sense of solidarity began to make itself felt among the brothers in race and religion.

Feudal Squabbles

William-Jordan proved an energetic leader. In three years, despite all the efforts of Ibn Ammar, Tripoli was almost reduced to starvation by the ever tightening blockade by land and at sea, where Pisan fleets gave chase to the Egyptian ships trying to revictual the city. The Provençaux now held nearly all the country. In April 1108, William-Jordan took by storm the castle of Arqa which the Turk Toghtekin, atabeg of Damascus, had seized from the vassals of the Banū Ammar, while Ibn Ammar himself found himself dispossessed of his city of Tripoli by an emissary from the Vizier of Cairo. Egypt was taking advantage of her unruly vassal's distress to annex the great city on the pretext of better defending it against the Christians.

In fact the Egyptians, although they possessed a formidable fleet, did not do a great deal to save Tripoli, and the fall of the city, where food supplies were running lower and lower, was no more than a matter of months or weeks. The siege had been going on for five years. "A pound of dates," says the book of *Kamil at-Tawarikh,* "was worth a gold piece. . . . The poor migrated, the rich were reduced to poverty." No expeditionary force was sent against the little Provençal army from the hinterland, where the rulers were the Seljuks of Damascus and Aleppo, much less from the atabegs of Mosul, the Caliph of Baghdad, or the Sultan of Persia, all of whom possessed excellent armies. The loveliest Moslem city of the coast, a great intellectual, artistic, and commercial center, for so long governed by a dynasty of peaceful and liberal cadis, was being slowly strangled by the indifference of the Moslem princes, none of whom felt any concern for the fate of a city which had made the mistake of clinging too closely to its independence.

William-Jordan was concentrating with splendid obstinacy on carrying out Raymond of Saint-Gilles's design when someone disembarked at Tortosa who had come East to claim from him the land he held by right of conquest. This was Bertrand of Toulouse, Raymond's eldest son by his first wife, who had been repudiated for reasons of consanguinity. Since Bertrand was consequently considered a bastard and had been excluded from the inheritance of Toulouse in favor of little Alfonso-Jordan, he had come to lay claim to his father's possessions in Syria. William-Jordan, however, not unreasonably considered his own rights superior to those of the newcomer.

Bertrand arrived in force with an army of four thousand men and a Genoese fleet. Before embarking for Syria, he had concluded a treaty with the Republic of Genoa, promising her large concessions in Tripoli. In Constantinople he had come to a further agreement with Alexius Comnenus, who in memory of Raymond of Saint-Gilles had welcomed him like a son and had promised him aid in return for an oath of fealty to Byzantium. Bertrand therefore had strong assets on his side. In other respects he was not a very attractive character. He was a man of middle age, the father of a grown-up son, compelled to live from hand to mouth and embittered by being undeservedly branded with illegitimacy, which had made him arrogant and difficult. He had already fallen out with Tancred by inviting him to give up to him the part of the city of Antioch which the

Count of Toulouse had occupied ten years before. When he failed to evict his cousin William-Jordan from a place which he had won by the sweat of his brow and the blood of his men, he addressed himself to the King of Jerusalem, Baldwin, meanwhile using his fleet to threaten the Provençal troops as well as the forces besieged in Tripoli.

For the first time, the King of Jerusalem was called upon to act as sovereign arbiter in a conflict between two Frankish princes. He seized the opportunity and arrived outside Tripoli with five hundred knights, feeling the more disposed to uphold Bertrand's rights because William-Jordan, on his side, had appealed to Tancred. Bertrand willingly accepted the King of Jerusalem's suzerainty and swore fealty to him for his lands already conquered and those he might acquire in the future. In return, Baldwin pledged himself to help him capture Tripoli. When William-Jordan heard of this, he was on the point of rushing to arms and asking his ally to do the same. In the end, Baldwin and Tancred succeeded in calming the two rivals, and it was decided at a public trial of the case that the cousins should divide the Provençal possessions in the Lebanon between them. Bertrand was to have Tripoli (still to be captured) with the title of Count, as well as Mount Pilgrim and Jebail, while William-Jordan was to keep Arqa and Tortosa. The first paid homage for his lands to the King, and the second to Tancred, Prince of Antioch.

Tripoli fell shortly after this agreement—the first official agreement passed between the Frankish fiefs in Syria. In early July 1109, the inhabitants of Tripoli negotiated a surrender, bargaining for respect of persons and property and permission for those who wished to emigrate into Moslem country. On July 12, the Franks entered Tripoli. It is known that the clauses of the surrender were not observed, but there are no grounds for blaming Baldwin and Bertrand, who did their best to keep order. The Genoese sailors, whose fleet had played a large part in the fall of the city, did not consider themselves bound by the promises of petty Frankish princes. They scaled the walls with ropes and ladders while the King's army was entering through the gates and set about sacking the town. In addition, the Republic of Genoa was well rewarded for its share in this episode in the holy war: Bertrand granted Genoa the entire city of Jebail, which was given as a hereditary fief to the admiral of the fleet, Hugh Embriaco.

William-Jordan died not long afterward, wounded in the heart by an arrow fired "accidentally" during a sergeants' brawl when he tried to separate the combatants. All the chroniclers are unanimous in finding something suspicious about his death, although they do not dare to accuse Bertrand openly. Tancred at all events had put his money on the wrong horse: William-Jordan had died without heirs and all Frankish possessions in the Lebanon went to Bertrand, Count of Tripoli. The county of Tripoli became the first great fief of the kingdom of Jerusalem, and in fact, Bertrand acted in concert with Baldwin and was present at his side during all his campaigns.

A year before the fall of Tripoli, the King of Jerusalem's position had also improved in a somewhat unexpected manner, thanks to the reappearance of someone who had not been heard of for four years. His cousin Baldwin of Le Bourg emerged from captivity, dressed in sumptuous clothes and riding on a horse belonging to the emir whose prisoner he had been. What had happened was that the atabeg of Mosul, Jekermish, who would never have done the Franks the service of liberating the Count of Edessa, was dead, and his successor, Jawali, had inherited the captive as his responsibility. Jawali was a rebellious vassal who had made war on Jekermish and then been attacked in turn by the Sultan of Rum, Kilij Arslan. Jawali appealed to Ridwan, King of Aleppo. Kilij Arslan was defeated and killed. But the people of Mosul revolted against their new atabeg because his wife, to whom the regency had been entrusted while Jawali was at war, had driven the people to desperation by her despotism.

Driven out of his city, Jawali took his Frankish prisoner along and reached an understanding with him, promising him his freedom in return for sixty thousand dinars, the release of Moslem prisoners, and a treaty of alliance. In this way Baldwin—and with him his relative and faithful companion Joscelin of Courtenay—found themselves free. The citizens of Edessa, only too delighted to have their old Count back and to be delivered from the Norman Richard of the Principate, got together the money for the ransom. But the return of Baldwin of Le Bourg had not yet put an end to the rule of Richard, and although Tancred contributed something toward paying the Count of Edessa's ransom, he refused to reinstate him in his lands except in return for an oath of fealty. Baldwin only recovered his city thanks to the assistance of his ally Jawali and of the Armenian prince Kogh Vasil, who lent him a strong army of Armenians and turcopoles.

Once more installed in Edessa, Baldwin of Le Bourg still felt more at one with Jawali than with Tancred; and the two Frankish barons were soon engaged in open war, either with the aid or on behalf of their respective Turkish allies: Baldwin of Le Bourg and

Jawali against Tancred, who in the event summoned to his aid his
former enemy Ridwan of Aleppo. Tancred, with his Normans and
the Turks of Aleppo, was victorious after a fierce battle which, according to Matthew of Edessa, cost the lives of two thousand Christians—to say nothing of the Moslems. The fiercest fighting was
between Tancred's and Baldwin's knights, each of the two barons
seeking at all costs to kill the other. Defeated, with their chivalry
decimated once again, the two Frankish rulers of Edessa, Baldwin
of Le Bourg and Joscelin, barely escaped with their lives. Baldwin
was again besieged by Tancred in the castle of Dulak and was only
saved by a threat that Jawali's army was about to return. Meanwhile, the Armenians in Edessa, fearing as they said to find themselves once more governed by Richard of Salerno, revolted and
planned to adopt one of the local Armenian princes as their ruler.
(Baldwin, on his return, decided that the Armenians were altogether
too strong and unruly an element and expelled them from the city.
It was Joscelin of Courtenay who later became the champion of
Franco-Armenian collaboration.)

After four years of Norman domination, Edessa became once
more the fief of Baldwin of Le Bourg, and Baldwin of Le Bourg
was the relative and ally of the King of Jerusalem. But as we have
just seen, the principality of Antioch recognized absolutely no ties
with the kingdom, and the two Frankish chiefs of northern Syria
were more inclined to make alliances with the Moslems than to live
on good terms with one another.

When Baldwin, King of Jerusalem, had assembled the somewhat
reluctant barons of Frankish Syria outside Tripoli in order to settle
the matter of the Provençal inheritance, Baldwin of Le Bourg and
Tancred had found themselves face to face in a feudal assembly very
like those in the West. The King, because he was the King, could
speak as a master or at least as supreme arbiter, as befitted a feudal
monarch, and assumed by right the role which had hitherto been
denied him—although this denial was never specific, since the question of the submission of the principality of Antioch to royal suzerainty had never arisen. Now Tancred found himself compelled to
be reconciled before a parliament of barons with Baldwin of Le
Bourg and Joscelin of Courtenay. He did not go so far as to swear
fealty to the King, but he was obliged to bow to his authority.

This gave the King firm allies in Tripoli and Edessa, in the persons of the two Counts. But Baldwin of Le Bourg, who in the course
of the last five years had lost, in his wars against the Turks and later
against Tancred, the better part of his chivalry, was in such a critical

situation that he could do little to help his cousin. Bertrand of Saint-Gilles was certainly the King of Jerusalem's vassal, but at the same time he was the vassal of Alexius Comnenus. This was in no sense to slight Baldwin, but it annoyed Tancred, who had been busy repelling attacks by the Greeks in the west at the same time as those by the Turks in the east and regarded any alliance between Franks and Greeks as an act of treachery. The war between the Prince of Antioch and the Count of Edessa in which both had fallen back on Moslem help appears to have shocked not only the men of the Frankish armies but also the knights, for even when Tancred found the three other Frankish princes to some extent ranged against him, he no longer dared use Ridwan's armies against them. As inheritors of the "holy war," the Franks were compelled to some form of solidarity despite themselves.

In 1110 the new Sultan of Persia, Mohammed (second son of Malik Shah, who had succeeded his elder brother Barkiyarok), was finally alarmed by Frankish progress in Syria and made up his mind to equip a powerful army and organize his own "holy war" against the infidel. His army, led by Sharaf ad-Daula Mawdud, atabeg of Mosul, was reinforced on the road by the troops of Soqman el-Qutbi, Emir of Khilat (in Greater Armenia) and those of Ilghazi, the Ortoqid Emir of Mardin (in Diarbekir). Mawdud intended to begin the reconquest of the lands lost by Islam. Edessa, the most vulnerable of Frankish possessions, was the first to feel the effects of the counter-Crusade. In May 1110, the great Turkish army reached the gates of the city and started to lay siege to it.

At that time, Tancred had still so little idea of coming to the assistance of his neighbor Baldwin of Le Bourg that Baldwin openly accused him of having provoked this expedition against Edessa by his intrigues with the Turks. (Matthew of Edessa, on the other hand, claims that Baldwin of Le Bourg and Joscelin of Courtenay had themselves appealed to the atabeg of Mosul, inviting him to make war on Tancred.)

In the end it was King Baldwin who, learning of Edessa's desperate situation, gathered all his troops and those of Tripoli led by Bertrand of Saint-Gilles, and succeeded, not without difficulty, in bringing about a reconciliation between the two Frankish princes of northern Syria (Albert of Aix). According to the chroniclers, Tancred only decided to join the royal army after strong pressure from his barons. With great misgivings, the Norman came to meet the King with his army, and found himself subjected to a somewhat humiliating call to order. Baldwin gave him to understand that their

cause was the same, that they had all come to this country to fight
the infidel, that the Christian community of Outremer had chosen a
king "who would serve as leader, protector, and guide" and that he,
Baldwin, as that king, had the right to demand of Tancred a complete
reconciliation with Baldwin of Le Bourg and all his assistance in the
fight against the Turks. "Otherwise," added Baldwin, "you cannot
continue one of us and we shall fight against you without scruples."

Such language had the merit of being reasonable and unequivocal.
But Tancred was not beaten yet. He was still the young man who, at
Constantinople and at Nicaea, had categorically refused, despite his
uncle's objurgations, to swear fealty to the *basileus*. Scarcely had
the Frankish army re-formed, ready to march against the Turks,
when the entire Norman force wheeled about and withdrew, thus
depriving King Baldwin of a good quarter of his fighting strength.
The army of Mawdud and his allies had fallen back on the country
along the Balikh, watching for a favorable opportunity to give battle.
Seeing that he could not rely on the Normans, and in a hurry to
take his army southward again because the Egyptians were taking
advantage of his absence to attack his possessions in Judaea, Baldwin decided not to venture against an army he knew was vastly superior to his own.

Massacres in Armenia

What finally happened was one of the greatest disasters in the history of the Crusades. The responsibility for this catastrophe belongs
to the Franks, to the two Baldwins in particular, and also indirectly
to Tancred and his somewhat equivocal attitude. The massacre of
the inhabitants of the region of Edessa surpassed in horror the sack
of Jerusalem and the massacres of the Crusading armies in Anatolia.
This time it was literally a case of genocide.

The Franks had had the unfortunate idea of evacuating the entire
civilian population of the region (including that of the fortified
cities) to the right bank of the Euphrates, in order to protect the
Armenians against the incursions of the Turkish armies and so that
they would be better able to defend the strongholds. It had not
occurred to them to consider the unwisdom of this mass exodus at
a moment when the great Turkish army was in the neighborhood.
So hopeless were they at directing and organizing the countless
hordes of peasants and townspeople, and so badly organized was
the transport by boat to the other side of the river, that Mawdud's

army found it child's play to fall upon the wretched people gathered on the plain beside the Euphrates. The Armenians were slaughtered in their tens of thousands before the very eyes of the Franks who, having already crossed the river, watched powerless while the hideous butchery took place. "The Franks," wrote Matthew of Edessa, "shed bitter tears as they contemplated this scene of desolation. After this signal success, Mawdud returned to Harran with masses of captives and incalculable booty." The captives were young women and children, whom the Turks generally spared. The men were killed. Those who flung themselves into the boats were drowned, because the boats were overloaded, and the majority of those who tried to cross the river by swimming did not reach the further bank. The carnage, says Matthew of Edessa, was such that "the waves of the Euphrates ran red with blood. . . . This day saw the depopulation of the whole province of Edessa."[9] This is no exaggeration. A whole rich and fertile province was transformed overnight into a ruined and wasted land—a desert. It never recovered.

Clearly the Franks cannot be held responsible for atrocities committed by the Turks, but it must be admitted that the great exodus undertaken at their suggestion constituted a direct provocation to atrocities which, but for that, the Turks would never have committed on such a vast scale. It is also fair to say that the whole operation must have been very badly conducted, and that the least the Franks could have done was to use their army to cover the retreat of the civilian population. Yet the Franks had crossed the river first, knowing full well that the Turkish army was on the other side. Lastly, the flight of the local Christians from the Turks, like the Turks' anger against the Christians, was the direct consequence of the Crusades themselves, which had led the Moslems to regard Christians as enemies by definition. Although the history of the Armenian people has produced more in tragic episodes of this kind than any other, on this occasion it can reasonably be said that massacre might easily have been avoided. With the best of intentions, the Franks had brought disaster on the heads of their subjects.

After this disaster, from which the Franks emerged intact, having lost neither men nor arms, it is understandable that the already faltering confidence of the Armenians of Edessa in their new lords was badly shaken. Indeed, their cherished wish was to have a prince of their own race once again. On the other bank of the Euphrates, the Armenian Kogh Vasil, lord of Raban and Kaisun, commanded a strong army, dependent on neither Greeks nor Turks, still less on the Franks. In Cilicia, Oshin and Thoros I ruled at Lampron and Vakha as distant vassals of Byzantium but in practice virtually independent. The Armenians' want of "loyalty" to Baldwin of Le Bourg is therefore quite understandable. But the county of Edessa was still the first rampart of Frankish Syria against Turkish attack.

Enforced Unification of Frankish Syria

Frankish Syria was beginning to form slowly and painfully, if not a state, at least a feudal unit like those in the West. The King, as official suzerain, received more than nominal respect. There were the two Counts as vassals of the kingdom, one principality not yet a vassal but inevitably bound to become one, and within each of the four states, fiefs great and small held by vassals of the King or the Counts. Tancred himself, in spite of his old grudge against Baldwin I and his hatred of Baldwin of Le Bourg, was not long in realizing that even they were still surer allies than the Turks. Hardly had he left Antioch in answer to the King's summons when his ally Ridwan came and sacked his lands. It is true that once again the Norman had the upper hand and inflicted a crushing defeat on Ridwan, and also that Ridwan was a useful neighbor with whom, in spite of everything, Tancred always managed to come to some understanding since the Seljuk, suspected of Shiism and not on good terms with the Sultan, preferred to unite with the Franks in their wars against the Turks of Mosul or Baghdad. All the same, when Mawdud launched an attack on the lands of Antioch in 1111, Baldwin I hurried up with his whole army, and Tancred's great enemy, Baldwin of Le Bourg, did the same. Short of becoming a Moslem, the great Emir Tankridos had no choice but to make common cause with the other Franks.

Tancred died in 1112 at the age of thirty-six after a full life in which every year held more battles than it contained months. His life was typical of that of any feudal lord in a land where there was never a want of causes for fighting. His tireless energy made him respected even by the Moslems: like his uncle Bohemond, he had the gift of leadership and the gift of inspiring confidence in his men. He had continued Bohemond's anti-Byzantine policy and had maintained the independence of his principality of Antioch against hell and high water, and long cherished the idea of uniting it with the county of Edessa. When he proved unable to extend his possessions at the expense of either Turks, Arabs, or Franks, he finally resigned himself to a state of semisubmission to the suzerainty of the King of Jerusalem, the man who had been his first enemy and his rival in Cilicia and who, in the end, had succeeded better than himself.

Tancred died without issue, but before he died he arranged for his wife, the Princess Cecilia of France, to marry the son of Bertrand of Tripoli, a young man named Pons, thinking in this way to extend Norman influence over the county of Tripoli. (William of Tyre further suggests that he had guessed that there were already some tender feelings uniting the two young people.) The heir to the principality of Antioch was—as feudal custom demanded and as the Norman barons of Antioch decided—Bohemond's son, the boy born to the first Frankish Prince of Antioch by his marriage with Constance of France. But the boy Bohemond was only three years old and living with his mother in Italy. In order to safeguard the province during his minority, Tancred's companions summoned his nephew Roger, the son of Richard of Salerno, to act as regent. Roger was an Italian Norman and, like Bohemond and Tancred, a valiant fighter. He was still young (about twenty-five), and possessed neither the intelligence nor the experience of his two predecessors. He quite naturally accepted Baldwin's suzerainty over the lands of Antioch and was a loyal auxiliary to the King.

Bertrand of Saint-Gilles died a few months after Tancred. He had been Count of Tripoli for only three years, and even if he had obtained possession of the whole county as the price of the murder of his cousin William-Jordan, the Holy Land had brought him no happiness. He was succeeded by his son Pons, who had married Tancred's widow. Pons was a very young man with no experience, and the government of the county came in practice under Baldwin's guardianship since he, as suzerain, had the right to intervene in the affairs of Tripoli.

Not long afterward, Baldwin of Le Bourg gave his sister in marriage to Roger of Salerno, regent of Antioch. In this way the houses of Edessa and Antioch were united by the family ties which feudal customs made almost obligatory between neighbors who were not enemies. Since the Count of Edessa was also, in addition, a first cousin of the King of Jerusalem, the reigning houses of the four Frankish states were beginning to look like one great feudal family; and in the next generation, these family ties were to be strengthened still further.*

---

* For the relationships between the ruling families of Frankish Syria, see the genealogical tables at the end of the book.

CHAPTER

VI

The Kingdom and Its Neighbors

(1 1 1 2 – 1 1 3 1)

Religion and Politics

The position of the Frankish kingdom of Jerusalem—for after Tancred's death it may truly be considered one kingdom—can be compared, in broad outline, with the present situation of the State of Israel today. Both states were created artificially in the same land, and faced with problems of a roughly similar nature. Israel, too, is a state founded as a result of a current of opinion of an ideological or religious nature, created by groups of volunteers sustained by active sympathy—some of it disinterested, some less so—from the outside world, constantly replenished by fresh volunteers from the West and materially dependent on the West. (Although Western interest in the Frankish kingdom in medieval times was, quite naturally, much greater and more active than that which the State of Israel enjoys.) Finally, in the Moslem world where this kingdom was carving itself a place as best it could, it was bound to arouse feelings of the same kind, to act as a catalyst, a factor for unity or discord, an excuse for settling old scores or, at times, for an ambitious ruler to win popularity or extend his frontiers.

As we have seen, the idea of a holy war, or *jihad,* was quite foreign to the Moslem princes of the period. This does not mean that they did not feel themselves bound out of deference to public opinion to display a certain zeal for the holy war. As we have seen, after years of a policy of goodwill toward the Franks, Ibn Ammar, the Emir of Tripoli, became a hero of Islam despite himself, thanks to the fierce energy with which he defended his city for five years, and was welcomed in Baghdad by the Sultan of Persia, Mohammed, with the greatest honors. The Sultan even sent him his own personal barge "with the cushion upon which he was wont to sit." In the capital of Islam, the Sultan and the Caliph loaded the lord of Tripoli with every sign of friendship and respect, feasted him, promised him aid—and did precisely nothing. Meanwhile another Moslem potentate, the Vizier of Cairo, was taking advantage of the Emir's absence to deprive him of the city he had so valiantly defended. This he did in the name of the holy war, and the better to defend Tripoli against the Franks. But it was easier for the fleet in Cairo to take possession of a city which opened its gates to the Vizier's emissaries than to dislodge the Crusaders of Provence from the coastal region and drive the Italian fleets from the sea. The battle fleet sent by the Vizier arrived after the city had fallen, having taken a year to get under way.

To the heads of state, the idea of a holy war against the Franks was as yet merely a pious wish, without any real political significance. But none of them would have dared stand out against the idea, and gradually, as the Franks took root in the land and the people grew more accustomed to their presence, public opinion in the Moslem countries became familiarized with the idea of a holy war.

In 1106 the chief of the Ismailians in Syria, Abu Tahir, decided to seize the fortress of Apamea on behalf of Ridwan, King of Aleppo, who favored the Ismailians. Accordingly he laid a trap for Khalaf, the Emir of Apamea. The cadi of the city of Sarmin, which had been stormed by Tancred, came to Khalaf with "some Frankish heads." He claimed to have vanquished these Franks in battle, and proposed a mutual alliance with a view to communal action against the infidel. Khalaf agreed and allowed his new allies to enter his castle. He was slain the same night. The cadi and Abu Tahir delivered Apamea to Ridwan, though not for long. The son of the Khalaf who had been so traitorously assassinated promptly went over to Tancred's camp with his troop of Bedouin, and with those reinforcements the Norman was able to take the town.

On this occasion a Sunnite emir had made common cause with the infidels to avenge his father, and the Shiite Abu Tahir found himself on the opposite side from the Franks. In general, however, a tacit agreement was already growing up between the Ismailians and the

Franks, an understanding which neither side could admit. The Ismailians were anxious not to be suspected of tolerance toward the enemies of their religion, and the Franks, aware of the reputation of this redoubtable sect, were not anxious to be regarded as accomplices of the Assassins. But that an understanding should have existed between the Franks and this heterodox sect, at the same time powerful and persecuted, is only too comprehensible from a political point of view. From a religious point of view there could be no understanding, or not officially, at least.

By a remarkable piece of good fortune for the Crusaders, the King of Aleppo, Ridwan, the Seljuk whose lands ran closest to those occupied by the Franks, was as we have seen so strongly influenced by the Shiite heresy that he almost openly protected the Ismailians, and therefore, in spite of the periodical skirmishes indulged in by the two princes as a result of their proximity, his relations with Tancred were on the whole good. When the atabeg of Mosul, Mawdud, returned to attack Antioch in 1111, his soldiers were often attacked and taken prisoner by Ridwan's. And yet, even while the King of Aleppo was consciously playing the Frankish game, the people of the city, who were either more orthodox or less sensitive to political combinations, were in open revolt, denouncing the King's weakness in the defense of Islam and sending deputations to Baghdad. There the revolutionaries from Aleppo stirred up public opinion, appealing to "men of the law," preaching the holy war, and even going so far as to interfere with the celebration of public worship on Fridays and hacking to pieces the preacher's *minbar,* or pulpit (this in sign of mourning and protest, of course, and not from any disrespect for religion). The rioting reached such proportions that the Sultan and the Caliph could only appease the mob by promises of an immediate campaign against the Franks. Ibn al-Athir tells us that again the following Friday no prayers could be held, because Moslems inflamed with pious zeal had broken the grilles in the mosque of the Caliph's court and once again torn the *minbar* to pieces. It was the pressure of public risings of a religious nature which compelled the Sultan Mohammed, in 1111, to send a fresh army against Edessa and Antioch.

Some enthusiasm for the holy war was beginning to kindle in Islam, but it was a feeble flicker as yet. Not only Ridwan but the atabeg of Damascus, Toghtekin (whom no one suspected of Shiite leanings), still preferred to keep the Franks in check by their own means rather than submit to the direct control of the sultans of Persia. In the words of Kemal ad-Din: "The reason for all this was that the princes of that time were anxious to prolong the occupation by Frankish troops in order to keep themselves in power." But since they could hardly proclaim themselves openly the Christians' friends, propaganda for the holy war continued to work silently among the Moslem people, only waiting for the emergence of energetic leaders capable of exploiting it.

The policy of the Crusader barons was in general determined more by their mutual disagreements than by loyalty to their religion, but the relations existing between these barons were idyllic compared to those reigning among the Turkish princes. At least there is some evidence that members of the same family among the Crusaders usually managed to get on reasonably well, but in the great families of the Turkish ruling aristocracy the fiercest hatreds were those between brothers. Often the sons of different—and rival—wives of the same sultan were only waiting for their father's death in order to indulge in merciless wars. The sons of the great Seljuk Sultan Malik Shah spent fifteen years quarreling over the Sultan's throne and title, and Malik Shah himself had a no more formidable rival than his own brother Tutush. Ridwan and Duqaq, Tutush's sons, quarreled to the death, and even then, before becoming King of Aleppo, Ridwan had had two of his brothers murdered. Relations between vassals and sovereigns were hardly better, and often an atabeg was no sooner invested by the Sultan with the government of a province than he was scheming to win his independence, feeling free to make war on the Sultan himself and, at all events, to ally himself with the Sultan's enemies.

If we add to these fraternal, dynastic, and feudal hatreds the hatred of the Arabs for the Turks and, to crown it all, the murderous religious fanaticism of the Ismailians, it becomes clear that the idea of a holy war against the Frank was pretty well the only point on which the divided Moslems had some chance of agreeing on some single course of action—action, at that time, meaning making war. It was not a very secure ground for agreement, but it had at least the advantage of resting on a simple, concrete idea and one which would give everyone a clear conscience.

In the spring of 1113, Mawdud, the atabeg of Mosul, whose bloody exploits on the Euphrates in 1110 had not been forgotten, joined up with Toghtekin, atabeg of Damascus, with the intention of crushing the Franks once and for all. This time the two powerful allies attacked from the direction of Galilee. King Baldwin gave battle without waiting for his allies and vassals (Pons of Tripoli and Roger of Antioch) and was defeated and put to flight. This in itself was not a disaster. The two vassal princes arrived to the rescue, and confronted by the united forces of the chivalry of Jerusalem, Tripoli, and Antioch, Maw-dud dared not risk a second battle and withdrew to Damascus. He did not lead a fourth campaign against the Franks; he was slain by an Assassin in Damascus as he was coming out of the mosque. Rumor accused Toghtekin of this murder (which caused the greater sor-row because the old atabeg died like a real Moslem saint). It was too well known that the atabegs of Damascus distrusted those of Mosul and the Sultan's plenipotentiaries. Whether or not Toghtekin was guilty, Baldwin I, who could not but rejoice at the death of his power-ful enemy, felt obliged to write a letter of reproach to the atabeg of Damascus, "a letter saying among other things that a people who cut down their allies, and *that on a feast day and in the house of their God,* deserve to be exterminated by God from the face of the earth."[1]

Baldwin's highly diplomatic indignation shows how far this Frank-ish prince already felt a moral solidarity with the other Oriental princes, Christian or Moslem. Moreover his policy toward Toghtekin had long been one, if not of actual alliance, at least of frequent truces which were faithfully observed. When the atabeg of Damascus was defeated by William-Jordan in 1108, Baldwin hastened to write him a letter couched in the most friendly terms: "Do not believe that the defeat which you have suffered tempts me to violate our truce. Princes are exposed to much more cruel trials than that which has just struck you, and this does not prevent them from reordering their affairs."[2] Even the letter of reproach on the subject of Mawdud's murder is a proof, if not of friendship, at least of understanding on a human level, and at a later date these good relations were to develop into a real alliance. Toghtekin became the King of Jerusalem's ally and fought at his side against the forces of the emir Bursuq, governor of Hamadan, in 1115. On this occasion, the Turkish prince and the Frankish king rode side by side "like good and faithful com-panions."[3]

Baldwin's desire to create the closest possible ties with those of the Moslem princes who might have some common interest with him is too evident not to appear as the result of a conscious and deliberate policy of assimilation. As an indomitable warrior, the premier Frank-ish prince and the defender of the Holy Sepulcher, he was the great promoter of that political alliance with Islam which alone could make his kingdom viable. This reasoning was a politician's, but Baldwin seemed to have forgotten—although he had not in fact done so—that not only was his own position in the Holy Land due primarily to re-ligious motives, but the whole fate, the whole future of the Frankish kingdom depended not on political alliances but on religious feelings, whether purely altruistic or exploited for political ends. On the one hand was the gradual recrudescence of the warlike instincts of pious Moslems after the first impact of the Crusade; on the other, the religious zeal of the West for the cause of the Holy Land.

Frankish Syria and the West

Officially, religion was inseparable from politics. A statesman, whether Greek, Latin, or Moslem, could undertake no important action without first finding a religious motive and justifying and explaining it from a religious point of view. This was not demagogy but a universally recognized moral necessity. When the Germans broke out in open warfare against the Pope, they could do so only by setting up an antipope and declaring themselves the real champions of the Church. The Turks, in laying hands on Ispahan and Baghdad, were working for Sunnite orthodoxy, while Alexius Comnenus, in Syria and Asia Minor, was defending the cause of the Greek Church. A people's material and temporal interests could not be conceived of apart from its religious interests, and this was a fundamentally logical attitude. These interests did not always coincide, but the second were rarely deliberately and officially sacrificed to the first.

Now in the case of the Frankish kingdom of Jerusalem, there was the unusual feature that, to Western eyes, the kingdom was a kind of theocratic state, a state whose religion was its real reason for existence and which, by its very existence, symbolized a great victory for Christianity. The wave of popular enthusiasm for the Holy Sepulcher abated just as swiftly as it had been aroused, leaving an aftertaste of bitterness and disappointment, even though Jerusalem was now in the hands of Catholic and Latin Christians, and more precisely, of Frenchmen. But this annexation by a Western people of the real Holy of Holies of Christianity was a source of joy and pride whose importance should not be underrated. The distant, inaccessible Jerusalem, a legendary land that was a symbol of the glory of paradise, had become to some extent a French possession, and this in itself was enough to create strong feelings of national pride even in people who had never stirred outside their native town or held a sword. For nearly half a century, even though there were no actual Crusades, there was a growing awareness that possession of the Holy Places was the inalienable right of Latin and French Christendom. The peoples of Europe, who were all in all very little affected by these distant battles and adventures, found their horizons strangely enlarged by the thought of Jerusalem delivered and of God's *gesta per Francos.*

Little by little, the popular imagination took hold of the Crusades, insisting on raising the great Crusading leaders, Godfrey, Bohemond, Tancred, to the level of legendary heroes. Paradoxically enough, these very real heroes never supplanted figures like Roland, Oliver, or the multifarious William of Orange, or the greatest of them all, Charlemagne with his hoary beard, who were already lost in the mists of the past. The people—and this includes the knights—still preferred the dream to the reality, and with the exception of Godfrey of Bouillon, whose memory survived in a curiously altered form, the heroes of the First Crusade did not become legendary characters in the West. But from the beginning of the twelfth century, there did grow up a form of historical and epic-historical literature, written in Latin, French, Provençal, and German, relating and celebrating the exploits of God's armies.

The Western public had a lively curiosity about events in the East. The majority of the evidence available today was written down in Latin and therefore meant for a relatively limited audience. The spoken word, on the other hand, had an importance hard to imagine today, because in those days even the aristocracy were very often unable to read or write. The spoken word, however inaccurate, was the great source of information. Witnesses of the events in question were numerous, and if they did not fill their hearers with any great desire to follow the example of the Crusaders, they did succeed in arousing in their own countries feelings of pride, of devotion to the Holy Places and hatred for the Saracens.

The Crusaders' exploits helped to appease the conscience of the Latin West, but the general feeling of people in Western countries was to leave the kings of Jerusalem and the princes of Antioch to fight for the glory of Christendom in their far-off Oriental realms. It was easier to believe that God had granted the Franks possession of Jerusalem once and for all.

If there was one power which continued to take an active interest in the cause of the Holy Places, this was the Roman Church, in the persons of the popes, who considered, not unreasonably, that the reconquest of the Holy Land was a great work for which the Church had, at least partially, assumed responsibility.* The Church was the first to profit from the reconquest of Palestine, by the increase in

* The fight which the popes were waging against the Empire in the twelfth century did not allow them to give active support to the kingdom of Jerusalem. Nevertheless, they did encourage all moves toward a Crusade.

prestige. Another advantage was that it enriched the Church of Rome with two of the most venerable patriarchates: Antioch and Jerusalem, snatched, so to speak, by force from the Greek Church. These phantom patriarchates, ruled by patriarchs appointed by the local secular authorities, did not add a great deal to the real power of the Church, but their existence, like that of the eighteen bishoprics they controlled, very quickly became a matter of prestige on which the popes would brook no argument. Paschal II does not appear to have been greatly disturbed by the fact that the Patriarch of Jerusalem was an unscrupulous cleric who had attained that dignity by means of intrigue. In fact, it mattered very little because the important thing was to create the kernel of a Latin Christendom in the East which might, with time, develop into something that could bring external Roman influence over the Eastern provinces into which it had not so far penetrated. (The Pope could not be unaware that this would lead to insoluble conflicts with the Greek Church, and he had taken the risk. Prejudiced against the Greeks to the point of having meditated sending a Crusade against them, he had no intention of taking seriously any rights the Byzantine Empire might have in Syria.)

We have only to read the *Itineraria Hierosolymitana* to realize the extent to which the Holy Land merited its name in the eyes of medieval Christians, East or West. Not only Jerusalem, the strength of whose attraction was obvious, but the whole land, every village, every spring, and every rock, had been transformed into a holy place by the pious workings of Christians' minds. During the first centuries of the Christian era, and especially after the conversion of the Emperor Constantine, archaeologists who were more concerned with the edification of the faithful than with historical exactitude had unearthed the very places where the nails of the Passion were forged, where Judas's thirty pieces of silver were coined, even the spot where David found the stone which killed Goliath. The smallest facts about Christ's life on earth and about the lives of the Apostles, Saint John the Baptist, the Virgin, and the prophets and patriarchs of the Old Testament as well were documented with meticulous precision and localized by this or that rock, chapel, or well. Even the star which had guided the Magi was discovered trapped in the bottom of a well in Bethlehem, into which it was supposed to have fallen on the day of the Epiphany. Pilgrimages of primary and secondary importance to the places that were all, in their different ways, holy had transformed the land that warriors like Baldwin, Tancred, the rulers of Damascus, and the Vizier of Cairo trampled under their horses' hoofs into a kind of immense shrine, a miraculous country studded with invisible stars. The longing to go on a pilgrimage had already been an important factor in people's lives in the eleventh century: by the twelfth, after the deliverance of Jerusalem, the Holy Land and the restless, pious wandering that constituted a pilgrimage had become a pole of attraction more powerful for pious Europeans than ever.

The Crusades had made the ancient overland route by Constantinople, the Bosporus, Asia Minor, and Syria impracticable. This was the road which less wealthy pilgrims had once taken in more or less numerous bands, crossing three thousand miles of friendly or hostile country with all its risks and dangers, seeking Jerusalem at the end of the journey. In the future no Christian pilgrim could venture along this road, since four great armies had been annihilated there. There remained the sea route, and this too was made unsafe by pirates. (Albert of Aix states that in the course of the year 1102 alone, three hundred pilgrim ships, carrying a total of 140,000 people, fell into the hands of the pirates, and however exaggerated these contemporary figures may seem, nevertheless they do give an idea of the terrible scourge which pirates represented at the time.) The danger of capture by pirates was very real, and just as real was the risk of shipwreck. Many pilgrims would have much preferred to travel on dry land for months rather than set foot on a ship. In addition, the sea voyage was very expensive, at least in the twelfth century, and only the relatively well off could afford it.

A pilgrimage to the Holy Land was therefore a difficult and dangerous undertaking and one which demanded many sacrifices. But in the twelfth century the fact that the country, from Jaffa to Jerusalem at any rate, was in Christian hands meant that a pilgrim disembarking at one of the ports on the Syrian coast could consider himself almost certain of reaching the Holy City without further trouble. In particular, he could visit Jerusalem and all the sanctuaries of Judaea, Galilee, and Samaria in the happy certainty that he was in a Christian land and would no longer see the crescent of Islam on the domes of churches, but would find instead each place of pilgrimage properly honored, served, and maintained by Christian and Latin clergy. Christian Jerusalem, the Jerusalem of the Crusaders and the Frankish kingdom, had become a temple city, the city to which pilgrims flowed from all Christendom, Latin and Greek, orthodox and heretic, vying with one another in their fervor, crowding to the Holy Sepulcher, to Golgotha, and to all the shrines of the city and its environs with a freedom that they would never have known in the days of Moslem domination.

The ability to worship Jesus Christ in the places where he had lived on earth, in freedom and propriety, with all the pomp and fervor which such a serious act demanded; the chance to adorn and enrich the churches, to build new ones, to found convents close to the Holy Places; and altogether the privilege of seeing the holiest place in the world at last become a true center of pilgrimage: this was Christianity's debt to the Crusaders and the kingdom of Jerusalem, and this, in the eyes of the Christian West, was the real function and the great merit of those who held this kingdom.

Baldwin I, as guardian of the Holy Sepulcher, was thus to some extent one of the high dignitaries of Christendom, a man charged with a sacred mission. Not only did this kingdom guarantee freedom of pilgrimage, but the very fact that the country was held by Christians was a pledge of divine approval to Christians in general and the Roman Church in particular. Up to the time of the Crusades this is a fact which seems to have been somewhat neglected by Christendom, although in the ninth and tenth centuries the Byzantines had made serious efforts to win back the Holy Land. In the twelfth century, and especially in the West, no one any longer doubted the immense spiritual advantages which the possession of Jerusalem conferred on Christians.

From the beginning pilgrims, both soldiers and civilians, came in large numbers, but both made their pilgrimages to the Holy Sepulcher and then went home. The soldiers served their time in the King of Jerusalem's army while they waited for the chance to take ship once more, and felt that they were serving God directly, serving their *"quarantaine"* under His banners as they might under those of some terrestrial lord. In 1110 Sigurd, King of Norway, brought with him a whole fleet, and the pious Vikings, after worshipping at the Holy Sepulcher, rendered Baldwin useful assistance in conquering the city of Sidon. The Crusaders who came every year with the warlike Italian merchant fleets from the great republics of Pisa and Genoa were, like the Norwegians, sailors first and foremost, and they made it possible for Baldwin, Bertrand of Tripoli, and Tancred to make themselves masters of the coast. But apart from this infinitely valuable but limited aid, the Frankish states received little reinforcement. Men died quickly in the Holy Land: battles were murderous, even for knights, and the climate of the country did not agree with everyone. The Crusader knights brought their families and friends from oversea, but the new arrivals were just enough to fill the gaps left by battle in the ranks of their companions in the Holy Land. According to Ibn al-Athir, the Turks had little difficulty in procuring "Frankish heads" even when there was no real military operation in progress.

The new Crusaders arrived in small bands and were promptly enrolled in the old guard of the Holy Land and rapidly assimilated; but early in the twelfth century a certain difference of mentality was already making itself felt between the Crusaders who had arrived first and the rest. With the years, this difference was to become still more apparent. During the reign of Baldwin I it had not yet reached the stage of open antagonism, for the pioneers of the holy war were in a morally stronger position. Yet even men like Baldwin I, Baldwin of Le Bourg, and Tancred, men whose merit and blame it was to have stood fast and survived, suffered in the eyes of the world by comparison with the great dead such as Godfrey and Bohemond. This can be clearly felt in the accounts of historians of the period. The new generation of Crusaders found more and more numerous grievances against the old guard.

Whatever his claims to be so, Baldwin I was not the master of his kingdom; affairs in the Holy Land were the concern of Western Christendom as a whole, as the kings of Jerusalem would have many occasions to realize. They were to a great extent dependent on the West, and they were compelled to adapt their policies to fit in with the needs of the various Western powers. These powers were not necessarily the Western *states*. The real powers were international, like the Church, and simultaneously supranational and particularist like the merchant republics. In addition, there was the very real power of public opinion, at least of the outwardly divided and inwardly homogeneous class formed by Western chivalry, and all these forces with their various interests in what was happening in the East had to be constantly considered by the Franks who were carving out a kingdom in Palestine with their help, for the benefit of Catholic Christendom.

Among the early Frankish princes, Tancred had been the most independent, the greediest, and perhaps the most ambitious. In fifteen years of holy war he had finally realized that his principality of Antioch could only be held and quite modestly extended at the cost of daily efforts and by a continual policy of holding a balance between his non-Christian neighbors. The man who boasted to the envoys of Alexius Comnenus that he was a "new Ninus, the great Assyrian," strong enough to pierce the ramparts of Babylon (Baghdad) with his lance, was actually quite well aware of the immense force represented by Islam, and that it was a considerable success even to have succeeded in carving himself a fief at all in a semi-Christian province on the frontiers of the Seljuk empire. But this the Crusaders who disembarked at the Syrian ports did not know or did not want to know. Their program was in fact a merciless struggle against Islam, a struggle intended to end in the total and definitive triumph of Christianity.

The knights of high or moderately high rank who decided to emigrate to the East were by no means all fanatics determined at all costs to exterminate the Arab and the Turk to the greater glory of God. But it is somewhat strange to realize that such a state of mind should have been more widespread among the later Crusaders than among those who came with the First Crusade. There was a particular spirit of warlike exaltation which, originating in the West *after* the Crusaders' victories, was an imported product in the East. In two decades a mythical Turk or Saracen became the traditional enemy of God and of all Christian knights, and this myth spread through Europe, whereas in the Latin Orient where the Saracen, whatever else he was, could not be considered a myth, it had never existed. Toward the middle of the century, the second (or rather the third, if we include the expedition of 1101) great Crusade, the first Crusade of the Kings, demonstrated in a spectacular fashion the difference between the attitude of Christians in Europe toward the Holy Land and the policy of the Franks in Syria.

End of the Reign of Baldwin I

In the course of his reign, which lasted for eighteen years, Baldwin had ample time to take stock of the difficulties, complexities, advantages, and disadvantages of the particular state which was his kingdom. Like every energetic sovereign he was concerned primarily with his independence, a precarious independence needing Western support and reinforcements in the shape of men, money, armaments, and even provisions, since Palestine did not produce enough meat or grain. The very fact of this material dependence meant that the King of Jerusalem was not really the master in his own house. He paid his Pisan and Genoese allies by granting them commercial privileges in the ports and cities he occupied, and this impoverished his own treasury. As far as the Church was concerned, he had succeeded in carrying through the election to the patriarchate of a man he could look on as his own creature, and he had very adroitly managed to make use of his privileges as protector of the Holy Sepulcher. Never before had national politics been so involved with the service of God.

The kingdom of Jerusalem derived considerable benefits from

pilgrimages: for although the King's government did not, as the Moslems had done, levy a tax on visits to the Holy Sepulcher, it made up for that by collecting its share—a quarter—of the cost of the sea voyage to pilgrims, to say nothing of various taxes and dues. The government also had the right to a share of the gifts which pilgrims made to the churches and religious houses. The flow of pilgrims naturally encouraged trade, but here the government did not share in the benefits, or only to a very small extent. The commercial republics were jealous of their monopolies.

Baldwin, it will be remembered, had married an Armenian, the daughter of Prince Thatoul (or Taphnuz), whose name was Arda. Now since Armenian influence in Palestine was practically nil and her dowry had long been spent, the Armenian princess had become a useless burden. Baldwin repudiated her and compelled her to enter a convent, claiming that she had been violated by pirates on a sea voyage from Lattakieh to Jaffa. (The Queen's subsequent behavior does indicate that she was not a model of virtue, but with a husband who was continually away and not notoriously faithful, she had some excuse.) The King of Jerusalem was looking for a rich wife.

His choice fell on the Dowager Countess Adelaide of Sicily, mother of Roger, the Norman Count of Sicily. She was one of the wealthiest women in Europe, a woman of middle age, and she accepted Baldwin as much to serve her son's interests as for the glory of being Queen of Jerusalem. She was no longer of an age to bear more children, and it was agreed that if she failed to give Baldwin heirs the crown of Jerusalem would go, after Baldwin's death, to Roger of Sicily. The King's betrothed arrived in the Holy Land, bringing with her two triremes and seven ships laden with gold, silver, and other treasures as well as fabrics and magnificent armor. The splendor of her clothes and her entourage and the magnificent reception Baldwin gave in her honor, splendors of which Albert of Aix and William of Tyre have left awed descriptions, made a strange contrast with the persons of the bridal couple themselves, who were very far from a fairytale prince and princess. Although somewhat put out to discover that her betrothed already had a wife living, the princess of Sicily was solemnly united to the King of Jerusalem by the Patriarch Arnulf Malecorne, and Baldwin hastily transferred to his own coffers the treasure his new bride had brought as her dowry. It was not until four years after Adelaide's arrival in the Holy Land, when he had finally spent all her dowry—in defense of the Holy Sepulcher—that a serious illness encouraged Baldwin to some feelings of remorse for his bigamy.

Arnulf, the person who had first advised and later blessed his marriage, gave him to understand that he could not continue to live in a state of adultery. In reality, the fear of imminent death had made the King realize the imprudence of leaving his inheritance to Roger of Sicily. The unfortunate Adelaide was sent home again in the most humiliating fashion, without her fortune, which Baldwin, having spent it all, would have been hard put to it to return. Having been made a laughingstock for the whole of Europe, her only course was to go and weep on her son's shoulder. Roger quarreled with Baldwin and refused to provide him with any more supplies or transports to carry merchandise to the kingdom of Jerusalem. Even so, Baldwin preferred this rupture to the risk of seeing his work destroyed, or at any rate falling into the hands of a stranger, and allowing his kingdom of Jerusalem to become a dependency of the Norman principality of Sicily.

He seems to have calculated his marriage deliberately, taking over Adelaide's treasure as he had once threatened to take over all the wealth of the Holy Sepulcher in the belief that the defense of the Holy Land justified and covered everything. In this he was sincere. His passion for his country, for the little kingdom at once so weak and fearfully menaced, and so great because of its name and the shrines it enclosed, seems to have been beyond any doubt. It had become a second vocation, and Baldwin of Boulogne had been so thoroughly transformed into the King of Jerusalem that it might have been said of him, as Fulcher of Chartres said of the colonists of the Holy Land: "We have already forgotten the land of our birth; who now remembers it?" Baldwin had been conquered, heart and soul, by Jerusalem.

In March 1117, during one of his expeditions against the Arabs of the hinterland, Baldwin received a spear wound in the groin and hung for a long time between life and death, and it was then that he made up his mind to send away his third, "illegitimate," wife. He was then between fifty-five and sixty years old and, although he recovered from his wound, was never fully to recover his health; but he did not give up his wars, the chief object of which was to extend his kingdom to the south and southeast. Sometimes on horseback, sometimes carried in a litter, he continued to harry the Fatimid possessions on the coast, even carrying his expeditions as far as the Nile delta.

Ibn al-Athir credits him with the design of conquering Egypt at this period, but the Arab chronicler was unaware of the extent to which the kingdom of Jerusalem was short of men. Baldwin's campaigns were no more than raids intended to deceive the Cairo government and discourage them from attacking Frankish territories. The King of Jerusalem's days were numbered, although he probably did not know this himself, or else refused to admit it. In March 1118, he penetrated into Egypt with his little army of two hundred knights and four hundred foot soldiers, and took the city of Farama without a blow being struck, the inhabitants having hastily evacuated it at the approach of the Franks. From there, he reached the Nile delta.

"He was much amazed at the sight of this river," says William of Tyre, "and gazed upon it gladly because it was said that this branch [of the Nile] comes from one of the four rivers of paradise."[4] This brief salutation to the great river was the King of Jerusalem's last pleasure. Aware that he was growing weaker, he decided to hasten his return to Judaea, but he died on the way at al-Arish, a little over a hundred miles from his capital, on April 2, 1118. His companions had his body embalmed and carried it back to Jerusalem.

Baldwin had not named a successor before his death, and this neglect is somewhat surprising on the part of a man who had known for a year that he was dying. Although he had taken the necessary steps to keep Roger of Sicily from the throne of Jerusalem, he had not thought (even in March 1117, when he believed he was dying) of officially regulating the matter of his succession. It is nevertheless clear that he could only have considered leaving his throne to a member of his own family: his knights and his court would have accepted as legitimate sovereign only one who succeeded the King by right of inheritance.*

The first idea of the Hierosolymitan barons was naturally to summon the defunct King's closest relative, his elder brother Eustace, Count of Boulogne. Eustace had come on the Crusade with his two younger brothers but had returned to Europe after the capture of Jerusalem. For the past eighteen years he had governed his county of Boulogne and had never shown the least desire to settle in the Holy Land. Furthermore, this baron was now over sixty and it was by no means certain that he would be prepared to set out on a life of adventure in his old age. Nevertheless, a deputation was sent to Count Eustace: the barons of Jerusalem informed him of the death of his brother and invited him, in the interests of Christendom, to accept the crown of Jerusalem.

There was, however, another party, a candidate not so closely

* Baldwin may very well have intended his brother Eustace to be his heir, but he did not express this wish in a sufficiently categorical way to impress it on his barons.

related to the dead King by blood but one who had the advantage of being on the spot and even—by an extraordinary chance—actually in the city of Jerusalem, where he had come to spend Easter. This was Baldwin of Le Bourg, Count of Edessa and a first cousin of Baldwin I. Rather than leave the kingdom without a king, perhaps for months, while they waited for the problematic acceptance of the Count of Boulogne, it seemed better to elect a king on the spot who had already proved himself very adequately in the Holy Land. Baldwin of Le Bourg's principal supporters were the Patriarch Arnulf Malecorne and Joscelin of Courtenay. The latter appears to have been disinterested in the matter, since his cousin (Baldwin of Le Bourg) had, five years earlier, driven him out of the county of Edessa and deprived him of his fief.

Baldwin of Le Bourg was therefore elected, not strictly in accordance with the laws of legitimacy but—according to the chroniclers—with the unanimous agreement of all the barons present. Count Eustace, who had accepted the crown he was offered more from duty than from personal ambition, did not learn the news of his cousin's coronation until he had traveled solemnly and at great expense halfway to the Holy Land. Messengers reached him with the news in Apulia in southern Italy, and Eustace's followers took it rather badly. The old baron himself, an easygoing individual, declared that he had no intention of going to war "out of covetousness," "in a land for whose defense his two brothers had died in such a saintly fashion."

The Count of Edessa, Tancred's former enemy, the husband of the Armenian princess Morphia and oppressor of the Armenians, mounted the throne of Jerusalem. Whatever else he may be accused of, he was a fearless warrior of great experience and an old campaigner in the Holy Land. Joscelin of Courtenay was rewarded for his contribution to the election with the county of Edessa.

Four years later, when Joscelin of Courtenay was taken prisoner by the Ortoqid emir Balak, he gave the emir, who had promised him his freedom in exchange for the county of Edessa, the following answer: "We are like camels bearing litters: when one camel perishes, the burden passes to another. Just so has that which we possess now passed into other hands." Thirteen years earlier, acting in concert with Baldwin of Le Bourg, this same Joscelin had been so little resigned to the sight of his fief passing into Norman hands that he had made an alliance with the Turks in order to make war on Tancred. That time was over. Frankish feudal lords in the Holy Land had learned by experience and were beginning to realize the importance of the solidarity of race and religion, which they had lacked at the outset simply because in the West it had not yet occurred to anyone that it existed. Baldwin I was undoubtedly the first to conceive the idea of this solidarity and set the example. This great ruler had succeeded, insofar as his means allowed him, in assuming the role of protector toward his greater vassals in northern Syria and had never treated them as rivals. The policy of the Frankish princes was never to become a model of co-operation and understanding, but for the kings of Jerusalem the path was laid down: they became, by right and in fact, the real overlords of all Frankish Syria.

Baldwin II

Baldwin of Le Bourg, now Baldwin II, did not have to impose his authority. As the successor of a man who had been supremely authoritarian, he inherited some of his cousin's prestige, and because his manner was more agreeable he was personally more popular. Chroniclers praise his great piety (his hands and knees were calloused from kneeling and prostrating himself), the exemplary dignity of his private life, his sobriety, and the simplicity of his manners and bearing. To these estimable virtues in the eyes of the clergy, he joined the qualities of a general and an almost excessive physical courage which won him the admiration of his knights. From the early years of his reign (1120), he acquired great popularity with the civilian population, Latins as well as natives, by suppressing all taxes, levies, and customs duties on trade in the city of Jerusalem. But what was to establish and reinforce his authority more than anything else was a succession of tragic events which left the principality of Antioch for long years without a master. Until his death Baldwin II had to assume the regency and take responsibility for the defense of the principality, so that the Franks of Antioch found themselves compelled to turn to the King as their natural protector.

The Count of Tripoli, who had from the outset refused to swear fealty to the new King, was forced into submission both by the threat of war with Baldwin and by the Hierosolymitan loyalties of his own knights. Later, two of Baldwin II's daughters were married to the heads of the two great vassal houses: one to the Prince of Antioch, and the other to the Count of Tripoli's son. Baldwin's policy was constantly aimed at establishing a better understanding between Latins in the East, and at his death this veteran of the First Crusade left his Oriental kingdom firmly established on dynastic legitimacy, already possessing its own traditions, an illustrious if not a lengthy history, and a personality all its own.

This was not due entirely to Baldwin II's own merits, but the still half-formed kingdom leaned on the personality of the King like a plant on a stake, and it is no small virtue in Baldwin to have succeeded in maintaining an appearance of order in a state so scattered and precarious, faced with so many contradictions within and perils without, and in making possible the creation of a real order.

"Ager Sanguinis"

Ever since the death of Tancred in 1112, Antioch had been governed in the name of the infant Bohemond II by Tancred's nephew Roger, the son of Richard of Salerno. Roger was not like his father a "veteran" of the Holy Land. He had spent his childhood in Sicily and had come East at the request of Tancred's vassals. He was a young man of impetuous character, already famous for his courage in battle. He was called upon to face such formidable deployments of Turkish troops that he can hardly be accused of having adopted a policy of aggression, but he was a lover of war for its own sake. William of Tyre describes him as "extremely luxurious, no respecter of marriage, either his own or anyone else's; greedy and covetous more than befitted a man of his rank; but he was, beyond all possible doubt, a faithful and valiant knight."[5] Roger of Salerno was one of the most brilliant generals the Latin East ever knew; he defended the land of Antioch against Mawdud's armies and later against those of Bursuq, governor of Hamadan, with an energy which earned him the admiration and terror of the Moslems themselves; he fought with a Viking's ardor, a crusading fervor, and the joyous ferocity of a man who enjoys risking his life in the shedding of blood. A man like this had no need for the pretext of a holy war to make him fight, but among the Frankish princes he was the first to incarnate the "Crusading" spirit, the intoxication with the holy war which the great leaders of the First Crusade had never known.

After repelling the attacks of the Turks of Mosul and the atabeg of Hamadan and winning a signal victory over the army of Bursuq at Tel-Danith in September 1115, Roger had to all intents imposed his rule on the kingdom of Aleppo, which had been governed after Ridwan's death in 1113 by a mentally defective young prince and his tutor, an ambitious eunuch. He conquered the castles of Azaz and Biza'a and then Marqab in Lesser Armenia, and had every intention of continuing his conquests.

In 1119, his truce with the people of Aleppo having expired, he set about the conquest of Aleppo. So far he had done only too much to make the Moslems fear him. Even the victories he had won with his relatively feeble armies against the much more numerous troops of Bursuq had made his position more dangerous. Before the threat to Aleppo, one of the greatest cities of Moslem Syria, Ilghazi, Emir of Mardin, and Toghtekin, atabeg of Damascus (the former ally of Baldwin I who had quarreled with Baldwin II), gathered all their forces and marched hastily toward the city which seemed likely to fall victim to the boldness of the Franks. They summoned to their aid Tughan Arslan, Emir of Bitlis in Greater Armenia, and obtained an alliance with the Munqidhite emirs of Shaizar, the Arab neighbors of the principality of Antioch. This time, Roger of Salerno's rashness had roused a real coalition of Moslem forces against Antioch.

Roger appealed to King Baldwin II and to the Count of Tripoli, both of whom assembled their forces and hurried to the Prince of Antioch's assistance, but Roger did not have the patience to wait for them. With his entire army, his Frankish knights and foot soldiers, his Syrians and turcopoles, he went out to meet the great Turkish army. He carried with him into battle the great cross, studded with precious stones, which was venerated in the basilica of Antioch, and hoping to meet Ilghazi's army before the Emir of Mardin could join up with the atabeg of Damascus, he set up his tents at the entrance to a "narrow gorge between two mountains" (to use the words of Kemal ad-Din), halfway between Aleppo and Antioch, near a place called al-Balat.

Admittedly, it was not entirely of his own free will that Roger of Salerno had chosen the perilous honor of confronting the adversary alone. He had wanted to wait for the King's troops, but his own vassals in the region of Antioch begged him to take his army out of their lands, for fear of having them ravaged by the Turks. The Prince of Antioch had no alternative but to go to meet the enemy. The position he had chosen was a good one in case of a sudden attack, but dangerous if there was a long wait. After eight days, when the Frankish army was beginning to suffer from hunger and thirst, Ilghazi attacked with his forty thousand (?) Turkomans, without waiting for his allies—or for those of the Prince of Antioch.

Roger of Salerno had seven hundred knights and three thousand foot—these last mostly recruited from among the local population. After encircling the little Frankish army and cutting off every avenue of retreat, Ilghazi attacked. Roger and his men already knew that all was lost and that their only hope was now to "sell their lives dearly." The entire army was destroyed, and those who were not killed in the battle or slaughtered on the spot later had cause to envy their comrades' fate. Prince Roger was killed at the foot of the great cross, and the victors carried away as trophies his head, his armor, and the cross studded with precious stones. Roger of Salerno was the first Prince of Antioch to be killed in battle. He was not to be the last.

Of his army (according to Walter the Chancellor) only 140 men escaped by flight. Reynald Mazoir, the constable of Antioch, after driving off the Turkomans from the rear of the army, was surrounded in the tower of Sarmeda and put up such a fine show of resistance that Ilghazi spared his life. Some of the prisoners were slaughtered on the spot; others were taken to Aleppo, where they were led in triumph through the howling mob which had waited anxiously for the outcome of the battle and now was celebrating the great victory for Islam. Half the captives were lynched on the spot by the crowd on the day after the battle.

The Turkoman emir Ilghazi, a minor vassal of the Seljuks, had inflicted singlehanded on the Franks a defeat such as they had never known since they first settled in Syria. This was a great day for Syrian Islam, the greater because Roger of Salerno, the heir of Bohemond and Tancred, had an immense reputation. In his seven years' reign at Antioch, "Sirojal" (Sire Roger) had made his uncle's exploits pale beside his ferocity and brutality. To Latin chroniclers and to history as a whole, the field where the battle took place was known ever after as the "Field of Blood," *Ager Sanguinis.*

When the Caliph of Baghdad, al-Mustarshid, heard the great news, he bestowed on Ilghazi the title of "Star of Religion," *Najn al-Din,* and poets celebrated him in song. "The Koran rejoiced at the triumph you have won for it, and the Evangelist wept for the death of his children!"[6] Ilghazi's triumph might have had incalculable consequences if the Turkoman general had hurled his army on Antioch immediately after the battle, when it was empty of defenders and plunged into horror and mourning.

But he wasted time—getting drunk, as the Munqidhite emir Usama ibn Munqidh asserts. "Ilghazi contracted a fever from drinking fermented liquors which lasted twenty days. He drank after exterminating the Franks and suffered a violent attack of fever. By the time he was better, Baldwin the King had reached Antioch."[7] The Patriarch of Antioch, Bernard of Valence, had taken the government into his own hands, and his chief concern was to prevent the native population from rising in revolt. But the city was not surrounded and was able to open its gates to the King of Jerusalem. The day after the disaster, Baldwin II was welcomed as a savior by the few Franks who remained in the city. He could not fail to realize the extent of the catastrophe. The Norman chivalry, which had been the most bellicose and the most numerous in Frankish Syria, no longer existed. His own army and that of the Count of Tripoli together numbered 250 knights, for half his knights had remained behind to garrison Jerusalem and Judaea. With the men Joscelin, Count of Edessa, was able to bring and those still left in Antioch, the King collected seven hundred knights. Meanwhile, Ilghazi's troops were joined by the large army of the atabeg of Damascus who, having arrived too late for the first great battle, was determined not to lose the benefits of the second.

On the fourteenth of August, six weeks after the extermination of the Norman army, Baldwin II fought a decisive battle: decisive because if it was not a victory, since each side claimed to have defeated the other, neither was it a defeat for the Franks, who in spite of severe losses remained masters of the battlefield and did not withdraw until the next day, while the bulk of the Turkish army gave ground on the same day. The second battle of Tel-Danith, four years after the first (Roger of Salerno's great victory), saved Antioch and with it the whole of the north of Frankish Syria. It had taken all the Crusaders' desperate courage and the help of the True Cross which the Archbishop of Caesarea, Evremar (a former patriarch of Jerusalem), had borne aloft in the thick of the fight, brandishing it over the heads of the combatants to raise their courage.

It had taken the ardent prayers of the Patriarch, the bishops, the knights, and Baldwin himself, who before setting out had gone barefoot, clad in the robes of a penitent, around all the churches in Antioch. This was no longer a war of conquest but a struggle for survival. The men fought that day with the memory of the thousands of dead on the *Ager Sanguinis* fresh in their minds, haunted by the horrors of the massacre, the wailing of widows, and tolling bells and tocsins, prayers of supplication and cries of terror and revenge still ringing in their ears. Baldwin II succeeded in saving Antioch and some of the castles in the neighborhood. He stood firm in the face of armies superior in numbers to his own. If it was not a victory, it was at least a respite. The situation of Antioch and, by extension, that of Edessa were so dubious that there was reason to wonder if the Frankish states could continue their precarious existence for much longer. And in the direction of Jerusalem, the kingdom was at that time menaced simultaneously by Egypt and Damascus.

It was not Baldwin's fault that the kingdom at present included the atabeg of Damascus among its enemies. From the time of his accession, the King had attempted to renew the treaties of alliance, or at least the truce which Toghtekin had concluded with Baldwin I. The Turk, probably hoping that the new King would be less energetic than his predecessor, preferred to ally himself with the Fatimid heretics, who seemed to him less dangerous than his own overlord, the Sultan of Persia. This was a fairly bold change of alliance on the part of an orthodox Sunnite because the Fatimids were, if not more hated in Syria than the Franks, at least better known and judged with more passion. The former "free and loyal ally" of Baldwin I had become the champion of Islam against the Franks and, perhaps because he had been generally blamed for his tolerance toward the Christians, the fiercest enemy of his "allies" of yesterday.

The battle of the *Ager Sanguinis* had not been a bloodier affair than the massacres in Armenia or the extermination of the Crusading armies in Anatolia. On the military scale, it was a disaster for the Franks, but not an absolute disaster since in spite of everything their position improved again fairly quickly. It marks a turning point in relations between the Franks and Islam. Frankish history did not need this episode to make it a tragedy, and even the most frightful tragedies are quickly forgotten. The Franks, who for their part wanted nothing more than to cling to the Syrian soil where they had already taken root, preserved the memory of that day as a magnificent and terrible harvest of martyrs. The last thing they felt was surprise or indignation. Albert of Aix saw it as a just punishment for the dissolute life of Roger of Salerno, and all the chroniclers are unanimous in censuring the Prince of Antioch's rashness for insisting, despite the King's orders and the entreaties of the Patriarch, on facing the enemy alone. But ultimately, the rivers of blood shed had been to the glory of God. It is not the Franks but the Turks whose hatred of the infidel seems from that day on to have grown more bitter.

The Turkoman War

Ilghazi's Turkomans had acted on the field of battle according to their custom, just as their brothers in Anatolia had acted toward the Crusaders of 1101. They were still half-savage nomads and Ibn al-Athir's description of them is merciless: "Cupidity alone enrolled them under their banners. They came one by one, each with a bag containing flour and strips of dried sheep's flesh. Ilghazi was obliged to count the hours while the campaign lasted and turn back as soon as possible. Indeed, if the campaign was a long one, the Turkoman would disband his army because he had no more money to give them."⁸

These men, little admired by the Turks themselves, were far from ardent champions of Islam. They slaughtered the already defenseless enemy on the battlefield out of pure savagery and deliberate ignorance of the rules of war. One of their favorite amusements was to place jars of water before prisoners already half-mad with thirst and then kill any who came forward to drink. Some of the prisoners on the *Ager Sanguinis* perished in this way.

The prisoners who were taken to Aleppo became the objects of a veritable surge of popular hatred. It was not the Turkomans or even the Turks who were most violent against them, but the Arab citizens. All Islam still remembered the massacre at Jerusalem, and this was the first time that several hundred Frankish captives had been brought into a Moslem city. Aleppo had suffered for twenty years from the proximity of the Franks. The men who were dragged, chained, naked, and bleeding, through the city like trophies, with their horses and armor, the severed heads of their companions carried on spears, the cross and the vestments of their priests, and all the treasures of the camp of Antioch, men already reduced to the last extremities of wretchedness, were tortured to death with savage delight by a crowd which was at last learning the taste of Frankish blood.

Those who escaped this fate (for Ilghazi had kept back some of the captives with a view to ransom or exchange) survived until the day after the second battle of Tel-Danith, when the two allies Toghtekin and Ilghazi returned to Aleppo full of disappointment at their failure to crush Baldwin II's army (although according to Kemal ad-Din they presented the outcome of the battle to the people as a victory). The remaining Frankish captives were brought out of prison and put with those captured in the last battle. It was Toghtekin who gave orders for the execution of the Franks, or of all those Ilghazi would let him have. (Walter the Chancellor claims that the atabeg of Damascus went so far as to offer the Turkoman chief forty thousand gold bezants in exchange for all the Frankish prisoners.)

Usama, who as a very young man took part in this war as an ally of the Turks, describes the following scene:

Robert, lord of Sahiyun, had been made prisoner. Robert himself estimated his ransom at ten thousand pieces of gold. Ilghazi said, "Take him to the atabeg. Perhaps by frightening him he will manage to extract a larger sum from him." He was accordingly taken to where the atabeg was drinking in his tent. When the atabeg saw him coming he stood up, tucked the panels of his robe into his belt, and drawing his sword, went out to Robert and cut off his head. Ilghazi went to the atabeg and reproached him, saying, "We lack even one gold piece to pay the Turkomans and here was a prisoner offering us ten thousand gold pieces for his ransom. I sent him to you in order that you should frighten him into offering a larger sum, and you have killed him!" The atabeg answered, "For my part, I know of no better means of exciting terror!"[9]

Not only was Toghtekin personally acquainted with Sahiyun; they were, according to Usama, "old friends."

This was the beginning of a deliberate policy of intimidating and terrorizing the Franks on the part of Toghtekin. Possibly equally deliberate was his policy of stirring up the Moslem crowds to frenzy by the sight of blood. The two Turkish chiefs vied with one another in cruelty. Ilghazi clearly insisted on sparing only wealthy prisoners. The blood of Franks who had been mutilated, beheaded, tied to stakes, and used as targets by the archers taught the people of Aleppo the meaning of hatred more surely than all the rapine, pillage, and murder committed by the Franks on their own lands. The cadi of Damascus, to whom Ilghazi offered the honor of personally beheading a noble prisoner, declined to do it and preferred to yield the honor to a soldier. Sixty years later, holy men "devoted to prayer and meditation" were piously soliciting the favor of beheading prisoners.

For the Turks it was not yet a question of a real counter-Crusade, in the sense of a phenomenon comparable to the Crusade itself—that is to say, of a war provoked by motives of a religious nature. The atabeg of Damascus was quite as interested in securing control of Aleppo as he was in fighting the Franks, and this was also Ilghazi's secret wish. The kingdom of Aleppo, which already in Ridwan's lifetime had been reduced to the level of a Frankish protectorate, was now in a state of complete anarchy as a result of the incompetence of the Seljuk's successors. After the tragic death of Ridwan's son, the young halfwit Alp Arslan, who was assassinated by his tutor, the eunuch Lulu, and after Lulu's own assassination, another eunuch, the renegade Armenian Yaruqtash, seized power, and Aleppo placed itself under the protection of the Franks of Antioch for fear of being annexed by Toghtekin or by the Sultan of Persia. In these circumstances, to attack Aleppo had been the most monumental idiocy on the part of Roger of Salerno.

Now installed as liberators in the great city, the atabeg of Damascus and the Emir of Mardin felt themselves masters of it and were looking forward to extending their conquests still further at the expense of the Franks. Ilghazi, as the leader of a band of nomads quite indifferent to the interests of religion, roamed the country with his army which, forever on the point of disbanding, gave itself up to plundering, burning, devastating the land, massacring such peasants as fell into its hands, "burning and roasting infants with unprecedented barbarism," in the words of Matthew of Edessa. For more than a year he terrorized the region between Edessa and Antioch. As master of Aleppo after the departure of his ally Toghtekin, Ilghazi was determined to exploit the prestige he had won by his victory to aggrandize his new kingdom.

Ilghazi had been officially awarded the title of Star of Religion, but in actual fact what he was fighting for was possession of Aleppo. To all appearances nothing had altered; the Franks attacked on one side and the Turks on the other. The war went on in the same way. There were raids, castles captured and recaptured, burning countryside, pillage, and the capture of prisoners. In the end the Franks had the upper hand, because Ilghazi never possessed regular troops; his Turkomans were not used to living long away from their families, and as soon as they decided they had collected enough booty they would go home again. The Franks, however, stayed where they were, and because they were defending their own property they were much more tenacious and much better organized. In 1121, Ilghazi's son, who had been made governor of Aleppo, concluded a peace treaty with the Franks according to the terms of which the Franks retained all that they had possessed before their defeat.

Ilghazi's position was not such a strong one as it might appear. His own son took no time in revolting against him, and at the same time he himself was defeated by the Georgian King David II in the north, near Tiflis. Out of hatred for his father, the rebel son, Suleiman, was ready to conclude a real treaty of alliance with the Franks. The old Turkoman chief finally died in 1122, three years after his victory of the *Ager Sanguinis*. His sons divided his domains of Diarbekir between them and his nephew Suleiman inherited Aleppo. Despite the annexation of Aleppo, the division of Ilghazi's inheritance made the Ortoqids of Diarbekir actually less dangerous than they had been before 1119.

The King in Captivity

Even so, the situation of the Frankish kingdom was far from hopeful. After the annihilation of the Norman chivalry of Antioch and the death of Prince Roger, Baldwin II had more or less redistributed the fiefs of castellans who had been killed, found new husbands for their widows, and seen to the defense of their castles by taking what soldiers he could spare from his already inadequate army in Judaea. He was already King of Jerusalem and regent of Antioch. In 1122, when his cousin Joscelin of Courtenay was taken prisoner by Ilghazi's nephew the emir Balak, lord of Kharpurt, he also became regent of the county of Edessa. The King, who was continually being forced by the successive misfortunes of the counts of Syria to play the part of providential savior, faced up to his responsibilities and even succeeded in recapturing the key fortress of Athareb from the Aleppans. Unfortunately, he set out on an expedition to rescue Joscelin, Count of Edessa, from captivity and was himself taken prisoner by Balak. In 1123, three of the Frankish states of Syria— the kingdom, the principality of Antioch, and the county of Edessa —found themselves simultaneously without a master, and Baldwin went to join his cousin in the dungeons of the castle of Kharpurt.

Having captured the two Frankish princes, Balak marched on Aleppo, seized it from his cousin Suleiman despite frenzied resistance by the populace, and then, like his uncle Ilghazi four years earlier, set out to invade the principality of Antioch. But in spite of enormous loss in terms of human life, four years spent in a constant state of alertness appear to have done much to stiffen Frankish morale. Faced with this crisis, they displayed a remarkable spirit of cooperation and even a sense of discipline that was in itself exceptional in feudal society. The constable of Jerusalem, Eustace Garnier, was appointed to govern the provinces in the King's absence, and during the two years of the King's captivity the Franks succeeded not only in beating off Balak's attacks on Antioch and driving back the Egyptian army's assaults on Jaffa and Jerusalem, but (with the help of Venetian fleets who played a decisive part in the affair) in undertaking and carrying to a successful conclusion the siege of Tyre, which was the last great Moslem port on the coast with the exception of Ascalon.

It would be impracticable here to describe in detail all the events of Baldwin II's reign and those of his successors. They constituted an almost uninterrupted and in itself monotonous series of campaigns, sieges, and battles; a *chanson de geste* lasting for many years, a day-to-day account of which would take up thousands of pages and any account, however abbreviated, overwhelm the patient reader with endless repetition of place names (often the same) and the names of men, many of them also the same, or coming and going so fast that any attempt to keep track of them is doomed to failure. Even an analysis of the situation in its broad outline is almost inextricable in its complexity. Any such analysis can be little more than an attempt to highlight, with the aid of the most significant facts, the principal human aspects of the situation. Given a basic knowledge of conditions of warfare in those days, all battles with a few variations become very much alike and the same applies to sieges, skirmishes, and even massacres. The endless catalogue of their exploits makes all the men seem like pawns in a curious game of chess, played with no rules and no object, or following some almost indecipherable plan in which a great deal is left to chance.

As we have seen, Ilghazi, the Ortoqid emir whose forceful intervention in Syrian affairs earned the gratitude of all Moslems, had extended his dominion over Aleppo only to disappear from the scene almost at once. His nephew Balak, lord of Kharpurt and later governor of Aleppo, was a great general who in his turn was beginning to build up a powerful Turkoman kingdom at the expense of his cousins and later of the Franks, when he died in 1124, killed by an arrow fired by a rebellious vassal. He is reported to have exclaimed as he pulled the arrow from the wound, "This is a mortal blow to all Moslems!"[10] But this was still no more than the cry of an ambitious chieftain for whom the holy war was an excuse to extend his own domains. Balak had spent much more of his time fighting his own cousins than he had against the Franks, and it was not a Frank who killed him. Nevertheless, galvanized by the peril in which they found themselves owing to the absence of their proper leaders, the Franks at that time were becoming an increasingly real power.

When Jaffa was besieged by the fleet from Cairo, the entire population, the local Christians and even women included, defended themselves so fiercely that in spite of an inadequate garrison the attack was beaten off. When, as a diversion from the siege of Tyre, the Egyptian army from Ascalon marched on Jerusalem, which had been left undefended, the citizens of the Holy City armed themselves with improvised weapons and went out to meet the enemy. Since they had not come in force, the Egyptians prudently withdrew.

In the assembled Frankish forces of Jerusalem and Tripoli, Count Pons of Tripoli, who had once attempted to refuse homage to Baldwin II, served willingly under the orders of the Patriarch of Jerusalem "as though he were the least of his soldiers." When, after the Venetian naval victory over the Egyptian fleet, the question arose of laying siege to one of the two great Moslem cities on the coast, Tyre or Ascalon, and a difference of opinion arose among the various barons of the country (those from Judaea favoring Ascalon and those from Galilee saying Tyre), it was decided to draw lots rather than prolong the dispute. The names of the two cities were written on slips of paper and a child was given the task of choosing one of the two pieces. In this way the siege of Tyre was decided, and this peaceful and innocent ceremony was enough to restore accord among the barons.

Tyre, a formidable fortress situated like Tripoli at the end of a narrow peninsula, was captured after a long and difficult siege. The Egyptian fleet, which had just suffered a crushing defeat by the Venetians off Ascalon, was helpless to intervene. Toghtekin, the governor of Damascus, did not possess enough forces to dislodge the Franks by himself, and since he was not on good terms with the Fatimids they did not send him an army. Balak was killed just as he was preparing to fly to the assistance of the great Phoenician port. Reduced to starvation, Tyre capitulated on July 7, 1124, and the new constable, William of Bures (Eustace Garnier having died in 1123), planted the King of Jerusalem's banners on the towers of the citadel. Tyre was occupied in the name of the captive King, Baldwin II, with the agreement of the Count of Tripoli and the Venetians.

All historians, Moslem as well as Latin, agree in acknowledging that the surrender was conducted in an orderly manner and that there was no plundering or violence, in spite of a mutiny among the foot soldiers of the army, who were angry at being cheated of their spoils. "There was," writes William of Tyre, "a great quarrel between rich and poor." The surrender had been negotiated with Toghtekin, whose garrison had been sent from Damascus to defend the city—the very man who, five years earlier, had slaughtered his Frankish prisoners without mercy. In a quarter of a century the Franks had learned to behave with caution, even after a victory, and at the capitulation of Tyre there was, if not fraternization, at least a peaceful meeting between the former adversaries. The defenders of Tyre were curious to see the "Christians" at close quarters, and they walked about their camp examining their arms and equipment with interest. When the Frankish soldiers entered the city they were amazed to learn that there were no more reserves of food in the stores, and "much praised the besieged for having held out so long under such conditions."[11]

When Baldwin II was released in August 1124, just after one of the greatest Frankish successes since the capture of Jerusalem, he was able to see that his kingdom was already so firmly established that not even the King's absence could seriously upset it. Baldwin obtained his liberty from Balak's successor, Timurtash ibn Ilghazi—a peace-loving prince who preferred a good ransom to the advantage of leaving the Franks without their leader. Baldwin promised eighty thousand dinars (twenty thousand to be paid in advance) as well as ceding a large portion of the principality of Antioch on the right bank of the river Orontes, and pledged his assistance in the war which the present master of Aleppo was waging against the Bedouin chief Dubais.

He was no sooner free than he promptly broke his promise, in spite of the fact that he had left behind him as hostages his youngest daughter Joveta, aged five, and a number of young nobles, including Joscelin of Courtenay's son. He was quite willing to pay his ransom, but not to hand over territories which, he argued, did not even belong to him, since he was merely the regent in the name of Bohemond's son, Prince Bohemond II (who was still only fifteen years old and living in Italy). "The Patriarch [of Antioch]," Baldwin wrote to Timurtash, "whom we cannot disobey, wished to know the nature of our concessions. . . . When he learned that I was to yield up Azaz, Athareb, Zerdana, the Jasr, and Kafartab, he flatly refused to agree and commanded me to repudiate this clause, adding that he would take the blame for violating the oath upon himself. I cannot go against his wishes." Timurtash cannot have altogether appreciated these pious scruples. As for the hostages, he apparently put to death one of Joscelin of Courtenay's nephews, and William of Tyre's continuater claims that little Joveta was raped by the Saracens while in captivity. (There is no other evidence for this, but if unfounded, it would be a curious story to circulate concerning a venerable abbess who died in an odor of sanctity.) Baldwin II was too much a statesman to hesitate between his daughter and the interests of his kingdom.

He did, however, commit a more serious error—the same as that which had led to the death of Roger of Salerno. Not only did he fail to support the atabeg against Dubais, he actually did completely the reverse and concluded an alliance with Dubais with the object of conquering Aleppo, being well aware that Timurtash was too lazy to be able to defend his city.

The Frankish King was now thoroughly committed to the game of alliances with a view to conquest which had been the policy of the Moslem princes in Syria for the past thirty years. Taking the young Sultanshah, the son of Ridwan with whom he had a kind of agreement, to some extent under his protection, he became the champion of Seljuk legitimacy against the Turkoman usurper. With the troops of the Bedouin Dubais—a formidable adventurer who was sweeping through the whole of the Near East with his army of nomads, spreading terror as far as the province of Baghdad—as well as those of the Seljuk Sultanshah and a cousin of Timurtash, he surrounded the city of Aleppo and subjected it to such a rigorous siege that the people in the city were reduced to eating dogs and dead bodies.[12] But although Dubais and Sultanshah might play this game with impunity, since they had nothing to lose, matters were rather different for Baldwin.

The Atabegs of Mosul

Abandoned by the feeble Timurtash, who had deserted his city and taken refuge at Diarbekir, the people of Aleppo appealed in desperation to the man from whom they would until then have made any sacrifices to avoid accepting help: the atabeg of Mosul.

The man who was occupying this important position at the time was a great Turkish captain named Aqsonqor il-Bursuqi. He had been appointed atabeg of Mosul by the Sultan Mohammed, but had already held the post before 1114. At that time, his failure in an expedition against the Franks had led to his disgrace. Il-Bursuqi immediately assembled his army in response to the appeal of the chief citizens of Aleppo. (He was so delighted when he heard of this unexpected opportunity to make himself master of Aleppo that he recovered instantly from an illness which had kept him to his bed.) The Franco-Bedouin army melted away before him, and he entered Aleppo, where he was welcomed with open arms, and installed himself as ruler. Baldwin II had lightheartedly taken the initiative in an action whose effect was to place Aleppo under the direct control of the atabegs of Mosul—one of the chief military powers of Islam, and regularly appointed officers, if not always very docile ones, of the sultans of Persia.

It is true that the Frankish chivalry, whose spirit of cohesion was at the time not the least of its virtues, succeeded in triumphantly repulsing the combined forces of il-Bursuqi and Toghtekin (Azaz, June 13, 1125; Saqhab, January 25, 1126), but, all things considered, the kingdom owed its safety at that moment, or at least a precious respite, to il-Bursuqi's death at the hands of an Assassin on November 26, 1126.

The atabegs of Mosul had already laid claim to Aleppo, and the most irreconcilably hostile Turkish power to the Franks was now consolidated in no uncertain fashion. It should not be forgotten that the atabegs of Mosul, as governors appointed by the Sultan and officially dependent on the caliphate of Baghdad, were morally in a much better position to wage a holy war than were the emirs and kings of Syria, and this remained true even when they were working toward the aggrandizement of their own empire.

Il-Bursuqi was succeeded in Mosul, after the brief reign of the mameluke Jawali, by a man still young but already renowned for his indomitable energy. This was Imad ed-Din Zengi, the son of Aqsonqor, one of the chief lieutenants of the Seljuk conqueror Malik Shah. Zengi belonged to the Turkish military aristocracy, which in the time of Malik Shah had imposed its dominion nearly everywhere in the Moslem East. Aqsonqor (the name means "White Falcon") had been nominated governor of Aleppo by the great Seljuk in 1094 while Zengi was still a child. Tutush, Malik Shah's brother, had killed Aqsonqor and taken possession of Aleppo. Zengi had taken refuge in Mosul, where he served under the atabegs of that city. In 1113, during one of Mawdud's wars against the Franks, young Zengi had particularly distinguished himself. According to Ibn al-Athir, finding himself before Tiberias "at the head of only a few men and seeing the Franks make a sortie, he charged them, thinking that his companions were following. . . . The Franks hastily retreated into the city and Zengi, who had advanced as far as the gates, beat on them with his lance so that he left a mark there. He remained there, fighting the enemy and hoping that his companions would come to his aid and take the city. When he saw no one coming, he fell back with resignation."[13]

Zengi's courage and loyalty to the Sultan earned him the appointment of governor of Basra. In 1126, when the Caliph al-Mustarshid rebelled against the Sultan, he defeated the Caliph's army at Wasit and for this he was rewarded with the appointment as high commissioner for Iraq (governor of Baghdad under the Sultan's orders). After the murder of il-Bursuqi, the Sultan Mahmud, wishing to ensure a strong government at Mosul and at the same time remove an overambitious military leader from Baghdad, made Zengi atabeg of Mosul, with orders to carry the holy war into Syria and drive out the Franks.

Zengi (called by the Franks, with a play on his name which may not have been altogether an accident, "Sanguins") was neither a fanatic of the *jihad* nor a docile plenipotentiary of the Sultan. He was working for himself. He was the toughest, boldest, most fearless, and most unscrupulous of all the Turkish conquerors, and he possessed two great assets, his mission to wage the holy war and his ability to carry out the Sultan's wishes, which he used with consummate skill. As the champion of Islam he earned a legitimate popularity with the people, and as the Sultan's plenipotentiary he covered his aggressions against the Moslem princes with a semblance of legality.

His aim was to found a vast kingdom stretching from Mosul as far as Armenia in the north and Egypt in the south, a kingdom which would include Syria, Palestine, Damascus, and Aleppo. Great soldier as he was, he was a victim to the lust for power, incapable of retreat in the face of any opposition and as harsh, if not harsher, toward his rival Moslems as toward the Christians.

When he was appointed atabeg of Mosul he hastened to take possession of Aleppo (of which his father had been governor thirty-four years earlier). The population welcomed him "with such an outburst of joy and gladness that God alone could measure its extent."[14] Next, strong in his role as a champion of the holy war, he made an alliance with the atabeg of Damascus, Buri, the son of Toghtekin. He promptly took advantage of this alliance to treacherously deprive Buri's son of his city of Hama, and then, after seizing his province, to imprison and torture Khirkhan, the Emir of Homs, luring him into an ambush undeterred by the fact that he had just concluded an alliance with this very Khirkhan "against the Franks."

From the moment he appeared in Syria, Zengi became the terror of the Moslem princes. He was sufficiently aware of his strength to risk imposing his rule by terror. Timurtash, the Emir of Mardin, formed a league with his cousins to escape Zengi's dominion but was defeated, and Zengi became master of these provinces which belonged rightfully to the Ortoqid emirs. As master of Mosul, Aleppo, and all the land north of the Euphrates valley, Zengi's principal rivals were now the Franks and the atabegs of Damascus (as well as the Armenian princes of Cilicia to the east and the Arab emirs of Shaizar and Homs). All of these, with the exception of the Franks and the Armenians, could be lured by threats or persuasion into entering into an alliance which would amount in practice to a vassal state.

Baldwin II's fatal mistake, as we have seen, had been in his first expedition against Aleppo at a time when this city was already weakened and would gladly have accepted a Frankish alliance. Driven to extremities, Aleppo had given itself up to the atabeg of Mosul and no longer possessed a prince of sufficient energy to win back its independence.

Not content with installing a powerful rival in Aleppo, at the gates of Antioch and Edessa, Baldwin II was now considering nothing less than the conquest of Damascus. The death of his old enemy Toghtekin made him think that this, the first city in Syria, was now wide open to attack. He made an alliance with the Ismailians, who were extremely powerful in the province of Damascus and openly favored by the Vizier, and negotiated with Abu'l Wefa, chief of the Ismailians, and with the Vizier of Damascus for delivery of the city by treachery —in exchange for a promise to hand over Tyre to the Moslems. The plot was discovered and the Ismailians, of whom there were a great many in Damascus, were lynched by the inhabitants, who remained faithful to the Sunnite tradition. Damascus was saved.

Baldwin did not give up. He sent to the Grand Master of the Knights Templar (an order of which more will be said later) in Europe, asking for reinforcements, and in 1129 he marched on Damascus. His army was very weak and the city very large. The attempt failed and the army withdrew with considerable losses. Indeed, the only person to have benefitted from Baldwin's plan had been Zengi, since Buri's son still preferred to come to at least a temporary agreement with the atabeg of Mosul rather than see his province overrun by the Franks.

Fulk of Anjou

While Moslem Syria was succumbing to the threat of a Turkish domination harsher even than that of the first Seljuks had been, the King of Jerusalem, who was having trouble enough maintaining himself in the lands he already possessed, was contemplating an invasion of the chief Moslem kingdom of Syria. Such political irresponsibility on the part of a man who, as king and suzerain of the Frankish provinces in the East, showed great deliberation and good sense seems somewhat surprising. From a military point of view, the occupation of Aleppo and Damascus, cities with a strong Moslem majority in the population, would have demanded of the Frankish kingdom an effort it could not possibly have sustained; and even with armies ten times the size, holding all the territory on the other side of the Jordan and the Orontes, which were constantly exposed to Turkish attacks and where the local population was hostile, would have been an undertaking doomed to rapid failure. The conquest of the kingdom of Aleppo, which was too close a neighbor of Antioch and Edessa for comfort, might have been justified from the angle of defensive strategy. Moreover, as we have seen, Baldwin had only undertaken the siege of Aleppo under cover of an alliance with Moslem princes and with the avowed intention, at least, of restoring a son of Ridwan to the throne of Aleppo. This might have been a sound calculation had thirty years of incessant war not made the people of Aleppo, of all Moslems, those who most hated the Franks.

As far as the move against Damascus was concerned, it is possible that Baldwin was not entirely responsible. His first expedition against Damascus—in 1126—was less a straightforward attempt at conquest than an episode in his long struggle against Toghtekin. After his victory at Tel es-Saqhab, the King failed to march on Damascus, but this was the first time the Frankish armies had penetrated into the huge fertile plain of Damascus, and this gave them plenty to excite their greed. It is a fact that after his captivity the King of Jerusalem became more powerful than ever before, thanks to the great victory represented by the capture of Tyre, and had reason to feel proud of his kingdom. The whole of the coast was now in his possession and he had kept it intact, and even enlarged the province of Antioch, which had suffered so severely before it was entrusted to his regency. His chief vassals, the Count of Tripoli and the Count of Edessa, were loyal to him and ready to back him up on all occasions. Finally in 1126, Bohemond II, the son of Bohemond, the minor in whose name Antioch had been governed for fourteen years, arrived in Syria to take possession of his lands. The moment he landed, Baldwin II married him off to his second daughter, Alice, and he had every reason to hope that his son-in-law would also prove a loyal and courageous vassal.

At this time, Baldwin II was already a man of sixty, worn out by thirty years of constant warfare (indeed, the only time he stopped fighting was during his two sojourns in Turkish prisons, amounting to six years in all), and he was beginning to look for a successor. He was a man of unusual vigor, and possessed the strength of mind of a soldier who has grown old in arms, indifferent to danger, as hard on himself as he was on others, shouldering the most fearful responsibilities with cool courage. He had seen so much that it seemed as though nothing more could shake him or take him unawares. As a king, he had to consider the welfare of his kingdom.

Baldwin had no sons, but he had four daughters: Melisende, Alice, Hodierna, and Joveta, the last two still children. He was naturally anxious to ensure his succession according to feudal custom in France, and his eldest daughter was the heir to the throne. For this reason, he had given his second daughter in marriage to the Prince of Antioch, since he had no desire to make Bohemond II King of Jerusalem. The eldest had to have a husband who possessed all the qualities and prestige necessary for such a high destiny. To this end, in 1128 Baldwin sent his constable, William of Bures, to the court of the King of France (Louis VI, the Fat), beseeching the King, in the interests of the kingdom of Jerusalem, to choose from among his barons the man in all points most worthy to undertake the government of the Holy Land.

By this step Baldwin, if he did not actually make submission to the house of Capet, at least placed himself under its moral guardianship. According to feudal custom, it was the king's privilege to choose a husband for the heiress to an important fief, and although the King of Jerusalem was not the vassal of the King of France, Baldwin meant to remind Louis VI that Palestine was, to some extent, French territory. Louis VI chose a husband as requested and he chose well: he advised Baldwin II to offer his daughter and his crown to Fulk V, Count of Anjou.

Fulk was a very great baron, as powerful as the King of France himself. He was lord of Anjou and Maine and had recently married his son, Geoffrey Plantagenet, to the heiress of England. Moreover, he was already acquainted with the Holy Land, having been there on a military pilgrimage in 1120. He was a formidable warrior, a stern and able administrator who had broken the resistance of his principal vassals on his own domains and paralyzed all attempts at emancipation by the townspeople. Forty years old, a seasoned soldier, and experienced in peacetime administration, Fulk V was precisely the successor Baldwin needed, quite apart from the fact that his fortune and nobility would unite Baldwin's somewhat haphazard dynasty to a family related to the most aristocratic houses of France.

A short, fat, coarse, red-haired man of forty was not the ideal suitor for the young and lovely Melisende, but she was sacrificed to political necessity. The nuptials were celebrated with great rejoicing on June 2, 1129. It was a marriage which did honor to both father and son-in-law. The title of King of Jerusalem was a not unfitting crown to the career of such a man as Fulk of Anjou, and the Count of Anjou was a great enough lord in his own right to show his father-in-law an almost filial deference. He never made the aging King feel that he was in undue haste to take his place.

All the same, the great warrior who, in his lands in France and Normandy, had successively confronted the kings of France and England, and had fought at the side of Louis VI against the Emperor of Germany, seemed unlikely to want to spend the rest of his days in petty local skirmishes, and the initiative for the campaign against Damascus probably came from him rather than from Baldwin. Fulk too was anxious to conquer a great Moslem city for the benefit of Christendom. Baldwin, with his natural love of adventure, had only been constrained to relative caution by extreme danger, and he considered the attempt worth risking. Toghtekin had died in 1128 and Damascus was suffering from religious upheavals that almost amounted to civil war. If Fulk's influence may possibly have predominated in the decision, it can be said that he, as a stranger to the country, had more excuse than the King of Jerusalem.

The attempt failed miserably, as we have seen. Fulk realized that he was to be king of a country which only existed by means of its army, an army numerically too weak even for a country which enjoyed peace on all its frontiers.

Young Bohemond

The son of Bohemond of Taranto and Constance of France inherited the principality of Antioch from his father, or more accurately, from Tancred, who had named him as his successor on his deathbed. With what impetuosity Roger of Salerno had defended, enlarged, and then almost ruined this inheritance has already been seen. At the cost of considerable labor, Baldwin II straightened out the affairs of the province, doing more fighting on behalf of Antioch than he did for his own kingdom, and he was anxious to see the heir of the great fief come to take possession of his own at last.

Bohemond II himself was certainly impatient to leave his home in Sicily and take up his paternal inheritance. In Europe, and especially in Italy, the name of Bohemond was still haloed in glory, and the child who could scarcely remember his father must have been brought up on the memory of the exploits of the great leader of the First Crusade. But he would have lost nothing by waiting a few more years before taking up the task of ruling a province like the principality of Antioch. Indeed, when he landed in Syria in 1126 he was still little more than a child, not quite eighteen years old. Trained in all the exercises of the profession of arms and physically tall and strong, he does not seem to have lacked spirit, and he succeeded in creating a reasonably good impression. It has been often said that men matured early in those days and boys of fifteen often behaved like adults, but this does not seem to have been the case with young Bohemond.

The chroniclers on the whole deal kindly with him. They describe him as possessing great charm, the charm of extreme youth, joined to a natural grace of manners and a gift of eloquence. Matthew of Edessa (who did not like him) admits that "his personality was irresistible." The facts indicate that the boy's character was somewhat unfortunate: he was domineering, conceited, and insolent, as touchy as a young fighting cock and given to tantrums like a spoiled child. We know that—for all his irresistible charm—he did not succeed in winning the love of his young bride, Alice of Jerusalem. No sooner was he master of Antioch than he managed to quarrel bitterly with his neighbor and ally Joscelin of Courtenay, Count of Edessa, and the quarrel reached such proportions that Joscelin appealed to the Turks for aid and invaded the lands of Antioch, pillaging towns and burning the harvests. (Michael the Syrian somewhat vaguely explains this quarrel by saying that "Bohemond appeared vain and proud and desired to dominate all the Franks," the implication being that he had asked old Joscelin to swear an oath of fealty. The great soldier, hero of so many battles and one of the premier barons of Frankish Syria, must have been irritated beyond measure by the young man's arrogance to have been provoked into such acts of hostility.) It took the intervention of the aged and venerable Bernard of Valence, Patriarch of Antioch, and of King Baldwin II and a serious illness on the part of Joscelin himself to put an end to the war between the two Frankish princes.

Bohemond II, who had already had his first taste of warfare in Italy, rushed into battle against the Saracens with a childish unawareness and the wild courage of an overgrown schoolboy to whom war was still a lovely game. He began his reign in Antioch by recapturing the castle of Kafartab (which the atabeg of Mosul had taken from the Franks two years earlier) from il-Bursuqi's troops. "He found there," says William of Tyre, "rich and noble prisoners who were willing to give a great deal of gold and silver to save their lives, but he [Bohemond] would take none of it and had them all beheaded, saying that this was the fashion in which he meant to wage war on the Turks."[15]

All "Saracens" were grist to his mill, Arabs and Turks alike, and he would dash in wherever there was a chance of a fight. Usama describes his attack on the emirate of Shaizar, when he set up his tents right outside the city of Shaizar itself and challenged every Arab horseman he encountered. During one of these skirmishes, the young Munqidhite emir happened to come up against Bohemond, and he describes the battle on the river bank for us with his usual vivacity. Bohemond, "a knight no more than a youth," charged straight for a group of Arab horsemen without waiting for his companions, and then retired after having his horse killed under him. It is Usama again who reports the Prince of Antioch's words to his knights: "A single Moslem horseman can beat off two Franks. You are not men, you are women!"[16] If a Moslem prince could overhear such a speech, then there are grounds for believing that the knights of Antioch were often treated to similar or worse, and they were certainly not men who lacked either courage or military experience.

In 1129 the Armenian principality of Cilicia, which was governed by the Roupenian dynasty, found itself dangerously weakened by the death of its Prince, Thoros I. After a plot in which Thoros's son was done to death, the crown went to Thoros's brother, Leo I, who was having a good deal of trouble in establishing his authority and was in no condition to defend his frontiers. Bohemond II was quick to profit from this state of affairs. In February 1130, he invaded Cilician territory and tried to take the Armenian city of Anazarbus, which he knew to be without defenders. But Leo's neighbor to the north, the Danishmend Ghazi, had had the same idea and he too was descending on Anazarbus with a fairly considerable army. Bohemond had taken with him only a handful of men. Michael the Syrian states that "the Franks knew nothing of the presence of the Turks nor the Turks of the Franks, but both Franks and Turks had a grudge against the Armenians."

Somewhat surprised at finding themselves face to face, the Franks and the Turks engaged in battle and the Franks, with their small numbers, were surrounded on a hill and massacred. The few who escaped the Turks were finished off by Leo I's soldiers. Bohemond II had ruled the principality of Antioch for three years and five months.

Michael the Syrian says also that "when the Turks brought Bohemond's head to the emir Ghazi, he had it embalmed and sent it with divers presents of weapons and horses to the Caliph of Baghdad."[17] Once severed, the handsome blond head was worthless. Ghazi was later to regret bitterly that he had not captured the Prince of Antioch alive. Even his horsemen were sorry for it, but it had never occurred to them that the Frankish ruler of Antioch might venture so far away from his own province with so small a company and he had been killed by mistake.

It is hard to say whether the sudden death of the boy soldier was really a misfortune for Frankish Syria. As we have seen, Roger of Salerno, with more experience and military talent than Bohemond, had already brought an unprecedented catastrophe upon the principality of Antioch. The Prince's youth still gave every reason for hope, and his death plunged the Franks of Antioch into consternation. They found themselves leaderless once more—and once more had no alternative but to appeal to King Baldwin II, asking for aid and advice. The old King, who had thought for some time that he was rid of the problem of Antioch, gathered his knights together and once more took the road to the north.

Princess Alice

Baldwin II was now doubly responsible for the fate of the principality: as suzerain and former regent, and as the father-in-law of the late Prince and grandfather of the heir of Antioch. Young Bohemond had had a daughter by his marriage to Alice of Jerusalem, Constance, who was about two years old at the time of her father's death. It was natural for the child's maternal grandfather to assume the regency in her name, but the right of regency also belonged, by custom, to the heiress's mother.

Historians are silent on the subject of Alice's relations with her young husband, although they do say that Bohemond II's private life was irreproachable, which suggests that he must have been a faithful husband. But the facts demonstrate that he must have inspired in the young princess he had been given in matrimony feelings very close to hatred. At all events, Princess Alice no sooner learned that she was a widow than she leaped at the chance to seize power, wasting no time in tears.

She wanted to keep Antioch for herself alone. But however strong her rights, she could only be regent in her daughter's name and share the power with her father the King and a council of barons. To avoid this, Alice hastily sent a secret message to Zengi, who, in his capacity as governor of Mosul and Aleppo, was at the time in the latter city and thus only about sixty miles from Antioch. Alice offered him an alliance if he would help her make herself sole mistress of Antioch. (William of Tyre says: "She sent a messenger with a very fine palfrey whiter than snow, shod with silver; the reins and harness were finely wrought and the saddle richly covered with white silk."[18]) Zengi was not a man to allow himself to be swayed by courtesies of this kind and he would probably have laid hands on Antioch without a thought for the young woman's rights. It is hard to see how Alice thought she could come to an agreement with him. Zengi never received her message; the messenger was arrested and taken to Baldwin II. The King, who was just about to set out for Antioch with half his knights, hanged the messenger and continued his journey.

The Princess refused to allow him to enter the city.

The young woman's rebellion was swiftly quelled. Most of the Frankish knights declared against her, and they represented the armed forces. They opened the gates to the King and his son-in-law, Fulk of Anjou, and the Count of Edessa. Alice and her supporters hastily took refuge in one of the towers of the citadel, and then, seeing that the game was up, she finally surrendered and threw herself at her father's feet. Baldwin II forgave her, but the culprit was sent to live in more or less enforced retirement in the city of Lattakieh, which had been part of her dowry.

It is curious to imagine how a young woman of twenty, simply because she wanted to rule a state over which she had in any case some official rights, had been able to embark on such an extraordinary escapade. But the mere fact that she could bring herself to do it seems to show that her design was not actually as strange as it might appear. What Alice was trying to do was essentially to revive the old Armeno-Syrian policy of thirty years back, calling in the Turks against the Franks, the Greeks against the Turks, and the Franks against the Greeks or the Turks, all with the object of maintaining, with the help of first one and then another, a precarious independence which had to be constantly purchased at a cost of blood and money. Alice may well have been a monster of ambition, but she was not mad; she knew the uselessness of appealing to the governor of Mosul without possessing firm backing and even a great many supporters liable to prefer the Turkish to the Frankish yoke. This revolt on the part of one so young and apparently so sheltered from the miseries of life must have been the result of fierce hatred and long-concealed bitterness.

Historians do not tell us much about Queen Morphia, the daughter of Gabriel of Melitene; they are content to state that she was a good wife to Baldwin II. She was an Armenian, brought up in Greco-

Armenian surroundings (Gabriel belonged to the Orthodox Church) and probably accustomed to the retired life of Oriental women, who were relegated to the women's quarters and spent their time in prayer and in feminine employments. We know that her daughters were brought up in the Frankish manner, which is to say that they enjoyed greater freedom than was allowed by Eastern etiquette. But given the continual absence of their father, their mother's influence over the princesses' education must have been paramount, and with Armenian as their mother tongue, the girls were undoubtedly more Armenian than Frank. Moreover they were—like most Frankish ladies— surrounded by Armenian nurses and maids and a whole household of Eastern servants, who were perhaps closer to them in spirit than the Frankish nobility. At the time when Baldwin II was still Count of Edessa, they had relatives in the country, and must have gone with their mother to the services of the Armenian Orthodox Church and certainly been acquainted with the local clergy.

The princesses' father, Baldwin of Le Bourg, had already robbed the Armenian nobles in his county of everything he could. In this he was following the example of his cousin Baldwin I, who had established himself in Edessa by treachery and violence. Baldwin and the other Franks had been indirectly responsible for the fearful massacre of the Armenians by the Euphrates. In 1111 and in 1113, learning of plots against him in the city, Baldwin of Le Bourg had had a great many Armenians, rich and poor, tortured, mutilated, and expelled from the city and had even contemplated putting out the eyes of their bishop. Matthew of Edessa, although he is generally favorable to Baldwin, conveys some echo of the sufferings of the Armenians of Edessa and their natural indignation against the Franks who, "as a reward for the benefits which Edessa had lavished upon them, subjected them to the most unworthy treatment."[19] In 1116, Baldwin of Le Bourg punished his ally the Armenian Vasil Dgha for communicating with the Turks by depriving him of the castles of Raban and Kaisun. Then he robbed another Armenian lord, Abu'lgharib, lord of Birejik, of his lands. Next he turned against Bagrat, the brother of Kogh Vasil and the very Armenian who had formerly opened the way to Syria to Baldwin I. Not content with seizing Bagrat's possessions, Baldwin of Le Bourg also took those of Constantine, lord of Gargar, in 1117 and flung Constantine into prison where the wretched man later died. "We could have wished," writes Matthew of Edessa, "to enumerate the countless misdeeds of the Franks, but we dared not, because we lived under their authority."[20]

This makes it seem likely that Morphia's daughters, the granddaughters of the ferocious Gabriel of Melitene, heard more complaints and curses directed against the Franks than was good for them. They had good reason not to love the father whom they never saw and whom they knew as a great oppressor of their people. The three sisters' behavior (the fourth, Joveta, took the veil and retained few links with the world) shows that they had a great affection for one another and an almost equal indifference to the welfare of the Frankish kingdom. Their lifelong display of sisterly solidarity is itself evidence of a sullen hostility to the world in which they lived.

Alice's attitude cannot be altogether explained by burning Armenian patriotism. First and foremost, she was greedy for power at all costs. But she undoubtedly did feel some Armenian patriotism and this was her principal asset; it was not only by plundering her dead husband's treasure chests that she succeeded in winning supporters among the civilian population of Antioch. This population had always been hostile to the Franks and the Latin Church, and had reason to hope that Alice's rule would at least give them greater religious freedom, even if this was under Turkish control. The Princess was popular with the local Christians, who regarded her as one of themselves. She herself had probably never regarded her young husband as anything more than one more Frankish oppressor, and it should not be forgotten that Bohemond II had been killed in a war against Armenians.

Living in retirement at Lattakieh and later restored to her rights as regent in Antioch through the intercession of her sister Queen Melisende, Alice remained, as long as she lived, one of the principal champions of the opposition to the King's power. She did not possess a great talent for politics, and furthermore she was a woman and therefore unable to make her way by military talents. There was no possible outlet for her thirst for power, her dreams, and her grievances. When she appealed to Zengi, she had been planning to destroy Frankish power in Antioch. Later she attempted, more modestly, to guarantee her rights by an alliance with Byzantium. But Alice died young and never enjoyed the benefits of this alliance, although it was very much in accordance with the interests of the Frankish kingdom. Although the chroniclers have deliberately sought to minimize the significance of her rebellion, explaining it as merely the action of a capricious woman, Alice's revolt nonetheless caused a considerable shock and was much more than simply a thorn in the flesh of the old King of Jerusalem. It was a brutal revelation of an already deeply rooted trouble: the impossibility of any real understanding between the Franks and the native Christians.

The Death of Baldwin II

Less than a year after her marriage, Melisende, the heiress to the kingdom and the wife of Fulk of Anjou, gave birth to a son who was christened Baldwin. The old King did not live to watch the future King of Jerusalem, the first Frankish king to be born in the Holy Land, grow up, but he had at least the joy of knowing that he was a healthy child and likely to live. The future of the dynasty seemed assured.

Baldwin II died in August 1131, after ruling for thirteen years. He left his kingdom in good hands: Fulk was a strong man and, as the husband of the future Queen, he could count on the loyalty of the vassals of the kingdom (if not on that of the Counts of Tripoli and Edessa). After the death of Bohemond II and the Princess's withdrawal into retirement, the principality of Antioch was directly dependent on the King, to whom the Frankish nobles of Antioch were the more devoted because they knew how serious was the threat from their redoubtable neighbor Zengi. Baldwin II could die in peace—insofar as the word "peace" had any meaning in that war-torn country.

The old warrior made an edifying end—the end, to use the words of the period, of a *prud'homme*. He did not let death take him unprepared and had time to repent his numerous sins. So that he could die nearer to the Holy Sepulcher, he had himself carried to the house of the Patriarch, and from there he summoned his daughter and his son-in-law, together with their infant son, and solemnly bequeathed his kingdom to them in the presence of the Patriarch and the chief barons of the land. Then he put on the habit of a canon of the order of the Church of the Holy Sepulcher, because he wished "to die in poverty for the honor of his Lord, who had been poor in this world for his sake and that of other Christians."[21] The ancient custom of turning to God in this way at the hour of death, reminiscent of the baptism *in extremis* of the first-century Christians, was very widespread in Europe and even more so in the East. The traditional solemnity of the King's last moments crowned his work: it was a work, if not of peace, at least of settlement in the Eastern land which under Baldwin II had become, incontestably, the kingdom of Jerusalem.

Thirty-five years earlier, in 1096, Baldwin of Le Bourg, the son of the Count of Rethel, a baron of a noble but somewhat obscure family from the Ardennes, had taken the cross and set out on the holy war in the army of his cousin Godfrey, Duke of Lower Lorraine. He was a professional soldier, more ambitious than devout, like the majority of the Crusader knights, though he was devout as well. His devotion was sincere, narrow, and dogmatic, and it coexisted in him with an unconscious amorality. Altogether he was a very simple man, able to believe himself a good Christian while committing the worst injustices, because he performed his devotions regularly and was faithful to his wife. This was probably why he succeeded better than Baldwin I had done in inspiring the kind of respect due to a *prud'homme*. Baldwin I had never been a *prud'homme,* and had had no desire to be. Baldwin II, though just as tough, ferocious, greedy, and unscrupulous as his cousin, left behind him the reputation of having been the wisest of men.

Indeed, in the course of his thirteen-year reign, he had often behaved like a wise man—had been compelled to because of the terrible difficulties he faced. He had performed his work of kingship with the honesty of a good soldier entrusted with a perilous mission, but because he was a soldier first and foremost, the moment the danger lessened his demon drove him on to fresh, perilous adventures.

When he died he left his throne to a man of great valor but a newcomer to the country. He also left Fulk of Anjou a singularly redoubtable adversary in the person of the first great Moslem leader who had consciously and methodically sought to exploit the idea of the holy war against the Franks. Only the resistance of the other Moslem princes to Zengi's tyranny made it possible for Frankish rule in Syria to be consolidated and take root.

Fulk of Anjou, King of Jerusalem

The great Angevin baron who, as the husband of the heiress to the throne, succeeded Baldwin II was a genuine Frenchman from France, and in his reign the court of Jerusalem finally became a proper court, like the royal courts of Europe, with a little more Eastern luxury. And Fulk meant to conduct his kingdom as he had conducted his province of Anjou. He was a good administrator, but he needed time to familiarize himself with the extremely complex situation of his new kingdom. In Anjou he had succeeded in establishing a kind of feudal monarchy much more centralized than the domain of the kings of France at the same period, and he must have felt somewhat irritated by the "organized chaos" of states where people talked four

principal languages, to say nothing of other minor ones, and professed
six different religions; where the King's Italian subjects owed allegiance only to their respective republics, and where knights of the
military orders (who made up a good half of the chivalry of the
land) owed obedience only to their Grand Master and to the Pope;
where the local population, while they remained subjects compelled
to submission by force of arms, declared themselves either for the
Emperor of Byzantium or for the leaders of their respective Churches;
and where, to crown all, the great vassals, even with the Turks at their
gates, were every bit as jealous of their independence as they were
in Europe, although the Turks were very much more dangerous
enemies than the most powerful of neighboring kings could be in the
West.

In accordance with a more or less general rule on the death of a
king in the Middle Ages, Fulk had to quell revolts by the great vassals,
Pons, Count of Tripoli, and Princess Alice of Antioch. The old Count
of Edessa, Joscelin of Courtenay, missed this opportunity to revolt
(although he had actually declared his intention of doing so) because he died on a campaign against the Turks in the neighborhood
of Edessa two or three months after the death of Baldwin II. (There
will be more to say about the life of this man, who was one of the
most original personalities of Frankish Syria.) Joscelin left the county
to his son, Joscelin II, a young man who was a long way from equaling his father in warlike valor and who did not suffer from an excess
of loyalty to the King. Princess Alice, who had no business leaving her
domains or meddling in the affairs of Antioch, was not in the least
resigned to her gilded captivity. She came to an understanding with
Joscelin II (to whom she was related and who, like herself, was half
Armenian) and with William, lord of Sahiyun (Saône), and the
Count of Tripoli, the three of whom had been negotiating with the
inhabitants of Antioch, the local Christians, and a few of its Frankish
barons after the death of Baldwin II and were plotting to restore
Alice to her rights as regent.

In doing this, the Counts of Tripoli and Edessa were hoping to
undermine the power of the King. When Fulk heard of the plot being
hatched at Antioch and attempted to set out with his knights to re-
establish order in the city, Pons of Tripoli refused to allow him to
pass through his lands. The King had to take ship from Beirut almost
unaccompanied and reached Antioch by sea, through the port of St.
Symeon. There the Frankish barons who opposed the Princess re-
affirmed the oaths of fealty they had sworn to King Baldwin and

made Fulk regent in the name of the infant Constance, who was the heiress to the principality.

Pons was furious and invaded the territory of Antioch with the intention of making war on the King. Fulk gave battle, routed him, and brought back some of the Provençal knights as prisoners to Antioch. The Count of Tripoli soon regretted his rebellion. He was attacked by the Turkomans and besieged in Montferrand, and had no alternative but to appeal to the King's clemency. His wife, Countess Cecilia (who happened to be Fulk's half-sister*), had to cast herself at the feet of the King her brother and beg him to come to her husband's aid. Out of pity for his sister and a sense of Frankish solidarity, Fulk set out at the head of his army to relieve Montferrand. This time Pons had given up all idea of withholding his homage.

Joscelin II was also fairly hard pressed by the Turks of Aleppo (led by Zengi's lieutenant Sawar) in his lands of Turbessel. The Princess Alice, no longer possessing either an army or allies, had no alternative but to stay quietly where she was.

After this almost obligatory demonstration of independence on the part of his great vassals, Fulk was officially recognized by the whole country.

Joscelin of Courtenay

The county of Edessa had been Baldwin of Boulogne's first fief in the East and he, it will be remembered, had seized it somewhat treacherously from the Armenian Thoros. It was a Christian country where the Armenians and Syrians did not live together on good terms, the Armenians having reduced the Syrians more or less to a state of vassalage. To these two rival Christian communities were now added the Franks. Baldwin, by force of arms and sheer mercenary greed, had brought them together. The people of Edessa bowed before this new scourge of God, praying for some plot to rid them of him. Baldwin of Boulogne's reign in Edessa lasted for only three years before he was summoned to the throne of Jerusalem. He was succeeded by Baldwin of Le Bourg, who continued his policy of oppression and extortion, only occasionally regularizing matters a little out of regard for his wife and his father-in-law, Gabriel.

With his retinue of Walloon and Ardennais knights, among whom

---

* Cecilia of France was the widow of Tancred by her first marriage. She was the daughter of Bertrada of Montfort, who had been the wife of Fulk IV of Anjou and later of Philip I, King of France.

he generously distributed all the fiefs of the county, he managed, while waging an incessant war against the Moslems, to keep the local population subdued for four years. Then for four years his place was taken by the Norman Richard of Salerno, whose severity and greed made the exploits of the two Baldwins pale by comparison. When Baldwin of Le Bourg returned to Edessa, he had to put down a number of Armenian revolts, and this he is known to have done with somewhat unnecessary brutality in the calmest conviction of his own right. He remained Count of Edessa for a further ten years, until 1118, the date of his accession to the throne of Jerusalem. In these ten years he enlarged his domains considerably, at the expense not of the Turks but of his Armenian neighbors. He had entrusted one of the principal fiefs of his county, Tel-Basheir, or Turbessel as it was known to the Franks, to one of his cousins, a man still young and poor whom he had brought from his native Ardennes after settling in Edessa.

Joscelin of Courtenay, whose wealthier and more noble cousin had decided to make his fortune for him, was a brilliant knight. Although not one of the original Crusaders, he was one of those ambitious younger sons more tempted by the reputation of the Orient than by the honor of serving God. When he became lord of Turbessel, he fought loyally at the side of Baldwin of Le Bourg, was taken prisoner at the same time as his cousin, and then worked so loyally for Baldwin's release that his attitude compelled the admiration of the atabeg Jawali. Joscelin made all Baldwin's quarrels his own and was at his side throughout all his campaigns, sharing with him in the cruel suppression of the Armenian rebellions. He acquired such a reputation for strength and courage that he was everywhere regarded as almost the equal of his suzerain.

After 1112, when the county of Edessa itself began to suffer from famine (the land having been completely laid waste after the massacre of the rural population by the Turks in 1110), Joscelin found himself richer than his cousin and benefactor. Seeing that the lands of Turbessel were rich and fertile, Baldwin of Le Bourg accused his cousin of ingratitude and brought him to Edessa on a false pretext. He then flung him into prison and only released him in return for a promise to yield up the fief of Turbessel. Deprived of all he possessed and expelled from the county, Joscelin's only course was to go and seek refuge with the King of Jerusalem, Baldwin I, who was only too glad of the services of such a good knight and granted him the fief of Galilee, which had been left vacant by the death of the preceding holder of the title, Hugh of Saint-Omer.

After the death of Baldwin I, Joscelin was, as we have seen, the principal architect of Baldwin of Le Bourg's rise to the throne. In gratitude for this service, the new King settled the county of Edessa on his cousin. Joscelin returned to Edessa where, like everywhere else, there was no shortage of opportunities for fighting. He was taken prisoner but escaped to continue defending his lands at Edessa without respite, and sometimes those of Antioch as well. All his contemporaries agree that his strength and courage, his knowledge of the art of war, and his fine presence made him one of the first knights of Frankish Syria.

According to Michael the Syrian, when Joscelin, while waiting for the arrival of Baldwin of Le Bourg's ransom, offered to remain a prisoner in his stead, Jawali was so struck by the Frankish knight's pride, beauty, and courtesy that for his sake he remitted the remainder of Baldwin's debt (a sum of thirty thousand dinars, amounting to almost half the ransom). The Syrian chronicler may be suspected of some romantic exaggeration here, but even so, the story proves that Joscelin of Courtenay's personality impressed even the Moslems themselves, less by his purely military virtues (which in a Frank were generally accepted as natural) than by his native charm and spontaneous gift for establishing human contact even with his enemies. Nothing in Joscelin's conduct suggests that he should be regarded as a hero of the faith. He was simply a landless knight with ambitions to enrich himself. This, in the age in which he lived, was considered a virtue and he fought valiantly for his overlord and for the lands entrusted to his care. He was not a gentle character. When the Armenians of Edessa rebelled in 1112, he is known to have acted with a cruelty in the suppression of the revolt which even exceeded that of Baldwin of Le Bourg. He was a loyal vassal to Baldwin, as he was to Baldwin of Boulogne, but then he was related to both. All in all, he possessed the ordinary vices and virtues of the good knight.

His conduct during his quarrel with Baldwin of Le Bourg is presented by William of Tyre in a rather unfavorable light, but we must not forget that William was writing at the time when the descendants of Baldwin of Le Bourg were occupying the throne of Jerusalem and that Joscelin's grandchildren (Joscelin III and Agnes) were our historian's personal enemies. To prove his accusations, the Archbishop of Tyre can produce nothing but vague gossip among Baldwin's and Joscelin's servants. Admittedly, Joscelin was in no undue hurry to supply his cousin's troops with victuals and preferred to keep his corn and his money for himself: this, at least, is the principal charge against him, but his avarice can certainly never have reached scandalous proportions, since relations between the two men appear to have been excellent. However, the story of the famous quarrel, as it is told by William of Tyre, is worth recounting.

Baldwin, having heard it said that the squires of Joscelin, lord of Turbessel, mocked at his poverty and vaunted the wealth of their master, became violently angry (the squires went so far as to say that Baldwin would do well to sell his county of Edessa to Joscelin and return to France) because he thought that "by the words of the servants, one may divine the thoughts of the masters." He feigned illness and summoned Joscelin to Edessa. Joscelin believed that he was summoned in order to be entrusted with the government of the county. From his feigned sickbed, Baldwin loaded Joscelin with the bitterest reproaches: "You, who owe me everything, yet do nothing to help me when I am in need, you make my poverty a reproach to me, and you seek to drive me out of my lands," and more in the same vein. At last, refusing to listen to his cousin's protestations, he had him seized and flung into prison. "He kept him in a very wretched prison, and made him suffer many torments, until he, [Joscelin] gave up to him all the lands he held." This kind of behavior, even to a Turkish chieftain, would have deserved the name of treachery pure and simple. But, in the words of Matthew of Edessa, the *wise* Baldwin of Le Bourg showed "an ingenious avidity in possessing himself of the property of others," and he treated his cousin and friend no better than he treated the Armenian princes of Cilicia. The lands of Turbessel were fertile. There was also another thing: Joscelin was greatly loved by his native subjects. His presence in the neighborhood of Edessa was undoubtedly damaging to Baldwin.

We know that Joscelin spoke up very eloquently in favor of Baldwin of Le Bourg when the throne of Jerusalem fell vacant. "You may well imagine," he said, "that I do not speak thus for love of him who has done me wrong enough and has made me suffer so many insults; but I say it in the interests of the country and for my conscience' sake. . . . I know him and I bear witness that he is a wise man, a man of great good sense . . . no man could come from any country who would be more proper than he to fill this office." William of Tyre, probably not without reason, suspects Joscelin of serving Baldwin's interests in the hope of getting the county of Edessa out of it: "It is quite possible that the intentions of the Patriarch [Arnulf] and Joscelin were not very pure on this occasion."[22] It is possible, even probable, that in spite of everything their intentions were pure, because the advice they gave was common sense and answered to the real needs of the kingdom.

Joscelin had married an Armenian princess, the sister of Thoros I, lord of Vakha and grandson of Roupen I, the founder of one of the principal Armenian dynasties in Cilicia. At the beginning of their stay in the East, the two Baldwins had tried to lean on the support of the local Armenian nobility and had both taken Armenian wives. Baldwin of Le Bourg had also given one of his sisters in marriage to Leo, the brother of Thoros I, who ruled Vakha after his brother's death (it was during an expedition against this same Leo that Bohemond II met his death). Joscelin, whose reputation from the beginning was almost as great as that of his relative and suzerain, thus became the brother-in-law of the powerful Armenian prince, and unlike Baldwin, he took this new family tie seriously.

He may be accused of excessive severity at the time of the revolt of Edessa, where, however, he was acting on behalf of Baldwin of Le Bourg. At Turbessel, whose lord he was for thirteen years, he made himself loved, and Armenian historians have neither cruelties nor extortion to reproach him with. He seems to have had a talent for adapting himself to his local environment without effort, almost unconsciously, simply by treating his Armenian vassals as he would have treated Frankish knights—as equals. When he became Count of Edessa in 1118, he found himself the lord of a fairly large principality whose population, thanks to the conquests of Baldwin of Le Bourg, was largely Armenian. The territories which Baldwin had conquered somewhat brutally Joscelin found no difficulty in holding. All the Armenians loved him and acknowledged him as their lawful lord, almost as their national hero.

He must have known enough Armenian to communicate with his subjects without too much difficulty. He is known to have formed ties of friendship with prelates of the Armenian Church, as also with those of the Jacobite Church. He tirelessly defended cities with a local population in which the Franks were only represented by small garrisons against Turkish aggression, and he took the welfare of their people to heart exactly as though they had been Franks.

When he was taken prisoner in 1122, the people of Edessa never thought of profiting from his absence to rebel. They were plunged in grief and submitted to Baldwin II while they waited for their Count's return. But when Baldwin in turn was captured, Joscelin thought of a way of escape. Part of the population of Kharpurt, where the two Frankish leaders were imprisoned, was Christian, and more important, Armenian. Joscelin of Courtenay's popularity with the Armenians had apparently spread beyond the confines of his county, and he found friends even in Kharpurt. He managed to send messengers to Edessa summoning his Armenian subjects to his assistance. It did not occur to the Armenians to let the Frankish knights into the secret of their plans. They made up their minds to liberate *their* Count in their own way. Fifty men of proven courage set out for Kharpurt variously disguised as monks, merchants, and beggars, with weapons hidden under their clothes. Succeeding in making their way into the castle, they assured themselves of the complicity of the Armenian laborers employed there, and these laborers, subjects of the Emir Balak, were ready to risk their lives to save the Frankish Count of Edessa. There was a rising of the entire Armenian population of Kharpurt; they forced the gates of the prison, murdered the guards, and freed the prisoners, who were many because Balak was a notable warrior. Before long the capital of the Ortoqid emirs was in the hands of the Armenians, Baldwin of Le Bourg, and Joscelin.

It was an extravagantly heroic attempt, but it was doomed to failure. No relief army could reach them at once and Balak's troops were very close. Joscelin with three Armenians from the district left the already besieged city to seek reinforcements. Disguised as a beggar and half-dead from hunger and thirst, he was recognized on his way to Edessa by an Armenian peasant. Joscelin feared to be betrayed and sold to the Turks, but he had nothing to fear. The peasant rejoiced at the opportunity to serve the Count who he said had once "given him bread when he had none for himself." There was nothing lucky about this meeting: Joscelin was known throughout the land, and many were the peasants who, like this one, would have offered to kill their only pig to make a meal for the Count and guide him to Edessa, at the risk of their lives, disguised as a peasant and carrying a baby in his arms. (Fulcher of Chartres describes the Count for us, on this strange journey, completely bemused and desperately worried because he did not know what to do to stop the baby's crying.)

The Kharpurt adventure had a tragic ending. Joscelin hastily assembled all the available knights, some from Edessa and others from Antioch and Jerusalem, with the object of rescuing the King, but he did not arrive in time, and the True Cross, which he had taken with him on his expedition, did him no good. Baldwin II with his companions in captivity and the Armenians defended themselves heroically, but Balak's troops finally took the citadel by storm. All the Armenians inside, women included, were savagely put to death. "Some," says William of Tyre, "were tied to stakes and fired at like targets, others were flayed alive, and the remainder hanged, burned alive, or flung from the ramparts."[23] The Frankish prisoners, with the exception of Baldwin himself, one of his nephews,* and Waleran of Le Puiset, suffered the same fate. Joscelin's freedom was dearly bought.

To avenge those who had been sacrificed for his sake, Joscelin sacked the neighborhood of Aleppo and ravaged the outskirts of the city. The people of Aleppo avenged his desecration of Moslem tombs by turning nearly all the churches inside their city into mosques.

Joscelin died in 1131, not long after Baldwin II, when he was not yet an old man, probably under sixty. He was inspecting the work of the sappers undermining one of the towers of a fortress he was besieging when the tunnel collapsed, and the Count was rescued from the debris with several broken limbs, mortally injured. While he lay on his deathbed, the Danishmend Turks (other sources claim that it was the Sultan of Rum) came to attack the castle of Kaisun on the northeast frontier of the county of Edessa. The old Count ordered his son Joscelin to assemble his knights and go to the relief of the fortress, but the young man refused, saying he had not enough troops. Thereupon, the dying man had himself carried in person on a litter at the head of his army. When the Turks saw the litter bearing the banners of the Count of Edessa coming to meet them, drawn by horses and surrounded by the Frankish knights, they raised the siege and fled. This was the last time in his life that Joscelin of Courtenay saw the Turks.

The litter was set down on the ground. The Count, says William of Tyre, "raised his arms to heaven and spoke these words: 'Good lord God, I praise and thank you as best I can that you have so honored me in this world . . . that you have been so merciful and generous to my end as to make my enemies fear me so that even when I am half dead, an impotent hulk unable to help myself, they dared not wait for me but fled at my approach. Good lord God, I know that this comes of your goodness and your courtesy.' When he had said this, he commended himself to God with all his heart and immediately gave up his soul. He died there, in that very place, among his own people."[24]

Out of all the great men of the First Crusade, Joscelin of Courtenay had been the only one to conceive and create something resembling a brotherhood between local and Latin Christians. This he

* Probably Manasses of Hierges.

did, not as a result of calculation, still less from humanitarian ideals because notions of this kind did not exist at the time, but simply by the strength of a generous nature, able to make itself loved because capable, perhaps even without knowing it, of giving love. Joscelin of Courtenay's great glory was not that he made the Turks flee at the mere sight of his litter, but that he inspired such affection that even sixteen years after his death the citizens of Edessa still looked on his son as their master and their savior.

This son, Joscelin II, was also loved, chiefly because he was his father's son but also because he was closer to the Armenians than any other Frankish prince was ever to be. He failed to keep his paternal inheritance, but although he himself was guilty of serious errors, his fall was probably partly due to his Armenian sympathies. The Frankish kingdom was aligning itself more and more against the native Christians, and was increasingly oriented toward the rule of a purely Frankish Latin and Catholic aristocracy. Those who became "Armenianized," like Joscelin II or Princess Alice, and showed a capacity to understand and encourage the interests of the local Christians to the detriment of those of the Franks appeared as traitors. Not that they would ever have tried, consciously, to embrace the native cause. They merely envisaged other solutions besides Frankish dominion pure and simple. They were subject to other influences and they had a different outlook. They were always foreigners in Frankish circles.

The experiment of uniting the Latin and indigenous communities by marriage, which had been inaugurated by the first kings of Jerusalem, proved unworkable—on the highest level, at least. The poorer Franks, soldiers or artisans, were actually obliged to take native wives for lack of women from their own land, but even so the latter, because less common, were more highly prized. The wealthy preferred to bring out wives from home, or to marry the daughters of local barons. Many had brought their own families with them to the Holy Land. Warriors died here more quickly than elsewhere. Young men married the widows of their dead comrades, some of whom might have outlived two or even three husbands. Except in the county of Edessa, the barons would no longer ask for the daughter of a local Roupen, Thoros, or Leo in marriage. Although the Frankish nobility in Edessa was to some extent Armenianized, and that of Antioch ultimately absorbed Oriental influences up to a point, these attempts at assimilation seem to have been made to the detriment of the Frankish community as a whole. To the local Christians, the kings of Jerusalem, the princes of Antioch, and the counts of Tripoli remained foreigners and masters. There was to be no second Joscelin of Courtenay.

The Military Orders

In 1118, the year of Baldwin I's death, a knight of Champagne named Hugh of Payens (or Payns) with eight companions founded in Jerusalem a brotherhood, simultaneously religious and military, the object of which was to protect poor pilgrims coming to the Holy Land. The strength of this brotherhood increased rapidly, and the Patriarch and the King granted it a house attached to the royal palace, the former Temple of Solomon; henceforth the institution was known as the "militia of the Temple."

Ever since 1070, another religious brotherhood had also existed in Jerusalem, devoted to the service of poor pilgrims of Latin origin. This had been founded by pious merchants from Amalfi in the vicinity of the Church of Saint John the Almoner. This brotherhood, which was open to monks and laymen, maintained a hostel and a hospital and did great service to the numerous pilgrims who visited Jerusalem at all times. Naturally, it enjoyed gifts of money from wealthy pilgrims and clergy, and once the Crusaders had settled in the Holy Land the head of this pious brotherhood, a native of Amalfi whose name was Gerard, set about organizing it along the lines of a real independent religious order which, while observing the Benedictine rule, had its own government and statutes and was known by the name of the Order of the Hospital of Saint John of Jerusalem, or simply the Order of Hospitalers. It was only from 1119 onward that this order, which at first had been devoted solely to works of charity, also undertook the duty of protecting pilgrims and began to include soldiers among its members, following the example of Hugh of Payens's "militia of the Temple."

The idea of a force that would be at the same time military and religious sprang from the same wave of popular piety which had led to the First Crusade. Although the enthusiasm of the mob was ephemeral and subsided so quickly that it barely survived the first terrible years of the great adventure, a burning, active piety still lived in the hearts of a few men for whom the Crusade had never been an excuse for conquest.

The great barons, busy with their wars, seemed to have forgotten that the reason they had come to the Holy Land was for pilgrimage. The Holy Places stood in such need of defense simply in order that

God might be better served there and the greatest possible number of Christians be able to pray there undisturbed. The "Knights of the Temple" were no sooner founded than they found countless recruits among the chivalry of the Holy Land, and still more among pilgrims landing from Europe. Pious souls, however warlike, no longer found satisfaction in the constant campaigns waged by the King of Jerusalem and the other Frankish princes against the Turks and Egyptians.

Spiritual heirs of men like Walter Sans-Avoir or the Count of Tübingen, the companions of Hugh of Payens dedicated themselves directly to the service of God, of God as they saw Him represented on earth in the persons of His poor. Indifferent to the political interests and territorial ambitions of the Frankish states, they devoted themselves solely to the service of pilgrims, of those of God's poor who came to the Holy Land to worship Jesus Christ and who also cared little for the kings and barons of Jerusalem.

It has already been shown that in the Middle Ages poverty was something of a cult, harking back with a simplicity, which has been forgotten in modern times, to the parable in the Gospel according to Saint Matthew (25: 31–46). Christian piety (and Koranic piety as well) made love of the poor an absolute duty and poverty a supreme ideal. In practice, the strong and the wealthy were content to buy God's pardon by distributions of alms, and almsgiving actually formed a substantial part of the budget of secular as well as ecclesiastical lords, but truly devout men, and even those not so devout, felt themselves somehow inferior to the poor. Genuine piety did not go well with wealth. Men who wished to serve God without having a vocation for the monastic life frequently pledged themselves to the service of the poor and this, in a time of great inequality and social injustice, created a certain equilibrium. The fact that private charity was obligatory and taken for granted went some way to counterbalance the harsh conditions of the common people.

In the Holy Land, the poor were chiefly pilgrims, and especially pilgrims of Latin origin, but pilgrims from all countries and belonging to all sects enjoyed the same prejudice in their favor. There were a great many of them, at all times and under all regimes, people who were vagabonds for the love of God, and the more respected in that their prayers contributed not only to their own salvation but also to the salvation of those in a position to help and protect them. They were deserving of respect just because they had made the greatest sacrifices and faced the greatest dangers for their faith. These people came from every corner of Christendom, often accompanied by wealthy pilgrims with an escort of armed guards, often disembarking in more or less organized bands, flanked by men armed merely with knives and cudgels. Monks came to worship at the Holy Places, in small groups which joined up whenever they could with more numerous companies. There were long caravans, in which the people traveled on horseback and in carts drawn by donkeys and mules, together with pedestrians of all ages and sexes, led by bearded monks clad in homespun, carrying crosses and singing psalms in chorus.

Such had been the companions of Peter the Hermit and their countless predecessors in the quest for salvation, and such now and for centuries to come were the crowds (in greater or smaller numbers from year to year) of pious vagabonds, repentant sinners, people who had suffered a cruel bereavement or been involved in a public scandal, fugitives from justice, fanatics seeking martyrdom, or simply adventurers and people with lively minds eager to see new lands. A Christian Jerusalem, offering hospitality to all Christians, was a magnetic pole for the kind of popular piety which cared little for what princes, kings, and barons might conquer or lose in the Holy Land, because their affairs had very little importance in comparison with the Holy Sepulcher.

A pilgrimage to the Holy Land had never been easy and since the Turkish conquest had become actively dangerous. It was this very fact which had been one of the original causes of the Crusade. Since the capture of Jerusalem, although the country was officially controlled by the Frankish armies, the danger remained, on account of the Bedouin tribes which, in spite of Baldwin I's continual vigilance, still made frequent raids on the countryside of Judaea and Galilee. Moreover, the permanent state of war which the country sustained had made the Moslem peasants much more hostile to the Christians than they had been before the Crusades. Armed bands of Egyptians and Arabs traveled the roads on haphazard military expeditions and often treated the pilgrims as enemies.

This meant that pilgrims who wanted to visit the Holy Sepulcher or Bethlehem, to be "baptized" in the Jordan, to visit Christ's home at Nazareth, and so forth, were risking their lives twenty times over in their pious wanderings. Inspired by a praiseworthy evangelical zeal, the knights of the Order of the Temple placed their arms and their courage at the service of the "poor," acting as guides and escorts, driving off or intimidating attackers, and forming what may be described as a police force to patrol the pilgrim routes. This was a public utility, the necessity for which could be clearly seen by everybody.

Under Baldwin II, the current of opinion among the military aristocracy which led to the rapid growth of the two pious brotherhoods reached such proportions that the two new institutions became transformed into actual religious orders modeled on the monastic orders, with their own rules, hierarchical organization, and administration. These orders were recognized by the Pope—the Hospitalers in 1120 and the Templars in 1128—and came under the direct authority of the Holy See, and by the end of Baldwin II's reign their ranks included hundreds of knights and sergeants.

Having chosen the Tower of David for his own residence, the King gave over the whole of the Temple of Solomon to the Templars, while the Hospitalers considerably enlarged their house which was situated close to the Holy Sepulcher. Even before 1130, these two military orders had such a reputation in the West that a great many knights from every Catholic country came to request the honor of being admitted to them, and both were going from strength to strength all the time.

It is not difficult to see that in feudal society the military orders constituted a kind of pietist or puritan reaction against the too openly secular attitude of the first Crusader barons. By what seems an odd coincidence, none of the great leaders of the First Crusade, for all its quasi-mystical character, had been in any sense idealists, mystics, or fanatics. That its leaders should have been the men they were was undoubtedly a blessing for the Crusade. Some of them were content to shed their blood for the greater glory of God, but this was never their primary object and when they were cruel, it was with the cruelty of wild animals who kill because they must. In addition to the exploits of the principal barons, the chroniclers have plenty of stories to tell about those of lesser knights. But although there are countless descriptions of swordplay and individual acts of heroism and prowess which testify to immense physical strength, we are told very little about the mental attitude of these knights. Sometimes, in moments of great danger, they rise to a state of religious exaltation, and sometimes their wild, fierce courage carries them to the point of actually seeking martyrdom. The majority of stories are probably founded on fact, but already they are tinged with legend and heightened to serve the needs of the cause. The *Anonymi* makes Count Eustace of Boulogne die a martyr's death when actually he is known to have outlived both his two brothers and died in France at a ripe old age.

For all the knights who went on the First Crusade for love of the Holy Sepulcher, there were at least as many who were perfectly content with a life of battle and rapine in Edessa, Antioch, and Tripoli, and those present at the capture of Jerusalem cannot have been so very different from their fellows who remained in northern Syria. Most of the genuinely pious, the "pure," who had not come to the country to seek their fortune, left the Holy Land once Jerusalem had been won back and their pilgrimage was over. Those who remained enriched themselves as and when they could because this was a soldier's natural right. But even so, a minority stayed quite simply for love of Jesus Christ and the defense of the Holy Sepulcher, asking nothing more than the honor of fighting against "God's enemies" and winning a martyr's crown. They were undoubtedly a minority, but quite a strong one, and morally in particular. It was they who joined Hugh of Payens's companions, and in the time of Baldwin I they still do not seem to have been very numerous, if only because men of this stamp were always the most ardent in battle and the first to get killed. Hugh of Payens himself did not reach the Holy Land until 1110.

By 1120 or thereabouts, the Frankish chivalry in the Levant, which was getting itself slaughtered so consistently on every front, included only a few survivors from the heroic days of the First Crusade. New recruits arrived regularly, but in small contingents. Most of the conquered land had already been given away and there did not appear to be a great deal of fresh country to conquer. Fiefs which fell vacant went to the newcomers whenever the holder died without issue; otherwise the successor married the widow and was merely the temporary master of the fief under his protection. A land which had once been open to conquest had now become, like Europe, a country amply provided with lords. Baldwin of Le Bourg had gained little by plundering his Armenian neighbors because their lands were soon given away and then, according to custom, they became inalienable fiefs which could benefit no one else.

In fact, although in the years 1120 to 1130 the Holy Land did gain a fairly large number of new military recruits, this was chiefly due to the expansion of the orders of chivalry. Volunteers willing to accept poverty, chastity, and even obedience came from northern and southern Europe, from Germany, England, Spain, Italy, and above all from France, knights who were prepared to fight to the death and asked nothing for themselves beyond the privilege of crossing swords with the infidel.

What made this such a remarkable innovation was the fact that these knights were actually monks. Their rule had been approved by the Pope and what is more, by one of the most revered and admired men of the time, one of the highest moral authorities of the Church, a man already acknowledged as a saint in his lifetime: the Abbot of Clairvaux, the new reformer of the Cistercian order, the man who was to go down in history as Saint Bernard. Hugh of Payens's idea seemed to him a possible means of regeneration by faith for a class which he considered worldly, impious, and greedy. He became an ardent supporter of the cause of these "soldiers of God," who succeeded in uniting in their persons the supposedly incompatible virtues of military valor and monastic humility.

It was certainly a good idea, and a new one; until the creation of the military orders, knights who practiced poverty and chastity could only set their consciences at rest by renouncing their military careers and entering a religious order. For men such as these, sterner and more serious than the general run of Crusaders, men who were genuinely torn between a need for the religious life and the desire to use their weapons to protect the weak, the Orders of the Temple and the Hospital were a providential solution to their dilemma. Naturally the chivalry of Europe did not rush in their thousands to embrace this new life. The orders demanded great sacrifices and their rule was strict: to begin with, at least, only men who possessed real monastic vocation entered the orders.

Unlike the majority of monastic orders, the military orders were divided into classes defined by the monks' social origin: the knights, who must all be noble (the reason for this being that only members of the nobility received a complete education in military matters); the sergeants, who might be of bourgeois origin; and last, the clerks, who alone were able to perform the holy office. The warrior monks bore arms and were consequently debarred from the priesthood. They were expected to observe absolute poverty, chastity, and obedience, an unconditional obedience to their local commanders and to the Grand Master of their order. The order was ruled by the Grand Master and his staff: the constable, treasurer, and marshal, and only knights attended meetings of the chapter. From 1130 onward they wore a uniform (this was something of a novelty in military costume—a novelty inspired by the monastic rules), the Templars a white tunic with a red cross and the Hospitalers a black tunic with a white cross.

There is a justly famous letter by Saint Bernard contrasting the vain, frivolous secular knights with their love of luxury, with the tough and austere chivalry of God. The Abbot of Clairvaux's words, dating from the first quarter of the twelfth century, could almost make us believe that feudal warriors of this period looked something like Molière's little marquises, with their long, carefully tended curls half covering their faces and "soft, delicate" hands which they hid in their wide, flowing sleeves. They loved finery: their shields and lances were painted in bright colors, their horses' harness encrusted with precious stones, and they wore silk tunics over their armor. The love of fine clothes, which was one of the principal characteristics of medieval knights, was increased to a remarkable extent by contact with the East and the possibility of obtaining silk, gold, and precious stones at bargain prices. Saint Bernard was not the only one to denounce this worldly vanity; and the current of opinion which finally led to the foundation of the military orders was, to some extent, a reaction against the insolent display of wealth which was one of the consequences of the Crusade.

This is what Saint Bernard has to say about the Templars:

> They come and go at a sign from their commander; they wear the clothes which he gives them, seeking neither other garments nor other food. They are wary of all excess in food or clothing, desiring only what is needful. They live all together, without women or children. No idlers or lookers-on are to be found in their company; when they are not on active service, which happens rarely, or eating their bread or giving thanks to Heaven, they busy themselves with mending their clothes and their torn or tattered harness. . . . Insolent words, vain acts, immoderate laughter, complaints and murmurs, when they are perceived, do not go unpunished. They hate chess and dice, and they have a horror of hunting; they do not find the usual pleasure in the ridiculous pursuit of birds. They shun and abominate mimes, magicians, and *jongleurs,* light songs and foolishness. They crop their hair close because the Gospels tell them that it is a shame for a man to tend his hair. They are never seen combed and rarely washed, their beards are matted, they reek of dust and bear the stains of the heat and their harness.[25]

Saint Bernard never went to the Holy Land, but he encountered Templars in Rome and in France, and he had heard a great deal about their life in Outremer. He admired these men, "rarely washed, their beards matted, reeking of dust," for their virile asceticism and their obvious contempt for worldly wealth. He may have forgotten that although they had no wives or children, hated good cheer, fine clothes, hunting, shows, and all sociable games, laughter and chat-

ter, they were still men. He was too deeply imbued with the prejudices of his age to imagine that the holy hatred of God's enemies
which was a consequence of this life of excessive austerity could be
a sin. Nor did he foresee that before very long this exemplary militia of God would be contaminated by the monkish vices of pride,
avarice, and sectarianism. The Templars and Hospitalers, these purest of the pure devoted to the service of the poor and the protection of the weak, once united in communities and provided with a
rule and a uniform, were not slow to view themselves as the salt of
the earth.

Later, toward the end of the century, the orders developed into a
kind of aristocratic foreign legion, including among their members
not only seekers after God and heroism but also—and in increasing
numbers—the failures, the disappointed lovers, restless, ambitious
men, and even repentant criminals. It took character to endure the
harsh discipline of the orders and the trials of a life compulsorily
dedicated to daily peril. The military orders were made up of strong
men, as hard on themselves as they were fearless in battle. Contemporary authors are not always kind to them, but all acknowledge
their exemplary courage and the austerity of their lives.

Hugh of Payens, like Gerard, the first Grand Master of the Hospitalers, and his successor Raymond of Le Puy, began on a relatively
modest scale. Their activities were confined simply to patrolling the
roads and giving assistance to poor pilgrims. The Order of the Hospital had the dual function of rendering practical help to the poor
and escorting bands of pilgrims, while the Order of the Temple was
content with the second of these two duties and was exclusively
military. The soldier monks waited in the coastal cities (Jaffa and
then more frequently Acre) for civilian pilgrims to land, and acted
as an armed escort, guiding them to all the places of pilgrimage
which the new arrivals wished to visit. If there was a rumor of
Bedouin bands in the vicinity of this or that major route, a corps
of Templars or Hospitalers was immediately dispatched there. These
kindly guardians patrolled the roads continually, watching at crossroads and from towers built to command deep valleys, always
ready to fight, one against ten, the moment an enemy band menaced
the safety of the way.

Trained in their difficult task, the first of these soldier monks
(most of them old Crusaders) had an amazing knowledge of the
country and of the tactics of the enemy. Before 1128, the orders cannot have numbered more than a hundred or so knights between
them, and probably fewer. (The Hospitalers had had a constable

since 1126, but this was an honorary title and bore no relation to the strength of the order.) In 1128, when Baldwin II had the idea of using these elite troops for his own purposes, Hugh of Payens was sent to Europe to recruit new brothers for his order and ask for assistance for the Holy Land. The founder of the militia of the Temple brought back a number of volunteers from this voyage and the Pope's confirmation of his rule. He had also succeeded in arousing public interest in the West, where the military orders had hitherto been little known. Saint Bernard had promised his help, and he was not a man to make airy promises; he made the merits of the new institution known throughout Christendom. A few years later the orders already represented a real force and were receiving gifts of money which they employed in building new forts and even castles along the roads. They were entrusted with the task of manning frontier posts, and were called in whenever there was a battle fought in defense of the realm. On this point their rule had no restrictions: the defense of the realm could be a task as urgent, and as pleasing to God, as the protection of pilgrims.

These two pious brotherhoods were not, properly speaking, a part of the kingdom. Initially approved by the Patriarch of Jerusalem, they very quickly freed themselves from obedience to him and came under the direct authority of the Pope. Owing no allegiance to the Patriarch of Jerusalem, they owed still less to the King.

Once they were entrusted with the defense of castles, they promptly declared the fiefs depending on these castles ecclesiastical property and refused to pay tithes to the bishopric to which the lands belonged. If a man living on their land had been excommunicated by the local prelates, the officers of the order were capable of ignoring this and receiving the culprit in their churches. William of Tyre tells that the Hospitalers, filled with an overweening zeal for the glory of their order, had erected such tall, massive buildings all around the Church of the Holy Sepulcher that it had become difficult to reach the church, which was completely hidden by the new buildings. Furthermore, in order to annoy the Patriarch, the monks had their bells rung as loudly as possible while he was preaching a sermon "so that people could not hear the worthy man, and he had to shout to make the word of Our Lord heard." As time went on, matters were to go still further, so far indeed that one day the Hospitalers actually burst into the Church of the Holy Sepulcher, armed with bows, "and fired a great quantity of arrows."[26]

The reason that these religious men had such a curious way of settling their monastic quarrels may have had something to do with

the principles on which their organization was founded. It was natural for them to be tempted to use their weapons when, even between
ordinary monastic communities, quarrels were often so bitter that the
monks came to blows and insults.

Inevitably, the spirit of competition between the two orders very
soon degenerated into open hostility, so that as time went on, if the
kings of Jerusalem managed to assure themselves of the support of
one of the orders, they were certain not to be able to rely on the
other, except in cases of extreme urgency. The knights, although
they were sworn to obey their Grand Master and did in fact obey
him without question, owed no obedience to the local princes, while
the Grand Masters were only disposed to serve the King as and when
it suited them.

For obvious reasons, the orders rapidly became extremely rich.
They were very popular with the nobility in the West, who, as soldiers
themselves, could imagine nothing more admirable than a soldier
monk and did not stint their gifts and bequests to such pious institutions. Moreover, constrained to poverty by their rule, the Templars
and Hospitalers spent very little on themselves. In addition each
brother, on entering the order, made over all his possessions as a gift
to the community. Their probity was legendary. While the Hospitalers
built huge buildings in Jerusalem and the Templars—and the Hospitalers also—were building dozens of castles at their own expense, the
orders also received castles and lands in fief and from these they
drew substantial benefits which they did not share with either the
King or the Church. All the money they received went into the treasury of the order and was used by the Grand Master and his officers
with a view to increasing the power of their house. But a Templar
or Hospitaler who was taken prisoner could never purchase his
freedom by paying a ransom. ("A Templar," said Odo of Saint-
Amand, one of the Grand Masters of the Temple, "who falls into the
hands of the Moslem can offer nothing as ransom but his belt and
his dagger." He himself died in captivity, and he was the head of
the order.) This was one of the clauses of their rule and it was
rigorously respected. But it will be seen that at the time of the fall
of Jerusalem, the Grand Masters refused to use the treasure to pay
the ransoms of the poor.

The proportion of Hospitalers and Templars killed in battle was
much higher than that of lay knights. Courage and the duty never to
retreat or seek safety in flight were also part of the rule of the
brotherhoods, and only those who put little value on their lives joined
the orders. They were formidable soldiers, always in the forefront

of the battle, ready to take hopeless risks and make desperate charges. The orders attracted a great many fanatics and men seeking martyrdom, because no institutions could have been better suited to men of that temperament—who can be found in every age and land —than those of the Templars and Hospitalers. By the middle of the century, each of the two orders formed an army of several hundred knights and at least a thousand squires and sergeants. In a fight, their military virtues made every man of them worth two ordinary combatants, and furthermore these elite troops did not have to be paid. The Grand Master could place them at the disposal of anyone he wished, only reserving the material benefits of their conquests for the profit of the order and retaining the right of pillage also for the benefit of the order. The kings of Jerusalem were always short of soldiers and it was in their interests to encourage the military orders. But by allowing them to develop, they were creating a new "state within a state" to add to the other far from negligible ones of the Church and the merchant colonies. The knightly monks lived on the fringes of Frankish society in the East, and because they were monks they despised it for its love of luxury and comfort, for the freedom of its morals (which were, in fact, considerably less strict even than those of secular society in Europe, not notoriously puritanical), and for its easy adaptation to an Oriental environment. New recruits came from oversea—from Europe—and if even secular pilgrims were shocked by the Oriental way of life adopted by their countrymen in the Holy Land, the disapproval of the soldier monks was more forceful still.

René Grousset has remarked on a contrast between the "Crusading spirit" and the *"esprit poulain"* (the word *poulain* was used to describe Franks born of mixed marriages and was applied in a pejorative sense to all Franks born in the East or those who had adopted Eastern ways). The "Crusading spirit" implied a certain attitude of intolerance, fanaticism, and a lack of understanding of local conditions. On these grounds, it could be said that the puritanical and aggressive orders of chivalry shared this spirit to the extent that a large number of their brethren were newcomers to the Holy Land. But they very quickly bowed to the discipline of the order and ceased to be either "Crusaders" or *poulains,* but became simply brothers of the Temple, or brothers of the Hospital of Saint John of Jerusalem, and as such more attached to their order than to their respective countries, the Holy Sepulcher, the Frankish kingdom, or any other social group whatever.

Although nominally monks, they were practically independent of the Church, for the Pope was a long way off and they recognized no other spiritual authority. The brothers of the two orders, or at least those among them who had the time and the taste for reflection, seem to have been more susceptible to Eastern influences than the other Franks. There were certainly intellectual and spiritual currents among them which were radically opposed to the Crusading spirit. It is not easy to establish the existence of a direct connection between the Templars and the Ismailians, those other voluntary dealers in death and murder by obedience to God, but it seems probable that the Assassins' brand of asceticism, deeper, more ardent, and more charged with mysticism than that of the warrior monks, did succeed by underground methods in infiltrating into an order whose members were also seeking for salvation by means of bloodshed and total obedience. That political alliances existed between the Franks and the Ismailians is well known, but any influences of a spiritual order can only be guessed at. When the Templars were put on trial early in the fourteenth century, certain "heresies" emerged which were never fully explained, and even allowing for the part played by slander pure and simple, they are still somewhat disturbing.

When Usama found himself rudely tackled by a Frankish knight, a recent arrival from oversea, who was shocked to see a Moslem praying in a Christian church, we know it was the Templars who defended him. The Templars' action proves that they could be courteous to an Arab guest, and also that religious fanaticism was not one of the Templars' vices. Yet they were monks, while the discourteous knight was a layman.

The two powerful military orders played a considerable part in the history of the Frankish kingdom, principally because of the number of soldiers they provided. Their members fell fighting in the front line in every battle and frequently decided the outcome of a combat by their indomitable spirit. Socially, their role was somewhat negative. They kept themselves ostentatiously to themselves and were not loved by nobles, clergy, or people, and they gained a reputation, no doubt deserved, for brutality and greed. Politically, the influence of the orders varied with the Grand Master of the moment, and an inefficient or overambitious master was enough to tip the kingdom toward disaster, because ultimately the kings of Jerusalem were heavily dependent on these elite troops of the powerful and practically independent orders. The reason they represented a terrible force was that although a great vassal could not necessarily command the obedience of all his men, a Grand Master could count on the total allegiance of his entire order, and could himself disobey the King with impunity, because the King could not afford to alienate the help of the military orders.

The Italians

The kingdom of Jerusalem was a *Frankish* kingdom, which by reason of the predominating French element in the First Crusade meant that it was largely French. Pilgrims and Crusaders from other lands (Germans, English, Scandinavians, Italians, and others) came to join in the great mutual enterprise of the defense of the Holy Sepulcher, but it did not occur to them to dispute control over the Holy Land with the French (or, in Tripoli, with the Provençaux).

But as we have seen, the Crusader barons also enjoyed the help of other allies, and thus a valuable assistance saved the kingdom time and again from the greatest perils and made possible its continued grip on the coast and the conquest of most of the great coastal ports. During the siege of Jerusalem, it was the Genoese ships of the Embriaco brothers which brought the Crusaders provisions and supplies for the war, and it was to Genoese sailors ("very good carpenters") that the chroniclers attribute a great part of their ultimate success, since without their movable towers and machines the town would not have fallen. In return for this important service, the Genoese had the honor of seeing their lofty deeds engraved in letters of gold in the Church of the Holy Sepulcher itself.

In the following year, the fleet from Pisa, bringing the Archbishop Daimbert, appeared off the ports of Palestine and besieged Lattakieh. Their Archbishop was elected Patriarch of Jerusalem, and the Pisans provided both gifts of money and ships ready to repulse the attacks of the Egyptian fleet.

In 1108, Bertrand of Saint-Gilles reached the besieged city of Tripoli, bringing a Genoese fleet, and this valuable reinforcement was instrumental in swaying Baldwin I's feelings in Bertrand's favor. The blockade at sea finally made possible the capture of the city, which had been holding out for five years.

In 1123, during Baldwin II's captivity, a large Venetian squadron inflicted a severe defeat on the Cairo fleet which allowed the Frankish armies to take Tyre the following year.

A recital of these few facts is enough to show that the fate of the kingdom was not decided only on land. The war at sea had its importance, and without the help of powerful fleets the Franks of Syria would never have been able to gain possession of the coast. Without this, their possessions would have been limited to a narrow strip of land surrounded by Moslem countries, and they would have been swiftly crushed. Possession of the coast was a vital necessity to the Franks, as the great leaders of the First Crusade had realized at once.

The Crusaders possessed no fleet of their own. The Egyptian fleet, which was built for war as well as trade, controlled the southern Mediterranean, and this gave Egypt certain rights over the cities of the Palestinian coast. The coasts of Syria and Asia Minor were held by Byzantium, also a great maritime power. For reasons which have already been outlined, relations between the Franks and Byzantium were somewhat strained, and the Crusaders had the less reason to expect help from the Byzantine fleet because they had taken a number of Syrian ports from the Empire and refused to return those they had captured from the Turks.

The eleventh century had seen the rapid growth of the trading fleets belonging to the great merchant ports of Italy: Amalfi first and then Pisa, Genoa, and Venice. These cities were wealthy commercial republics with dreams of supplanting Byzantium in the Mediterranean market, and they were looking for new outlets on the trade routes to the East. It is possible that the intervention of Genoa and later that of Pisa in the affairs of the Crusade were equally due to the republics' eagerness to serve God's cause—but it is certain that the first consideration of the captains of the Italian fleets was always to win concessions for their home cities in the lands they conquered, beginning with Jerusalem. The Genoese were not satisfied with having their name in letters of gold; they wanted their own street, and so did the Pisans in Jaffa. After the capture of Tripoli the Genoese earned themselves, as well as a street in the great city, the whole town of Jebail. At the time of the First Crusade, the Venetians were allies of Byzantium and lent, or rather hired, their fleet to her. Alexius Comnenus, being pressed for money, had made vast concessions to the Republic of Venice in Constantinople itself and given the Venetians exorbitant privileges which ruined his own trade. Constantly on the verge of financial disaster and resorting to one expedient after the next, he then, in return for the loan of huge sums of money, and incidentally also hoping to counterbalance the influence of Venice by means of her rivals, Pisa and Genoa, conceded whole districts in Constantinople, together with monopolies and tax exemptions, first to Pisa and later to Genoa. The Empire was becoming more and more materially dependent on the three republics, and in the course of the twelfth century they were almost totally to obliterate Byzantium as a commercial power.

Early in the century, however, Alexius Comnenus still felt himself strong enough to exploit the rivalry between the great Italian cities. When the Pisans began to settle in Constantinople, this was a bitter blow for the Venetians. Hitherto, they had been prepared to support the Greeks against the Crusaders should this become necessary; now, in revenge, they began to take an interest in affairs in the Holy Land. It was in the Venetian interest to weaken their old rival, the Egyptian fleet, and they were not anxious to see Pisa and Genoa take over the Frankish ports in Palestine. On May 30, 1123, the great Venetian fleet of three hundred ships, led by the Doge Domenico Michiel, destroyed the entire battle fleet of Egypt off Ascalon in one of the long succession of famous naval battles which became the glory of Venetian history. After assisting the Franks in the capture of Tyre, the Venetians demanded and obtained such privileges in the kingdom that when Baldwin II emerged from captivity, one of the first things he did was to repudiate the treaty which had been signed with Venice on the grounds of impracticability. Even then, he left his new allies with immense advantages, including a quarter of the city of Tyre, a district of their own in every Frankish city, total Venetian autonomy over the lands conceded to them, and exemption from customs dues.

Genoa, who as a result of her part in the siege of Tripoli had supplanted her rival Pisa in the Palestine market, had long enjoyed similar privileges. It was not long before Pisa returned to the attack. Another great merchant republic, which played a more modest part in the Holy Land despite having stronger links with France and Languedoc than her Italian rivals, was Marseilles, but she too obtained trading rights in Jerusalem, a church at Acre, and another market at Jaffa.

What the Italians were hoping for was nothing more or less than a stranglehold on the entire trade of the country where they established markets, and this meant both the ruin of local trade and the elimination of foreign rivals. Moslem, Jewish, and Syrian traders had been impoverished by the war and did not enjoy the same privileges as the Italians, while under Frankish rule the local population was chiefly employed in craftsmanship or the production of manufactured goods for which cities like Tyre, Tripoli, Acre, and Jerusalem were famous. Such trade as there was remained on a small scale. Venice's real rival was Genoa, and Genoa's rival was Pisa, and these Italian nationals were divided by an implacable enmity more violent than

any between Christians and Moslems or Greeks and Armenians. They
lived in a state of armed neutrality in separate, fortified districts,
chained off from one another, and in a land where the military
power was not in their hands they were unable to settle their disputes by fighting. (Moreover, with the exception of the city of Acre,
the Palestinian ports in the twelfth century were never major Italian
colonies. The "quarter" allotted to each republic generally contained
only a few hundred or possibly a thousand people.)

The Italian colonists retained a permanent contact with their native cities through the fleets which came to anchor in all the great
ports, dropping and picking up pilgrims, and they still thought of
themselves very much as citizens of Venice or Genoa rather than of
Acre, Tyre, or Jaffa. Their districts were vast warehouses stuffed
with all the merchandise of the East which for centuries had been so
highly prized in Europe: silk, both raw and elaborately worked,
costly fabrics from China and the Indies, carpets from Persia and
Arabia, precious stones, perfumes, spices, exotic fruits, candied or
dried. Some of these things were made on the spot, others imported
from still further east: vessels of gold and glass, weapons, stamped
leather, enamel, ceramics, and objects made of ivory and ebony.
Once they had a foothold in the great trading cities of the East, the
Italians were able to acquire all this merchandise and sell it at a far
lower price than before the Crusades. This was especially true of articles manufactured in the Holy Land itself. Their object was to ruin
the trade of Byzantium with the West. The Italian colonists were
officials appointed by the republics to watch over the interests of
their native cities and were, understandably, no more than mildly interested in the fate of the Frankish kingdom.

What they were doing was actually benefitting the West, and already as early as the first half of the twelfth century an appreciable
rise can be discerned in the standard of living of the wealthier classes
in Western Europe, with the appearance on the market of products
which were formerly rare and costly, such as silks and spices. This
sudden enrichment was not the result of the Crusades themselves,
which were a source of expense rather than profit to the West. It was
the trading activities of the Italians and the ruthless competition existing between the rival cities which made it possible for Europe in
the space of a few decades to enjoy some of the riches of the East.

The letters patent held by the great merchant seamen were a good
deal more ancient than those of all the great imperial, kingly, or
feudal families which had been in control of military power since
ancient times only to vanish one after another. Phoenicians, Greeks,

et aussi sams lieus la cimtou.
Et les xpiens phibitaus z demou
rans . z que les austres par eulx
tyranniquement z Justiumaint
ment tues . Ils auoient resceu
en Justissieuse bie a fin que sur
eulx en loprobze du saint nom
xpiens paissent continuer plus
longuement leurs Justatables

mautistes . Et comment Il
les tenoient en trop opprobzieuse
captiuite z seruage . ou tressaint
deshoneur z opprobze de tous
les xpiens . Consuiant z mon
strant par diuerses raisons tre
euidentes que le saint peuple
xpien ne debzoit plus souffrir
nendurer que les sains lieux et

The Council of Clermont. Fifteenth-century miniature, from
"Livre des passages d'outre-mer," by Sébastien Mamerot

I

ABOVE: Battle before Jerusalem. Fourteenth-century miniature, from "La très noble et excellente ystoire des saintes chroniques d'outremer"

Godfrey of Bouillon in a siege tower. Fourteenth-century miniature

Crusaders' entry into Jerusalem. "La très noble et excellente ystoire des saintes chroniques d'outremer"

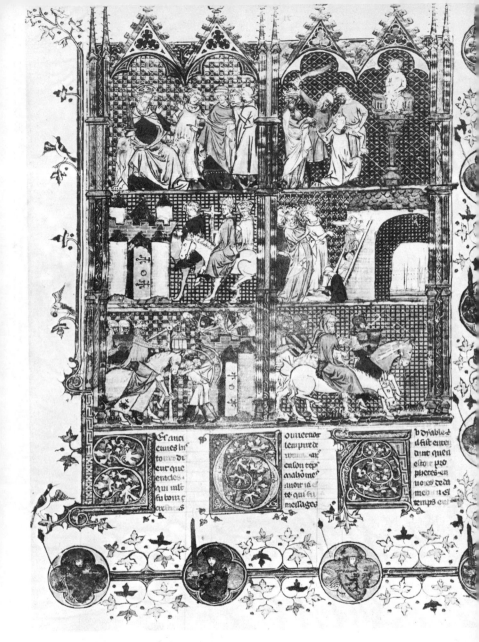

Scenes from the First Crusade. Fourteenth-century miniature, from "Romans de Godefroi de Bouillon et de Salehadins"

Godfrey of Bouillon cutting off a camel's head. "Romans de
Godefroi de Bouillon et de Salehadins"

Death of King Baldwin I. "Romans de Godefroi de Bouillon et
de Salehadins"

V

Entry of Conrad III and Louis VII into Constantinople. Fifteenth-century miniature, from "Grandes chroniques de France"

Saladin hanging Christians. "Romans de Godefroi de Bouillon et de Salehadins"

Plan of Rome. Fifteenth-century miniature, from the "Très riches heures du duc de Berry," by Pol Limbourg. Chantilly Museum

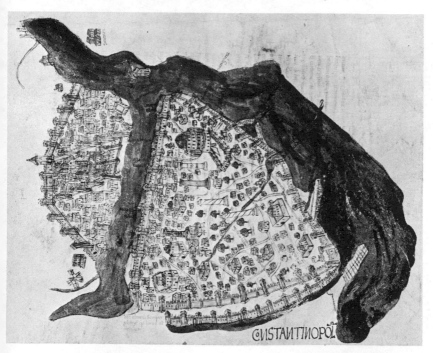

Plan of Constantinople. Thirteenth-century drawing

View of Antioch. Late sixteenth-century engraving

... iew of Jerusalem from the east. Late six- ...enth-century engraving

... Church of Calvary at Jerusalem, with tombs ...f Godfrey of Bouillon and Baldwin I. Seven- ...eenth-century engraving

Church of the Holy Sepulcher at Jerusalem. Seventeenth-century engraving

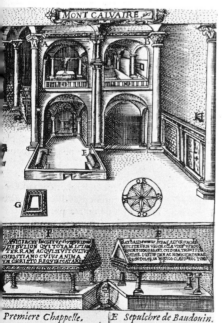

Premiere Chappelle.
Seconde Chappelle.
Fente du mont de Caluaire.
Où se void la teste d'Adam.

E Sepulchre de Baudouin.
F Sepulchre de Godefroy.
G La pierre de l'Onction.
H Entree de l'Eglise.

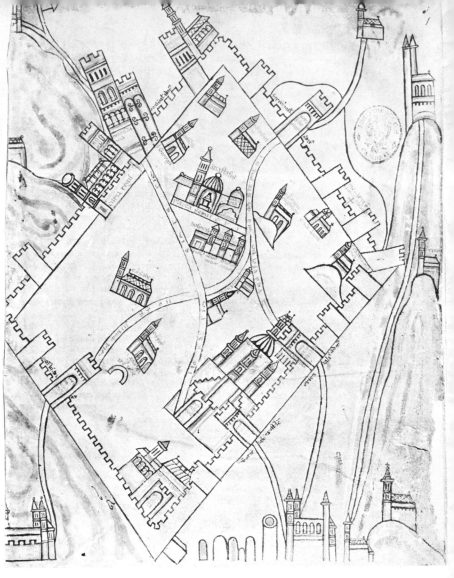

Plan of Jerusalem. Twelfth-century drawing

ABOVE RIGHT: View of Damascus. Seventeenth-century engraving

BELOW RIGHT: Castle of the Templars at Margat. Seventeenth-century engraving after a contemporary miniature

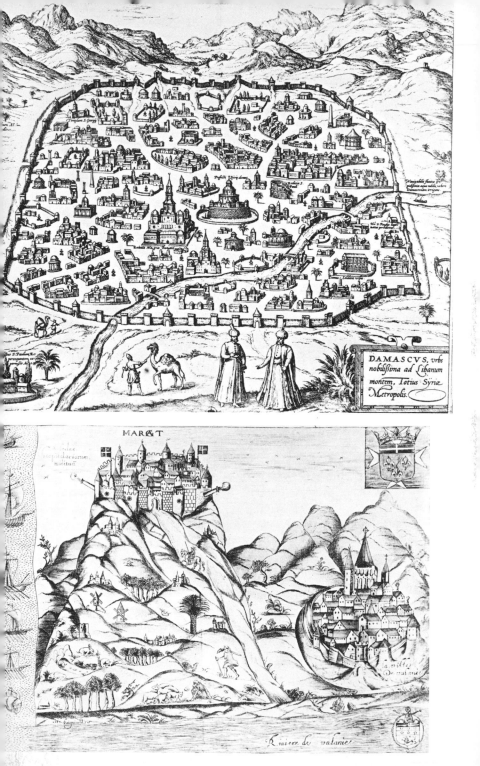

Plan of Jerusalem and its environs. Seventeenth-century engraving

Effigy of Robert Curthose, Duke of Normandy, one of the leaders
of the First Crusade

Portrait of Emperor John Comnenus. Twelfth-century mosaic from Hagia Sophia, Constantinople

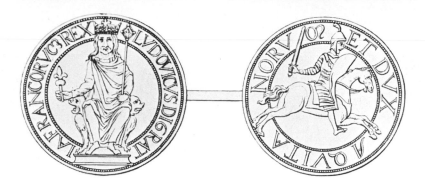

Seal of Louis VII before 1148,
after a seventeenth-century engraving

Portrait, presumed to be of Saladin. C. 1180

Portrait of
Frederick I Barbarossa.
Twelfth century.
Vatican Library:
"Roberti Monachae
Historiae Hierosolymita

Richard Coeur-de-Lion
and his mother,
Eleanor of Aquitaine.
Effigies in the
Abbey of Fontevrault

Crusader's cross:
the First Crusade.
Cluny Museum, Paris

Lead seal of a
Prince of Antioch
(Bohemond).
Twelfth century

Coins of Bohemond I,
Prince of Antioch.
Eastern Latin coins

Coins of Baldwin I,
Count of Edessa:
between 1098 and 1100

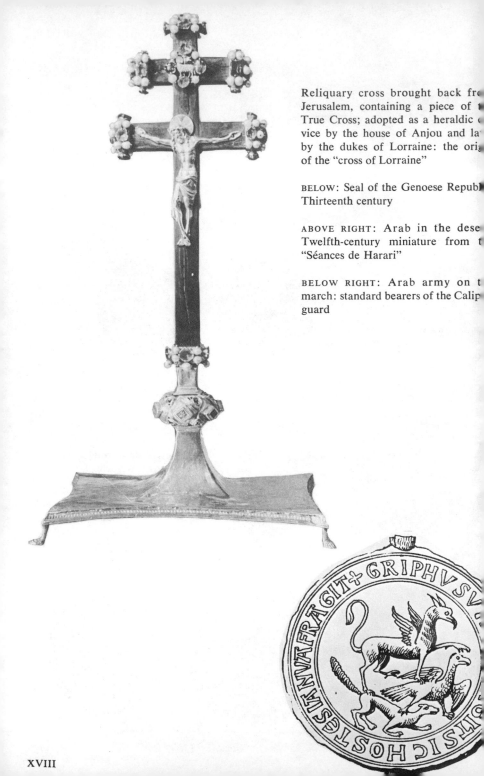

Reliquary cross brought back from Jerusalem, containing a piece of the True Cross; adopted as a heraldic device by the house of Anjou and later by the dukes of Lorraine: the origin of the "cross of Lorraine"

BELOW: Seal of the Genoese Republic. Thirteenth century

ABOVE RIGHT: Arab in the desert. Twelfth-century miniature from the "Séances de Harari"

BELOW RIGHT: Arab army on the march: standard bearers of the Caliph's guard

وارى أديم فدفر وفدفر بلدفد ● وافعى بالسع عند المورد

وأثرهم الصواب والغلط وإن جلية الحكم عندي فارتبوا بنقدي وكلاستفوا العمل

Arab vessel. Thirteenth-century miniature

Saladin's horsemen. Fourteenth-century miniature, from "Romans
de Godefroi de Bouillon et de Salehadins"

Turkish lord with his flocks. "Romans de Godefroi de Bouillon et de Salehadins"

Laying siege to a city. Thirteenth-century Spanish fresco, Casa Aguilar, Calle Montcada, Barcelona

Scene from a campaign of James I of Aragon. Thirteenth-century
Spanish fresco, Casa Aguilar, Calle Montcada, Barcelona

Medieval seamanship: Crusader fleet in the Bosporus. Fifteenth-century miniature, from "Livre des passages d'outre-mer"

Warriors. Mosaic from floor of Church of St. John the Evangelist, Ravenna

ABOVE RIGHT: Death of Roger le Preux in battle. Fourteenth-century miniature, from "Romans de Godefroi de Bouillon et de Salehadins"

BELOW RIGHT: A Crusader knight. Twelfth-century fresco from church of Cressac

LEFT: A pilgrim. Fresco in the crypt of the church of Tavant

RIGHT: Portrait of Geoffrey Plantagenet. Twelfth-century enamel, Le Mans Museum

BELOW: Warrior. Twelfth-century sculpture from St. Martial, Limoges

Portrait statue
of Count Timo (?).
Thirteenth century,
from Naumbourg
Cathedral

Tombstone of Gerard I,
Count of Vaudémont,
Crusader,
and his wife(?).
Twelfth century,
Chapelle des
Cordeliers, Nancy

Arabic mural decoration. Twelfth century

Decorative inscriptions from tombs of Seljuk sultans (Konya)

ABOVE: The Pope and the Emperor. Thirteenth-century Byzantine-Romanesque mosaic in Chapel of St. Sylvester, Rome

LEFT: Twelfth-century Byzantine mosaic from Norman Sicily. Chamber of King Roger in palace at Palermo

RIGHT: Frankish Syrian sculpture: remains of a church capital from Nablus

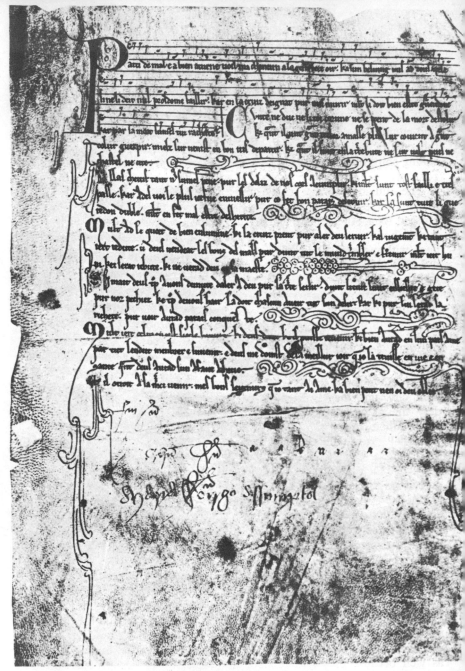

Manuscript of a Crusader song. Twelfth century

Romans, and after them the Arabs, Byzantines, and Italians who sent out their ships on the spice routes from the great Mediterranean ports all belonged to one race, the great and terrible race of maritime adventurers and seekers of fortunes. They were daring, ruthless, and cunning, a proud and greedy race matured by a long tradition of the cult of money and the power money bestows. In the days of sailing ships and camel caravans, the life of a merchant on the spice route was no sinecure.

The Italian republics dealt with markets as far afield as China and the Indies. Their ships circumnavigated Africa and their caravans crossed Asia. An ordinary sailor from Genoa might know a great deal more about the wide world than all the savants: he rubbed shoulders with people of all colors and all religions, traveled in many different climes, and rarely died in his bed. On their long voyages the captains followed itineraries which had been handed down to them by their predecessors in deadly secret, and they used endless ingenuity to send the ships of their competitors astray.

Travelers by land and sea would never reveal the routes they followed or the names of their suppliers to anyone. Trade secrets were like secrets of state and men would rather die than betray them. The great armorers and the heads of the merchant houses in each great city would meet in council or parliament to direct the interests of their city, and they represented a power which had every right to defy the great barons of the land. They were not always united among themselves, but they would make common cause to defend the privileges of their republic, indifferent to any considerations other than their trading prosperity and motivated by a keener and more conscious local patriotism than any displayed by the aristocracy. This patriotism might be directed at the exploitation of a new trade route or the annihilation of a rival. Almost unknown to the princes of Europe, the great Italian merchants of the twelfth century were already a force to be reckoned with.

The aristocracy despised the "bourgeois" on principle. Citizens were not allowed to bear arms, but in those cities that were ruled by a "commune" there was nothing to prevent important citizens from walking out surrounded by an armed bodyguard, and sometimes even laying hands on the person of a noble. The nobility of the great cities were merchants as well, and great merchants rose to titles of nobility. Frequently, the merchant adventurers went on trading expeditions in person. Commercial fleets were equipped as battle fleets as well because they had to defend themselves against pirates and the ships of powerful enemies. Hundreds of ships were lost at sea with all hands, and in this way huge fortunes could be reduced to nothing overnight. Merchants had the gambling instinct in their blood, and this only added to their nose for profit. Business took no account of Greeks, Turks, or pagans, and a Genoese would more willingly strike a bargain with the Egyptians than with the Pisans. We find the Pisan merchants of Antioch sending supplies to the people of Tyre and Tripoli while these cities were under siege by the Franks.

This is not to say that the wealthy merchant class was indifferent to religion. The magnates of Italian trade gave generously to endow pious foundations, to adorn churches and build new ones, and offered jewels of great price to the Virgin of their district. Few had more need of divine protection than these men whose lives were constantly at the mercy of a tempest or a pirate raid, and few had greater need of divine mercy on their deathbeds. They also regarded this pious generosity as yet another means of increasing the glory of their city and their family. But the interests of their city, and therefore of their trade, were undoubtedly more important to them than those of religion under whatever aspect they appeared. These people had settled in the Holy Land for the greater prosperity of their own cities, and it never occurred to them to regard the Frankish kingdom as their native land or to risk their own possessions in defense of the Holy Sepulcher.

It must be said that the Frankish chivalry did nothing to facilitate the assimilation of Italian notables into a land where both were foreigners. The descendants of Hugh Embriaco, who became lord of Jebail after the siege of Tyre, were an exception to this rule, and even so, it was not until the second half of the twelfth century that these wealthy Italians became completely ennobled and were adopted by the Count of Tripoli's Provençal nobility as Franks, the lords of Embriac and able to regard themselves as Frankish barons of Outremer. William of Tyre's continuator is very explicit on this point: eighty years after the first exploits of the Italian fleets in the Holy Land, the Italians were still looked on as an inferior race: "Those from France held those of Italy in contempt, and an Italian, however rich or valiant he might be, was held to be a *vilain:* since the majority of those from Italy were usurers [bankers] or corsairs and merchants, and men who were knights despised them on this account."[27]

The difference in culture, traditions, and way of life between the bourgeois, who were generally of Latin origin, and the nobles, largely of barbarian descent—Germanic or Norman—was too great to allow of any real collaboration between them. The wealthy citizens, who

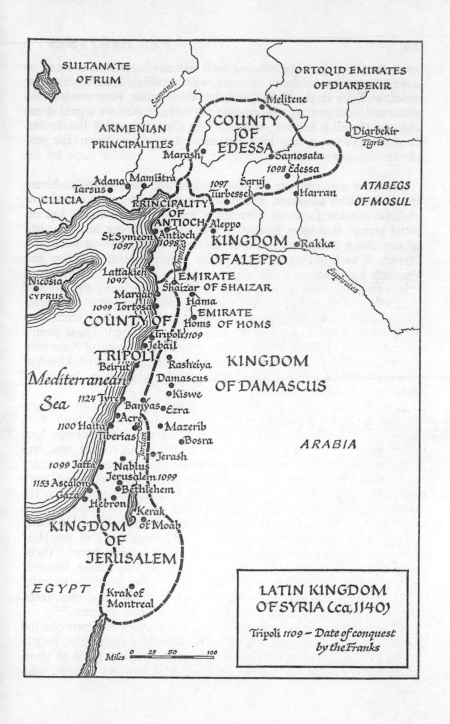

SULTANATE OF RUM

ORTOQID EMIRATES OF DIARBEKIR

Samanti

Melitene

ARMENIAN PRINCIPALITIES

COUNTY OF EDESSA

Diarbekir
Tigris

Marash

Samosata
1098 Edessa

ATABEGS OF MOSUL

Adana
Tarsus
Mamistra

1097 Saruj
Turbessel

Harran

CILICIA

PRINCIPALITY OF ANTIOCH

St.Symeon
1097
Antioch
1098

Aleppo

KINGDOM OF ALEPPO

Rakka

Orontes

Lattakieh
1097

EMIRATE OF SHAIZAR

Euphrates

Nicosia
CYPRUS

Shaizar

Maraab
1099 Tortosa

Hama

EMIRATE OF HOMS

COUNTY OF

Homs

Tripoli 1109
Jebail

TRIPOLI

Beirut

Rasheiya

KINGDOM

Mediterranean

Damascus

OF DAMASCUS

Sea

1124 Tyre

Kiswe

Banyas
Ezra

1100 Haifa
Acre

Mazerib

Tiberias

Bosra

ARABIA

Jordan

Jerash

1099 Jaffa

Nablus

1153 Ascalon
Gaza

Jerusalem 1099
Bethlehem

Hebron

Kerak of Moab

KINGDOM OF JERUSALEM

EGYPT

Krak of Montreal

LATIN KINGDOM OF SYRIA (ca. 1140)

*Tripoli 1109 — Date of conquest
by the Franks*

Miles 0 25 50 100

throughout Europe were winning their independence by the force of money and often by force of arms, were hostile to the knights on principle. Even in the Holy Land, Italian colonists were much more concerned with gaining new trading advantages than with getting on with the Frankish barons, who although Christian and Catholic like themselves, were in the long run more foreign to them than the Moslem merchant class.

This brief note may provide some insight into the internal problems of the Frankish kingdom, where even subjects of Latin origin and Catholic religion (a small minority in the total population) formed social groups that were foreign to one another. There will be more to say about the third and not the least important element, the Church. Now it is time to return to the political development of the Frankish kingdom.

CHAPTER

VII

The Franks Between Byzantium and Islam: Aleppo, Damascus, and Cairo

(1 1 3 1 – 1 1 7 4)

The Zengid Threat and the Policy of Fulk I

In the course of his twelve-year reign (1131–1143) King Fulk reaped the benefit of the political and religious troubles which turned the Moslem world upside down during these years. Baghdad, Damascus, and Cairo suffered palace revolutions and popular risings, and even Zengi himself was compelled to abandon his plans for conquest because his tyrannical behavior was, not unreasonably, disquieting to the Arab and Seljuk princes.

Zengi, the apostle of the holy war against the Franks, found himself at war with the religious leader of Sunnite Islam, Mustarshid the Caliph. This warlike Caliph was not one to resign himself to the role of puppet king which the Turkish sultans had imposed upon the Commander of the Faithful, and aimed at reviving the glorious traditions of Harun al-Rashid. Al-Mustarshid was a brave man and—as a religious leader—popular, and he had taken advantage of the death of the Sultan Mahmud and the ensuing interregnum to declare war on Zengi who, as atabeg of Mosul, was the principal general of the Persian empire. Defeated by the Caliph's armies and besieged in his capital of Mosul, Zengi had reason to fear a revolt of his own subjects, who as good believers favored the Caliph. Even when Mustarshid had been defeated by the Sultan Mas'ud and later assassinated, and Zengi was finally triumphant, he had still too many Moslem enemies to deal with to be free to attack the Franks.

Summoned to Damascus by the atabeg Ismail ibn Buri (a grandson of Toghtekin), he did not succeed in taking possession of the city. In spite of the chaos caused by palace revolutions, Damascus was still able to resist the formidable atabeg of Mosul, and after Ismail had been assassinated, a former mameluke of Toghtekin's named Unur took over command of the Damascene armies and Zengi was forced to abandon the attempt in the face of the city's energetic resistance. Zengi did not resume operations against the Franks until after the Caliph's assassination in 1135.

Thus, after a few years of only comparative peace, the Frankish kingdom found itself once again in the most critical situation. The Franks of Syria suffered defeat after defeat, and this time they must have realized that they would not be able to maintain themselves in the country by their own efforts. They had to do two things: appeal for help to the West and look for allies on the spot. Unfortunately, these courses of action, both equally necessary, were not easily reconcilable.

When, on the French King's advice, Fulk of Anjou came to take possession of Baldwin II's inheritance, he may not have foreseen that in addition to the manifold responsibilities of the kingdom of Jerusalem, he would also have to reckon with the person who brought him the royal crown as her dowry. Fulk was a mature man, hardened by long experience of power and the profession of arms, yet he seems to have fallen genuinely in love with the young Eastern princess who had been given to him for his bride. However, Melisende of Jerusalem did not love her husband. She loved another man, a young knight named Hugh of Puiset, who was her childhood friend and her second cousin. This love, which may or may not have been perfectly innocent, provoked the King's jealousy and led to a scandal at court. It was a long and complicated story, and Hugh of Puiset did not play a very impressive part in it. Fulk was probably not directly involved, but the affair ended with the young man being challenged to defend himself in the lists against a charge of treason. He failed to appear, was condemned in his absence, and took refuge with the Egyptians in Ascalon. Although disgraced by his dealings with the infidel, Hugh nevertheless obtained his pardon in return for a promise to return to Europe as an exile. On the eve of his departure, he was stabbed by a knight from Brittany, and he died in Sicily not long afterward as a result of his wounds.

To clear himself in the eyes of his wife and the general public, Fulk had the murderer put to the torture, and he denied to the end that the King had anything to do with the crime. It is impossible to say whether Queen Melisende was convinced. William of Tyre credits her with plotting to kill her husband, or at least, asserts that "the King . . . many times believed himself in danger of his life." According to all the evidence, the young Queen was utterly desperate at the death of the man she loved, and dreamed of nothing but murder and revenge. "None of those who had been the Count's [Hugh's] enemies were safe; they dared not go out without weapons and a great company, and could not venture among crowds for fear of receiving a thrust from a dagger."[1] For William, who had a great respect for the Queen, to speak in this way, Melisende's despair must have been truly obvious and terrible.

Her extreme grief gave the young woman a great hold over the King. Fulk's behavior shows that he did not know what to do to comfort the Queen and win her forgiveness. William of Tyre also says that he "submitted all the affairs of the kingdom to the Queen to know her advice and her desires; he did not hold even the smallest reception without her presence."[2] This shows that when time had assuaged her grief, Melisende was not slow to take full advantage of her aging husband's genuine affection for her, and she possessed an autocratic disposition. Indeed, it was lucky for Fulk that she was not really interested in politics.

In 1135, the Queen persuaded the King to rehabilitate her sister Alice. Very much against his better judgment, it seems, the King reinstated the dangerous princess in her rights as regent of Antioch. Just at the very moment when Zengi had his hands free on his eastern frontiers and was able to concentrate his efforts on the conquest of Frankish Syria, the principality of Antioch fell once more into the hands of a woman who had previously been prepared to hand the city over to Zengi himself. It was not long before the King, who was not utterly blinded by love, took back with one hand what he had given with the other.

Princess Alice had gained some supporters among the Franco-Norman nobility (William of Tyre says that she did this by means of lavish gifts of money). She had given up any idea of an alliance with the Turks, but relied instead on the support of Joscelin II, Count of Edessa, and governed with the aid of the Patriarch of Antioch, an intriguing and ambitious prelate named Radulph of Domfront. Alice was regent, but the real Princess of Antioch was her daughter, little Constance. Her mother is said to have disliked the child so much that she considered shutting her up in a convent, or marrying her to some baseborn man. In 1135, Constance was seven or eight years old and consequently almost of marriageable age. Since she could not risk getting rid of her, Alice decided to make use of the young Princess and offered her in marriage to Manuel Comnenus, the young son of the Emperor of Byzantium. In this way she hoped to exchange Frankish protection for the more distant and therefore more malleable suzerainty of Byzantium. This the Frankish barons of Syria wished to avoid at all costs. Fulk sent ambassadors secretly to France to find a husband for the young heiress of Antioch.

The selected bridegroom was Raymond, younger son of William IX of Poitiers, Duke of Aquitaine. Raymond was a man of thirty-six, already renowned for his courage and military experience and famous also for his physical strength, which was exceptional, and his handsome appearance. Such was the complexity of diplomatic relations at the period, and so uncertain the routes by land and sea, that the great French baron had to travel much of the way disguised as a "poor pilgrim" in order to escape being captured and imprisoned on the way. Furthermore, the object of his journey had to be kept deadly secret since it was important not to awaken the suspicions of Princess Alice, whose spies were everywhere. Moreover, Alice had a certain ally in Roger II of Sicily, who had hated the kings of Jerusalem ever since the affront offered to his mother by Baldwin I, and who also, as Bohemond's cousin, had a claim to the inheritance of Antioch. Roger II possessed a considerable fleet and it would not have been difficult for him to capture the unwanted suitor. In the end, after a voyage packed with adventures, Raymond of Poitiers reached Antioch, but before he could get inside and lay hands on young Constance, he still had to deal with the Princess Alice.

The princess was betrayed by her ally, the Patriarch Radulph, who summoned Raymond to his presence and made him swear an oath of fealty, even asking for his "liege homage" (unheard-of pretension on the part of a cleric). Raymond promised everything that was asked of him. Next the Patriarch made Princess Alice believe that it was she and not her daughter that the Duke of Aquitaine's son wanted to marry. In fact, Alice was not yet thirty and this would have been a more appropriate match than the other. Alice does not appear to have suffered from an excess of naïveté, but even so she was silly enough to believe the Patriarch and allowed Raymond of Poitiers to enter her city. She welcomed him cordially and withdrew to her palace to prepare for the wedding. While she was doing so, Radulph of Domfront was solemnizing the marriage between the baron from the West and little Constance in the church of Saint John. Alice's regency was at an end. Raymond, as the lawful husband of the young Princess, was the rightful Prince of Antioch.

The Patriarch regretted his perfidious treatment of the Princess Alice. Raymond of Poitiers had no intention of keeping the oaths which the wily Radulph, whose own part in the affair seems remarkably guileless, had made the mistake of taking literally. The new Prince of Antioch raised a cabal against him, had him accused of simony and various other abuses, and finally obtained his deposition.

At last, after the tragic disappearance of her two Norman Princes, Antioch had a new master—a man from Europe, like Fulk the King, and a baron of the highest nobility of France. He was brave, ruthless, and a man of few scruples, but he really meant to be a good vassal to the King of Jerusalem. Raymond may have made an enemy of Joscelin II of Edessa from the outset, but Fulk at least had nothing to complain of from him, and it was high time the principality of Antioch had a head.

During the short reign of Princess Alice in 1135, Zengi had succeeded in recapturing from the Franks the castles of Atharcb, Zerdana, Tel-Aghdi, Maarat al-Numan, and Kafartab, all of which belonged to the principality of Antioch. In the same year, Zengi's lieutenant in Aleppo, Sawar, was ravaging the principality's lands, pushing his incursions as far as Lattakieh. Two years later, Pons, Count of Tripoli, was killed on an expedition against Bazawash, the mameluke commanding the armies of Damascus, and on this occasion it is important to note that there were in the Moslem army "pious Moslems who desired to earn their salvation."[3] Their zeal was such that they actually killed the Count of Tripoli when he was an unarmed prisoner, and in full knowledge of who he was, although they could have expected a considerable ransom for him. At this time, Frankish power appeared to be so much weakened that the Syrian Christians of the mountainous hinterland of the Lebanon rose and made common cause with the Turks. Unable to avenge himself on the Turks, Pons's young son, Raymond II, at least succeeded in torturing and slaughtering a great many of these rebellious peasants. "Thus he consoled himself as best he could, and consoled others who had lost their friends."[4]

In the same year, Zengi personally led an attack on the Count of Tripoli's possessions. King Fulk, who came to the young Count's assistance, was defeated before Montferrand and shut up and besieged in the citadel with what was left of his army. The situation was so serious that this time the Count of Edessa and the Prince of Antioch forgot their quarrels and gathered all their knights to come to the King's assistance. They came too late. Fulk surrendered after a desperate resistance, and was then extremely surprised when Zengi allowed him to depart freely, with full honors of war. Zengi had his reasons. He had accepted an honorable surrender because the Frankish relief army was only a few days' march away and he did not want to risk being caught between two fires.

But the King's defeat showed that the Franks were losing ground more and more seriously, and there was an urgent need to revise the kingdom's whole political policy. Fulk at least seems to have realized this. A new test arrived in the nick of time to point the Franks of Syria a new way of coping with their difficulties.

John Comnenus

It has already been seen that the Normans' hold over Antioch irritated Alexius Comnenus beyond bearing and had turned the *basileus* against the Crusaders since the early years of the century. That a city regarded by Byzantium as one of the most venerable in her Empire should have fallen into the hands, of all people, of Bohemond and his successors seemed to Alexius disgustingly unfair, a crime deserving the worst possible punishment. After defeating Bohemond and seeing to it that he ended his days in humiliation and obscurity, Alexius had requested Tancred to carry out his uncle's promises. Tancred's reply had been an insolent refusal, which provoked the Emperor very nearly into abandoning his other wars and all the affairs he had in hand in order to take his army and chastise the audacious barbarian who dared to flout him. Only the open opposition of his own followers prevented him. But for the great Comnenus, the matter of Antioch had become a real obsession, and his hatred of Bohemond, which even his adversary's death had not appeased, made him regard Tancred, and any Frank who was likely to take Tancred's side, as the worst enemy of his Empire. He was prepared to resort to any means to drive the Normans out of the ancient Byzantine city. He roused the court of Egypt against the Franks. He even wrote to the Caliph of Baghdad and the Sultan of Persia, urging them to take up the holy war against the Christians who had settled in Antioch. (In 1111, the citizens of Baghdad reproached their Sultan with the words, "Do you then not fear God's anger, that you suffer the King of Roum to have more zeal for Islam than yourself?") Not content with this diplomatic warfare, Alexius tried to win back the coastal cities belonging to the principality of Antioch from Tancred by force of arms. In this he could rely on the sympathies of Christians belonging to the Greek rite, and the Normans had almost as much trouble defending themselves against the Greeks in the west as against the Turks in the east.

Alexius realized that the other Franks—the King of Jerusalem and even Count Pons of Tripoli—were ultimately on the same side as the Normans of Antioch and were not anxious to see the principality revert to the possession of the Empire. Consequently, Alexius Comnenus was compelled to regard all Franks as his enemies, and worse, as traitors. Henceforth, he pretended to consider them nothing more than rebellious and ungrateful mercenaries for whose sake he had emptied his coffers, lavishing on them sums of money "beyond all reckoning," and yet they had not only refused to do the job "for which they had been paid" but had insolently turned their weapons against him.[5] In short, as far as Alexius was concerned there was no longer any question of Christian solidarity: men who trampled other people's rights underfoot as they did and whose policy was actually anti-Christian (because anti-Greek) no longer deserved the name of Christians.

This meant that as far as the Crusaders were concerned, Byzantium was a hostile power, although she was not invariably and openly so. Constantinople at that time was still something of an international metropolis of Christendom, a crossroads on the major trade and pilgrim routes, a center of cultural enlightenment—in short, a second Rome, setting herself up as an arbiter among the barbarians. Even when her stature was no longer adequate to maintain this role, she retained toward the people of the West a haughty, outwardly benevolent, and somewhat paternalistic attitude which annoyed them a great deal but to which they nevertheless subscribed. Altogether, since it was his mission to reward the good and punish the bad, the Emperor was within his rights whatever he did, and he was still ready to heap his favors on the Latins if they showed themselves worthy of his confidence. (Alexius' ambassadors are to be found telling Bertrand of

Tripoli, "You must not show yourself inferior to your father Isangeles [Saint-Gilles]"[6]—"inferior" in this case meaning less loyal to the Emperor. It is therefore difficult to accuse Alexius Comnenus of perfidy: his conduct was highly moral according to his own lights, dictated solely by the interests of the Empire and the struggle against the Empire's enemies.

Alexius died in 1118, in the same year as Baldwin I. He was succeeded by his son John, who was to reign for twenty-five years, his reign corresponding exactly in point of time to those of Baldwin II and Fulk I of Jerusalem. He was an only son and his birth had shattered the hopes of his elder sister, Princess Anna, who had dreamed of the imperial crown since she was a child. She was an ambitious woman, and while her father lay dying she was still making a bid for the throne and scheming to imprison—some even said to blind and put to death—the unwanted younger brother, whose praises she is careful not to sing in her *Alexiad*. Other Greek* and even Latin historians speak of him with admiration as a proud warrior, praising his courage and steadfastness, his exemplary morals and great piety. In fact, though less able and less of a statesman than his father, John was first and foremost a soldier monarch, the "emperor-knight." He spent his life in camps and on battlefields, continuing with a fine tenacity his father's work of reconquering the Greek provinces of Anatolia from the Turks.

He did not forget the matter of Antioch, which had been one of his father's principal preoccupations, but since he was busy with more pressing wars he hoped to be able to find a peaceful solution to the problem by means of a matrimonial alliance. His attempts failed. Roger of Salerno might possibly have agreed to marry his daughter to a prince of the imperial family in order to strengthen his own claim to a principality of which he was merely the regent, but he was killed. A projected marriage with one of Baldwin II's daughters came to nothing. Finally, when Princess Alice was thinking of marrying her daughter to John's young son Manuel, Raymond of Poitiers was summoned by the barons of Antioch and King Fulk, and came and took both the girl and the principality by surprise. Seeing this, John Comnenus was finally convinced, if he had not been so already, that the Franks of Antioch intended him no good, and made up his mind to try force.

In 1137 he appeared before Antioch at the head of an army, just at the very moment when the King of Jerusalem had been defeated

---

* John Cinnamus and Nicetas Choniates.

by Zengi at Montferrand (Ba'arin). Raymond of Poitiers had been compelled to abandon his capital, which was already under siege by the Greeks, in order to go to the King's assistance, and when it became obvious that his help was useless, he returned to continue the defense of his city. John Comnenus took this war, as he did all his other wars, very seriously. It was a bitter siege. The Emperor set up powerful siege engines and bombarded the walls without intermission, and was preparing to undertake mining operations.

Raymond and a number of his barons decided to negotiate. John demanded that the city should be handed over to him. Raymond sent emissaries to his suzerain, King Fulk, asking for help and advice. The King, after consulting the records on the matter, replied that Byzantine rights over Antioch were undeniable and the Emperor's claims consequently fully justified. Fulk was clearly reasoning as a diplomat and not as a lawyer, since the rights which the Byzantines had been claiming for thirty-five years became valid in the eyes of the Franks only when the Greek army was actually at the gates of Antioch. But Fulk's decision was not merely an expedient; it indicated a real wish to revise the policies of Frankish Syria with regard to Byzantium.

John Comnenus was dreaming of a great Crusade against Zengi. Delighted to find that those he was treating as rebellious vassals were ready to become his allies, he did not allow his troops to occupy Antioch and did not even insist on his right to make an entry into the town. Instead he went on immediately to discuss plans of campaign. His armies, together with those of the Latin princes of Antioch and Edessa, were to seize possession of the kingdom of Aleppo in the east and the emirate of Shaizar in the west, and later, carry the Crusade on toward Damascus. Once the united armies were in possession of Aleppo, Raymond of Poitiers would receive this city in fief and then hand over Antioch to the Byzantines.

Now that for once they had a Byzantine emperor who was inspired by the most authentic Crusading spirit, the Frankish princes of Syria suddenly displayed a curious indifference to the idea of a holy war. The reason could have been caution: they might have reckoned that operations on such a vast scale would leave them open to fresh dangers. It might have been fear of the growing power of the Greeks and reluctance to fall under their control. The fact remains that Raymond of Poitiers and Joscelin II of Edessa (who had formerly been at daggers drawn) suddenly found themselves allies in their mutual reluctance to support the efforts of John Comnenus.

Raymond of Poitiers was obviously anything but anxious to conquer Aleppo if by doing so he was to lose his claim to Antioch. In the end, however, the first assault by the Christian armies was not launched on Aleppo but against Shaizar, the Arab emirate which had been by turns the ally and the enemy of the Franks. This was one of the small, independent principalities whose existence was more of an advantage than an inconvenience to the Latin kingdom. John Comnenus was less closely involved, and as he had dreams of subduing the whole of Syria, it seemed as though he might as well start with Shaizar. But while he was spending himself recklessly taking part in the siege work and exposing himself to danger like the humblest of his soldiers, he saw the two Frankish princes, Raymond of Poitiers and Joscelin II, openly mocking at him, spending their time drinking and playing dice in their tents, and discouraging their knights from taking part in the fighting.

In the end, when he had actually taken possession of one of the suburbs of the besieged city, the austere emperor-knight, heartbroken at the princes' lack of seriousness, opened negotiations on his own. He obtained an oath of vassalage from the Munqidhites and the promise of an annual tribute, after which he broke camp and finally made up his mind to deal with the matter of Antioch without waiting for the capture of Aleppo.

He called on Raymond of Poitiers to hand over the city, but Raymond, who had in theory been pledged to do this ever since the Greek army had raised the siege of Antioch, was not expecting to be taken at his word. His one idea was clearly to think how to get out of performing his promise. With the help of Joscelin II, he organized a real uprising of the Frankish population of Antioch. (At that time the city included a great many French and Italians among its citizens.) The revolt reached such proportions that it was judged impossible to hand the city over to the Emperor in such a state. John Comnenus was probably not deceived by the two princes' plot, but he was compelled to withdraw, with fury in his heart.

When Zengi saw John Comnenus leave the country, he took heart again. He had been terrified when the imperial armies appeared on the Orontes, and by the alliance between John Comnenus and the Franks, and had left no stone unturned in his attempts to sow discord between the allies, including sending letters to Raymond and Joscelin charitably putting them on their guard against the Emperor's perfidy. Now, one after another, he recaptured from the principality of Antioch the frontier castles of Biza'a, Athareb, and Kafartab, possession of which was the Norman state's guarantee of safety, and which John had recaptured only a little while before.

King Fulk's only course was to seek a fresh alliance with Damascus in order to check Zengi's advance by a new coalition. The Damascenes were no more anxious than the King of Jerusalem to fall under the domination of the atabeg of Mosul, whose reputation for cruelty was already firmly established. This alliance saved the independence of Damascus and avoided for Frankish Syria the catastrophe of having such an adversary as Zengi as their immediate neighbor.

While this Franco-Moslem pact was still being consolidated, John Comnenus appeared once again in northern Syria, determined this time to force the Frankish princes to honor their promises. Once again he was compelled to withdraw having obtained nothing. Once again Raymond of Poitiers fell back on the unconquerable repugnance of the citizens of Antioch to accept Greek domination, talking about the rights of the Pope and declaring that he could not dispose of land which belonged, not to him, but to his wife, and altogether offering a total block to John Comnenus's demands (1142), although in fact he himself had summoned the Emperor to his assistance when Zengi's troops were threatening his lands.

Winter was approaching and John was not anxious to undertake a siege, but since he was determined not to give up, he resolved, while waiting to commence operations against Antioch, to make a pilgrimage to Jerusalem. He informed King Fulk of his intention and Fulk replied that he would be delighted to welcome him, but begged him to come with only a small escort since the country was too poor to support the entire Byzantine army. John answered that he was accustomed "when riding outside his Empire, to cover all the land with his army" (William of Tyre). He did not go to Jerusalem. There is no knowing whether he would in the end have imposed his will on the Franks by force of arms. He died in the spring at his camp in Cilicia, having been wounded by a poisoned arrow while out hunting. There was no longer any need for Raymond of Poitiers and the Count of Edessa to fear the annexation of their lands by the Greeks —or for King Fulk to fear the interference of the *basileus* in the affairs of his kingdom. But in John Comnenus, Zengi lost his most formidable adversary.

In 1137, after the Emperor had concluded his alliance with the Frankish princes of Syria, it did appear that some common action would be possible. John Comnenus was a sincere Christian and once he had decided to carry out his Crusade, he relied on Frankish collaboration. In exchange for certain religious concessions and a formal acceptance of his suzerainty, he would have left them the enjoyment of their lands. He would in fact have been a valuable ally for them. It is possible also that by mid-century, Greek power had already been too severely shaken to be able, even with the help of the Franks, victoriously to outweigh that of Turkish Islam. There was a risk that the conquest of Syria, Damascus, and even Egypt would have proved to lead nowhere. The Frankish princes may have considered the *basileus*'s plans too impractical and preferred to maintain a precarious status quo rather than embark on an adventure in which they risked everything. However this may be, once again it seemed that real collaboration between Greeks and Latins was impossible.

The Greeks' demands for recognition of their claim to Antioch were fair enough in themselves and, from the point of view of the interests of Christendom, perfectly reasonable. The interests of the Frankish colony suffered a little, as did those of the Latin Church in the East, but ultimately it was the actual existence of an irreconcilable hostility between Greeks and Latins which created such a divergence of interests between the two Christian communities. There had grown up gradually, in the course of nearly half a century, so much bitterness and distrust between Eastern and Western Christendom that all peaceful coexistence had become impossible, even when they were faced with a formidable common enemy whose power was continually increasing.

The Greeks may have been to blame for this. John Comnenus appears to have come forty years too late. With this warlike Emperor at its head, a great Greco-Latin Crusade could have resolved the Eastern question to the advantage of Byzantium. There would have been no Frankish kingdom, although a number of Frankish barons might have held fiefs from Byzantium. Yet it is doubtful whether under Byzantine leadership, and without the powerful stimulant of Frankish national pride, the enterprise would have been possible at all. But John Comnenus was pursuing ultimately the same goals as the Franks. He came in time to save them from disaster, halting Zengi's advance by his mere presence. He was sincerely anxious to collaborate with them, and he cannot be accused of either perfidy or weakness. John Comnenus was a valuable ally, but he was treated as an enemy.

William of Tyre's account of the siege of Shaizar suggests that Raymond of Poitiers and Joscelin II behaved like spoiled children, rude and disobedient, like schoolboys playing tricks on their teacher. (This attitude is so characteristic that the historian of the Frankish kingdom excuses the two princes by saying they were "young." Raymond was going on forty and Joscelin not much under thirty.) It has been seen that while the battle was raging fiercely on the Greek front, these two rested in their tents, dressed in "silken robes," playing dice and chess and mocking those who were wounded in the battle. The Emperor himself came to beg them to behave differently: "He prayed them gently to show a little more energy in the work they had undertaken, since he, who was wealthier than they and had kings and great princes under his dominion, did not rest but exposed himself to pains and dangers in the service of Our Lord; they ought not to do less than he." But it was this very awareness of the Emperor's superiority, his official superiority due to the wealth and glory of his Empire, which annoyed the two Frankish princes. They were petty feudal lords, jealous of their independence and constantly ready to tear one another to shreds, as indifferent to "the service of Our Lord" as they were to vast plans of conquest.

Joscelin II was clever and intelligent, but he was a man of pleasure rather than of action. His attitude in this affair has frequently been explained by the fear of seeing Raymond take possession of Aleppo and become too powerful. Raymond of Poitiers was not a man of great intelligence or will power; he was despotic rather than authoritative and vain rather than proud, and so easily influenced that he even listened to advice from Joscelin, whom he detested and who detested him. The strange thing is that these two rather ordinary men were perhaps, in their mischievous way, wiser than the proud and valiant John Comnenus. It was not in the interests of either the Franks or Byzantium to destroy buffer states such as Shaizar, Aleppo, and Damascus. Even the conquest of Aleppo by itself would have been a mistake; it would have been enough to eliminate Zengi, who was the real enemy of the moment. John Comnenus had nothing to gain by recovering Antioch from the Franks, who regarded it as their property and were better able to defend it; all he needed was a friendly collaboration. If the projected Franco-Byzantine alliance failed in 1137, it was because John Comnenus was still insisting on his idea of a "Crusade," while for the Frankish barons—even for a new-comer such as Raymond—this idea was already out of date.

Events will show that the kings of Jerusalem were thinking more and more seriously of a Byzantine alliance, and that John Comnenus's successor, who also realized the need for such an alliance, did his best to get the Frankish kingdom of Syria under his influence. No real understanding was ever achieved: the prejudices on both sides were too deep and the conflicting interests too irreconcilable. Above all, there was the conflict between the ancient pride of Byzantium and the young pride of the West. This conflict was of a kind over which no practical considerations could triumph.

When John Comnenus made a triumphal entry into Antioch after the failure of his campaign against Shaizar, Raymond of Poitiers and Joscelin II walked on foot in front of him, holding his horse's reins. John believed he was merely acting as a lawful suzerain; he was much too aware of the sacred character of imperial majesty to understand that the two princes and their barons regarded this ceremony as a real humiliation.

King Fulk survived John Comnenus by only eight months and he, like the emperor-knight, died as a result of a hunting accident. He fell from his horse and was fatally injured. His death was a great loss to the Frankish kingdom. Fulk had been a strong man, gifted with both common sense and a sense of duty, a good organizer, an agile diplomat, and a strong, reliable warrior. He had succeeded in winning the respect both of his major vassals and of the barons of the kingdom. In the kingdom of Damascus, he had managed to raise a still-solid bulwark against the danger threatening the Frankish lands, creating a real pact of alliance with this neighboring country which made himself and the people of Damascus together strong enough to resist Zengi. Thanks largely to his wife, he had succeeded in establishing a climate of understanding and mutual esteem with the local Christians, Armenian and Syrian. He extended the Frankish possessions in Transjordan and to the east of the Dead Sea, and built castles there to command the caravan routes. In Judaea, he built castles to protect the surrounding countryside, which he repopulated with Christian colonists; in a short while this countryside became a rich, well-cultivated land.

At a time when the power of Zengi was an ever increasing menace, Fulk was the only really strong man in Frankish Syria. The three great fiefs were ruled by incompetents and were moreover divided by irreducible misunderstandings. With the death of the King, Frankish Syria lost its head: the regency fell into the hands of the Queen, a woman by no means devoid of initiative but completely ignorant in matters of politics and dreadfully jealous of her authority. Fulk of Anjou's natural successor was his eldest son, Baldwin III, who was thirteen at the time of his father's death.

Melisende

Queen Melisende remained regent for as long and longer than her son's age demanded. She had not forgotten that her husband had become King of Jerusalem through her, and that she was Baldwin II's eldest daughter and heir. She mourned her husband's death with every appearance of sincere grief, but for her its greatest importance lay in the opportunity it offered her to satisfy her craving for power at last.

It is true that even while Fulk was still alive, she had attempted to interfere in matters of government as much as her influence over her husband allowed her. Not content with playing a merely advisory role, she had busied herself in founding religious houses and had also taken steps toward attempting to bring about a reconciliation between the Frankish community and the local Christian communities. The fact that she herself had been born in the country and was herself only half Frankish put her in an excellent position to do this. She introduced the Jacobite Metropolitan, Ignatius of Edessa, into her husband's circle of friends, and Michael of Syria tells us that Fulk, though a Frank from Europe, was happy to see the prelate and regarded him as "an angel from heaven." The Queen's youngest sister, Joveta, had entered the Church, and Melisende set about building a new convent especially for her and enriching it with generous gifts. She very soon used her influence to have Joveta nominated abbess of the community.

Melisende was a pious woman, with the stern, mystical piety of the East. She had a lifelong passion for churches and emptied her treasury in pious donations. But once regent, she showed a much greater eagerness for worldly honors than for spiritual perfection and quickly made herself, in the words of William of Tyre, "feared" by the barons of Jerusalem. She also made herself feared, or at least respected, by her two sons. Young Baldwin III remained under his mother's tutelage until the age of twenty-two, and only freed himself under pressure from the barons and public opinion after a hard struggle. Melisende's piety was not altogether disinterested. She was an ambitious woman, and she hoped to use the support of the clergy and the native population to control the barons' party, which held the military power.

Melisende seems to have loved power for its own sake. She did not possess a political turn of mind or any real sense of her responsibilities, or show any desire to impose a particular ideal or party. She knew how to make herself obeyed, but she was incapable of turning the authority she wielded to good account. Her regency was marked by military disasters and political errors caused by her inability to rise to a crisis. In the end, for important decisions involving peace or war, she was obliged to fall back on the Hierosolymitan barons who formed her immediate entourage, and on the most aggressive and intriguing section of these. Mistrustful of any whom she suspected of acting in the interests of her powerful vassals, she listened to the advice of men whose ambitions were limited to security and the growth of the "kingdom" as such, even if this were at the expense of other Frankish states. Her chief confidant was her first cousin, Manasses of Hierges, her father's nephew, whom she had appointed constable. Manasses was no less personally ambitious and no less politically incompetent than his cousin.

Thanks to the deaths of John Comnenus and of Fulk, Zengi could now congratulate himself on having his hands free as regarded both Byzantium and the kingdom of Jerusalem. He took advantage of the situation: a year after Fulk's death he laid siege to Edessa, the most isolated and exposed of the capitals of the Frankish states. It must be admitted that Melisende did her best to get together an army to relieve her native city, which had been her father's first fief, but she was not able to act quickly enough or stir up the enthusiasm of her knights. Her army arrived too late and, when it learned of Zengi's victory, made no attempts to retrieve the situation. Instead, after a brief skirmish with a body of Turkomans, it turned back, a fact which suggests that the army was neither very numerous nor very aggressive.

Edessa

Edessa, the first great city of the East to fall into Frankish hands, Baldwin of Boulogne's first conquest, which had been held by Baldwin of Le Bourg and later by Joscelin of Courtenay, had been a "Frankish" city for forty-six years. Now it had fallen into the possession of the Turks, who even before the Crusades had never occupied it except for a few years. But it was probably thanks to the Franks that this important Byzantine and Armenian stronghold, one of the most threatened by Islam, had remained under Christian control for longer than it would have done under Armenian princes.

As we have seen, at the beginning of the century the inhabitants, finding the Franks no easy masters, had several times conspired to deliver the city up to the Turks. But Joscelin of Courtenay, and also his son Joscelin II, had succeeded so well in establishing a climate of understanding between the Franks and the local population that by the time Zengi came to lay siege to the city there was no longer any question of the Edessans conspiring to surrender to the enemy: the entire population, Syrians and Armenians as well as Franks, were solidly determined to resist.

Unfortunately the Count himself, Joscelin II, was not in the city, as he usually lived on his domain of Turbessel, which was situated in a more rich and tranquil and pleasant part of the country. There he led a life of pleasure, heedless of Zengi's intentions. To distract him, Zengi had been leading a campaign against the Ortoqid emirs in Diarbekir.

Joscelin II was so improvident that he had not even thought of supplying his capital with reserves of food or a strong garrison. Latin and Oriental chroniclers tell us that he openly favored the native Christians—especially, and understandably enough, the Armenians —above the Franks, and was not anxious to antagonize his subjects by forcing on them the military protection of the Franks. As a result, the defense of the city of Edessa was entrusted primarily to the Armenians, who were good soldiers but did not—at least this is the fault William of Tyre has to find with them—possess the military discipline of Western soldiers.

When Joscelin heard that his city was being besieged, he appealed to the regent, who did in fact take steps to send him reinforcements, and to his neighbor and enemy Raymond of Poitiers, who was in a better position than Melisende to help Edessa. Raymond was deaf to Joscelin II's appeals. As William of Tyre puts it, "the Prince of Antioch saw that the Count of Edessa was in great anguish and peril to lose his inheritance, and this gave him great joy." Left on his own, Joscelin could do nothing against Zengi's army. He remained at Turbessel waiting for reinforcements.

Edessa was a strong city with high, thick walls, well able to drive off attacks and withstand bombardment by machines. The entire population manned the ramparts to help the defenders. In spite of shortage of food, the defense was fierce and caused terrible losses in the ranks of the besieged. Zengi's sappers succeeded in undermining one of the towers, which collapsed, opening a passage to the besieging army. The Turks swarmed into the city and a fearful carnage followed, in which all the Franks perished, including the Latin Archbishop Hugh, who had been directing defense operations in the Count's absence. A great many native Christians were also massacred, or were trampled to death in the crowds which rushed to the gates of the citadel at the entrance of the Turks.

On December 26, 1144, Zengi entered the first great Christian city to be reconquered from the Franks, and not a single Frankish army so much as attempted to dispute his victory.

It was a catastrophe for the whole of Frankish Syria, and Raymond of Poitiers, rejoicing at the downfall of his enemy Joscelin, was now the first to be threatened. The Latin barons did not at first realize the magnitude of the danger, for the very reason that the victim of the disaster was Joscelin, half native himself and accordingly despised as such—the only Frankish prince who had aimed at winning the support of the native element and had broken the ties of solidarity which bound the Franks among themselves. Although he was not a bad soldier, Joscelin certainly lacked initiative and the capacity for decision. But the ruin of the county of Edessa strengthened Zengi's position and he had no intention of interrupting his run of good luck.

Once master of Edessa, the terrible atabeg, who two years earlier had had the Moslem garrison of the city of Baalbek crucified, put a stop to the carnage, called a halt to the sack, and made his soldiers return all the property they had taken from the inhabitants. He also returned all prisoners and generally made it clear to the Christian inhabitants of the conquered city that he meant to treat them with humanity and had only come to liberate them from Frankish tyranny. He meant to use Edessa as an example to attract the sympathies of the populations of other cities of Frankish Syria. By these sensible measures he succeeded in ensuring the help of the Syrians of Edessa. (Michael the Syrian states this explicitly in the words he puts into the mouth of the Jacobite Archbishop Basil Bar Shumana: "What has happened is very good. . . . For you [Zengi], because you have carried off a brilliant victory, for us, because we have deserved your esteem; for just as we have not failed in our oaths toward the Franks, so we shall keep the faith we have sworn to you, since God has permitted us to become your slaves."[7])

The Armenians of Edessa, however, were in no mood to admit that "what had happened" was "very good." They had always been much more hostile to the Turks than the Syrians. However, Zengi appeared to have made up his mind to win the support of the native element, and he heaped his favors upon the vanquished. He allowed Edessa to continue under its own government, completely respecting its character as a Christian city, and satisfied himself with leaving a

Turkish garrison there which was expressly forbidden to oppress the population.*

After this great victory, Zengi proceeded to take away from Joscelin his stronghold in the county on the right bank of the Euphrates.

Zengi could undoubtedly have taken possession of the entire county of Edessa with very little trouble, because no Frankish army came to the help of the unfortunate Joscelin and Raymond of Poitiers was still rejoicing at the defeats suffered by his enemy. But a rebellion broke out at Mosul, and the atabeg had to strike camp and take his armies hurriedly back to his capital. The great Moslem general was no prophet in his own country and had to be constantly fighting against his brothers in religion. He was meditating the conquest of Damascus, and had just laid siege to a small Arab fortress, Qalat Jabar, when he was assassinated on September 15, 1146. This does not appear to have been a political act, but simply the revenge of a slighted servant.

Ibn al-Qalanisi says that "Zengi had gone to sleep, after drinking some wine. He awoke suddenly and saw the eunuch (a man named Yaruqtash) drinking the remains of the wine with some pages. He threatened them with punishment and went back to sleep. Then they killed him."[8]

The man who had for fifteen years been the heaviest threat to Frankish and Moslem Syria was no more. His opponents thought they could breathe again. Zengi's courage had inspired immense admiration among the Franks. Contemporary Latin historians, while execrating the cruelty of "Sanguins" as it deserves, portray him as tireless, intrepid, and omniscient, always ready to seize a favorable opportunity to do some harm to his enemies. There was even a rumor, in Europe as well as in Syria, that the atabeg of Mosul was of Frankish origins. His mother was supposed to have been Ida, the lovely Austrian Margravine who was taken prisoner and ended her days in the harem of Zengi's father, Aqsonqor. Only a great lady of Europe was worthy to have given birth to such a hero. (The legend was none too well founded, seeing that Zengi's father died seven years before the tragic events of 1101, and if the Margravine had survived the battle she would undoubtedly have succeeded in obtaining her release at the cost of a ransom.)

With Zengi dead, it seemed as though anything might happen.

* Here however the Syrians were clearly favored, which explains the dissatisfaction of the Armenians.

His enemies had no reason to suspect that his successor would prove even more formidable to them. In fact, the kingdom which the remarkable atabeg had scarcely begun to found quite naturally split in two after his death. His eldest son, Saif ed-Din Ghazi, inherited Mosul, although before he could do so he had some trouble in putting down a revolt by the local Seljuk prince. The younger, Nur ed-Din Mahmud, inherited Aleppo. This division, while it apparently weakened Zengid power, was a fresh danger for Syria. Nur ed-Din was young and energetic, and since he was not, like his father, forced to keep one eye constantly on Mosul, he was able to devote himself with redoubled ardor to the conquest of the territory around Aleppo. While he waited for an opportunity to deal with Antioch and then with Damascus, he turned his attention to what remained of the county of Edessa.

But Nur ed-Din was still young and unknown. As soon as the news of Zengi's death reached Edessa, the Armenians in the city believed that their hour of liberation had come. Joscelin II had not given up hope of winning back his capital, and discouraged by the lethargy and hostility of the Frankish princes, he decided to attempt to recapture it by his own efforts. With what remained of his knights he launched an attack on Edessa, and the population opened the gates to him. He was given a triumphal welcome, massacred the Turkish garrison (some of whom succeeded in taking refuge in the citadel), and sent messages to Antioch and Jerusalem to ask for reinforcements.

William of Tyre tells us that the reconquest of Edessa caused great joy throughout the land. If so, it was totally disinterested: no reinforcements were forthcoming. Nur ed-Din marched on the city with his whole army. Edessa, which had been disarmed by Zengi two years earlier and possessed only improvised weapons, had no troops to speak of except for the handful of Franks that Joscelin had brought with him.

Joscelin gave up all hope of assistance (and in fact neither Melisende nor Raymond of Poitiers had made any attempt to raise Nur ed-Din's siege of Edessa). He made up his mind to a desperate course of action, which turned out to be criminally rash. Rather than leave the population shut up in the city at the mercy of the Turks, he undertook to help the inhabitants escape in one massive sortie, hoping to get them through the enemy lines and dispersed about the countryside. He had insufficient troops to protect an exodus of tens of thousands of civilians with their wives and children and sick, and after a bloody and furious battle in which the Turks, an-

gered by the "treachery" of the Edessans, spared no one, the city
was captured a second time. This time it was punished unmercifully.
The city was sacked wholesale, and those of the people who were
left alive were reduced to slavery or expelled. Joscelin himself fled
and took refuge in the castle of Samosata on the other side of the
Euphrates.

Michael the Syrian estimates that the two sieges (the second more
murderous than the first) cost Edessa thirty thousand human lives,
as well as a further sixteen thousand sold into slavery. He says that
a thousand men managed to escape by flight, but not a single woman
or child. "Edessa was left deserted, a hideous sight, infested with
the bodies of its children, the home of jackals."[9]

This disaster was due as much to the lack of interest shown by
the heads of the other Frankish states as to Joscelin's rashness and
the impatience of his Armenian subjects. At that time, the states
were not even at war, and it would have been easy for them to take
advantage of Zengi's death to undertake a unified offensive against
his successor, who was still only shakily established in Aleppo. This
did not even occur to them and they left Joscelin to fight and be
destroyed all alone, feeling free to heap their scorn on him later.

All the same, because of the horror of the massacre and the wreck
of the city, this second fall of Edessa did cause great feeling in the
country, feeling which was all the greater because people were realizing, with some consternation, that Zengi's son was no less fierce
and warlike than his father. It will soon be apparent that he was, if
possible, still more dangerous. William of Tyre said that he was
"a pious and wise man, and one who, according to the superstitious
tradition of his people, *feared God.*" He feared Him only too much.
Zengi had been a man of great ambition, but Nur ed-Din was a fanatic. His hatred of the Franks was a religious hatred, and his love
of the holy war the result of sincere piety.

The Second Great Crusade

In Europe, and in France especially, there was still a good deal of
interest in what was going on in the Holy Land, although this was
not a particularly active interest. Ever since two great French lords,
Fulk V of Anjou and Raymond of Poitiers, the son of the Duke of
Aquitaine, had become princes in the East, French feudal society
felt joined to that of Syria by ties of family solidarity. French barons, like those of the Empire, went on pilgrimage to Jerusalem and

became Crusaders for a few weeks, sometimes a few months, at a time. Diplomatic and commercial relations were becoming increasingly important. For more than half a century, the Holy Land had been a kind of French Catholic province, although this did not prevent other Catholic countries, Germany, England, and the Scandinavian countries in particular, from feeling an interest in the Holy Land. People in Europe already regarded the situation as a perfectly natural one and one destined to last indefinitely, while Frankish conquests in Syria could only go on increasing. In granting victory to the Christians, God had made it clear that He wished them to triumph over Islam by force.

Consequently, the fall of Edessa in 1144 had already caused some anxiety among the European nobility. As early as 1145, King Louis VII was thinking of taking the cross and going to the aid of the Holy Land, which, as the facts proved, was more than ever threatened by the infidel.

Louis, an inordinately pious young man, dreamed about the Crusade in very much the same way as the pilgrims of 1096, and indeed, as pilgrims at all times. To him, taking the cross was a mystical adventure rather than a political move. But after half a century of French rule in Jerusalem, he was convinced, as King of France, that the French crown had a messianic role to play and believed that he was following in the footsteps of Charlemagne, who, according to a generally accepted tradition, had made the pilgrimage to Jerusalem.

The German Emperor, Conrad III, was also cherishing the same hopes and ambitions. Certainly when Saint Bernard, an ardent advocate of the new Crusade, preached before the Diet of Speyer, the Emperor was inflamed by a wholly religious zeal for the Holy Places and was not keen to leave to Louis of France the honor of being the first great European ruler to set foot in Jerusalem.

One popular legend had it that a Christian king or emperor, a descendant (or reincarnation) of Charlemagne, would bring about the arrival of the millennium, the thousand years of peace and prosperity preceding the final triumph of Jesus Christ, by taking possession of Jerusalem. Certainly at about the time of the Second Crusade there was a fresh current of popular excitement which gave rise to the appearance of preachers and "prophets" who based great hopes on King Louis's Crusade, saying that he would be the "King of the Last Days" of the apocalyptic prophecies.

Saint Bernard, who cannot be suspected of being influenced by these somewhat anarchic trends in popular piety, nevertheless saw the Crusade as a work for the salvation of souls rather than as a purely political and military enterprise. His preaching reached a wide audience. There is no doubt that it was his passionate eloquence over and above any political considerations which made the Emperor Conrad and his barons decide to take the cross. Saint Bernard preached at Vézelay, and crowds gathered to hear him. Great barons took the cross in a wave of enthusiasm, and just as at the time of the First Crusade, there were numerous poor pilgrims. The regular armies made it a point of honor to allow these, God's poor, to follow the army, and the barons supported bands of civilians by alms-giving although these were a source of trouble and even danger to an army in the field.

It is known that both armies, the French and the German, took the road separately as far as they could, and on the few occasions they met displayed the most open hostility and outrageous contempt for one another. Moreover, since they both had to travel through Byzantine territory and pass Constantinople, the two armies had serious trouble with the Emperor Manuel Comnenus, who, like his grandfather Alexius before him, distrusted and feared them even more than he feared the Turks. The two armies were strong (although less numerous than those of the First Crusade), their knights well equipped and disciplined, their infantry—partly made up of civilian pilgrims—turbulent and somewhat disorganized, a source of continual conflict with the populations of the countries through which they had to pass.

At the very moment when the King of France and the Emperor of Germany were nearing Constantinople, Manuel Comnenus had just made peace with the Seljuks of Anatolia. True, the Seljuks were not exactly the Turks the Crusaders had come to make war on, but even so the Sultan of Rum was not disposed to allow the Frankish armies to cross his territory, and Manuel Comnenus's action looked like a deliberate act of hostility toward the Latins. Later events were to show that the Franks really represented a greater danger to Byzantium than the Turks, in the twelfth century at least, but it is possible to aggravate a danger by overapprehension. Manuel's first thought was to get the Crusading armies across to the other side of the Bosporus as quickly as possible. Once he had seen them land in Asia Minor he lost interest in their fate, and there are even some grounds for accusing him of complicity with the Turks as far as King Louis's army was concerned. (It is a fact that Louis VII's arrival in the East accompanied by his wife, Eleanor of Aquitaine, raised the question of Greek claims to Antioch, the Queen of France being a niece of Raymond of Poitiers. Manuel, who could not have cared less about the interests of France and Westerners in general, would still have preferred to see the French army beaten by the Turks than see it settled in Frankish Syria as a Latin force hostile to Byzantium.)

Never before had such a brilliant gathering of European princes crossed the Bosporus. With the German army, besides the Emperor Conrad III, were Bishop Otto of Freisingen (the Emperor's half-brother), Conrad's nephew Frederick of Swabia (later Barbarossa), Henry, Duke of Austria, Welf, Duke of Bavaria, Herman, Margrave of Baden, Henry, Bishop of Toul, Stephen, Bishop of Metz, William, Marquis of Montferrat, and many other great lords of the Empire.

Some of the greatest vassals of France had taken the cross with the King's army: Henry, Count of Champagne, Alfonso-Jordan, Count of Toulouse, Thierry, Count of Flanders, and Robert, Count of Dreux and brother to the King. Most of the great lords took their wives and daughters with them, accompanied by a suite of noble attendants, ladies in waiting, chaplains, and servants, as well as the poor they had taken under their wing.

The fate of these two great armies was a little less sad than that of the armies of 1101, but the civilian pilgrims, the "poor," seem to have been fated never to set eyes on the Holy Land, even from a distance. It can be assumed that nearly all of them suffered the fate of Peter the Hermit's companions and the hosts of the poor from Lombardy, Germany, and Aquitaine.

The Emperor Conrad was the first to land in Asia Minor and was defeated by the troops of the Seljuk Sultan of Rum, Mas'ud I, in the region of Dorylaeum. Once again, as in 1101, the heat and the Anatolian desert were the Turks' best allies. The Germans, dying of heat and thirst, were surrounded and, since they were unable to crush their opponents by a massive cavalry charge, were either slaughtered on the spot or put to flight. William of Tyre reckons that in this battle of October 26, 1147, Conrad lost nine-tenths of his army. Even if this is something of an exaggeration, it is certain that he lost nearly all his foot soldiers, all the pilgrims, and a large number of his knights. All the leaders managed to escape, but for practical purposes the army no longer existed. Thousands of fugitives were captured and sold into slavery. Conrad returned to Constantinople and from there took ship directly for the Holy Land. The others who had escaped the disaster could only fall back on Nicaea and pursue their journey under the protection of the French army. They had lost everything in the debacle. Michael the Syrian says that the Turks collected so much booty after their victory that overnight the value of silver in the country "became as the price of lead."

The King of France was more fortunate. After marching through mountainous and desert regions where he lost many of his men, in falls from cliffs and from starvation as well as in attacks by Turkish bands, he succeeded in cutting his way through to Attalia, a coastal city belonging to Byzantium. From there, the French took transport on Greek ships, in small groups, as far as St. Symeon, the port of Antioch. Some of the infantry and civilians were unable to find transport, and these unfortunates were expelled by the Greeks and nearly all of them perished in Turkish attacks.

Once again the poor people were attracted by foolhardy if not actually criminal propaganda and paid dearly for it. This Crusade, like the earlier ones, distinguished itself by a ridiculous and terrifying waste of human lives, the lives of poor, humble folk. A great many knights and wealthy people also lost their lives, especially among the Germans. A great many more were taken prisoner—ten thousand, at least.

Of the German army, nothing remained beyond the great barons and a hundred or so knights, but the French army had, all things considered, lost only the least useful fighters and useless mouths. With traditional feudal selfishness, the rich soon consoled themselves for the sufferings of the poor. It could still be said that the Franco-German army—or rather the French army accompanied by the remains of the German—was still a strong force. It was strong enough, at all events, to delight the Franks of Syria and to intimidate Nur ed-Din. The inhabitants of Aleppo regarded themselves as already on the eve of disaster when they learned that a great king of the Frankish lands was almost at their gates.

Westerners and "Syrians"

With the help of the Frankish armies in Palestine, or even with those of Antioch and the military orders alone, the royal army could at that moment easily have taken Aleppo and dealt a decisive blow to Nur ed-Din. It did not do so. Louis VII stopped short at Antioch, the first great Frankish city on the way to Jerusalem, but he seemed in no hurry to make war. This, after the exhausting and murderous crossing of Asia Minor, is sufficiently understandable.

The Prince of Antioch, Raymond of Poitiers, had hastened to welcome these providential guests with banquets and all honors. He thought they came to save him simultaneously from the grasp of Byzantium and the Turkish attacks and was highly delighted, believing himself already rid of Nur ed-Din and master of Aleppo, to say nothing of the provinces which he had lost along the Orontes. He was doubly fortunate in having, in the person of his niece Queen Eleanor, the best of advocates with the King. It is a known fact that Louis VII was passionately in love with his wife, who was a beautiful, clever, flirtatious, and willful princess. Unfortunately, what Raymond thought was his greatest asset did him more harm than good.

There has been a good deal of argument about the nature of Eleanor of Aquitaine's relations with her uncle. Raymond, although he was getting on for fifty, must still have been a handsome man and was certainly more attractive than the dull, morose Louis. On the other hand, the Prince of Antioch was reputed to be a most faithful husband, and considering that he had not shown much interest in amorous exploits so far, it seems hard to believe that he should have tried to seduce his own niece. Whatever the truth of the matter, by explaining to the Queen the advantages of a campaign against Aleppo, Raymond of Poitiers drew on himself the jealousy of the King.

The King and the great Crusader barons, although they had recently discovered to their cost what the Turks were like, cannot have realized the dire threats hanging over the flourishing province of Antioch and the wealthy, apparently peaceful city where the Franks of Outremer led a life of greater luxury than that of kings in the West. In his desire to be pleasant to his hosts, Raymond of Poitiers had not neglected to display before their eyes all the refinements of the Oriental hospitality which had already become a legend about the Franks of the Levant. Probably all this luxury of sumptuous palaces, rich with mosaics, silken hangings, and splendid gardens filled with fountains and marble-tiled pools, merely antagonized the Crusaders from the West rather than winning their admiration. A luxury which astonished no one in the East must have filled them with envy and scorn for their compatriots who, far from "defending the Holy Sepulcher," were leading a life of pleasure in dreamlike cities. Raymond's earnest pleading could not impress them. Yet the Prince of Antioch himself was only too well aware that he was living on the edge of a volcano, and a year later his severed head went to join those of his two predecessors in Baghdad.

Depressed by Louis VII's attitude, Raymond promptly thought up a plan to change alliances which, in the circumstances, could do him nothing but harm. He turned to the Queen. Eleanor of Aquitaine was undoubtedly a woman of considerable personality. Although, being a woman, she was bound to submit to her husband's tutelage, she was nevertheless Duchess of Aquitaine in her own right, suzeraine of a larger and wealthier province than the domain of the kings of France. Raymond of Poitiers had some excuse for believing he could rely on her. He tried to detach her from the French alliance, and the only way of doing this was to get the Queen's marriage annulled and so bring Aquitaine under the rule of a different suzerain. In the event, the most obvious choice seemed to be Henry Plantagenet, the heir to the throne of England, a nephew—through his father Geoffrey, the son of Fulk of Anjou—of the young King of Jerusalem. The English marriage was certainly agreed to between the uncle and niece at the same time as the breach of the French marriage. At all events, we know from William of Tyre[10] that Raymond's advice was behind the young woman's decision. Eleanor told her husband that she intended to leave him and asked for an immediate divorce. Since he could not obtain Louis VII's help, the Prince of Antioch at least revenged himself by instigating the divorce which was to leave the kingdom of France in danger for centuries. Louis VII's immediate reaction was to leave Antioch secretly by night, taking the Queen with him, still protesting her wish for a divorce. He made for Jerusalem, followed by his army and the rest of the barons.

Raymond of Poitiers saw his last chance of triumphing over Nur ed-Din vanish after a momentary glimpse. Louis, deeply embittered by his wife's behavior, could console himself with the prospect of seeing Jerusalem and the Holy Sepulcher at last.

This Second Crusade was certainly unlucky: after the heavy losses suffered in Anatolia, after the abandonment of the projected campaign against Nur ed-Din at the very moment when a campaign of this kind was most wanted, and after the semipolitical, semi-emotional drama which ended in the breach between the royal couple, a new tragedy was to disrupt relations between the Crusader barons and the Count of Tripoli's Provençal nobility.

Alfonso-Jordan, Count of Toulouse, the son of Raymond of Saint-Gilles, who was born in the Holy Land and taken to Europe as a child to reign over Toulouse, came with his wife and two of his children to visit his birthplace and the Holy Places at the same time, and to see his father's tomb. Count Raymond and his followers in Tripoli were none too pleased at this double pilgrimage on the part of the Count of Toulouse. Raymond II's grandfather, Bertrand of Saint-Gilles, had come to Palestine in the same way in the past to claim the county of Tripoli from his kinsman William-Jordan of Cerdagne. It was possible that the Count of Toulouse, the late Bertrand's half-brother, would do the same and try to seize Tripoli from his grand-nephew. The memory of Raymond of Saint-Gilles was still revered in the Lebanese Provence, and the arrival of his son, born in the country, the distant, lawful lord of the Oriental Provençaux, who were more attached to their mother country than the men from the north of France, was awaited with great impatience. If he had wanted to, Alfonso-Jordan would certainly have had no trouble in getting rid of young Raymond II and having himself proclaimed Count of Tripoli. Probably he did not want to, but that Raymond II feared him is a fact.

The Count of Toulouse died suddenly at Caesarea, where he had halted on the way to Jerusalem. He had been in good health only the night before, and there was talk of poison. In fact, poisoning is not always easy to prove, even in our own times, and was even less so in those days. William of Tyre, who regarded the crime as a certainty, says only that "a son of the devil, no one knows who or why he did it," slipped some poison into the Count's food. Even if Alfonso-Jordan's death was an accident, as is very likely, no one believed it.

Naturally, the men of Toulouse and the other Crusader barons blamed the Count of Tripoli. For lack of evidence, no one could be either accused or proved innocent. Even the regent, Queen Melisende, was suspected of having done it to protect the inheritance of her younger sister Hodierna, who was married to Raymond II. This may seem to be carrying sisterly affection rather far, but the Queen was well known to be passionately fond of her sisters. Whatever the truth, the consequence of the unexplained tragedy was that the Provençal nobility, indignant at the suspicions which fell on their young Count, refused to go to Jerusalem with the Crusading army.

The Crusaders' meeting in Jerusalem was saddened by mourning for the Count of Toulouse. The Emperor Conrad had arrived there to join the French army with what barons were left to him, and all the chivalry of the kingdom of Jerusalem gathered to welcome the noble pilgrims. Louis VII was at last able to prostrate himself before the Holy Sepulcher and visit Bethlehem and Golgotha, and to one of his pious temperament these satisfactions may well have compensated for the fatigues and sufferings he had endured and even for his disappointment in love. He was a man for whom Jerusalem was an object in itself. He had actually rejected Raymond of Poitiers's proposals on the grounds that he had not come to fight for Antioch but to worship Jesus Christ at Jerusalem. But the Crusaders had not come to the East merely to pray.

The presence of the French King's army and so many great European lords (not to mention the Emperor Conrad) in Jerusalem was an extraordinarily providential event, an unexpected piece of good fortune for all the Franks of Syria. It was something which had never happened before and was never likely to happen again. In fact, although after the losses it had suffered in Anatolia this army was no stronger than the rest of the local armies together, it nevertheless appeared a formidable force. People had been hoping for a *real* Crusade for so long. Now the King of France and the Emperor of Germany had actually arrived. But they had not come to spend their lives in Syria, only for a warlike pilgrimage, and it was vitally urgent to make the most of this one chance. Raymond of Poitiers had already tried to enlist the King's aid and had failed. Joscelin II was hoping to reconquer Edessa and Raymond of Tripoli wanted to win back Montferrand. While the King was still in Antioch, these two princes had sent the King and the Emperor letters full of entreaties and expensive presents. Their ambassadors besieged the Crusader princes with arguments in favor of one or the other plan of campaign. Badgered by requests from four separate directions, and not very well informed about the real position of the Frankish states, Louis VII had obeyed the dictates of his conscience, regarding Jerusalem as the most important city to be defended. Unfortunately, at that particular moment Jerusalem was in no danger and stood in no need of defense.

The Westerners were understandably more than a little bewildered by this feverish competition, the rivalries and conflicting local interests, and they decided that the Franks of Syria were thinking a great deal more about the safety of their own lands and very little about the glory of God, and that each one seemed anxious to profit by the help of the Crusaders to the detriment of his neighbors. In Antioch, Louis VII had been visited by the Patriarch of Jerusalem, Fulcher of Angoulême, who had been sent by the regent. The prelate had tried to make the King understand that it was his duty to go to the Holy Places first, and Louis had easily allowed himself to be convinced. But in Jerusalem, the King found the same atmosphere of intrigue and distrust, and the same desire to make use of his presence for purposes of conquest—conquests which he was quite willing to believe were necessary for the defense of the Holy Places. The trouble was that all parties were urging this necessity with the same assurance.

In Jerusalem at that time there was an aggressive party which, imagining the strength of the royal army to be greater than it was, believed that the time had come to seize Damascus. In the end, because they were in Jerusalem, the Crusading princes were won over to the opinion of these Hierosolymitan barons. It is hard to see that Baldwin III had any say in the plan to conquer Damascus, for at the time he was only a youth of eighteen and still very much in awe of his mother. Neither did the regent have any great territorial ambitions. It is already clear that, in matters of foreign policy, Melisende allowed herself to be guided by her constable, Manasses of Hierges, and the constable and his party were among the feudal lords who were eager to annex as much land as possible, with no ideas beyond the immediate interests of the kingdom itself. For them, the Counts of Tripoli and Edessa and the Prince of Antioch were rivals and not allies. There can be no doubt that the campaign against Damascus, just because it was an aggressive campaign, appealed to the Crusaders more than the defensive, or semidefensive, campaigns envisaged by the heads of the other Frankish states. There were more lands to acquire, and more than one among the Crusader barons must have had dreams of the laurels won by Godfrey or Bohemond, while in Frankish Syria itself there was no longer any land without its lord.

As we have seen, Fulk of Anjou had established a firm treaty of alliance with the kingdom of Damascus. This pact was broken, four years after his death, at the instigation of the constable and barons of Judaea, who came to the assistance of the Emir of the Hauran in his revolt against the atabeg of Damascus in the hope of winning new lands in the region. This amounted to a declaration of war. The Frankish army, led by the youthful Baldwin III, was defeated by the Damascenes and narrowly escaped disaster. The regent of Damascus, Muin ed-Din Unur, had formerly been one of Toghtekin's lieutenants and he favored the Frankish alliance in preference to a pact with Nur ed-Din. He was a formidable warrior and an able politician, jealous of his country's independence, and while he was prepared to offer steadfast resistance to the Franks in case of attack, he was also ready to renew an alliance which offered him a guarantee against the inroads of the atabeg of Aleppo.

It was consequently the most monumental political blunder to allow the Crusading army and the Frankish army of Syria to attack Damascus, which asked nothing better than peace, while in the north the very existence of the Frankish states was being threatened by Nur ed-Din. But Damascus had a greater attraction for the Crusaders than the unfortunate cities of Edessa or even Aleppo. The siege of Damascus was therefore agreed upon almost unanimously. Moreover, it was an undertaking which concerned only the Hierosolymitan nobility. Neither Raymond of Poitiers nor the Count of Tripoli came to Jerusalem.

The Crusaders had been in Syria for four months, and in Jerusalem for over a month. They had not yet had an opportunity to use their weapons against the infidel, which was the only reason they had taken the cross and endured such tribulations in Asia Minor. The attack on Damascus was carefully planned and undertaken with the utmost seriousness, but to judge by the results, without much enthusiasm. The siege began on July 24, 1148, and ended four days later on July 28. After some initial success in the outskirts of the city, an awkward maneuver led to the army's camping in a sterile region without water. Then, after a great deployment of siege works, digging trenches, throwing up fortifications, and after more or less open negotiations had been going on between the Syrian barons and the besieged, a misunderstanding (which had admittedly been building up for a long time) broke out between the Crusaders and the Syrian Franks. It was decided that the siege was going to be too difficult and that it would be better to strike camp.

The barons of Jerusalem were openly accused by their allies from the West of treachery in the affair and of being corrupted. It was claimed that some of the barons had been bribed by Unur. Michael the Syrian states in so many words that the court of Jerusalem received 200,000 dinars and the lord of Tiberias 100,000. (The same historian asserts that the greater part of this tribute was paid in counterfeit coin.)[11] This in itself is not at all unlikely, but it does not justify an accusation of treachery. Ibn al-Athir explains the attitude of the Frankish barons by considerations of elementary political caution. Unur, he says, had sent them the following message: "Saif ed-Din [the atabeg of Mosul, and eldest of Zengi's sons] has just arrived in the neighborhood. If you do not raise the siege and I know I am too weak to defend the city against you, I shall deliver it to him. And you cannot be unaware that on the day he possesses Damascus, it will no longer be possible for you to remain in Syria."[12]

In the face of the Frankish threat, the atabeg of Damascus had actually appealed to the two Zengid brothers, Saif ed-Din and Nur ed-Din, who were naturally enough only waiting for the opportunity to lay hands on Damascus. This was what Unur feared most of all, and he would only have turned to the Zengids in desperation and with the object of frightening the Franks.

It is understandable that even those of the Syrian barons who had the greatest thirst for conquest should have realized the gravity of the threat. Once they heard that the armies of Mosul were in the vicinity, they had no alternative but to retreat and renew their good relations with the people of Damascus. They had to explain this to King Louis and to Conrad III, and the two princes returned to Jerusalem full of indignation. According to William of Tyre, they "talked together . . . saying that they had put their persons and their men in trust with these people [the Franks of Syria], and they had falsely betrayed them, and had brought them to a place where they could not fight for Christendom and for their honor." It was only too true that the barons of Jerusalem had given the King and the Emperor very bad advice: they would not have had to be prophets to foresee the possibility of Zengid intervention a little earlier than they did. It seems reasonable to accuse them of being rash and foolhardy, but not of any idea of treachery.

In the end, the united armies returned to Jerusalem, humiliated and made ridiculous in the eyes of the Moslems, and terribly disappointed. It is hard to say on which side the disappointment was greater.

"Until these events," says William of Tyre, "the men of France gladly remained in the kingdom of Jerusalem, and they did much good there; but afterwards, they were no longer on good terms with the people of this land as they had been before; and although they sometimes come here on pilgrimage, they depart as soon as they can." He adds also that "matters in this country [Syria] were beginning to displease the great princes [Louis and Conrad] more and more, and they wanted to have nothing more to do with them." In fact, there was very nearly an open split between the Oriental and the European Franks. There was a mutual lack of understanding and, on the part of the Europeans, an expressed contempt for the *poulains*—the half-castes—who from their point of view were people softened by too easy a life, disloyal, unreliable, and evasive, always ready to come to an understanding with the Turks. This, with very little difference, had been the attitude of the first Crusaders toward the Greeks. Only the knights of the military orders inspired the Westerners with any admiration and respect.

The Frankish barons could not be accused of inability to fight: their lives were much more dangerous and exciting than those of the greatest warriors in the West, and perhaps for that very reason they knew what life was worth and had no taste for useless martyrdom. Usama, while he recognizes that the Franks were braver and more aggressive than the Moslems (he compares them to wild beasts), admits that in battle the Franks were "the most cautious of all men." Their small numbers compelled them to think before entering any engagement, and to calculate and maneuver in battle just as in diplomacy. Hence, probably, the impression of comparative softness which they managed to give to their Western allies in the skirmishes outside the walls of Damascus. In Christian countries, knights were more frequently released upon payment of a ransom.

"The humble people of France," wrote William of Tyre's translator, "would say openly to the Syrians [the Franks, that is] that it would not be a good thing to conquer cities for their profit, since the Turks were worth more than they were." These "Syrians," who regarded themselves as the bulwark of Christendom and the defenders of the Holy Sepulcher, must have bitterly resented such words from the lips of people who lived "in comfort" in a good Christian land. They were forgetting what the pilgrims had suffered in order to reach Jerusalem. And neither Franks nor Crusaders could forgive one another the mortification of the siege of Damascus. The kings departed with their barons and armies, having done, quite literally, nothing except cause a great deal of trouble and raise false hopes and genuine quarrels, and make themselves a terrible nuisance to the Frankish princes.

Only one Crusading baron remained in the Holy Land. This was Bertrand, the son of Alfonso-Jordan, Count of Toulouse, who had died so mysteriously at Caesarea. The young prince and his sister were not concerned with fighting the Turks. They wanted to avenge their father and they began by making war on their cousin, Raymond II of Tripoli, who appealed to both Nur ed-Din and the atabeg of Damascus for assistance. The Crusaders of Toulouse were defeated and Nur ed-Din took Bertrand and his sister into captivity in Aleppo, where they remained for twelve years.

Nur ed-Din, who at one moment had been seriously afraid for his principality of Aleppo and for the future of his holy war against the Franks, realized that the Franks were people who could never come to agreement among themselves. They were doomed by God to perdition and fated to perish by the Moslem sword.

For the Franks of Syria, this abortive Crusade was a terrible blow, even though they had not, like the Emperor Conrad, lost tens of thousands of men and vast wealth all to no avail. They now realized that they had little to hope for from the West, and that this foolish and vain demonstration of force had only emboldened their enemies and ruined the Franks' credit with the Moslems forever. Hitherto, even the boldest of Turkish conquerors had lived with the idea that somewhere, far away to the West, there were great kings who had formidable forces in reserve, forces which nothing could resist if they were ever to march. Nur ed-Din had been terrified by the approach of the great King of the Franks. Dazzled by the title, he had not realized that this was simply a vast expeditionary force already greatly reduced by losses sustained on the way. The Turks, with their swift, seminomadic armies perpetually on the road, were incapable of envisaging the hardships involved in marching a Crusading army across Europe. All they understood was that the Frankish kings had brought all their forces and after four days had shown themselves incapable of capturing a single Moslem city. It did not take a prophet to realize that, after such an experience, there was nothing more to fear from the intervention of the European states— at least, not for a very long time to come.

The Franks who remained had gained nothing, and had spent a great deal of money to no effect. Now they could only continue to defend themselves as best they might.

Edessa, Antioch, Jerusalem, and Tripoli

They were to defend themselves for a long time yet. But although it was an unequal struggle, such was the tenacity of the Franks and so unconquerable their will to keep the land they had won that the final disaster was due at least as much to their own mistakes as to the strength of their adversaries.

After the departure of the Crusaders, the Prince of Antioch, in a furious rage, set about making war on Nur ed-Din on his own account. He launched his offensive alone, since neither the regent nor the Count of Tripoli—still less Joscelin II—would have anything to do with him. He attacked the province of Aleppo intending to wage, as every Prince of Antioch had done since 1100, an incessant struggle, pillaging, capturing and recapturing castles, ravaging the countryside. Raymond of Poitiers was a good feudal lord, the kind of man who was always ready to fight without calculating his chances of success too closely. He had once refused to aid his neighbor Joscelin II because he was not keen to engage in a war which would bring profit to an enemy. Now he rushed headlong into battle with his four hundred knights and one thousand foot against an adversary much more powerful than himself, betrayed by this same Joscelin, who had made an actual treaty of alliance with Nur ed-Din. He had no real need to do so. He acted out of sheer bravado, as if to prove that he could fight, all by himself, the enemy whom the Crusaders had refused to attack.

Unable to believe that the Frankish leader could have the effrontery to attack him with such feeble forces, Nur ed-Din was at first convinced that Raymond was bringing with him only the advance guard of a much larger army. Contemporary historians (William of Tyre and Gregory the Priest) are unable to explain the Prince of Antioch's action. It was clearly suicidal. Surrounded with his troops near the Fountain of Murad—Fons Murez (Ma'arratha)—and seeing that all was lost, Raymond refused to abandon his army and save himself as his ally, a leader of the Ismailians, advised him. There was a battle and some of the Franks escaped by flight, but Raymond, with a group of faithful knights, fought on to the bitter end. It will be remembered that he was a man of immense stature, possessed of a Herculean strength still undiminished by age. "He made a clear space around him," says William of Tyre, "cutting down all who came near him. But in the end he was overcome."[13] "The body of this accursed prince was found lying amid the corpses of the most valorous knights among his followers. His head was cut off and carried to Nur ed-Din. He was one of the knights most renowned among the Franks for his great courage, his extreme vigor, and his mighty stature."[14] Also killed in the same battle was Reynald of Marash, lord of Kaisun, a former vassal and son-in-law of Joscelin II, Count of Edessa (June 29, 1149).

The Prince of Antioch's death was celebrated as a great victory throughout Moslem Syria. Once again the principality of Antioch was without a head. The government fell into the hands of Raymond's young widow, Constance, who assumed the regency in the name of her infant son, Bohemond III. Taking advantage of the consternation caused among the Franks by the Prince's death, Nur ed-Din ravaged the province and pushed on as far as Antioch, which he very nearly captured, only abandoning his siege on the approach of the King of Jerusalem's armies. This time, however, he did finally recapture and occupy all the lands across the Orontes which had formerly belonged to the princes of Antioch. The principality still existed, but reduced by half and now wide open to attack by its immediate neighbor, the atabeg of Aleppo.

Joscelin II was delighted to learn of the death of his old enemy, but it was a joy not unmixed with bitterness because, though Raymond's death avenged him, it only made his own position still more dangerous. The Count of Edessa was, in fact, no longer lord of any

lands beyond Turbessel. He had been abandoned by all. His back
was to the wall and he was compelled to swear fealty to the Seljuk
Sultan of Rum in order to preserve what remained of his lands.
Even so, he lived in the expectation of imminent disaster.

He had not abandoned all hope. Even when attacked simultaneously from the north by the Ortoqid Turkomans and in the southeast
by Nur ed-Din, he fought on. Little by little he lost his northern
provinces, but at the end of 1149 he succeeded in defeating the
atabeg of Aleppo's troops and actually captured Nur ed-Din's own
personal squire. Not long afterward, he fell into an ambush and was
taken to Aleppo as a prisoner in May 1150. His end was a tragic
one: refusing to abjure the Christian faith, he had his eyes put out.
(According to the Syriac *Anonymi,* which cannot be suspected of
sympathizing with Joscelin. It is not easy to understand why Nur
ed-Din should have imposed this test on the Count of Edessa when
the general run of captive Christians were spared it. His severity
may be explained by Joscelin's habit of making alliances with the
Turks and breaking them as soon as he got the chance.) Joscelin
was flung into prison, where he died nine years later. As far as his
own people and the Franks of Syria were concerned, he was dead
from the day he was taken prisoner: they knew only too well that he
would never be released on payment of a ransom, and no attempt to
secure his freedom was made.

His wife, or his widow, a Frankish lady named Beatrice who had
been the widow of the lord of Sayihun (Saône), mourned him bitterly, and since she could no longer defend her lands, finally sold
what little she still possessed—Turbessel and its surroundings—to the
Byzantines. She was a brave woman, but she was terrified and at the
end of her resources. When she appealed to the young King Baldwin
III, he advised her to accept the Greek offer. Knowing that the lands
were indefensible in any case, the court of Jerusalem decided that
"it was better that this land should be lost by the Greeks than by us"
(William of Tyre). Countess Beatrice resigned herself to accepting
sacks of gold and an annual pension from the hands of the Byzantine
envoys, left her domain, and went to live in Jerusalem with her
three children.

A part of the indigenous population, Armenians and even Syrians
who could have borne to live under the Turkish yoke, still preferred
exile to Greek dominion, and when Baldwin III's troops came to
Turbessel to wind up the affairs of the vanished Count, these requested to be escorted to Frankish territory. The young King crossed
the land infested with bands of Turks and Turkomans, his little

army escorting the band of voluntary exiles: a caravan of people on foot, carts, and mules loaded with such belongings as the refugees could take with them. "As they departed there was such weeping and wailing that those who saw it wept for pity."[15] Baldwin III succeeded in fending off the Turkish attacks and leading this melancholy exodus into the territory of the kingdom of Jerusalem.

The following year, Nur ed-Din seized from the Greeks all the lands they had bought. All the territory which had formerly made up the county of Edessa was now in his hands, with the exception of that in the north which had been conquered by the Ortoqids.

The annihilation of the county of Edessa and the threat hanging over the principality of Antioch finally made the barons of Palestine realize that they could not in their own interests confine themselves any longer to the affairs of their own kingdom. In the north they had a singularly aggressive neighbor whose avowed object was to drive the Franks out of Syria, and who had begun so well that more than half of northern Frankish Syria was already in his possession. Although Antioch was the first to be threatened, it would not be long before it was the turn of Tripoli and Jerusalem. Quite naturally, the government of the regent and her constable was held responsible for the constant succession of failures occurring in the nine years which had passed since the death of King Fulk. In 1152, the young King Baldwin was nearly twenty-two and his barons were endeavoring to make him understand that it was unworthy for a man of his age to allow himself to be ruled by a woman, "as though he were a child."

The King was certainly a docile son. Although from a very early age he had assumed the frequently dangerous task of leading his armies and had acquitted himself with courage, he does not seem to have been in the least troubled by the thirst for power. His character was likable and easygoing, and even a quite serious one despite his fondness for fun and flirtation. He was educated, literate, and possessed a considerable knowledge of the law. His piety was unimpeachable. Yet the young King, so admirably fitted for government, had to be forced by his courtiers to take over the power which Melisende seemed determined to keep as long as she lived.

However great Baldwin III's respect for his mother, he had no reason to harbor the same feelings with regard to the constable Manasses of Hierges, the nephew of the late Baldwin II. William of Tyre describes him as a man of unbearable pride who had nothing but "ugly words and rude answers" for his fellow barons. The young King disliked him, and his friends did their best to encourage the mild young man in his antipathy to the constable. They succeeded so well that Baldwin, who was probably anxious to prove that he was no longer a child, finally agreed to turn the tables on his mother. When the day came for his official coronation, Melisende was determined that she too would be crowned at the same time and so keep her right to power, but Baldwin had himself crowned alone, unknown to the Queen.

Next he asked his mother to resign all power into his hands. The Queen would only agree to a somewhat curious division of responsibility by which she was to keep Jerusalem, Nablus, and the provinces belonging to them, that is to say, the principal lands of the kingdom, while her son was dispatched to "reign" over Acre and Tyre. Baldwin agreed. His barons had other ideas. A time when the whole of Frankish Syria was in danger of collapse was hardly the moment to set up two kingdoms of Jerusalem in the place of one. Finally realizing that the situation was contrary to the real interests of the country, and supported by his own constable, Humphrey of Toron, and the majority of the Palestinian barons, the young King marched on Jerusalem with his army. The people of the capital rose in his favor and opened the gates to him. After a pitched battle in which Melisende and Manasses of Hierges, supported by the Patriarch and the clergy, defended themselves "as though this were a war between Christian and Saracen,"[16] the Queen Mother finally surrendered. She was obliged to renounce all claim to power and withdraw in retirement to her dowry of Nablus.

Whatever William of Tyre may say of this strange conflict, the Queen was quite clearly in the wrong. She was clinging to power when she was not capable of wielding it. Her political views were shortsighted, and she ruled the royal domains as though they were a palace or a convent. It is true that despite the praises later heaped on him by the Archbishop of Tyre, the young King Baldwin III seems to have been on the whole a weak character, but he was much more conscious of his responsibilities than his mother. Melisende, a woman with so little maternal feeling that she was prepared to make war on her own son when he claimed a power that belonged to him by right, showed in all her actions a real hostility toward the *Frankish* society of the country as such, that is, to the nobility and bourgeoisie of French origin. This does not mean that the Queen lacked supporters. Only a minority among the barons had embraced her cause, but she could count on the support of the Church; the Patriarch Fulcher of Angoulême was fully on her side, and he had the bishops and clergy of the kingdom behind him. The Queen had won them over by her generosity, by what could even be called the wild prodigality with which she exhausted the treasury of the state to provide alms and donations and in particular to finance the work of building and restoring religious edifices. It was her ambition to transform Jerusalem into one vast temple, a single magnificent house of God. At the end of the century Moslems described the works executed by the Franks with admiration, and the majority of these buildings dated from the time of Melisende's regency.

The Queen made up for her lack of political intelligence by her talent for patronage, and her ideas were grand enough when it came to adorning the City of God. Consequently she was popular with the clergy. To judge by her attitude toward clashes between the various religious communities, she was presumably also liked by the local Christians, and she may have felt closer to them than to the Franks. She used her power somewhat clumsily, but she did represent a party which was by no means negligible, that of the nobility which had become fairly closely assimilated with the wealthy classes of the indigenous population. To this clan had belonged the Princess Alice, who had not long survived the humiliation inflicted upon her by Raymond of Poitiers (one good reason why Melisende had never been very keen to help the Prince of Antioch), and also Joscelin II of Edessa and his half-Armenian vassals. In the quarrel which divided the regent and her eldest son, her second son, Amalric, then aged seventeen, took his mother's side against his brother. Amalric married one of the daughters of the unfortunate Joscelin II, Agnes, the widow of Reynald of Marash, and he remained all his life, in spite of the pressure put upon him by the barons, to some extent under the influence of the "Edessan" clan, more orientalized than the majority of the Frankish nobility.

After his victory over his mother, Baldwin III had driven Manasses of Hierges out of the country and now enjoyed the complete support of his vassals. The barons, having reluctantly submitted to a woman's orders for so long, were prepared to support this agreeable and courageous young man through thick and thin. Even supposing him to have been somewhat idealized by the historian, it seems probable that the King was very much as William of Tyre describes him, with a "fresh and vermeil" complexion, fair hair, a silky beard, a tall, slender figure, and graceful carriage. Baldwin III's equable temper, his cheerfulness and good manners were as attractive as his physical appearance. He was to prove, if not an outstanding head of state, at least an honorable and competent one. The credit for the victorious wars he undertook belongs largely to his constable, Humphrey of Toron. The fact that he had no great inclination to impose his will on others only made him the better loved, and surrounded by his council of barons, he was an excellent constitutional monarch.

Like his grandfather, and like his father, King Fulk, the young King had to undertake, besides the government of his own kingdom, the regency of the two other Frankish states, Antioch and Tripoli. Antioch had been governed since the death of Raymond of Poitiers by the Princess Constance and by the Patriarch Aimery of Limoges. Tripoli, which had been governed by Raymond II, the son of Pons, was to be left without a head in the very year of Baldwin III's coronation.

The cause of Raymond II's death remains a mystery to this day, for if this was a political murder, both the motive and for whose benefit it was committed are still unknown. The King of Jerusalem and his mother were both in Tripoli at the time of the Count's death, having gone there with the object of reconciling Raymond II with his wife, Melisende's sister, the Countess Hodierna. Raymond had been married for thirteen years and is known to have displayed the most extreme jealousy of his wife. This jealousy was not a recent development. He had refused to recognize their first daughter, the infant Melisende, as his own child, and the Countess complained bitterly of the "life of boredom" her husband forced her to lead. Queen Melisende lectured her brother-in-law at great length to no effect and then decided to take her sister to her domain at Nablus, to which Raymond agreed. As he was returning to Tripoli after taking leave of the two princesses, he was assassinated by an Ismailian at the city gates.

There seem to be no grounds for accusing Melisende or her sister, who were never suspected of any dealings with the Ismailians. It will be remembered that Raymond II had once appealed to Nur ed-Din, the declared enemy of the Ismailians, for help against his cousin Bertrand of Toulouse, but what Raymond II's exact relations with that curious sect may have been is not known. The fact remains that this was the first time a Frankish prince had fallen to the Assassins' knives.

Raymond II left one son and one daughter. The son, Raymond III, also destined to meet a tragic end, was only twelve years old at the time of the murder. Inevitably the young prince's cousin, Baldwin III, became his guardian, coregent, and protector of the county.

This was the situation in Frankish Syria in the middle of the twelfth century. Jerusalem was governed by a young king, full of good intentions but without great initiative. The county of Tripoli and the principality of Antioch were both without heads and governed by women and minors, and the county of Edessa no longer existed. In Aleppo, a vigorous atabeg inspired by a passion for the holy war had already made himself master of a large part of the Frankish provinces of northern Syria. However, the Frankish kingdom was not yet in its decline. On the contrary, despite political and military reverses, despite the differences with the West which resulted from the Second Crusade, the Franks were taking root in the country to an increasing extent and were looking for fresh solutions to their problems.

Ever since Zengi's rise to power, and in particular since Zengi's son Nur ed-Din had installed himself in Aleppo, the Franks of Syria were beginning to be aware that a strong power was developing in Islamic Syria, a strong power sworn to their destruction. In future they could only fall back on alliances with Byzantium, with the kingdom of Damascus, or with Egypt. The Byzantine alliance precluded the Egyptian one, and since in any case the Egyptian court was in a state of total decadence, the Franks were more inclined to take advantage of this state of affairs in order to extend their kingdom to the south at the expense of their Fatimid neighbors.

As far as the Byzantine alliance was concerned, this was only possible if the Franks would accept the effective suzerainty of Byzantium over Antioch and in particular the restoration of the Greek patriarch of that city. The succession of minorities and regencies which had occurred in the principality since 1119 had made the Latin patriarchate particularly strong in Antioch, and it was fiercely opposed to the coming of a "schismatic" patriarch. The factors which made it more difficult to reach agreement with a Christian power than with a Moslem one were therefore primarily religious. There remained the alliance with Damascus. As will appear, this soon became impracticable for reasons which were not entirely the fault of the Franks.

The Marriage of Constance

Baldwin III had no intention of wasting his time and the forces of his kingdom defending territories of Tripoli and Antioch which were not properly speaking a part of the kingdom. His aim was to enlarge the kingdom at the expense of the Egyptians and to capture the one important stronghold which the Fatimid caliphs still retained on the coast of Palestine. The possession of Ascalon was a real advantage to the Frankish kingdom, a guarantee of safety for the people of southern Judaea and for the ships of merchants and pilgrims alike. There was no need to fear a counter-Crusade from Egypt, and the other Moslem powers were bound to rejoice at the weakening of the Fatimids.

In order to have his hands free of Antioch, Baldwin III was anxious to marry off his cousin Constance to some powerful baron who would undertake the defense of the principality. Constance, however, was not at all anxious to remarry. She was a pretty young widow who had been married, while still a child, to a middle-aged man, and she had scarcely acquired a sense of the responsibilities involved in her situation. As regent in the name of her little son Bohemond, she was perfectly happy enjoying her freedom, leaving the government in the hands of the Patriarch, and taking a mischievous pleasure in annoying her cousin the King by refusing the succession of suitors he proposed to her.

She rejected Yves of Nesle, Count of Soissons, a high baron who had come from France on a pilgrimage; she rejected Walter of Saint-Omer, lord of Tiberias and Galilee, and she also rejected the general John Roger, a Byzantine prince of Norman origin whom the Emperor Manuel had sent to Antioch. None of these great lords was young or handsome enough to please the Princess. While few young girls would have been asked for their opinion, a widowed princess who was the mother of four children and regent of a great fief was free to set up her rights to love and happiness in opposition to those who talked to her of the interests of the country. Nevertheless she was abusing her power, since what was at stake went far beyond the mere question of young Constance's happiness or unhappiness. Baldwin III had insufficient authority to force a husband on his young cousin, while the Patriarch Aimery of Limoges was greedy for power and encouraged the young woman's willful independence. The King appealed to his mother and to his aunt, the Countess Hodierna of Tripoli, and the two dowagers lectured their niece at considerable length, "begging her to have pity on her lands," but got nothing for their pains.

Having made up her mind to marry only a man she loved, Constance finally made her choice. Baldwin III was so impatient to see her married off that he gave his consent as soon as he heard that the Princess had finally deigned to approve of a suitor. The man was utterly obscure, a newcomer to the country without name or fortune, a young knight with nothing to recommend him but his youth, courage, and good looks.

Constance's choice scandalized the nobility of the entire country and caused a furor in ecclesiastical circles. "Many people," says William of Tyre, "could not behold without amazement the sight of a woman so illustrious, so distinguished and powerful and the widow of such a noble husband, deigning to bestow her hand on a simple knight."[17] The man's name was Reynald of Châtillon; he was the penniless younger son of an Angevin family of no great nobility, and had come to the Holy Land with the intention of entering the service of some wealthy baron of the country. He was not only brave, he was a warrior of such unbridled ferocity, a creature so inordinately pugnacious, that beside him men like Bohemond, Baldwin I, or Zengi seem like angels of moderation. He was crude, thick-headed, and stubborn, but he did possess an extraordinary vigor, for the simple reason that the extreme simplicity of his character left him deaf to the elementary considerations of prudence, principle, or expediency which generally rule the conduct of even the strongest and most ambitious men. It seemed doubtful whether Constance, once married, would have long to enjoy her choice.

The Patriarch Aimery of Limoges, who wielded great power during the Princess's widowhood, could not be expected to take with equanimity the sight of a petty knight of no fortune setting himself up as master of Antioch. This prelate had no great reputation himself, having raised himself to the patriarchal seat by means of intrigues against his predecessor and benefactor, Radulph of Domfront. He was extremely proud and dictatorial, but he was no weakling and had been capable of organizing the defense of Antioch after the death of Raymond of Poitiers. A proud man and secure in his great wealth, he did not conceal his contempt for the new Prince. When Reynald heard the things the Patriarch had to say about him, and probably hoping to lay hands on the Patriarch's fortune, he had Aimery seized by his soldiers, and not content with flinging him into prison, had him flogged until he bled and then exposed on a tower in full sunlight, smeared with honey to attract wasps and flies.

When Baldwin III heard of this barbarous behavior he may have realized—rather too late—the kind of prince into whose power he had delivered the province of Antioch when he agreed to his cousin's marriage. He demanded that Reynald release the Patriarch and restore him to his office. Reynald obeyed, but the Patriarch showed no further desire to remain in Antioch and took refuge in Jerusalem. Henceforth, the new Prince of Antioch was undisputed master and lord of his province. He encountered no further resistance on the part of his subjects and no further interference in his plans from the King.

Nur ed-Din

From his youth, Baldwin III had proved that he would not shrink from the fatigues, dangers, or responsibilities of a military leader. As his father and grandfather had done before him, he spent a great deal of his life in camps and on the march, in battles, sieges, raids, and skirmishes. His actual reign, which was fairly short, was little more than a succession of military operations, more often than not successful. During his reign, the Frankish kingdom was swelled by the capture of the city and province of Ascalon, and this was a considerable success, since it gave the Franks control of the whole of the coast of Palestine and allowed them to threaten Cairo. In the same reign Damascus fell into the hands of Nur ed-Din, but although the Franks were well aware of the scale of the disaster, they were powerless to prevent it.

Syria in the mid-twelfth century was the scene of a clash between two rival powers of unequal strength, both essentially aggressive and imperialist, who faced one another with no possibility of compromise. The Franks, who held the coast and all of Palestine from the Arabian Desert along the valley of the Jordan and the Orontes as far as Cilicia, were divided into three states which were, if not exactly united, at least in agreement for a large part of the time. In the hinterland, running parallel to the Frankish kingdom along the right bank of the Jordan and the Orontes as far as the mountains of the Anti-Taurus, stretched the Zengid kingdom of Nur ed-Din, independent, but supported by the Turks of Anatolia and the Ortoqid Turkomans to the north and by the kingdom of Mosul, also Zengid, in the east. These states were not necessarily allies of Nur ed-Din, but they were Sunnite Moslems and as such ready to help him in case of need. Up to 1154, the kingdom of Damascus, which had fallen from the hands of the Seljuks into those of the descendants of the atabeg Buri, formed a separate enclave within Nur ed-Din's possessions and favored the Franks in order to preserve its independence.

Nur ed-Din, continuing his father's work, had succeeded in wresting a large part of northern Syria away from Frankish control—the territory lying furthest inland; the county of Edessa and all the lands to the east of the Orontes were firmly under Zengid control and lost to the Franks forever. On the other hand, the Franks were establishing themselves more and more firmly on the coast and in the south, at the expense of Egypt and the Arab tribes of the desert. Nur ed-Din, it has already been said, was an almost fanatically pious Moslem, convinced that a holy war against the Frankish infidels was absolutely necessary. Nevertheless, he did not persecute native Christians, the autochthonous inhabitants of the country. He was willing to let them live in peace provided they remained subject to Islam. What he, like other pious Moslems, found intolerable was the Christian domination of lands once held by Islam, with Christian government, mosques turned into churches, and the impious Christian faith taking official precedence over the Law of the Prophet even in the Moslem holy city of Jerusalem.

Nur ed-Din pursued his methodical conquest of Syria in the name of a united Islam and the triumph of the true faith. He preached aloud the brotherhood of all believers and was almost ready to forget differences of doctrine and go to the assistance of the Egyptians of Ascalon, who were Shiite heretics. Ascalon fell to Baldwin III in 1153 (August 19). Several months later, on April 25, 1154, Nur ed-Din took Damascus.

When Ibn al-Athir writes of this event that "Islam recovered Damascus," he is speaking as a Mesopotamian, not as a Damascene, for although the kingdom of Damascus had for half a century preferred the alliance and even the protection of the Franks to the dominion of another Moslem power such as the sultans of Persia or the atabegs of Mosul or of Aleppo, this did not mean that the people regarded themselves as unfaithful to Islam.

Nur ed-Din actually wrote to the atabeg of Damascus, Mujir ed-Din Abaq (Toghtekin's grandson), begging him to accept his "aid" in the interests of the faith, but the Damascenes showed little response to his arguments. "But," wrote Nur ed-Din, "since God has given me the power to protect Moslems and fight the infidel by means of my wealth and the great number of my soldiers, it is not permitted that I should remain idle and not come to the aid of your people when I know you to be powerless to defend and preserve your own territories. Indeed, it is this powerlessness which has compelled you to ask for Frankish help against me, and to lavish on them the riches you have extorted by violence and iniquity from your weak and unfortunate subjects. Such conduct can be approved neither by God nor by any Moslem." The government of Damascus answered these pious exhortations: "It belongs to the sword alone to decide between you and us. We find a sufficient support among the

Franks to drive you off should you attack us."[18] It is obvious what is going on: one state, jealous of its independence, is defending its rights against a too powerful neighbor, while an ambitious conqueror is resorting to ideological arguments to justify his intervention in the affairs of a weaker neighbor.

But Nur ed-Din was terribly sincere. His use of violence and the cunning he employed to go the atabeg of Damascus one better were all dictated to him by the interests of religion, and when, by his cunning, he had weakened his adversary and succeeded in taking Damascus by surprise before the defenders had time to appeal to their allies the Franks, what enabled him to establish himself was his obvious good faith in defense of Islamic interests. He cannot be accused of either extortion or an abuse of power: the great unifier of Moslem Syria left to posterity the image of an exceedingly just and pious prince, a kind of warrior saint. With him, the "counter-Crusade," the *jihad* against the Franks, finally took its real direction and ceased to be merely an excuse for local conquests or settling of personal scores.

In 1164, during the siege of Banyas by the Moslem armies, Nur ed-Din's brother had an eye put out by an arrow. Far from sympathizing, Nur ed-Din told the wounded man, "If you could see the recompense awaiting you in paradise, you would beg to lose the other eye!"[19] After the city's capture, he told Unur's son, a former ally of the Franks, who had surrendered the place to them, "This conquest is a matter for joy to all Moslems, but yours should be double." "How is that?" asked the other. "Because," Nur ed-Din answered, "today God is giving relief to your father who was burning in the fires of hell."[20] This is only one of many indications showing the kind of a man this Islamic Crusader was. He was to rule Moslem Syria for thirty-one years, Aleppo from 1146 onward, and Aleppo and Damascus together from 1154 to 1174. Under his leadership, and thanks to the tireless and infectious ardor of his religious zeal, the war took on increasingly the character of a sacred work, and the ideal of the *jihad,* which had been somewhat neglected by Arabs and was quite foreign to the Turks, acquired in the reign of Nur ed-Din a force never before known in Islam.

The Franks who were the excuse for all this pious aggression were no longer the fanatical pilgrims or brutal soldiery of Godfrey of Bouillon who had profaned mosques and burned Jews and plunged Jerusalem into a sea of blood. They were princes and emirs very similar to the Moslem princes and emirs, no more warlike and ferocious than they, and conscientious and reasonably humane administrators of the territories over which they ruled. They lived on good terms with their Moslem and Christian subjects, and were perfectly prepared to make alliances with neighboring Moslem princes.

After the unfortunate incident of the Second Crusade, Baldwin III had done his best to make up the quarrel with Damascus and had twice saved the city from Nur ed-Din's attacks. Between 1149 and 1154, Damascus and Jerusalem so successfully made common cause against their powerful adversary that for both parties their religious differences seemed to have become an entirely secondary factor. Nur ed-Din had taken Damascus by surprise, it would not be too much to say by treachery. The Franks of Jerusalem accepted the fact, and to begin with tried to live in peace even with Nur ed-Din. By a kind of tacit understanding which they hoped would prove lasting, they made tentative advances in the direction of Egypt, leaving the atabeg of Aleppo in possession of the territories he had conquered in northern Syria. But there was now no possibility of maintaining a status quo between the two forces. Nur ed-Din wanted war, and the Franks, although they did not want it, lacked the will to avoid it.

William of Tyre is the first to condemn Baldwin III's foolishness (or rather that of his advisers, for the young King generally appears to have let himself be guided by others), a foolishness which was to call down God's anger on Frankish Syria and finally to prove one of the causes of its downfall.[21] The people of Damascus and the Turkomans were in the habit of pasturing their flocks near the forest of Banyas (Paneas) in Frankish territory, and they had obtained the King's express permission to do this. However, these flocks were very large and included, besides sheep and cattle, a large number of horses. In the days of his alliance with Damascus, Baldwin III had certainly never thought of touching these animals, but, says the chronicler, he was in debt and "so persecuted each day by his creditors that he did not know what to do." Finally in February 1157, persuaded by "evil counsel," he laid hands on the flocks and slew the Turkomans who were guarding them. "Those who knew the truth," says William of Tyre, "regarded this deed as treachery and not as prowess."

Nur ed-Din was only waiting for an excuse to declare war. He inflicted on the French in the vicinity of Banyas a number of defeats in succession, and his victories as well as his speeches and his example aroused popular feelings to fever pitch. From Damascus, the city which had resisted him for so long, "a considerable crowd of young men, volunteers, lawyers, Sufis, and pious men joined him."[22]

The atabeg of Aleppo and Damascus was on the way to becoming the great hero of Islam. In June 1157 the King of Jerusalem's entire army was surrounded and cut to pieces before Banyas. Most of the knights were taken prisoner and Baldwin III was only saved by a miracle. Ibn al-Qalanisi describes Nur ed-Din's triumphant return: "The prisoners and severed heads reached Damascus on Monday [June 24]. On each camel were two of their warriors with a standard unfurled and still matted with blood and brains and hair. Each captive lord, and governors of castles or regions, advanced on horseback dressed in coats of mail, helmets on their heads and standards in their hands. The foot soldiers were tied with ropes in groups of two or three. The inhabitants of the city, old men, young men, women, and children, flocked out to see the spectacle which God graciously bestowed upon the Moslem world after this brilliant success." The historian then quotes a poem composed for the occasion:

We have never seen, in times past, a day of such perfect beauty and such great brilliance.

A day like that on which the Franks were covered with the shame of captivity, disaster, and ruin.

Mounted on red camels, their standards in their hands, they were led through the streets captive and ashamed.

They who had been so powerful, and whose fame had sown terror in the ranks of armies and on the field of battle.

The infamy they committed in seizing the flocks will cover them with shame by night and day.

In their blindness they broke their sworn truce, after vowing to observe it faithfully.

May God scatter their people and let them never be reunited, even to the end of time.[23]

"This time," says William of Tyre, "Our Lord visited upon the King and his men what they had done to the Turkomans and to those of Arabia, when they treacherously killed and robbed those whom they had guaranteed upon oath."[24]

William of Tyre was a Latin colonist of Italian origin who had been born in the country, and here as elsewhere, he echoes the opinion of the Franks in general (or at least of a section of them). In the second half of the twelfth century there was a very real sense of solidarity among people of the same country, whether they were Christians or Moslems, and this feeling was stronger among the Christian Franks than among the Moslems and the local Christians.

Coming from the pen of the Archbishop of Tyre, who was generally favorable to Baldwin III, such a sentiment shows a breadth of spirit which is never found in the Syrian or Armenian and much less in the Moslem chroniclers.

At a time when Islam was becoming increasingly fanatical and intolerant, a certain humanitarianism, in the modern sense of the word, was beginning to infiltrate into Frankish society in Syria. This was a cause of weakness, since there was no strong power or great ideal to defend in the democratic state, or rather the aristocratic republic, which the Latin kingdom was gradually becoming. The most turbulent and aggressive elements were coming out on top simply because of the comparative lack of opposition from those who had completely settled down in their new country and asked nothing more than to live there in peace.

They thought they could live in peace with Nur ed-Din at their gates, and they left action to anyone who wanted adventure. The disaster of Banyas had amply demonstrated the Franks' weakness in the face of their powerful neighbor. Baldwin III was not a man of action, but he was not devoid of political sense and he tried to set the kingdom on the way to find new alliances. His successor, more intelligent and more self-willed than Baldwin, did his best to govern alone and enforce his own policies, which in the end proved a failure. Sixty years of Frankish rule in Syria had already, with the growth of new generations, created a local feudal society, more divided and more independent even than those in Europe, too confident of its own right to exist to measure the seriousness of the threats hanging over it.

The Byzantine Alliance

Frankish Syria, cut off at present from its territories in the north, was now reduced to little more than a broad coastal strip, about thirty miles wide in the region of Antioch and Tripoli and some sixty miles in the south near Jerusalem, and menaced on its eastern frontiers by a dynamic and aggressive Moslem power. To the south was the desert of Arabia and Egypt; to the north, the Seljuk Turks of Anatolia, and Byzantium. Since there was no longer any hope of substantial reinforcements from the West, new alliances must be found if the Franks were to stand up to Nur ed-Din. Since the Seljuks were excluded as potential allies, this left Byzantium and Cairo.

Egypt was a broken reed and in the mid-twelfth century did not seem able to provide her allies, whoever they might be, with effective military aid. The court of Cairo was caught in a web of harem intrigues and palace revolutions,* and despite the Franks' evident Ismailian sympathies, the caliphs of Cairo evinced no desire to make an alliance with the infidels.[25] As for Byzantium, in over half a century the Franks had learned to beware of her policies, which always appeared to be perfidious and occasionally were so. But considering the magnitude of the danger, the court of Jerusalem found itself compelled to turn to Constantinople.

The failure of the attempt at a Franco-Byzantine alliance at the time of John Comnenus's Crusade has already been described. After this failure, Raymond of Poitiers had spent his time wavering between two contradictory attitudes: appeals to Byzantium and fear of Greek intervention. Terrified by Nur ed-Din's progress, he actually went in person to Constantinople, acknowledged himself the Emperor's vassal, and made honorable amends before the tomb of John Comnenus; but he consistently refused to satisfy the Greek demands. However inconsistent, the policies of this unfortunate prince had been logical, dictated simultaneously by the dangers of the time and an understandable desire for independence. But the new Prince of Antioch was not even capable of this elementary policy of self-defense. He was guided solely by the needs of the moment and the prospect of immediate profit. Otherwise, he was a brave soldier and a great leader of men, able to communicate to his soldiers his own superabundant energy.

Reynald of Châtillon, who by his marriage with Constance had become the official leader of the Frankish forces in Antioch, had begun by making war on the Armenians of Cilicia for the benefit of Byzantium. Thoros II, son of Leo I, had won back the greater part of Cilicia from the Greeks, and the *basileus* appealed to Reynald (theoretically a vassal of the Empire) to suppress the Armenian revolt. Later, the Prince of Antioch changed sides without a moment's hesitation and allied himself with Thoros against the Greeks.

Acting in concert with the Armenian, whose hatred of Byzantium was well known, Reynald of Châtillon, in the spring of 1156, organized an expedition against the island of Cyprus, which lay not far from the Syrian coast and belonged to Byzantium. Now Cyprus had

---

* After the assassination of the Caliph al-Zafir (in which assassination Usama was one of the prime movers), viziers governed in the name of boy princes (1154–1163). After several *coups d'état* in which three successive viziers lost their lives, Shawar assumed power.

always maintained good relations with the Franks and regularly sold them provisions. The troops of Reynald and Thoros II made a surprise landing, and the inadequate Greek garrison had no time to organize the defense of the island. The governor of Cyprus, John Comnenus, a nephew of the Emperor Manuel, and Michael Branas, the general commanding the Greek troops, fought bravely, but they were overcome, vanquished, and taken prisoner. Reynald gave over the whole island of Cyprus to fire and slaughter, plundering and laying waste, burning towns, and sacking churches and convents. Priests and monks were mutilated, women raped, and men who tried to defend themselves slain without mercy.

After causing as much damage as was physically possible, forcing the Cypriot peasants to buy back their stolen flocks at exorbitant prices, collecting all the gold and valuables he could find, and levying an enormous tribute of war on the inhabitants and forcing them to give hostages as a surety of prompt payment, Reynald returned to Antioch with enough booty to make the province wealthy for years, although he and his companions squandered it almost immediately.

The sack of Cyprus, accompanied as it was by atrocities such as even the Turks never allowed, aroused not only the indignation of Byzantium but the anger of the King and court of Jerusalem as well. Baldwin III managed to convince Manuel Comnenus that he had had nothing to do with this act of piracy, but he was never able to make Reynald obey him. For that matter, Reynald was never to obey anyone in all his life.

As a vassal he was a valuable auxiliary in battle, but he behaved with such arrogance toward the King that he acted as if he were sole master in Antioch after God—and not only in Antioch. In October 1157, when the combined armies of the King of Jerusalem, the Prince of Antioch, and a great baron, Thierry of Alsace, Count of Flanders, who had come from Europe with a contingent of Crusaders, were on the point of taking the city of Shaizar, capital of the Munqidhite emirs, the Franks never occupied the city. By common consent of the whole army Shaizar was to become the property of Thierry of Alsace, but Reynald refused to countenance this except on condition that the Count did homage to him for the city, which bordered on his own province. Thierry declared that such a man as he could do homage only to a king. That a knight of humble birth such as Reynald of Châtillon should lay claim to the homage of a count of Flanders was so scandalously contrary to all feudal custom that it was decided to abandon the town, which was already all but captured. Nur ed-Din took possession of Shaizar almost immediately.

(This Arab city, which had guarded its independence for so long, was never actually conquered by either the Franks or the Turks. In 1157 the entire region was devastated by a terrible earthquake and Shaizar suffered more than any other city. Half the houses were destroyed, and a large part of the population—the entire family of the Munqidhite emirs included—perished. The only surviving members of the noble and ancient family were one princess, who escaped the disaster by a miracle, and Usama, who was in Cairo at the time and whose memoirs were all he could do to save the glory of his ancestors from oblivion. Nur ed-Din had the castle rebuilt, and installed his foster-brother and faithful companion, Majd ed-Din Abu Bakr, there.)

Reynald's attitude during the siege of Shaizar had annoyed Baldwin III, offended Thierry of Alsace, and set the whole of the Latin chivalry against the Prince of Antioch. It had prevented the creation of a new Frankish county and left a place of the utmost importance wide open to Nur ed-Din. Reynald himself appears to have been as oblivious of the disapproval of his comrades in arms as he was of the military and political consequences of his behavior. He was not even the King's vassal, though when he pleased he did him the kindness of joining his forces. When in the following year Baldwin III and Thierry of Alsace won a brilliant victory over Nur ed-Din at Butaiha, northeast of Tiberias, it was without Reynald.

When his war against the Petchenegs on the Danube finally came to an end, Manuel Comnenus returned to Syria, determined to exact vengeance at least for the hideous attack on Cyprus. The Prince of Antioch was compelled to change his attitude.

Baldwin III had long been hoping to establish good relations with Constantinople, a policy which his father, Fulk of Anjou, had already attempted. Baldwin aimed to continue it, not because he liked the Greeks but because the Greeks were the last allies on whose support the kingdom could hope to rely. Thierry of Alsace, his Crusade accomplished, had left the country, and there was no other prospect of a Crusade led by a great baron. The young King, who was twenty-seven and still unmarried, made up his mind to ask for the hand of a princess of the house of Comnenus, and with the help of this union to set the seal on a treaty of alliance with the Byzantine Empire.

Approached by the Frankish ambassadors, the constable Humphrey of Toron and William of Barres, Manuel Comnenus after some hesitation agreed. Baldwin's emissaries gave him to understand that their King was no friend of the Prince of Antioch. This was the first time that a king of Jerusalem had taken the initiative in an openly friendly step toward the Empire. The *basileus* chose for Baldwin III one of his nieces, Theodora, the daughter of his brother Isaac. She was a girl of thirteen, and she proved to be the best possible ambassador for her country at the court of Jerusalem. She was very tall for her age, and with her white and gold prettiness and youthful grace she seems to have quite literally conquered not merely Baldwin himself but also his followers, for whom William of Tyre speaks.[26]

Theodora was brought to Jerusalem in great pomp with a princely escort and a magnificent dowry, and she was welcomed by the acclamations of the crowd. The Frankish colonists were not backward in expressing their joy, for the Franks still had great faith in the power of the Greeks in spite of everything, and the royal marriage was a pledge of a real alliance. Frankish Syria would have the much needed protection of the Byzantine Empire.

Baldwin III, says the chronicler, fell in love with his child bride the moment he set eyes on her and forsook all other women for her. Hitherto something of a Don Juan, he was in future absolutely faithful to Theodora. Theodora herself, on the other hand, as events will show, must have felt more than a little out of place in the society of "barbarians" to which her uncle's policy had exiled her.

Since he was now the King of Jerusalem's uncle by marriage, Manuel Comnenus had no longer anything to fear from the King's intervention on behalf of the Prince of Antioch. He marched on Cilicia (whence Thoros and his family fled precipitately in fear of the imperial anger) with his army and advanced on Antioch. Well aware that Manuel was determined to avenge his Cypriot subjects, Reynald of Châtillon could not hope to try and defend his province against the Emperor's formidable army. In his terror he decided to go in person to Manuel's camp at Mamistra and beg his pardon.

Yielding to the entreaties of the Bishop of Lattakieh, the *basileus* agreed to forgive him. Reynald had to appear before him as a suppliant, barefoot and bare-armed, and prostrate himself in the dust at Manuel's feet as he sat on his throne. Chalandon, in his history of the Comneni, remarks that the *basileus* "was pleased to prolong this ignominious scene for so long that the spectators were sickened by it."[27] "Many Frenchmen," says William of Tyre, "were indignant at this, and greatly blamed the Prince for having failed to stand up at that moment." It might be thought, however, that Manuel Comnenus had at least the right to allow himself this mild revenge in return for the destruction of a whole country and its thousands of slaughtered men and violated women. At last he raised up the culprit, kissed him on the lips, and forgave him. Feudal law, not unlike that of our own time, was strangely gentle to war criminals. Cyprus had been so devastated by Reynald that it was never to recover its former prosperity.

Manuel, like a good prince, contented himself with the homage of Reynald of Châtillon and with formal promises which, in the event, Reynald did not even keep. He had made a demonstration of force and was not anxious to anger or weaken the Franks of Syria, since they constituted an important bulwark against the power of the Turks.

King Baldwin III also came to visit the Emperor's camp, as a relative and ally. He was received with the most friendly courtesy, and the Greek and Latin chroniclers, John Cinnamus and William of Tyre, tell us that the Emperor was so delighted with the young King's good manners that their relations were of the most cordial; so cordial, indeed, that Baldwin succeeded in bringing about a reconciliation between Manuel and his former enemy, Thoros II, who in turn paid homage to the Emperor and was confirmed in his possessions in Cilicia (1158–1159).

In the minds of Baldwin III and the Frankish barons, this meeting outside Mamistra should have been the prelude to a Crusade by all the Christian forces of the East against Nur ed-Din. Manuel Comnenus does not appear to have seen matters in this light: in the event the combined armies, Manuel's Byzantine forces with the Franks of Baldwin III and Reynald of Châtillon, and the Armenians of Thoros II, marched against Aleppo, and Nur ed-Din once again trembled for the continuance of his power, fearing the capture of Aleppo and the loss of northern Syria, and with more reason this time than on the occasion of the Crusade of 1147. Then, when the Franks were quite ready to continue the campaign, the *basileus* opened negotiations with Nur ed-Din and agreed to raise the siege in return for the release of all Christian prisoners the Zengid was holding in his prisons. These were very numerous, certainly more than six thousand, and the great majority of them were either Syrian Franks or survivors of the Kings' Crusade who had been languishing in Turkish fortresses for more than ten years. Among the captives were Bertrand, the son of Alfonso-Jordan, Count of Toulouse, and the Grand Master of the Temple, Bertrand of Blancfort.

The Franks were immensely disappointed by this peaceful victory. Chalandon, the great historian of the Comneni, explains Manuel's action by the desire to keep the Franks at his mercy under the permanent threat of danger provided by the Zengids. It would not have been in his interests to wipe out the archenemy of the Franks and so make them strong enough to go back on their promises of alliance. A calculation of this kind, which appears to reduce the Franks to the level of barbarians who could only be held in check by fear, implies that Manuel was convinced he could never really agree with his new allies, yet we know that he was in favor of the West and that his policy was always one of some friendliness toward the Franks. It is true, however, that in 1159 Reynald of Châtillon was still Prince of Antioch.

It is also true that the Emperor of Byzantium might very well have been reluctant to involve all his forces in a war against an adversary who offered no direct threat to himself when he was already engaged in what he regarded as a more important struggle with the Seljuk Sultan of Rum. In fact he defeated Kilij Arslan II the next year and forced him to swear an oath of fealty. Also, it should not be forgotten that in the eyes of the Byzantine Emperor, procuring the safety of several thousand Christian prisoners, even if they were Franks, was a work more agreeable in the sight of God than making war. Manuel may in all good faith have regarded his negotiations with Nur ed-Din as a victory and hoped that the Franks of Syria would be glad to see their lost friends again.

To the Franks, however, these liberated prisoners, most of whom were Germans from Conrad's army in a hurry to get back to their own country, constituted no reinforcement on a military level. They saw only one thing: that they had thought themselves on the point of getting rid of their most dangerous enemy and now their powerful ally and protector was betraying them by withholding his assistance. Consequently, Manuel's withdrawal led to a cooling of the relations between the Greeks and the Franks, which had so recently begun to grow more friendly. Baldwin III continued his campaigns against the Turks unaided, resigned to nothing more spectacular than border raids and small frontier skirmishes. Reynald of Châtillon, for his part, wished no more large-scale undertakings and returned to plundering the surrounding country.

A year after his humiliating scene with Manuel Comnenus, the Prince of Antioch was taken prisoner by Nur ed-Din while engaged in pilfering some cattle, the rightful owners of which were actually Christians. He was taken to Aleppo and flung into prison. Baldwin III did not miss him and made no attempt to set him free. There is reason to suppose that Constance's feelings were much the same, for she seems to have been perfectly satisfied to rule alone for the future.

Aimery of Limoges, the Patriarch who had formerly been so mal-
treated by Reynald, returned to Antioch where he was restored to his
position and privileges. Reynald remained a prisoner for sixteen
years.

Meanwhile, Antioch was left once again without a master and was
in great danger from the indomitable enemy of the Franks, whose
one idea was to make the most of his latest victory. Princess Constance, delighted at regaining her independence, seized power and
was determined to govern alone, taking no account either of her
young son, Bohemond III (who was now sixteen or seventeen), or
of the Frankish barons. These appealed once again to the King of
Jerusalem, while the dowager, on her side, attempted to consolidate
her position by leaning on Manuel Comnenus. She actually sent a
message to the Emperor, promising to surrender the city as though
to its suzerain and protector. Despite his treaty with Manuel, Baldwin
III took the side of the Frankish barons and exerted his rights as
suzerain to place Antioch under the regency of the Patriarch. Ousted
definitively from power, Constance was forced to be content with a
life annuity, and in fact died three years later. Aimery of Limoges
could consider himself avenged.

It is already clear that the affairs of Frankish Syria interested the
Emperor only insofar as they gave him a chance to recover Antioch.
Baldwin's behavior annoyed Manuel considerably, although he did
not at first allow himself to show it. He did, however, permit himself
a small diplomatic revenge. He had recently become a widower, and
contemplating taking a Frankish princess to wife, he courteously
asked the King of Jerusalem to suggest the person he thought most
suitable to become Empress of Byzantium.

Baldwin III was flattered, but his choice clearly did not correspond
to the Emperor's wishes. There were only two possible candidates:
the Count of Tripoli's sister Melisende, and Maria, eldest sister of the
Prince of Antioch. Manuel was obviously thinking of the second.
The King of Jerusalem, who still feared above all else that Byzantium would lay hands on the principality, offered the Emperor the
princess of Tripoli. He was so definite about this that the engagement
was regarded as official and young Raymond III, delighted at the
idea of his sister becoming an empress, literally ruined himself to
hastily provide a magnificent dowry. He had twelve handsome galleys built and equipped to transport the princess with her treasure
and her suite, while King Baldwin, who was the girl's first cousin,
also contributed handsomely toward the future empress's trousseau.

Manuel, who was by no means unaware of these preparations, blandly changed his mind and fixed his choice on the princess of Antioch instead. Baldwin was indignant and the young Count of Tripoli, angrily burning for revenge, armed the galleys he had made ready for the dowry and promptly sailed across the sea to spread terror in the unfortunate island of Cyprus, which was once more subjected, through no fault of its own, to attack by its Frankish neighbors. The rejected fiancée, young Melisende, never recovered from the affront. She fell into a decline and finally retired to a convent, where she died young. Maria of Antioch's subsequent fate was a still more cruel one.

Maria was the daughter of Constance and Raymond of Poitiers, but since she had two brothers and one sister still living, she was obviously not the heiress to Antioch. Nevertheless the marriage did give Manuel certain rights which he thought he could turn to some advantage. Moreover, if Greek historians are to be believed, this princess was a veritable miracle of nature: ". . . beautiful, more than beautiful, so great and so remarkable was her beauty that beside her all the legends of Aphrodite of the lovely smile and Juno of the white arms and Helen of the soft neck seem so much fantasy."[28] The marriage was arranged almost without the knowledge of the King of Jerusalem and in such haste that Princess Constance had not even the time to prepare a suitable trousseau. Baldwin III was highly displeased, but he made no objection: he did not want to stand in the way of his young relative's good fortune, and in any case there was nothing he could do to thwart the Emperor.

The marriage between Maria of Antioch and Manuel Comnenus was celebrated in December 1161 in Constantinople. Married to a man too old for her, surrounded by admirers—some disinterested, others not so—Maria, once Empress of Byzantium, plunged into palace intrigues, seized power after her husband died, and finally paid by a frightful death for the dangerous glory for which she had been so envied. By this marriage, Manuel Comnenus gained a young and lovely bride and a voice in the government of the principality of Antioch, which remained a Frankish possession. This is not to say that the Emperor did not take his role as suzerain of the province seriously, and thanks to Byzantine protection Antioch was to escape Moslem domination for another hundred years.

King Amalric

Baldwin III died two months after Maria of Antioch's marriage. He was only thirty-two and his premature death on February 10, 1162, was sincerely mourned throughout Frankish Syria. As the King's body was being taken from Beirut, where his sudden death had occurred, to Jerusalem, the people of the villages came down from their mountains to the road and wailed around the coffin. The Arabs, says William of Tyre, showed as much grief as the Christians. By his gentleness, good looks, and obvious care for the people's well-being, Baldwin III had made himself loved, better probably than he made himself obeyed.

Nur ed-Din's friends advised him to take advantage of the resulting consternation among the Frankish chivalry to deliver a decisive blow to his enemies. The pious atabeg nobly refused, saying it was unworthy to attack men suffering such affliction at the loss of their king.

Baldwin III left no children. His young Queen Theodora, widowed at eighteen, left Jerusalem and went to live in her own city of Acre, which she had received as a dowry. She lived there in comparative solitude, which she probably preferred to the excitement and intrigue of a court whose manners must have seemed crude to her, and only emerged from her retreat five years later in the company of her kinsman Andronicus Comnenus (later Emperor) to become the heroine of one of the most celebrated love stories of the time.

Baldwin III's natural heir was his younger brother Amalric. Amalric was twenty-five at the time of the King's death. He possessed neither his elder brother's beauty nor his charm, had not received such a careful education, and was not unduly loved by the Frankish nobility of Jerusalem, partly on account of his arrogant disposition and partly because of his connections with what might be called the opposition party. He was married to the daughter of Joscelin II of Courtenay, and had surrounded himself with barons of the former county of Edessa, several of whom were half Armenian. Furthermore, all those who had previously revolted against the despotic Queen Mother Melisende knew that Amalric had remained faithful to his mother's party. However unpopular this prince may have been, his rights were incontestable; but the barons of the land, whom Baldwin III's natural weakness had already accustomed to treating the kingdom as a kind of feudal republic, hesitated for some time before swearing fealty to Amalric, who they knew would be much less biddable than his brother.

The upshot was that Amalric was not acknowledged as King until he had been confronted with a veritable ultimatum. This ultimatum was strange enough in itself: he was asked to repudiate his wife. The demand (according to the *Chronique d'Ernoul*) was formulated in somewhat insolent terms: "Sire, we well know that you ought to be King, and yet we can by no means accept that you shall wear the crown until you are separated from that wife you have. For she is not a woman who should be a queen, and the queen of such a lofty city as Jerusalem." Was Agnes of Courtenay's behavior already so notoriously reprehensible? At all events Amalric agreed amiably enough, and it is possible that the person really aimed at in this was not Agnes herself but her brother, Joscelin III, a man devoted to intrigue and machination and one whose influence might well have been feared. The fact remains that Amalric agreed and had his marriage annulled on the usual pretext of "consanguinity." (The relationship was not in this case a particularly close one: the couple's grandfathers had been first cousins.) When he repudiated his wife, Amalric saw to it that the two children she had borne him were declared legitimate, and by this act Baldwin and Sibylla became heirs presumptive to the throne of Jerusalem. But it was understood that the children were to be taken away from their mother. Baldwin was given into the care of tutors qualified to instruct him in the profession of kingship, while Sibylla was brought up by her great-aunt Joveta, the abbess of the convent of Saint-Lazare at Bethany. Agnes, who deserved some compensation, consoled herself by marrying Hugh of Ibelin, one of the principal barons of the land.

Amalric had a head for politics and a conqueror's temperament. His ambitions were vast, but he was clear-headed enough to understand that he did not possess sufficient forces to realize them. He seems to have been more admired by the Moslems than by the Franks. Ibn al-Athir wrote of him: "Never since the Franks first appeared in Syria had there been a king to equal him in courage, cunning, and cleverness." The prince, who had been born in Syria and was more influenced by the indigenous element than his brother, had an admirable knowledge of what was going on in the country and was able to evaluate at their true worth the political and religious factors which, in Frankish Syria as well as in Islam, might serve or damage the interests of the kingdom. He was not a particularly zealous Christian or a notorious Frankish nationalist, and was much more like the atabegs of Damascus and Aleppo who had been supplanted by the Zengids than like the first Crusaders. He was deeply curious about the manners and customs of non-Christian lands, even going so far (so William of Tyre implies) as to doubt the pre-eminence of the Christian revelation over other religions.* He had a natural understanding of the Moslems—the ordinary Moslems, not fanatics like Nur ed-Din. He was cynical and calculating, and he organized the policy of his reign like a game of chess. He was good at taking risks, at aiming high and losing without being discouraged. Naturally autocratic, he still had some difficulty in imposing his wishes on others, and he had to deal with considerable anarchic elements which he was forced to humor. And, possibly because of his cold, proud temperament, he never succeeded in inspiring sufficient confidence to make himself spontaneously obeyed.

Amalric was extremely fat, even obese (although he was not a great eater or drinker), but in spite of this he was an intrepid fighter, able to bear the labors and fatigues of a campaign as well as the least of his soldiers. His cupidity was notorious and he found money wherever he could, levying heavy taxes and trying—though this was not easy—to lay hands on ecclesiastical benefices. He also intervened personally in the courts of justice and, as supreme judge, insisted on his profit. He lived very simply and wanted money only for the needs of the state. Considering the situation in which the kingdom found itself, these needs could be reduced to a single source of expenditure, namely, war. Fully aware of the danger to Frankish Syria represented by the united kingdom of Damascus and Aleppo, and hesitating to place himself under Byzantine suzerainty, Amalric carried on the Egyptian policy laid down by his brother, but on a much vaster scale.

His great idea was the conquest of Egypt. In the years from 1160 to 1170, the Fatimid caliphate was in such a state of decadence that Egypt seemed to be a prize just ripe to fall into the hands of a new master. Two powers in the north coveted it equally: the Franks and Nur ed-Din. Now the competition between the two had come into the open, and each was hoping to steal a march on the other. Nur ed-Din and Amalric were both driven less by greed than by the fear of seeing the other's position too strongly reinforced.

After the assassination of the Caliph al-Zafir and a number of bloody palace revolutions, the governor of Upper Egypt, Shawar, seized power in 1163 and governed with the title of Vizier in the

* See below, pages 527–28.

name of the young Caliph. Dethroned by his rival Dhirgham, Shawar took refuge with Nur ed-Din and urged him to march on Cairo in the hope of regaining power. Only too glad to intervene in Egyptian affairs, Nur ed-Din sent an army led by his best lieutenant, a Kurd named Shirkuh, an extremely capable man who had no difficulty in restoring Shawar to the vizierate. Meanwhile Dhirgham, on his side, had appealed to the King of Jerusalem, and Amalric arrived with his army only to find that his ally had already been defeated. Then, as was to be expected, Shawar turned about and himself concluded a treaty of alliance with Amalric in order to protect himself against the ambitions of Shirkuh and Nur ed-Din.

The King of Jerusalem had just defeated Nur ed-Din at Buqaia (al-Buqai'a al Hosn) in 1163, thanks to the assistance given to his army by two great French barons who were then on pilgrimages to the Holy Land, Hugh VIII, Count of Lusignan, and Geoffrey Martel, the Count of Angoulême's brother, and also by the Byzantine governor of Cilicia, Constantine Coloman. The vigor of the Greek warriors had impressed the Franks as much as the Moslems, and Amalric had reason to believe that northern Syria, protected by the troops of Byzantium, no longer needed his help and that he was free to devote himself to the matter of Egypt.

Consequently, the two adversaries, Amalric and Shirkuh, confronted each other for several weeks on the outskirts of Cairo without daring to engage in battle. Shawar had got what he wanted, because when Nur ed-Din's lieutenant saw that the Franks were determined to drive him out of Egypt, he retired of his own accord. In this way the ambitious Vizier regained power without compromising his country's independence to the advantage of the Zengids. It is true that at the same time he became dependent on the Franks, but they themselves were much too seriously threatened by Nur ed-Din to waste their efforts on invading Egypt.

At the very moment when he was forcing Shirkuh to strike camp, Amalric himself was preparing to beat a retreat and hurry north again. He had just learned that Nur ed-Din had inflicted a heavy defeat on the Frankish forces near Harenc on August 10, 1164.

This defeat was the more serious because on this occasion the Eastern Christians, not only the Franks but the Armenians and the Greeks of Cilicia as well, had actually risen in a body to protect the castle of Harenc, which was under siege by Nur ed-Din. In this great army, the Prince of Antioch and the Count of Tripoli and also the son of the former Count of Edessa rubbed shoulders with the Roupenian prince Thoros II and the Greek Constantine Coloman.

Even monks had been mobilized to provide a powerful infantry. Their superior numbers gave the Christians an initial advantage, but then, deceived by a clever maneuver on the part of Nur ed-Din, the cavalry rashly set off in pursuit of the Turks and found itself surrounded and cut off from the foot soldiers, who were badly led and were cut to pieces. After a desperate struggle, the knights were forced to admit defeat and all those who had not perished on the field of battle were led into captivity. Kemal ad-Din, to enhance the story of the victors, insists that the Franks defended themselves with exemplary courage, while William of Tyre, on the contrary, accuses them of behaving like cowards and of having "flung down their swords and cried mercy."²⁹ Only the Armenian Thoros, who had foreseen the Turkish maneuver and had not set off in pursuit, escaped from the disaster. The Greek general Coloman and the three young Frankish princes whose titles all included the figure III (Bohemond III, Raymond III, and Joscelin III) were taken to Aleppo with their knights, led in triumph through the streets of the city, and then flung into prison. Northern Syria was left without defenders and exposed to the mercy of the Turks.

This was why Amalric abandoned Egypt in such a hurry and led his troops northward to defend the Syrian provinces, which were once more masterless. Antioch, however, was not to remain so for long. Bohemond III was released a year later. And although Nur ed-Din did capture the strategic strongholds of Harenc and Banyas, he had no idea of exploiting his victory by marching on Antioch. The Franks could see that the situation had changed a good deal since the time of Roger of Salerno and Raymond of Poitiers. Antioch was well and truly under Greek protection, and the mere threat of the Emperor's intervention forced the fearless Nur ed-Din to respect the Frankish principality. The atabeg answered those who reproached him for his apparent lack of initiative, "I would rather have Bohemond for a neighbor than the King of the Greeks!"³⁰ (He was afraid that the Franks, unable to hold Antioch themselves, would hand it over to the Emperor.) The same considerations enabled Bohemond III to regain his liberty. The Prince was a young man, lacking either experience or authority, and only too well aware of the weakness of his position, he relied heavily on his alliance with his suzerain and brother-in-law, the Emperor Manuel. Not long after his release he went to Constantinople, and when he came back he brought with him a Greek patriarch for Antioch. The solemn enthronement of this prelate consecrated the re-establishment of Greek suzerainty over the city in the eyes of Byzantium.

The two other Frankish princes, Raymond III of Tripoli and Joscelin III of Courtenay, with most of their knights, remained prisoners for eight years or more. Joscelin III, whose father had died five years earlier in the same prison in Aleppo, and Raymond III, the same young man who had earlier ravaged the coasts of Cyprus to avenge his sister, were of no interest in the Emperor's eyes. Consequently Nur ed-Din did not have to treat them carefully, since he was not in the least afraid of Amalric's anger.

In fact the Greeks, who had long been regarded by the Franks as a soft, effeminate, and unwarlike people, now inspired more fear than the Franks themselves. Belatedly realizing that the "perfidy" and inexplicable lukewarmness of the Byzantines over the past sixty years had been based on nothing more than Frankish lack of response to the Empire's claim to Antioch, Amalric turned, more resolutely than his brother had done, to Byzantium and dreamed of the creation of a vast Franco-Byzantine condominium, stretching from Cilicia to the valley of the Nile.

The Struggle for Egypt

Somewhat reassured about the state of affairs in northern Syria, and still drawn overwhelmingly to Egypt, the King of Jerusalem took the road to Cairo once more. He was too good a soldier not to be obsessed by the idea of conquering a land of whose weakness and wealth he was very well aware and which, if he did not take it, was bound to fall into the hands of his worst enemy. At the beginning of his reign he had written a long letter to Louis VII, outlining in detail the position of the Fatimid empire, its political isolation, and the ease with which he was confident he could make himself master of it if only the King of France would send him ships and an army. He offered the Capet in advance suzerainty over Cairo and the Nile valley, but Louis VII, who was thoroughly fed up with the Holy Land, did not take the offer seriously. Amalric therefore addressed himself to Manuel Comnenus. The conquest of Egypt offered Byzantium advantages more immediate and real than it did France, and Manuel, though he was still absorbed in his wars in Anatolia and the Balkans, was quite willing to lend his fleet and some of his army with a view to an expedition against Egypt.

However, the King of Jerusalem was playing a tricky game with Shawar and Shirkuh. The latter was still trying, in the name of Nur ed-Din, to awaken the Vizier to a sense of Moslem solidarity, while

Shawar wavered between the Frank and the Zengid, hoping to out-
wit both and so safeguard his country's independence. The religious
schism dividing Shiite Egypt from the rest of Islam, which was subject to the caliphate of Baghdad, should not be forgotten. The reason
that Nur ed-Din wanted to conquer Egypt was largely in order to
re-establish Sunnite orthodoxy there, and there were many Egyptians
who feared this religious annexation almost as much as Frankish
domination. When Shirkuh suggested to him that he unite with Nur
ed-Din against the Franks for the triumph of Islam, Shawar answered, "No, for they are not *Firenj* [Franks], but *firej* [salva-
tion]!"

Shirkuh, a powerful Kurdish chieftain who was wholly devoted
to his overlord, was on the way to becoming the strong man of Moslem Syria. Nur ed-Din, after a serious illness which in 1157 had left
him hovering for a long time between life and death, was giving
himself up more and more to prayer and meditation with only spasmodic eruptions of his former energy. Shirkuh, a rough warrior,
without culture or education but gifted with an intelligence as great
as his courage, was a terrible opponent for Amalric. After the treaty
of alliance had been officially ratified between Egypt and the Franks,
Shirkuh invaded Egypt with his troops, defeated Amalric's army at
Babain, in the Nile valley two hundred miles south of Cairo, and then
marched back up the river and took Alexandria. Amalric, with his
Frankish knights and some Egyptian troops, closely blockaded the
city, which was defended by Shirkuh's nephew Salah ed-Din Yusuf,
and forced it to surrender. Once again Shirkuh evacuated Egypt
with bag and baggage, while the Franks marched into Alexandria
as liberators.

It was at the surrender of Alexandria that the King of Jerusalem
and his knights met for the first time the man who was to be the future conqueror of Frankish Syria. Salah ed-Din was the son of Ayub
and a nephew of Shirkuh. Though still young, he was already a gallant captain and a Moslem inflamed with zeal for the holy war, and
like his uncle, he had not abandoned hope of conquering Egypt.
Meanwhile, defeated and fearing the anger of the people of Alexandria, he had been compelled to take refuge in the camp of his enemies the Franks, who treated him with the greatest courtesy. Amalric
even went so far as to intercede with Shawar on behalf of those
Egyptians who had embraced Shirkuh's party, reminding him of the
clauses of the surrender. The future Saladin must have been considerably mortified to see a Frank acting as arbiter between Moslems,
but he could also give Amalric's honorable behavior its due.

Indeed, it seems that the King of Jerusalem did actually make a point of behaving as honorably to the defeated as to his allies in this affair. William of Tyre describes him as facing urgent pressure from his barons to profit by his victory by taking possession of Cairo, and he even states that the bishops had proposed to the King to "take the sin on themselves and have it absolved by the Pope." Amalric replied that he would never have himself or his heirs accused of such treachery. He made an agreement with Shawar, who in return for military assistance promised an annual tribute of 100,-000 gold pieces. This, for the Franks of Syria, was very good business. In practice it meant that Egypt became a vassal of the kingdom of Jerusalem. Whether Shawar was motivated by personal ambition or Fatimid loyalty, he salvaged what could still be salvaged of his country's independence; but by one compromise after another he drove the patience of his subjects, the fragile loyalty of the Franks, and the interested indignation of Nur ed-Din and Shirkuh to their limits.

A year after the Frankish protectorate had been set up in Egypt, Amalric made an alliance with Manuel Comnenus with the avowed object of conquering Egypt for Christendom. In 1167, the year of his Egyptian campaign, he followed his brother's example and married a grandniece of the Greek Emperor, Maria Comnena, the daughter of Manuel's nephew John Comnenus. This marriage was the prelude to a military alliance. The person entrusted with negotiating plans for this alliance in Constantinople was the future Archbishop of Tyre and historian of the kingdom, William, then Archdeacon of Tyre and of Nazareth. The object was a great Franco-Byzantine campaign against Cairo. It was agreed that in 1169, a year after the ratification of the treaty, the Greeks would send their fleet and an army to join up with the Frankish forces on the Egyptian coast.

Amalric was undoubtedly tempted by the fabulous wealth of the Fatimid empire, wealth of which his ambassadors had given him dazzling descriptions. Cairo was one of the wealthiest cities in the world, and William of Tyre's account of the Caliph's reception of the Frankish ambassador (Hugh of Caesarea) shows that even an austere churchman could not help but be overwhelmed by the almost fairytale splendor of the Caliph's palace.[31] Greed was the ruling passion of the Frankish knights, and the kings of Jerusalem were always desperately short of money. All the same, Amalric's policy seems to have been primarily determined by the fear of seeing Nur ed-Din lay hands on Egypt. He was certainly quite happy with his annual tribute of 100,000 gold pieces, and was not a man to chase after shadows. But circumstances made the treaty with Shawar a precarious one: the knights whom the King of Jerusalem had left in Egypt to keep an eye on the payment of the tribute behaved insolently and rapaciously, and aroused the anger of the population against both the Franks and Shawar. The Vizier, constantly in terror that the Franks would break their promise and invade Egypt, was secretly negotiating with Nur ed-Din, not to bring him into Egypt but to rouse him against the Franks. The situation was in fact becoming more and more explosive, and Amalric still preferred to see Cairo in Greek hands rather than in Shirkuh's.

Apparently the barons of the kingdom, and the military order of the Hospitalers in particular, were very conscious of the fact that in the event of a Franco-Byzantine conquest of Egypt the Greeks would take the lion's share. They advised the King to begin the campaign in 1168, without waiting for the arrival of the Byzantine ships. Indeed, they did more than advise: they enforced their decision. Ibn al-Athir, as the voice of Moslem opinion, depicts the King as categorically opposed to any such plan:

> The Franks urged their King, Murri, to undertake the conquest of Egypt. In spite of the representations of officers of the most distinguished ranks and experience, he would not agree to it. "It is my opinion," the King said, "that we ought not to undertake this thing. Egypt gives us supplies, all her wealth comes to us and furnishes us with the means to fight against Nur ed-Din. If we enter there with the object of taking possession, neither the sovereign nor his army nor the people of the cities or the countryside will agree to deliver them to us; they will fight us in their own defense, and the fear that we shall inspire will decide them to yield the country up to Nur ed-Din. Now if this prince takes it and if he acts there as Ased ed-Din [Shirkuh] has done, then it will mean the ruin of the Franks and their expulsion before long from the land of Syria."[32]

Amalric, however, is known to have been planning the conquest of Egypt, but with Byzantine help, for he wanted to strike only when he could be sure of victory. He may have feared that Nur ed-Din would not wait for the Christian forces to unite, and he wanted at all costs to prevent the occupation of Cairo by his enemy. The fact remains that this campaign was decided against his wishes. The Knights Hospitaler, whose opinion appears to have been decisive in this, pledged everything they possessed to equip the troops of their order, seeing to it that the entire province of Bilbeis was promised to them in advance as their fief. "The great ones," says Michael the Syrian, "did not adopt the King's advice. 'We shall go,' they said, 'and take Egypt before Nur ed-Din has even time to prepare.' Thus the King was defeated by them." William of Tyre, for his part, accuses the King and his barons in so many words of breaking their given word and even of treachery (to Shawar).

Once in the field, Amalric himself explained to Shawar's emissary, with a good deal of embarrassment, that "people from oversea have come among us. They have prevailed in our counsels and set out to take your country. Fearing that they would succeed, we also came to act as mediators between them and you."[33] There may have been a few Crusaders from Europe with the army, but there is no doubt that those chiefly responsible for the campaign were in fact the Knights Hospitaler.

In his heart of hearts Amalric might have been genuinely anxious to temporize, keep the ardor of his army in check, and withdraw after levying fresh tribute, but neither the Franks nor the Egyptians saw matters in this light. There was a real war and one which ended exactly as Amalric had foreseen.

This campaign of 1168 constituted a political blunder of the utmost importance. In attacking Egypt when he had insufficient forces to maintain himself there, or even to conquer the country completely, Amalric was doing Nur ed-Din's work for him and hastening the encirclement of his kingdom by a Moslem power whose avowed object was the annihilation of the Franks of Syria. What he could not have foreseen was that he was also at the same time making himself the architect of the rise to power of a man yet more dangerous than Nur ed-Din.

The Franks were expecting to enter Egypt as a land already conquered and incapable of resistance—such, at least, had been their impression on previous campaigns. This time they met with furious resistance on the part of the garrisons and the people. When the city of Bilbeis was taken by storm they behaved with extreme savagery, slaughtering even women and children. Their intention was to terrorize the populations of the other cities and leave them no will to fight, but all they did was to arouse an even stronger spirit of resistance. "If the Franks had behaved with humanity toward the inhabitants of Bilbeis, they would certainly have taken Fostat and Cairo afterward, but it was God who, for His own ends, drove them to act thus."[34]

In the end the Franks failed to take Cairo and were compelled to withdraw from Egypt after demanding, for form's sake, a tribute of one million dinars. Terrified by the Frankish threat, Shawar had been forced to appeal to Nur ed-Din, who promptly sent him Shirkuh at the head of a vast army.

Seeing that he could not stand against the Egyptians and against Shirkuh at the same time, King Amalric did not wait for payment of the tribute, but struck camp and returned to Palestine, "reproaching bitterly those who had advised him on this expedition."[35] He had in fact plenty to reproach them with. In January 1169, immediately after the departure of the Franks, Shirkuh entered Cairo in triumph and became almost the official master of Egypt. A few days after Shirkuh's troops had marched into Cairo, the wretched Shawar was assassinated—or summarily executed—by Salah ed-Din and his friends at the instigation of the Fatimid Caliph himself. Two months later Shirkuh also died, leaving everything to his nephew.

It is easy to see to what extent these events compromised the future of Frankish Syria. One of Nur ed-Din's lieutenants ruling in Egypt meant first and foremost the end—officially at least—of the religious dissidence in the heart of Islam. Three years after Shirkuh had seized Cairo, the young Fatimid Caliph, al-Adid, died. For a long time his power had been no more than a shadow, and Saladin had not even waited for his death to compel Egypt to acknowledge the religious authority of the Caliph of Baghdad.

The end of the schism meant that the whole of the Moslem Middle East was united under the rule of Nur ed-Din. Now the atabeg of Aleppo and Damascus (who was already generally referred to by the title of Sultan) controlled Egypt, and in 1170 he also became master of Mosul through the death of his brother Qutb ed-Din, who had succeeded Saif ed-Din. In the face of this formidable power, the Franks, with their insignificant army of at most a few thousand knights and their already shrunken territories without natural frontiers, could not hope to hold out for long. (Admittedly, Nur ed-Din was no longer young and his death might put the whole situation back in the melting pot.)

Horrified by the consequences of his march on Cairo, which he had foreseen only too clearly, Amalric appealed in vain to the West. Although a few great barons did occasionally bring contingents of armed pilgrims, this military aid contributed at the most to the success of a few defensive campaigns. There was no real Crusade. Where they needed tens of thousands of men, the kingdom of Jerusalem now saw them arriving two hundred, five hundred, or a thousand at a time, and even these never stayed long in the country.

In 1169 the Byzantine aid, which had in fact been arranged for that year, actually arrived, but Manuel had not forgiven the Franks for their rash expedition of the previous year and the barons of Palestine on their side seem to have been more jealous of the possible success of the Greeks than worried about the advancing Moslems. The allies laid siege to Damietta, but the siege dragged on for a long time and ended in failure. To add to their misfortunes, a large part of the Byzantine fleet was destroyed by a storm.

Amalric, who was barely succeeding in holding off the attacks of Saladin in the south and Nur ed-Din in the north, made up his mind, possibly in spite of his barons, to place his kingdom under the official protection of the Byzantine Empire. In 1171 he went in person to Constantinople and there concluded a treaty of alliance with Manuel which implied some sort of recognition of Byzantine suzerainty. In spite of the loss of his fleet, for which the inertia of the Latin barons was principally to blame, Manuel was genuinely anxious to collaborate with any Christian kingdom bordering on his own territory and especially one which enjoyed regular aid from the West. He was already having difficulty enough in keeping the Seljuks of Asia Minor in a state of semivassalage without tolerating the creation of a powerful Moslem state in Syria. Neither he nor Amalric had given up their plans to conquer Egypt. It seemed to them that all was by no means lost on that front.

Egypt had certainly fallen into the power of Nur ed-Din's lieutenant, but this lieutenant was ambitious and his rebellion against his suzerain not inconceivable. Left to his own devices in a land where the population was hostile to him (or so at least the Christian monarchs believed), Saladin could easily be crushed.

It was a fact that the Shiite subjects of the new governor of Egypt were anything but resigned to the official suppression of the Fatimid caliphate and only too inclined to look for support from the Franks. But where a vizier governing in the name of the Caliph had failed, a clandestine subversive movement, quickly discovered and harshly put down, could achieve very little. Saladin was now undisputed master of Egypt and although he was not quite thirty-five years old, his renown and prestige almost equaled that of Nur ed-Din. By a policy combining firmness and adaptability he had brought about in three years what Sunnite Islam had been hoping for in vain for a hundred and sixty-eight: the end of the Shiite schism and the suppression of the heretic caliphate. In the eyes of pious Moslems this victory was more important than any military conquest. All that remained for the Franks and Greeks was to pin their hopes on the rivalry between the new master of Egypt and the powerful atabeg of Syria. Hence the unexpected sympathy the Franks initially showed for

Saladin who, however warlike he appeared, was still a lesser menace than Nur ed-Din.

Once again Amalric found himself faced with the same dilemma. He had to decide whether to attempt the straightforward conquest of Egypt with the aid of Byzantium. (With the Emperor's support, the project did have some semblance of legality and feasibility. Before the Arab conquest Egypt had been part of the Byzantine Empire, and possessed a strong though not orthodox Christian population in the mountains to the south. The kingdom of Ethiopia was a Christian kingdom adhering to the Coptic Church, and a return to Christian rule over the Nile valley was not in itself such a farfetched idea.) The other alternative, to foster further misunderstandings between Nur ed-Din and Saladin and bid for the alliance, or at least the neutrality, of the latter, was perhaps more prudent, but there was a chance that Nur ed-Din's power would crumble on his death, while Saladin was still young. Consequently the King of Jerusalem was in a very delicate position, and one for which he himself was partly responsible. He was hesitating between two equally dangerous courses of action, insofar as he still had time to hesitate and reflect at all. Nur ed-Din's troops were attacking constantly in the north, near Antioch, and Saladin's in the south, near Ascalon. This was not the moment to alarm Saladin and drive him into the arms of his suzerain by threatening him with a great Franco-Byzantine Crusade.

At this moment another cruel and totally unforeseeable misfortune placed the future of Frankish Syria in still greater jeopardy. In addition to the external perils, Amalric's only son, the heir to the throne of Jerusalem, fell victim while still an infant to a mysterious disease which resisted every remedy. When the child reached his tenth year, the young prince's doctors and attendants were finally compelled to acknowledge the truth: little Baldwin was a leper.

Amalric died on July 11, 1174, of dysentery which he contracted at the siege of Banyas, at the age of thirty-nine. He had had every reason to hope that he himself would live longer, but he had known for years that his son was doomed. Paternal affection and the anxiety for the continuation of the dynasty prevented him from disinheriting Baldwin, the more so because he had no other male heirs. Sibylla was not yet of an age to marry, and by his second wife, Maria Comnena, the King had only a daughter.

In principle the laws of the time enforced the strict exclusion of lepers from all aspects of social life, making them virtually dead in the eyes of the law. Leprosy, especially in the East, was not a rare disease, and it was legislated against in exactly the same way as theft, civil offenses, and crimes against the faith. Once a leper's condition was confirmed, he forfeited all his rights and was confined to the society of those in the same plight as himself. These measures were dictated solely by considerations of public health and implied no kind of religious taboo. The little prince of Jerusalem was never regarded as "unclean" or unfit to rule, but it was only too easy to forecast what his life would be like and everyone knew that he could not live for long.

Knowing that young Baldwin would never marry, Amalric cast around to find at least a husband for his daughter, a husband rich and powerful enough to be a defender for the kingdom. But Jerusalem, once such a coveted prize, now that it was in danger and almost on the point of falling into Moslem hands aroused only the most lukewarm interest in the rest of Christendom. People thought that if matters were going badly for the King of Jerusalem, this must be the fault of the Franks of Syria, who were "half Moslem" (William of Newburgh) themselves, bastardized, dissolute, poor guardians of their splendid heritage. Stephen, Count of Blois, the son of the Count of Champagne, whom Amalric considered as a potential husband for the Princess Sibylla, came East in 1171 and left at the end of four months because, says William of Tyre, "it did not please him to stay in the land [Palestine] any longer because he did not get on with the people of that country." The young French baron had no wish to be merely the brother-in-law and constable of a leper king. A leper could take many years to die. Amalric, on his side, had no wish to disinherit in favor of a stranger a child whose sickness only made him dearer still.

Young Baldwin seems to have possessed a naturally strong constitution, and he was also gifted with undeniable qualities of character and a strong, lively intelligence. William of Tyre, who was his tutor, says that "in his childhood he was very handsome, with a quick and open mind, and he rode very well, better than his forebears had done." "Never forgetting an injury, and still less a kindness," he had "a retentive memory, was well educated with an excellent memory for tales and a fondness for telling them." The child must have realized very early that his disease was incurable, and his reaction shows great strength of character. He wanted to forget and make everyone else forget, right up to the end, that he was sick. But by the time King Amalric died, young Baldwin's disease had made such progress that it was already beginning to show, and "the people of the kingdom felt great grief when they looked at him."[36]

Thus the King of Jerusalem died while still young, leaving his throne to a child who was already doomed and his kingdom a prey to the aggression of Saladin and the feudal anarchy that always accompanied the accession of a minor. Amalric's great plan for the conquest and vassalization of Egypt had failed lamentably, not altogether through his own fault, and the Byzantine alliance toward which he had wisely been working was to be compromised first by the latent hostility of the Frankish barons and especially of the Crusaders from Europe, and then by the defeat of Manuel Comnenus at Myriocephalum, a defeat which once more put the whole question of Byzantine power in the East in the balance.

The Latin kingdom's only chance of survival lay in the misunderstandings between the Moslem states surrounding it. Saladin had actually moved into almost open revolt against Nur ed-Din, and Amalric, while endeavoring to remain on good terms with the new governor of Egypt—by periodical truces between two campaigns—had done his best to achieve friendly relations with the Ismailians and the Shiite faction in Egypt in order to undermine Saladin's power from within.* If he had lived, Amalric would certainly have given Saladin a run for his money even now, not so much by his talents as a military leader as by his increasingly close relations with Moslem dissidents. But his clever if not entirely chivalrous tactics were to be undone almost at once by the insubordination of the King of Jerusalem's own subjects (or rather by men who, although belonging to the kingdom, did not acknowledge themselves the King's subjects): the Templars. At one time Amalric even considered sacrificing the order to the Ismailians and dissolving them, wanting to have no more soldiers in his own lands who flouted his authority.

Amalric did at least have the satisfaction of seeing the old enemy of Frankish Syria go before him. Nur ed-Din died in Damascus on May 15, 1174, leaving his states to his eleven-year-old son Malik as-Salih Ismail. The Franks would probably have preferred an older heir who would be better able to defend himself, but Amalric did all he could to impress upon the young prince's guardians that he was prepared to support him against the claims of Saladin. After one attempt to win back Banyas, Amalric signed a truce with the government in Damascus, to the virtuous indignation of Saladin, who knew quite well that this truce was in fact the beginning of a Franco-Damascene

---

* The King of Jerusalem had succeeded in reaching an understanding with the partisans of the former Fatimid caliphs and was planning to restore the Caliph's son to the throne after the assassination of Saladin by conspirators. The plot was discovered and brutally suppressed.

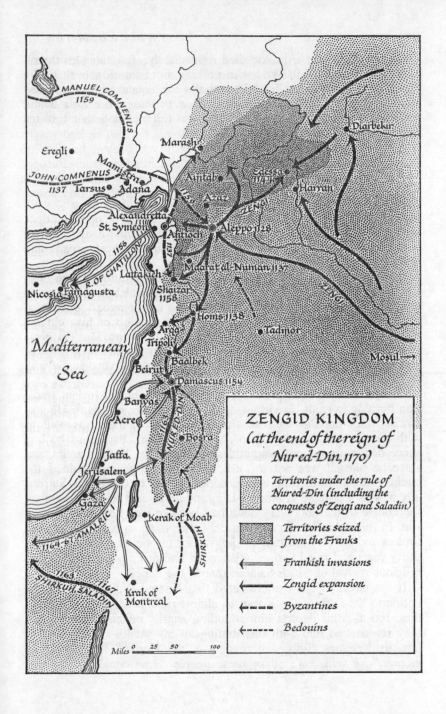

MANUEL COMNENUS
1159

Eregli

Marash

JOHN COMNENUS
1137 Tarsus

Mamistra

Adana

Aintab

Diarbekir

Azaz

Edessa

Harran

Alexandretta
St. Symeon

Antioch

ZENGI

Aleppo 1128

R. OF CHATILLON
1156

Lattakieh

Maarat al-Numan 1137

Shaizar
1158

Nicosia Famagusta

Homs 1138

Tadjior

Arqa

Tripoli

ZENGI

Mosul →

*Mediterranean
Sea*

Baalbek

Beirut

Damascus 1154

Banyas

Acre

NUR-ED-DIN

Bosra

Jaffa

Jerusalem

Kerak of Moab

SHIRKUH

Gaza

1164-67 AMALRIC I

1163   1167
SHIRKUH, SALADIN

Krak of
Montreal

ZENGID KINGDOM
*(at the end of the reign of
Nur ed-Din, 1170)*

Territories under the rule of
Nur ed-Din (including the
conquests of Zengi and Saladin)

Territories seized
from the Franks

⟵ Frankish invasions

⟵ Zengid expansion

⟵--- Byzantines

⟵----- Bedouins

Miles 0 25 50   100

alliance against him. Amalric died immediately after this agreement.

Saladin was faced in Syria with nothing more formidable than two states both a prey to the feudal squabbles consequent upon the accession of a minor. He could see no reason to fear either little Malik as-Salih, or the young leper King who was thirteen at the time of his father's death.

Saladin

Saladin—Salah ed-Din Yusuf—was one of the few Moslems who were famous enough in the West to enjoy a westernized version of their name. Saladin was one of the great figures of Islamic history. There is no need to stress his fame, which has persisted across oceans and across centuries, or his great reputation for justice and wisdom, a reputation which made Dante place him in the paradise of the non-Christian Just. His was a complex personality which is not easy to analyze, and there will be time to return to it when the sequence of events makes it possible to get a better appreciation of his achievements. At the time when, as virtual master of all the Moslem Near East, he was preparing to seize the two headless kingdoms of Moslem and Frankish Syria after the death of Nur ed-Din and Amalric, Saladin was thirty-seven years old.

He had not yet been glorified, even beatified, by a Moslem tradition burning to exalt his virtues as the great unifier of Islam. He was already very popular with all the more pious elements as well as with the army of Sunnite Islam. As Nur ed-Din's lieutenant he had succeeded in winning the sympathies of some of the Turkish emirs, and since he himself was not a Turk but a Kurd, he also gained the backing of the Arabs, who were generally hostile to the Turks. Spiritually he was a disciple of Nur ed-Din, and all he had to do was follow the course of the holy war which had been so well begun by Zengi's son. In this field, Saladin owed nearly everything to Nur ed-Din: the tireless and ardent preaching of the warrior mystic who for more than thirty years had ruled Syria singlehanded had made possible the great religious revival of which Saladin reaped the benefit.

It has already been demonstrated that Nur ed-Din carried his devotion to the faith of the Koran to almost ridiculous limits of exaltation. Ibn al-Athir depicts him rounding angrily on his officers when they reproached him with distributing all his wealth to "doctors of law, to dervishes, Sufis, and readers of the Koran." "My hopes of victory," he said, "are all in these people. How could I cease my gifts of alms to those who fight for me with their prayers while I sleep, and that with arrows which never miss their mark?"[37] Having heard that the Prophet traditionally carried his saber in a scabbard, he was shocked to see Moslem warriors wearing theirs in their belts: the proper course was to imitate the Prophet in the smallest details of behavior. The army was promptly made to adopt the practice of carrying the saber in a scabbard.[38]

Ibn al-Athir also quotes the words of a prayer of the pious atabeg which was revealed in a dream to an imam who had asked God for a sign to convince Nur ed-Din that his vision was authentic: "Lord, it is the faith which must be protected and not Mahmud [Nur ed-Din]. Is this dog of a Mahmud worthy of Thy protection?"[39] With his burning, inextinguishable zeal for his faith, Nur ed-Din was working for Moslem unity as the cleverest politicians had never been able to do. He irritated his followers and invited the mockery of emirs who were tired of his excessive devotion, but at the same time he won the hearts of the crowd.

Ibn al-Athir reports a significant remark by Kara Arslan, the Emir of Diarbekir, a Moslem with little zeal for the holy war:

Nur ed-Din adopted such a policy toward me that if I did not provide him with troops my own subjects would rebel against me and drive me out. Even in my own household he kept up a correspondence with ascetics and holy men, explaining to them the sufferings which the Franks imposed on the Moslems of Syria, death, captivity, and plunder. He entreated them to help him with their prayers and asked them to rouse the faithful to the holy war. Each of those to whom he wrote would go and sit in the mosque with their followers and friends and there give them Nur ed-Din's letters to read. When they had read them they would burst into tears and curse me, calling God's vengeance on me. This is why I cannot help but march against the Franks.[40]

Nur ed-Din was quite right to prefer the invisible arrows of holy men's prayers to what he termed the "frequently uncertain" arrows "of men who only fought when [he] was there." When he was ill in 1157, his vassals and closest friends, believing that he was dying, were already preparing to quarrel over his inheritance, and even Shirkuh, who was dedicated to unconditional loyalty to his suzerain to the end, had done so cautiously in collusion with his brother, keeping a foot in both camps. (Nur ed-Din was in fact never aware of this and reposed full confidence in Shirkuh.)

To keep the ideal of the holy war intact, Nur ed-Din relied not on his vassals and an army but on public opinion throughout Islam, and in this he was successful. The great letter writer who flooded the Moslem capitals with missives full of imprecations against the Franks and invocations to God was the educator of a whole generation, even of two generations, of God's warriors, and these warriors were not recruited solely from soldiers but from among the people and the servants of religion as well. He set about creating a spirit of holy war with a seriousness and tenacity which the pontiffs of the West might well have envied. Indeed, there was no preacher of the Crusade in Christian lands to equal this great Moslem leader.

Yusuf, surnamed Salah ed-Din—Protector of the Faith—was the son of a Kurdish emir, of fairly humble extraction but a valiant soldier, appointed by the Sultan of Persia to be governor of the little town of Tekrit in the province of Baghdad. Najm ed-Din Ayub had earlier distinguished himself by his loyalty to Zengi when he was fleeing in defeat before the Caliph's troops in 1132. Ever since then Ayub and his family had figured among Zengi's foremost companions, and later among those of Nur ed-Din. Ayub and his brother Shirkuh were rough soldiers whose indomitable courage was equaled by a kind of peasant cunning, and they were quite capable of advancing their careers by parading their devotion to the person of their chief, Nur ed-Din. Young Yusuf was given a careful education; he spent several years of his youth in a monastery, where he began the study of the Koran, and his piety was firm and sincere. However, it was not from the monks and dervishes that he learned his enthusiasm for the holy war, but in Nur ed-Din's court and his armies, where the atmosphere was one of exalted devotion and ardent, warlike mysticism: the desire to imitate the Prophet by fighting for the faith as he had done.

A serious-minded boy, Saladin became so imbued with the teachings of his master and the pious men who surrounded him that he actually came to regard the holy war as his first duty. "The fight for God's cause," wrote Beha ed-Din, "was a veritable passion with him. . . . He talked of nothing else, and all his thoughts and preoccupations were with weapons of war and with soldiers. He gave all his attention to those who talked of the holy war and exhorted the people to take part in it."[41] But the young mountain-bred emir who served with such exemplary loyalty under the command of his father and his uncle had too balanced a temperament to fall into excesses of piety and the mystical-warrior illuminism which was Nur ed-Din's strength. It would be fairer to say that he regarded the holy war as a duty and that his real passions were elsewhere.

In 1168 he set out with his uncle, on the orders of his sovereign, to defend Cairo against the Franks. With the modesty often affected by great men, he himself describes the reluctance with which he embarked on the affair:

"By God, if I were given the whole kingdom of Egypt I would not go again. I suffered too many pains and fatigues in Alexandria ever to forget them." Then my uncle said to Nur ed-Din, "He must come with me. Order him to go . . ." Then Nur ed-Din told me, "I command you take the road with your uncle." I answered him with complaints of the sad case in which I found myself, having insufficient steeds or equipment to make the journey. He gave me all I needed to equip myself and I set out like a man who is sent to his death. Thus I made the journey with my uncle, and no sooner had he established his site in Egypt than he died. Then God gave me rule over this land, although I had not expected it.[42]

In fact things were not quite so simple as this. To begin with, Shirkuh and Saladin had no more right to the country than the Franks themselves. The Fatimid Caliph and his vizier had asked for their help and opened their gates to them. The Franks departed and the Egyptian authorities loaded their deliverers with presents and honors and promises of money, promising to yield up a quarter of Egypt to Nur ed-Din in the hope that their armies would withdraw. Power was still in the hands of Shawar. It was the Caliph al-Adid who treacherously delivered up his vizier to Shirkuh, or more accurately, to Saladin. Saladin and his knights fell upon Shawar while the Vizier of Cairo and the young Syrian captain were riding together to a place of pilgrimage. They struck him down and then, acting on the authority of the Caliph, cut off his head. The Caliph hated Shawar as weak monarchs always hate too powerful ministers, but in fact Shawar carried Egyptian independence with him to his grave.

Saladin's action can no doubt be excused by the customs of the society in which he lived, the more so in that Shawar appears to have been contemplating the assassination of Shirkuh and his nephew during a banquet. Moslem courts were ruled by the law of the jungle, and at that moment Saladin merely happened to be the swiftest and most agile; but it cannot be said that his part in the affair was a glorious one.

The weak and treacherous Caliph bestowed on Shirkuh the title of "Victorious King," the office of vizier, and immense riches, and he was able to distribute fiefs in Egypt to all his emirs and set up a powerfully organized military dictatorship. When he died suddenly, three months after the murder of Shawar, Saladin naturally took his place. "God," he said afterward, "gave me rule over this land, although I had not expected it." It is true that he could not have anticipated his uncle's death, but God had certainly very little to do with the whole adventure.

Saladin was what could be called a self-made man. Inheriting the vizierate after Shirkuh's death, he applied himself highly efficiently to extirpating, either by persuasion or the threat of armed force, the Shiite heresy which had existed in the kingdom of Egypt for over a century and a half. (In doing so he was obeying the demands of the Caliph of Baghdad.) According to the chroniclers (who were all orthodox Sunnites) the revolution took place quietly and almost of its own accord, and reading between the lines this suggests the atmosphere of an extremely well-organized police state.

Some of the Caliph's mamelukes were intriguing with the court of Jerusalem in the hope of driving out the foreign master and attempted to provoke a revolt of the Caliph's personal guard, a powerful army corps of fifty thousand Negro soldiers from the Sudan and Nubia, men renowned for their strength and courage and fanatical devotion to their lord and religious leader. In the belief that their Caliph was a prisoner (which to some extent he was) the Negroes launched an attack on Cairo in August 1169. Seeing that his army could not get the better of men who rushed into battle with a complete disregard for death, Saladin had the idea of setting fire to the camp where the soldiers of the guard had their families. When the Negroes learned that their wives and children were being burned alive, their morale broke. Some rushed to the burning camp, while others made their way to the Caliph's palace only to have their master, terrorized by Saladin's threats, basely disown them: "Hunt down these dogs of slaves and drive them from the land!" Totally demoralized, the Negroes fled. In this way the entire guard was gradually wiped out. The Caliph's Armenian Guard could not intervene because the gates of their barracks had been shut before the Armenians could get out, and then they too were set afire. The slaughter and the burning lasted for days.

The Caliph, now a defenseless prisoner, dragged out a miserable life for another two years. On September 10, 1171, an official envoy from Baghdad offered up prayers in the name of the Sunnite Caliph al-Mustadi, Commander of the Faithful. "None dared raise a murmur of disapproval. On the following Friday, on Saladin's orders, all the preachers of Cairo and Fostat also replaced the Abbasid *khotba* [official prayer] with the Alid *khotba*. This came about peacefully, without so much as a clash between two goats."[43] However blasé and indifferent the twelfth-century Egyptians may have become, knowing the Moslems' ardor in religious argument and their readiness to quarrel over the slightest infringement of tradition, this allusion to the "peacefulness" of the people is enough to make one shudder.

The man who assassinated the Vizier who had asked for his help and had thousands of women and children—to say nothing of the soldiers—burned alive, who oppressed and terrorized the population of a land he had come to defend, did not even have the excuse of fanaticism carried to extremes or of a blind devotion to his sovereign's orders. First and foremost, Saladin was an ambitious man. He had become master of Egypt and he meant to remain so. Nur ed-Din, anxiously watching the assurance with which his young lieutenant was settling in his new dignity, and jealous of the growing popularity of the new champion of Islam, did his best to treat Saladin as a subordinate, merely granting him the title of Emir and never forgetting to remind him that he was only the temporary governor of Egypt.

After the proclamation of the Abbasid *khotba* in Cairo, the tension between the aging atabeg and his young rival became so obvious that in September 1171 Saladin gave up a campaign against the Franks for fear of increasing Nur ed-Din's power. His advisers told him, "If Nur ed-Din invades the territory of the Franks in their present state, attacked by you on one side and the atabeg on the other, he will take it. And once the Franks have disappeared from the land and their kingdom has been conquered, you will no longer be able to stand against the atabeg in Egypt."[44] Obviously the holy war was not Saladin's first preoccupation or the prospect of the Franks' "disappearance" would certainly have filled him with delight rather than anxiety. Nur ed-Din saw through his erstwhile protégé's plans, sent indignant letters to Saladin, and then decided to march in person against Egypt with the intention of driving out the person he henceforth regarded as a rival.

Alarmed, Saladin gathered all his clan—his father, uncle, brothers, nephews, and cousins—for a council of war. His father, old Ayub, lectured him as though he were still a young man too inexperienced to do what was necessary. He began by protesting his feudal loyalty: "I declare to you before God that if I or your uncle saw Nur ed-Din here, we could not prevent ourselves from falling on our faces before him. Should he order us to cut off your head with a sword, we would do it without hesitation. If Nur ed-Din should present himself, even alone, before us, none of his emirs, not one soldier, would dare remain in the saddle. This land of Egypt is his, and you are here only as his lieutenant." These sentiments, worthy of a samurai, did not express the old Kurdish chieftain's real feelings. Left alone with his son, Ayub advised him to be cunning, to feign the most abject submission, and write, "Let my master send a courier to put a rope around my neck, and I will suffer myself be led before him unresisting." Temporarily reassured, Nur ed-Din did not enter Egypt. But without moving into open rebellion, Saladin still remained an unsubmissive vassal, more anxious to support the Franks than to help his master fight them.

His fame was still less than Nur ed-Din's. However great his personal popularity, he was compelled to put on a show of submission and keep the atabeg happy with false excuses, sending letters full of flattery and protestations of loyalty, but always avoiding having to meet him face to face. Nur ed-Din was not taken in, but his strength was declining, all the more quickly because of the strict fasting and constant prayer he imposed upon himself. He would still rather make war on the Franks than on his own vassal. However, even on the eve of his death he was meditating an expedition to Egypt to drive Saladin out, and he certainly cannot have foreseen that the ambitious Kurdish emir would inherit not only his states in Syria but also the great cause of the holy war to which Zengi's son had devoted his life, or that the interests of the faith would only gain from this.

After Nur ed-Din's death, Saladin quite naturally cast his eyes on Damascus, which had become the capital of the Zengid kingdom. Since his suzerain had left only a child of eleven as his heir, he demanded that he should be given the guardianship of the young prince, "his master's son," and claimed, with apparent shamelessness, the office of regent. "If death had not taken the atabeg he would not have left the education and defense of his son to another! I shall come to the court of my master's son, and repay to the child the benefits which I received from the father."[45] Saladin's hypocrisy is obvious. Later events demonstrate that his feelings toward Nur ed-Din's son were anything but fatherly. But he was a man for whom the end justified the means, and who genuinely confused his own interests with those of the ideal they served.

Nur ed-Din's death disturbed the balance of political power in Syria. Saladin, who had so recently been anxious to bolster up the Franks, now emerged as their worst enemy and violently denounced the actions of the court of Damascus, which for its part was inclining toward a Frankish alliance for fear of Saladin. It was an unequal struggle. Against a kingdom governed in the name of a minor by regents who could not agree among themselves was set the rising master of Egypt and the champion of Islam, a hard man who would stop at nothing, supremely intelligent, a great general, a great politician, and the kind of man that appears only once in a blue moon. Whatever reservations should be made about his moral stature (there are many, and it would be childish to attempt to excuse all his faults on the grounds of the influence of society and the time), it is certain that in his own sphere of activity Saladin was a person of real greatness. There was nothing low or mean about him, no vanity, and even in his cunning he retained the innocence of a man who knows that when he demands the first place he is asking for no more than his due. All his life, even when at the height of his power, he retained the natural simplicity of manners and behavior which belong to a man who has never felt the need to appear greater than he is.

To have such a man as a neighbor was a disaster for Frankish Syria. If Zengi had begun the unification of Moslem Syria, and Nur ed-Din had filled the Moslems with enthusiasm for the holy war, Saladin was the incarnate image of the awakening of Islam and became, almost in spite of himself, its hero and paladin. Even his enemies were to feel a superstitious awareness of his superiority over them.*

* For the changing situation of the kingdoms of Aleppo and Damascus, see the genealogical tables at the end of the book.

CHAPTER

VIII

The Fall of the Frankish Kingdom

(1 1 7 4 – 1 1 8 8)

The Leper King

Saladin knew that the Franks would be no easy adversaries to subdue. All the same, at the time of the King's death, he still did not suspect that he would have a great deal of trouble in triumphing over them. In the end his success was the result of an extraordinary series of lucky accidents. The Franks were stronger than he thought and perhaps than they themselves believed.

Of the two regencies facing Saladin after the deaths of Nur ed-Din and Amalric, the first to be dealt with was obviously Damascus. This task was made easier for him by the fact that he had allies already inside the city, thanks to his popularity in the Moslem world. Nur ed-Din's successors made his job easy for him. Nur ed-Din's nephew Saif ed-Din Ghazi, atabeg of Mosul, had taken advantage of his uncle's death to seize part of this inheritance—northern Syria, with Nisibin, Harran, Edessa, and Saruj. The governor of Aleppo, Ibn ed-Daya, was jealous of the governor of Damascus, Ibn al-Muqaddam, and the discord between the two cities grew fiercer when the emirs of Aleppo obtained the guardianship of the young sovereign, as-Salih Ismail, for themselves. The Damascenes summoned Saladin to their assistance and he delightedly seized the opportunity to enter Damascus and install himself as master of the city, while proclaiming himself the young Zengid's faithful subject (mameluke) and accusing the Aleppans, he said, of keeping him in their city unjustly.

Now the emirs of Aleppo, and young as-Salih in particular, were so little taken in by this show of loyalism that when they saw Saladin's army before Aleppo they appealed to the Franks. The child king harangued his troops and his people from on horseback, begging them to protect him against the perfidy of Saladin. The resolute bearing of the people of Aleppo and the approach of the Frankish army compelled Saladin to raise the siege and fall back to Damascus. The atabeg of Mosul, little as-Salih's cousin, attempted, with the help of the troops of Aleppo, to drive Saladin out of Syria and was defeated at Qurun Hama on April 23, 1175. Abandoning his show of loyalty, Saladin had himself proclaimed King of Damascus and openly declared his hostility to Nur ed-Din's son. Aleppo's only hope of guaranteeing what remained of its independence now lay in the support of the Franks. Even if he remained nominal ruler, as-Salih was now doomed in practice to be no more than a vassal of Saladin, who was already the master of Moslem Syria in all but name.

The Franks, however, were more difficult to get the better of; but after King Amalric's death the kingdom of Jerusalem, like that of Damascus, was in a very precarious situation, with no stable government and a prey to intrigues and struggles for power.

On the King's death, power passed into the hands of the seneschal, Miles of Plancy, a French knight who had been a personal friend of Amalric's. All things considered, this man's ideas on the necessity for a strong government were quite reasonable, and he assumed as of right the powers of a dictator. But what the barons had unwillingly accepted from a lawfully crowned king they were not prepared to tolerate from one their own equal, and a foreigner to boot. The majority of the nobility and the Franco-Syrian population set up another candidate for the regency in opposition to the seneschal.

Miles of Plancy was very unpopular (William of Tyre draws a most sinister picture of him, and one in which loathing predominates over the wish to be fair), but he believed himself so formidable that, when warned of a plot being hatched against him, he answered, "Even if they [his enemies] found him asleep, they would not dare to wake him."[1] He was attacked in the street one night by a band of conspirators who killed him with their daggers.

One man who possessed an official claim to the regency was the Count of Tripoli, Raymond III. It would have been hard to dispute his rights: he was the late King's first cousin (through his mother,

Hodierna of Jerusalem) and the premier baron of the Latin kingdom (since Bohemond III, Prince of Antioch, had definitely become a vassal of Byzantium). The time was long past when royalty might permit itself to stand out against the great vassals as in the West, and the little kingdom, harried on all sides, reduced to half its former size, was struggling to gather what remained of its strength. Jerusalem feared to lose the support of the Count of Tripoli and its inhabitants were glad to be sure of the Count's support.

In 1174 Raymond III was thirty-four. Two years earlier he had emerged from the dungeon in Aleppo where he had been a prisoner for eight years. His captivity had left its mark on him; he was no longer the turbulent and quick-tempered young man who had rushed off to plunder Cyprus in order to avenge his sister. He was ambitious, but the little we know of his character does not make it seem likely that it was he personally who gave orders for Miles of Plancy's murder. He laid claim to the regency on his own account, letting it be known that he would regard a refusal as an act of hostility. The great barons had the greater interest in humoring him because he had recently married the widow of the lord of Tiberias and Galilee, and had consequently become the tenant of one of the greatest fiefs of the kingdom. After Miles of Plancy's death he became regent and promptly set in motion a policy of caution. He did not quarrel with the young King of Aleppo or with Saladin and was particularly anxious to avoid letting both Damascus and Aleppo fall into the hands of Saladin at the same time. "The enemy," wrote Saladin (and by this he meant the Count of Tripoli), "has placed the people of Aleppo under the protection of the Cross and has infected them with his hatred of Islam."[2]

Fearing, however (mistakenly, as it turned out), that the atabeg of Mosul would have designs on Aleppo, and by driving Saladin from Syria become too powerful in his turn, Raymond III made a truce with Saladin, even obtaining the restitution of all Frankish prisoners. This was in May 1175. Well aware that it would not be long before Saladin extended his power over the whole of Moslem Syria, and thinking that in any case it was better to live on good terms with him, Raymond III and the constable Humphrey of Toron continued cautious hostilities, punctuated by truces and courteous exchanges. They knew that their opponent was too powerful for them to contemplate his complete annihilation, and their one idea was to make him realize that they were still a considerable enough force for it to be in his interests not to drive them too far.

From 1175 onward, the regent and the barons of Jerusalem were able to count on an unexpected ally, and a more valuable one than might have at first been thought. At fourteen years the young King Baldwin emerged as an intrepid fighter, capable of leading his troops into battle and later on of commanding them personally in the field. He was seen at the side of the constable and the Count of Tripoli, riding at the head of his troops and taking part in raids and diversionary campaigns, attacking first Damascus and then Aleppo, plundering, taking prisoners, and even in 1176 routing the armies of Saladin's brother Shams ad-Daula.

At this time the King was still too young to actually command his army, and his principal function was as a symbol and an inspiration for his men. They were all happier marching under the command of their lawful King. Young though he was, he was like the flag, to be protected and followed through the thickest of the fight, and he was not afraid of personal danger. At that time he was still an excellent horseman, if we are to believe William of Tyre, who says that he rode "better than his forebears." But even so, going to war meant riding miles at a time, often in full armor, with hauberk and helmet, in the blistering heat, and then hurling oneself upon the enemy, shield on arm and lance in hand. Even a healthy child of fourteen or fifteen might have had some trouble in sustaining such an effort.

Baldwin's disease must have appeared very early, at an age when, according to the evidence of William of Tyre, he was still incapable of understanding that there could be anything abnormal in his insensitivity to pain (he felt nothing when his young playmates pinched or scratched him). When he came to the throne, he had therefore been a leper for ten years, and although the disease did not begin to make rapid strides until puberty, it must, even in early adolescence, have weakened and exhausted him. It is unlikely that anyone would have dared to reproach him had he wished to consider himself an invalid, yet he behaved as though he were perfectly well.

He had been educated, as became a prince, by knights and masters of arms and also by churchmen (one of whom was the historian William of Tyre), and these had not failed to teach him patience and prepare him for the harsh trial that was to be his life, and to arouse in him a sense of duty and pride in being, despite his infirmity, King of Jerusalem and Defender of the Holy Sepulcher. Whether as a result of education or temperament, Baldwin IV seems to have had little inclination to self-pity. The young King overcame his illness with all the determination of an adolescent who knows he is physically weak and is bent on proving to everyone, himself included, that he can equal and even surpass others. He may have been a king who had the misfortune to be a leper, but he was also a leper lucky enough to be a king.

He loved power because it was all life had to offer him, and he very early evinced a wish to govern by himself, and would not tolerate disobedience. A temperament of this kind can easily degenerate into tyranny and capriciousness in one so young, but Baldwin IV had a lively and precociously mature mind, and was sincerely concerned to do his best for the good of his kingdom; and this right up to the time when his sufferings began to drive him out of his mind.

This descendant of Baldwin II and Fulk of Anjou, of Gabriel of Melitene and Joscelin of Courtenay, was born for action, and however genuine his piety he was never, even at the end of his short life when his limbs were literally falling from his body, to find consolation in the mystic's exaltation or the peace of prayer. Up to the last moment he wanted to be a king and a general, and he wanted to be obeyed. It was his way of clinging to life, and he was a terrible fighter.

Brought up in a busy, frivolous, and somewhat dissolute court, where people thought at least as much about amorous adventures and political intrigue as they did about war, he was intelligent enough to know that his birth had placed him in the very center of this great game of hatreds, jealousies, ambitions, and calculations both interested and disinterested. He knew that his death had been reckoned on by everyone in advance and the succession coveted, that he himself would never have an heir, and that while he was alive all those around him would try to guide and dominate him, and this made the young King naturally suspicious, with little inclination toward friendship and relaxation, for who would want to be friends with a leper? After the death of his father, who adored him and whom he had certainly loved very much, he found himself surrounded by men whose loyalty must always, rightly or wrongly, be suspect. He seems to have trusted his constable, Humphrey of Toron, a man as brave as he was upright, but Humphrey was a soldier and meddled little in politics. Too young to govern himself and of an independent nature, Baldwin finally fell at least partially under the influence of a person so stubborn and egotistical, and so absolutely indifferent to the public good, that she unscrupulously abused the undoubted rights she had over him.

This was the King's mother, Agnes of Courtenay, the repudiated wife of Amalric, who had never been Queen and was therefore never known by the title of Queen Mother. She had been separated from her children while they were still young, had been married again to Hugh of Ibelin, and then, a widow, had been married for the fourth time, to Reynald of Sidon, whom she left not long afterward to live her own dissolute life. It is only fair to add that her youth had not been a happy one. While still very young she had watched the ruin of her father, Joscelin II of Edessa; she had seen her first husband killed,* her father a blinded captive, and her mother compelled to sell the remainder of the paternal domain. Then, as a princess she had been deprived and humiliated. At the death of Baldwin III she saw the barons arrogantly forbidding her accession to the throne, while her husband repudiated her and took away her children. Her brother had been taken prisoner the same year. As a result, Joscelin of Courtenay's granddaughter was an embittered, cynical woman with only one idea: to get as much out of life as she possibly could. Her life appears to have been already something of a scandal even at the time of Amalric's death, for though she was forty years old, she showed no signs of giving up her amorous adventures, and later she was still to be found shamelessly flaunting her amours.

But with Amalric gone, she also became someone of considerable importance in the kingdom. She was the King's mother and the mother of the heir presumptive, the Princess Sibylla, and now no one could stop her from seeing her children. There is no telling whether it was maternal affection or self-interest which led to her reunion with them, but it seems likely that the two children, who had hitherto been deprived of maternal affection, clung eagerly to the tenderness she offered them, and Agnes's hold over her son and daughter was very great.

Agnes of Courtenay had a rival at court: Amalric's widow, the Byzantine princess Maria Comnena. Maria took no part in the government and lived on her dowry at Nablus, but she had a daughter, Isabella, who was still very young. Maria could claim the inheritance of Baldwin IV for her daughter since Baldwin and Sibylla, being the children of a marriage which had been annulled by the Church, were in theory illegitimate. Baldwin might reign because he was a boy. Sibylla's claim was more doubtful, but on the other hand Sibylla had the advantage of being already of marriageable age and of being able to provide the kingdom with an heir. In addition to his problems of external politics, the young King had to cope with these domestic quarrels, clan rivalries, and court intrigues which all, directly or indirectly, had the same object: the seizure of power on the day when

---

* Baldwin, lord of Marash, was killed at Fons Murez in 1149, at the same time as Raymond of Poitiers.

he himself should no longer be there. Yet he was barely out of adolescence and seems to have had an insatiable lust for life.

In order to establish his sister's claim and regulate the whole matter of the succession once and for all, Baldwin IV decided to marry Sibylla off at the earliest possible moment. In 1176, he brought to Palestine a noble Italian baron, the son of William III, Marquis of Montferrat. This young man William, known as William Long-Sword, was related to both the King of France and the Emperor of Germany. He was handsome and brave, but unfortunately, says William of Tyre, he was also extremely irascible, and he seemed well able to defend the kingdom when the time came that Baldwin was no longer able to do so. William Long-Sword married the Princess Sibylla, but he died eight months after his wedding, in June 1177, of malaria. He left his young widow pregnant. The King and the barons of Jerusalem found themselves in worse difficulties than ever, for if the child turned out to be a boy (as in fact it did) he would be the heir to the kingdom, and Sibylla had become much less attractive to barons from Europe now that her future husband could not hope to be anything more than a temporary tenant of the land.

In the course of the same year, a very great lord of northern France, Philip, Count of Flanders* (the grandson on his mother's side of King Fulk and consequently Baldwin IV's first cousin), landed in the Holy Land with a substantial army of Crusaders. The King and his knights were happily convinced that the Count was motivated by a pious zeal for the Holy Sepulcher and by family feeling—the more so in that his mother, the Countess Sibylla, had become a nun in a convent near Jerusalem. They were quickly disabused. Philip of Flanders had come to marry off the two sons of one of his cousins, Robert of Bethune, to the two princesses of Jerusalem. One of these princesses was a widow of only three months standing and pregnant, and the other was no more than seven years old. Moreover, Philip refused to take on the responsibility for the defense of the kingdom, despite the entreaties of Baldwin IV who—such was his faith in the valor and prowess of those who came from Europe—was ready to nominate his cousin regent of the kingdom and put his armies, his treasure, and his lands at his disposal. The offer did not tempt the Count of Flanders in the least; what interested him was marrying off the two heirs of Bethune in order to obtain from their

* He was the son of the same Thierry of Alsace who had already undertaken two campaigns in the Holy Land and taken home the precious relic of the Holy Blood. Thierry's wife, Countess Sibylla, daughter of Fulk of Anjou by his first marriage, had remained in the Holy Land.

father the cession of the county of Bethune to his own advantage. Mortified to see their land of Jerusalem sunk so low that it had become a bargaining point for the King of France's vassals, Baldwin IV and his counselors rejected these offers.

They had nothing to hope for from Philip of Flanders. Even when they asked him to march against Saladin, he answered that he was not sufficiently familiar with the country; and when they suggested that he take command of the Frankish army for the Franco-Byzantine expedition against Egypt which had been arranged in the treaties made with Manuel Comnenus, he replied that he was afraid his soldiers would run short of provisions. The Byzantine fleets, which had been relying on the Flemish troops, went back to Constantinople. Finally Philip, in response to continued entreaties to mark his stay in the Holy Land by some valiant action, decided to go with Raymond III of Tripoli to lay siege to Hama. Having failed to take Hama, he then went with Bohemond III, Prince of Antioch, to lay siege to Harenc in northern Syria. His behavior here was such that Bohemond preferred to raise the siege, after extracting a financial tribute from the besieged, because far from fighting, the Crusaders from oversea thought of nothing but making pleasure trips to Antioch, where they haunted gaming houses and places of ill repute.

Meanwhile, while the Count of Flanders was wasting his time in northern Syria (whither he had taken some of the Hierosolymitan chivalry and the Knights Hospitaler), Saladin was attacking the kingdom in the south, near Ascalon.

He thought it would be so easy to get the better of a land without defenders that he allowed his army to disband and ravage the countryside. Baldwin IV, hastily gathering his remaining knights and taking the True Cross with him, first barricaded himself into Ascalon with all speed and from there harried the enemy. But the country already believed it was on the point of being invaded by the irresistible force of Saladin's troops, which had come in vast numbers—27,000, according to William of Tyre.

The King of Jerusalem had with him 375 knights, eighty of whom were Knights Templar led by their master, Odo of Saint-Amand. He was also accompanied by "Prince" Reynald of Châtillon* and the King's uncle Joscelin III of Courtenay, both of whom had recently emerged from Turkish prisons; as well as the Ibelin brothers, Reynald of Sidon, and Aubert, Bishop of Bethlehem, who carried the True

---

* Reynald had been liberated in 1175 and had married the chatelaine of Kerak of Moab, which again gave him a right to the title of Prince.

Cross. The foot soldiers hastily recruited even from among the ordinary citizens were more numerous than the knights, but numbered a few thousand at most.

The numerically inferior Frankish army took Saladin by surprise in the rear. "The army's equipment which was arriving at that moment blocked the way," says Abu Shama. "Suddenly the Frankish companies appeared. They rose up, agile as wolves and howling like dogs, and full of a fiery ardor they attacked in a mass. The Moslem troops were scattered through the neighboring villages, intent on pillage. Thus the fortune of battle turned against them."[3] The Moslems did not succeed in re-forming and they were systematically routed and hacked to pieces. Saladin himself only narrowly escaped thanks to the devotion of his personal bodyguard of mamelukes, who were killed around him almost to a man.

It was a terrible defeat for the great Moslem leader, as even the Arab chroniclers admit.[4] The remnants of Saladin's great army were compelled to flee across the desert to Egypt, dying of thirst, losing their horses and mules, and harried by the Franks in the rear. Even if the defeat was due principally to Saladin's own carelessness, for being too sure of himself that day, the King of Jerusalem's decisive spirit and the desperate valor of the Frankish troops succeeded in what appeared to be a miracle. A powerful Moslem army, led by Saladin in person, had fled before the Franks, who possessed only half their normal strength and were led only by a youthful leper and the True Cross.

Baldwin—and the Cross—returned to Jerusalem in triumph. The victory of Montgisard (November 25, 1177) was regarded by contemporaries as a miracle, and it saved Frankish Syria from the greatest danger it had been in to date. At that moment it seemed as though nothing was yet lost. The King made a truce with Saladin, and the Frankish lords set about strengthening their fortresses and building new ones, determined to carry on indefinitely fighting a defensive war which might enable the kingdom to continue its existence even with such a neighbor as Saladin. Saladin would not live forever, and what mattered was to keep Jerusalem for Christendom.

The leper King continued to organize warlike expeditions and to lead them in person. Two years after Montgisard he suffered a defeat in a forest near Banyas, and in the course of a ferocious battle the constable Humphrey of Toron was literally studded with arrows as he protected the King's person with his own body. The King barely escaped with his life and the constable died of his wounds. He had been the commander in chief of the royal armies under Baldwin III,

Amalric I, and Baldwin IV, and had been the greatest warrior of all three reigns. His death was an irreparable loss. Ibn al-Athir says of him: "It is impossible to convey an impression of Humphrey. His name became a synonym for bravery and good sense in battle."[5]

On June 10 of the same year Saladin again defeated the Franks on the plain of Marj Ayun, where his troops beat the entire Frankish army before the Count of Tripoli and the Templars could effect a junction with the King. The kingdom lost half its knights, dead or captive. One of the prisoners on that day was the Grand Master of the Temple, Odo of Saint-Amand, whom the chroniclers blame for the disaster. Two months later, Saladin took the castle of Jacob's Watchtower and destroyed it by undermining and fire, after slaughtering the greater part of the defenders.

At the same time Saladin was arming his fleet in Egypt to go and plunder the Frankish coasts, and reached Acre, where he took all the ships that were in the harbor.

Baldwin IV asked for a truce. Saladin, who was having some difficulty in keeping both Egypt and Syria under control, agreed to allow the Franks a breathing space. This was only a postponement. By now the King of Jerusalem was entering his twentieth year and was beginning to be really incapacitated by his disease. He was badly disfigured and had almost lost the use of his hands and feet, so that he could no longer hope to sit a horse and lead his armies into battle. It was the beginning of the end, for the kingdom as well as for the King.

Baldwin fought fiercely, no longer against Saladin, because he hoped to maintain the truce for as long as possible, but against those he suspected, rightly or wrongly, of seeking to remove him from power. One day the Count of Tripoli and the Prince of Antioch decided to go and perform their devotions in Jerusalem, and when the King heard of it he got the idea that they were coming with the object of dethroning him, and tried to prevent their entering the kingdom. Despite the arguments the two princes produced to reassure him, he was still suspicious of them and set about marrying off his sister Sibylla again as quickly as possible, not in order to have an heir (for the young princess had given birth to a son, christened Baldwin, in 1178) but so as to have a defender at his side.

He made a somewhat hasty choice, or rather allowed his mother and sister to choose for him. While suggestions were being put forward to marry the young widow to the Duke of Burgundy (who never came) and then to a great baron of the country, Baldwin of Ramleh, of the family of Ibelin, Sibylla herself fell in love with a young French knight whom her mother and her lover, Amalric of Lusignan, had brought from France with exactly this in mind.

Amalric of Lusignan belonged to one of the noblest families in France. The Lusignans were counts of La Marche and Poitou, and as a landless younger son, he had come to seek his fortune in the Holy Land. There he had made quite a good marriage with the daughter of Baldwin of Ibelin or Ramleh (the same who was a suitor for Sibylla's hand) and had then become the lover of the King's mother. An intelligent, ambitious, and somewhat unscrupulous young man, Amalric was too much a Frenchman to understand the real interests of the kingdom of Jerusalem, but he wanted power. He gained great influence over Agnes of Courtenay, who in turn had great influence over her daughter. The lovers resolved to marry Sibylla as they thought best, and Amalric summoned his younger brother Guy from France. Guy was a gallant knight, but still more famous for his good looks than for his courage. Urged by his mother and sister, and in any case in a hurry to provide the latter with a husband, the King finally agreed to this suitor. Guy of Lusignan married Sibylla and received the lands of Jaffa and Ascalon in fief and the title of Count.

It has often been said that Guy of Lusignan was a simpleton and Sibylla a fool for her determination to marry a handsome boy at all costs. But if this marriage was a blunder from a political point of view, the responsibility lies squarely with Baldwin IV, whose intentions, whatever else may be said of them, were by no means silly and were in any case quite explicable. He wanted to stay in power and he preferred to have as his brother-in-law a man like Guy who was noble enough to enjoy, if necessary, some support from Europe (the Lusignans were related to the King of England), poor enough not to be personally dangerous (Guy brought no contingents of Crusader knights to support his claim), and insignificant enough to be merely the docile instrument of the King's will. Naturally generous himself, one who "never forgot an injury and still less a kindness," Baldwin was not expecting ingratitude from the man whose fortune he had made. He persisted in his refusal to understand that in the eyes of healthy men a leper was no longer a man and that, king or no, men took no notice of his wishes.

Baldwin had more or less quarreled with the Count of Tripoli, who was the most powerful man in the kingdom, the former regent, and who, in the opinion of Moslem chroniclers, openly coveted the succession. He distrusted the Palestinian barons, who were very influential in Jerusalem and whom he suspected of espousing the cause of the Dowager Queen Maria Comnena and her daughter (Maria Comnena had married one of the leading local nobles, Balian of Ibelin). By marrying his sister to a penniless foreigner, Baldwin IV annoyed the entire nobility of the land, but at least he thought to find in Guy a faithful and loyal auxiliary. The young baron from Poitou was only too notoriously a handsome lad, but he lacked neither courage nor military experience.

The King's other sister, little Isabella, was also provided with a husband. Wishing to honor the family of the heroic constable who died to save his life, and judging the grandson by the grandfather, Baldwin married his sister to Humphrey IV of Toron, the son of Humphrey III of Toron and Stephanie of Milly, chatelaine of Kerak of Oultrejourdain. This marriage was a big mistake for a number of reasons. First, Humphrey IV was a child of fourteen, a gentle boy "more like a woman than a man";[6] and second, his mother and the mother of his bride-to-be loathed one another to such an extent that the marriage became a cause of fresh discords and new intrigues. Lastly, Stephanie of Milly was a widow who in 1175 had married for the third time,* the former Prince of Antioch, Reynald of Châtillon, and consequently this already sufficiently troublesome individual now became the father-in-law of one of the heirs to the throne and consequently a future candidate for power.

The court of Jerusalem, like the leper King himself, seemed to be decomposing and falling apart and would almost have been qualified for light opera had its position not been so perilous, the passions that raged there so fierce, and the reason for the disorder that reigned there so desperately sad. This reason was the slow and painful agony of a young man who was defying death and fighting hopelessly for his life, his rights, and his realm.

He did not have the sense to hand over his power in his own lifetime to the Count of Tripoli, who, whatever his faults, was still the only man capable of keeping at least comparative order. (Admittedly Raymond III had many enemies, but the King was able to impose his wishes when he wanted. Yet instead of making a bid for the Count's support he did everything he could to keep him out of power.) The influence of Agnes of Courtenay and her brother Joscelin III can be divined in this, but more important was the young King's own tenacious desire not to let go of his post. He had patiently endured Raymond's regency during the early years of his reign and had no wish to

---

* Stephanie of Milly's first husband had been Humphrey of Toron, and her second, Miles of Plancy, was murdered in 1174.

submit to his guardianship again although, as events will show, he
had a real esteem for the man.

Agnes of Courtenay and her brother made their wishes law at
court, thanks to the King's favor. Joscelin III, a prince deprived of
his inheritance of Edessa, was an intelligent and energetic man, but
terribly embittered by ten years of captivity and jealous of everything
and everyone. He hated the Hierosolymitan nobility, who would do
nothing for his father or himself (he had only been liberated through
his sister's influence), and he seems not to have cared about the
possible ruin of the kingdom. He held one of the highest positions at
court, having been appointed seneschal, and he used it to plunder
the treasury shamelessly with his sister's connivance. Joscelin desired
only one thing: to get his nephew to name him regent during the
minority of the future King, Sibylla's infant son Baldwin. Sibylla's new
husband, Guy of Lusignan, also coveted the regency, or more accurately it was coveted through Guy by Guy's brother, Amalric of
Lusignan, who had recently been appointed constable. In other respects the two men, Joscelin and Amalric, got along very well in their
common anxiety to put a stop to the claims of the Count of Tripoli.

The Patriarch of Jerusalem, Amalric of Nesle, died in 1180. The
Patriarch's personality had been a great influence, especially in time
of trouble or of serious danger from outside. The province of Antioch,
it has been seen, had several times been saved from disaster by
patriarchs strong enough to take over control in the absence of a
secular government. The candidate proposed by the clergy and nobility for the patriarchal seat of Jerusalem was an eminent and generally
respected man who had enjoyed the favor of Amalric I in the past
and was now maintained by the Count of Tripoli. He had formerly
been the tutor of the leper King and was a former royal ambassador
to Constantinople. This was the Archbishop of Tyre, a child of the
land, with an admirable knowledge of Syrian customs, able to speak
Greek, Hebrew, and Arabic and altogether a man who seemed made
for the office of patriarch. He was also the historian of the kingdom,
William of Tyre. He never had to undertake the grave responsibilities
in which he would most probably have acquitted himself honorably.
He was passed over in favor of the candidate proposed, or rather
imposed, by the King.

Heraclius was a poor cleric from Gevauden, of little education and
more than doubtful morals, but he was extraordinarily handsome and
not without a certain eloquence, and had been fortunate enough to
attract the interest of Agnes of Courtenay. He had enjoyed the
favor of the King's mother for a considerable time, and through her

support became Archdeacon of Jerusalem and later Archbishop of Caesarea. He must have had other qualities besides the knack of pleasing ladies: he was cunning and ambitious and he succeeded so well in manipulating his greatest asset, Agnes's favor, that the canons of the Holy Sepulcher adopted him as a candidate for the patriarchate. Finding himself opposed by such a rival, William of Tyre offered to resign his candidacy and begged the chapter to select some other prelate, or even to bring in one from abroad, rather than elect a man so notoriously unworthy. ("If you nominate him, know that the city will be lost and all the land with it!"[7]) But the canons would not listen to him, and Baldwin IV put in his word on behalf of his mother's lover, against the respectable prelate who had formerly been his tutor. It seems incredible that the young King should have made up his mind to such a serious action solely to gratify his mother. More probably the thing that damned William of Tyre in the King's eyes was his evident attachment to the Count of Tripoli's cause.

Heraclius was elected. He was an uncommon type for a patriarch, so openly debauched that he kept a concubine in his palace in Jerusalem, an Italian merchant's wife who used to walk the streets dressed in such fine clothes and surrounded by such a splendid suite that strangers took her for a countess and were told, "No, it's the Patriarchess." The Patriarch coveted money more than power, but he needed power to satisfy his luxurious tastes.

But if these were the seneschal, the constable, and the Patriarch of Jerusalem toward the end of Baldwin IV's reign, there was worse to come. The kingdom was constantly on the defensive and primarily dependent on its army, or rather on the most disciplined and experienced part of that army, the shock troops—that is to say, the two military orders of the Hospitalers and the Templars, who obeyed the central authority only when they felt like it, openly opposed the King's policy when they did not agree with it, and moreover, lived on extremely bad terms with each other.

There was worse yet: the man whom Baldwin III and Amalric I, not without some relief, had seen imprisoned in the castle of Aleppo had regained his freedom after sixteen years in captivity and was intent on making up for lost time. Reynald of Châtillon has been seen fighting at the King's side at Montgisard. He was still present at every battle, and Baldwin IV had thought of putting him at the head of the army to attack Egypt. In spite of his long period of enforced inactivity he was still a first-class fighter, and all the fiercer because he had his lost youth to avenge. He was no longer Prince of Antioch, because Constance had long been dead, but he was still known as Prince Reynald and this title and his reputation for bravery were useful in his marriage to the widow of Humphrey III of Toron and Miles of Plancy, the Stephanie of Milly who has already been mentioned as the chatelaine of Kerak of Oultrejourdain. Once again, Reynald found himself master of a great fief. His lands bordered Egypt and the trade routes for the great caravans to and from the Indies, they overlooked the Arabian desert and the Red Sea and the pilgrim road to Mecca, and it was Reynald of Châtillon's duty to see to the safety of this outpost of the kingdom.

In sixteen years the Frankish barons must have forgotten what kind of man Reynald was. They knew he was active, but he was much too much so. With the simplicity of all great dreamers, Reynald believed himself capable of seizing all that his eager imagination could conceive of as within his grasp. From his impregnable fortress on the edge of the desert he organized forays, or more accurately raids, on the caravan route, joining with the Bedouin tribes to plunder and pillage. In 1181, in time of peace and in contempt of the King's sworn truce, Reynald penetrated into Arabia with his troops, attacked the road to Medina, and when driven off by Turkish troops, consoled himself by taking a caravan on its way to Mecca from Damascus. He captured an enormous amount of booty. Saladin asked Baldwin to restore the stolen property, reproaching him for the violation of the truce, but Reynald answered the King's envoys that "he would not give up the caravan, whatever the King might do, and that it was useless to entreat him further for he would not do it."[8] Raging inwardly, Baldwin IV was compelled to admit to Saladin that he could not make his own vassal obey him.

He could do nothing against Reynald, but Reynald was not the only one to oppose the King's will. Baldwin had begun his reign too young and now that he had reached the age of manhood—he was twenty-one —he was already a helpless invalid. He was not easy to get on with, for his terrible sufferings, both physical and moral, made it hard for him to be patient with those around him. The mere sight of him struck men with terror, and his presence infected the air with the smell of decay. Nevertheless, he continued to attend all sessions of the council of barons: he could still make his voice heard, but he was doomed to see opinions contrary to his own carried almost invariably. It seemed that he was only King now to command his troops. Such as he was, his enemies feared him more than his own subjects.

The result of Reynald's rash provocation was that Saladin marched on Oultrejourdain with the intention of laying siege to Kerak of Moab and exacting justice on his own account. The council of barons decided to send the Frankish army to bar his way, and Baldwin himself led the army, carried in a litter. Meanwhile Saladin's nephew Faruk-Shah, governor of Damascus, was invading Galilee. When the news reached the royal army, it turned around and met the great Moslem army, led by Saladin, on the road to Lake Tiberias. Although numerically inferior, the Franks succeeded in repelling their adversaries. Saladin changed his tactics, marched for the coast, and embarked on a siege of the port of Beirut, with the intention of cutting off the kingdom of Jerusalem from the county of Tripoli. The Frankish army, which was still encamped near Sephoria, also marched on Beirut, and this time Saladin did not wait before raising the siege.

Until the end of the year 1182, the royal litter traveled the length and breadth of the country, surrounded by troops and accompanied everywhere by the True Cross. The Frankish army ravaged the province of Hauran, south of Damascus, besieging castles and threatening Damascus itself, in an attempt to protect the province of Aleppo, whose governors and people were still loyal to the Zengid dynasty, against Saladin.

Baldwin IV and Raymond of Tripoli asked nothing better than to lend their armies to help the atabeg of Aleppo, Imad ed-Din Zengi II, Nur ed-Din's nephew; but it was the prince himself who, to the indignation of his subjects, sold Aleppo to Saladin. This was a fresh disaster for the Franks. Now their continued existence depended on armistices granted by Saladin's favor. In the course of a year of almost uninterrupted campaigning, the leper King had exhausted what little strength remained to him. By then, according to William of Tyre, he could no longer use his hands or feet and had lost his eyesight, although in actual fact he was not yet totally blind.

His friends advised him to give up all his activities and retire to "live honorably" on his income in a palace on the coast. He refused. A terrible attack of fever which almost killed him forced him temporarily to resign his duties. He entrusted the regency of the kingdom to his brother-in-law, Guy of Lusignan, keeping only the city of Jerusalem in his own hands. He probably thought that Guy would show him respect and be ready to follow his advice.

He must soon have realized his mistake. Guy had no respect for his royal brother-in-law and little enough for the Franks of Syria in general. The young European aristocrat had not adapted himself to a half-Oriental and somewhat provincial court, given over to intrigue and absorbed in problems he was incapable of understanding. It has been said that his behavior was proud and arrogant, but it had no reason to be. He simply shared the native Frenchman's scorn for the "Syrian" nobility. He was, quite naturally, loathed by this nobility, who moreover also held him in contempt. On his side he had only the King's immediate followers, Agnes of Courtenay, who was still under the influence of Amalric of Lusignan, the Patriarch Heraclius, and Joscelin III of Courtenay. It will appear that Guy also enjoyed the support of two other great men of the kingdom, Reynald of Châtillon and the Grand Master of the Temple. Sibylla's husband was notoriously weak and inexperienced, and he was made use of as a tool to block the Count of Tripoli's path.

Baldwin IV had made a bad marriage for his sister (although admittedly Sibylla at least was perfectly content with her husband), and he had chosen his regent badly. He had long been made to believe that the Count of Tripoli was seeking to seize the kingdom, and distrust of the Count was the real motive behind most of his actions.

In October 1183, the year in which for the first time the King failed to march at the head of his troops, the Frankish army was surrounded and very nearly wiped out by Saladin's troops. It was only saved by the calm good sense of its leaders, who managed to avoid a battle in spite of every provocation. All the great barons were there: the Count of Tripoli, and Reynald of Châtillon, Guy of Lusignan and his brother Amalric the constable, Joscelin III of Courtenay, and the lords of Ibelin. Completely bottled up near the foothills of Mount Tabor, tormented by hunger, crammed into a narrow space and constantly on the defensive, the Frankish army held out for several days against the attacks of their adversaries and the temptation to engage in an unequal combat. In the end it was Saladin who, not daring to attack the compact mass of the Frankish cavalry, struck camp.

Once the danger was past, a rumor went around among the ranks of the humbler soldiers accusing the barons of cowardice, and some Italian Crusaders, newcomers to the land, believed there was a plot afoot against Guy of Lusignan and that his compeers wished to deprive him of a victory. The local people, on the other hand, blamed Guy's incompetence. Guy of Lusignan himself, enjoying the sympathy of the Western pilgrims, behaved as though he were already master of the land. He was becoming increasingly unpopular.

Whether angered by his brother-in-law's behavior or merely tormented by his disease and anxious for a change, Baldwin asked Guy to hand over to him the city of Tyre, where the climate was better than it was in Jerusalem. He offered Jerusalem in exchange, but

Guy was suspicious, aware that the King was more popular in the capital than he was himself. He refused. Baldwin realized that he was being regarded as already dead and buried, and reacted fiercely by depriving Guy of his title of regent and heir to the crown. Instead he had the throne officially assigned to his nephew, Sibylla's five-year-old son, who was proclaimed King on November 20, 1183, under the name of Baldwin V. After the leper King's death the regency was to go to the Count of Tripoli, the man Baldwin had hitherto regarded as his rival. Now, knowing that he had not long to live, the King was beginning to resign himself to the passing away of his powers. He would have accepted a loyal and submissive brother-in-law; he would not accept the arrogant upstart which Guy had become.

Reynald of Châtillon, meanwhile, had organized a massive offensive against Arabia and had armed a fleet which early in 1183 sailed down the Red Sea coast from the Gulf of Akaba, pillaging and spreading terror among the coastal cities. To crown all, the lord of Kerak of Moab was planning to make himself master of all the pilgrim roads to Mecca and to capture and plunder Mecca itself, and far from concealing the fact, he took care to publish it widely.

Not even the boldest Frankish king had ever dared to cherish such plans, and now, at a time when the kingdom's very existence was hanging by a thread, a mere vassal of the King, whose strength lay only in his boldness and a few hundred soldiers, was literally lighting the fuse that would send a shock of terror and anger throughout Islam. "People believed," writes al-Fadil, "that the hour of Judgment had come, that the preliminary signs were appearing and the earth would return to oblivion."[9] Nothing better could have been found to cement complete Moslem unity and create a climate of holy war to the death. If Reynald had been Saladin's paid agent, he could not have thought of anything more effective.

Saladin's reaction was one of amazement and indignation such as he had never felt before: from a cool politician he was transformed once and for all into a paladin of the holy war. Saladin's brother Malik al-Adil, the governor of Egypt, sent his fleet to destroy Reynald's ships in the Red Sea. Eight months later Saladin himself went in person to lay siege to Kerak of Moab, the powerful fortress from which Reynald of Châtillon was threatening the desert roads.

He laid formal siege to the castle in November 1183. Reynald and his wife, Stephanie of Milly, were at that moment celebrating the marriage of Stephanie's son Humphrey to the Princess Isabella of Jerusalem. There was a great banquet in the castle and the most noble knights and ladies of the kingdom were assembled there. While the feasting, music, singing, and dancing were proceeding in the keep, there was fierce fighting on the battlements. Saladin had brought up his siege engines and was bombarding the towers with his missiles. In vain did the lady of Kerak send Saladin roast beef and mutton so that he and his army might also partake of the wedding feast. Saladin ordered his men not to fire on the tower where the young couple were lodged, but he continued merrily bombarding the other towers. The defenders could not hope to hold out for long on account of the great numbers of people in the castle, but the siege was raised. The royal army was approaching under the command of the Count of Tripoli and accompanied by the King himself. Saladin did not wait for it, and on December 4 he destroyed his siege engines and withdrew.

The leper King, blind now and completely bedridden, was carried into the relieved castle on his litter with the curtains drawn. Once again, and for the last time, Baldwin IV had put Saladin to flight.

He died a little over a year later. To the end he behaved in such a way that no one could consider him yet gone from the world of the living. On the contrary, it seemed as though his physical decay had even increased his need for activity.

Now, determined not to allow his brother-in-law any share in the power, he gave free rein to his anger against Guy of Lusignan. He even talked of having his sister's marriage annulled. Guy, already deprived of his *"baylie"* (regency) and seeing the leper King resume control of the whole kingdom, proceeded to open rebellion, barricaded himself into Ascalon with his wife, and refused to allow Baldwin to enter. Baldwin promptly confiscated all his lands at Jaffa. Guy, furiously angry, took a mean revenge: in defiance of the truce and the King's word, he charged out and massacred the Bedouin who were pasturing their flocks near Ascalon. When Baldwin heard of this his anger was terrible. He immediately convened a council of barons, and had Guy definitely set aside and Raymond of Tripoli elected to the *"baylie"* of the kingdom. Then he made the barons swear fealty to his nephew, little Baldwin, and had him solemnly crowned in the Church of the Holy Sepulcher.

Baldwin IV died in March 1185, after a reign lasting eleven years, when he was not quite twenty-five. The Arab historian al-Imad wrote of him: "This leper child made his authority respected."[10] For once a spark of sympathy for a Frank can be seen from the pen of a Moslem. In the face of such a terrible destiny, religious and national prejudice was mute, and there is nothing to say of this life but that it was exemplary. Baldwin IV was not, as he has been called, a saint. He was a passionate, dictatorial, sensitive, and intelligent young man, frightfully mortified in the flesh, but who in the last extremities of physical decay could still be "in great torment" wondering how he could help those who were besieged in Kerak of Moab. This mutilated creature who, without hands or feet or face, could still summon his barons and dictate his will to them, is one of the greatest examples of moral fiber in all of history.

The Kingdom Divided

Once again, as it had in 1143 after the death of King Fulk and in 1174 after the death of Amalric I, Jerusalem became a city whose king was a child. Baldwin V was seven. The chroniclers do not have a great deal to say about this prince who was the son of Sibylla of Jerusalem and William of Montferrat (William Long-Sword). This was in fact more than simply a period of royal minority, because the fatherless child, neglected by his mother, who preferred the children of her second husband (two daughters), seems to have been, like Baldwin IV, an invalid whose early death was expected. The Count of Tripoli, to whose guardianship the leper King had meant to entrust the care of the little sovereign, had refused the honor, saying that if the child were to die he, the Count, would be accused of having poisoned him. An argument of this kind would not have been recognized as valid had the prince's health not given grounds for fearing the worst.

The man in power, by Baldwin's wishes and those of the majority of the barons, was the Count of Tripoli, who had been named regent of the kingdom. However, the leper King's last wishes had offended what were to all appearances perfectly legitimate susceptibilities. The child had been taken away from his mother and her husband, and Sibylla herself had been practically disinherited by her brother. Under the will of Baldwin IV, if the child were to die, the Count of Tripoli was to remain regent until 1195, after which the Pope, the Emperor of Germany, and the Kings of France and England were to decide between them the rights of the King's two sisters, Sibylla and Isabella. This was to place the kingdom squarely under the protection of the international powers of Western Christendom, which Baldwin, not unreasonably, regarded as morally responsible for the defense of the Holy Sepulcher. In actuality, the real heir to the throne was the Count of Tripoli. This testament does honor to the leper King's political good sense, but under the existing conditions it was not easy to put into practice because the Count had too many enemies in Jerusalem.

While the child King lived, Raymond III did actually govern, since no one could dispute the formal will of the late King. All Frankish Syria, the natives as well as the Latin colonists, regarded the Count of Tripoli as a lawful master, the strong man on whom to rely. The Frankish chroniclers, who have many tales to tell of intrigues at the court of Jerusalem and of the clashes between the various parties, have somewhat neglected this highly important fact, although it is recorded by Moslem historians. Ibn Jubayr, an Arab of Spanish origin who made a journey to the East in 1181, is an excellent witness because he wrote without bias, as a disinterested observer of the complications of local politics. According to him it is the Count (*al-Coummes*) who is the real lord of the country and "worthy of the throne for which he seems to have been born." It is the Count to whom "all revenues are paid" and who has "power over all." This was the impression of a foreign traveler, curious about the situation of the country and admitted into the indigenous society of Frankish Syria.

Raymond III of Tripoli, as we have seen, had spent a long time as a prisoner of the Turks. William of Tyre observes that he made use of his captivity to educate himself, for he was fond of reading and talking of the Holy Scriptures "when he found someone able to converse with him." The Archbishop of Tyre was, in fact, an obvious person for him to talk to. William does not conceal his sympathies for the Count, and whatever the verdict on Raymond's actions, the esteem of such a man as the historian of the kingdom is a valuable testimony of character. During his captivity, Raymond had learned other things besides the Holy Scriptures. He loved and understood the Moslem world, and perhaps even admired it. Moreover, he had developed a conviction that the Frankish kingdom could only endure at the price of close collaboration with the Moslems and even with the acceptance of Moslem suzerainty. He envisaged a policy of caution, but what was caution to him easily took on the appearance of treason to the Frankish cause. The Moslems as yet might give him only moderate praise for recognizing the Sultan (Saladin) "as his lord and liberator," but his Frankish enemies could not fail to be indignant at such an attitude.

Raymond III had barely become regent before he hastened to conclude a four-year truce with Saladin. The excuse for this truce was an exceptional drouth which had endangered the harvests in 1185.

Thanks to the truce, Frankish Syria was able to obtain supplies from her Moslem neighbors, and the Count, according to William of Tyre and Ernoul, was "loved and honored by the people of the land." Saladin, on his side, was having serious difficulty in maintaining his power, which was now being disputed by members of his own family who, once he had installed them as provincial governors, were attempting to free themselves from his authority. The truth, as later events were to show, was that the Count of Tripoli's goodwill toward Saladin was by no means returned. Saladin had not given up hope of conquering Frankish Syria. He was merely playing for time, but Raymond III hoped to disarm him by a policy of friendship, and in any case there is no reason to doubt the sincerity of his admiration for Saladin.

Little Baldwin V died in September 1186, after a reign of only one year, at Acre in the palace of his great-uncle on his mother's side, Joscelin III of Courtenay. This was a serious blow for Raymond III. The question of the succession to the throne arose once more, and now that the legitimate, crowned heir of the leper King was dead it was all too easy to present the late Baldwin IV as a tyrannical prince, semi-irresponsible and too enfeebled by illness to be capable of deciding the fate of the kingdom. According to dynastic law, the heir was Sibylla. Although the majority of the barons, the people, and the citizens of the larger towns asked nothing better than for Raymond III—who at least seemed to promise peace—to continue as regent, the population of Jerusalem and the surrounding countryside stood firm for Sibylla, the daughter of Amalric I and the direct descendant of the kings of Jerusalem, whereas Raymond was only a distant cousin.

Sibylla herself was a person of small importance, utterly devoted to a husband as insignificant as herself. Guy was a weak man, easily influenced and eager to reign out of sheer vainglory rather than ambition. He had energetic and even devoted supporters. Reynald of Châtillon was one of the first, because the lord of Kerak, conscious that the Count of Tripoli was a man capable of standing up to him, thought that he would easily get the better of Guy of Lusignan. Others were Agnes of Courtenay and her brother; the constable Amalric of Lusignan, naturally enough; the Patriarch Heraclius; and finally, Gerard of Ridfort, Grand Master of the Temple. It is worth saying a few words about this individual. Gerard of Ridfort was a Flemish knight who had once been a friend of the Count of Tripoli but had conceived a violent hatred against him because the Count had given the hand of the heiress of Botrun to another man after he had promised it to Gerard. For a sum of ten thousand bezants, Raymond had given preference to a wealthy Italian merchant. In his disappointment Gerard of Ridfort had become a Templar and was not long afterward elected Grand Master. What is known of the man makes his election seem somewhat surprising. The mastership of the Temple was one of the most important positions in the kingdom, and the order enjoyed the highest repute even in Europe. Gerard was simply an adventurer, and furthermore he was mean, incompetent, and arrogant.

Sibylla therefore made her solemn entry into Jerusalem and was led to the basilica of the Holy Sepulcher to be crowned amid the acclamations of the crowd, while Raymond III was kept away from the city on a false pretext. The coronation could be said to have been carried out somewhat highhandedly, as a surprise maneuver, in spite of the vehement protestations of the Grand Master of the Hospitalers and some of the clergy and knights. The part played by the Patriarch on this occasion was decisive. Heraclius forced his wishes on the local clergy and crowned Sibylla. Only when he had solemnly consecrated the Queen did he invite her to "bestow the crown on a man able to govern [her] kingdom." She bade her husband come forward and placed the crown on his head. (According to William of Tyre's continuator, the Grand Master of the Temple was heard to murmur at that moment, "This crown is a fair return for the inheritance of Botrun." Raymond III had in fact lost the crown, but Gerard of Ridfort's hatred was not appeased for all that.)

The coronation of Sibylla and Guy caused consternation among the barons of Jerusalem and the whole kingdom, who were assembled in parliament at Nablus preparing for the solemn session at which they intended to proclaim the Count of Tripoli King. Seeing that he was powerless to fight against a legitimate heiress who was moreover already crowned, Raymond III had the idea of setting up Sibylla's younger sister Isabella, daughter of the Queen Dowager Maria Comnena and wife of Humphrey IV of Toron, in opposition. Humphrey belonged to the ancient nobility of the land, and his candidature might attract Reynald of Châtillon (who was married to Humphrey's mother) to the barons' party.

The parliament rallied to this suggestion, but it was Humphrey himself who, when he heard of the plan, hastened to warn Sibylla. He had no desire to be made King. The conversation between Humphrey and Sibylla is recorded by Ernoul: "My lady, I couldn't help it, for they have held me and would make me King by force, and today they would have crowned me. And I fled because they wanted to make me King by force." Sibylla answered, "My brother Humphrey, you were quite right. Those who wished to make you King have put a great shame upon you. But since you have acted properly, I forgive you."[11] It was useless to rely on Humphrey any further, or to dispute Sibylla's rights.

Presented with a *fait accompli,* the barons had no alternative but to swear fealty to Guy of Lusignan, though they did so with a very bad grace. One of the most powerful, Baldwin of Ramleh, head of the family of Ibelin (the same who had long coveted Sibylla's hand), preferred to leave the country rather than swear an oath of homage to the new King. Raymond III retired to his county of Tripoli, officially breaking all connection with the court of Jerusalem.*

In future he meant to steer his own course without worrying himself about the fate of the kingdom. He was so confident of Saladin's friendship that at the "parliament" he had promised the barons the aid of the Saracen against Guy of Lusignan, and the suggestion had not been considered at all improper. Now that he no longer had to govern the kingdom but only the county of Tripoli, with the fief of Tiberias and Galilee, Raymond openly went over to Saladin's party.

Historians of Frankish Syria who favor the Count have little to say of this aspect of his policies. The Norman Ambroise, a supporter of Guy of Lusignan, accuses the Count of treachery in so many words. Moslem historians are scarcely less explicit. They paint Raymond III's conduct in the blackest colors, almost taking the part of the other Franks against him. Ibn al-Athir declares that the Count had appealed to Saladin in order to gain his help in obtaining the throne of Jerusalem, and he adds, "Then there was discord among the Christians. This was one of the principal causes leading to the conquest of the country." (Ibn al-Athir may not have known that the "discord" among the Franks dated from long before.) Al-Imad states, "The Count's zeal for the Moslems merely increased. He swore only by the power and fortune of the Sultan, and even performed base acts to the detriment of his religion. . . . The Count had loyal servants who helped him in his undertakings just or unjust, and they led to serious embarrassment for the Franks."[12]

Raymond III certainly had no intention of "betraying" anyone. His previous conduct is sufficient indication of this. He was a man of political ideas and clung to his belief in peace with Islam. Angered by

* Guy of Lusignan and Sibylla asked him to account for the money he had spent during his regency and the Count, outraged at the rudeness of the request, used it as an excuse to break with the new King.

his failure in Jerusalem, he continued to practice his policy, but in conditions which did in fact make it treason, because the kingdom of Jerusalem was not to remain at peace with Saladin for long, and once war was declared the Count, as Saladin's ally, became the enemy of his countrymen.

When Baldwin of Ramleh heard of the coronation of Guy of Lusignan, he exclaimed, "He won't be King for a year!" Guy, though a gallant soldier, was no firebrand. He knew, as everyone else knew, that his kingdom only existed by reason of the truce which Raymond III had negotiated in 1185, and he undoubtedly hoped for a renewal of this truce. Saladin was known to be a man of his word and never broke an agreement he had made.

Reynald of Châtillon was living on his lands across the Jordan as an independent lord and sole master of his wife's lands after God. Devoted to pillage as others were to the profession of arms, he had made sure of the complicity of the nomadic Bedouin who held the merchant caravans to ransom. At the end of the year 1186 he and his knights, with the Bedouin, fell upon a large caravan traveling from Cairo to Damascus.* Reynald took an enormous amount of booty and threw the travelers into prison. Saladin sent to ask the King of Jerusalem for the return of the caravan. Guy, as Baldwin IV had done before him, vainly entreated Reynald to do so. Reynald retorted that he "was master on his land like the King on his." "The capture of this caravan was the cause of the fall of the kingdom of Jerusalem."[13]

The truce was broken. This time Saladin had made up his mind to finish with the Franks. He mobilized all the armies of Damascus, Aleppo, Egypt, and the whole of northern Syria. According to al-Imad, his army swarmed over valleys and hills and stretched for several leagues in all directions, and "the day on which it was reviewed made men think of the Last Judgment." It was known that the Franks were redoubtable warriors and their castles strong, and that it would not be easy to reduce them. The holy war which had been preached so many times before, and each time with a greater degree of exaltation, was now like a mass rising of the faithful against the cohorts of the devil.

The fervor of the army, sustained by the preaching of ulemas and dervishes, was at its height. Saladin, determined not to tolerate the slightest weakness or slackening of morale, meant to bring all his

---

* Ernoul claims that Saladin's sister was with the caravan.

armies together and triumph over the Franks once and for all by crushing numerical superiority.

Meanwhile, the King of Jerusalem was contemplating a war against the Count of Tripoli to punish him for his refusal to join him. His barons managed to prevent him, but in fact Raymond III, bound by his truce with Saladin, was playing the Sultan's game. He even went so far as to allow an armed body of Moslems to cross his lands, when he cannot have been unaware that their object in wishing to cross Galilee was to attack the kingdom.

This armed body was supposed to make a reconnaissance trip and then turn back toward the Jordan, and Raymond III made it known that the Moslems were there with his consent and that they were not to be attacked. As was to be expected, such extraordinary tolerance was not approved of by the Knights Templar who were in the neighborhood. The Grand Master of the Temple hastily assembled all the brothers he could find, as well as a few knights who did not belong to the order (the Grand Master of the Hospitalers among them) and set out to meet the Moslem army. They were a hundred and fifty against several thousand.

Brave as they were, even the Templars hesitated for a moment. Gerard of Ridfort ordered them to attack, and he is reported to have said to his marshal, James of Mailly, "Do you then love your blond head so much, that you are so anxious to keep it?" James answered him, "I shall die like a knight, and you will be the one to flee."[14] They attacked, says Ibn al-Athir, "with such ferocity that the blackest head would have turned white with terror."[15] It was a spectacular suicide: all but three were killed. One of the three who fled was Gerard of Ridfort.

When he heard of the disaster, Raymond III forgot all his grudges against the King. There could no longer be any question of peace or friendship with Saladin when Turkish and Kurdish warriors were riding across his lands carrying the heads of Templars on the ends of their spears. He let it be known at the court of Jerusalem that he wished for a reconciliation with the King.

Guy, who was in desperate straits, had no intention of reproaching the Count for his equivocal behavior and, when he saw Raymond coming to meet him, was the first to dismount. When the Count saw this, he too dismounted and knelt before the King. The reconciliation was apparently complete, but it came too late. The vast enemy army was already in control of the land.

Hattin

The Franks knew as well as the Moslems that this was the decisive trial of strength. They had never before seen an army to compare with the one Saladin was assembling on the far side of the Jordan. They knew, too, that if they ever succeeded in withstanding this army they would not see another like it for a very long time. But to drive back such a tide of men they needed an army that was not ludicrously inferior to Saladin's.

This meant gathering all the Frankish forces. The troops of Jerusalem and all the great fiefs of the kingdom were summoned together, leaving only the minimum of defenders for each castle. The Count of Tripoli brought all the troops at his disposal. All the knights of the military orders joined the royal army, except for the small garrisons left to guard their castles. The Temple had recently been bled white, having lost almost a third of its knights in Galilee. Gerard of Ridfort enrolled mercenary troops and equipped them hastily. Guy of Lusignan and Raymond III sent an appeal to the Prince of Antioch, Bohemond III, who for twenty years had lived in comparative peace under the protection of Byzantium, making truces with the Turks and taking no part in Frankish affairs. Bohemond did not come himself, but he sent his eldest son Raymond with fifty knights.

At that moment the kingdom also had a number of passing guests, pilgrims and sailors, who were invited to join the army. The *Historia Regni Hierosolymitani* estimates the Frankish forces assembled that summer at a thousand knights, twenty-five thousand foot, and four thousand turcopoles (mercenaries of Moslem origin), together with twelve hundred knights and seven thousand foot equipped by the Templars and paid for by the treasure entrusted to the Temple by Henry II of England, who had given a substantial gift to the order in expiation for the murder of Thomas Becket. If these figures are accurate, the army comprised three or four thousand cavalry, including the knights (if one includes the turcopoles, some of whom were mounted, and the mounted squires who attended the knights). There were also between thirty and thirty-five thousand foot, whose military effectiveness varied considerably, since besides the professional soldiers this included a number of sailors who were good soldiers but more accustomed to sea battles, and pilgrims or local volunteers with more enthusiasm than experience.

It was an impressive army, one of the greatest the Franks had ever assembled in the East. Not since the time of the First Crusade had there been such unity in the armies of Frankish Syria, or such determination to fight back. The reconciliation between the King and the Count meant a rebirth of hope in Jerusalem and throughout the country, because it was to Raymond III that the Franks of Syria looked for their salvation. Raymond had placed himself at the service of a king whom he had hitherto refused to recognize, but he was neither able nor willing to claim the supreme command for himself. Had he tried, he would have met with too much opposition. This would not have been from Guy himself, for he was terrified by the weight of responsibility placed on his shoulders, and might well have agreed to put an older, more popular, and more experienced man than himself at the head of the armies. But neither Reynald of Châtillon nor Gerard of Ridfort, whom a king with more authority would have compelled to total obedience by reminding them of their previous disastrous rashness, had any idea except to get their own way. Even at that moment, with an armed enemy on the point of invading the country, these two—and Gerard in particular—were thinking first and foremost of the harm they could do to the Count of Tripoli.

Consequently this powerful army, with its elite cavalry and strong infantry and, as the Moslem chroniclers testify, its high morale, was to all intents without a head. The king who was officially in command had no authority; he was a foreigner and neither liked nor respected. His only asset was the crown he wore. It was better than nothing, but it was not much.

The great Frankish army gathered near Sephoria toward the end of June 1187. Saladin, on his side, was rallying his forces on the frontier of Galilee, and not wishing to waste his strength in forays and skirmishes, he waited patiently until the Franks had finished assembling in one place. However formidable their army, he had numerical strength on his side, as well as his gifts as a general, the blessing of Allah, and the prayers of all Islam. He knew that the cities and strongholds had been milked dry of defenders and that if he succeeded in annihilating the army he would be master of the whole of Syria in a few days.

Saladin wanted a battle, but he also feared one, for the experience of eighty years of Franco-Moslem wars had shown that numerical superiority was sometimes a feeble weapon against the Franks. Though chroniclers are vague on this point, his cavalry was almost certainly at least twice as strong as the Franks', but once again it was light cavalry against heavier armed troops. The morale of his troops was very high, but the Franks had brought the True Cross with them, and knowing that they were staking the survival of their kingdom on this battle, they seemed determined to fight to the last ounce of their strength.

On July 2 Saladin, having finished his preparations, moved his forces across the Jordan at a point just south of Lake Tiberias, and advancing along the shore, laid siege to the city of Tiberias. The city, with its back to the lake and surrounded on every side by a huge army, could not hope to hold out for long. "The Sultan's army surrounded Lake Tiberias like the ocean, and great plains vanished beneath their spreading tents."[16]

The principality of Galilee and Tiberias belonged to Raymond III's wife, the Princess Eschiva, Countess of Tripoli. Saladin's first act of aggression was directed against the Count of Tripoli because the Sultan meant to punish him for breaking his treaty of alliance. It must be said that Saladin, in common with the majority of the Moslems, still regarded Raymond III as the real leader of the Franks, but if he thought that by laying siege to a city in which his wife was shut up he would force Raymond to take the initiative and attack, he knew little of the Count's character. Although al-Imad implies the reverse, it was not Raymond who was responsible for the march on Tiberias.

At that time the Frankish army was encamped near Acre. It remained in readiness, awaiting fresh reinforcements or the choice of a favorable field of battle; but it was not wise to leave the soldiers for long in a state of enforced inactivity. Learning that Saladin was outside Tiberias, the hotheads in the army—Reynald of Châtillon and Gerard of Ridfort—advised the King to set out to relieve the city. The Count of Tripoli was against the idea, judging the operation too risky, but he was promptly accused of treachery by his opponents, and forced to acquiesce. The army therefore marched on Tiberias and halted near Sephoria, less than twenty miles from the besieged city, in a good defensive position, amply supplied with water and with a wealth of springs. There, despite the alarming news sent by the Countess Eschiva, who when the city fell had taken refuge in the citadel with her women and a handful of soldiers, Raymond III set his face firmly against marching on Tiberias. "A cry went up among the knights of the army: 'Let us go and rescue the ladies of Tiberias!' "[17]

The Count pleaded urgently with the King: it was *his* land and *his* wife and his wife's children (whom he loved, says William of Tyre, as though they were his own), and no one in the army stood to lose more by the fall of Tiberias than he himself. This they could believe. "I would rather Tiberias were taken and destroyed, and that my wife and my men and all my goods were lost, than see the whole land lost. For if you go to the aid of the city, I know that you will be captured or killed, you and all the army, I will tell you why. There is no water between here and Tiberias except one small spring, the spring of Cresson, and that is nothing to a whole army. . . . And if you are forced to make camp there, what will your men and your horses do with nothing to drink? If they remain without water they will die of thirst. And the next day the Saracens will take you all." This is probably an exact report of his speech, because Ibn al-Athir also credits Raymond with the same words. "As for my wife and children," said the Count, "I will ransom them afterward, and as for the castle, we can recapture that later. . . . If you go there, all is lost!"[18]

Shaken, Guy of Lusignan took the Count's side. Then, when he was left alone with Gerard of Ridfort, he allowed himself to be persuaded that Raymond was betraying him, that he had gone over to Saladin and sought to dishonor him, Guy, before all of Christendom. Once again the weak King allowed himself to be persuaded, and in the middle of the night he sounded the alert and ordered the army to march on Tiberias.

"At the news that the Franks were on the move," says Abu Shama, "the Sultan felt a deep satisfaction. 'That is just what we want!' he exclaimed. . . . His sole design in laying siege to Tiberias was to lead the Franks to abandon their positions at Saffuriya [Sephoria]. The Moslems had set up camp near the water [Lake Tiberias] and the summer was very hot."[19]

Once the campaign was under way Raymond III, who had so clearly seen through the adversary's tactics, was one of the architects of disaster. A rapid charge would still have given the army a chance to break the Moslem ranks and hack their way through to the lake, but instead, on the Count of Tripoli's suggestion, the army camped for the night on the hill of Hattin.

This was a bare rocky hill, without water, and the early July heat was stifling. During the night, the Frankish army on its hill was surrounded by Moslem troops. It had fallen into the trap. Taking advantage of the wind which was blowing into the enemy camp, Saladin set fire to the dry grass of the plain. Half-dead with thirst, exhausted by the heat in their metal armor, the Franks found themselves enveloped in smoke and flames. Half the infantry surrendered in the first few hours of the battle, and the rest gradually followed, most of the men being in no condition to fight. The cavalry stood firm, hoping

somehow or other to cut its way through to the water. The lake was
about five miles from the site of the battle.

The cavalry charged with such ferocity that for a moment Saladin
thought he was beaten. His son, Malik al-Afdal, said that he had
seen his father at that moment "a prey to despair. He changed color
and clutched his beard as he advanced, crying, 'Let the devil be con-
victed of lying!' " Guy of Lusignan did not disgrace his rank: he
fought with exemplary bravery and was among the last to surrender.

Raymond of Tripoli and the Syrian barons who fought at his side,
the Prince of Antioch's son Raymond, Balian of Ibelin, Reynald of
Sidon, and their knights attempted a desperate charge in the direction
of Sephoria, and succeeded in breaking through the enemy ranks and
escaping. Their conduct was judged in various ways. Ibn al-Athir
presents it as an act of bravery: "The charge of the Franks was a
charge of desperate men and . . . there was no way to stand against
them." They were allowed to pass simply because all resistance
seemed vain. Al-Imad describes the Count's action as desertion in
the midst of the battle, a desertion which led to the moral collapse
of the rest of the Frankish army. William of Tyre's continuator is
somewhat evasive; Ambroise speaks in no uncertain terms of treason. The fact remains that in this way some of the army and a few
of the chief leaders escaped death or captivity.

They were the only ones. According to eyewitnesses the carnage
was terrible. But there were more prisoners and wounded than dead.
The knights sold their lives dearly, fighting until the last of their
strength was exhausted. They were well protected by their armor.
Among the prisoners were all the leaders, many knights of high or
moderately high rank, and at least three hundred Templars and
Hospitalers (some of them ordinary sergeants). In this, as in all
medieval battles, the infantry paid infinitely more heavily than the
cavalry. The number of Moslem dead was also great, and the hill of
Hattin and its surroundings on the eve of that day resembled a
gigantic charnel house of men and horses.

The True Cross, which had been carried not by the Patriarch
Heraclius, a man of small courage, but by the Bishop of Acre, was
captured before the end of the battle. Al-Imad attributes the final
despair of the Franks to the capture of the Cross. "When they knew
that the Cross had been taken from them, none desired to escape
from peril."[20] For a Moslem observer to have noticed this, the effect
on the Christian soldiers must have shown itself in a very obvious
and spectacular way. Suddenly in the midst of this hell of thirst and
blood and defeat the Crusading spirit reasserted itself: the defeated

army became once more the soldiers of the True Cross, a True Cross profaned, outraged, and lost.

All was lost. The King's army was no more and the defenseless cities lay at Saladin's mercy. On that one day, July 4, 1187, the power of the Franks in Syria was shattered once and for all, and the kingdom of Jerusalem to all intents ceased to exist.

Hattin was Saladin's greatest victory. It was a victory due chiefly to Saladin himself and the courage of his soldiers, but also to a great extent to the rashness of the Frankish leaders, a rashness which had been foreseen and condemned in advance by the Count of Tripoli. But the great victors of the day were heat and thirst, because once again, despite their numerical inferiority, the Franks were essentially the stronger side. Even in the state of intolerable physical suffering in which they found themselves, there was a moment when they almost drove Saladin back.

What this battle meant to the Moslems will appear later. It was their own private Crusade, and the accounts of Moslem historians testify to the state of mind in which they embarked on it. Filled with joy and giving thanks to God, Saladin immediately had tents set up on the field of battle, installed his lieutenants, and summoned forth the most noble captives. It was a very fine haul, including the King of Jerusalem; his two brothers, Amalric the constable and Geoffrey; Reynald of Châtillon, lord of Kerak of Moab; Gerard of Ridfort, Grand Master of the Temple; Humphrey of Toron, husband of the Princess Isabella of Jerusalem, and the old Marquis William of Montferrat, grandfather of the late child King. There were still a few great names missing, most illustrious among them that of the Count of Tripoli. Al-Imad, in his account of the battle, is unduly severe on the Count. In fact, far from betraying the Frankish army, Raymond III had saved as much of it as could be saved, and it is just this which the Arab historian cannot forgive him: he had made Saladin's victory incomplete.

A few months before the great campaign in Galilee, Saladin, when suffering from a serious illness, had made a solemn vow to sacrifice to God with his own hand the Count of Tripoli and Reynald of Châtillon. Raymond of Tripoli, busy making alliances with Saladin, had been unaware of this detail. Reynald, however, had good reason to fear Saladin's anger, but he also had some excuse for thinking that his head was valuable enough to be spared.

On the evening of that great day, after setting up his tents on the field of battle, saying his prayers, and offering thanks to God, Saladin summoned his principal captives to his presence. He is said to have

received only Guy, the King, and Reynald of Châtillon in his own
tent. The wretched Poitevin gentleman who, when he came to the
Holy Land to marry the heiress to the kingdom, had certainly never
suspected that he would one day become the man to lose the True
Cross for Christendom, appears to have been completely broken
by shame as well as by physical suffering. According to Moslem
chroniclers he was reduced to complete speechlessness and on the
point of fainting. Reynald, a much older man, approaching sixty,
had not fought as energetically and was by nature impervious to
moral suffering. All accounts describe him facing Saladin with a
sullen arrogance. He listened while the Sultan enumerated his crimes
and reproached him for violating his sworn oath, and then asked the
interpreter to translate his reply: "But this in truth is the custom of
kings and I have only followed the beaten path."[21] Of all the answers attributed to Reynald on this occasion, this is the one which
rings truest. It is the kind of thing no reporter would have invented,
whatever his feelings toward Reynald. But when he propounded his
brief and not unreasonable political philosophy to Saladin, Reynald
of Châtillon was forgetting one thing: that he had never mastered
the art and manner of practicing the "custom of kings," and that a
bandit chief is not the same thing as a head of state.

"The King was suffering from thirst and dizzy from the intoxication of terror. The Sultan spoke to him gently, calming the fears
to which he was a prey and soothing the terror which was making his heart pound. Then he had iced water brought to him. When
the King had drunk and quenched his thirst, he offered his cup to
Prince Arnaud [Arnât = Reynald], who drained it and slaked his
thirst."[22] According to Beha ed-Din, "Saladin, seeing this, said to
the interpreter, 'Inform the King that it is he who has given this man
to drink, and that I give him neither food nor drink.' It is indeed one
of the noble customs of the Arabs that if a captive has eaten or
drunk at the table of the person who has taken him prisoner, he shall
have his life spared."[23] Even so, it is worth noting that Saladin had
not the heart to snatch the cup from the hand of an old man who was
dying of thirst.

Reynald drank for the last time in his life, and afterward Saladin
executed him. He struck the prisoner on the shoulder with his sword,
almost shearing off his right arm from his body. His lieutenants finished the job and then dragged the body from the tent, before the
horrified eyes of Guy of Lusignan. Judging the King already sufficiently punished by terror, Saladin spoke to him kindly, saying, "One
king does not kill another."[24]

Those noble prisoners who were able to pay a ransom or were useful as hostages were taken to Damascus in chains. The others—and there were thousands of them—were herded together in one place, like cattle. (Al-Imad quotes the number of thirty thousand prisoners, but this figure must be cut by at least half.) The hosts of Frankish captives must have been an impressive sight. "Those who saw the dead said, 'There can be no prisoners!' Those who saw the prisoners said, 'There can be no dead!' "[25] A single strategic error and a waterless piece of ground had destroyed the entire forces of Frankish Syria at one blow. Nearly every man who was able to fight had been recruited for the battle. In the city of Jerusalem only two knights remained.

The Moslem Holy War

On the day after his victory (July 5), Saladin took the citadel of Tiberias. He showed the greatest courtesy to the Countess Eschiva, granting her a safe-conduct to go to Tripoli with her ladies and her household and take with her all her household goods. Then he assembled all the Templars and Hospitalers who could be found among the prisoners. Many of them had already become the prize of Moslem warriors and Saladin purchased these from their captors, offering fifty gold pieces per head. More than two hundred were brought to him, in addition to those falling to the Sultan's share of the booty, making nearly three hundred men in all. Some others had already been taken to Damascus at the same time as the most important prisoners. All the brothers of the two orders, knights and sergeants, were executed, the majority of them on the spot outside Tiberias and the rest in Damascus. Only one was spared: Gerard of Ridfort.

After performing what he regarded as an act of justice pleasing to God, Saladin had only to continue his victorious progress. Nothing remained of Frankish Syria but cities empty of soldiers, and terrified people. Before the year's end he had captured more than fifty major strongholds, cities or castles, including Jerusalem.

The Frankish army had marched to Hattin, in the words of al-Imad, like "a mountain on the move, a sea of tumbling, foaming waves." It was a magnificent and terrifying army, with its ironclad cavalry bearing a thousand brightly colored banners, surrounding the cortege of the Bishop of Acre, who brandished the True Cross high over his horse's head. The True Cross under its canopy, its banner raised on high in the midst of the monks and priests who formed its escort, was in some sense the heart and head of that army, as the Ark of the Covenant was to the Hebrews. It was the most precious treasure in Christendom, the living sign of the presence of Jesus Christ. For eighty-six years, ever since the day Baldwin I had had it carried before his troops as he hastened to repulse the army of the Egyptian Vizier at Ramleh, the True Cross had been at all the kingdom's great battles, a sign of great peril and a pledge of victory. Although not all the battles in which it played a part had a happy outcome, it had been nonetheless, for the soldiers and their leaders, the Holy of Holies to be defended to the bitter end, giving victory or comfort in defeat.

Those who carried it to Hattin knew that this was the battle at which the fate of the kingdom would be decided, and they prayed for victory as their ancestors had done. But this was not an army going to fight for the Cross: its leaders were divided among themselves and motivated by personal grudges and ambitions which made them forget the greatness of what was at stake. The soldiers were not going out to conquest and martyrdom for God; they were going to defend their land against an enemy who they knew already was stronger than they.

On the other side was an army making ready to invade a land which certainly did not belong to it, but to which it believed it had an inalienable right, an army of God's soldiers, moved by a wild desire to triumph over the infidel or to welcome martyrdom, sure in the triumph of the true religion. This holy war, which the Moslem princes had practiced as a matter of policy for so long and which fanatics had demanded without result, the war which Nur ed-Din had prepared for, preached, and dreamed about for thirty years with all the ardor of his insatiable piety, had come at last. It had matured and been tempered by contact with the Franks, whose own warlike piety seems to have penetrated Islam in some underground way. The holy war had changed sides. In the Christian chronicles it was no longer a matter of miracles, illumination, and the joy of martyrdom, but only of that soldierly piety which was found also in the West. True, the enemy was the infidel, but this was only a minor detail—he was simply the Enemy. Reynald of Châtillon (to whom, according to Beha ed-Din, Saladin offered the chance to embrace Islam) was never regarded as a martyr to the faith.

It is the Moslem chroniclers whose tone gradually changes from war in general to the idea of a holy war. Not that the theme of the *jihad* was unknown to those who later wrote down the history of the first decades of the twelfth century, but they make it clear that the powerful and aggressive Franks of that period aroused no real anger or religious hatred. In the time of Nur ed-Din and still more in that of Saladin, Moslem warriors could no longer be killed without becoming martyrs; their soldiers were no longer merely Moslems, or the army of this or that prince; they were soldiers of Islam, the soldiers of God. "God sent down victory from heaven to those who are faithful to his law here below. He granted this favor to those who did their duty in the *jihad*."[26]

One description of Moslem warriors on the occasion of an unsuccessful attempt to surround the Frankish army in 1186 runs: "Here were warriors who, saber in hand, were surrounding the enemy in the hope of being themselves surrounded with golden vessels:* here were brave men marching to their deaths like bridegrooms in a wedding procession."[27] The Franks were no longer hated for their cruelty and injustice. (And if the truth be told, with the exception of Reynald of Châtillon, and even he was associated with the Bedouin who were "oathless men, hateful to our religion," the Franks displayed neither cruelty nor injustice.) They were hated for their false doctrine. They were the "worshippers of Satan; blasphemers against nature human and divine." Saladin's private secretary, al-Imad, an educated man whose letters, even when they are guilty of an excess of zeal, probably convey the real feeling of the army, gives us a vivid picture of the struggle between heaven and hell.

"The night came, and placed a barrier between the two armies [this is the night preceding the battle of Hattin], but our cavalry occupied both roads. On the one side were the steps to hell, and on the other, the ladder to heaven. *Malek* [the angel of death] was waiting, and *Ridwan* [the guardian angel of paradise] was joyful. It was the night of *Kadr,*† a night valued above a thousand months, on which the angels and Gabriel come down to earth, a night whose dawn announced the victory which the morning was to bring true. Great was our happiness during that glorious night, for we were those of whom God has said, 'God shall bring them a reward in this world, and a greater in the next.' (Koran, III, 141) On this night heaven appeared to us with the holy law to accomplish; the cupbearers of the celestial spring were ready, the eternal gardens promised us their fruits, the spring of life was opening before us."[28] It is a fact that they

* A quotation from a verse in the Koran: "On all sides they shall be offered golden vessels and cups filled with all that their tastes could desire."

† The night of predestination and ineffable mystery, celebrated on the twenty-seventh of Ramadan.

had water in plenty, while the encircled Franks had drunk nothing since the previous day.

Dawn came. "The Dog Star shed its beams on the men clad in iron [the Franks] and the rage did not go down in their hearts. The burning sky sharpened their fury; the cavalry charged in wave after wave among the floating mists of the mirage and the torments of thirst with fire in the wind and anxiety in their hearts. These dogs hung out their parched tongues and howled under the blows. They hoped to reach the water, but before them was hell with its flames and intolerable heat overcame them."[29]

Al-Imad describes the Sultan, "full of trust in God's help, going up and down the ranks of his soldiers, arousing their ardor, promising that heaven would aid them as always, and hurling them a hundred against a thousand." This was hardly necessary, seeing that his army was the more numerous. "One of the sultan's mamelukes, a man named Mangouras, rushed forward the foremost . . . he found himself alone in the midst of the Franks, and in the bottom of this abyss of death he stood firm and fought until he was overwhelmed by their numbers. The Franks took his head, believing that they had the head of one of the Sultan's sons: he was a martyr rising to the home of the merciful."[30] The wind was blowing toward the Franks and "one of our pious volunteers set fire to the grass, so that it caught fire and enveloped them. In this way the worshippers of the Trinity endured, in this life, the torments of a triple fire: the fire of the burning field, the fire of thirst, and the fire of the biting arrows."

Al-Imad had every incentive to describe the Franks as terrible fighters whose defeat was only due to the manifest protection of God, but we know that in fact the Frankish cavalry very nearly succeeded in breaking through the adversary's ranks and making a passage through to the lake. There is one melancholy fact about the story of this battle, the battle which decided the fate of the Latin kingdom. This is that tens of thousands of men were fighting *for water,* "tormented by the thought of the lake." Facing them was an enemy with no lack of water. The knights, studded with arrows until they looked "like hedgehogs," were invulnerable while they remained on horseback, not because their armor could not be penetrated by a sword or spear but because their swords and spears made a clear space around them and no one dared attack them except with arrows. Toward the end of the day, Guy of Lusignan and his chief barons, having lost their horses, retreated on foot with their banners to the summit of the hill and there hastily dug trenches. Saladin's son wrote: "I cried again, 'We have put them to flight!' But my father said to me, 'Be quiet, we have not beaten them until that banner [the King's] has fallen.' Even while he was speaking to me, the banner fell."[31]

There were no more men left to fight and "the lions had turned into timid sheep." Our reporter reviewed the battlefield: "I went over the battlefield and I found it full of information. I saw what the elect had done with the reprobates. I saw heads flung far from motionless bodies, eyes plucked from their sockets, corpses trampled in the dust, their beauty vanished under the talons of birds of prey." There follows a detailed description of the human wreckage, a description of macabre and fantastic lyricism. "And what a warning for those who think on it! At the sight of these faces pressed against the earth, no longer animated by any desires, I recited this passage from the book of God: 'Then shall the infidel say: would to God that I were dust!' (Koran, LXXVIII, 41) But what a sweet scent of victory was exhaled by this charnel heap! What flames of vengeance flickered over these corpses! How men's hearts rejoiced at this hideous spectacle!"[32]

The prisoners were another source of joy. There were vast crowds of them, men so exhausted that they were no longer capable of any reaction, bound thirty or forty together with one rope and led by a single horseman: a hundred or two hundred men assembled in one place with a single guard to watch over them. "There they were, the insolent ones, humiliated, the rebels, naked men who possessed thrones led into captivity." Obviously the men who were tied thirty and forty to a rope were only poor folk who had nothing to lose but their freedom, but in the intoxication of victory the Moslems saw every prisoner as Reynald of Châtillon. "How many arrogant masters caught as though in a hunt, kings brought low and free men reduced to slavery, imposters delivered up to the true believers!"[33]

There were many dead in the battle, but there is no knowing how many died fighting and how many were slaughtered when they were already in no condition to fight. The evidence shows that the infantry did not hold out for long. Presumably the four thousand turcopoles were all killed, for Saladin gave no quarter to renegades to Islam. There was not a systematic massacre: Saladin's armies were much less ferocious than the bands of Turkomans. Even so, it was in blood that Saladin signed the triumph of the true faith.

The murder of Reynald of Châtillon was Saladin's own personal vendetta, the fulfillment of his vow (he himself wrote to the Caliph of Baghdad, on the subject of the lord of Kerak: ". . . and it was your servant who slew him with his own hand to accomplish his vow"), and al-Imad's anger—a reflection of the Sultan's own—against

Raymond III is understandable enough, for by his flight he prevented the Sultan from keeping the promise he had made to God. The chronicler consoles himself by observing that the Count of Tripoli, tortured by "fearful dreams," did not long survive the battle. Reynald's death seemed an extraordinary triumph in itself, as though the man's very existence was an outrage against Islam—he who had talked of coming with his band to plunder Mecca and had told the travelers he captured, "Let your Mohammed get you out of prison." (That such a commonplace insult on the part of an old soldier should have seemed so shocking infers that the Franks of Syria must have become remarkably tolerant and polite.)

Saladin's exploit was sung by poets:

Oh, noble and pure sword which slashed the head of the prince, and pierced infidelity in its most infamous place!

When that head fell it was bathed in its own blood like a frog diving into a marsh.

Troubled by his perfidy, he lunged like a wild beast, but death is the only answer to the attacks of a traitor.[34]

So, glorified above his deserts until he became almost an incarnation of the devil, the poor knight who had once been loved by Constance of Antioch to the misfortune of Frankish Syria made his solemn entry into the pantheon of hell, from which it occurred to no Latin historian to rescue him. But to mark "the triumph of truth over lies," there had to be other victims.

It has already been said that on the day after the capture of Tiberias, Saladin ordered all the Templars and Hospitalers to be killed. This was a political gesture. The Sultan knew that even as prisoners the brothers of the two orders were still to be feared because they were more talented escapers than their fellow countrymen. "I wish," said Saladin, "to purify the land of these two monstrous orders, whose practices are of no use, who will never renounce their hostility and will render no service as slaves. Both are all that is worst in the infidel race." (Later he is known to have insisted on calling on the brothers of the Temple to ratify an agreement with the Crusaders because he knew that the Templars were incapable of violating an oath. On the day after Hattin he proved his esteem to them, in his own way.) As we have seen, his warriors were not particularly anxious to cut off their prisoners' heads and only gave them up in return for the promise of a handsome recompense. But it does seem as though the army's state of exaltation demanded a hecatomb especially dedicated to God, and other victims besides those who chanced to fall in battle.

"Now," writes al-Imad, "there were in the gathering a number of volunteers, people of pious and austere habits, holy men, Sufis, men of law, savants, and initiates in asceticism and mystical intuition. Each of them drew his sword, rolled up his sleeve, and begged for the favor of executing one prisoner. The Sultan was seated, and his smiling face contrasted with the surly bearing of the miscreants. The troops were drawn up in their ranks and the emirs in two lines."[35] There were about three hundred of the condemned, and the allusion to their "surly" bearing shows that the brothers of the two orders bore themselves with some dignity. It would have been asking a good deal to expect them also to have smiling faces. The holy men, initiates of asceticism and mystical intuition, came forward to show their skill. "The swords of some cut and slashed miraculously, and these were congratulated. The swords of others remained refractory and blunt, and they were excused. Others were ridiculous and had to be replaced." "Ridiculous" probably means that they hesitated, or were terrified at the sight of so much blood and so many severed heads.

Saladin, at any rate, enjoyed the spectacle. Al-Imad goes on: "And for myself, I contemplated this great smiling warrior, and I marveled that here was the master of words and deeds, who had fulfilled so many promises, had won such glory. What a host of rewards was reserved for this shedding of blood, how much merit he acquired by causing these heads to fall!"[36] These lines, written by an eyewitness, cast some doubt on Saladin's humanity, yet he could be humane to the poor and to women and children. But his piety and the piety of his companions was of a kind which could also delight in watching the slaughter of unarmed men, a slaughter carried out in cold blood, if the bloodthirsty exaltation of these "holy men" can be called cold blood. Whatever the atrocities committed by the Crusaders, whatever their ardor to "avenge the injuries to Jesus Christ in the blood of the infidel," they can never be accused of such a frightful compound of piety and cruelty. It is true that here the victims were soldiers already resolved to face martyrdom, but the executioners were neither soldiers nor ignorant and fanatical brutes, nor were they outlaws disguised as pilgrims.

One single Templar, as we have seen, escaped the massacre. The Grand Master had been sent to Damascus with the other important captives. Strange rumors were later to circulate on his account. On the occasion of the great trial of the Templars in 1307, the brothers explained the abjuration of Christ and the practice of spitting on the cross, which were part of the initiation ceremony of the order, by the fact that a "bad master" who was taken prisoner by the Sultan had once saved his life by promising to introduce this practice into the ritual of the order, and the man referred to is clearly Gerard of Ridfort. Even if he did make this strange promise to Saladin, the Master of the Temple would not have failed to get the Pope to relieve him from the necessity of keeping it. In fact, Saladin spared Gerard for political reasons which are very easily understood. There were still some Templars left in the land, and castles held by brothers of the order. Two months after Hattin, Gerard of Ridfort purchased his freedom by delivering up these castles to Saladin. Bound by their oaths of unconditional obedience to the orders of their master, the brothers obeyed in this too. Saladin's perfectly natural clemency nevertheless seemed surprising because of the religious hatred the Sultan professed with regard to the two orders. In fact, this was the last time he ever spared one of the brothers who had been taken prisoner.

Joy reigned in Damascus. The army brought back rich spoils and thousands of slaves and sold them in the marketplaces to the cry: "The price of prisoners has fallen to three dinars in Damascus!" "Every day," writes Mohammed ibn al-Kadersi, "Christian heads were seen arriving, as numerous as watermelons. The spoils of oxen, sheep, and goats and mules were so great that no one wanted any more."[37] An "image of the Crucified" made its entry into the city, fastened to the stem of the cross and carried upside down by the cadi Ibn-Arroun.

Al-Imad again: "A splendid and beneficent year, a blessed age, looked to by previous ages as they passed as a glad fulfillment. Then was the holy place purified and all the shrines hailed the sanctity of it. Then divine grace delivered the Holy Land from so many tribulations. God destroyed the evil work of polytheism and decreed that infidelity should be drowned in waves of blood. The Nacerite dynasty triumphed over the ruins of the Nazarene sect, monotheism avenged itself on the doctrine of the Trinity, and the glory of the reign of Salah ed-Din spread throughout the world."[38]

The Dissolution of the Kingdom

The war was not over. It was indeed very far from over, because in his wish to drive a small colony of Christians from oversea out of Syria, Saladin did not foresee that ten times more Franks than all those he had fought in the previous fifteen years would come against him. Frankish Syria still existed, even if the kingdom of Jerusalem did not.

The Moslem army marched toward the coast, taking one city after another. Acre, governed by Joscelin III of Courtenay (one of those who had escaped from the battle of Hattin), surrendered without a fight, because immediately after the great defeat no one had any thought of resistance. But Saladin could not be everywhere at once or take every city in two weeks. The Franks were endeavoring to re-form and rearm. Ascalon, emptied of soldiers, held out for several days defended by a citizen army, despite the pleas of Guy of Lusignan, who was led on foot beneath the walls and entreated the defenders to surrender the city to purchase his freedom. "The people of Ascalon," says Ibn al-Athir, "answered him in the most disobliging manner, and said many things to him that were painful to hear."[39] Ascalon only surrendered after a fierce resistance and with full honors of war, on September 5.

Saladin was now master of the entire coast (Acre, Jaffa, Beirut, and Ascalon) and of Galilee and Samaria, and the only one of the great coastal cities still in Frankish hands was the formidable stronghold of Tyre, so effectively isolated on its narrow-necked peninsula that even in the absence of a strong garrison it was not an easy place to which to lay siege.

After consolidating his position on the coast and in the interior of the country, Saladin finally marched on Jerusalem—al-Quds the Holy —the holy city whose capture was to set the seal on his fame in the eyes of Islam.

Jerusalem, as we have seen, had been left without defenders, but it had a very large Frankish population which had been still further increased since the defeat by the influx of refugees fleeing before Saladin. While the Sultan was conquering the remainder of the country, the capital, terror-stricken but determined to resist, was organizing its defense. The soul of this resistance was Balian of Ibelin, who by good luck had escaped from the disaster of Hattin with Raymond III of Tripoli and had then obtained from Saladin a safe-conduct to Jerusalem in order to fetch his family. Once inside the city, he was kept there "by force" (as he was later to explain to Saladin) by the Patriarch Heraclius.

Circumstances compelled the incompetent prelate to evince some signs of energy. Balian of Ibelin was one of the premier barons of the kingdom and the husband of the Dowager Queen. He was spontaneously accepted as their leader by the entire population. Queen Sibylla was now regarded as having forfeited her rights and kept out of public affairs—so great was the anger of the Hierosolymitans against the man who had lost the battle and allowed the True Cross to be captured.

Balian and the Patriarch took over the charge of putting the city in a state of defense, melting down the ornaments of the Holy Sepulcher to make money, enrolling in their impromptu militia all men of an age to bear arms, granting a knighthood to every young noble of fifteen and over and to the sons of important citizens. With the money obtained from the Holy Sepulcher they recruited mercenaries. When, on September 20, two and a half months after Hattin, Saladin appeared outside the Holy City, he found it equipped for resistance and prepared to stand a siege.

Knowing the city's complete lack of soldiers, he had obviously not expected this. He had already, three weeks earlier, offered the citizens of Jerusalem an honorable surrender with respect for persons and property. The offer had been rejected. Confident of his victory, the Sultan had written to Queen Sibylla inviting her to join her husband, who was a prisoner at Nablus, since he wished, he said, to spare her the perils of a siege. (Sibylla, having no further reason for remaining in Jerusalem, took advantage of the offer.) Saladin also allowed Queen Maria Comnena to leave the city, with the children of the Ibelin family, whom he received in his tents with every mark of kindness, even giving the young boys "jewels and costly garments." In fact, after his triumph he was anxious to appear as a magnanimous victor. He treated the conquered people with greatest gentleness, especially the indigenous population, to whom he wished to convey the impression that he was liberating them from the tyranny of the Franks.

In the Holy City itself, one section of the population was praying for the Sultan's victory: these were the Christians of the Greek rite who had always found the domination of their Latin coreligionists hard to endure. Consequently, while the Franks were defending themselves against the Moslems they also went in fear of a rising of the Greeks inside the city. Nevertheless, the siege was sustained with great vigor and the attackers encountered stubborn resistance. Al-Imad, who describes the siege, says of the Franks: "They fought like demons, prowled like wolves, and acted like evil spirits. When their warriors drew their swords it was like the tumult of a raging sea. The priests urged them on, their leaders inflamed their spirits, their hearts rose to the fight. . . . They set up an engine on every turret, dug deep trenches, and raised solid pillars on all sides. . . . They put up a host of obstacles and blocked all the broad streets to make them impassable. Each one undertook a task that would formerly have been beyond his strength."[40]

The people of Jerusalem knew very well that there was no longer an army and that no help could reach them. The few men available had flung themselves into Jerusalem: some, like Balian of Ibelin, who had escaped from Hattin, others the defenders of castles which had been reduced by Saladin, among them a certain number of Templars and Hospitalers, but they were still only a handful of men. Balian of Ibelin said later that there was "one man for every fifty women and children" inside the city. (He must have meant the Latin colonists, since the Greeks took no part in the defense.) Al-Imad, in a curious passage of which more will be said later, attempts to explain the reasons for this heroic resistance which was doomed to failure in advance. The Moslems were beginning to realize that this city was a holy city for the Christians also, and that there might be good reason for their desire to keep it at all costs.

"Islam," writes the Arab chronicler, "went in search of its bride, offering her thousands of lives as a dowry, bringing her happiness in place of wretchedness." But Jerusalem was not the "bride" of Islam, nor even the first among the Moslem holy cities, and Saladin, addressing his troops before the attack, preached a long sermon explaining the reasons why al-Quds should be specially venerated. "The home of the prophets, the station of the saints, the oratory of the pious . . . it is here that the human race shall be gathered and reborn. . . . This is the rock whose surface has remained smooth and without stain, the road of the ascension [of the Prophet], the sublime dome which forms a crown above the rock; there the lightning shone and Borak took his flight [*Borak*—lightning—was the name of the celestial mare which carried Mohammed through the air]."[41]

In enumerating the virtues of the Holy City, its countless shrines, the verses of the Koran it had inspired, and so forth, Saladin was probably telling the faithful nothing they did not already know, and very little perhaps to the bulk of the soldiery, for the most part extremely pious, but in the end he himself admitted that this was only the third among the holy cities of Islam. No Christian preacher had any need to remind even the most ignorant believers, in the West as well as the East, of the reasons why Jerusalem should be venerated, just as no Moslem would have taken the trouble to make a speech explaining why Mecca should be defended. The mere idea that Reynald of Châtillon's bands were planning to attack the road to their Holy City sent a shiver of horror throughout Islam and made people think that the Last Judgment was upon them.

Looking at things, therefore, from the point of view of the holy war, the Christians had by far the strongest right to Jerusalem, and furthermore theirs was the more ancient. "How great and noble it [the Mosque of al-Aqsa] is, how glorious and splendid, sublime and venerated! Fortunate are its blessings, blessed its prophecies! What a combination of beauties, what graceful perfection, how brilliantly decked and with what dazzling ornament. And by thus enumerating the virtues and privileges of the mosque, the Sultan affirmed the imminent return of these pacts and benefits."⁴² Saladin's soldiers were well assured that in conquering Jerusalem they were fighting for their faith, but they were not inspired by the mystical madness of the "poor" of the First Crusade and did not feel the fierce despair of the besieged in 1187. However great their zeal for religion, their reasons for fighting were in fact less powerful.

The Franks of Jerusalem, on the other hand, were fighting to save their honor, and al-Imad is quite wrong in supposing that there were sixty thousand Frankish *warriors* inside the city. There were not even six thousand, but "they faced the arrows and stood firm in the face of death, saying: one of us will fight against ten, and ten of our men will resist two hundred."⁴³ In the end, seeing that Saladin's engines were about to batter down the walls and that the fall of the city was inevitable, the defenders decided on a mass sortie, by night, in order to try and take the enemy by surprise. It was the Patriarch who opposed this plan, which was in fact a sufficiently desperate one considering the number of the besiegers, saying that they had no right to leave the women and children to Saladin's mercy. It would be better to negotiate a surrender.

Balian of Ibelin, with several other knights, went to Saladin's camp. The Sultan demanded an unconditional surrender. "I mean," he said, "to treat Jerusalem as the Christians dealt with it when they took it from the Moslems ninety-one years ago. They drowned it in blood without leaving it a moment's respite. I shall slaughter the men, and the women I shall take into slavery." At this Balian of Ibelin threatened to destroy the city: "When we see that death is inevitable we shall kill our sons and our wives, we shall burn our wealth and our goods, and we shall not leave you so much as one dinar or one dirhem to plunder, nor one man or woman to carry into captivity. When we have finished this work of destruction we shall tear down the Qubbat al-Sakhra and the Masjid al-Aqsa, and the other holy places of Islam. After that we shall slaughter the five thousand Moslem prisoners we have, and we shall slaughter all our cattle and pack animals to the last one, and then we shall all come out to meet you. And thus not one of our people shall die who has not already slain several of yours. We shall conquer or we shall die covered in glory."[44] (Al-Imad attributes to Balian a similar, rather longer version of the same speech.) Saladin was not anxious to lose the moral effect of his victory, or its more material advantages, by leaving the Holy City a heap of ruins. He negotiated.

It was agreed that the population of Jerusalem should have their lives spared and be permitted to ransom themselves at a price of ten dinars for a man, five for a woman, and one for a child. Those able to pay would be allowed to leave, taking their belongings with them, but the price was very high. "For one man able to pay," said Balian, "there would be a hundred who would not have so much as two dinars. . . . For the whole city is full of peasants, and humble people and children, and women whose husbands and fathers you have killed."[45] Saladin agreed to accept a lump sum of 100,000 dinars as the ransom for twenty thousand of the people unable to pay.

The surrender of the city was agreed to on these conditions: the Sultan pledged himself to keep order and not allow the bulk of his troops to occupy the city until the fate of the population had been decided. Balian and Heraclius took charge of the collection of the ransom money. Once the excitement of the siege was over and it had become apparent that Jerusalem was really lost, no one seems to have thought of anything but themselves. Balian of Ibelin had great difficulty in collecting that promised third of the ransom for the poor (he had not dared promise all of it). The Patriarch took great care not to sacrifice his personal fortune nor to give away the church treasures he had appropriated. The Templars and Hospitalers, more generous of their blood than their deniers, refused to delve into the coffers of their orders, and the Master of the Hospital was only made to pay up by the threat of a popular rising. "The Templars and Hospitalers," says William of Tyre's continuator, "gave, but they did not give as much as they should have."

Saladin had installed himself in the Tower of David, where Balian of Ibelin and Heraclius took him the thirty thousand dinars which was the agreed ransom for seven thousand people. There were still sixteen thousand of the poor unransomed. Saladin magnanimously yielded to the prayers of the Patriarch and granted their liberty to another five hundred, while his brother, Malik al-Adil, not to be outdone in generosity, liberated a further thousand of the poor, after having them allotted to him as his share of the spoils. The rest were taken into slavery.

According to al-Imad the population of Jerusalem at that time

(including refugees and peasants from the surrounding countryside
who had taken refuge inside the walls at the approach of the enemy
army) had swollen to more than 100,000 people. Those who were
completely unable to pay were laborers and workmen, peasants, beggars, poor craftsmen, and a great many widows and orphans. Many
must have benefitted from the private charity of wealthy citizens, or
from ecclesiastical help. In the final reckoning, more than three-
quarters of the inhabitants were able to purchase their freedom
(assuming that the estimated figure of 100,000 is something of an
exaggeration).

That this fall of Jerusalem bore no resemblance to the previous
capture of the city in 1099 is greatly to the credit of Saladin and his
army. It was a peaceful and a melancholy occasion. Saladin made
sure that his word was kept, to show the Christians the superiority of
his faith over theirs. The dissolution of the Frankish rule in Jerusalem was carried out as an administrative operation, under the super-
vision of a bureaucracy supported by military force.

"Supervisors were appointed to count out the population and
reckon up the value of the tax. At each gate an emir and other high
officials held back those who were departing and prevented the
crowds from forcing their way out. When a man had paid he was
allowed to leave, and those who could not pay were flung into prison
with no hope of deliverance. If the sum accruing from taxes had been
kept as it should have been, it would have enriched the public
coffers considerably. But this had been completely neglected and all
was complete confusion. Anyone able to produce a bribe was released, and the officials left the way of integrity for that of connivance."[46] Here the chronicler seems to be describing the actions
of people anxious to evade a lawful tax rather than recording a
panic-stricken people fighting for their lives, and yet: "Some slid
down the walls on ropes, and others got out by hiding in the baggage; yet others escaped clandestinely by disguising themselves as
soldiers, while others were the object of intervention from a higher
source which could not be disobeyed. The highest and most respected officials allowed their places to be taken by lesser men to
whose irregularities they turned a blind eye, and amassed great
sums for themselves."

In the end, the Sultan's brother, Malik al-Adil, managed to instill
a certain amount of order into this administrative chaos, and also
granted the poorest easier terms of payment. "There is not one
among us," says al-Imad, "who has not had a large share in these

benefits and has not profited from great fees." Many of those who paid had to part with everything they possessed. Compared to the things the rules of war gave them reason to fear, they were lucky to have even the chance to part with it voluntarily and then to depart in safety, armed with a receipt to be shown to the officials stationed at the gates.

Most of the Christians left Jerusalem. Saladin allowed those who so wished to remain, on condition that they paid a capitation tax. This permission chiefly affected the indigenous Christians, Greeks or Syrians, who tilled the fields and vineyards around Jerusalem. If al-Imad is to be believed, the ransom money, which was demanded more as a symbolic gesture than anything else (although the sum involved was an extremely large one), seems to have been largely embezzled by greedy emirs and unscrupulous officials. Saladin was the most disinterested of men; money flowed through his hands. He cheerfully allowed himself to be robbed and exploited, distributed alms unstintingly, and died a poor man.

What is certain is that during this campaign, which ended in the almost complete conquest of Palestine by the Moslem army, Saladin behaved in a consistently generous fashion toward the vanquished, and except for the massacre of the soldier monks he cannot be accused of a single atrocity. Far from making him drunk with triumph, his brilliant initial victory seems to have increased his awareness of the responsibilities he was taking on with regard to the lands he was bringing to Islam. Rarely in the accounts of a defeated people has there been such a general paean of praise addressed to the victor, disinterested praise coming from witnesses who had no reprisals to fear for their frankness. Rarely has a general who has won an overwhelming victory on all fronts been found to show such consideration, courtesy, and even sympathy for his adversaries of the previous day, especially when those adversaries were the enemies of his religion.

The Sultan not only distinguished himself by his chivalrous treatment of the great Frankish ladies, he not only behaved with great clemency to all who came to him as suppliants, readily granting their freedom to captive fathers and husbands; he even took a personal interest in escorting the emigrants to Christian lands, giving them protection and supplying them with food at his own expense, and instructing the officials at the gates to see to their transport in good condition, and seems to have tried, as far as possible, to limit the damage and avoid causing needless suffering to the tens of thousands of innocent victims whom his victories plunged into misfor-

tune. Admittedly, he did allow the fifteen thousand poor Franks of
Jerusalem to be taken into slavery, bewailing their fate, but this fate
no longer depended on him: they were property which did not belong to him. His efforts to cause the least possible misery are so
obvious that it is hard not to admire—as indeed the Frankish chroniclers did—a magnanimity rare in a conqueror.

Saladin had everything to gain from winning the sympathies not
only of the indigenous Christian population but of the Franks also.
The county of Tripoli and the principality of Antioch were still holding out, thanks to the proximity of the Byzantine provinces of Asia
Minor. They were no longer a threat, but Saladin could hope that
by treating the vanquished humanely he might find it easier to
achieve his design to overcome these provinces. After his recent
striking success the Sultan had no need to fear accusations of weakness, and the greater the generosity he showed, the more he would
be respected. Furthermore, as a pious and fanatical Moslem he could
find no better way of proselytizing, and the wish to give the Christians
a lofty idea of his religion certainly played a large part in his en-
deavors to display magnanimity. It is nonetheless true that history
provides few examples of great conquerors who have been so careful
not to abuse their power.

The refugees, who comprised very nearly the entire Frankish population of Jerusalem and its environs, had an opportunity of making
a melancholy comparison between the generosity of the Moslem
prince and the severity of their own coreligionists. Those who reached
the county of Tripoli were ill-used by the local nobility and robbed
of their possessions—or of the little they had left—almost as soon as
they entered Christian territory. Those like the people of Ascalon
who wished to take ship for Europe met with little sympathy from
the captains of the Genoese ships at Alexandria, who refused to
take passengers aboard without payment. The cadi of Alexandria
had to intervene on behalf of the emigrants and use threats and force
to ensure the poor wretches' return to Europe.[47] According to the
evidence of Ernoul, those of Saladin's soldiers who had been ordered
to escort the hosts of refugees behaved admirably throughout the
journey, taking care of the sick and of those exhausted by the
march, themselves carrying children and giving up their horses to
old men and women. However strict the Sultan's orders, such conduct on the part of soldiers shows that the care taken to treat the
defeated with humanity was the result of long discipline, and a genuine re-education of Nur ed-Din's army by Saladin.

The Franks who still remained in Syria—those in Antioch and Tripoli, in Tyre, and in the castles along the Jordan, together with a minority of poor people left in the conquered cities—were too scattered and cut off from one another, and also too discouraged, to have any idea of reorganizing. For a long time Bohemond III had only survived by means of compromises and truces with Saladin and the Turks of Anatolia. Furthermore, he had married a woman of unsavory reputation who was a secret agent of Saladin's. He was not altogether an ineffectual prince, but he lacked initiative and gradually allowed his inheritance to be nibbled away, losing lands and castles on his northern and eastern frontiers while still remaining master of the great city and its environs, together with the port of St. Symeon.

The county of Tripoli was also very much diminished, having been reduced to a narrow coastal strip some sixty miles long and twelve wide, and lived from one day to the next in the constant expectation of being in its turn swallowed up by Saladin's conquests. Raymond III had managed to salvage a considerable number of his knights and the county's military situation was therefore, in itself, less disastrous than that of the kingdom. But the Provençal knights were not well thought of by the other Franks in Syria, and as invariably happens after a defeat, there was a hail of mutual recriminations and accusations of treason and cowardice; and the unfortunate Raymond was only too open to accusations of this kind. His treaties of alliance with Saladin had not been forgotten, and if the Moslems themselves regarded him as a traitor to his religion, the people of the kingdom of Jerusalem were inclined to judge him more harshly still. He, the strong man to whom they looked for salvation, had been able to do nothing, had thought only of saving his own domains and had extricated himself on the day of the great battle. . . . He did not lack defenders, but his share in the responsibility for the disaster is hard to deny. He himself was only too well aware of this, and it is a fact that he never recovered from the day of Hattin.

His life dragged on for a few more months in which he was literally consumed by remorse and regret and too discouraged even to join in some movement toward armed resistance. This time the bridges between him and what still remained of the kingdom were well and truly down. He survived the fall of all the Frankish cities of the kingdom and the fall of Jerusalem, and it is not difficult to imagine the nature of the "fearful dreams" which al-Imad says troubled him. He succumbed to an attack of pleurisy at the end of 1187, at the age of forty-eight. Raymond had never had any children. He was succeeded by the second son of Prince Bohemond III of Antioch, young Bohemond, who after the death of his father and elder brother was to reign over both Antioch and Tripoli.* With the death of Raymond III the direct line of Raymond of Saint-Gilles died out in the East. This unhappy prince who, in the almost unanimous opinion of Franks and Moslems alike, had been the obvious master of all Frankish Syria, a man "intelligent and perceptive above all," "worthy of the throne for which he seemed to have been born," ended his life disgraced and dishonored by the accusation of treachery, disappointed in his hopes—which were undoubtedly sincere—of possible Franco-Moslem friendship, utterly defeated in everything for which he had striven. What had been lost—and lost partly through his fault—was no ordinary country; it was Jerusalem and the True Cross.

Saladin could rejoice at the death of his enemy, who had not really escaped him and whom he had no need to strike with his sword to put out of action. He believed himself already master of the kingdom. After the capture of Jerusalem he wrote: "The only obstacle in the way of this design [that is, the conquest of the whole country] is the capture of Tyre. This is nothing to disturb us since the name of the Prince of the Faithful, En Nacer el Din illah, is proclaimed from thirty pulpits in the land of the Franks."

But Tyre was in fact an obstacle worth worrying about, and one of considerable magnitude. Immediately after the battle of Hattin, a baron from Europe landed in Syria accompanied by a band of knights intending to join the King of Jerusalem's army. He came from Constantinople and had not yet heard of the Frankish defeat. Surprised to see the Moslem banners floating from the towers of Acre, he set sail for Tyre and barricaded himself in there. His name was Conrad of Montferrat, and he was the brother of that William Long-Sword who had been Sibylla's husband for such a short spell, and was consequently the paternal uncle of the short-lived little King Baldwin V. The garrison and people of Tyre promptly elected him their leader. Conrad was an Italian, related to both the Emperor of Germany and the King of France, and one of the bravest generals of the period. He was stern, dictatorial, and ambitious, and in the face of an apparently desperate situation he reacted with all the courage of a great man of action. All was not lost. Help would come from

* Raymond III had designated his godson Raymond, the eldest son of Bohemond III, as his heir, but the Prince of Antioch had refused to be parted from his firstborn.

the West: a Crusade would be preached, and Saladin would swiftly be driven from Syria. Meanwhile the most important thing was to stand firm in those places which were still in Christian hands.

Saladin had believed that Tyre would drop into his hands like a ripe fruit once the rest of the country had been subdued. Defended by a man like Conrad of Montferrat, the city, which was almost impregnable to landward and strongly fortified on the seaward side, resisted all attacks. Hoping to break the resolution of this Frank from Europe, the Sultan brought out the old marquis, William III of Montferrat, Conrad's father, who had been made prisoner at Hattin, before the walls and threatened to leave the old man in the front line of battle, exposed to the heaviest fire. Conrad answered that he would shoot his father himself rather than surrender the city.

Guy of Lusignan was still a prisoner, and no one seems to have been sorry for the fact except Queen Sibylla, who inundated Saladin with prayers and polite reproaches, begging for the restoration of her husband's liberty. In the end the Sultan allowed himself to be persuaded, less out of gallantry, say the Latin chroniclers (even those in favor of Guy), than out of a wish to embarrass the Franks. He had so low an opinion of the King of Jerusalem that he did not think it could do the Moslems any harm to set him free, while it would spread discord among the Franks and weaken them still further. As we shall see, King Guy was less harmless than Saladin thought, although his release did in fact lead to divisions among the Franks of Syria. As soon as he was released, Guy immediately decided to go with his wife to Tyre, where all the barons and knights of the country who still had any freedom of movement had assembled, but Conrad refused to allow the King and Queen of Jerusalem to enter the city.

Saladin was methodically pursuing his conquests. In 1188 he took the cities north of Tripoli and south of Antioch (Banyas, Valania, Jabala, Sahiyun, Lattakieh, Burzey, Qosair, Baghras, and Darbsaq) and only abandoned the idea of marching on Antioch, despite the evident inertia of Bohemond III, because his troops were exhausted by two years' incessant campaigning. The Krak des Chevaliers—the formidable fortress belonging to the Order of Hospitalers—proved impregnable. In Palestine, the castle of Beaufort, and Kerak of Moab and Montreal to the south of the Dead Sea, held out stubbornly for a long while and finally had to be starved into submission (Montreal in 1189).

The Franks were organizing their defense. After the floodtide of 1187, those fortresses which had held out became less easy to capture. The garrisons, which at first had been almost nonexistent, were being reinforced by the training of young recruits and volunteers. Soldier pilgrims were disembarking in increasing numbers at Tyre or St. Symeon, running the gauntlet of Saladin's Egyptian fleets. Soldiers who surrendered and were allowed to go free with their lives immediately hastened to fling themselves into such strongholds as had not yet fallen. Overcoming the Franks was decidedly no easy task, especially when waging a humane war and respecting persons and property as far as possible, as Saladin was trying to do.

In 1189, Guy of Lusignan, who had succeeded in acquiring a following of a few hundred knights and sergeants newly arrived from France or escaped from captured castles, went to lay siege to the city of Acre. Acre was a formidable stronghold, a great seaport, defended on the landward side by nearly a mile of high walls flanked by towers, and the garrison alone was more numerous than the erstwhile King of Jerusalem's small army. When Saladin heard the news, he thought it must be a joke, or merely a diversionary maneuver. Guy's action was so improbably foolish that it forestalled any reaction on the part of his adversary. When Saladin finally realized that Acre was actually under siege and arrived with his troops, the Franks had already dug themselves into a fortified camp as impregnable to the army from outside as it was to the men of the garrison. They had succeeded in blockading the city by land, and in gaining a foothold on the shore whence they could obtain reinforcements by sea. They replied to all Saladin's attacks with such vigor that it was impossible to dislodge them from their camp.

The third great Crusade was about to begin.

CHAPTER

IX

The Crusade of the Kings

(1 1 8 8 – 1 1 9 2)

Jerusalem and the West

When he assumed the task of successfully continuing the holy war against the Frankish infidels in succession to Nur ed-Din, Saladin knew that he was fighting a religious war. For more than thirty years an intensive propaganda campaign had been in progress throughout the Moslem Near East against the heresy and impiety of the "polytheists"—and in particular against the Frankish, Latin polytheists who had dared to seize Palestine and Jerusalem from the Moslems.

The first Crusaders, who had inundated Jerusalem in blood and perpetrated countless other massacres, profaned mosques, and tortured Moslem holy men, had aroused the horror of ferocious wild beasts on the rampage, but in fact Islamic Syria had reacted very tamely. The sultans of Anatolia, who had wiped out several Crusading armies on their own account, were motivated by no particular religious zeal and would have been equally likely to attack any invader, even a Moslem. At the beginning of the century, religious fanaticism had been the province of religious zealots and pietist sects, and only occasionally of the mass of the people, when this was stirred up by a particular preacher. Princes, emirs, and the army were quite ready to reach an understanding with the Franks if they found it to their advantage, while the Franks, on their side, had very quickly realized this. Baldwin II, while still only Count of Edessa, can already be found executing a Moslem convert to Christianity for allowing himself to speak ill of his former religion. For nearly ninety years, the Franks who settled in Syria had behaved like a military occupying force, differing little from autochthonous military governments, scrupulously honoring their own faith but tolerant toward the religions of the natives, although their relations with the local Christians, and the Greeks in particular, were sometimes worse than with the Moslems.

From Zengi to Nur ed-Din, and from Nur ed-Din to Saladin, the Syrian princes' desire for conquest had drifted—with the help of public opinion in general—toward a real enthusiasm for the holy war and a reawakening of Pan-Islamism. The Franks were to blame for this only insofar as they were an alien element: however holy Jerusalem, and however deplorable the Christian profanation of the Mosque of al-Aqsa, Palestine was nonetheless merely a frontier province, and the deeper life of Islam was not affected by its loss, while the Christians had always possessed undisputed rights over the Holy Places. The troubles of the First Crusade had receded into the past and the Christian kingdom which had been established in Syria was one political factor among others, the less dangerous because it was on bad terms with Byzantium. It was also useful because its existence neutralized the ambitions of kings or atabegs eager for conquest. By systematic, tireless, and passionate preaching, Nur ed-Din had finally succeeded in awakening Moslem public opinion by demonstrating that Christian dominion over a land which had formerly belonged to Islam was a scandal. And yet it was frequently the Franks' immediate neighbors who, although they engaged in constant skirmishing against them, found it easiest to tolerate this scandal and were the most reluctant to see the end of it.

By using politics in the cause of religion and religion in the cause of politics, Saladin made himself the apostle of reconquest, demanding that every one of his soldiers become a soldier of God. It was not the Franks in themselves who were hateful; it was their status as infidels. They were guilty of the error of the Trinity, of polytheism, the deification of the human being, and idolatry. The Moslems believed they were fighting against a barbarous and backward faith, dissipating the shades of error, and letting the Truth shine forth. Against this somewhat abstract enemy, Saladin was waging a war that was simultaneously relentless and chivalrous.

Motivated entirely by the conviction of the superiority of his faith, and of the inevitable triumph of God over the devil, Saladin may not altogether have understood that the Franks might be motivated by exactly the same feelings. He believed that he was setting up the forces of the spirit against brute force, but the Franks, however crude their superstitions, clung to them with such force as to reveal themselves capable of miracles of energy. Saladin might have foreseen that the fall of Jerusalem would not be readily accepted by the Franks from Europe who possessed powerful kingdoms beyond the sea, although the experience of 1147 and of the various private Crusades like that of Philip of Flanders may well have given the Moslems grounds for believing that the West was not unduly interested in the Holy Land. Saladin may have thought that by allowing Christians to make pilgrimages to Jerusalem and by a general policy of tolerance and goodwill, he would make the distant Christian monarchs understand that they had not lost a great deal.

He had refused to have the Church of the Holy Sepulcher demolished as his lieutenants asked him to. "What is the good of wrecking and destroying when the seat of their adoration is the site of the Cross and the Sepulcher and not the external edifice? Even were it razed to the ground, the various Christian communities would not cease to come there!"[1] He had the Holy Sepulcher kept for the use of the Christian religion, as well as a number of other churches, and installed Greek Orthodox clergy in them, thus restoring to them the privileges they had lost in 1099. He also tolerated a Latin clergy. He solemnly returned the Mosque of al-Aqsa to the Moslem faith. This was the third in holiness of all mosques and had been occupied during Frankish times by the Knights Templar. Naturally, "all traces of Christianity" that were found there were removed. But he did permit Christian pilgrims to make pilgrimages and have access to the Holy Places on payment of a tax, as had been the custom of Moslem princes in previous centuries. Christians, both East and West, had been after all quite content with this state of affairs for almost five centuries.

The Crusaders of 1189–1190

As was to be expected, the news of the battle of Hattin, and even more that of the fall of Jerusalem, aroused immense feeling and had still greater reverberations than the conquest of Jerusalem in 1099. In the days between 1160 and 1185, when Amalric I and Baldwin IV were begging the kings of Christendom to send them help and the Holy Land might still have been saved for Christendom by a massive intervention of Western forces, Catholic Europe had remained quite indifferent to calls for aid, even though some great barons did become Crusaders on their own account from time to time.

Western Crusaders in general were unfavorably impressed by the way of life and the mentality of the Franks of Syria. They made their pilgrimage and gave an occasional helping hand to the local armies, but without great enthusiasm and without feeling that they were taking part in a genuine holy war. Then they left, taking with them indulgences and relics. Some, like Philip of Flanders, went so far as to refuse their aid, considering that there was little profit in the undertaking. Count Stephen of Blois and Henry the Lion, Duke of Saxony, in 1171; the Norman King of Sicily, William II, in 1174; Henry the Liberal, Count of Champagne, in 1180; Godfrey III, Duke of Brabant, and Ralph of Mauléon in 1183; William III of Montferrat in 1185—all were great lords who, according to their energy and their means, had taken part in the wars that the kingdom of Jerusalem was compelled to wage in its own defense. The military and merchant fleets of Genoa, Pisa, and Venice landed periodically on the coast of Syria, and once they had accomplished their devotions in Jerusalem their sailors took service in the King's armies for the duration of one or two seasonal campaigns; the part played by these fleets in protecting the coasts against the Egyptian fleets was considerable. Pilgrim soldiers also came in a private capacity, in small groups, and some, like Amalric of Lusignan or Gerard of Ridfort, settled in the country hoping to make their fortunes or simply, like those who entered the military orders, to serve God. The constantly diminishing ranks of the Frankish armies were fairly regularly strengthened by new arrivals from Europe who, if they were reasonably valiant, had some hope of marrying the widow or heiress of a local baron who had been killed in battle. But from beginning to end of the kingdom's history, Frankish Syria was always up against the same problem: inadequate armed forces and a shortage of knights and professional soldiers. This is an indication of how little the Eastern adventure attracted the feudal warriors of the European countries.

It was true that the journey was dangerous and expensive, and the profit to be gained from it very fleeting and chiefly of a spiritual nature. In the circumstances, the number of feudal lords who did take the cross in the course of the twelfth century is, in spite of everything, quite remarkable and proves that "pilgrimage" had become a habit and enjoyed general popularity. But ultimately, the Crusaders from the West seem to have been deceived by appearances and to have regarded Jerusalem and the other Frankish territories as the inalienable fief of Catholic Christendom. They were more inclined to criticize the conduct of the Franks in the East than to share their hopes and fears.

Since they could not rely on substantial aid from the Western powers, the Franks were thrown back, reluctantly enough, on alliance with Byzantium, and this in turn set a chill on their relations with the Catholic princes. Manuel Comnenus was known to favor a reconciliation with the West, and relied heavily on his alliances with the Franks on the one hand and with the Italian merchant republics on the other. His defeat at Myriocephalum in 1176, where his army was surprised in a narrow defile by the Turks of Kilij Arslan II and completely wiped out, struck a decisive blow at his policies and his prestige, and after his death in 1180 and the short regency of his widow, the excessively beautiful and unpopular Maria of Antioch, Manuel's cousin Andronicus seized power and broke with the "Latins." His reign began with terrible popular uprisings, in the course of which almost the whole of the Italian colony at Constantinople (over fifty thousand people) was massacred. Andronicus himself perished tragically, two years later, in 1185. He was overthrown by the aristocratic party and lynched with unprecedented savagery by the populace, despite the fact that in him the people lost one of the few emperors who would really have taken their side against the nobles. With the elimination of the Comneni the imperial throne was wide open to the intrigues of the nobles and occupied by individuals possessing neither authority nor prestige: Isaac Angelus, and after him his son Alexius. Frankish Syria could no longer rely on the assistance of the Greeks, who were too taken up with intestinal struggles, their wars against the Normans, and the growing hostility of Venice.

As we have just seen, Saladin had had little difficulty in crushing the Frankish kingdom, and he was confident of his ability to reduce the remainder of the Frankish states in Syria before very long. But his army was tired, and unaccustomed to long campaigns. In theory his emirs, like feudal barons, owed him a service which was limited to a certain number of days in any one year, and it had taken the enthusiasm for the holy war and the intoxication of a great victory to keep them with the flag for nearly two years. On the other hand, the people of Damascus and Aleppo grew impatient, regretting their former Zengid masters, and the Ismailians were less than ever inclined to abandon their holy war against triumphant Sunnism. The Seljuk Sultan of Rum, having nothing more to fear from the Greeks for the time being, was looking askance at the growing power of the Kurdish chief who posed as an apostle of the faith. Saladin had every reason to fear the arrival of a great Frankish army from the West and did everything he could to prevent a new Crusade.

He had taken risks already: in his desire to reconquer Palestine and Jerusalem for Islam he was attacking much more than one small Christian kingdom which happened to be in possession of a holy city of Islam. He was striking all Christendom to the heart. (Western Christendom, at least, because Saladin's conquest of Jerusalem was only a semicatastrophe for Byzantium.)

It has been seen that the great Sultan was doing his best to win the sympathies of the indigenous Christians. He behaved with equal magnanimity toward the Jews, who had not been particularly well treated by the Franks and could only congratulate themselves on the change of masters. With the Franks, Saladin adopted a policy of gentleness, of chivalrous honor, which earned him the personal admiration of his enemies. But if he had subjected Jerusalem to fire and slaughter, the effect produced in the West by the capture of the Holy City could not have been any greater.

Moslem chroniclers record this with some surprise. Ibn al-Athir tells the story of one Frankish prisoner who came from Europe after the fall of Jerusalem: "A Christian prisoner told me that his mother was a woman who had no other sons besides himself: all their wealth consisted of a single house, which his mother sold and used its price to equip him. Then she sent him off to reconquer Jerusalem, and he was made prisoner. This was the strength of the religious and spiritual motives driving the Franks, as I have just revealed it."[2] Here, in a few words, the Arab historian tells the story of tens of thousands of poor people who sold all they had and left everything, not this time for an unknown Jerusalem to be conquered, but for a Jerusalem which had been lost and must be saved. Love of Jerusalem awoke anew, more painful and more exalted than ever. People had little wish to know whether its conquest had been humane or not; they knew only one thing: that the True Cross was in Moslem hands and Jerusalem lost.

The Patriarch Heraclius left Jerusalem, with all his own wealth and a good deal of that belonging to the churches of Jerusalem, and set sail for Europe. However unworthy and discredited he might be, his title gave him certain obligations. He went first to Rome and from there made a tour of the capitals of Christendom, describing the sufferings of Jerusalem and preaching a fresh Crusade. (Ibn al-Athir describes the Patriarch and his escort, dressed in black, holding aloft for the contemplation of the faithful a "representation of the face of the Messiah, adding the figure of an Arab striking it, and they soiled the image of the Messiah with blood. This image, they said, is that of the Messiah. Mohammed, the Prophet of the Moslems, is striking it and has already wounded and killed him. This sight was painful to the Franks."[3] The Latin chroniclers give us no details about this eloquent popular imagery, but it is very likely that propaganda of this kind was employed, among other means, to arouse the indignation and grief of the crowds.

Even before the fall of Jerusalem, Conrad of Montferrat, from his seat in Tyre, had sent Josias, the Archbishop of that city, to Europe with an urgent request for help. William II, the Norman King of Sicily, was so moved that he made a hasty peace with his constant enemy Byzantium and armed a fleet; but even this prince, like the other Christian sovereigns, was ultimately too taken up with the affairs of his kingdom to devote himself heart and soul to the reconquest of the Holy Land. The news of the fall of Jerusalem caused great mourning throughout Christendom, but the heads of state, however sincere their grief, took some time to react. They had to be forced into it by pressure of public opinion and the appeals of the Pope.

Ever since the beginning of the century, the kingdom of Jerusalem had appeared in two different lights. In the first place it was an actual state with a precise location in time and space and faced with the problems affecting all nations: the need to defend its frontiers, ensure its economic equilibrium, achieve internal stability, and so forth. Its other aspect, which is more difficult to define, was what the possession of Jerusalem meant to Western Christendom. The kingdom was in practice a French state by language and tradition; its princes, its aristocracy, and the greater part of its Latin population were French; but even so, an unwritten law made it an international state, and the Holy Places entrusted to its care were the property of all Christendom and of Western Christendom in particular. Englishmen, Italians, Germans, Scandinavians, all came on pilgrimages to Jerusalem and took the cross, under the banners of the kingdom, without in any way feeling that they were taking service with the French. Over there, every man was in the service of God. National rivalries and differences which existed in Europe were in theory subordinated to the interests of religion. For Europe, Palestine in the twelfth century was the Holy Land first and foremost and a Christian nation second, and as the Holy Land it belonged to everyone. People in general were much less interested in its real situation than in what might be called its spiritual and everlasting nature.

Possession of the Holy Land did have undeniable mystical value, and was to some extent an assurance to the Catholic peoples of God's physical presence among them. Because of this the kingdom of Jerusalem was a great unifying factor among Christian nations, all of whom felt, to a greater or lesser extent, that they were sharing in a great common undertaking. Gifts and donations reached Jerusalem from every corner of Europe, and men of all nations entered the military orders.

Even so, collective enthusiasm for the cause of the Holy Land was little in evidence (after the Crusades of 1096 and 1101) except in 1146, and then partly thanks to the preaching of Saint Bernard. We know that the Crusades of Louis VII and Conrad III were a failure, and that the attempt at a holy war in Syria only led to a quarrel between the Crusaders and the Franks in the East. On a psychological level, the failure of this great undertaking, which was nevertheless the result of a real current of opinion, can be explained by the apparent insignificance of the goals in view: this was not a question of taking Jerusalem, or even of defending it against immediate danger. Saint Bernard had realized, quite correctly on the whole, that the Holy Land was in real peril and that the growing power of the Zengid dynasty must be checked at all costs. But his extraordinarily eloquent preaching placed greater emphasis on the spiritual side of the affair than on its practical aspects; he spoke of the birthplace of Jesus Christ, and of the Christian's obligation to abandon everything for the land where God had ransomed men. If he had spent his time explaining to his audience the necessity of preventing the atabeg of Aleppo from seizing Damascus and of driving the Turks back across the Euphrates, he would probably not have filled the crowds with such enthusiasm. The Crusade was based on a terrible misunderstanding: not only was Jerusalem not in need of defense; in addition, the barons of the place preferred to disband the Crusade hastily rather than quarrel with their Moslem neighbors. The Crusaders neglected to attack the real enemy because his possessions lay far from Jerusalem.

Louis VII probably felt some remorse when he heard, after his return to France, of the tragic death of Raymond of Poitiers, whose entreaties he had so roughly rejected, but in any event it was too late to embark on a fresh Crusade. Too much money, too much energy and enthusiasm—to say nothing of human lives—had been wasted for nothing.

The Holy Land was a great center of pilgrimage, but it was not, in the twelfth century, the central preoccupation of Christians, any more than Rome was. It was only when the news of the fall of Jerusalem reached the West that Europe realized what possession of the Holy Land meant to Christendom. While no king had actually taken part in the First Crusade, it was now generally recognized and acknowledged by all that the reconquest of the Holy Places was an absolute duty for every Christian, and for heads of state first and foremost. The papacy, whose prestige had been greatly enhanced by the First Crusade and which regarded the Holy Land as a fief of the Church (although it had never exercised its rights of suzerainty), reacted most vigorously, making it a duty for the clergy to preach the Crusade, promulgating the creation of a special and quite substantial tax—the *dime saladine*—aimed at financing the equipment of a Crusading army. Propaganda in every country was intense and well organized, and organized spontaneously because it answered a deep feeling among the people.

There could be no doubt that the Holy Land was now synonymous with general salvation: no man had the right to stand aside; the insult to the Christian religion was too bloody and it was Jesus Christ himself who had been struck at, humiliated, and trampled underfoot in the person of his country, and it was he who summoned Christians to his aid.

Kings had no right to evade the duty of the Crusade. They could not produce excuses such as the interests of their kingdoms or the safety of their subjects; not even the most obvious reasons to prevent them would be considered valid. They must take the cross or be regarded as traitors to Christendom. It was the same for the great barons, and in fact, although not all became Crusaders, the least they could do was to send a son or a brother with a suitable body of knights, or suffer the dishonor of seeing their banner absent from those of the armies of God.

Frederick Barbarossa

From the beginning of the year 1188, the King of France and the King of England, who as Frenchmen were the Christian sovereigns most directly concerned in the affairs of the Holy Land, were compelled to publicly renounce their own quarrels and together make a vow to take the cross (at Gisors on January 21). Both Kings were equally reluctant to leave their own countries and set out to wage war in the East. Henry II Plantagenet was old and ailing, and had long been busy with the war he was waging simultaneously against the King of France and against his own sons. The King of France, young Philip II (Philip Augustus), had such good reasons to fear for his kingdom that he had little room left to worry about the troubles of the Holy Land. Ever since the divorce between Louis VII and Eleanor of Aquitaine had given the Plantagenet possession of lands three times as extensive as the kingdom of France itself, the Capet family, who in theory were the suzerains of the kings of England, had been in danger of sinking definitively to the status of minor powers on French soil. Their tactics consisted in entertaining Henry II's sons and encouraging them to rebel against their father and quarrel among themselves, as well as stirring up revolts among the great Plantagenet's vassals. At the same time they were having natural enough difficulty in controlling their own vassals. Consequently, Philip Augustus felt reluctant to go on a Crusade, even if Henry II did so at the same time, because it would mean leaving his kingdom wide open to the King of England's son Richard, who was as unreliable as an ally as he was unsatisfactory as a son. Admittedly Richard also took the cross and even displayed a great zeal for the holy war, although more for effect than from conviction. Altogether, the French Kings did everything they could, despite the threats and accusations of the Pope and the pressure of public opinion, to postpone fulfilling their vow. However, they were compelled to equip themselves and set out because their abstention was becoming more and more of a scandal and making them increasingly unpopular.

Henry II was in fact never able to fulfill his vow. He died in 1189, and the English King who led the Crusade was Richard.

A number of great French barons set out between 1188 and 1190 without waiting for the Kings. These included the Count of Bar, the Count of Champagne, and the Count of Brienne, not to mention lords of lesser importance from the north and south of France. The whole of French chivalry rose in a body, and it is no exaggeration to say that this time those who went were in the majority. Never before had anything like this assembly of Frankish forces set out for the East.

This time, although very many of those who went were Frenchmen, the knights of other lands were at least as eager to share in the war of reconquest. Fleets from Pisa and Genoa first, and then Normans from the Mediterranean, English, Danes, Norwegians, and Flemings appeared during the two years that followed the fall of Jerusalem, and rapidly acquired control of the coast of Syria.

Tyre was still in the hands of Conrad of Montferrat, and the Crusading knights were able to land unhindered outside Acre where Guy of Lusignan was still maintaining his siege of the city. The army laying siege to the castle now included only a handful of Syrian Franks, but there was an impressive body of Crusaders and the Frankish camp was growing every day. Caught between the besieged city and the sea on the one hand, and Saladin's army on the other, this monstrous camp, overflowing with people and crawling like an ant-hill, had become the rallying point for the military forces of the whole of European chivalry.

There was a third Christian monarch, who was putting more ardor into the fulfillment of his vow to go on the Crusade than the Kings of France and England. This was the German Emperor, Frederick of Hohenstaufen, known as Barbarossa. He also had taken the cross in 1188 and with the help of his vassals and the German bishops had fitted out an army estimated by chroniclers at 100,000 men (this means there were probably 50,000). This was a real army, with no civilians and no hangers-on. Frederick I was a good organizer and forty-two years earlier he had taken part in the second great Crusade with his uncle, the Emperor Conrad. This time he was determined to avoid the mistakes which had led to the loss of the German army in 1147.

While the armies from France, Italy, and the Nordic countries took the sea route, the Emperor found it more practicable to travel through Hungary and the Balkans and then via Constantinople. He himself did not cherish any hostile feelings toward the Greeks, who were the traditional enemies of his own traditional enemies, the Normans, but the inevitable friction between his army and the people of the Byzantine Empire, and especially the fears and blunders of the new Emperor of Byzantium, Isaac Angelus, almost led to armed conflict. Less of a diplomat than his predecessors, the Comneni, Isaac had little idea how to cope with this redoubtable Emperor and his impressive army. The Greeks at that time were hard pressed in Anatolia by Kilij Arslan II and were trying to preserve their alliance with Saladin, and they were afraid to allow Frederick to cross over into Asia Minor in case this effected a reconciliation between the Seljuks of Rum and the new master of Syria. On the other hand, it would have been child's play for the German army to take possession of Constantinople at that moment.

But Frederick Barbarossa had set out to defend the Holy Sepulcher and he was not interested in taking Constantinople. Although his relations with Isaac were vitriolic enough to suggest the possibility of a Crusade against the Greeks, he finally contented himself with threats in order to obtain a passage into Asia for his army and then continued his way to the Holy Land.

This time the situation was very different from that in 1147; the Greeks, threatened by Kilij Arslan II, were intriguing with Saladin and keeping him informed of the German army's movements, and as a result the Seljuk, who had little love for Saladin, far from attacking Frederick as his forebear had attacked Conrad III, succeeded in coming to an understanding with the German Emperor whereby he allowed him to pass through his territory without hindrance. There was an engagement outside Konya which resulted in a victory for the Crusaders, and the Sultan was compelled to open the gates of his capital to Frederick. The two princes got on very well together and went so far as to conclude a mutual treaty of alliance against Saladin. It seemed as though Saladin must be lost. With his army almost intact and still strictly disciplined, Frederick entered Cilicia, confident of a swift and easy victory. But the great Emperor was seventy years old. One day, reaching the banks of the river Cydnus and tired after a long day in the saddle, he unwisely decided to bathe and dropped dead of heart failure.*

Frederick had been a great general and his powerful personality had earned him the almost superstitious reverence of his troops. His sudden disappearance was felt as a disaster by the whole army, and it was as though immediately after his death the army virtually ceased to exist. His son, Frederick of Swabia, had little authority and was not able to maintain the discipline of an army already exhausted and thrown into despair by the death of its leader. Ibn al-Athir wrote: "If God had not condescended to show his goodness to the Moslems by making the King of the Germans perish at the very moment when he was about to enter Syria, men would write today that Syria and Egypt had once belonged to Islam."[4]

The German army was no more. The troops disbanded; some of the barons returned to Europe and others took the road southward toward Antioch. A great many fell into the hands of Saladin's soldiers and were sold into slavery. Those who escaped reached Antioch but were soon decimated by an epidemic, and Frederick of Swabia reached Acre with only a mere one or two thousand men. It was said the Germans were fated never to reach the Holy Land. Their first great army was massacred in 1101, the second by the Seljuks in 1147, and the only one to succeed in avoiding a clash with the Turks of Anatolia (an unprecedented exploit for a Crusading army) foundered miserably as a result of an accident as senseless as it was unforeseeable. Frederick, old man though he was, had seemed full of

* According to other chroniclers, he fell from his horse while attempting to cross the river. In any event, his death seems to have been due to heart failure.

vigor and cut out to ride at the head of his troops for years to come. His son had his body carried to the Holy Land for burial at Jerusalem, but it had been clumsily embalmed and decomposed on the journey so that only the skull was preserved and did in fact reach Jerusalem three years later.

In Germany there was a legend about him which spread rapidly and continued for a long time (popular tradition further confusing his name with that of another great emperor, Frederick II). It said that the old Emperor had not died but had disappeared and was living inside a mountain in Swabia, whence he would one day emerge to lead the Germans to a decisive victory over all their enemies. The Moslems, in any event, had good reason to believe themselves the object of God's especial favor: the battle of Hattin and the conquest of Jerusalem, Christianity's great effort before Acre and on the coast of Syria, the tens of thousands of dead on either side—all this would have been to no avail or would have had a different meaning if, on June 10, 1190, an old man had been better able to stand the shock of cold water. No philosophy of history can correctly estimate the incalculable, inexplicable importance of the human personality in the case of a great leader of men.

The Siege of Acre

Frederick, the only Christian monarch really to have taken his role as a Crusader seriously, was dead. The other kings had finally decided to make the journey, but they had not yet landed in the Holy Land. They were certainly in no hurry, since neither was anxious to leave before the other or lose sight of the other. They stopped in Sicily, where Richard had to settle a family quarrel concerning the position of his sister Joanna, William II's widow. Then at last Philip, the more conscientious of the two monarchs, made his way to the Holy Land and landed at Acre on April 20 (three years after making his vow to go on the Crusade) together with two great vassals, Hugh III, Duke of Burgundy, and Philip of Alsace, Count of Flanders (the same who had formerly made such a bad impression on the leper King and his barons). As for Richard Coeur-de-Lion, he first spread terror throughout Sicily and then embarked on the conquest of Cyprus from Byzantium. This was hardly difficult since he arrived with a formidable armada, and the Byzantine army, like its government, was in a state of complete decay. This conquest did in fact help the Crusade because as master of Cyprus, Richard was in a

better position to supply the besieging army. At last he turned up
in person, and although he had made everyone wait a long time for
him, he was given a most enthusiastic welcome. He had an immense
reputation for strength and courage and was said to be the first
knight of Christendom.

The son of Eleanor of Aquitaine and the Plantagenet Henry II
was a descendant of the counts of Blois and the dukes of Aquitaine,
but he seems to have chiefly inherited the brutal energy of his distant
Norman ancestors. He belonged to the same race as Bohemond and
Robert Guiscard, and although he had less intelligence and tenacity,
he possessed their gift of arousing the enthusiasm of his troops and
making his soldiers obey him. During the siege of Acre he displayed
real qualities of generalship and conducted operations with remarkable dash, despite a serious illness which kept him out of the front
line for a long time. Philip Augustus was also ill, and the two Kings
were not the only ones. Ever since the beginning of the siege in
1189, as the army's strength increased, it had been proportionately
reduced by terrible epidemics which were aggravated by lack of food,
cold and damp in winter, and excessive heat in summer. But new reinforcements were arriving all the time, morale was still very high,
and the presence of the two Kings gave the army confidence of imminent victory.

The garrison of Acre, cut off from the outside world for over a
year, was still holding out with a gallantry which compelled the admiration of its assailants. Saladin, who had set up his camp around
the Christian camp, found himself powerless, for if the Crusaders
were immobilized outside Acre, he himself was equally so. He could
neither strike camp nor reduce his strength because the vast Christian army would have seized the opportunity to take him in the rear
and invade the country.

Acre fell, its towers in ruins from fierce bombardment and its garrison exhausted by hunger and at the end of its strength, on July 12,
1191, after a siege lasting two years. It was a great victory and was
followed by a pitched battle which the Crusaders won and then by
the recapture of a number of other major coastal cities. Even so, it
was a Pyrrhic victory.

The siege of Acre (August 1189–July 1191) was by far the most
murderous military operation ever undertaken by the Franks in
Syria. It can be compared, from the point of view of the number
of human lives it cost, to the disasters in Anatolia of 1101 and 1147,
but these were militarily and psychologically on a different level.

They were comparatively swift, almost accidental defeats, in which hunger and thirst led to the collapse of the army and their slaughter by half-savage hordes. The situation at Acre was altogether different. The Crusaders had gained a foothold in the Holy Land, and possessed undisputed mastery at sea, and they simply sat there, barricaded into their vast encampment, with no intention of moving until they had taken the city. Reinforcements flowed in constantly from the sea, and with these reinforcements came new reasons for hope. While it is difficult to estimate the strength of the Crusaders who landed at Acre in the spring of 1189 and during the siege, this can be reckoned at over 100,000 men, to judge by the number of Genoese fleets bringing successions of Genoese, Venetian, and Pisan Crusaders (from April 1189) and later on the Danes, the Frisians, the men of Champagne in September, the North Italians and Germans at the end of the same month, the French from all parts of the country, Italians, and Scandinavians in October. Then, in the summer of 1190, came the armies of the Count of Champagne and his chief vassals, followed by those of the King of France and the Count of Flanders, and lastly of the King of England. With these must be included the forces led by Frederick of Swabia who, in spite of everything, had managed to keep with him the pick of his knights.

The siege had begun with ridiculously feeble forces, and one can only admire the nerve of the former King of Jerusalem who had been released by Saladin because he knew that "King Guy was unlucky and was neither fierce nor terrible in war."[5] Guy had been determined to belie this well-established reputation in the belief that he now had nothing more to lose. It was Acre and not Tyre, the impregnable stronghold of his rival Conrad of Montferrat, which became the rallying point of the reconquering army. Toward the end of 1189 the Crusading camp had become a vast canvas city, with its countless districts divided according to nationality, where men spoke twenty different languages and dialects among which, on this occasion, French did not predominate. The whole of Christendom was represented by knights and barons of the best families as well as the countless and anonymous host of civilian volunteers. Even these volunteers were already equipped and trained for war, for this was not, as it had been in 1096, a mass movement of God's poor aspiring to a great pilgrimage. This Crusade was a frankly military undertaking, and the kings and barons had no time for useless mouths.

The majority of the Crusaders were therefore soldiers, whether professional or impromptu: citizens, rich or poor, artisans, peasants

who had sold all or part of their possessions to obtain weapons and
money for the voyage. There were even women among the combatants—as witness the woman "covered in a green mantle" (described
by Beha ed-Din) who was an expert at the longbow, and the three
women who fought on horseback dressed as men, mentioned by Ibn
al-Athir.[6] Other women, who did not actually join in the fighting,
still rendered considerable service in an auxiliary capacity, while others, if Ibn al-Athir is to be believed, carried piety to the length of
giving themselves to the soldiers for nothing, in order to keep up
their morale (these were probably more or less repentant courtesans). Nevertheless, women seem to have been no more numerous
here, in any capacity, than they were in any other army of the period,
and probably rather less so, since the Norman chronicler Ambroise
mentions a catastrophic shortage of women.

This great army, cramped into a comparatively small space owing
to the failure of all attempts to force Saladin's blockade, rapidly became a prey to epidemics. The men, Northerners for the most part,
found the climate of the country hard to bear, especially in the
wretched conditions in which they were forced to live. During the
winter of 1189–1190, and to a still greater extent in the winter and
spring of 1191 (when their numbers had at least tripled), there was
actual famine. The fighting, on the two fronts of the besieged city
and in Saladin's camp, was sufficiently murderous, but privation and
sickness killed more men than the war.

In July 1190 a company of foot soldiers mutinied and hurled
themselves—ten thousand of them—against Saladin's tents. The cavalry, which did not approve of the attack, failed to support them
and the majority of the unfortunate men were slain. Their bodies remained in the gully dividing the two camps and for weeks the smell
of decomposition made the air unbreathable, while clouds of flies
bred new diseases. In the full heat of August and lacking proper
food, the soldiers had little resistance to disease and the death rate
was terrible. The constant arrival of reinforcements compensated for
the losses, but the newly landed men also fell victims to disease in
their turn. Philip, Count of Flanders, died a few days after his arrival at Acre, and Philip Augustus and Richard Coeur-de-Lion also
nearly died in the holy war before they had a chance to do any fighting. Both in turn were ravaged by a strange disease which made the
skin fall from their bodies, and they almost lost their sight. The two
Kings were young, strong, and well cared for and they recovered;
there is no knowing how many soldiers died.

Among those who died in battle were Count Andrew of Brienne,

Aubrey Clement, Marshal of France, and Gerard of Ridfort, the Grand Master of the Templars. (Gerard was taken prisoner again and was then decapitated, which seems a sufficient indication that there were no grounds for accusing him of any hidden treachery; moreover he fought with great courage.) The garrison of Acre fought back with exemplary vigor, bombarding the attackers with missiles and pouring flaming naphtha down on them. Saladin, on his side, launched frequent attacks on the camp, but it was in the sorties mounted by the Crusaders themselves that most of the soldiers lost their lives.

Moslem losses were much less than those of the Franks, since they were generally on the defensive and had the whole of the hinterland to maneuver in and obtain supplies. Their troops also fought less keenly, since for them the initial *élan* of the holy war had somewhat abated and there was nothing particularly dramatic about their actual situation. For the Franks, clinging to their scrap of land, it was a matter of life and death. Ambroise, who was an eyewitness of the siege, shows that in spite of the inevitable demoralization caused by sickness and starvation, the Crusading army had little doubt of ultimate victory, and that it had a real feeling of holy war, the desire to conquer or die for the recovery of Jerusalem and the True Cross.

At the highest level, among the leaders, intrigue was rife throughout the siege in spite of sickness and battles. They wanted to recover Jerusalem, but they also wanted to be sure on whose behalf they were doing so. Of the two candidates for the throne, Conrad of Montferrat and Guy of Lusignan, the first was supported by the Frankish barons of Syria and the second by the Crusaders from abroad. Frederick Barbarossa, had he lived, would probably have settled the matter in favor of Conrad, who was related to him. The two Kings, Philip and Richard, each in turn campaigned for their own candidate, Richard being in favor of Guy of Lusignan, and Philip, of Conrad of Montferrat. Both invoked ties of kinship but were in fact motivated by sympathies of a political nature.

Richard was actually related to the family of Lusignan, and Guy and his brothers had helped him to conquer Cyprus, having crossed the sea to meet him when they learned that he had landed on the island. By supporting Guy, the King of England was hoping to gain reliable allies in the Holy Land and to be able to establish his own hegemony there. Philip Augustus, seeing that Conrad enjoyed the support of the local nobility, thought it better to back the Italian and so put a stop to Richard's ambitions. During the siege of Acre, Guy had in fact lost what little right he still possessed to the crown of Jerusalem. Queen Sibylla and her two daughters had died in October 1190. Guy's only claim was through his wife. He had no legitimate claim at all, but he had been crowned in Jerusalem and could not renounce his title without appearing a coward in the eyes of his followers. Conrad of Montferrat, on the other hand, had no other claim beyond his presence in Tyre and his unquestionable military prowess.* The Syrian barons had joined forces with him in 1187 because, although a foreigner, he seemed to be capable of making the cause of Frankish Syria his own, while Guy was doomed to remain a pawn in the hands of Crusaders from oversea.

The legitimate heir to the throne was Amalric I's second daughter, Isabella. There was only one way of making Conrad the lawful King, and that was to marry him to Isabella. Isabella's husband was fortunately a man whom no one took seriously: the same Humphrey of Toron who had so feebly wriggled out of the baron's attempt to make him King in spite of himself. He was handsome and educated, but his manners were so effeminate that people wondered whether he was able to fulfill his conjugal obligations. Such as he was, Isabella loved him. Humphrey protested but was silenced, not a very difficult matter. Isabella's mother Maria, who was married to Balian of Ibelin, succeeded in overcoming the girl's resistance. The marriage was declared null on the pretext that the bride had never given her consent to the marriage (she had in fact been only eight years old when betrothed to Humphrey of Toron). The pretext was of course pure fiction, for in the present case the whole trouble came from the complete consent of the young woman to her marriage. Once divorced, Isabella of Jerusalem was promptly married off to Conrad of Montferrat, who thus became by dynastic custom, if not actually King of Jerusalem, at least the first legal candidate to the title.

Those Crusaders who took any interest in politics and the future of the kingdom were therefore divided into two camps: those supporting Lusignan and those for Conrad of Montferrat. This did nothing to diminish the army's effectiveness in battle. Before they could argue over the kingdom, it had first to be reconquered, and the supporters of both claimants displayed a fine solidarity against the Moslems. There was even an incident in which, during a sortie against the enemy camp, Guy of Lusignan plunged into the fray in order to rescue Conrad, who was surrounded by enemy soldiers and on the point of succumbing. (There is no knowing whether Conrad, in similar circumstances, would have done as much for Guy; he was

---

* Conrad, it will be remembered, was the brother of Sibylla's first husband. This relationship clearly did not confer any rights on him.

the more able of the two claimants, but he was also the tougher and more unscrupulous.)

Richard Coeur-de-Lion

After the fall of Acre, the Crusading army was exhausted and terribly reduced in numbers. So many soldiers died before Acre that it can be estimated that one in four, possibly even one in every two, perished either in battle or from disease. The mere recital of the barons and knights of high estate who died during the siege gives an idea of what the mortality rate as a whole must have been. To an entire generation of Christian knights, the siege of Acre was to remain *the* siege. It can be compared to the memory of the battle of Verdun for those who fought in the 1914–1918 war, for although the number of victims was smaller, so too were the numbers of men involved in the fighting, and the losses, for the period, were appalling. Contemporary chroniclers mention over 100,000 dead and testify that epidemics and famine claimed many more victims than the Saracen armies. The survivors, too, were mostly in pitiful condition.

The fortress which had held out so magnificently for almost two years fell at last, after the surrender of the garrison who, their strength exhausted, had negotiated against Saladin's wishes. The defenders, who numbered about three thousand, were hailed by the Crusaders themselves as heroes and placed in a prison camp to wait for the ransom which the Sultan was to pay for their release. This ransom was a huge one: 200,000 gold dinars, with the release of 2500 Frankish prisoners and the restitution of the True Cross. The fall of Acre was a triumph for the Crusaders and a cause of despair to the Moslems, because Saladin had appealed in vain to all the powers of Islam in an attempt to follow the example of the Franks and set in motion a mass movement of volunteers for the *jihad,* from Baghdad to Granada. He must have realized that Jerusalem did not mean to the Moslems what it did to the Christians. His own emirs were weary and supplied him with only seasonal contingents, and he was having difficulty in maintaining a sufficient force in the country.

Acre, which had been a Christian city for eighty-three years, had become one again after four years of Moslem rule, and although there was still a small Moslem minority in the cities of the Syrian coast, Islam had no vital interest in retaining possession of these cities. For the Christians, however, the capture of Acre had been a necessity because of the huge sacrifices demanded by the siege. All the same, the great port, though one of the keys to the great pilgrimage to Jerusalem, was far from being Jerusalem itself.

Consequently, once installed in the suburbs of Acre and the outskirts of the city, the army very quickly relapsed into a state of pleasurable inertia. The victory which had cost so much was not living up to expectation. Rivalries and intrigues among the leaders were growing keener, and Richard Coeur-de-Lion was making the most of his popularity with the soldiers and the immense wealth he had acquired in Cyprus* to behave as though he were undisputed leader of the Crusade. As this was really an international venture, most of the princes and leaders of the Crusade bitterly resented the King of England's haughty attitude. Richard's insolence toward his comrades in arms had no limits. When Leopold, Archduke of Austria, had planted his banners on one of the towers of Acre— as he had every right to do—Richard had it publicly torn down and flung into the latrines, and Leopold tried in vain to obtain compensation for the outrage.†

Philip Augustus, who had not had the good luck to conquer Cyprus and who moreover was seriously ill, could do nothing against his rival's dictatorial tendencies. The competition between Guy of Lusignan and Conrad of Montferrat divided the victors' camp into two parties which no longer bothered to conceal their mutual hostility. Richard did his best to worsen the situation by affecting not to recognize in the Holy Land any other authority than his own. A spirit of jealousy was arising between the Syrian barons, dispossessed owners of the Eastern provinces, and the new Crusaders— by far the more numerous. Philip Augustus, in order to check Richard's policy, insisted upon Conrad's rights. Finally, Richard's opinion prevailed; an agreement was reached by the terms of which Guy kept his title of King of Jerusalem and Conrad was made his heir presumptive and kept Tyre and also Beirut and Sidon (the two latter cities being still to conquer). Conrad quite clearly had not much to gain from this position of "heir": he was older than Guy.

All in all, the Frankish barons considered themselves slighted and no longer concealed their distrust of the Plantagenet. Then Philip Augustus, whose state of health was giving rise to the most acute anxiety, decided to leave the insalubrious land of Syria and return to France. It is only fair to say that his departure was by no means

* He had sold Cyprus to the Templars and consequently possessed plenty of ready money.

† Leopold's revenge is well known. Richard's captivity after his departure from the Holy Land was to contribute greatly to his legend.

a desertion: he left his entire army behind him, entrusting its command to Hugh III, Duke of Burgundy, and specifying that every stronghold that was conquered with the help of the French should belong to Conrad of Montferrat. This shows how far Richard's behavior had annoyed him. Nevertheless, whatever the King of England's faults, the army at that time clearly needed a single strong leader, and Richard was the only man capable of filling the role.

The departure of the King of France left a certain uneasiness in the camp, especially among the French and the vassals of the crown. Richard's popularity among the troops increased, and his arrogance with it. Less than six weeks after the capitulation of Acre, Richard ordered all the prisoners to be beheaded because Saladin was slow in sending him the 200,000 dinars and the True Cross. The massacre took place outside the city, on an open space facing Tel Keisan, where a part of Saladin's army was still encamped. The victims numbered three thousand (2700 according to Ambroise who, however pro-English, does not seem proud of it). This was the first time the Crusading armies had indulged in such a cold-blooded slaughter of prisoners, and there is no doubt that Richard was responsible, because the crime was carried out on his express orders.

Saladin had not refused to honor the agreement (signed without his consent) between the Crusaders and the garrison of Acre. He had merely asked for time to collect the demanded sum, and since Saladin had not even been informed legally, Richard's action was consequently a violation of his oath. The *Estoire d'Éracles* shows that the Franks of Syria were horrified and angered by this barbarous act, which did them more harm than it did the passing Crusaders. Saladin's indignation is easy to imagine. The True Cross, which was already in his camp, all ready to be solemnly restored to the Christians, was sent back to Damascus where the Sultan had it tossed into store. There was naturally no further question of the release of the Frankish prisoners, although Saladin had the generosity not to have them killed as reprisals. But he let it be known that in future he would take no prisoners.

Richard was first and foremost a general. From a strictly military point of view the execution of the prisoners can be explained quite easily: he wished to continue the campaign as quickly as possible, before the morale of his army disintegrated completely, and also for fear of allowing Saladin to reorganize his forces. He had no wish to leave three thousand prisoners—redoubtable warriors, as he was only too well aware—in a half-disarmed city guarded by weakened and demoralized troops, yet neither could he take the prisoners with him, nor be sure of keeping them fed and guarded. The simplest way out was to eliminate them. The continuation of the war was more important than the gold of their ransom. As for the lives of the captive "dogs," as Ambroise describes them, the Plantagenet does not seem to have regarded them as in the least important. He had not even the excuse of being motivated by hatred or fanaticism, but by a moment's irritation at the very most. (The *Éracles* claims that the number of the slain amounted to sixteen thousand, which is clearly untrue. But Richard would no doubt have massacred sixteen thousand men just as readily.)

Richard was determined to embark on the conquest of the coast, and after he had to some extent shaken the soldiers out of their lethargy by presenting them with the spectacle of this bloodbath, he gathered together willy-nilly as many troops as he could find in a condition to fight and left Acre with quite a strong army, and one at least in a good state of discipline. Thanks to their discipline and the strength of their armor, the Franks were able to withstand all Saladin's attacks on their flank. Before Arsuf, on September 7, 1191, the courage of the Crusading chivalry, and Richard's strategic gifts above all, enabled the Franks to defeat Saladin's numerically greatly superior army. Once again, it was to be seen that when the Frankish chivalry was well commanded and able to take the initiative in a charge, nothing could stand against it.

Saladin had to fall back in despair, with enormous losses. The Franks advanced along the coast, spreading terror wherever they went, for the cities which had been held by Moslem garrisons for four years did not risk holding out for long. The emirs told Saladin, "If you want to defend Ascalon, go there yourself, or send one of your elder sons; otherwise not one of us will go after what happened to the defenders of Acre."[7] Richard's brutal policy was bearing fruit. With death in his heart, Saladin decided to destroy the walls of Ascalon, so as to prevent the Franks from using the fortress. He also destroyed Jaffa, the second most important of the coastal strongholds still in his hands. Richard reached Jaffa, which had been abandoned by the Moslem troops, and set about rebuilding it. Meanwhile, Saladin was organizing the defense of Jerusalem.

Distinctly discouraged despite the brilliant victory of Arsuf, the Crusading army lingered on the outskirts of Jaffa where, as at Acre, there were a great many women of loose morals (brought by sea from Europe by specialists in the white-slave trade who had decided to take their own part in the Crusade). "Ah, mercy," sighs Ambroise, "what evil weapons with which to reconquer God's heritage!"[8] In fact, the Crusading army had lost a good deal of its enthusiasm and will to fight outside Acre. Although it marched against Jerusalem twice (at Christmas 1191 and in June 1192) it was never to take it. It was already too diminished and pulled in too many different directions by conflicting interests, and the passion for "God's heritage" only returned spasmodically—as it did at Beit Nuba (Betenoble), twelve miles from Jerusalem, at the end of 1191, where, according to Ambroise, the soldiers' fervor and excitement reached its peak. They believed themselves really on the eve of laying siege to Jerusalem. There, those who had never seen the Holy Sepulcher were in the majority, and they were almost like Godfrey of Bouillon's Crusaders.

But acting on the advice of the Franks of Syria and the military orders, who were more familiar with the situation, Richard drew back before the perils of a siege which would have been tougher than that of Acre and carried out under much less favorable conditions. Saladin had made a desert of the whole region, so as to prevent the Franks from settling there again. From a strategic point of view, the retreat was fully justified, but the army's morale suffered dangerously as a result.

Richard himself, realizing the difficulties of any attempt to reconquer the place, opened negotiations with Saladin and proposed to give his sister Joanna (the widow of William II of Sicily) in marriage to Saladin's brother Malik al-Adil. The couple would reign jointly over Jerusalem, which would remain under Moslem control but with ample privileges for Christians. This in itself amounted to abandoning all hope of the reconquest of the Holy Places. The King of England, who was not the most logical of men, suddenly found himself full of sympathy for Saladin, when only a few months before he had been slaughtering his faithful warriors. Saladin could hardly feel any sympathy for Richard, but he had to admire his military talents and respected his royal title. The curious compromise—which in fact pledged Saladin to nothing—almost came about, but Queen Joanna refused to marry a Moslem.*

Richard's sudden friendly feelings toward the enemies of Christendom can be explained by his violent dislike of the Franks of Syria. It was they and not the Crusaders who really had something to gain from the reconquest of the kingdom. While Richard was

* Both sides concerned appear to have been anxious for the negotiations to be successful. Richard was known to be extremely fond of his sister, and this proves his good faith in the matter. When it was suggested to Malik al-Adil that he should become converted to Christianity, far from rejecting the idea indignantly he asked for time to think about it, an unheard-of thing to do. In the end, however, he did not agree.

negotiating with Saladin, Conrad of Montferrat on his side was doing the same. Each was trying to win the Sultan's support in order to frustrate the ambitions of the other. This was a far cry from the climate of the holy war which had existed during the first months of the siege of Acre. In April 1192, Richard summoned all the Frankish barons of the kingdom and the leaders of the Crusade to Ascalon (which he had recaptured and partially rebuilt), and asked them to settle the differences between Guy of Lusignan and Conrad of Montferrat once and for all. Whether or not he thought that his candidate would get the majority of votes, the fact remains that the barons almost unanimously chose Conrad. This was a blatant insult to the King of England, but he was obliged to bear it with a good grace. Conrad was to be crowned at Acre and become, with the consent of the Western powers as well as of the Franks of Syria, King of Jerusalem, or more accurately, of Tyre, Acre, Jaffa, and Ascalon.

There was general rejoicing in what remained of the Frankish colony in Syria. Much was expected of Conrad. He was a man of strong will and great ambitions, capable, stubborn, cunning, and fearless. His joy, like that of his supporters, was short-lived. He died from an Assassin's dagger a few days after his election.

According to Beha ed-Din, the murderers accused Richard of instigating the murder. Ibn al-Athir, however, expressly incriminates Saladin. The chroniclers of Frankish Syria believed that this was the Ismailians' vengeance on their own account. Given the facts presented by Ibn al-Athir, the second theory seems the most plausible. From Saladin's point of view, this was not actually an assassination in the modern sense of the word: the Ismailians owed him the blood of an enemy of the faith, and he was paying the heretics to perform a ritual murder of the kind that he himself had perpetrated upon the person of Reynald of Châtillon. He had every reason to fear the rule of a man like Conrad in Frankish Syria. The same act on Richard's part would have been surprising. It would have been easier for him to use as his instrument one of his own knights, among whom Conrad had no shortage of enemies. What is known of his character suggests that he was not a man to make arrangements with Moslems for the killing of a Christian prince, and the evidence of the murderers means nothing in itself beyond the fact that the master of the Assassins had his reasons for wishing to add to the discord among the Franks.

Whatever the truth of the matter, the death of Conrad of Montferrat must have made both Richard and Saladin very happy. The latter was rid of a vigorous Frankish leader who had been deter-

mined to remain in the country and fight to the end for the recovery of the Holy Places. Richard now had no rival in the Holy
Land and became once again the supreme head of the Crusade.
For the Franks of Syria, this Crusade was the last chance of winning
back their lost provinces, while basically the King of England was
only thinking of getting the whole thing over with as quickly as possible without loss of face. News was already reaching him from
France and England of the rebellion of his brother John and of
Philip Augustus's attacks on his provinces in Normandy, and he was
realizing that the Crusade was a long-drawn-out affair demanding
greater resources of men and money than he would ever possess.

After Conrad's death, Richard gave up any idea of forcing Guy
of Lusignan on the Syrian barons. He found a more innocuous candidate, and one who was, for lack of an alternative, able to unite
all votes. This was the Count of Champagne, Henry II, who was both
his own nephew and the nephew of the King of France.* In this
way the French and English factions could both consider themselves
satisfied. The young Count was not particularly anxious to end his
days in the Holy Land; he accepted the crown of Jerusalem as a duty,
but without enthusiasm: in order to become King he would first
have to marry Isabella of Jerusalem, who (according to Ibn al-Athir
and Ernoul) was pregnant at that time, and the crown would go by
right to this child if it were a boy.

Consequently, Isabella was no sooner widowed of her second
husband than she was united to a third, in spite of her resistance
and objections. It was necessary for reasons of state and in the
interests of Christianity. Isabella was twenty-two and, Ambroise asserts, very pretty; it seems that neither she nor Henry of Champagne
ever regretted their hasty marriage.

The wedding was celebrated with great pomp in Tyre, a week
after the murder of Conrad of Montferrat. There were "processions,
the streets were hung with carpets, and censers full of incense hung
at every window and outside all the houses." With barely time to
mourn for the Marquis who had been crowned less than a fortnight
before with banquets and acclamations, another man had already
taken over his crown and his wife. Henry II was neither a great warrior nor a strong personality and had nothing to recommend him
but a great feudal title and his royal connections. He was a young
man of gentle and placid disposition, adequately brave and with a
fair amount of common sense.

The real reason for the delight shown by the Latin barons and citi-

---

* Henry was the son of Marie de France, the daughter of Louis VII and
Eleanor of Aquitaine.

zens of the Holy Land at the coronation was that both were hoping that Richard, now that he finally had a candidate of his own choice on the throne of Jerusalem, would waste no more time in setting out to conquer the Holy Places. Richard, however, had not the slightest wish to do this, and the army had literally to force his hand. Ambroise, who was very much in favor of Richard, is precise on this point: there was no one, he says "who did not show uncontrollable delight [at the idea of marching on Jerusalem], excepting only the King. He did not in the least rejoice and went to bed, thoroughly upset by the news he had received."[9] Richard's one thought was of how he could manage to set sail for Europe, and while the army was advancing on the Holy City in a state of indescribable enthusiasm, weeping with joy and convinced that the real Crusade was beginning at last, the King was hesitating, temporizing, and setting up camp twelve miles from Jerusalem. Saladin had had all the springs and wells poisoned and Richard foresaw the difficulties of a siege in a desert country with no drinking water in the height of summer (June 1192). He had the idea of causing a diversion in Egypt, maneuvered his army between Beit Nuba and Ramleh, and despite the insistence of the barons, and of the Duke of Burgundy, leader of the French contingents, in particular, he refused to undertake the siege of the Holy City.

According to Beha ed-Din, Saladin's camp was in complete confusion and he himself the only person anxious to defend Jerusalem at all costs. His emirs were weary and disgruntled; they knew from experience what the energy of the King of England and the tenacity of the Christians could be like, and they almost advised him to give up the struggle, saying, "For a long time our armies were able to defend the Moslem empire without need of Jerusalem."[10] If Richard had really wanted to, he could at that moment have launched a decisive attack on the city, which the Moslems had held for only five years. It was underpopulated and defended reluctantly and without conviction. Saladin, himself half inclined to give it up, lay prostrate in the Mosque of al-Aqsa, shedding bitter tears. On July 4, Richard struck camp and ordered a retreat, to the great indignation of the entire Crusading army.

There was consternation among the Crusaders and joy in Saladin's camp. Once again the King of England negotiated, and in the most courteous terms. What Richard offered Saladin was the setting up of a kingdom of Jerusalem as a Moslem protectorate. Henry of Champagne, as King, if not of Jerusalem, at least of the coast of Syria, would become a vassal of the Sultan and fight for him against his

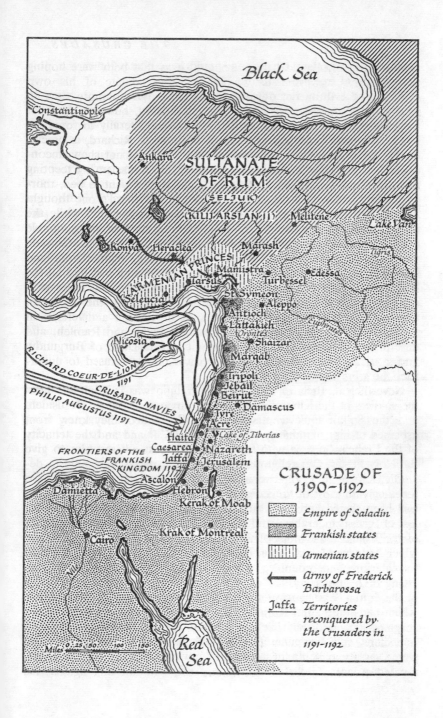

Black Sea

Constantinople

Ankara

SULTANATE
OF RUM
(SELJUK)
(KILIJ ARSLAN II)

Melitene

Lake Van

Konya

Heraclea

Marash

ARMENIAN PRINCES

Mamistra

Tarsus

Turbessel

Edessa

Seleucia

St Symeon

Aleppo

Antioch

Lattakieh

Orontes

Shaizar

Nicosia

Marqab

Tripoli

Jébail

Beirut

Damascus

Tyre

Acre

Haifa

Lake of Tiberias

Caesarea

Nazareth

Jaffa

Jerusalem

Ascalon

Hebron

Damietta

Kerak of Moab

Cairo

Krak of Montreal

Nile

RICHARD COEUR-DE-LION 1191

CRUSADER NAVIES

PHILIP AUGUSTUS 1191

FRONTIERS OF THE
FRANKISH
KINGDOM 1192

Tigris

Euphrates

Red
Sea

Miles 0 25 50 100 150

CRUSADE OF
1190–1192

Empire of Saladin

Frankish states

Armenian states

Army of Frederick
Barbarossa

Jaffa Territories
reconquered by
the Crusaders in
1191–1192

enemies. In Jerusalem, Christians should have possession of the Holy Sepulcher and free access to the Holy Places.

After successfully recapturing Jaffa, which had been stormed by Moslem troops, and giving up hope of holding Ascalon, Richard signed a peace treaty with Saladin. There was an exchange of civilities which says less about the spirit of mutual comprehension between the two princes than about their haste to put an end to hostilities. For Saladin, Richard's attitude was an unexpected piece of luck, and he was only too glad to make the English King's task easier by loading him with protestations of esteem and even of admiration. For Richard, who was no diplomat, it was a matter of saving face by flattering his opponent and so appearing to be giving up his plans less out of weakness than from motives of humanity and sympathy for the great Moslem leader. "I want your friendship and affection," he wrote. "You are no more permitted to send all your Moslems to their deaths than I am all our Franks."[11] It goes without saying that the Duke of Burgundy and his French barons did not approve of this policy in the least and were disgusted to find themselves unwilling accomplices in what they regarded as a shameful desertion. Their discontent showed itself in accusations, bitter jokes, and satirical songs, but it did not reach the point of armed rebellion: they too were tired of the war.

Nevertheless, Richard did attempt to influence Saladin to forbid the soldiers of the King of France to make pilgrimages to Jerusalem, and the Sultan took a mischievous delight in making the King ashamed of his unkindness. "There are here," he answered—speaking of the French—"people who have come from far off in order to visit the Holy Places. Our religion forbids us to prevent them."[12]

On October 9, 1192, Richard Coeur-de-Lion left the Holy Land, together with most of the knights and soldiers of the Crusade. Peace had been signed and the Crusade was over. This peace ratified the loss of Jerusalem, Galilee, Judaea, and Transjordan. All that remained of the Frankish kingdom of Jerusalem was the coastal cities: Tyre, which had never fallen, Acre, Haifa, Caesarea, Arsuf, and Jaffa, and in the interior of the country, half the lands of Lydda and Ramleh. A "King of Jerusalem" ruled at Acre, under the accepted protectorate of the Sultan. The county of Tripoli and the principality of Antioch, which had stood apart from the Crusade, were no more than narrow strips of land wedged in between territories held by the Armenians, Ismailians, and Aleppans. Though still Frankish provinces, they too were vassals of Saladin's empire, governed by quite pacifically minded princes (Bohemond III at Antioch and his younger son,

Bohemond IV, at Tripoli), and the two former great fiefs of the kingdom had fallen to the level of the small Armenian principalities of Cilicia, halfheartedly attacked and equally halfheartedly defended, caught up in the monotonous shifts of petty feudal wars and inspiring neither the hate nor fear of the Moslems, the greed of the Greeks, who had other things to worry about, nor the interest of Europe.

The End of the Crusade

This was not the end of the Crusades. Italian fleets and German armies were still to attempt to take up the war in the East again on their own account. Christians and Moslems would still win and lose strongholds in Syria. But the fact was that there was no longer a Frankish Syria nor a kingdom of Jerusalem, but only a kind of Frankish colony, closely dependent on the West, and a few trading posts.

Richard's conquest of Cyprus proved a lasting one. The great island, repurchased from the Templars and given to Guy of Lusignan as a kind of compensation, went after his death to his brother Amalric, the former constable of Jerusalem and lover of Agnes of Courtenay, who was to become the chief beneficiary of the troubles of which he had to some extent been the cause. After the accidental death of Henry of Champagne, Amalric, King of Cyprus, became the fourth husband of Isabella of Jerusalem and bore the title of King of Jerusalem under the name of Amalric II.

The "kingdom" had become a legal fiction, an excuse for ambitions and struggles for power in the West and for political dreams at once too large and too vague because basically lacking in a real object. Twelve years after the winding-up of the great Crusade of 1190–1192, a great Crusading army took Constantinople (1204). This was the tragic end to the long rivalry between the Christian East and West, a rivalry which had been reawakened and sharpened by the Crusades. Twenty-five years later, in 1229, the Emperor of Germany, Frederick II, obtained a treaty ceding Jerusalem to him, only to lose it fifteen years later in 1244. In 1249 Saint Louis attempted the reconquest of the Holy Places without success, and attempted to return there in 1270 by the roundabout route through North Africa, where he died. During the second half of the thirteenth century, the fate of Palestine and Syria was actually decided in the East. In 1291, nearly two hundred years after the preaching of the First Crusade, the last Frankish strongholds, trading ports with a Latin population, fell to the mamelukes.

The idea of the Crusade and of the reconquest of Jerusalem were to remain, for another two centuries, as a collective myth, one of those obsessive ideas which make up the conscience, or rather the guilt complex, of a civilization. Great popes like Innocent III and Gregory IX continued to see in the deliverance of the Holy Places one of the primary objects of their policies. Right in the middle of the Hundred Years' War, great lords were still setting out on armed pilgrimages, not to reconquer the Holy Land, which was lost forever, but at least to confront the infidel and suffer—or die—for Jerusalem. In 1212 there was a "children's Crusade," which was the most useless and tragic of all, and in 1290, on the eve of the fall of the skeletal "kingdom," a people's Crusade. Throughout the thirteenth century, despite the double distraction of the Crusading impulse—first against Constantinople and then against the heretics of Languedoc (not to mention the Spanish Crusades)—it was Jerusalem that remained the real object of pious warriors in the West.

But it was a goal which became—at first unconsciously and then almost consciously—more and more dreamlike and inaccessible, the symbol of a great longing for heroism which was doomed, by definition, to failure.

After this attempt to throw some light on the political and military history of a kingdom which was unique of its kind, it is time to describe briefly the kingdom of Jerusalem itself and the attempt to set up a Western state in the Holy Land. The actual history can be reduced to the eternal game of holding the balance between several rival powers, and the work of a few great statesmen or a few great adventurers; but what makes the history of the kingdom particularly interesting is the specific nature of the double religious war which led on the one hand to the foundation and destruction of the state, and on the other, to the clash on predestined soil of two civilizations and traditions hitherto unknown to one another.

CHAPTER

X

Frankish Syria, a Doomed Kingdom

The Death of Saladin

The Frankish kingdom of Jerusalem had endured for eighty-eight years—a long lifetime. At the time of the capture of Jerusalem by Saladin, there was still an old man who had come to Syria as a child with Godfrey of Bouillon's troops and been present at the capture of the Holy City by the Crusaders.

Jerusalem had had eight Frankish kings (nine, if we include little Baldwin V), eight kings the first of whom was merely the Advocate of the Holy Sepulcher and was so for barely a year, and the last of whom reigned only a year before losing the kingdom and died six years later as King of Cyprus. Six were actual ruling kings. If there was a decline in the royal line itself, this was due to the health of Baldwin IV. If he had not been a leper, there is every likelihood that he would have kept a firm grip on a kingdom that was seriously threatened but not yet lost, and sired sons to carry on his work. Common though leprosy was in the Middle Ages, the case of a leper king and one who had been a leper from earliest childhood is unique in history, and this remarkable exception had to occur in a kingdom which was already sufficiently remarkable on other counts.

Saladin had reconquered Palestine, leaving the Christians only a section of the coast, despite all the tremendous effort provided by the Crusading armies of the West. Richard of England had hurriedly disbanded an international undertaking which was not his work, in which he was not directly concerned, and whose importance he could not properly estimate. Less than six months after Richard's departure, Saladin died. The vast Ayubid empire was broken up and the great Sultan's sons, brothers, and nephews quarreled over the inheritance. If the Crusading army, however demoralized, had remained in the country it could easily have reconquered Jerusalem at that moment. Moreover, this army, with an abundance of supplies brought in by all the navies of the West, would have run little risk if it had camped within reach of the Syrian ports. But no one could have foreseen the death of Saladin, who was only fifty-six years old and apparently full of vigor.

The third great Crusade had been cut short, condemning what remained of Frankish Syria to an artificial existence with no real future and with no independence or identity of its own. Once again the little colony in the East, clinging firmly to the Syrian coast, was to spend a century fighting for survival. Right up to the end the remnants of the former population of the kingdom, and in particular the erstwhile Frankish nobility, constituted its most stubborn, intelligent, and lively element.

As we have seen, Saladin himself only escaped by a narrow margin from being swept away by the wave of enthusiasm for the Crusade. Moslem dominion over Syria was only made possible at that moment by the death of Frederick Barbarossa and later by the incompetence of Richard Coeur-de-Lion. In Palestine more than anywhere else, a cosmopolitan province which for a thousand years had lacked any kind of religious or national unity and had always been a prey to conquerors, the destiny of the country had been closely linked to the outcome of battles and the character of the great leader of the moment. (Admittedly, it can be said that if the German barons and Frederick's army had been motivated by a real Crusading zeal, they would have constituted a redoubtable force even without the Emperor, and that the Crusaders of 1192 could have done without Richard and continued the holy war in spite of him if they had really wanted to. This is a difficult point to answer, but there are other examples to show that the will of the people alone has never conquered or created anything. It can be a determining factor, but it remains ineffectual unless expressed in the actions of a leader.

The disappearance or the incapacity of a leader condemns movements that are perfectly viable in themselves to failure.)

The hosts of pilgrim Crusaders of 1189 were certainly animated by a more fervent and disinterested zeal than that which had impelled the soldiers of the First Crusade along the road to the East. Their numbers were greater and their reasons for fighting stronger. They were not facing a unified and organized Islam, but only a temporary conqueror, not very well established in the possession of an overgrown empire. (The idea of Islamic solidarity had undoubtedly made great strides in the preceding hundred years, but it still remained subordinated to the interests and ambitions of princes, and Frederick Barbarossa had had little trouble in reaching an understanding with Kilij Arslan II against Saladin.) Once again, the Crusade had been played out like a game of chess, or even poker, with luck taking the place of skill among the players. When Saladin saw the English and French Crusaders take ship in the wake of Richard Coeur-de-Lion, it must have been the happiest day of his life. It was only on that day that he could regard the conquest of Palestine as final, or at least lasting. Time was to have a chance to work for Islam.

The interior of the country had already been swept virtually clear of Latin colonists, and Saladin had demolished castles, burned farms, and destroyed orchards and vineyards in order to prevent the Franks from settling again in their former possessions. Judaea, which until the twelfth century had been relatively prosperous, was never to recover from the blow. The one thing that was a vital necessity to the kings of Jerusalem, the wealth of the land, was of no importance in the eyes of the great Kurdish warrior, who was temperamentally and atavistically a nomad. For Islam, Palestine was and remained a minor province.

The war was over. Pilgrimages were made safe for all, Christians and Moslems alike. At last Saladin was making preparations for his own pilgrimage to Mecca, the great religious duty which every year he had put off until later, for lack of time and money. He was a man of exemplary piety, but he never had the supreme consolation of beholding Mecca. He died after a short illness on March 3, 1193. In fact, we cannot be sure that he would ever have made the journey even had he lived to be a very old man. He was one of those men who are always absorbed in some urgent business, incapable of thinking of themselves, even in a matter of such necessary and legitimate satisfaction as the great pilgrimage. After his death all that was found in his treasury was "forty-seven Nacerite dirhems and one Syrian gold piece. He left neither goods, nor houses, furniture, gardens, village, nor plowed land, nor any kind of property."[1] "He who had possessed such riches," says his biographer, but in fact he had never had any possessions, because he coveted none.

He was a man of great ambitions, but simple and modest in his private life, careless of protocol and so good-natured as to be almost weak. Beha ed-Din describes him, at an officer's meeting, asking several times for a drink without anyone troubling to bring him a glass of water. Nothing does a great leader more honor than a trait of this kind. The Caesars never wanted for flatterers to hang on their lips and tremble in case they should fail to forestall their slightest wish. For the powerful Sultan to be so badly served he must really have inspired a trust that was complete and unthinking.

As we have seen, this extraordinary man's behavior was, to begin with, anything but saintly. He was not incapable of cruelty or duplicity, and as a politician he was a determined opportunist, calculating, cold, cunning, and unscrupulous; he also possessed the art of manipulating people to a remarkable degree and managed to put a good face on even his most questionable actions (such as his treatment of Nur ed-Din and his son). It was only after his decisive victory over the Christians at Hattin that he appeared in his true stature and, as a man of petty origins, seemed to be trying to eclipse kings and emperors by his greatness of spirit. This was more than merely the luxury of a parvenu: he seems to have been naturally direct and impulsive, and to have cared little for the opinions of others. To support this there is an unexpectedly childish incident quoted by Ibn al-Athir. After the capture of Menbij a certain number of precious objects were found in the city engraved with the name Yusuf—the name of one of the defeated sheik's sons. Saladin took the things for himself, exclaiming, "I am Yusuf, and I shall take what has been kept for me."[2] He did not keep it for long. The man who could take a gold vase because he found it amusing to see his name engraved on it gave away everything he gained in war, gave it to the conquered, to women and children, and the thing for which Moslems and Christians chiefly praised him was his "almsgiving."

He was so consistent in his policy of executing the knights of the military orders that this must really have been the result of a religious scruple or the fulfillment of a vow. Where his other opponents, whoever they were, were concerned, it must be said that his humanity usually exceeded that of more "civilized" epochs. But when he heard that a "young man named Sohraouerdi was failing to acknowledge prescriptions of the law and setting at nought the dogma of the faith," he ordered his son to put the culprit to death at once.[3] There is no doubt that he was a fanatic, but he was so much a man of action and so conscious of the human realities behind his actions that in practice he was able, as if in spite of himself, to rise to a magnanimity of spirit rare enough in his time, or indeed in any time.

The Franks of Syria and the European Christians could offer themselves the sad consolation that they had not been vanquished by any ordinary adversary, and this consideration had a great deal to do with Saladin's posthumous fame in the West, although if the great Sultan hoped by doing good to demonstrate the excellence of his religion he did not convince the Franks, who were content with including him among those infidels almost worthy of being Christians. He died, and they admired him for his humanity and simplicity. The joy of those Franks left in Syria must have been somewhat bitter: the great empire was now broken up and divided between the Sultan's sons, who were young and incompetent, and whom their uncle, Malik al-Adil, was concentrating on keeping under his thumb. This was the perfect opportunity for the Franks to recover the kingdom, but there was no longer any Crusading army, and the opportunity would not come again.

The kingdom which for practical purposes had been dead for five years was now dead in sober earnest. It would be ten or twenty years before fresh hosts of Crusaders decided to take the road to the Holy Land once more.

The Latin Kingdom of Jerusalem

In the days of its prosperity the kingdom of Jerusalem had covered the whole of the Syrian coast from Gaza as far as Cilicia, all the hinterland as far as the valley of the Jordan and beyond, and had stretched for about thirty miles to the east and southeast of the Dead Sea. In area it was larger than the kingdoms of Damascus and Aleppo (if the great fiefs of Tripoli and Antioch are included as part of the kingdom); militarily it was powerful enough to provide a counterbalance to the ambitions of states like the kingdom of Mosul and to act as arbiter between Egypt and Damascus. The growing importance of its commercial ports and the flow of pilgrims to Jerusalem made it comparatively wealthy. The question remains whether it was ever a viable proposition, whether its existence answered to local or international needs, whether, in fact, it was a *nation* in formation or simply a historical accident of no real significance.

The Holy Places, as Saladin had realized, would never cease to be *the* Holy Places of Christianity, and nothing would ever be able to stop Christians from going there on pilgrimage. But as we have seen, from the point of view of the pilgrim's interests the kingdom of Jerusalem was a great acquisition for Christians, and it was chiefly from this angle that the majority of people in Europe regarded it. The year 1187 brought a harsh awakening: people realized that God had not granted Christians the guardianship of the Holy Places forever. Jerusalem had been lost again—and it was the Christians in Syria, the Syrian Franks, who were naturally held responsible for its loss.

The only explanation for the scandal of the occupation of the Holy Places by Moslems had to be that the Franks had become unworthy of divine protection and that Saladin's virtues made him worthy to be the instrument of God's anger. A section of Franks in Syria—and the clergy in particular—shared this view. But the kingdom was also something more than a place of pilgrimage entrusted to the keeping of European Christians, good or bad. It was a state: a medieval, feudal, and consequently particularist state, jealous of its independence, proud of its traditions, and developing, with a speed which would seem surprising in our own time, a lively and complex national sentiment.

It has been shown that the kings of Jerusalem appealed on a number of occasions to the Capet kings of France, thus implicitly acknowledging themselves the King of France's vassals. In fact they were nothing of the kind. Godfrey of Bouillon had been a baron of the Empire, and Baldwin I had sworn fealty to no one (or to no one but the Patriarch of Jerusalem: an oath which was purely a legal fiction). The nobility of the kingdom was largely of French origin (Picards, Walloons, Ardennais, Champenois, and Burgundians, Normans in Antioch and Provençaux in Tripoli), and their traditional attachment to the royal house of France seems natural enough. The King was a long way away, and had he raised any claim of a practical nature to the Frankish lands of Syria it would obviously not have been well received. The Baldwins, and even Fulk of Anjou, wore the crown of Jerusalem to be masters there after God. And so their subjects understood it.

Frankish Colonization and Its Nature

Colonists of Latin origin preferred to settle in the cities, except in Judaea and in Galilee, where Frankish peasants gradually took the place of the Moslem peasantry which had emigrated in 1099. But even here the peasantry remained largely indigenous, either Moslem or made up of Christian immigrants from the provinces of Oultrejourdain.

It was in the cities that the East was gradually to have its effect on the Western immigrants, gradually modifying their habits and outlook and, in consequence, exerting an influence on the distant West itself.

As early as 1098, the Crusaders took over one of the greatest cities in the Near East: Antioch. A year later they captured Jerusalem, although the circumstances admittedly left them little leisure to contemplate its beauties. Ten years later they took Tripoli, the principal city on the coast and famous for its wealth and its commercial, industrial, and intellectual activity. Even less important cities, like Jaffa, Arsuf, Tortosa, Arqa, and others, surpassed the greatest European cities in comfort and cleanliness. All in all, the Crusades gave huge numbers of people from Europe the chance of coming into contact, for the first time, with another way of life and with a civilization richer, more complex, and more highly developed than their own.

It is a fact that, from the very first contact, the Crusaders behaved like real barbarians, a fact which can perhaps be attributed to the particular character of their anarchic and fanatical infantry. But at that period even troops not on a Crusade regarded the right of pillage as their natural prerogative. Antioch does not appear to have been too severely plundered, since it was after all a Christian city and belonged, in principle, to the Byzantine Empire.

The way in which Jerusalem was delivered over to fire and slaughter has already been seen. The victors barely spared Christian shrines such as the Tower of David and palaces in which their leaders had billeted themselves on the first day. The city was not destroyed, but so ravaged and depopulated that at first kings of Jerusalem found great difficulty in restoring a certain degree of prosperity. Tripoli, where the Crusaders had not even the so-called excuse of being driven by motives of fanaticism, is known to have been partially sacked and pillaged by Genoese sailors in direct violation of the treaty of surrender. The library of the Banū Ammar in particular, the greatest in Syria for the quality as well as the quantity of the books which were kept there, was scattered and destroyed. This was a treasure whose value the Crusading soldiers were completely incapable of appreciating.

The soldiers plundered and their leaders set them an example, while as we have seen, the representatives of the Church had no scruples about robbing their Eastern colleagues. The True Cross, the most revered relic of all, which was to play such a mighty part in the life of the kingdom up to the fall of Jerusalem itself, had been seized by threats and force from its original owners, the Greek monks of the Holy Sepulcher. It is not to be deduced from this that every city was systematically plundered and all the inhabitants deprived of their property; there were not enough Crusaders to do this and they had nothing to gain by it. The capture of Jerusalem and Caesarea remain fearful exceptions. Other cities in fact suffered no more from the Crusades than any city was bound to suffer in time of war and at a period when the soldiery was naturally brutal, but where the greater number of the inhabitants took no part in the war and were content to bow their heads and wait for the storm to pass.

Occasionally, when a city was taken by storm, there was street fighting in which the civilian population was not spared, and women especially, since they were regarded as part of the justly acquired spoils of war. But even in these cases most of the people escaped, and after a few days life returned pretty much to normal. Although impoverished by war, by plunder, and by the departure, voluntary or otherwise, of a part of their population, those Eastern cities occupied by the Crusaders remained busy, wealthy centers of commerce, industry, and craftsmanship considerably more intense than that of Western cities, and the Latin colonists—French or Italian—formed only a minority of their population.

There was a fairly striking contrast between any Western city, even the capital of a kingdom, and an Eastern city such as, for example, Antioch (to say nothing of Constantinople or Baghdad). This was not merely a difference between two kinds of civilization; it was an unquestionable superiority of culture and living standards, a superiority which, on an intellectual and moral level, the Westerners were unable to appreciate. (This was not out of natural boorishness, but simply because they did not understand the language.) On the level of technical achievements, refinement of manners, and the outward comforts of life, they realized it very well and—understandably—adapted very quickly.

This adaptation took place all the more quickly in that the contrast between the two civilizations was much less great than it would be today. Both were the heirs, directly or indirectly, of Greco-Roman and later of Byzantine civilization, and the Eastern and Western civilizations were still united by fairly close ties of kinship. It must not be forgotten that buildings for religious or military use in Syria and Palestine were frequently the work of Greek architects, while early Romanesque churches in France, Germany, and Italy were completely Byzantine in inspiration. Moorish influences penetrated through Spain into southern and central France, while in southern Italy and Sicily, Greek and Arab traditions existed side by side. The sacred art of Europe was still almost entirely derived from the Byzantine and its decorative art strongly influenced by the Moslem East, and by Persia in particular. At this period Europe still regarded the East as the land not only of wealth and luxury but also of technical and artistic progress. It was in general a model to be imitated as far as possible, but one which people had as yet no idea of equaling.

In this, the Latins can be compared to people in the so-called underdeveloped countries today, who envy Western technological superiority without any conception of its moral superiority, and very often seeing only the technical side of a civilization whose spiritual content escapes them. This is of course a very approximate comparison: in other respects relations between the medieval Latin West and the Greek or Moslem East were of course by no means comparable to those existing today between Western civilization and the rest of the world. And neither East nor West attributed to this purely material side of civilization the importance that is generally given to it today. An Arab in the twelfth century would have thought the fact that his city possessed water mains and houses of more than one story a curious thing to be proud of; and to an inhabitant of Troyes or Chartres the comfort of the East was an undoubted advantage but one of quite minor importance. The Arab on the other hand admired a refined thought or a poetical style or the religious fervor of a dervish above all else, while the Latins, illiterate though they were, also had their spiritual traditions which they regarded as superior to all others.

Nevertheless, the Crusaders could hardly fail to be impressed by the comfort and even more by the wealth of the land in which they had settled, and since these riches were theirs for the asking they wanted to take all the advantage of them that they could. We know that very early on, Crusaders coming to the East were shocked by the "effeminate" behavior of those of their countrymen who had become citizens of Syria: effeminate because they had got into the habit of taking frequent baths, using scents and perfumes, wearing shirts of fine cloth, sleeping in sheets, eating from vessels of metal or precious woods, and being served with meals consisting of various exotic dishes flavored with different spices. They surrounded themselves with numerous slaves, wore jewels, garments of cloth of gold, and sometimes even turbans. In doing all this they were merely imitating Eastern lords, and would have thought it strange not to live as the people of the country did.

The great cities of the East possessed conduits of running water fed by cisterns and springs in the mountains. Antioch is known to have had water brought all the year round by miles of underground pipes. Everywhere were numerous pools and public baths, which were a necessity in Islamic countries because frequent washing (four times a day) was a religious duty for Moslems as well as highly advisable in a hot country. The streets were paved, and many were actual mosaics of different-colored stones. The houses were large buildings several stories high, housing numerous families, with terraces on the roofs, internal galleries and balconies, and fountains in the center of the courtyards. Every city had its countless gardens, and on the outskirts were great orchards full of orange and lemon trees, apples, pomegranates, and cherries. A glance at a few Persian miniatures is enough to give an idea of the gracious refinement of Oriental life as it could be lived by the wealthy and noble, for although Syria was not Persia, the same civilization had long created a kind of uniformity in people's way of life. The Latins were discovering an art of living of which at home they could only have had the remotest idea in the form of stories and the fantastic travelers' tales whose echoes come through in poems like the *Pèlerinage de Charlemagne* and the later *Floire et Blancheflor*. It is a fact that the courts of Western princes also presented the spectacle of a luxury which today would deserve to be called Oriental (as indeed it was—the fine carpets and fabrics and even some of the golden ornaments were nearly all imported from the East). Luxury was not entirely the prerogative of the Church, but riches in the West still had a certain hieratic and ceremonial quality, and even the King of France would not have thought of having a marble swimming pool with hot and cold fountains built for himself, or of having gardens laid out filled with carefully cultivated blooms and exotic birds.

Not even Christian women in the East would go out unveiled, and

FRANKISH SYRIA, A DOOMED KINGDOM

the wealthy were more or less completely cloistered in their houses, surrounded by numerous slaves, eunuchs, and bodyguards. They bathed every day, sometimes several times a day, anointed their bodies with sweet-smelling oils, dressed in silk and muslin and in veils woven with gold and silver, and wore bangles and chains of precious metals, worked until they resembled lace and studded with pearls and precious stones, around their necks, wrists, and ankles. Some of these noble ladies fell victims to the soldiers, but on other occasions the Franks were given the opportunity of discovering, in the luxurious creatures whom chance put in their way, an aspect of woman of which they had hitherto been unaware. They married Armenians, and learned to treat captive Moslem ladies with courtesy.

Frankish women very quickly adopted Eastern dress or Eastern styles and also began to wear veils. They vied in elegance and refinement with Arab and Armenian ladies while still retaining their freedom of movement and society, although their menfolk, getting the idea from local customs, seem to have made sporadic attempts to keep them secluded. The changing attitude of men with regard to women, otherwise not easy to explain, which led, in fiction and also in social behavior, to the phenomenon usually known as "courtly love" may well have been a product of the Crusades. It could have been due to Moslem influence, and to that of the Arabs in particular. If Arab influence was at work here, it could also have come from Spain; but it is certain that among the other virtues of Eastern civilization, the Crusaders discovered a kind of respect for women which did not exist in the West.

They could not have appreciated the mystical and love poetry of the Arabs, because Franks who knew and admired Arab literature were few and even those lived in the second half of the century. But they were able to realize that women to the Moslems were the object of a respect that was complete, unconditional, and jealous and which made them almost sacred beings. They could also realize that the origin of this seclusion of Eastern women lay not simply in the wish to keep them in a state of servility, but also, and perhaps to an even greater extent, in a recognition of the sacred character of womanhood, although theoretically this was denied by their religion. The Arabs were polygamous but they, like the Turks, always showed toward women, and toward their mothers in particular, a respect which had no equivalent in medieval Europe. In spite of her officially dependent position, a Moslem woman often found herself entrusted with important tasks such as the regency during her son's minority or taking over the government or defense of a city in the absence of her husband, exactly as women did in the West. Women were not considered servile, although they were protected from impure looks and contacts which might have sullied them.

As we have seen, the Syrian Moslems were extremely shocked by the free behavior of the Frankish woman, and their indignation was based partly on a misunderstanding. But the Oriental cult of woman's austere and somewhat mystical modesty was not without its nobility. The Crusaders may have felt and understood this. There is no existing evidence that this was so, since insofar as the writings of the historians of Syria mention women at all, their attitude toward them is exactly the same as in the West. However, something of the Oriental concept of woman did undoubtedly enter their ideas. At all events, it seems highly probable that the ideal of the inaccessible beloved which was so dear to Arab poets, whether mystical or not, did actually exert an influence, however indirect, on Western poets.

During the earliest years of their establishment in Syria, the Crusaders—or those at least who chose to remain in the Holy Land and so were no longer, properly speaking, Crusaders—showed neither curiosity nor intolerance at being confronted with a new way of life, another civilization, and peoples whose race and religion were alien to their own. They were too preoccupied with the urgent business of keeping their place in the land, whether attacking or on the defensive. They treated the natives more or less as they would have treated the inhabitants of a Christian country in the same circumstances. Little by little, and in fact fairly quickly, this attitude to some extent forced them to acquire an understanding of the conflicts which were splitting the Moslem world as well as the Christian communities. A few years after his accession to the throne, Baldwin I was already, on the political chessboard of Middle Eastern politics, an Oriental prince not so very different from the Turkish and Arab emirs of Syria, making alliances, humoring first one and then another of his neighbors, finding ways to exploit the mutual rivalries of adjoining states, and bowing to the customs of local diplomacy and courtesy, just as though he had been born in the country. Tancred and Baldwin of Le Bourg adopted the same attitude, simply because it was the only possible one.

Differences of language and customs did not prevent the various great feudal barons of Syria from understanding one another and especially from coming to agreements to further their own interests. What remained insoluble was their religious antagonism. As we have seen, the only class whose interests and way of life were comparable to their own was that of the Moslem military aristocracy, and the Latins could not unite with them on a basis of the marriage ties which formed the foundation of feudal alliances.

On the side of the Franks, therefore, there was a somewhat superficial adaptation to local customs, and comparatively good relations with the indigenous peoples combined with an almost total indifference to them. This was an indifference of caste, and the Moslem aristocracy felt no closer than the Franks to the common people of Syria. The Franks were trying to create in this new land an Orient of their own in the image of the West, but it was reserved for their own convenience, in other words for the convenience of a fairly restricted community.

They were remarkable builders of churches and castles, and the building frenzy which had overrun Europe at the end of the eleventh and during the twelfth century reappeared in Frankish Syria on a scale that is somewhat surprising when one remembers the small density of the Latin population of those countries. The builders and masons were of course local workmen—who were even worse paid than their equivalents in Europe—and prisoners of war. As early as 1098, the victorious Crusaders began building a church at Albara, near Antioch, which was finished within a few years. There were, however, plenty of Christian churches in the country, most of them having been transformed into mosques, and almost everywhere these were restored to the Christian cult. But the Crusader princes were possessed by the ambition to build new churches and to embellish and enlarge those already existing, to say nothing of erecting private houses, convents and monasteries, country houses, and above all, castles.

Although they were constantly at war and chronically short of money, they spent, if the number and splendor of the buildings they erected are anything to go by, enormous sums. In provinces which were threatened incessantly on all sides by the enemy—Edessa and Antioch had the Turks at their gates on more than one occasion and Jerusalem was three times seriously in danger—in a foreign land held precariously by force of arms, the Franks built as they had never been able to do in Flanders, in Provence, or in Italy, because what their Oriental adventures had given them above all was the will to power, a taste for luxury and splendor, and pride in being the liberators of the Holy Land. A great many of these buildings—especially the castles of the military orders and religious institutions— were financed by gifts from the West. The kings of Jerusalem, however, and Queen Melisende and her two sons after her, are known to have devoted a large part of their personal budget, meager though it was, to the embellishment of Jerusalem and its surroundings. The prestige of the Holy City demanded it.

What Jerusalem was for the Franks at that time it was never to be again for its successive occupants.

Population

We have already seen that the Franks constituted only a small minority in the kingdom. The works of recent historians (Waas and Runciman) suggest that the dominant class—the nobles—of the Franks in the East never rose much beyond the number of five thousand persons: immigration was small and mortality high, while the birth rate was comparatively lower than in the West at the same time. The number of colonists of bourgeois or peasant origin must have been greater, but no accurate estimate is possible. The same goes for the *poulains,* the half-castes born of mixed marriages but speaking French and regarded as Franks. Even including the Italians, the number of colonists of Latin origin in the four states taken all together must have been less than fifty thousand. The actual population of the country was about one million. In this Frankish kingdom, even the Jewish minority (very much reduced after 1099) was numerically stronger than the Frankish.

According to texts quoted by Reinaud in his history of the patriarchs of Alexandria, it was estimated at the time of the capture of Jerusalem by Saladin that the majority of the population of the Holy City was made up of Greeks. This seems to be an exaggeration, but Greeks and Syrians belonging to the Orthodox Church were evidently sufficiently numerous to make such a statement sound plausible. We know from al-Imad that at that time there were also at least several thousand Armenians in Jerusalem (the majority of them refugees from the county of Edessa). All the same the bulk of the population was made up of Syrians belonging to the various Christian sects. Greeks were numerous in the principality of Antioch, and Armenians in Edessa and Cilicia. All these communities lived side by side, as some of them had done for centuries, mingling very little and having no more to do with one another than was strictly necessary. Their mutual feelings were rarely very cordial and more often frankly hostile. But in the majority of cases the various communities had nothing to do with one another, each leading their own lives in their own villages or districts. The phenomenon of the ghetto, which in our own time has become a symbol of racial persecution and reactionary fanaticism, was more or less general in the Middle Ages and seemed perfectly natural, as it still is in the big cities of Black Africa, where people usually live among those of their own tribe or from their own village.

The Syrians—Maronites, Jacobites, Nestorians, Greeks (or Melkites), and Copts—all had their own villages, or in the great cities, their own district. The same was naturally true of Moslems and Jews, and also of the Italians, who were further divided by the fact that Pisans would take care not to mingle with Genoese. The Franks themselves were less exclusive because they were the most willing to enter into matrimonial alliances with the local inhabitants, but they too had their villages around Jerusalem and quarters in the cities where they gathered according to their trades. The lay clergy was mostly of French origin, but there was also a strong Italian element. The regular clergy was more truly cosmopolitan, although naturally German and Scandinavian religious institutions enjoyed fewer gifts than the French and their houses were smaller and less wealthy.

Even the Frankish population was not entirely of French origin and also included Flemings and Germans who had come with the first Crusades, while among the pilgrims who decided to settle in the Holy Land there were naturally people of all nations. However, French—a French which seems to have become somewhat diluted with various local words, if Fulcher of Chartres is to be believed—very quickly became the common language of the Franks, and was also the official language spoken by the nobility and the leaders.

Provençal was spoken in the county of Tripoli, and in spite of the presence of knights from other lands (like Gerard of Ridfort) who had come to take service there, the county remained Provençal to the end, and more conscious than the other Frankish states of belonging to a distant motherland. (We have seen the fears provoked by the arrival of Alfonso-Jordan, Count of Toulouse. If he had so wished, the Count could easily have obtained the support of the local Frankish population. Raymond III, who died without issue, did not willingly resign himself to leaving his county to Bohemond IV of Antioch and stated specifically in his will that the county was to remain at the disposal of the counts of Toulouse, if they wanted to reclaim it.)

With the exception of the county of Tripoli, the Frankish states of Syria were within a very short time of their formation definitely "Syrian" states and had quite forgotten their Western past. William of Tyre, the only native-born historian of the Frankish kingdom to have left a lasting record of the life of the realm, writes as a Syrian.

The noble families rapidly abandoned their family names—the names of their fathers' castles—in favor of those of their own possessions in the Holy Land. In future these men from Picardy and Champagne were to bear the names of Toron, Ibelin, Jebail, Marash, Kerak, Sidon, and Ramleh. Joscelin of Courtenay became Joscelin of Turbessel and later Joscelin of Edessa, and the lords of Saint-Omer thought it more glorious to be called lords of Tiberias. These nobles, the majority of whom had not been great lords in their own country, had no snobbish feelings about the ancient names they bore. On the contrary, they loved their new possessions with the age-old passion of landowners which was common enough in the West but was quite unfamiliar to the Turkish emirs.

The clergy retained their original names—the names of their native cities: Radulph of Domfront, Aimery of Limoges, Fulcher of Angoulême, Bernard of Valence. There were no great names among the prelates of Outremer, and although Western custom frequently devoted the younger son of a princely family to a bishopric, the great dignitaries of the Frankish Church in Syria were recruited from clergy of humble origin. There will be more to say of the part played by the Frankish Church in Syria, but first it is necessary briefly to recall its position in the kingdom. Officially the Church included two of the most venerable patriarchates in Christianity, those of Antioch, which was as old as the patriarchate of Rome, and Jerusalem. The Church was wealthy, wealthy out of all proportion to its real importance to the life of the country, and powerful insofar as it was the Church of the ruling class. It was also to some extent dependent on the secular power, but on the other hand it enjoyed a considerable degree of independence from the Holy See. Papal influence in the affairs of the kingdom was never actually very strong, because the prelates of Outremer, whether saintly men or adventurers, all seem to have shared the same dislike of submitting to instruction from a distant foreign power, while the popes, for their part, evinced a curious lack of interest in these ecclesiastical provinces with their all too glorious names. The protection accorded by the papacy to the military orders, who were notoriously antagonistic to the local Church, is a sufficient indication that this Church was not taken too seriously in Rome.

Patriarchs and bishops were subject to the secular power, whose choice determined the election of prelates, and although they sometimes clashed with the royal authority, they had no real political influence: the number of their supporters was so small that they owed their privileges only to force of arms, and consequently to the Frankish chivalry. They were much more unpopular with the local population than were the secular lords. On the whole the Frankish clergy in Syria, which was as numerous in the major centers as in Western cities, also formed a kind of autonomous and all but self-sufficient society. The patriarchs of Jerusalem and Antioch ruled over cities the majority of whose population had nothing to do with them and recognized the authority of other prelates. Even among faithful Catholics they found themselves thwarted by the military orders, who were a quite considerable power in the kingdom. The influence of the clergy could be great in periods of interregnum or in the absence of the secular power, but in general the Church was dependent on royalty. (The period of Melisende's regency shows the extent to which the clerical faction found this dependency hard to bear: incompetent though she may have been, the Queen Mother enjoyed the absolute support of the clergy because to her the affairs of the Church took precedence over affairs of state.)

Franks of humbler degree, such as soldiers, tradesmen, craftsmen, and peasants, made up, especially in Jerusalem, a sufficiently powerful colony for their opinions and interests to be taken into consideration by those in power. What the chroniclers refer to in their accounts of events as the *people* generally means primarily this Frankish minority, which was the only one to take an active part in public life, at least by its need to demonstrate its joy or discontent. The Jacobite and Armenian Christians and the Italian colonists also shared this spirit of citizenship on occasion, although to a lesser extent. The Greeks, Jews, and Moslems remained an irreconcilably alien element, and of the three it was the Moslems who were least hostile to the Franks.

What is known as Frankish Syria was actually a country governed by a Frankish aristocracy, and this was the class which had control of the land, of the government of cities, of the administration of justice and finance, and most important of all, of military power.

Organization

At the head of this aristocracy was the King or, in the major fiefs, the count or prince. As in the West, the King's personal domain was only quite a small one. In the kingdom the royal domain consisted of Jerusalem, Acre, Tyre, Jaffa, and at a later stage, Ascalon, and the lands lying immediately around these cities. The remainder of the country was given out in fiefs to the major vassals, who in turn had vassals of their own. The same was true of Antioch, Tripoli, and

Edessa. As in the West, all feudal lords, great and small, drew their wealth in principle from the land entrusted to their care. In actual fact this land did not bring in enough, because although the coast, the valley of the Jordan, the region around Antioch, and the hinterland of Edessa were fertile provinces, the Judaean highlands, the Lebanon, and the mountainous district of Cilicia were on the whole poor. The incident quoted in Chapter VI, when Baldwin of Le Bourg deprived his cousin Joscelin of the lands whose revenues had made him unduly wealthy, shows that in the East, as in the West, the Frankish feudal lords relied on their corn, vines, and cattle more than on the spoils of war to fill their coffers. The income from the land was often inadequate and princes and great feudal lords supplemented it with various taxes such as road tolls, customs dues, levies on contracts for buying and selling, taxes on pilgrimages, and so forth. In the event of a serious threat to the security of the country, the King was entitled to levy a special tax for purposes of war. Peasants were compelled to pay a capitation tax, over and above the produce of the land which they had to give to their lord (usually a half of the harvest).

All this did not amount to a vast source of wealth. It is a fact that the King of Jerusalem's treasuries were always empty and that the heads of state were constantly crippled with debts. Admittedly, they lived extravagantly and built a great deal, but where money matters were concerned the King, the first citizen of the kingdom, was no different from private citizens, and we have already seen that Amalric I, when presiding over a court of justice, was not above accepting bribes from the parties concerned. The heads of the native communities offered gifts to the Frankish princes in order to win their favor in their various differences with rival communities, and this shows that once settled in the country, the Franks showed no disposition to rob their subjects by violence.

Royal power was fairly limited: the King commanded the army, presided over the council of barons and the courts of justice, appointed men to the highest offices of the state, but he could take no important decision on his own initiative and in a court of law his wishes were subordinate to those of the jury. The government of the country was, theoretically, in the hands of a High Court made up of the great barons, ecclesiastical dignitaries, representatives of the foreign communities, and the heads of the military orders. In general, it was the soldiers' decision which carried the day. Knights (whether monks or laymen) were in the majority in the High Court. Feudal society had never subscribed to the idea of an absolute monarchy, and European knights found barbaric the Greek governmental system in which—at least in theory—the will of the *basileus* could have the force of law; they saw such a concept of government as a proof of the cowardice of the Greeks, an inexplicable denial of their dignity as free men. This was the reason why the Latin barons were so fond of arguing—the habit for which Anna Comnena blames them so bitterly. For them, no decision could be taken until the point of view of every great lord who meant to use his right—or duty—of counsel had been heard. In the kingdom of Jerusalem, even more than in European kingdoms, the High Court meant to keep its privileges, and it has been suggested that this was the most "republican," or at least parliamentary, of all medieval kingdoms. The King was only obeyed when his personality, intelligence, and powers of persuasion were strong enough to ensure the Court's agreement to his plans.

As the principal administrator of the property of the state, the King was empowered to distribute fiefs, which were taken from his personal domains, and—another aspect of the same privilege—to marry as he thought best the heiresses to fiefs which had been left to the distaff side. He could also prevent his vassals from selling their domains if the proposed sale seemed to him damaging to the interests of the state. As to his office as supreme judge, or president of the court of justice, the King's prerogatives extended no further than to the Frankish nobility, since feudal law prescribed that every man should be judged by his peers. Even so, high justice (for crimes involving the death penalty) was in the ultimate instance the prerogative of the royal officials.

Consequently feudal society—by which is meant the King, his major vassals, and their vassals—lived its own life, somewhat cut off from the rest of the population, very much as it did in the West, and its relations with the people were basically no different from those of the Western nobility, for whom the citizen and the peasant were almost as much foreigners as the Armenians or Syrians could be to the Frankish barons.

Relations with the Natives

On the level of personal relationships, however, the particular circumstances dictated that Latin feudal society was brought into frequent contact with local society. Not for nothing were the Latin lords accused of having become "arabized," even of being "half Moslem." For centuries the prevailing language, the administrative language of the country, had been Arabic, and the Franks had to be constantly surrounded by scribes, interpreters, and native secretaries, Syrian or Moslem. All their servants were natives, and a large proportion of the administrative work was in native and occasionally Moslem hands. Most of the Franks spoke some rudimentary Arabic or Armenian, according to the region, and some of them spoke these languages fluently. Toward the end of the century there were a few great lords who became considerable Arabic scholars—men such as Isabella's husband Humphrey of Toron, or Reynald of Sidon. But these were exceptions and it was rare to find any curiosity about Arabic or Syriac literature among nobles whose interest in French or Latin literature was already scant. William of Tyre certainly knew not only French, Latin, and Italian but also Greek and a little Arabic and Hebrew, but he was another exception. The clergy, whose secretarial functions brought them into some contact with their native colleagues, were often familiar with one or another of the languages of the country, but there were a great many languages and dialects, and although Arabic had long replaced Greek as the administrative tongue, the Franks had neither the time nor in all probability the wish to impose their own language on the country. Those official acts that were written in Latin, or occasionally in French, concerned only the Frankish colony.

This colony, governed as it was according to a feudal system like those of the West, was in fact a state within a state. The King, his principal ministers, and his vassals were responsible for the defense of the land and for the collection of taxes. In other respects the various local communities enjoyed almost complete autonomy. Jews and Moslems did not have the right to carry arms—the only exception to this being the turcopole mercenaries, the majority of whom were converts to Christianity. Syrians, and to an even greater extent Armenians, on the other hand, made up a considerable portion of castle garrisons and of the infantry, but except in the county of Edessa, they held only noncommissioned rank in the army. Latin chroniclers frequently blame the Syrians for their lack of courage in battle and the Armenians for their lack of organization. In fact, the native contingents were less well armed than the Franks, and were never more than second-rate troops because the Franks distrusted them and would not leave them in sole charge of the defense of a castle.

The Franks were effective protectors for the Christians of the country, even when these Christians were not particularly anxious to escape from the Moslem yoke. As we have seen, there were many who preferred the Turks. The Syrians, as the eternally oppressed natives of the country, had no real reason to prefer one or the other. Those who belonged to the Greek rite definitely preferred the Turks, whereas the "heretics" of various sects favored the Franks insofar as they were against the Greeks. Both lived quite comfortably under Moslem domination because the Moslems did not interfere with their religious lives, while the animosity between the Syrians and the Latins grew largely out of religious differences. The Frankish secular government may have shown tolerance, understanding, and goodwill, but this was clearly not at all the case with the ecclesiastical authorities or, on occasion, with the common people or soldiery. The local Christians regarded the pre-eminence given to the Latin rite and the taking over of their churches by Catholic clergy, and the often haughty behavior of Frankish prelates, as an insult. However, after the initial years—years of brutal conquest in which the Crusading troops committed many excesses—the population of Syria and Palestine had no greater reason to complain of the Franks than quarrels of a religious nature, quarrels which the head of state frequently decided in favor of the natives. Moreover the Latin prelates were by no means invariably intolerant: they are to be found enjoying the friendliest relations with the heads of the Maronite Church and with Armenian patriarchs. The Jacobite Syrians were Monophysites, but the Latin clergy in the East does not appear to have felt strongly enough about theology to attempt to fight the Jacobite heresy.

The Jacobite Michael the Syrian observes: "Although the Franks agreed with the Greeks on the duality of the two natures of Christ, they were nevertheless very far from them in their practices. They never raised difficulties on the subject of the faith or attempted to arrive at a single form of worship for all Christian languages and peoples."[4] In 1140 we find the Armenian Catholicus, Gregory III Bahlavouni, anxious to work toward a reunification of the Churches, even promising the Latin prelates to revise some points of doctrine on which the two Churches could not agree. In 1152, a saint of the Jacobite Church of Syria, Saint Barsauma, was credited with the miraculous cure of a Frankish child. Reynald of Châtillon and Constance, who were then ruling in Antioch, had a church consecrated to this saint and inaugurated it with great pomp amid the pious rejoicings of Franks, Syrians, and Armenians. In 1180, the Maronite Christians decided to turn to the Church of Rome, as a result of the intervention of the Patriarch of Antioch, Aimery of Limoges. After this the Maronites were authorized to frequent Latin churches and to celebrate their offices there with the ornaments of the Latin clergy.

It will become apparent that the attitude of the Latin clergy—who were often principally concerned to enrich themselves at the expense of other Christian communities—stood in the way of attempts at a reconciliation from which the Franks would have been the first to benefit. What is certain is that in general the Franks behaved toward the peoples they governed with a tolerance hitherto unknown to the Christian societies of the time.

Having neither the time nor the means to reorganize the life of the country according to their own customs, and being warriors rather than legislators and men of action rather than theoreticians, the Frankish barons left the natives to their old ways of government, specifying that each community was to be governed by its own laws, obey its own leaders in everything that did not concern military operations, be judged by its own judges, and so forth. Their tolerance, which even in the religious sphere was considerable, was in every other sphere complete. In the event of a lawsuit between members of different communities, the royal courts acted as arbiters and the parties were made to swear on the holy books of their respective religions (Christians on the Gospels, Jews on the Old Testament, and Moslems on the Koran). Moslem chroniclers testify to the impartiality of these courts, and in fact the Franks adapted sufficiently quickly to the customs of the country to make no difference in a court of law between a Christian and an "infidel."

Their small numbers made it necessary for them to remain on good terms with the natives, and apparently they seem to have done this with more tact than the Turks, who were too confident of their own strength and their rightness as Moslems.

As far as the peasants were concerned, the feudal Franks acted very much according to Western customs, which were less harsh than the usual practice in Oriental countries. In demanding from the peasants the same sort of payments in money and in kind that they would have extracted on their lands in Champagne or Provence, they were, without being aware of it, making the lot of the Syrian peasant more bearable than it had ever been. Ibn Jubayr, who visited Frankish Syria in 1181, testifies eloquently to this, and he cannot be suspected of bias.

We left Tibnin [he writes] on Monday at dawn by a road which ran past a series of adjoining farms, all inhabited by Moslems who live in great well-being under the Franks. The terms given them are to yield up half their harvest at the time of reaping, and the payment of a capitation tax of one dinar and five qirats. The Christians ask nothing more, excepting only a light tax on fruit trees, but the Moslems are the masters of their homes and run them as they like. Conditions are the same for all the *rastaq,* that is to say farms and small holdings inhabited by Moslems in all the territories occupied by the Franks on the coast of Syria. When they compare their situation with that of their coreligionists in cantons governed by Moslems, which is the very reverse of security and well-being, most of them are tempted by the devil. One of the misfortunes afflicting the Moslems is that under their own government they have always to complain of the injustice of those above them, while they have nothing but praise for the conduct of their enemies (the Franks) whose justice is to be relied upon.[5]

It must be added that conditions for Christian peasants were even better, since they paid fewer taxes and were not subject to a tithe as Moslems were. It was in the Franks' interest to treat the peasants well. The lands were sparsely cultivated after the great exodus of Moslem peasants from Judaea in 1099, and even the most fertile regions were not producing enough to supply the needs of the country. The Franks needed peasant colonists as much as they needed soldiers. But their policy was based principally on their concept of feudal law, and had they demanded three-quarters of the harvest their subjects would certainly have found it perfectly natural to give it to them. Under Moslem princes the peasants were entirely at the mercy of government tax collectors, who took what they could get without setting a legal limit to their demands. (Presumably if even a Spanish Moslem could remark that the Syrian peasants were "tempted by the devil," the Moslem princes of Syria must have found the terms on which the Franks treated the peasants altogether inadmissible. Considerations of the same kind in our own day have something to do with the attitude of the governments of the Arab countries toward the State of Israel.)

Faced with the necessity for coexistence between the two rival faiths, the Franks very quickly allowed the Moslems the right to practice their own religion, even in Christian territory. Ibn Jubayr tells of churches where a corner was reserved for Moslems to pray: for example, near the tomb of the Moslem prophet Salih in what had formerly been the mosque in Acre but was then converted into a church. Another building in the same city was a mosque in which the Christians kept a chapel: "In this way the Moslem and the infidel were united in this mosque, and each prayed there, turning toward the seat of his faith."[6]

We have already seen how Usama, praying in a church in Jerusalem with his face turned toward Mecca, was twice disturbed in his devotions by a pilgrim newly arrived from Europe who kept trying to make him turn toward the east and telling him, "This is the proper way to pray!" Some Templars who were in the church twice at-

tempted to pacify the intolerant individual, and finally they threw
him out and then apologized to their Moslem guest and begged him
to continue his prayers. Usama answered with barely concealed ill-
temper that he "had prayed enough for today." If the Munqidhite
emir was naturally shocked at the Frankish pilgrim's boorishness, he
had to admit that to Franks from Europe, the sight of an infidel sullying a Christian church with his prayers was infinitely more shocking:
"I departed, amazed at the expression of horror on the devil's face,
at the way he trembled, and what he had felt at seeing someone
praying in the direction of the Qibah."⁷ The Templars' behavior,
which Usama finds perfectly natural, might have struck Europeans
as so peculiar that later on the order was actually to be accused of
having a secret understanding with Islam. It is easy to imagine what
the pilgrim in question must have thought. But the Knights of the
Temple were only acting as polite hosts and keepers of public order.
From the first half of the twelfth century there was a gulf of mutual
incomprehension between the Franks of Syria and pilgrims from Europe, which was all the deeper because the former were unable to
explain to the latter the real causes of the misunderstanding.

An Apprenticeship in Tolerance

"Those of the Franks," says Usama, "who have settled in our midst
and who have frequented the society of Moslems are greatly superior
to those who have come among us more recently."⁸ The Arab writer
is wrong in attributing this "superiority" to Moslem influence. It
would be more accurate to talk of Armeno-Syrian influences, since
it was to the native Christians that the Franks owed their discovery
of religious tolerance toward Islam. In the East, centuries of living
side by side and the day-to-day contacts necessitated by administrative or commercial functions had given Christians and Moslems the
habit of a reciprocal esteem, if not of understanding. The Greeks
themselves, however intolerant they were toward Christian dissidents,
displayed toward the Koranic faith a respect which was made up of a
mixture of politeness and indifference. The emperors, who demanded
that their Armenian officials accept conversion to Greek Orthodoxy,
did not enforce baptism on their Moslem mercenary captains. They
maintained diplomatic relations with Moslem princes and treated
them the same as Christian princes. When, for example, Anna Comnena displays her hostility toward the Turks, she may indignantly

condemn them for their loose morals or their cruelty, but it never occurs to her to blame them for their "miscreance."

The Eastern Christians—Armenians and Jacobites as well as Greeks —were further than the Franks from any kind of indifference in religious matters. They were better versed in matters of dogma and in theological speculation than Western Christians, they were passionately attached to their rites and traditions, and in their mutual struggles they were capable of a fanaticism that would have been incomprehensible to the Franks. But even so, Islam in their eyes was an authentic religion, erroneous, certainly, but in itself respectable, a religion which had its own saints and sages and philosophers and with which it was possible to maintain brotherly relations. For centuries, the Christians of Persia, Mesopotamia, and Egypt had learned to honor the caliphs as lawful masters imposed on them by God's will, and granting the Moslems' real tolerance toward the Christians, these did not complain about the domination of Islam. It was only ambitious or aggressive men who might find themselves cramped by a government which reserved the chief places in the state and the army for Moslems. Apart from this, Christians and Jews were as much citizens as anyone else, and even the tax they paid to the state was not a real cause of irritation. It had become so much a matter of habit and non-Moslem communities were so large that it did not occur to people to complain of a legal measure which, as far as they were concerned, was the common lot. Those who were converted to Islam, whether genuinely or out of self-interest, were blamed in just the same way as people are today in a totalitarian state who go over to the ruling party, but it had long been understood that this non-Christian faith was a great religion.

The moment the Franks settled in Syria they found themselves rubbing shoulders with Christians whom they were tempted to regard as semipagan. Time and again, however, the attitude of these natives showed them that they were really brothers in the faith: in Antioch, Galilee, and Jerusalem and in all the cities reconquered from the Moslems, the local priests and prelates came to meet the Crusaders with crosses raised on high, with processions and hymns of joy, and led them into the churches where the cult of Christianity had been maintained since the earliest Christian times. Those who were not put off by the barbarism of the Crusaders became valuable allies and guides in their first contacts with the country. We have seen the part played by the Armenians in northern Syria. The Jacobite Syrians—who had a well-organized clergy but no military or bourgeois elite—had the advantage of speaking Arabic, and their hatred for their Orthodox compatriots made them the auxiliaries of the Franks (in the province of Jerusalem, at least, where Melkites were numerous). When Fulcher of Chartres mentions the number of marriages between Franks and local women, he is speaking particularly of the Syrians in the south and the Armenians in the northern provinces. A man who "lived among a whole new native family by marriage" easily fell into the habit of thinking in the same way as that family.

Whatever the Franks' natural pride, and whatever the superiority complex possessed by the conquering soldiery, the Crusaders were a mere handful of men in the midst of a local population rich in traditions, and they fairly rapidly adopted the "Oriental" mentality of which their countrymen from Europe were later to accuse them. It was not very difficult to discover that the Moslems—the infidels—were simply ordinary men. All that was needed was a little common sense, and the Franks in Syria had plenty of this. It was nonetheless a major discovery, and one which was scarcely appreciated at the time and was later to be forgotten by the West.

In an age when faith was the primary criterion by which a man was judged, it was not easy to talk about a brotherhood of simple humanity. Yet this kind of brotherhood genuinely existed in the East, although in an implicit rather than an explicit fashion. Religion remained an almost impassable barrier, and this was the stumbling block against which this first attempt at fraternization between Islam and the Christian West finally broke. The adventure had begun with war and violence, and however orientalized it might become, Frankish Syria was fated to live in an atmosphere of perpetual religious wars when it felt neither the wish nor the need to do so.

When the Franks first came to Syria, they knew very little about Islam, and with a few exceptions they learned very little during the short life of their kingdom. All contacts were never more than superficial. When they were not fighting, and sometimes even when they were, Frankish warriors were too busy fulfilling the obligations imposed on them by their own religion to show any curiosity about the religion of their neighbors on the other side. Twelfth-century Latin chroniclers—including the most eminent and perceptive of them all, William of Tyre—were all churchmen, and immovable on the subject of the faith. William of Tyre sets down the story of the schisms which rent the heart of Islam, showing a marked preference for Shiism. He asserts that Mohammed's son-in-law, Ali, was "the best knight, braver and more valiant than any of the other caliphs had been," and that the *Siha* (Shia) "is not so far from the true Christian faith" as the *Sunna*. Once they had begun to talk about distances nearer to or farther from the Christian faith, there was a possibility of discussion. The Eastern Christians, and the Franks after them, did finally come to consider the Moslems as strayed brethren, worshippers of the same God, God the Father, who had fallen, through the fault of Mohammed, into some lamentable errors but were genuinely pious and desirous of winning salvation.

Many shrines in the Holy Land, and especially those commemorating the patriarchs and prophets of the Old Testament, were revered by Christians and Moslems alike (as they were also by the Jews). Here there was a real brotherhood of faith and mutual understanding. When some patriarchal relics came to light, Franks, Syrians, and Moslems were all to be found participating in the excavations with the same fervor and sharing the same joy. In Syria, the two different religions were in direct contact with a common religious heritage, and the European Christians discovered that the Moslems venerated not only the prophets of the Old Testament but also the Virgin, Saint John the Baptist, and even Jesus Christ himself, who was popularly credited by pious Moslems with more miracles than were admitted by Christian canonical works. Moslems were in the habit of making pilgrimages to the various shrines of the Virgin, and although Christians might be surprised and indignant at the fact that men could have been led into error by Mohammed *after* the Christian revelation, they were also able to ascertain that Mohammed's precepts encouraged his faithful to charity, asceticism, respect for their given word, and altogether to a great many praiseworthy virtues very similar to the Christian virtues. Their "miscreance" was only hateful when seen from a distance.

The Moslems for their part—those of them at least whose testimony has been preserved—seem to have suffered from a greater incomprehension of the Christians than that shown by the Franks with regard to Islam. If Christians regarded the Moslems as dissidents who had been led away from the true faith by a false prophet, the Moslems regarded the Christians, and especially the Franks, who were the most barbarous of all Christians, as reactionaries and worse, as actual pagans, who were capable of believing in three Gods and making a divinity of a man. They were, in fact, less capable of understanding Christianity than the Christians were of understanding Islam.

CHAPTER

XI

Frankish Syria as an Eastern Province

The Moslem World

Islam in the eleventh and twelfth centuries was no longer a young religion. It possessed a tranquil pride in its glorious past as a conquering faith, the conqueror of a large part of the then known world, and a sense of its absolute superiority in all fields (here, only Byzantium still cast its shadow) and its inalienable right to dominion over other races. In its five hundred years of history, the religion of Mohammed had had plenty of time to become acquainted with schisms, heresies, and serious internal dissensions, to see developing in its midst schools of mysticism and philosophy varying from the purest contemplative piety to the most warlike and fanatical, from the loftiest exaltation to a skeptical pantheism bordering on atheism.

Islamic civilization was enhanced by the support of a number of other faiths which Islam had assimilated as it converted people of all races and all cultures: Eastern Christianity, Persian Zoroastrianism, Hinduism, and Judaism, even African totem worship and Mongol shamanism. All these influences gave Islam a great variety of different aspects according to the provinces it ruled, but all were brought within the otherwise rigid framework of the Koran, since only the Koran was admitted as being a revelation of divine origin and therefore not to be questioned.

In this, Moslem piety went further than Christianity with regard to the Gospels, because though Christians believed in the authentic revelations of the Apostles and prophets, they nevertheless admitted (in a small degree) the human origin of the Holy Scriptures, while the Koran was supposed to have been literally dictated by God directly to His Prophet. Each verse of the Holy Book was a miracle in itself; it was the very voice of God, revealed to the Prophet in a moment of ecstasy which came to him while he was praying. Moslems who accused Christians of the crime of idolatry (the divinization of a human being) easily incurred the same reproach from Christians and Jews, so total and fervent was their devotion to the Prophet.

From the first century of its existence, by a process analogous to the formation in Christianity of a Church which was the guardian of the sacred traditions and itself sacred by the same token as Christ himself, Moslem religion admitted the existence of a tradition, the Sunna, which was parallel to the inspired revelation of the Koran and completed or explained it. The majority of Moslems professed a devotion to the Sunna which certainly in no way diminished the absolute authority of the Koran but was regarded as obligatory for the true practice of the faith. Shia, which admitted the authenticity only of the Koran, which was the work of the Prophet himself, may be compared (if we ignore the difference between the two religions) to those currents of opinion in Christian thought which reject the authority of the Church and refer back directly to the Scriptures. Shiism, which also took different forms in the various countries where it predominated, had a general tendency toward a more rigid moral discipline, joined to a greater freedom of interpretation of the Koran. It was influential in Persia and had many followers in Baghdad and in Syria. In the tenth century, it has been shown, it gained official rights in one city and created in Cairo a caliphate independent of that of Baghdad. The Shiite (or Fatimid) caliphs claimed to be descended more or less directly from the Prophet's daughter, Fatima, who was married to Ali.

Although Sunna was the religion of the majority of Moslems (and the conversion of the Mongol peoples of tribes from the northeast, the Turks and Turkomans, in the tenth and eleventh centuries had further increased its power), Shia was fiercely disputing the ground with it in the Mediterranean provinces and in Persia. On an intellectual level, literary and philosophical as well as theological, the various Shiite currents of thought bear witness to a depth and vitality at least equal to those of orthodox tradition, and Ismailiya was a genuine movement toward a religious and intellectual revival, although all too often it tends to become confused with the militant sect of the Assassins.

Islam, which had started like a grain of mustard seed with an obscure tribe of Arab nomads, was in the eleventh century the greatest power in the world. It was a vast empire, united in principle by adherence to the same faith, stretching from the Indus to Gibraltar and constantly advancing southward among the black races of Africa and to the northeast among the Mongols and Scythians as far as China. Its influence was not due to its political power. The Islamic world comprised dozens of states, many of them rivals and many with no interest in one another at all. The Moslems of Spain, the Sudan, or Bengal had more in common with their Christian or pagan neighbors than they had with their brothers in religion on the other side of the world. But because the dominant aspect of any civilization is its religion, Islam was a moral and cultural power. Divided, torn, and heterogeneous, Islam—the sum total of those faithful to the Koran —after five centuries of existence formed an infinitely complex, vital, and original whole, rich in human values and eager for progress, which today, for want of a better word, we would call a great civilization.

It was a civilization that was at once Eastern and Mediterranean, in which the influences of Zoroaster and Manes, of Aristotle and Plato, of the Talmud and the Fathers of the Church had subtly undermined the primitive purity of the revelations of the Koran; in which, just as in Europe, the most ancient paganism still survived in popular folklore in the form of deeply rooted traditions and superstitions; in which a fierce and passionate struggle was constantly being waged by the learned theologians, of whom there were more than in any other religion, for the purification of the faith and absolute fidelity to the teachings of the Prophet. The Moslem conception of Islam was as one single great nation of the faithful—in theory, at least. We find medieval historians describing events in the various provinces of Islam—Syria, Asia Minor, Persia, Spain, North Africa, and Egypt —as though they were dealing with the history of a single people.

They were a ruling people, a sovereign people in their own right to whom God had entrusted the mission of conquering and then of regenerating the world, ardently proselytizing, especially among socially and economically backward nations, constantly gaining ground and confident of continuing to gain still more. Islam was so conscious of its superiority in every field that even in countries such as Spain or Sicily (where the indigenous population was still largely Christian), the Moslems felt themselves to be the lawful masters and regarded the Christian princes who were native to the country as usurpers when they made war on them. If they did not impose their religion by force, like Charlemagne, and in general behaved toward conquered peoples with tolerance and humanity, they nonetheless regarded non-Moslems as second-rate human beings, not worth much attention.

This attitude was on the whole common to all religions, and it was still more noticeable among the Jews, who had long ago lost all hope of becoming a ruling power and made little or no attempt to convert their neighbors (except where barbarians or pagan peoples were concerned) and had fallen back on an apocalyptic cataclysm to assure the triumph of their faith. The Christians for their part, more barbaric or more passionate than the Moslems, showed their interest in their neighbors by trying to save their souls by every means, sometimes even the most brutal. The Moslems (following in this the principles of Mohammed) generally showed more respect for their subjects and avoided enforced conversions. Mohammed, as we have seen, having prescribed the imposition of a *qurat,* or capitation tax, on infidels alone and not on true believers, religious toleration was to some extent allied to self-interest. It admitted the principle of a division of society into masters (Moslems) and subjects (infidels). It is true that the progress of the religion of Islam was such that within two centuries more than half of the subject infidels almost everywhere had become Moslems and citizens. This was true of Arabia, North Africa, Mesopotamia, Iran, and Iraq. Even so, non-Moslems were still sufficiently numerous in all these places for their presence to justify feelings of pride in Islam as a race of the elect, made to rule over other peoples.

From a cultural, economic, and artistic point of view, there was no possible comparison between Western Europe and the Moslem East. Compared to Baghdad, Paris, Mainz, London, and Milan were not even like modern provincial cities compared to a capital. They were little better than African villages or townships, where only the churches and the occasional princely residence bore witness that this was an important center. Baghdad, Cairo, and even smaller cities like Damascus, Aleppo, Ispahan, Alexandria, Tyre, Tripoli, Granada, Tunis, Mosul, and Hamadan were already modern cities, such as would not begin to flower in the West until the seventeenth or even the nineteenth century. These were cities whose populations ran into hundreds of thousands (the population of Baghdad in the eleventh century reached one million), with dozens, sometimes even hundreds of mosques, to say nothing of churches and synagogues. It will be remembered that in Aleppo, at the time of the Crusades, in the middle of a war and at a moment when the city was in an economic doldrums, there were still a number of Christian churches. In these cities there were schools for all, free for young children and sometimes even for university students; there were public baths at every street corner, as well as many private pools.

The majority of the houses were in blocks several stories high with a large interior courtyard, and many had running water, thanks to a system of drains and conduits which had been in wide use since ancient times. The streets were generally paved and often shaded with canopies stretched between the roofs of the buildings to give shelter from sun and rain, while in wealthy quarters the conditions of hygiene and comfort were closer to those at the close of the nineteenth century than to anything in the Middle Ages or even in the seventeenth century in Europe. Admittedly, while the luxury of palaces outdid anything which Western civilization has ever imagined since in this field, the poorer quarters were evil and squalid, but even there standards of cleanliness were relatively greater than in the West as a result of the obligatory use of the baths.

These cosmopolitan cities, in which different communities inhabited their own separate districts, were naturally great centers of commerce. Caravans flowed into them from all corners of the East and West. They were administrative centers employing thousands of clerks, cultural centers where sometimes tens of thousands of manuscripts were preserved in public and private libraries, where schools of literature and philosophy of all persuasions met, where the majority of the male population were able to read and write, and where men assembled in the squares and on street corners to discuss the Koran. They were great business cities, where everything from precious books and *objets d'art* to slaves could be bought and sold. They were pious cities with shrines that covered the tombs or relics of the saints of three faiths, and Moslem saints in particular, and with numerous seminaries and theological schools. They were cities of pleasure where whole districts were given over to courtesans of both sexes and all prices. Each of these great cities was a world in miniature. Even small cities, feudal strongholds like Homs or Shaizar, had an opulence and comfort which European kings might have envied.

Christianity and Islam

EASTERN CHRISTIANS

It is understandable that Europeans arriving in the East were over-come with awe at a civilization which, on a material level at least, was clearly superior to their own. The Moslems, on the other hand, regarded these Christians from distant lands as complete savages.

While retaining a conscious pride in being the guardians of the Truth and the people destined to rule over all others, Islam did ad-mit the existence of other rival religions. In the West, and in the Near and Middle East, the religions it chiefly encountered were the two other Biblical religions, Judaism and Christianity. Although the Jews were still a force on a religious and philosophical plane, po-litically they were no longer a threat to Islam since, like the Christians in Oriental countries, they had been deprived of any say in their gov-ernment for too long to be able to re-create a state of their own. The Jews formed a quite substantial minority, initially severely perse-cuted by Islam, but later tolerated and kept in a state of subservience. In Syria their condition was much the same as that of the Jacobites and Copts, and since they had always been oppressed by the (Greek) Christian government, they preferred the milder dominion of Islam. Islam made few converts among them, but outwardly their customs were very similar to those of the Moslems. They were regarded as loyal subjects, and the hostility between the two faiths never reached the point of open conflict, simply because of the Jews' considerable numerical inferiority.

In its dealings with Christianity, Islam had from the outset been confronted with one Christian power which was both politically for-midable and superior from a cultural point of view: the Byzantine Empire. In the ninth and also in the tenth century, Byzantium was still sufficiently powerful to outmatch the forces of Islam in Asia Minor and in Syria, and for four hundred years *Roum* (Rome = Constantinople) was the only real danger to the successive Moslem kingdoms, the great and powerful adversary before whom, despite its remarkable progress, Islam always retained an unconscious feeling of inferiority, as a still youthful civilization toward an old civilization which had once been mistress of the world and was still powerful. These Christians possessed a culture which, on a technical and scientific level, as well as in matters of refinement of manners and intellectual attainment, could rival the Moslem, and the Moslems were not forgetting all that they owed to it. However false the religion of the "trinitaries," it could not be despised while it took the form of such a considerable force. Even toward the end of the twelfth century, when the Empire, undermined from within and harried on all sides without, had in fact nothing but the appearance of its great past, Saladin still feared it more than he feared the princes of the West. He wrote to the Caliph of Baghdad, referring to Manuel Comnenus: "The master of Constantinople is a proud despot, a Goliath of infidelity, the sovereign of an empire which has lasted for many years, the head of Christianity, which everywhere acknowledges its supremacy and bows beneath its yoke."[1]

Byzantium was the great Christian power—the only one, in fact, worthy of comparison with Islam. There were of course other Christian states whose "mischief" the Moslems knew from experience: in the north of Syria, in the Caucasus, between the Black Sea and the Caspian, were the Georgians and Armenians, warlike mountain people with an ancient Christian culture influenced by Byzantium who were constantly attacking their Moslem neighbors. (Although the Armenians had been rendered partially harmless by the oppressive policies of Byzantium, which by trying to keep them in a vassal state had considerably weakened them, the Georgians, from their all but impregnable mountains, set out from time to time on holy wars in the hope of recovering the entire Taurus region.) In Spain, the kings of Catalonia, Murcia, and Aragon had been fighting spasmodically for hundreds of years with the Moslem princes of the country, and although the peninsula was deeply influenced by Islam, the Latin Christian princes were not resigned to Moslem domination and summoned Christians from the north and from Italy to their aid. Finally, and worst of all, the Normans, recent converts to Christianity, had set out in the tenth and eleventh centuries to conquer the Mediterranean which had hitherto been divided between Greeks and Arabs. They had seized Sicily and southern Italy and made merciless war on the Arab fleets. The appearance of these terrible sailor-warriors in the eleventh century dipped the balance of power in the Mediterranean, which had hitherto remained reasonably stable, in favor of the West. At that time the awakening of Maghrabin Islamism was becoming such a menace to the sea routes and coastal provinces of the Mediterranean countries that the Normans appeared as saviors. The Pope gave them his protection, and with the help of their battle fleets they founded formidable kingdoms at the expense of the Arabs and of Byzantium. (Saladin considered the King of Sicily the most redoubtable of all Christian princes after the Emperor of Byzantium.) When the first Crusaders arrived in Syria, the Moslems first took them for mercenaries in the pay of the Greeks and then for a new kind of Normans. Ibn al-Athir asserts that the Norman Roger of Sicily had sent them eastward so as to deflect them from the projected conquest of North Africa, which he coveted for himself.

FRANKS

Altogether the newcomers, barbarians who resembled neither Christians nor Moslems, at first made the impression on Islam of a horde of nomadic warriors not unlike the Huns, lusting after nothing but slaughter and plunder. Islam at that time was still shaken by the recent Turkish conquests—more shaken, in fact, than the historians (who were all writing at a much later period) give any idea of. Although they were champions of Islam and restorers of "order," the Turks themselves were still semibarbarians, foreigners, usurpers, to be tolerated reluctantly. However weak purely national feelings may have been at the time when compared to religious feelings, Turkish domination was felt by the Near East as a disaster made all the greater by the fact that incessant wars and forays by the Turkish and Turkoman armies ruined the countryside and impoverished the cities.

The ephemeral but formidable Seljuk empire was a source of legitimate pride to the Moslems in that it shook the power of Byzantium and crushed the small Christian kingdoms of Cilicia and the Caucasus, but it was not easy for the Arabs, who had once been masters of half the world, to submit to the tutelage of the descendants of pagan mercenaries. Ibn al-Athir attributes one of the causes of the First Crusade to the intrigues of the Fatimids of Egypt who, fearing the Seljuks, summoned the help of the Franks from the West. The attitude of Palestinian lords such as the cadi of Tripoli or the Emir of Shaizar toward the Crusaders in 1099 and 1100 shows that these Arab princes (even in 1100, after the sack of Jerusalem) were still more hostile toward the Turks than to the Latin conquerors.

Despite the fact that the Franks were notorious for their aggressive Christianity, the Moslems of Syria did not initially understand that the Crusade was a war undertaken for religious motives. They judged the Crusaders by the Normans, who were scarcely fanatical Christians and the sworn enemies of that leading power of Christendom, the Greek Empire. In 1098, when al-Afdal, the Vizier of Cairo, offered to share Syria with the Crusading leaders, leaving the north to them

and himself retaining the south, including Jerusalem, he does not seem
to have realized that the whole object of the expedition was in fact
the capture of Jerusalem. But when Jerusalem and, in the years that
followed, the whole of the Syrian littoral and hinterland were in the
hands of the Crusaders, the Moslems were able to see that this was in
fact a conscious and deliberate Christian reconquest, and that the
Franks had come to their country in the desire for a *jihad,* a holy
war, and were continually gaining reinforcements of pilgrims from
their own country who believed they were working for the salvation
of their souls in fighting for Jerusalem.

Nevertheless, Moslem historians are extremely reticent on this subject. They did not feel the least curiosity about the Franks: they were
there, they fought and oppressed the Moslems, and they either conquered, by their almost legendary bravery, or they were vanquished,
by God's grace and the heroism of the Moslems. The chroniclers
scarcely seemed to realize that the Franks were human beings. Those
dealing with later events (in the second half of the century) show
more interest in the "accursed" who were, as a matter of course,
doomed to the torments of hell. Some, like Humphrey II of Toron,
were frankly admired for their chivalric virtues. The King Amalric
(Murri) enjoyed an unspoken sympathy which comes through the
obligatory curses. This King of Jerusalem not only succeeded in com-
pelling the admiration of the Moslems, but almost made them admit
the legitimacy of his rule in Syria. The chroniclers, quoting freely
from contemporary documents of events, show that in the last thirty
years of its existence at least, the Frankish kingdom had become in
the eyes of its neighbors an integral part of Syria. At the very moment when the spirit of the counter-Crusade was developing most
rapidly, there was also growing up, parallel to it and perhaps in the
same surroundings, a spirit, if not of brotherhood, at least of understanding for the Franks, an unconscious admission of their human
dignity. It was an admission that was never or hardly ever formulated,
hardly even hinted at, but from the pens of Moslems it was still something quite remarkable.

ISLAM AND THE FRANKS: USAMA

Of all the Moslems who came into more or less frequent contact
with the Franks in the twelfth century, only one has left memoirs dealing, among other things, with a subject not generally considered deserving of the attention of true believers. Nearly all our information
about these contacts, which were nonetheless frequent and, if we are

to believe Latin historians, sometimes friendly, comes from the auto-biography of Usama ibn Munqidh, a descendant of the noble family of the emirs of Shaizar. Usama was a scholar and a soldier, a diplomat, and a man of an adventurous spirit if not actually an adventurer. Usama probably echoes the feelings of the society in which he lived, but this is not entirely certain; his was an original and in some ways unorthodox mind, and he was certainly more concerned with expounding his own opinions than with conforming to everyone else's.

Usama was clearly not unduly fond of the Franks. He was a son of an emir of Shaizar whose property had suffered considerably from the perpetual inroads of the Franks from Antioch, and when still a young man he himself had fought in the armies of Ilghazi and Toghtekin at the battle of the *Ager Sanguinis* in 1119. Nineteen years later he saw the powerful Franco-Byzantine army laying siege to his native city, although this also gave him an opportunity to note that the Greeks were infinitely fiercer in their attacks on Shaizar than the Franks. He was a man who was extremely attached to his lands and his family, but he was ambitious and, like the younger sons of great feudal families who entered the service of neighboring sovereigns, he served for some time at the court of the atabeg of Damascus. In the time of the Vizier Unur, the friend of the Franks, he paid a number of visits to the kingdom of Jerusalem, once in the company of Unur himself. He performed the duties of an ambassador and was treated with great respect on this account. He seems to have conversed quite freely with the Franks. Some, like the Templars, must have been able to speak Arabic, but in any case the use of interpreters was so widespread that intercourse between people who did not speak the same language presented no difficulties.

Relations between the Franks and the people of Damascus were at that time extremely cordial. Fulk of Anjou (Fulk ibn Fulk) meant to base his policies on a defensive alliance with Damascus against Zengi, and Unur (Muin ad-Din Unur) had formerly been one of Toghtekin's mamelukes and was governing the kingdom of Damascus on behalf of his master's grandson. He was a capable old man, jealous of his country's independence and particularly hostile to Zengi because at Baalbek (a city belonging to Damascus) Zengi had already distinguished himself by indescribable atrocities. He had had the governor, one of Unur's lieutenants, flayed alive, and had crucified the entire garrison, and this after making a promise "on the Koran and the divorce of his wives" that their lives should be spared. In comparison with Zengi, the Frankish King Fulk ibn Fulk seemed a model of honor and humanity.

Unur, whose wisdom and courage is praised by Moslem chroniclers such as Ibn al-Athir and Kemal ad-Din, saw nothing dishonorable in maintaining friendly relations with the Frankish *malik,* and went in person to Acre to negotiate with Fulk, although Usama is the only person indiscreet enough to mention the fact. Official historians prefer to remain silent about it in order not to compromise the old Vizier's memory. (This suggests that if other Moslems besides Usama had written their memoirs, we should be better informed about any understanding which might have existed between the Franks and the Moslems. Such understandings did exist, although the Franks say little about them and the Moslems only mention them to denounce them as treason.)

We do not know what Unur's (Latin historians call him, after the French fashion, Aynard) feelings may have been, but Usama, with all the pride of an aristocrat, an intellectual, and a Moslem, describes the Franks as though they were a race of savages. He observes them with a certain interest, but it never occurs to him to take them seriously. Of course, they had qualities which made them useful as allies: they were excellent soldiers. This was understandable because they were a primitive and uncultivated people whose courage was based on ignorance. "Anyone who has studied the Franks has seen in them wild beasts who have the merit of courage and ardor in battle, just as animals have superior strength and ferocity, but no other."[2] Even today Europeans can still be found holding similar opinions when speaking of the courage of a particular African tribe, or even of Moslems.

However, as we have seen, Usama himself was able to make a distinction between the Franks of the country and Franks who had recently arrived from the West, who were "more inhuman" than the others. The Vizier of Damascus's ambassador probably had reason to complain of the rudeness of some Crusaders who were shocked at finding themselves in the company of an infidel (quite apart from the incident with the Frank who had disturbed his prayers). Moreover, these Crusaders were probably more sympathetic than Usama gives them credit for being, because he seems to contradict himself when he says that he became extremely friendly with one of these newly arrived pilgrims, "a respectable Frankish knight who had come from their lands to make a pilgrimage and then return home again." It was clearly the respectable knight who took the initiative in this friendship and not Usama; the Frank even went so far as to refer to the Moslem noble as "my brother" and to propose taking charge of the education of his young son. According to feudal custom, this was a great proof of esteem and friendship between knights. "He will see our knights there," said the Frank, "and will learn the science of chivalry." (It is not said that the knight went so far as to entrust Usama with the care of his own son.) It is needless to say that our narrator was not in the least tempted by the offer. He could not, he says, have feared a worse fate for his son; it would have been as well to see him a prisoner in a dungeon. He refused very politely, saying that he could not send his son to such a distant land for fear of the affliction it would cause his aged mother. " 'Is your mother then still alive?' the knight asked me. 'Yes,' I answered. 'Then do not grieve her,' he told me."[3]

All the same, there is something rather pathetic about this story of the unknown Frank, won over by the charm of the noble Arab and no doubt taking his ordinary politeness for genuine friendship and obviously unaware of the glass wall against which he was beating. His own goodwill may have been only superficial (that we shall never know) but it was certainly quite sincere. Yet this was a Westerner, one of those who "have never seen anyone pray who did not turn toward the east," one of those accustomed to behave in a barbarous and inhuman fashion. Any inhumanity here is rather on the side of Usama, who could not for an instant imagine the possibility of human contact with a Frank.

If he regarded the Franks as such a deplorably inferior race, it was probably because what he saw of the kingdom seemed to suggest that this was true. He describes, not without some amusement, medical practices of horrifying crudeness, and notes the same primitive crudeness in a legal duel—a Judgment of God—in which the two parties literally knock one another unconscious with cudgels. He has one somewhat indelicate story to tell in which a Frankish knight displays a complete disregard for his wife's modesty. Incidents like this—which are taken from life, although often at second hand, and which amuse or shock the storyteller and perhaps tempt him to embellish the truth—do in fact show a considerable degree of barbarity. The Arabs, like the Greeks, are so unanimous in decrying the Westerners' savagery that it is necessary to make some effort of imagination to realize, at a distance of eight hundred years, the kind of gulf which must have existed between the two civilizations and how the rudeness of the Franks which so shocked the Orientals displayed itself.

Relics of the past, such as literary and artistic monuments, obviously tell us nothing or very little about this because they present an idealized picture of reality. Chronicles, histories, and collections of laws reveal streaks of savagery in the Orientals which seem to us as revolting as any we find in the West. What no one thought to describe, because they were taken for granted, were details of everyday life and habits of what were regarded as good and bad manners. It is only very occasionally that someone mentions them in order to show surprise. Usama, however uncomprehending and ill-informed, is therefore a valuable witness.

He is rightly shocked at the improper behavior of a knight who allows his wife to be attended by a Moslem manservant when she is naked in her bath. The Franks apparently had no idea of false modesty, or indeed of modesty in any form, and showed a completely Nordic freedom from shame at the idea of nakedness. The *chansons de geste* also reveal this aspect of their customs: it has already been seen that ladies, whether married or unmarried, might assist a man in his ablutions with perfect propriety; and twelfth-century storytellers do not consider that they are contravening any laws of decency in describing the beauty of a chaste and noble maiden in the most intimate detail. To a strict Moslem like Usama, certain manners which merely sprang from a different concept of life seemed barbarous and indecent. He observes that a Frank who is walking in the street with his wife and meets another Frank will allow his wife to give her hand to the other and talk freely with him. What is more, if she dallies too long in conversation he will leave her alone with the stranger and go about his business! (Western politeness actually went to the lengths of an exchange of kisses between men and women, but our Moslem apparently never witnessed this.)

Usama records this fact with horrified amazement, seeing it as outrageous contempt on the part of the husband for his wife's honor, while Frankish women would have regarded it as an outrage and an affront to their dignity if their husbands had behaved any differently. (One wonders what the Munqidhite emir would have said if he could have known that a few centuries later, Moslem women would be demanding, as a sign of progress, the same shameful freedom of manners, conceivable only among a backward people?) Frankish women, even when they were models of virtue, showed their faces unveiled in public. Actually wealthy women did wear veils in the street, but this was to protect their complexions from the sun. For Moslem women, as we know, showing the face was the height of indecency. Our author, who admires and venerates his mother and sisters and has an almost religious respect for the honor of the women of his family, can feel only pity for the unfortunate wives of the Franks. He believes that all or nearly all of them must be abandoned by their husbands to the first man in sight. The Franks, he says, don't know the meaning of jealousy, and to prove it he quotes a story[4] which, from a Western point of view, would have been regarded as a tale about a complaisant husband* (that, at least, would have been its funny side). Usama, however, comes to the opposite conclusion, that this is as far as jealousy could go with the Franks. He really believes in all good faith that he is being told the story of a jealous husband. There is no need to point out that the Franks were by no means strangers to jealousy. The social history of Western society in the Middle Ages is full of domestic tragedies in which husbands wreak sanguinary vengeance on their wives or their wives' lovers. But Usama knows nothing of this and has no interest in finding out. In fact, the subject interests him so little that it never occurs to him to worry in case he is basing his judgments on a misunderstanding. (Frankish society in Syria was admittedly notorious for the freedom of its morals.)

It is difficult for us today to regard women's freedom to mix with masculine society as a sign of barbarism, but there are other aspects, which even Usama does not describe, probably because they seem to him to be too obvious, which make the Franks seem every bit as boorish as the Orientals accused them of being. Visiting Europeans at least wore coarser clothes, and according to Anna Comnena their movements and speech were much more energetic. Presumably they used a great many gestures, raised their voices on any subject, and were not very adept at controlling their natural excitability. Their code of politeness, although it too had its shades of refinement, did not correspond to that of the Orientals. Consequently they frequently appeared rude, and often actually were so, because a great many of the Crusaders who came to the East were, like Reynald of Châtillon, rough soldiers whose lack of education was shocking even to the Franks themselves.

It can easily be imagined that the knights who accompanied Godfrey of Bouillon, and even those who came after them, of whom the rare portraits of the period show only a few crude and hieratic images in stone, were not very genteel characters with their long hair and flowing beards, their faces seamed with scars and tanned by the sun, their hands calloused and their gestures abrupt, smelling of horses and dirt like the Templars so much admired by Saint Bernard. They adapted readily enough to Oriental ways, but even so they spent most of their time at war. They were bloodthirsty men, trained to

---

* A Frank, finding another man in his wife's bed, allows himself to be drawn into an argument and reluctantly accepts his rival's unlikely explanation.

kill, flinging themselves at the enemy like missiles and howling like fighting beasts. Their armor alone and the weight of their weapons were enough to strike terror into men's hearts, and even more so was the impetuosity with which they hurled this mass of iron and muscle at the enemy. The Orientals had no desire to copy their battle technique despite its obvious effectiveness. Their own ways had other advantages, and it did not occur to them to compete with the barbarians on their own ground. It was as though this armor and method of making war belonged to the Franks in just the same way as their teeth and claws belong to wild beasts.

Fearsome in battle but otherwise unremarkable, dull, ignorant, and clumsy: there was a good deal of racial antipathy in this judgment. The Franks were a completely different ethnic type from the Orientals (Moslem or Christian). In general they were bigger, stronger, whiter-skinned, often blond and blue-eyed, more hairy, less agile—and much greater eaters and drinkers than the men of the hot countries (their apparently immoderate appetites made them seem still more savage). The Moslems must have been used to these racial differences, because the exploits of the pirates and after 1101 the Crusaders' battles had brought a great many slaves from the European races into the markets and harems. But all the same the sight of so many Franks gathering in Jerusalem, Acre, and the other Syrian cities must have created a quite remarkable feeling of disorientation.

Savage they undoubtedly were to some extent, but so after all were the Turkomans, and even more so. However, the Franks were Christians and, in their own way, clearly more barbarous and superstitious than the native Christians. Usama records, as a curious fact, how a Templar asked Unur one day when he was visiting King Fulk if he wanted to see the "infant God." Out of politeness, the Vizier agreed. His interlocutor showed him a statue of the Virgin with the infant Jesus. "The Templar went before us until he showed us an image of Mary with the Messiah (on whom be salvation) in her lap. 'There,' said the Templar, 'is the infant God.' May God rise above what these impious men say." The Arab emir lived in a land where there had always been a great many Christians and could not be unaware of the dogma of Christ's divinity, and his astonishment is therefore hard to explain. Probably no Syrian or Greek Christians (and he was acquainted with many) would have been sufficiently naive to claim to show him the infant God; even when the native Christians were trying to proselytize, their arguments must have been more subtle. As a good

Moslem, Usama saw in the holy image he was shown nothing more than a clumsy idol.

THE WORSHIPPERS OF THE CROSS

The addiction of the Greeks and other Eastern Christians to relics and holy images was a well-known fact. Strangely enough, this did not shock, even though it was thought extremely reprehensible. This was first because Moslems venerated these relics no less than the Christians, and people who visited the shrines of the Virgin (the pilgrimage to Our Lady of Tortosa was among those very much frequented by Moslems) were used to seeing Christians there adoring images which symbolized the earthly form of the Virgin Mary. The cult of images as it was practiced by the Franks seems to have appeared more shocking primarily because the Franks, once they had made themselves masters of the country, began putting up images everywhere and multiplying the number that already existed. They were, as we know, great builders and also great decorators. In the twelfth century, the period of the rise of Romanesque sculpture, the human figure was beginning to invade all the painted and sculptured decoration on religious and secular buildings, and Moslem observers visiting the cities of Frankish Syria were amazed at this proliferation of capitals, porches, and frescoes of Biblical and Gospel scenes representing an infinite repetition, and easily concluded from it that the Franks were the most idolatrous of men.

The Moslems' chief reproach to the Christians was that they were worshippers of the Cross—"the servants of a piece of wood"—and whenever they wished to insult the Christians the first thing they did was to abuse the Cross. The Franks of Syria, in particular, had an especial cult of the True Cross, the priceless relic found in Jerusalem. This is known not to have been the whole Cross but simply a part of it, set in a huge crucifix and venerated in the Church of the Holy Sepulcher. On great feast days it was carried in procession through the streets of Jerusalem, and it accompanied the King's army into major battles. This is what al-Imad has to say about it, after the battle of Hattin:

It is before this cross, whether it is reclining or standing erect, that every Christian prostrates himself in prayer. They claim that it is made of the wood to which was fastened the God whom they worship. They have covered it with a layer of fine gold encrusted with pearls and jewels. They keep it ready for days of great peril and for the celebration of their usual feasts. When it is taken out, escorted by priests and carried by their leaders, all Christians hasten to crowd around it. It is permitted to no one to desert it, and the life of anyone who refuses to follow it is forfeit. The capture of this cross is more important in their eyes than that of their king; it is the greatest disaster which they have suffered in this battle. . . . They are bidden to adore it: it is *their God;** before it they bow their heads in the dust and bless it with their lips. They swoon before it and dare not raise their eyes, and mortify themselves in its presence; they fall into ecstasy at the sight of it, and lament at the sight of it. They would lay down their lives for its sake, and they look to it for their salvation. They make other crosses *in its image** and address their homage and their oaths to it in the temples of their cult.[5]

The strange thing about this extract is the mixture of obviously accurate observation with an ignorance of Christianity which is astonishing in a cultivated man with an inquiring mind. Saladin's secretary here confuses the symbolic meaning of the Cross with the physical object that is the relic itself, and has the impression that all the crosses adored in every Christian country were nothing more than imitations of this one particular relic which was kept in Jerusalem. The Moslem writer appears to see nothing beyond the Cross itself, as though it had nothing to do with the Crucified (not to mention the mystical and theological implications of the Passion). As for the boundless devotion which the precious relic inspired, al-Imad is probably not exaggerating when he describes the prostrations, tears, and ecstasies of the Franks in the presence of the True Cross, especially in time of peril.

He is extremely hard on the idolaters who worship a piece of wood, but Moslem devotion to the *qibah* in Mecca would have seemed to Christians equally strange, or even stranger still, for the Cross was at least the tangible sign of the actual Incarnation of God and consequently an object far more meaningful than any other physical object; but it does not even occur to the Moslem historian that any such comparison could be possible or that the Christians' adoration could be directed, not to the relic itself, but to God. The Christians themselves were to blame for this because, instead of keeping such a sacred object in an inviolable Holy of Holies, safe from profane eyes and unveiled only in solemn ceremonial after a long ritual of prayers and purifications, they promenaded it in the open among the soldiers, exposing it to arrows and unclean contacts. Such imprudence combined with such fervor was enough to cast doubts on the good sense of the Franks. Their faith seemed superficial and crude, because its obsession with the Incarnation and its reaching after familiarity with

* Author's italics.

the sacred and perpetual miracle was even greater than that of Eastern Christians.

It appears, however, that at the time of Saladin's capture of Jerusalem, on the day the kingdom died, the Moslems themselves finally realized that this was something precious to the Christians and worthy of respect in itself, and that the faith of these polytheists, however erroneous, was not without nobility, at least on the human level. Al-Imad, again describing the siege of the Holy City, attempts in a moment of goodwill to *understand* the Christians, and in this way, even if only by an effort of the imagination, to feel for them. The desperate energy of this population, cut off and without regular troops but determined to fight to the end for Jerusalem, must have impressed the victors.

Al-Imad tries to understand that for these people this place was holy. He reports, or rather imagines, the words which passed between Balian of Ibelin, the Patriarch Heraclius, the Knights Hospitaler, and the rest.

"It is here," they said, "that our heads must fall and our souls go out with our blood; we are to die by the sword. Attacked again and again, covered with wounds, we shall have patience to endure and shall lay down our lives to save the home of our faith [Jerusalem]. It is here, our Holy Sepulcher [literally, "our *Komamah*"—shit—the name given to the church by the Moslems]; here we are to be born again, here our ghosts will flit and moan with sincere penitence . . . here is our burning desire and the payment of our debt. Our honor lies in paying homage to this holy place, and our salvation depends on its salvation. . . . If we abandon it, shame will be on us, and we shall merit dishonor. . . . Here are statues and images, memorials and likenesses, portraits and figures, columns and pictures, bodies and souls. Here is the representation of the Disciples in their meetings, of the Fathers in their teaching, monks in their monasteries, priests in their councils, and magicians in their enchantments. Here are present Our Lord and Our Lady, the altar of the Nativity, the table and the fish in carvings and sculptures, the disciple and the master, the cradle and the child who speaks; here is the picture of the ox and the ass, of heaven and hell, the bells and the psalms." And they added, "In this place the Messiah was crucified and the victim immolated at the sacrifice, here was divinity incarnate, God made man, the mingling [of the two natures] complete; here the Cross was set up, and light came down and dissipated the darkness, humanity was united with the divine hypostasis, and existence with nonexistence; here the Baptism of God took place, and the Virgin brought forth a child in pain." And to these lies which are the object of their cult, they added the illusions which turn men away from truth and cried, "We shall die before the tomb of Our Lord, and rather than lose it we shall lose our lives, because we are fighting for him as well as for ourselves. Should we be guilty of abandoning this tomb, suffering them to take it from us and ravish that which we seized out of their hands?"[6]

In this long passage, the author is clearly trying to bring out the errors of Christianity, which are then contrasted with the Moslem Truth proclaimed by Saladin, but the passage also suggests the genuine curiosity of an intellectual trying to come closer to an alien way of thinking. To some extent he succeeded. Although there are some phrases—"We shall die before the tomb of Our Lord" and "If we abandon it, shame will be on us"—which seem to be a direct echo of the words of the defenders of Jerusalem, the general tone is so improbable as to suggest that al-Imad had never heard Franks talking, even translated by an interpreter. By placing the ox and ass, the image of the Virgin, the columns and altars all on the same level, he assumes that the people of Jerusalem were art lovers (as he was himself) and chiefly sensitive to the beauty of the paintings and sculptures in their buildings. This they may well have been, but he also takes them for innocents who believed that there could be no representations of the saints and Apostles anywhere else, and for worshippers of vain images.

The images, sacred or profane, which covered the walls of the churches and palaces of Jerusalem were nearly all destroyed by the victors and were allowed to remain only in the Church of the Holy Sepulcher, which was retained by the Christian Church. Most of the monuments erected by the Franks in the other cities suffered the same fate because representations of the human body were forbidden by Moslem religion. But here the desire for plunder acted as a stimulant to religious fanaticism. Al-Imad, himself anything but a vandal, shows in this matter a completely modern sense of respect for the artistic and cultural treasures of the enemy race. "I once beheld Lattakieh," he writes. "It was a city rich in fine buildings; everywhere were houses with stone carvings, marble porticoes, and massive arcades. No house but had its garden. There were fruit trees on every hand, and broad markets. The light was dazzling and the climate salubrious. Our emirs have taken these fine marbles and transported them to their palaces in Syria. They have changed the beauty of the buildings and tarnished their brilliance. . . . Outside Lattakieh there was a great church, old and lovely, covered in porphyry and rich in pictures and figures of all kinds. . . . When our soldiers took the city, they took away the marbles and defaced its fine buildings, condemning that which had once been so rich to poverty and leaving it wretched and ruined. . . . Degraded and devastated, it seemed to cling to its pillars and hold fast to their bases."[7] Evidently there were cultivated men among Saladin's followers, men capable of regretting the destruction of works they could not help seeing were lovely, and this testimony makes it clear that Jerusalem and the other Frankish cities astonished the Moslems by their beauty. Yet a man like al-Imad had seen Damascus, Baghdad, and Cairo and cannot have been easily impressed.

What is particularly moving about his description of Jerusalem (as he puts it into the mouths of the Franks) is the involuntary admission of the uneasiness he, as a Moslem, brought up with an austere and semiabstract conception of art, must have felt at the sight of so many buildings, walls, vaults, columns, and hangings from which the "Disciples," "Fathers," "monks," and even "magicians" stared at him with their great Byzantine eyes, painted or inlaid, with a haunting inner life like the eyes of Romanesque effigies. He seems to be haunted by the memory of these figures: "memorials and likenesses, portraits and figures . . . bodies and *souls.*" Whatever the value of these sculptures and frescoes in the eyes of the Christians, the fascinated Moslem chronicler probably attributes to them a mysterious and magical significance that is even greater. The Christians were not worshippers of images; their devotion was to the holy place or relic and rarely to a figure, however beautiful; an image was revered to the extent to which it had proved itself by some miracle and could be connected with a relic. But the creative urge which took hold of Western civilization in the twelfth century was so resolutely humanist and representational that the human face appeared everywhere, in gargoyles and cornices, slipped in between leaves of stone, crowning the bodies of animals, representing vices and virtues, the months and the seasons, the stars and the forces of nature. Art used and abused allegory as though the better to transform the work into man's image.

Jerusalem was the royal city where there was no stinting either materials or ornament. Gifts flowed in from all over Europe, and in addition to the incomparable wealth of its churches the city boasted palaces with marble porticoes, rooms paved in marble, and walls covered with frescoes; fountains with marble carvings stood in the public squares, and the squares themselves resembled great gardens, while the colonnades which surrounded them, says al-Fadil, were like trees, so abundantly were the capitals carved with leaves.[8] The Franks had inherited some of their predecessors' technical skill and had set local artists, usually Greeks, to work to their specifications. When they saw how the cities of Palestine had been beautified while the Franks were there, the Moslems could scarcely call them barbarians. Or if they did, then these barbarians had adapted to civilization with surprising ease.

Failure of the Crusades: Losses and Gains

To pious Moslems in the second half of the century, the Franks had become a menace to the exact extent that they appeared as tolerant and tolerable neighbors, to the extent that people had grown accustomed to their presence and their dominion was beginning to seem perfectly natural. More than that: their Moslem subjects were considered more fortunate than those in neighboring lands and were "tempted by the devil." Saladin, who had his own reasons for denouncing the policies of Nur ed-Din's successors in Damascus and wrote off their ministers as "stupid mamelukes, born to obey and not to command," declared that in Damascus and in Aleppo "each of them [the mamelukes] is in communication with the Franks and seeking support from them. We are convinced that if we do not find some way to take Jerusalem, and if no serious steps are taken to stamp out the religion of the infidels, it will spread its roots and become a grave threat to the true faith."[9] Now the Franks were not generally accused of proselytizing. At the most they encouraged the conversion to Christianity of their Moslem mercenaries, who were generally recruited from prisoners of war and whose conversion was a pledge of faith. They were a threat to the true faith because they had taken root in the country to such an extent that they had friends in every camp and their presence made the political interests of the kingdoms of Syria seem more important than the interests of Islam. If Saladin meant to gain control of the whole of Syria, he needed a holy war; but the Moslems of Syria did not need one and had nothing to gain from it.

It is a fact that the kingdom's Moslem subjects, faithful to their religion, almost everywhere made common cause with Saladin and welcomed him as a liberator. The peasants did not gain much from this (in fact they lost), but at least they had the satisfaction of no longer paying their taxes to infidels, and people in the cities stood to gain a good deal. But the majority of the kingdom's population was Christian. The people of Aleppo and Damascus lost more than they gained by the elimination of the Frankish kingdom. The Frankish lands of Syria, which in the ninety years since the disastrous early years of the Crusades had reached a state of comparative stability and prosperity, never recovered from Saladin's campaigns. As for the *rights* of the Franks to the lands they had occupied in Syria and the viability of this attempt at a Western settlement in the East, this is a question which has been so often discussed and has given rise to so many contradictory answers that it is not easy to examine it impartially.

In the thirteenth century, the failure of the Crusades was a cause of legitimate pride to Islam. (Indisputably, the great Crusade of 1190–1192 had been a terrible setback for the West.) The Moslem world, which had always been politically divided but at the same time conscious of a spiritual unity, had won a great moral victory and recovered, in the Near East, the undisputed hegemony which had seemed shattered in the twelfth century. Twelve years after the end of the Third Crusade, the Europeans rid Islam (for a long time, at any rate) of its oldest and most tenacious adversary: the Empire of Byzantium.

There were no successful Crusades in the thirteenth century. The reason for this did not lie in any incompetence on the part of the leaders or in the numerical weakness of the armies. The Crusades failed because Islam now had a clearer awareness of the irreconcilable antagonism between itself and the Christians. In spite of Mongol invasions, Islam's numerical preponderance in the East increased only gradually, overcoming the resistance of the local Christians of Greece and Asia Minor; and by the fifteenth century, a good half of Eastern Europe had become a part of Islam, more Islamic and certainly more oppressed than Syria and Spain had been in the Middle Ages.

The Crusades and their failure were therefore a decisive step in the westerly progress of Islam. For Western Europe, a century of Christian rule in Palestine had contributed to the awakening of national pride and a considerable enrichment of intellectual and material standards, but the deeper life of the Christian countries had not been involved and the cause of the Holy Land was always something foreign to the vital interests of Christendom. The Crusade had been, first and foremost, a great dream. Even today the very word *crusade* is still used to describe an undertaking which, although praiseworthy in principle, is in no way dictated by necessity. No one would describe the defense of his country in time of peril as a crusade.

Syria as a Nation

The Franks of Syria, however, were already fighting for their own country. A Frankish nation had existed there for a good many years and although after 1190 it shrank to a few cities, a strong element of local patriotism still persisted there for another hundred years, side by side with increasingly powerful foreign influences.

The remarkable thing about the creation of this somewhat artificial state was the swift development of a new national consciousness based (rather like that of people in the State of Israel today) on the Christian Biblical past, the eternal past of the Holy Land. A man like Baldwin I, the kingdom's first king, was already the first scrvant and the first citizen of a country he had made his own, and he brought a genuine spirit of patriotism to its defense. Arriving in Jerusalem at the age of forty, and becoming king as the result of a series of happy accidents, he was an eminently practical man who seems to have suddenly become identified with all the kings, from Saul to Herod, who had ruled over and gone to war in the same land. So great was the power of the land and of the name of Jerusalem that for Christians Palestine could become quite spontaneously and unequivocally a real homeland.

Admittedly the majority of the Crusaders, homesick or discouraged, preferred to return home, but those who stayed were fully conscious that they had become citizens of the real home of all Christians. As we have seen, they adapted readily to their new land, first because when they were not busy fighting they were able to lead a life of greater wealth and comfort there than anything they had known in Europe, and secondly because they liked the land itself. The majority of those who decided to stay had no vocation for sacrifice. The barons who did not hesitate to make alliances with a Moslem neighbor to protect their lands did not feel that they were acting as traitors to their race. They believed they were defending their lawful rights. The question remains: To what extent did they remain foreigners, tolerated only because of their military might?

REASONS FOR THE FALL OF THE KINGDOM

Foreigners they undoubtedly were, because of their language and religion, their customs which remained partially unchanged, and their lasting dependence on a Europe which, however brotherly in principle, understood them less and less. The Turks were foreigners also, but they were already more adapted to the ways of Islam than the Franks were to those of the Eastern Christians. It has been suggested that the Franks had difficulty in getting used to the climate and conditions of life in Syria. As far as the participants in the First Crusade were concerned, those who survived the crossing of Asia Minor, the siege of Antioch, and the Palestine campaign must have possessed exceptional physical resistance. Of those whose names have come down to us through the chroniclers, for one like Godfrey of Bouillon who died of illness and probably of exhaustion, we find many more killed in battle, dying of wounds, or living to a respectable age like Baldwin II. The climate was much less murderous than the ordinary conditions of life, and for men war was an everyday affair.

In spite of frequent assertions to the contrary, the Frankish race of Outremer does not seem to have been in the least degenerate, and every mediocre son of a remarkable father is by no means an argument of degeneracy. Joscelin II of Courtenay was not his father's equal, but he was not without qualities and seems to have been somewhat maligned. Baldwin II's daughters were unlucky not to have been born boys, since the worst that can be said of the two eldest, at least, is that they were excessively spirited. Baldwin IV, a representative of the fourth generation of Franks in Syria, was in spite of his disease a model of physical and moral vigor. In the thirteenth century the families of Saint-Omer (Tiberias), Ibelin, and Sidon (descendants of Eustace Garnier) were among the liveliest elements of what remained of Frankish Syria. It is true that the heroic Humphrey of Toron, who was born in Syria and was the son of a friend of Baldwin I, had an effeminate and not particularly heroic grandson, but in other circumstances and another country this young man, whose fault was that he was too gentle and good-looking, would probably not have attracted the attention of historians, and he was by no means a typical representative of Frankish society.

What is certain is that the Franks of Syria were a small minority ruling a country which was under constant threats from without, and that they were faced with greater difficulties than any which an ordinary society would have encountered. It is not their faults, although these were unfortunately all too many, which have condemned people like Agnes and Joscelin III of Courtenay, Guy of Lusignan, Heraclius, and Gerard of Ridfort (the last three, in any case, not being Syrian Franks) in the eyes of posterity; it is the fate, banal enough in itself, which decreed that at such a critical moment in its history the state should have been governed by selfish and incompetent people.

One man at least played a decisive part in the fall of the kingdom. It is reasonable to assume, given the complexity of the political situation of the time, that the kingdom of Jerusalem would have been able to neutralize the threat represented by Saladin by means of diplomacy or intrigue. Saladin was neither invincible nor immortal, and his position in 1187 was far from being an easy one. But Reynald of

Châtillon, as we have said, could not have done better if he had been
a paid agent of Saladin's. His behavior was a real masterpiece, not
even of clumsiness, but of a diabolical brilliance in exacerbating the
enemy just at the very moment when it was most important not to
provoke him. Even so, Reynald had his supporters, his own vassals to
begin with, and others including the Grand Master of the Temple and
Joscelin III of Courtenay, both of whom saw in him first and foremost a man who was capable of standing up to the Count of Tripoli.
His other allies—and not the most negligible—were the Bedouin of
Transjordan. Reynald was well known to be an unreliable friend to
anyone, and he was a potential danger to all. They had already seen
him at work before his imprisonment, yet this irresponsible individual
was no sooner at liberty than he found himself in charge of one of
the greatest fiefs in the kingdom. If he had wished, Baldwin could
have disposed of the hand of the chatelaine of Kerak of Moab elsewhere: instead, he contemplated entrusting Reynald with supreme
command of the kingdom's troops and even with the regency. Consequently, it was an intrigue against the Count of Tripoli which
gave Reynald of Châtillon a fresh chance to exercise his talents.

There are grounds for saying that after the death of Amalric I and
the assassination of Miles of Plancy the court of Jerusalem had lost
all idea of the real interests of the country. The kingdom was led to
destruction by feudal squabbles and intrigues in which jealousy,
cupidity, and personal grudges played a major part. Baldwin IV's own
responsibility for this cannot be minimized. The leper King knew very
well how to make people obey him when he really wanted to do
so. He was intelligent and clear-sighted, but his extreme youth and
the touchy pride of an invalid drove him to fight to the end against
the one man who was still capable of saving his kingdom, and when
he finally resigned himself to acknowledging Raymond III's claims, it
was already too late. The Count of Tripoli could no longer regain the
ground that had been lost.

And so the government led the kingdom to its death, at the very
moment when, among the lesser nobility and the citizens, a fundamental Frankish patriotism was growing and taking on shape and
firmness, and when the Frankish society of Outremer was really beginning to take root in the country. The Franks might really have
succeeded in staying in the land and becoming, among the other peoples of Syria, a small nation of a new kind with its own right to existence, its own personality and traditions, and an internal wealth and
a future of its own.

THE "SYRIANS"

William of Tyre admits that the Syrians were not liked by those who came from Europe. They had their faults, certainly, faults which were denounced by their own local prelates as well as by pilgrims from oversea. Quite apart from the Italians, who were accused by everyone of being "either pirates or merchants or usurers," and who in any case remained faithful to their mother country, there were in every city and especially in the hinterland a Frankish population of French origin, whose chief reproach was their excessive moral freedom. Caesarius of Heisterbach accuses the citizens of Jerusalem—even the wealthy—of "offering their sisters, their daughters, and even their wives for the pleasure of pilgrims for money."[10] The pilgrims did not spend all their time in prayer when they reached Jerusalem. A pilgrimage was often a holiday and an excuse to travel on the one hand, and a source of both legal and illicit profit on the other. Many Frankish and native citizens lived off pilgrims in the same way that the people of Venice or Athens live off tourists today. As well as the excessive greed of certain citizens, Ernoul also notes the comparative frequency of instances of homosexuality, a phenomenon that was reasonably uncommon in the West but almost officially tolerated in the Moslem East. From the very earliest times of the Crusades, the ease with which Frankish soldiers could find themselves local women encouraged a slackening of morals. But the laws punished moral derelictions as severely in the kingdom as everywhere else.

In addition to the nobility—who were invariably soldiers—and a section of the bourgeoisie which lived by the luxury trades, by usury (banks), and by exploiting the pilgrims, there were in most cities and even in small towns Frankish colonies made up of craftsmen of all kinds, farmers, and cultivators: a working-class population not very different from the local population—and in fact Frankish farmers generally employed local labor for their heavy work. This Frankish population was a privileged minority, because the government was anxious to encourage Western colonists to settle in the country. Settlers were not liable to military service in the modern sense of the word, but they were expected to provide and equip a certain number of soldiers and, on some domains, to maintain lookout posts and even to be responsible for defense in the event of an attack from outside. Very little is known about the "poor Franks," the humble colonists who gained their living from the land, living very much as the natives did, speaking Arabic, and frequently married to native women, although they had their own laws and their own administration of justice just as all the other communities did. In some instances these founded "new towns" near the towns and villages of Nestorians, Samaritans, or Moslems. In time of war they were naturally the first victims, not because anyone had a real grudge against them but because they were the most obvious foreigners. It was their disappearance, after 1190, which marked the end of Frankish Syria as a nation.

After 1187, a large proportion of the chivalry—probably more than a third—finally reassembled in the cities and joined up with the Crusaders from Europe, for Saladin is known to have released a great many noble prisoners and allowed the defenders of those strongholds which surrendered to him to go free. The wealthy citizens, who had been ruined by the war, scattered, some taking refuge in Antioch, others setting sail for Europe, while still others tried to settle in the coastal cities which had been reconquered by the Crusaders in 1190. Room was scarce there, and there was a hard struggle for life. The bulk of the poor Franks disappeared without trace; apart from the few thousand who managed to take ship from Alexandria and a few more who joined the Crusading troops, the whole Frankish population sooner or later ended up on the great roads and in the slave markets. It is unlikely, considering Saladin's well-known clemency, that there were any systematic massacres. Certainly the Europeans—the colonists of Tripoli and the Italian seafarers—treated the hosts of refugees, who could be easily captured and sold because no one any longer thought of defending them, much more cruelly than did the Moslems.

The Franks, according to Usama, who is basing his assertion on events as early as 1140, were a "people accursed," reluctant to join in marriage with other races. Admittedly the examples he quotes concern marriage with Moslems, which suggests that the native Christians had a more tolerant attitude toward marriage with infidels. But for both Franks and local Christians, marriages of this kind must in general have been forced ones, brought about by the rules of war.

The country had been fought over constantly for hundreds of years and the fate of the people who were sold as slaves had shocked no one: slavery was almost as common a misfortune as unemployment, economic crises, or the enforced industrialization of a particular region in modern peoples' republics. In any event, the behavior of the Franks, as it is reported by Usama, would not strike us as particularly shocking. A woman sold as a slave when very young becomes the favorite of an emir and has a son by him. When the son grows up he inherits a castle, and the Frankish slave, as the castellan's mother, finds herself in charge of the castle. Suppose, then, that instead of congratulating herself on her good fortune, the woman were to leave the castle at night by sliding down a rope from the walls and hastily take refuge in the nearest Frankish town where she marries a fellow countryman, a shoemaker by trade. The height of folly, according to Usama, but even he is more inclined to laugh than to be shocked. There is also the story of another Frank, taken prisoner at the same time as his father and compelled to embrace Islam while very young. We are even told that he practiced the true faith with praiseworthy zeal, that his masters were fond of him, and that he was given a Moslem girl to wife. He had a number of children and lived very happily until one day when he suddenly departed for no reason at all, taking his wife and children with him. He went back to the Franks, became a Christian once more, and naturally enough led his wife and children into apostasy.

These examples certainly show that the Franks were regarded as people extremely attached to their religion and their own ways, but there is nothing astonishing about this in a land where there was actually a Frankish kingdom which could be reached on foot in a few days. The Frankish slaves (the majority of whom was not made up of converts to Islam or of fathers of families) must have always been potential escapees. Frankish girls, few of whom ever had the good fortune to become the mistresses of castles, rarely escaped but—as Usama's irritation suggests—must have annoyed their masters by their sullen and hostile attitude. It is perhaps excessive to blame people for not enjoying slavery, however mild, but what struck the Moslems about the behavior of their Frankish servants was their natural pride in the fact that they belonged to the kingdom of Jerusalem, to a master race.

It seemed as though the humble people, the *poulains* whom the Westerners accused of being "half Moslem" while the Moslems blamed them precisely for their lack of association with other races, were condemned to remain forever poised like this, halfway between East and West and alien to both. Whatever Usama's opinion, they appear to have been more like Orientals and "greatly superior" (as our author himself admits) to Franks recently arrived in the country. In other words, they had adapted to the Oriental environment, but remained faithful to their own religion and language and were endowed with a fierce and even aggressive national pride. (Usama's own, like that of Zengi or Saladin, was no less so, but it was a different matter to tolerate so much arrogance on the part of common people and a race of semisavages.)

The Franks, on the other hand, were neither astonished nor made indignant by Moslem arrogance. On the contrary, they appear to have approved of it. Their attitude even at a very early stage was one of simple respect, based on an implicit acknowledgment of their adversaries' rights. They knew that this adversary was the stronger numerically by ten to one, even when he was defeated (which happened on a number of occasions), and possessed domains ten times larger and richer than the Frankish states as well as inexhaustible reserves of men. The Moslems were also strong in their religion, the irresistible power of which the Franks soon realized. The champions of Christendom treated the Moslems as adherents of a rival faith but of one possessing almost equal rights with Christianity. This was a diplomatic attitude, but ultimately it became a moral one. The Moslems were undoubtedly hostile by definition, but it was only the fighting soldiers who were actual enemies. The peasants, merchants, travelers, nomadic shepherds, pilgrims, and craftsmen, whether they were citizens of the kingdom or of other lands, were not regarded as enemies, or only became so when it was a matter of the sack of a city whose population had resisted (and this was something which could happen just as easily in Christian countries).

"They were fighting for their lives, their land, and their liberty . . . they were honestly defending their wives and their little children whom these faithless dogs would slaughter to the last one if they succeeded in taking the city."[11] These words were written by William of Tyre. The people he describes are the inhabitants of Cairo, which was under siege by Amalric I's army in 1168, and the "faithless dogs" are the Franks. Though the kingdom's official historian, a churchman, and a Syrian patriot always ready to exalt the victories of his own side, William of Tyre may have possessed a greater moral sense than the majority of his countrymen, but there is nothing to suggest that his way of thinking was unusual or that he was in any sense a revolutionary. Words like this from the pen of a Moslem or a Western chronicler would be completely unthinkable. In this period, as in any other, it took an uncommon kind of moral strength to allow oneself to describe one's own countrymen who were guilty only of attacking the infidel as "faithless dogs." But strength of this kind is never the strength of conquerors.

The Franks were obviously not lacking in energy when it came to defending Jerusalem, or at Hattin where the knights were backed up by a considerable body of infantry recruited from the citizen militia and including the majority of men able to bear arms. With the exception of Acre, which surrendered in an access of panic immediately after Hattin, the Frankish cities all held out, even with the few defenders they had left, and although most of them were captured before long, the reason for this was the overwhelming strength of the forces brought against them. But everywhere, the Frankish civilian population, and often the Syrian as well, armed themselves hastily and hurried to the ramparts. Castles where there were any knights left held out for weeks, some even for months, when there was no hope of relief. Kerak of Moab resisted for a year, and the Krak of Montreal for a year and a half, while the Krak des Chevaliers was never taken.

It is true that these men had some hope of holding out until the arrival of fresh Crusaders from the West, but the fact remains that in many cases they stoically allowed themselves to be cut down on the walls rather than surrender, when Saladin had promised them their lives, their freedom, and respect for their property and they knew that he would keep his word. At Darbessac (Darbsaq), a castle held by the Templars, when the walls had been breached by the bombardment the soldiers crowded into the breach and stopped the gap with their own bodies. "I saw," observes Beha ed-Din, "that wherever one of them was killed, another took his place. They stood there like a wall completely unprotected."[12]

Reynald, lord of Sidon and Beaufort, was one of the premier barons of the kingdom and a grandson of the constable Eustace Garnier. Neither ambitious nor warlike, this lord (who was, among other things, Agnes of Courtenay's fourth husband) was a cultivated man, a rare occurrence among the Franks, and so orientalized that he could speak and read Arabic fluently and admired Moslem poetry. In 1188, seeing his domains threatened by Saladin's armies, he went in person to Saladin and told him that he was prepared to surrender his castle of Beaufort (Qalat al-Sharif), and asked in return for a house in Damascus and a substantial income. All he asked was that Saladin would grant him a short delay, long enough to get his family out of Tyre and out of the way of the Marquis of Montferrat's revenge. "His courtesy," said Beha ed-Din, "was truly engaging. . . . This lord came very often to visit him [Saladin]. He conversed with us on the subject of religion, and we argued with him to show him the vanity of his beliefs. He spoke very well and expressed himself with great moderation and politeness."[13] Finally it dawned on Saladin that the Frank was trying to deceive him and that he had no intention of surrendering the castle. Reynald was seized and taken before the walls of Beaufort. He gave orders in Arabic for the soldiers to surrender, and then in French ordered them to do nothing of the kind. On Saladin's orders he was tortured for a long time underneath the castle walls. In the end, according to William of Tyre's continuator, he gave way and gave his soldiers the command to surrender the castle.[14] But his men disobeyed him and, al-Imad asserts, Beaufort did not surrender until six months later when it was reduced by starvation.

Reynald ended his days peacefully. Saladin, who in spite of all had some respect for him, gave him back half his lands of Sidon, which remained Frankish territory under the protectorate of the Sultan. His descendants held Sidon and Beaufort until 1260. Among the Franks of Syria, Reynald was reputed to be one of those most in tune with his Oriental surroundings, and this he must have been to a very obvious degree if Saladin himself could have believed him ready to exchange his demesne for a palace in Damascus. But there were never any doubts about his loyalty to the Frankish cause. Saladin's clemency and his generosity to the vanquished aroused the admiration they deserved, but no defections or changing sides. The Frankish obstinacy, which so astonished the Moslems, was partly due to their hope of a rapid reconquest with the help of reinforcements from the West, but it can also be explained by a long, proud tradition of chivalry which forbade these men to come to terms with the victor. While the kingdom still stood, Raymond III of Tripoli could use the Sultan's support to undo his rivals' plans although he was, with some justification, accused of treachery. But the Franks of Syria were no longer Westerners. They were not hostile to Islam on principle, and from the very beginning of the century they had acquired a comparatively strong sense of national identity, based on the idea that their land was the land of Our Lord and that in the eyes of all Christendom they were its accredited guardians.

According to contemporary witnesses, they were by no means noted for an excess of Christian piety and were most conscious of being Christians when they were face to face with the enemy, for the Cross was in fact their banner. Even when they were fighting side by side with Moslem allies or scouring the countryside to relieve Damascus, they were always in principle fighting for the Cross and for Jesus Christ, because for Christian soldiers, especially in the Holy Land, there was no other way to fight. Because they were a race of soldiers, their faith was an additional stimulant: it was important not to lose face before people of another religion. They had long ago understood that God would not infallibly give the victory to their own side, and only the clergy explained their defeats by divine anger against the sins of the Christians.

Accustomed as they were to the sight of people praying to God and even to Jesus Christ in many different ways, the Franks were any-thing but fanatical, but they remained deeply loyal to their faith. Like the other Christian minorities, they were the more attached to it be-cause of their constant need to defend it. Historians quote few in-stances of soldiers becoming converted to Islam under the threat of death, although the century had its share of wars of all kinds, cour-teous and ferocious. Sometimes prisoners were treated well; at others they were slaughtered en masse or faced with the terrible choice of abjuration or death. Even to the Templars, Saladin offered this choice. The soldiers preferred death. Women and of course children who were captured in the course of the frequent raids were for the most part forcibly converted. The same thing sometimes happened to captive Moslems. There are few known instances of Moslem prisoners being slaughtered by the Franks, who were too much afraid of reprisals on their own captive countrymen for they had fewer men to lose. Because of this constant awareness of their terrible numerical inferiority, they succeeded in uniting a genuine tolerance toward their enemies with a fierce adherence to their own faith. Even for the least religious, their faith was the very symbol of their honor.

Consequently there was no likelihood that this ruling minority, which in many ways resembled the Armenian minority in Cilicia, would one day melt into the mass of the native population, Christian or Moslem. With their French language and their Latin ritual the Franks were fated to remain forever "foreigners." By their distance from Europe—with which, however, they always maintained contact —they found themselves cut off from the deeper life of their native lands. They remained strangers to the literary and cultural move-ments which in the thirteenth century gave rise to the poetry of trou-badours and *trouvères* and the chivalric and courtly romances. Their Romanesque art was always a compromise between new tendencies which had been half absorbed and Byzantine art. Yet in spite of everything, local culture, Greek or Arab, remained a closed book to them. All they took in was the outward or purely technical side of it.

Culture

The knighthood was a caste of men whose business was fighting. It was useless to reproach them for the luxury and softness of their lives, because they were people who never knew a moment's respite even if they wanted it, and even those who were reputed the most indolent and the most given up to their pleasures spent a great deal of their lives in the saddle, riding to sieges, forays, and battles. (The list of actions fought by a man like Joscelin II of Courtenay, who, according to William of Tyre, thought of nothing but "drinking," "objects of luxury," and other "delights," is impressive enough in itself. We find him taking part in all the kingdom's great battles, attacking here the Ortoqid Turks, there the Zengids, and losing his lands less through inertia than as a result of the apathetic behavior of his Frankish neighbors.)

Western nobility was already sufficiently boorish, for lack of time to be anything else, but the Frankish nobility of Syria was still more so. Baldwin III and his brother Amalric are known to have had a fairly advanced education, especially in the law, but they were king's sons. Raymond III of Tripoli had to wait until he was a prisoner to get his education, and could well have done without those eight years of enforced idleness. William of Tyre asserts that Raymond of Poitiers was illiterate, but at least he was very fond of poetry. He was a European, and not for nothing was he the son of the first of the troubadours. Men like Reynald of Sidon and Humphrey IV of Toron can be quoted as examples of cultivated men, but their culture was Arabic. Lords were familiar with the habit of taking baths and with running water, and in time of peace they dressed in silken garments, perfumed their bodies, ate from silver dishes, and were served by a huge staff of native servants, but intellectually they lacked refinement.

When a man like Usama, a Moslem feudal lord of an ancient and noble Arab line, mentions his family, he describes his father's virtues with tenderness and admiration. The pious and learned emir had, with his own hand, copied out the Koran forty-three times, adding at the end the fruit of his own meditations, which were different each time. "There was one copy in a large format, written in letters of gold, and containing at the end a dissertation on the relative sciences of the Koran, its variants, particularities, and language, what had been rescinded and what had lapsed, an elucidation, the reasons for its revelation, and its jurisprudence. This dissertation was entitled the *Great Commentary* and it was alternately sepia, red, and blue. My father wrote another separate copy of his commentary in letters of gold. As for the other copies, ink was used in them for the text, but gold for the decades, quintaines, new verses, the heads of the hundred and fourteen chapters, and the heads of thirty sections."[15]

Murshid ibn Munqidh, Emir of Shaizar, was, like the Frankish lords, a man of war. He too rode at the head of his troops and organized the defense of his castles. But these were secondary occupations compared to his great work of active meditation on the Holy Book, the chapters of which he copied out with such loving art. His object was not, as might have been thought, to make the faithful more familiar with a text which he assumed had no need of his humble contribution to be revealed to men. He intended to have all his manuscripts put into his coffin, and this was done. Only three (according to Usama) were not intended to be buried. Al-Imad said of the noble family of the emirs of Shaizar: "In literature, they were dazzling lights, delicious orchards, and overflowing cisterns. As for poetry, they are the riders in its hippodrome, the heroes among its knights, and the souls in its bodies."[16]

The Munqidhites, the great family so tragically wiped out in the earthquake of 1157, were an exception even among Arab nobles, but in general all these placed a very high value on intellectual attainment. Chroniclers describing a great personage whom they mean to praise naturally mention his piety first, but immediately afterward they eulogize the beauty of his style, his fine writing, and the art with which he expresses himself. Even leaders like Saladin and Nur ed-Din, whose origins were more or less obscure, were men very well read in the lore of the Koran and the great letter writers.

The Franks left theological speculation to priests and even the most literate among them confined their learning to matters of a practical nature. William of Tyre praises Baldwin III and to a lesser extent Amalric for being "scholars." Baldwin III was said to be the best lawyer in his kingdom (which is all to his credit but does not give a very high impression of the rest of the lawyers, because the young King had after all other things to do besides studying law). Otherwise, the education of Fulk's sons seems to have been poor enough.

William also reports a conversation he had with King Amalric one day when the King was sick and bored and had summoned the Archdeacon William to talk to him about "matters concerning divinity." Among other things, he asked the Archdeacon to "prove to

him by reason" the immortality of the soul. When William referred
to the Holy Scriptures, the King asked him to omit that argument as
it did not apply to non-Christians. William answered him:

"I will give you proof. Imagine that you are one of these miscreants
and answer me as he would do. You know that God exists." "That is so,"
said the King. "All Good resides in Him: otherwise, were He to lack any
attribute of goodness, He would not be God. Therefore He is just and
therefore returns good for good and evil for evil; otherwise He would
not be acting justly." The King said, "I do not doubt that it is so." Then
William continued, "Yet you see that it is not always thus in this world:
for good men suffer many torments in this life. . . . The wicked are rich
and powerful and enjoy all kinds of pleasures. . . . Thus you see that
Our Lord does not deal justly with men in this life. Now know that He
will do so in the next, for otherwise the wicked would be rewarded and
the good chastised. Therefore there must be another life in which those
who have done well shall receive their reward and the others shall pay
for their iniquity." When the King heard this, he rejoiced greatly and said
that none could stand against these arguments, or say that there was not
a life hereafter.[17]

This extract is interesting from the point of view of Amalric's
character; his serious and faintly skeptical mind comes through
clearly. The simplicity of William's argument and the easy way Amalric is satisfied show that neither the Archbishop nor the King was
inclined to philosophical and metaphysical subtleties. An Arab, if he
had reached the point of questioning the immortality of the soul,
would probably have added, "Prove to me that God exists, and that
He must necessarily be just," for at this very period Moslem think-
ers were carrying their melancholy doubts and fears for the destiny
of the soul to great lengths.

William of Tyre seems to have been one of the most refined and
cultivated men that Frankish Syria ever produced, and admittedly it
is not quite fair to judge the intellectual level of the Franks, even of
the clergy, by this example. Truly outstanding men must always be
regarded in a different light, and by his strong intelligence and noble
character William would have done honor to any country in any age.
He was the only talented writer Frankish Syria ever produced, and it
was her misfortune not to have this man at the head of the Church
at a time when the destiny of the kingdom was being played out.
Excommunicated by his successful rival, Heraclius, William went to
Rome in 1182 or 1183 to appeal to the Pope against the sentence
(and also probably in the hope of persuading the Holy See to intervene in the affairs of Jerusalem). He died shortly after his arrival in

Italy and there was some talk of murder. It was said that Heraclius was afraid of what the Archbishop of Tyre might reveal and had him poisoned by his doctor. The great prelate was not to be a spectator of the fall of the kingdom which he had so despairingly prophesied. (Ernoul credits him with these words, dictated perhaps by a legitimate anger against the strange Patriarch of Jerusalem: "Jerusalem was reconquered by a Heraclius* and in the reign of another Heraclius it will be lost!")

Little is known of William's origins, except that he is believed to have been the son of a citizen of Italian extraction and a native of Jerusalem. A cleric's only country is the Church, but William was nevertheless a Frankish patriot, proud of the beauty of Frankish cities and the wealth of the countryside and the ancient shrines, and of course of the "most sacred spot on earth"—the Holy Sepulcher itself. He had spent a number of years in the West, having been sent there by his superiors, who saw in him a particularly gifted subject. He returned to Syria at the age of about thirty-five and immediately rose swiftly. His intelligence and the breadth of his knowledge must have inspired the greater admiration because they were rare in ecclesiastical circles in Syria. William does not seem to have possessed a talent for intrigue or to have been devoured by ambition, and yet —quite apart from his great historical work, which was undertaken at the request of King Amalric—he found himself entrusted with the education of the heir to the throne and with diplomatic missions to Rome and Byzantium. In 1174 he was appointed chancellor of the realm, then Archbishop of Tyre—and had been within an inch of becoming Patriarch of Jerusalem. This was a great deal for one man when it is remembered that quite apart from his history of the kingdom of Jerusalem he also undertook two other works, and in particular a history of the Eastern princes in which he traced the history of the various Moslem kingdoms.† William of Tyre was neither a philosopher nor a theologian. He was first and foremost a historian, but he was also a moralist, gifted with a sure judgment, an extensive knowledge of men, and genuine breadth of mind. In this he is a witness for the defense of Frankish Syria, where the coexistence of different civilizations had made it possible to envisage a kind of humanism based on the mutual knowledge and respect of one race

---

* William of Tyre had begun his history of the Latin kingdom by an account of the wars of the Emperor Heraclius against the Persian King Chosroes; Heraclius had reconquered Jerusalem in 628.

† This work, now lost, was known and used by European historians in the thirteenth century.

for another. This is a rare achievement. This kind of comprehension existed between Christianity and Islam in Spain before the twelfth century, and in Frankish Syria it almost developed along still more obvious and richly productive lines.

Speaking of the (Latin) Christian monks of Saint John of Sebasta, Usama declares: "I witnessed there a spectacle which moved my heart, but I was saddened and pained never to have seen among Moslems a zeal such as theirs."[18] On a religious plane at least, the Franks—for all the falsity of their doctrines—could not have seemed to the Moslems to be mere barbarians, just as the Moslems could no longer be "miscreants" to the Latins. Genuine religious fervor speaks for itself and cannot lie. As we have seen, it was perfectly natural for Franks who were accustomed to the country to respect another man's prayers, and by implication admit that the prayer was genuine and that a church was not defiled because those faithful to the Koran worshipped God in it according to the precepts of Mohammed. It is also a fact that the Franks were not guilty of indifference to their own faith; their attitude was quite simply that of the native Christians, but in them it was the more praiseworthy because they were, after all, the conquerors. But the Latin West never understood this attitude and never shared it.

CHAPTER

XII

Eastern Christendom

Franks and Christians

The Franks were not "colonists" in the modern sense of the word. In modern times, and especially after the discovery of America, the word has taken on a derogatory or laudatory meaning according to the opinions of the person using it. It can be clearly defined to imply a conquering—and European—race which takes possession, generally by force, of lands inhabited by other races (non-European), and as far as possible imposes its own laws, exploits the wealth of the land for its own profit, and rules in the utter certainty of being the most civilized and superior, whether on racial, religious, or technological grounds. This is what it means to "colonize" a country. There has been colonization by violence, in which the autochthonous peoples have been almost entirely wiped out or reduced to slavery and robbed of everything they possessed. There have also been gentler colonizations which have left the natives in possession of part of their independence but deliberately treated as inferiors, and exploited as such.

The Christian sense of superiority was Roman and Byzantine in origin. In the twelfth century it did not yet exist in the West. The Franks were not strong enough to attempt to impose their own religion, too little civilized to impose their civilization, and too disorganized to exploit a conquered country efficiently: they were a ruling class, an army, an ethnic minority, but not a colonial power.

They were not loved because military powers never are, especially when they are foreigners, but they were not oppressors. They treated the peasants reasonably well, but these were always on the point of rebellion: the Moslems out of loyalty to their faith, and the Syrians for more complex reasons which included elements of both religious hostility and the fear of Turkish reprisals. The Greeks hated them, with all the pride of Christians of a superior race (i.e. religion) forced to submit to Christian barbarians. Only the Armenians, in spite of the countless robberies which, up to 1120, the Franks perpetrated on them, retained any awareness of an identity of interests between themselves and the Latins. During the thirteenth century we find the Frankish principalities of Tripoli and Antioch becoming progressively more Armenian, and even the Armenians becoming more Frankish, by means of a complicated policy of marriages, alliances, feudal wars, and reconciliations.

The reason for this is that a genuine Armenian feudal society existed in northern Syria whereas there was no kind of feudal system, Greek or Syrian, in either Syria or Palestine. The fact that the Franks in Palestine never succeeded in becoming integrated with the life of the country was due to the absence of any class of the population with which they could integrate; the feudal lords of these provinces were Moslems and consequently people with whom no matrimonial alliances were possible.

In the history of Frankish rule in Syria, one fact must never be lost sight of where the civilian population is concerned: the continual pre-eminence of the religious factor. It is true that the historians who describe these events were all churchmen (or if Moslems, then they were doctors of theology whose chief interest lay in the good of the faith). Theoretically at least, there was little distinction between religion and politics. Those who, whether consciously or not, adopted any other point of view were generally considered men without faith or laws: they were the great merchants and pirates, and the reason they can be put side by side in this way is because commerce at that time came nearer in spirit to piracy than to even the most imperfect feudal order.

We have seen how the Genoese merchants in Alexandria reacted toward the refugees from Frankish Syria with a total lack of human or Christian feeling; their attitude was that of fanatical disregard for anything but profit. Saladin wrote in 1175: "Among our enemies, there were also some soldiers from Venice, Pisa, and Genoa, but all these behaved at one moment like soldiers burning with implacable hatred and causing considerable damage and at the next like travelers who had come to Islam to trade and were not obliged to adhere strictly to the rules. . . . We established relations with them and concluded advantageous treaties of peace."[1] Contemporary historians of events generally neglect capitalism and commerce, whether Moslem or Christian, and they provide explanations of a moral and religious nature even for undertakings that were most unashamedly inspired by commercial interests, such as the Venetian attack on Constantinople. If there is some error of vision here, it is due to the fact that economic motives were genuinely thought to be of secondary importance and appeared less significant than questions of prestige, national pride, or religion.

The Crusaders—or a great many of them, at least—came to Syria with the hope of enriching themselves at the expense of the Orientals. This was the conquering soldier's right. It is a fact that the clergy who accompanied the army took advantage of this right to despoil the local Syrian and in particular the Greek clergy of most of its wealth. This wealth was part and parcel of Greek supremacy in the patriarchate of Jerusalem, and if the Latins had not taken a single penny, the Greeks would have felt just as bitterly humiliated at the sight of their offices treated with contempt and replaced in the majority of churches by the Latin services. This humiliation was a grave one and not easy to bear. Moreover, the Latins carried their initial arrogance to the point of suppressing all other Christian services in the Church of the Holy Sepulcher. According to Matthew of Edessa, it took a miracle to make the Franks adopt a more tolerant attitude. (The lamps of the Holy Sepulcher, which were supposed to light on Easter Saturday of their own accord, refused to burn at all in 1101, and this was interpreted as presaging ill fortune and a sign of divine anger. The lamps would not light until the Franks had restored to the native Christians some of their privileges.)

In actual fact, the Franks were on good terms with the local clergy, but these, especially the Greeks, nevertheless felt that they were being oppressed. The Syrians and Armenians could still congratulate themselves on the comparative tolerance of the Frankish bishops and princes, but the Greeks could ask for nothing less than complete equality, if not actual supremacy of rights. It is a fact that in 1187, the Melkite population of Jerusalem prayed for Saladin's victory and was on the point of rising and slaughtering the Frankish population. The only possible reason for this could be a religious hatred which must have been almost entirely disinterested since Christians of the Greek rite were not subjected to a tax, restricted in their freedom, or ill-treated or humiliated in any way; but their services were celebrated only rarely and as it were on sufferance in the principal churches. This was more than enough to justify the most bitter hatred.

The Syrians

The chronicles of Michael the Syrian and of Matthew of Edessa each trace the history of a people, or what amounts to the same thing, of a religious community. The Armenian chronicler lays a greater stress on the national aspect, the Syrian on the religious. The events they describe run parallel to Moslem and Latin chronicles, they relate the same facts, while never allowing it to be forgotten that the most interesting people, and the ones whose history is most important, are of course their own.

The Syrians (Jacobites) regarded themselves as the only nation with a right to call themselves Christians. The others, Greeks, Latins, or Armenians, were Chalcedonians, all heretics on account of their erroneous doctrines on the nature of Christ. This heresy was so serious in itself that even the Moslems were scarcely more odious. The Franks had the great merit of not encouraging too much discussion on the subject of faith, but their prelates were arrogant and greedy and tended to trample on the other Christian Churches. Fortunately the Frankish princes themselves were known on occasion to support Jacobite prelates against Latin bishops.

The Syrians' feelings toward the Franks evidently fluctuated constantly between sympathy and hostility, and since they were in any case a people destined to be underdogs, the rule of the Turks often seemed to them preferable. The Turks did not force a rival Christian Church on them; quite the reverse. In fact they tacitly acknowledged the primacy of the Jacobite Church over the rest in places where Jacobites were in the majority, and even in places such as Edessa where they were less strong and consequently less dangerous. "God aided our people" wrote Michael the Syrian on the occasion of the earthquake of 1170, when Jacobite churches in Antioch remained standing while Latin and Greek basilicas collapsed, "perhaps because there were no kings or rich men amongst us."[2] They had no kings or rich men; the only heads of the community were the prelates, who were in fact reasonably comfortably off. The Jacobites' only treasures were their churches, their seminaries and relics, their books and ornaments, and the sacred objects of their cult.

They were a race of peasants, craftsmen, and tradesmen who

owed no allegiance except to an aristocracy of bishops and monks, which in its turn was ruled by a patriarch. The inner life of this Christian community (one of the most ancient in the Christian world) and the events which excited its interest were primarily concerned with ecclesiastical disputes, the amount of influence their prelates could wield in public affairs, and the greater or lesser consideration accorded to their religion by the various governments. It would be unfair to accuse the Jacobites of "treachery" or of "defecting" every time they showed themselves hostile to Christian governments and in favor of the Turks. They, like the Jews, were a people denied a political existence and attached solely to their religion, and they were prepared to respect whichever power guaranteed them the maximum of moral independence.

It is a fact that after the first fall of Edessa, Zengi, whose reputation for cruelty was well established, was anxious to win over the Jacobite population of the city by a praiseworthy show of clemency, but he found that it was not easy for a victorious general to force his officers to part with the rich spoils they had taken. (Ibn al-Athir describes, by way of example, the discontent of one emir who was compelled to give up a lovely young girl he had selected as a slave. However, when Edessa was taken for the second time, the girl became his victim once again, and this time there was no getting her away from him.[3]) All conquerors understood what respect for their property and their religion could mean to a people who were constantly downtrodden, and the Moslems when they liked could be cleverer at making use of this tool than the Franks, because they did not have a Christian clergy jealous of its own privileges constantly at their elbows. "Seeing that the Bishop was a brave man and spoke Arabic quite well [community of language was another bond between Moslems and Jacobites because Arabic had practically become the everyday tongue of the Syrians], Zengi ordered him to be dressed in his tunic and summoned him to his tent. He consulted with him about the rebuilding of the city. . . . Zengi honored Basilius and entrusted him with the reconstruction and repopulation of the city. While Zengi ruled over Edessa, that is to say until his assassination, the venerable Bishop was very influential there. . . . Zengi went to Edessa and remained there for some time. He encouraged the Syrians who were there. He was wholeheartedly concerned to behave mercifully to the Christians [Syrians] who were gathered there."[4]

When they received such treatment from their Turkish masters, the Jacobites had little reason to prefer the Franks. The Franks also had their own archbishop in Edessa who took control of the government in the Count's absence. He had precedence over all other prelates and was immensely wealthy. During the siege of Edessa, the Latin Archbishop, Hugh, refused to dip into his treasury to pay the soldiers, thus arousing the legitimate indignation of the besieged. Both Armenians and Syrians were fighting gallantly and suffering heavy casualties on the ramparts. The Archbishop was killed in the fighting which followed the storming of the city, and the Jacobite Bishop, who had been dragged before the conqueror half-naked at the end of a rope, found himself given charge of the administration of the city. From the Syrian point of view, this was simply his due, which had always been denied him by the Christians.

It is worth remarking that the Syrian element was particularly favorable to the Moslems in places where there was a strong Armenian minority, and still more so where the Armenians were in the majority. In fact, the Jacobites hated the Armenians even more than the Franks. In the county of Edessa, where the Courtenay family —Joscelin I and Joscelin II—had managed to live on good terms with both, the Syrians nevertheless felt insulted by the Frankish princes' preference for the Armenians, and Joscelin II, who was more Armenian than Frank, was actually loathed *as an Armenian*.

Four years after the fall of Edessa, Joscelin II with his Frankish and Armenian troops descended on the Jacobite monastery of Mar Barsauma and plundered it from top to bottom, carrying off "silver vessels, patens, chalices, crosses, censers, candlesticks, flabella, copies of the Gospels and other books," as well as all the "gold, silver, copper, vestments, and carpets" he could find. Joscelin also carried off a number of the monks to Turbessel as slaves, after dividing the spoils among his companions. This was much more an act of vengeance on the part of an Armenian than it was a piece of Frankish brigandage. Joscelin blamed the Jacobite Syrians for their treachery to their Armenian compatriots, and he was determined to make a public display of his contempt for Mar Barsauma, the Jacobite saint. Saint Barsauma got his own back in the end, however. Not content with appearing to a number of knights in dreams and threatening the impious Count with the divine anger, the Syrian chroniclers assert that he pursued him to his deathbed. Joscelin was taken prisoner and his eyes put out. He lived for nine years in captivity, deprived of all the comforts of religion, and on his deathbed he was refused the presence of a Latin or Armenian priest. A Jacobite bishop gave him absolution, but first compelled him to make full reparation to Saint Barsauma.[5]

In general the Frankish princes were sensible enough not to espouse the cause of one local Church against another, and they tried to act as impartial arbiters in ecclesiastical disputes. Joscelin I is well known to have made repeated efforts to reconcile the Jacobite Bishop of Edessa with his patriarch who had excommunicated him. Joscelin was so careful not to favor the Armenians at the expense of the Jacobites that when the Syrian Bishop John Maudiana was elected Patriarch in 1130, he deliberately went to be consecrated in the Latin church at Turbessel in honor of the Count of Edessa, who had been influential in securing his election. In 1137, Queen Melisende intervened on behalf of the Jacobite community of Jerusalem in the course of a lawsuit between the Jacobite Bishop and a Frankish knight named Gauffier, who had earlier seized two villages belonging to the bishopric and returned to claim them after thirty-four years as a prisoner in Egypt. The Queen gave the villages back to the Syrians and saw to it that the knight had compensation. Not only Melisende but other Frankish kings and princes and even the military orders are to be found making gifts of land to local prelates and religious houses. The church dedicated by Princess Constance of Antioch to Saint Barsauma has already been mentioned. The Turks would certainly never have carried their leniency so far. The attitude of the Franks was not dictated purely by political expediency. They were Christians. The astonishing thing is not that they should have inspired hostile feelings in other Christians, but that they should have inspired so few.

Armenians, Greeks, and Syrians

To read the Armenian and Syrian chroniclers, one would think that the Greeks were the root of all evil. It is not so much the emperors and their generals who are to blame, but the patriarchs, metropolitans, Orthodox bishops, and ordinary local Greeks who are invariably perfidious and motivated entirely by hatred of other Christians. The Greeks are always present to rejoice at the misfortunes of the Jacobites and grieve when the Christians are happy. (Thus, Michael the Syrian on the subject of the miracle of Saint Barsauma and the celebrations arranged to solemnize the consecration of the church: "Present at this consecration were Thoros, Prince of Cilicia, the Princess of Antioch, the Frankish princes, the Armenian and Syrian people, and a multitude of priests, deacons, and monks, those belonging to the Franks and Armenians as well as our own. But the Greeks in their hatred and envy were grieved."[6] In Jerusalem as well as in Antioch, their dislike of the Greeks was the Franks' greatest asset with the Syriac population. The Armenians of the county of Edessa preferred to be exiled rather than submit to Greek rule.)

As we have seen, men like Thoros and Gabriel who, as officials of the Empire, had been obliged to adopt the Orthodox faith were disgraced in the eyes of their countrymen even though they were engaged in protecting their freedom. Yet the doctrines of the Armenian Church were not so very far removed from those of the Greek Church, and national sentiments were stronger among the Armenians than religious feelings. These Armenian princes were therefore doubly hated by the Jacobites, both as Armenians and as Greeks. In 1180, Gabriel had backed the election of the Jacobite Bishop John, despite the fact that another prelate had offered him splendid bribes, but when the prince approached the new Bishop to receive his blessing, John rejected him scornfully, saying, "Stand back! For you are a Greek and we are Syrians!" This scorn was the only luxury which an oppressed community could allow itself. Turkish princes would never have considered asking a Syrian prelate for his blessing, and they were not hated nearly as much. But Gabriel, "Greek" though he was, was still a genuine Armenian, and the Armenians hated the Greeks.

In 1179, the Armenian prince Kakig II (the brother of the Catholicus) took the Greek city of Caesarea, and seizing the Greek bishop of the city, put him to death by tying him up in a sack with a mad dog. Not long afterward, Kakig was lured into an ambush by the Greeks and killed. The Armenians waged a persistent war against the Greeks, a war which was continually complicated by temporary alliances against the Turkish aggressors. Dispossessed of part of their lands in Greater Armenia, from which the Greeks had evacuated them with the idea that this would help them to defend the country, the Armenians, as we have already seen, had migrated in great numbers to Cilicia in the eleventh century. There they pursued a policy which was both logical and contradictory. They were cleverer than the Franks and continually played off one side against the other, submitting first to the Greeks and then to the Turks, with only one real idea: to preserve their own independence and enlarge their domains.

They were that rare thing for the period, a people who were more devoted to their national individuality than to their religion. The Armenians hated Byzantium, the great centralized, bureaucratic empire which demanded religious unity in the name of the unity of the state.

Nevertheless, some Armenian leaders were converted for political reasons, whereas none have ever been found who were converted to Islam. It was rare for them to seek a Turkish alliance with any conviction, and the furthest they would go was to offer, like Thoros, to pay the Turks a tribute in return for being left in peace. They were not, like the Syrians, an eternally downtrodden people, but powerful rulers in their own right and often with a great deal more to lose by submitting to the Turks than they had by accepting the remote overlordship of the Greeks.

On a religious plane, their divergences from Orthodox doctrine were not insurmountable. Proof of this can be found in the relative ease with which they accepted union with the Church of Rome, whose doctrines were almost identical with those of the Greek Church. But they would never have considered submission to the Greek Church because such a submission, although dogmatically acceptable, would have seemed to them the height of humiliation. Neither Matthew of Edessa nor any of the other Armenians are guilty of an excess of religious fanaticism; for them the enemy is always the Turk first, the Greek after, and the Frank third, and this is not because of religious differences so much as because of their degrees of cruelty toward the Armenian people. In the end, political and military alliance with the Franks brought the Armenians at least officially into the fold of the Roman Church, and this, however superficial, was a gesture of immense significance. The Armenians were the only Near Eastern people to trust the West, and they did so out of hostility to the Greeks.

Rights of the Greeks

There is not one Greek Syrian author who has left either memoirs or a chronicle dealing with the rule of the Crusaders in the East. Byzantine historians from Constantinople or Asia Minor generally ignore events in Syria and deal mainly with the Empire's Western policies and the wars with the Seljuks. Anna Comnena was the only one to mention the Crusades, and she saw them as a phenomenon that was certainly disturbing, interesting, even amazing, but all things considered, of minor importance. To the Fourth Crusade, which took place in 1204, there are quite naturally plenty of Greek witnesses; but this was no longer concerned with the Holy Land, Jerusalem, or the Empire's interests in Palestine.

Events proved that Anna Comnena was right. This whole barbarian drive toward the East was simply various different aspects of one vast enterprise aimed at the destruction of the Eastern Roman Empire, and these supposed Christians were more dangerous than any Moslems.

This, on the whole, was the Greek opinion of the Crusades. It was not entirely unfounded, if events are considered in their historical perspective. Like every great empire, Byzantium regarded itself as the center of the world, the only really civilized country, sole guardian of Truth in matters of religion and the heir of Roman greatness, of Greek thought and Christian revelation, and naturally the Empire set up the care of its own interests as a moral right. The expression "Byzantine perfidy" would have been inconceivable to a Greek. The proudest of totalitarian states in our own day could never equal Byzantium in its calm awareness of its own sovereign rights and its ineradicable consciousness of superiority. This was largely a religious feeling, because the Church was a state Church and the Emperor was the secular head of the Church. Byzantium was not exactly a theocracy, but this was what it set out to be, uniting the theocratic ideal of Judaism to the absolutism of Rome, and mingled with reminiscences of Oriental despotism. It is true that in the eleventh and twelfth centuries, the reality gave the lie to this proud certitude, but nothing goes more against the grain for a great people than the recognition of its own weakness. It takes centuries of decadence followed by centuries of servitude to reach this point. Even when they were harried on all fronts, losing province after province, constantly in the grip of economic crisis and on the edge of collapse, the rulers of Constantinople still behaved like masters of the world. The Greek aristocracy attached more importance to court intrigues and quarrels between the factions which split the capital than to the battles being waged by their armies on the frontiers of the Empire.

In the Middle Eastern provinces which the Byzantine Empire had lost in the seventh century, Greek or Greek Orthodox minorities remained even after centuries of Moslem domination. This was true not only in Palestine and Syria but also in Mesopotamia and in Egypt. There were also one or two places in Italy and Sicily where Byzantium was still disputing the ground with both Arabs and Normans.

Heraclius in the seventh century and Nicephorus Phocas in the tenth had succeeded in driving back the Arabs in Syria, and if they did not reach Jerusalem, their goal had been nonetheless not merely the conquest of the Holy Land but of Egypt as well. This was not a Crusade; it was an affirmation by force of arms of the rights of the Empire. Alexius Comnenus, at the end of the eleventh century, was less ambitious. Kilij Arslan had set up his capital at Nicaea, almost opposite Constantinople. With the help of the Crusaders the Greeks succeeded in recapturing a large part of their provinces in Asia Minor, and even if the first blow struck at the Seljuks in Anatolia was the work of the Crusaders, Alexius Comnenus was the man who actually recovered the provinces. It goes without saying that his ambitions did not stop there. It is a fact that he never admitted the possibility of compromise on the subject of Antioch. He did not dream of the conquest of Jerusalem because he did not possess sufficient means to keep it, but as far as Byzantium was concerned Palestine was legally a province of the Empire, and in 1142 John Comnenus did not fail to assert his implicit rights over Jerusalem.

The Greeks of Syria were not all of Greek nationality. In the south, in the province of Jerusalem, the majority of Christians belonging to the Greek rite were in fact Syrians. There were many Greeks in the province of Antioch and in Cilicia. Byzantium regarded them all in principle as subjects of the Empire, subject—under a foreign government—to their bishops and patriarchs who were appointed from Constantinople. The Emperor, as temporal head of the Church, was directly responsible for this, and not for nothing were these people regarded as "Melkites" in their own countries. They were the subjects of the king and in consequence Byzantine, and their loyalty to Byzantium never faltered.

It has been seen that in the time of Tancred, the Byzantine armies were easily able to recapture many strongholds in Cilicia and the neighborhood of Antioch from the Franks, thanks to the local Greek population who spontaneously opened the gates to them and placed themselves under their protection. Even in Antioch, the Greek faction was still powerful; it supported the Princess Alice's rebellion, came down in favor of a reconciliation between Raymond of Poitiers and John Comnenus, and even won over a number of the Frankish barons to its own cause. It was understandably held in suspicion and the more persecuted because it represented a real force. The Turks, during their brief occupation of the city, had wiped out the Greek nobility, a numerically small and wholly military class. (It must have been numerically small indeed, for in 1078 the government had been entrusted not to a Greek but to the Armenian Philaretus.) Consequently the Greeks of Antioch were simply clerks, tradesmen, and artisans, if craftsmen and artists are to be included in the latter class.

It has been said there is little in the writings of the period to mark the presence of the Greeks, except when demonstrating their hostility either to the Franks or to the other Christians. They were nevertheless an important section of the population—important both numerically and because of their economic and cultural standards. There was a tendency to ignore them, and they kept very much to themselves as a matter of pride and prudence. Even so, they had one great consolation: Bohemond III, their Frankish Prince and the Emperor Manuel's brother-in-law, returned from Constantinople in 1165, accompanied by *their* Patriarch, the incumbent of the patriarchal seat of Antioch, who had been living at the Emperor's court and had never set foot in the city. The Empire had never recognized the authority of Latin patriarchs, and continued to appoint Greek patriarchs who inherited the title from the John IV who had once been driven out by Tancred; and the Greek population of Antioch was under the authority of exiled patriarchs. The Patriarch of Antioch, Athanasius II, had blessed the Emperor Manuel's marriage to Maria of Antioch, and by doing so had shown the Greeks' disregard for the Latin Patriarch. Bohemond III, who was held prisoner by Nur ed-Din and was released thanks to his ties of kinship with the Emperor, went to his powerful brother-in-law to ask him to pay his ransom. Manuel paid and heaped gifts on the young Prince. The restoration of the Patriarch was to set the seal on the good relations between the two courts, and Athanasius II was solemnly enthroned in his city, to the immense chagrin of the Patriarch Aimery and all the Latin clergy. In his indignation (which was quite legitimate since there could not be two patriarchs in the same city) Aimery placed Antioch under an interdict and retired to the castle of Qosair.

More is said about the anger of the Franks and the solidarity of the Jacobite clergy for the Patriarch in exile than about the delight of the Greek population. This delight was short-lived. In 1170 the province was ravaged by a terrible earthquake. With that of 1157, it was one of the greatest disasters of the century. Whole cities were reduced to heaps of rubble and thousands of people lost their lives. In Antioch, a large number of the stone houses and churches collapsed, burying all those inside. The shock happened so suddenly that no one had time to get out. The Patriarch Athanasius was celebrating mass in the Greek cathedral when the catastrophe occurred, and he was dug out of the ruins mortally injured. This was not all: Prince Bohemond, believing like all the Franks that the disaster was a divine punishment for the installation of a Greek prelate, "shaved his head, put on sackcloth, and assembling all the people, went up to Qosair to ask forgiveness of the Patriarch [Aimery of Limoges]. Dressed in hairshirts, they prostrated themselves at his feet and begged him to return to the city because his anathema had been the cause of the tragedy. He said to them, 'First drive out the Greek Patriarch who is an intruder.' When they went to carry out this order, they found the Greek Patriarch dying. Nonetheless the Prince ordered him to be carried on a litter outside the city. Then the Patriarch Aimery returned to Antioch, and the city was comforted."[7] It seems probable that the Greeks were the last people to feel "comforted" by this event, but the Franks were not interested in their grief and the Syrians were delighted by it. At all events, there was no further suggestion of putting a Greek on the patriarchal throne of Antioch.

In Jerusalem, the Emperor was a long way off and memories of Greek rule had long been forgotten. Consequently relations with the Frankish masters were less strained, although there was undoubted hostility. This was due less to the behavior of the Franks themselves than to mutual dislike between the various rival Christian communities which the Franks favored in preference to the Orthodox. (Even if they had behaved with strict impartiality, the Orthodox Greeks could not have failed to feel some annoyance at finding themselves put on a level with the heretics. In Moslem times, thanks to the Emperor's protection, they had enjoyed a privileged status. Under the Franks they, the members of a Church which was in principle the sister of the Church of Rome, were actually lumped together with the Jacobites, Armenians, and Nestorians and, after 1180, placed below the Maronites. Negotiations for a reunion between the Churches and an end to the schism were still going on, and until the Crusades the Latins had never disputed the authority of a Greek prelate.) Two of the Frankish kings of Jerusalem married Greek princesses, but these had no political influence. Maria Comnena had a certain amount, but this was not as a queen or a Greek but as the wife of one of the leading local nobles. Married very young, and queens for only a few years, neither Theodora nor Maria was in any position to alter the attitude of the court of Jerusalem toward the local Orthodox population. Oddly enough, Maria Comnena is mentioned by al-Imad (in his account of the fall of Jerusalem) as "a Greek princess who devoted her life to the Holy Sepulcher" and this was the reason she did not leave Jerusalem. In fact Maria, who was married to Balian of Ibelin, can hardly have been loved by the Greek population of Jerusalem. While this very Balian was defending the city with desperate energy, the Melkites were on the point of rebellion and hoping for a victory for Saladin. This fact alone shows clearly enough that a reconciliation between the Franks and the Greek population was practically an impossibility.

Faithful to his policy of goodwill to all Christian populations, with the exception of the Franks, Saladin after the capture of Jerusalem restored to the Greeks he found there the privileges which their forebears had enjoyed before 1099. It is true that the city became Moslem once more and most of the churches were converted into mosques, but the Greeks and Jacobites retained their seminaries and the Greek Orthodox Bishop became the official head of all Christians in Jerusalem. There were no Franks left, with the exception of a few priests and monks who were authorized to stay near the Holy Sepulcher. The Greek colony naturally reaped the benefit of the expulsion of the Latin population, since it took time to repopulate the city with Moslems. It is not easy to believe that it was really possible for Christians to rejoice sincerely at seeing the Holy City fall once more under the Moslem yoke. Here, the feelings of the Greeks were like those of the heretic minorities in Turkey which had been persecuted by Byzantium: preferring the rule of the infidel to that of a rival church. The Franks admittedly did not persecute anyone, but their clergy were arrogant and jealous of their privileges.

Only a far-reaching policy of reconciliation between the Churches, co-operation between the papacy and the patriarchate of Constantinople, and the forceful intervention of both in the affairs of Palestine might possibly have been able to put an end to this inevitable antagonism. But neither Rome nor Constantinople was interested in the fate of the Christian minorities in the East. Both were attempting, in the twelfth century, to find a strictly political or military solution to the problem of Syria. On this level, there was so little prospect of understanding between the Christian East and West that the kings of Jerusalem who, alone, attempted to bring about a reconciliation with Byzantium in the latter half of the twelfth century were systematically sabotaged in their undertaking both by their Western allies and by their own vassals. The Greeks of Judaea and Galilee had no hope of one day finding themselves under the dominion of Byzantine emperors. They had become accustomed, for centuries, to regard Moslem rule as normal and legitimate. In 1099, they too had welcomed the Latin liberators joyfully and come to meet them singing hymns and bearing banners and crosses, and they could not forget the insult that had been dealt them then.

Misfortunes of War: Fate of the Indigenous Christians

A LAND DIVIDED

All the chroniclers agree that the government of the Franks in Syria was generally humane and reasonable, that they treated the populations of the countries they occupied more or less as they would have treated the citizens and peasants of their own lands, and often more liberally. Here they had national and religious susceptibilities to deal with, and aware that they themselves were foreigners, they recognized their subjects' rights to live under their own laws. But it is a fact that their presence was in itself a source of serious trouble, even if not of real calamity, because they had come to the country as a conquering armed force and were constantly at war.

Nearly all these wars, both offensive and defensive, were rendered unavoidable by the very nature of Frankish society, but they seriously disrupted life in the regions where the wars were being waged. Palestine was not a very large country, and although there were cities and districts lucky enough to remain untroubled by military operations for many years at a time, many more districts were taken and retaken, besieged and laid waste, their harvests fired and cattle stolen, sometimes more than ten times in the course of one century. Whether the armies were Frankish, Turkish, or Egyptian, the damage they did was much the same. The Franks had not brought war to the country; it had been there already, for more than thirty years.

The Crusades were wars, and because of this they caused all the suffering that wars have always caused. Moreover they were, if not actually religious wars, at least wars between peoples of different religions, and this religious difference was an additional cause of suffering to the local population.

The Moslem civilians, naturally, suffered the most from the initial depredations of the Crusading armies. The soldiers were motivated by a real religious fanaticism and besides, as we have already seen, they did not always distinguish between Christian and "pagan." Christian civilians suffered almost as much, since the approach of a powerful Christian army quite naturally exacerbated Moslem governors against a population already suspected guilty of sympathizing with the enemy and openly accused of having brought this plague upon the country. (William of Tyre mentions that the Christians of

Palestine were severely persecuted because they were thought to have sent messages to the Pope and to the kings of Europe which gave rise to the Crusades.) The Christians of Antioch were expelled from the city at the news of the Crusaders' approach. The same thing happened to them in other cities, and although there were no actual massacres, many Christians lost their lives in the first years of the Crusades. Despoiled and disarmed, the refugees fell victims to the wandering soldiery, to vagabonds, nomads, and peasants who were eager to wreak vengeance on them for the defeats of Islam.

In Jerusalem, hatred between the two communities, Christian and Moslem, had not waited for the excuse of the Crusade before bursting out. Neither side had forgotten the terrible slaughter of Christians which had taken place in the Holy City on the orders of the Fatimid Caliph al-Hakim,* nor the massacre of Moslems by the Turk Atsiz in 1076 (when the Christians were spared). The Turks mistrusted the Arabs and protected the Christians. After Dorylaeum and to an even greater extent after the capture of Antioch, Christians of all sects naturally became odious to the Turks. Soqman, Atsiz's successor, a lieutenant of the Seljuks, lost Jerusalem in 1098, and the Fatimids who then occupied the Holy City regarded the Christians as allies both of the Turks and the Crusaders. During the brief occupation of Jerusalem by the Egyptians, the Christians, who were loathed by their Moslem and Jewish fellow citizens and regarded as enemies by the occupying military forces, fled in great numbers to the countryside or to the cities along the coast—where, however, they were not well received. The Crusading armies were to blame for this since, by coming to help these very Christians, they had made them appear suspect and traitors.

CHRISTENDOM BETRAYED

The more terrible the Franks appeared, when they were still an unknown, mysterious, and distant power, the more the Christians, as the supposed accomplices of the Franks, were oppressed. By the time the Crusaders actually arrived, there were so few Christians left in Jerusalem that after the massacre of the Moslem and Jewish populations the chroniclers were able to estimate that there were virtually no people left in the city. They had to be replaced by colonists

---

* Al-Hakim was a Fatimid (Shiite) caliph (996–1021) who pursued a bloodthirsty policy of persecution against the Christians. No such intolerance was practiced by any other caliph. Al-Hakim was a fanatic who believed that he was an incarnation of the Divinity.

(Melkites and Jacobites) brought in from Transjordan. The Crusade had been a disaster for the native Christians even before it became one for the non-Christians. Christians who were not killed, expelled, or reduced to slavery were the object of hostility and suspicion, whereas previously they had been citizens like everyone else—second class, it is true, but too accustomed to their status to complain.

There had been a time when the Crusade had offered them the promise of great hopes, as well as great suffering. The way in which the victorious Crusaders were welcomed everywhere shows that for once all the local Christian communities had forgotten their mutual animosity and joined together in the same spontaneous demonstrations of joy and pride. At last a Christian force was driving the infidel from the Holy Places and the Cross finally triumphing over the Crescent. It is impossible to say to what extent the native Christians took part in the massacre of Jerusalem, but they probably did all they could to help the victors. Even if the local clergy, which was almost the only Christian element remaining in the city itself, cannot be suspected of taking an active part, they cannot have stood out against the murderous frenzy which followed the capture of the city, and they certainly shared in the rejoicings, processions, and acts of grace which followed. The laymen who poured into the city in the wake of the Crusading armies knew where to look for the enemy and whom to strike, and they had plenty of outrages to avenge.

What is certain is that the Christians' simple, trusting joy turned sour after a very few days. Here, as in Antioch, the providential saviors first brought about the ruin of their brothers in the faith and then proceeded to treat them like a conquered people. Responsibility for this lies first and foremost with the clergy attached to the army. Adhemar of Monteil, had he lived, might perhaps have succeeded in preventing this inexcusable deterioration in the spirit of the holy war. At that moment it would still have been possible to establish a religious brotherhood—that is, if there was still a possibility of any genuine Christian movement after the frightful massacre of July 15. When the barons entered the blood-soaked city, they found the place virtually cleaned out. There was no one to dispute their laurels. The clergy found rival clergy. They behaved exactly as if it—or rather they—had not existed. It is not surprising that the native Christians should have felt they were losing on all fronts. They too had suffered for the cause of Jesus Christ, although they had not asked to do so. They had not taken the cross, but they knew they were being persecuted for their faith (and in this, according to the Gospels, they could consider themselves superior to the Crusaders).

The Franks behaved like soldiers who despise civilians on principle even when they treat them well. The bishops and clergy of the Crusading army were not soldiers, although some of them, beginning with the legate Adhemar, had not been above taking part in battles in person and all regarded themselves as members of God's army—an army which was not remotely spiritual or symbolical—and this affected their attitude toward the Eastern clergy. Just as the Frankish barons despised the Greeks and Syrians for their supposed softness, so the Crusading clergy seem to have blamed their Syrian colleagues for their lack of aggression. They treated them as though they had been somehow shamed because they had borne the infidel yoke for so long, and tended to regard simply as cowardice what the Orientals considered their heroic patience.

It should not be forgotten that the Oriental clergy, obeying a tradition a thousand years old (which until the Crusades had also been that of the great majority of Western clergy), was strictly pacifist and peace-loving. They might go so far as to pray for a Christian victory, and even to absolve the crime of murder if committed with pure intentions and in defense of the faith or native land, but it was their duty to hate bloodshed. (In this connection, it is appropriate to recall the tragic dialogue between Prince Gabriel and the Jacobite Bishop of Melitene: "Have mercy, O Prince, there is killing outside [the city], let there not be killing within!" "And you," replied Gabriel, "would you then deliver the city up to the Turks?") A Christian prelate might legitimately prefer the domination of the infidel to a war, even a victorious one, if it involved a great loss of human life. The Western Church had not lost this quite natural and altogether religious horror of murder, but it was less strong in the West than in the East, and it seems likely that among the prelates and priests with the Crusade it had practically ceased to exist. God in person had granted victory to their side, and a priest might take up arms without sullying himself when even the saints and angels descended from heaven to fight at the side of Christ's soldiers. It was natural for them instinctively to despise the meek, resigned clerics who refused to take part in the fight and used their sacerdotal duty as an excuse, and who, for centuries, had paid the infidel the honor due to masters imposed by God. This had certainly been the attitude of the primitive Church, but it had not been current in the West for a long time.

Admittedly, it might be said that the distinctly unbrotherly attitude of men like Arnulf Malecorne or Daimbert hardly needed explaining on a moral level: they were greedy, ambitious churchmen with only their own profit, or possibly the profit of their kind, in view. But a great many Latin churchmen took part in the Crusade, and although there were certainly bad ones among them, there were also good ones. The most ambitious and autocratic came out on top, but without great resistance on the part of the majority. This criminal betrayal of Eastern Christendom seems to have been committed in all innocence, and a serious and intelligent man like William of Tyre, relating the events to do with the installation of Latin Christianity in Jerusalem, mentions the intrigues and speeches which attended the election of the Patriarch, and the friction between the barons' party and that of the clergy, and severely censures Arnulf Malecorne's ambitions. But from what he has to say no one would imagine that there were Eastern bishops and abbots present, who might also have a voice in the chapter. (It is true that contemporary chroniclers such as Raymond of Aguilers denounce the cupidity of the first Latin Patriarch of Jerusalem[8] and the depredations of which he was guilty with regard to the native clergy, but it does not for an instant occur even to Raymond that there was any possibility of an equal collaboration between the victors and those they had come to "liberate.")

DANGEROUS PROTECTORS

It can therefore be said that as far as the local Christians were concerned the Crusades were first a source of suffering and then a great disillusionment. The suffering was to continue just as the wars did. In regions bordering on Moslem states, the life of Christians became unendurable, and in Moslem cities, difficult. Many migrated to Frankish territory where, protected by the Crusading armies, they took the place of the Moslem citizens and peasants who had been killed or had left. In 1115 Baldwin I embarked somewhat belatedly on an actual propaganda campaign to encourage the greatest possible number of Christians to come from the Hauran and Transjordan to repopulate Jerusalem and its environs. The Franks had long realized that there could be no question of treating these natives as a conquered people. From 1101 onward, the local religious communities recovered some of their privileges, and the immigrants which the country so badly needed found themselves provided with houses and land and exempt from the tax they had formerly paid to the Moslems. The patriarchate, whether from greed or from a desire to encourage conversions to the Latin faith, did, however, make several attempts to impose a tax on Christians of other sects, a tax from which Catholics were exempt. These attempts failed, but the Christians were nonetheless confirmed in their idea that the Frankish Church meant to treat them as an inferior race.

The country was constantly at war. Where the Turks were not far off, the lot of the Christian population was infinitely more precarious than it had been before the Crusades. At that time the Christians had at least had the advantage of being, in principle, neutral, whereas now they found themselves being slaughtered or sold into slavery simply *because* they were Christians. The massacre of the Armenians on the Euphrates in 1110 shows clearly enough what were the consequences of the Franks settling in lands under Turkish suzerainty. The great exodus, which was followed by a mass slaughter, had been decided upon because the lives of the Christians beyond the Euphrates had become a hell.

On a number of occasions during the wars which were being waged in northern Syria, the natives were found endeavoring to betray the Frankish governors at the approach of a powerful Turkish army, negotiating with the enemy, agitating, or even coming out in open rebellion. Their reason was generally fear of the Turks, but occasionally it was hatred of the Franks. The Franks reacted brutally. Matthew of Edessa, who favors the Franks, provides a number of examples of this. On the occasion of the first bloody capture of the city of Edessa by the Turks, it has been seen that Zengi had done his best to retain the sympathies of the Christians of the country. After the second siege of the city, all Christians indiscriminately were killed or sold as slaves. The majority of them only asked to be allowed to live in peace, whether under the Franks or under the Turks.

Paradoxically, even where they showed the best will in the world, the Franks were a danger to the Christians simply because they were Christians themselves.

CHAPTER

XIII

The Reckoning

Legends and Disasters

The Crusades have been glorified, discussed, decried, and judged by historians in many different ways, but they remain a great episode in the history of Western Christendom. A close examination reveals them as an extremely complex phenomenon, and yet, unlike most great historical movements, they grew out of an idea which was simple enough in itself. In spite of everything, the Crusades are still the symbol of a glorious, disinterested—and even chimerical—undertaking. Since the eighteenth century there has been no shortage of detractors to insist that in these holy wars there was little enough altruism and on the contrary a great many atrocities, to say that the whole affair was a piece of brigandage giving free rein to the basest instincts on the pretext of religious zeal, and to assert that only fanatics and narrow-minded nationalists could still approve of the principle of this succession of battles and massacres carried out in the name of Christ. (It is worth remembering here Simone Weil's remark that the Crusades were "the basest" of wars.)

As a military operation, the Crusades were a failure. Western Christendom lost Jerusalem ninety years later, after it had unwittingly helped to bring about the reunification of Islam in the Near East, had strengthened the warlike ardor of the Moslem world, had first weakened and then ruined the Empire of Byzantium and in so doing increased the danger from the Turks and Mongols. They were, however, a considerable moral triumph for the West, which is a good deal, and they were also an indirect source of both material and cultural wealth as a result of prolonged contact between the Western world and the East. The Crusades were part of a general movement in the West, an expansion which was then only beginning but which, in the course of several hundred years, was to assume altogether unexpected proportions.

The Crusades can be treated to a process of "demythification," as it should perhaps be called, but nonetheless they form an integral part of the myth of the Christian, barbarian West, all-conquering, unashamedly militarist, adventurous, and accustomed to confusing heroism with prowess in battle. The greatness of this conquering adventure, which was in other respects a failure, lay in the name of Jerusalem. Jerusalem delivered and Jerusalem lost: these are still significant pointers to the growing self-awareness of the Latin West. There was Jerusalem and there was an uninterrupted series of disasters: wars, massacres, murders, pillage, and devastation. The far from negligible benefits which the West obtained from the Crusades have also been used to explain and justify them in the history books. The Crusades are known to have involved a fantastic waste of human life, and it is this angle which deserves to be considered now.

It is a notorious fact that the Crusades were responsible for an immense amount of bloodshed, and the appalling massacre of the people of Jerusalem is enough to discredit the Crusades as "holy wars" forever. But the earliest victims of the Crusades were the Jews of Metz, Mainz, Worms, Prague, and Speyer in 1096, more than a thousand men, women and children and possibly even several thousand. Next were the Hungarians, Serbs, and Greeks who lived in the regions through which the bands of Crusaders passed, and then the inhabitants of the district around Chrysopolis in Asia Minor, all of whom were Christians. These crimes were expiated to the full and more, and the Crusaders who indulged in this orgy of violence were nearly all exterminated like wild beasts, some in Hungary and others near Nicaea in Asia Minor. "When the bodies of all the warriors who had been slain, which lay all around, were brought together they made, I will not call it a great heap nor yet a mound, nor even a hill, but as it were a high mountain of considerable size."[1] The "high mountain" may only have existed in Anna Comnena's imagination, but the dead numbered more than twenty thousand and not all of them were murderers; there were many women, children, old men, and sick among them, and their numbers, in Europe as well as in Asia, were far greater than those of their victims.

The regular armies, from Lorraine, Normandy, Provence, and France, who set out along the road to Asia Minor in 1096 were lucky enough to distinguish themselves by great victories and to reach Jerusalem. But contemporary accounts, with their endless recital of the misfortunes which befell the armies one after another, might have been written to discourage volunteers who were anxious to imitate the Crusaders' exploits. The holy war made many more martyrs than it did conquering heroes.

The First Crusade

After their victory at Nicaea, where they had been robbed of the fruits of their victory by the Greeks' agreement with the Sultan, the Crusaders narrowly escaped being wiped out at Dorylaeum when they were confronted by such multitudes of Turks that "all the hills, all the valleys, and all the plains, inside and out," were covered with enemy troops. The Turks ground their teeth, uttering resounding cries and demoniacal yells, and attacked ferociously, retreating and returning to the attack and overrunning the Crusaders' camp in a succession of waves so terrifying that their defeat could only be explained by God's help. "Who is wise enough to describe the sagacity, the warlike talents and valor of these Turks?"[2] For a long time the Crusaders withstood the terrifying charges, the hell of howling warriors, the thunder of galloping horses, the whistle of bows, and the dense, murderous hail of arrows and javelins. We are not told how many were the dead and wounded, and no one had time to count them. The foot soldiers crouched on the ground with their long shields and spears while the cavalry charged, and the women were "a great help," running into the front line and carrying drinks to the fighting men. There was victory, pursuit, and vast spoils of "gold and silver, horses, asses, camels, sheep, oxen, and many other things."

But the march was hard. They traveled for hundreds of miles through an arid landscape in high summer under a burning sun. They had to climb mountains (called by the chroniclers "the Mountain of the Devil"—the Anti-Taurus) "so steep and narrow, none dared go before the others on the path that was up the side. The horses plunged into the ravines, and one pack animal dragged down the others." Men and women died of heat stroke, thirst, and exhaustion and fell from precipices, while those who lagged behind were slain by the Turks. It took the army four months to cross Asia Minor in the heat of a summer such as the pilgrims had never seen in their own countries. Then there was the long siege outside Antioch, in winter, with icy, torrential rains. For lack of adequate shelter, they camped in the freezing wind, sleeping in muddy water, while the poor died of exhaustion and hunger finished off the sick who were already half dead with cold. Historians merely remark that "too many" pilgrims died.

The battles went on with their almost ritual exchange of severed heads: heads of Turks and heads of Franks, brandished on the ends of spears, flung from one camp to another, and carried as presents to the leaders. Then there were the heads of prisoners which Bohemond had roasted, to make people believe that he ate them, and the three hundred heads which the Franks sent to St. Symeon to the ambassadors of the Caliph of Egypt, who was the Seljuks' enemy. Victories were as bloody for the victors as for the vanquished. In one engagement at the gates of Antioch on March 6, "the swift waves of the river [Orontes] were red with the blood of the Turks."[3] Corpses were piled in heaps on the bridge. Antioch was captured and the Turkish garrison massacred. Kerbogha, the atabeg of Mosul, arrived to relieve the besieged, cut his way into the city, and slaughtered the Frankish garrison guarding the bridge. Then, when the fighting was over, the famine, epidemics, and despair came once again.

"Anyone who found a dead dog or cat ate it with relish. . . . There were to be seen knights and sergeants, who had been so brave and strong and valiant in all warlike enterprises, become so weak and wasted that they went about the streets leaning on sticks, their heads bowed, begging for bread."[4] If knights were reduced to this condition, it is not hard to guess what the state of the poor people must have been.

Even the most experienced minds, the leaders who had most accurately calculated the difficulties of the undertaking beforehand, must have felt that things were getting out of hand; only the physical impossibility of giving up the war which had begun so badly (in spite of its initial success) compelled the army to persevere in its design of conquest. Some deserted, and more would probably have done so if flight in disorder through hostile desert country had not been more dangerous than carrying on with the war. Even Peter the Hermit attempted to flee. When Count Stephen of Blois fled with his knights and placed himself under the protection of the *basileus*'s armies, he is known to have told them that the Crusaders had certainly been annihilated by Kerbogha already and that it was useless to go to their assistance. He was probably so crushed and the whole adventure seemed so cruel and absurd that he secretly hoped it was true.

Stephen had to pay dearly for his defection, but at least, as the richest man in France, he had the means to escape with the maximum chance of getting out alive. The bulk of the army, which stayed where it was, was saved by the miracle of the Holy Lance.

It was now a case of conquer or die. At Antioch, as at Dorylaeum, it was the energy of despair which worked the miracle and won the Franks immortal renown. Contemporary accounts make it clear how much of this access of almost mystical exaltation was due to the fierce refusal to admit defeat, to crude fighting spirit and to sheer heroism. The Crusaders' luck—if luck it can be called—in the critical situations in which they were always finding themselves always lay in their comparative weakness.

It can be estimated that about a quarter of the army which crossed the Bosporus set out again from Antioch on the road to Jerusalem. The proportion of those who deserted is unknown, but most of them, if they were not murdered on the spot, ended up as slaves. The number of dead must have been immense, and historians console themselves with the assurance that all these pilgrims had become martyrs and were even now praying God for their comrades, from the ranks of the celestial hosts which fought invisibly alongside God's soldiers. To any other army, losses like these would have meant defeat and the end of the war. But the Crusaders could not go home, or even sue for peace. A peace concluded at Antioch, for example, would have resulted in the immediate disintegration of the army and a retreat with heavier losses even than those already sustained. The Turks, though their courage was reputed to be without equal, could afford to be routed because they had somewhere to flee to.

The Frankish army moved on toward Palestine, weakened, reduced, desperate, and formidably inured to suffering and all the fiercer because of it. After what they had been through, God's soldiers had nothing more to fear and nothing more to lose. Neither the chronicles nor historical *chansons de geste* can convey what life in the Crusader camp must have been like, a mixture of misery and heroism, compounded of mud, blood, sweat, and tears. Occasionally, when a siege proved particularly severe, historians mention the intolerable smell exhaled by the dead and dying, the swarms of black flies, and the polluted food. For men at the end of their tether, cramped together in a narrow space, these things could be the cause of unbearable wretchedness, but the smells, flies, and vermin were at any rate ordinary, everyday plagues. Filth was everywhere in these camps, where water was always rationed in hot weather, where the animals had to be watered first, and where victuals and fodder were a perpetual source of anxiety. Men, horses, pack animals, and animals intended for slaughter trailed along the roads in convoys miles long and camped on broad open spaces surrounded by ditches, filling the air with the heavy stench of acrid sweat, dung, roasting meat, and rotten food, and leaving behind them ravaged fields and heaps of refuse.

Then there was the noise: braying and lowing, singing and swearing, children screaming, groans of the sick, beating of drums, martial music and psalms. . . . There were more processions, sermons, and public prayers in this moving city than in any other. The wealthy had their prelates and chaplains, the poor their priests and prophets. The smell of incense constantly mingled with the smell of blood and corpses, religious hymns with the shriek of battle cries. Before a battle the priests would walk along the ranks of soldiers, holding the cross above their heads and raising the chalice aloft, while the men flung themselves down in the dust, weeping and beating their breasts and stretching out their arms to the holy images, before they hurled themselves on the enemy, roaring and screaming and laying about them like men possessed.

At every charge, the foot soldiers were decimated by the enemy arrows, which flew in such numbers that the archers had scarcely need to take aim. Eyewitnesses say that the arrows rained down as thick as hail. When the battle turned into a general melee, the wounded, friend or enemy, were trampled under the horses' hoofs; mutilated horses, their bellies ripped open and spears stuck in their flanks, reared and fell, crushing their riders, while others, bleeding and panic-stricken, stamped and turned, biting and plunging in terror. Battles were a hell of thundering hoofs, shrieks and yells, and the clash of metal on metal, of swirling clouds of hot dust, choking and blinding. And in the midst of this deafening uproar, each combatant was doing his best to shout louder than the rest, because shouting was also a weapon, a means of intimidation and a rallying cry. A soldier on the point of collapse would feel his courage revive when he heard the shouts of his own side rising above the others and the cries of his comrades coming closer. There were always bishops and priests in the Crusading armies bold enough to hurl themselves into the thick of the fray, brandishing the cross high above their heads so that the soldiers could see it from afar.

After two and then three years of this cruel existence, even the mildest became so used to the sight of blood that it moved them less than that of water—which was often scarcer. Thirst, in these medieval wars and especially in the East, was one of the most fearful threats.

It was thirst which defeated the Frankish army at Hattin, and battles fought for water or campaigns which misfired for lack of water were commonplace. It was natural in time of war for both sides to use all their ingenuity to destroy what little water the poor land still harbored after months of drouth: springs were poisoned, carrion thrown into wells and into the beds of the trickling rivers. Even in fertile lands, water was precious in summer; but blood was easily shed, more easily than in any other war. The blood of an enemy was pleasing to God, and the blood of the faithful also, because it was the blood of martyrs. There was also the blood of horses, which no one wanted to shed because horses were the most coveted of all the spoils and the prime weapon of war. This taste for blood made itself felt even in peaceful recreations—it was a natural element of the soldier's life. There is a famous story of the Arab sheik who had a great camel brought before Godfrey of Bouillon and entreated the Frankish general to show his strength by cutting off its head, which Godfrey promptly did, as easily as if it had been "a goose's neck." The sea of blood as the sacrificial camel fell dead can be readily imagined.

The Crusaders of 1099

These filthy, verminous men, racked by fever and nervous excitement, brutalized and bewildered, were pitiful examples of God's soldiers but they were good soldiers for all that. They seemed strange and savage to the Orientals, and after what the Crusade had done to them they might well have seemed strange even to their own countrymen. During the siege of Antioch, the leaders decreed that any man caught in the act of "adultery or fornication," any man guilty of playing at dice, drinking, or swearing (taking the Lord's name in vain), was liable to the death penalty. Measures like this were authorized by the sanctity of their cause, but in practice they could not be maintained for long. Loose women were periodically driven out of the camp (to fall a prey to the Turks) and other women found in the next captured city, though never enough of them. The soldiers' obsession with sex took its simplest form in rape. Local women, and Moslems especially, would first be raped and then become soldiers' whores. But in a holy army, things were never so simple. There were plenty of honest pilgrims preaching purity and uttering frenzied denunciations of vice, although this did not prevent them from sometimes indulging in it themselves, like the visionary Peter Bartholomew. Bartholomew had the luck, or the genius, to unearth the Holy Lance and his visions gained credit with the army, but visionaries were always appearing in every corner of the camp, prophesying victory or disaster. Military brotherhoods grew up, like that of the Tafurs mentioned in the *Anonymi*. These were poor men so fierce and terrifying to look at that they even frightened the Crusaders themselves. They were intrepid and ferocious and so disinterested that they would kill any of their own comrades whom they discovered in the act of looting. Their aim was destruction, not to enrich themselves. It was known that they dug up the bodies of the enemy to eat them. They did it from hunger, but they boasted of it afterward as an exploit.

We have seen that it was a revolt of the infantry which compelled the Crusader barons to leave Antioch and march on Jerusalem. The leaders seem to have been more appalled than their men by the difficulties of the undertaking. They dawdled on, pausing to lay siege to the cities nearest Antioch, which seemed to them the most accessible and the most profitable to capture. They were afraid of the power of Egypt, and were in no hurry to engage in a campaign which promised to be simple suicide. In the end, they did reach Jerusalem and laid siege to it, realizing fully that it was now too late to draw back and that all that remained was to risk everything in the hope of gaining everything. This was the only way to keep up the army's morale.

The story of the siege of Jerusalem is in itself a long catalogue of suffering, privations, and murderous battles for the attackers. The heat was appalling; water was scarce and they had to go many miles to find it, and overwhelming quantities must be brought back to water so many thousands of men and horses and other animals. While the engineers and carpenters, directed by the barons, were building siege towers, the army, with the pilgrims, organized processions around the city, around the Mount of Olives, to the Jordan, and to Bethlehem, in a state of growing exaltation as their sufferings grew more intense. It was becoming increasingly clear that God could not refuse a miracle to His own people.

The capture of Jerusalem was in fact a miracle, and one for which the leaders of the Crusade had not perhaps, in their heart of hearts, dared to hope for. It seemed to them a clear manifestation of the divine will. Neither al-Afdal, the Vizier of Cairo, nor the Sultan of Persia nor his lieutenants, had bothered to send an army to relieve the siege of the Holy City, and the Franks, comparatively few and ill-armed though they were, found that to all intents they had no opponents in Judaea except the Fatimid garrison of Jerusalem. Godfrey of Bouillon and Raymond of Saint-Gilles were excellent soldiers, and they can hardly have expected this. Even so, the siege lasted for over a month.

However bitter the siege, it seemed astonishing that Jerusalem could be captured in so little time, like any ordinary city, when a much larger army had sat outside Antioch a whole year and been nearly wiped out by vastly superior Turkish forces. It is a disquieting thought that this astonishment—even wonder—should have expressed itself in unimaginably murderous frenzy. For so long the soldiers had become accustomed to the sight of blood, drunk with blood, that to mark such a victory as this they wanted more than the usual massacre which followed the capture of a city by storm. They wanted torrents and rivers of blood, the blood which in the Mosque of al-Aqsa rose to the men's ankles or even to their horses' chests,[5] inconceivable as this seems. The inside of the mosque was several hundred yards square; the bodies lay on the ground, drowned in their own blood, while the victors splashed through it and were soaked in blood with every step they took.

The leaders, or at least the bulk of the knights, cannot be entirely excused from responsibility for this. In the heat of battle, they must have lost their heads. Nevertheless, this vengeance belonged first and foremost to the poor, to the humble, obscure, and wretched, to the strayed, the mad, the desperate and exalted, to the whole mass of those so often dismissed as the dregs of humanity and who, if they were not so at the beginning, certainly became so after three years of misery. It was they who, taking vengeance for their poverty, for their centuries of wretchedness and degradation, indulged themselves with this gruesome festival because they had no claim to any other: theirs was the victory here, and they were God's justicers. Even to their own leaders and to the wealthy pilgrims, they were objects of respect and a pledge of divine favor; they were no longer the least of mankind, they were God's poor whose presence justified the war. It was for them that Jerusalem had been conquered.

The palaces and great houses were occupied by the barons and churchmen, but among the poor also there were those who became citizens of Jerusalem and settled down among the belongings of dead infidels. Most of the pilgrims are known to have taken ship again as soon as possible: Jerusalem was not a paradise. It was also a fact that ships' masters would not take passengers who could not pay; and the knights who were going home, however charitable, could not pay the passages of hundreds of poor people. Among those who stayed behind, only the strongest and cleverest stood a chance of survival. The country at that time was infested with robbers, and food was scarce and expensive.

The Pioneers of the Kingdom

A few hundred knights and sergeants remained behind, and as for the poor and the civilians, the chroniclers have little to say about them. Whatever their numbers, they were not combatants or people easy to classify as citizens. But fresh hosts were already streaming to the liberated Jerusalem from all the Christian countries of Europe. They never reached it. At Kastamuni in Paphlagonia, nearly fifty thousand Frenchmen, Lombards, and Provençaux were killed, while some fifteen thousand Nivernais perished near Heraclea. In this same vicinity, a further fifty thousand from Aquitaine and Bavaria were lost. These were whole armies, pilgrims and all. It took all the prestige of the holy war and all the Christian fervor for the Holy Sepulcher to make these expeditions seem, to contemporary eyes, anything but the most disastrous folly. Even after 1101 the idea of the Crusade still retained its popularity in the West: people no longer went to the Holy Land in great hordes, but they still dreamed of the Crusaders' victories and of Jerusalem delivered. Resounding failures were passed over in silence and blamed on accidental causes; what really mattered was the recovery of the Holy Places. Nevertheless, it can be said that the Crusaders themselves were the first and greatest victims of the war they had undertaken under the sign of the cross.

At least they had brought it on themselves, while those they were attacking asked for nothing but to be left in peace. The Turkish and Turkoman armies slaughtered thousands upon thousands of the intruders, mercilessly and at almost no risk to themselves. Kilij Arslan and Ghazi Gümüshtekin had no reason to behave with more clemency than the victors of Jerusalem. Once Islam had recovered from the initial shock, it realized that this was not an invasion, that they were not dealing with a race of conquerors but only with a few isolated expeditionary forces. The few survivors of these sacrificial armies found themselves in the Holy Land. They had the consolation of having accomplished the pilgrimage to Jerusalem and of placing their swords at the service of the Holy Sepulcher. No blame attached to these leaders for having escaped, practically alone, from an escapade in which all their soldiers and all the civilians who had set out under their protection had lost their lives. They were like the survivors of some natural disaster, and in a tragedy of such magnitude any who managed to escape were regarded as fortunate rather than cowardly.

They were men who had lived through a hell of hunger, thirst, heat, and Turkish arrows. First the arrows, and then the sabers, slicing off heads by the dozen; thousands of bleeding corpses and living men trampled underfoot by the charging horsemen. Bishops and counts could be seen running away on foot, half-naked, dragging themselves for days on end through rocky, waterless mountains to arrive, half-dead from exhaustion, at the gates of the nearest Christian city. Hugh of Vermandois, the brother of King Philip I, who was wounded in the battle of Heraclea, reached Tarsus in this condition and died there. William IX of Aquitaine was luckier: he managed to make his way back home, where he earned himself a reputation as a troubadour which eclipsed his exploits and misfortunes in the Holy Land. How many of the less illustrious escaped is unknown, but all historians state that their number was very small.

In Syria, where the Crusaders were dealing with adversaries less formidable than Kilij Arslan and the Danishmendites, war was possible, and they made war. The Egyptian armies came up the coast and attacked what was left of the first Crusading army. Baldwin I was a man to defend his own lands. Once again it was a case of conquer or die. "If you are killed you will have a martyr's crown. If you are victorious, immortal glory. All desire for flight is useless: France is too far away!" Accompanied by the True Cross, which was carried by the Bishop Gerard, the King, at the head of his knights, hurled himself against forces ten times greater than his own. At Ramleh he lost his best companions, Bervold and Geldemar Carpenel, who fell with all their men, but he won the victory. Eight months later there was another massacre of Frankish knights and a total rout. Hugh of Lusignan, Geoffrey of Vendôme, Stephen of Blois, to mention only the greatest of them, were killed there. "There had not been such a slaughter of knights in Syria before—and the power of Christendom in that land was greatly weakened thereby. Those who knew the land best were more shaken than the rest, and considered fleeing from the country because it was too dangerous to stay there," wrote William of Tyre. And this was in 1102, three years after the capture of Jerusalem. There was talk of two hundred knights slain, and although this is a ludicrous figure when compared to the strength of the great Crusading armies, for Frankish Syria it was enormous. It was indeed dangerous to stay, but they stayed all the same.

They not only stayed—those in Jerusalem and in the north, in Antioch, Edessa, and the Lebanon—they indulged in the luxury of making war among themselves. Not very often, indeed, but as often as was physically possible for them. There was no longer any great army, but there were always newcomers and seasonal reinforcements. Ten years after the great departure for the First Crusade, there was already a kernel of Franks in Syria who considered themselves at home there and were fighting for lands which were already their own. Some had lost friends and brothers there; others, like Baldwin I, their wives and children, and all shared in the pride of possessing the most glorious land in all the world because it was the holiest. They had other reasons, too, for being attached to it.

The Holy Land

It was a beautiful country, though too hot for men who came from Normandy and Flanders, and with some regions, like parts of Judaea and Galilee, that were barren enough. But there were also provinces like the coastal plain, the plain of the Jordan, and the lands around the Orontes that were so providentially fertile that three harvests could be gathered in one year and men could grow not only corn and vines and apples but other fruits, unknown in Europe, such as oranges and lemons, many varieties of vegetables, and sugar cane. There were also the forests of the Lebanon and Banyas, which produced the finest woods for building and were well stocked with game, and the prairies of Jordan and the coast of Lebanon. As good landowners, the Franks prized all this. They appreciated and admired the comforts and beauty of the cities, and the superb fortifications and defense works, which excited them so much that they began covering the land with castles.

With its wooded hills, calm white villages and cypress groves, stony tracks where donkeys passed to and fro laden with stone jars and baskets of olives, and broad roads along which the great caravans traveled, this land with its bluest of blue skies and cold, starry nights was a land a man could love, and would have loved even if it had not been the birthplace of Jesus Christ.

The original inhabitants—those of the cities, at any rate—were more or less roughly dispossessed. In Edessa and Antioch they were left where they were, but oppressed. In Jerusalem, and also in Caesarea, the other Palestinian city which suffered a massacre, they were wiped out. Moslems were expelled from other cities along the coast: Jaffa, Tripoli, Beirut, and Tyre lost their Moslem populations and only the poor remained. Every time a city fell there was murderous fighting, especially on the side of the attackers, but the brunt of the attack was shared by the Italian sailors who had well earned the privileges they obtained. The Crusaders gained a good deal of wealth from the spoils of victory, and a man who had not owned "so much as one village" might find himself in the East "the lord of a city." Fulcher of Chartres was telling the truth, but he forgot to mention that these fortunate ones were the minority and that most of the warrior pilgrims, far from becoming lords of anything at all, simply became "martyrs." There were not such vast numbers of cities or even villages in the East waiting to be picked up by adventurers from Europe.

In those first ten years the knights, eager for land and for glory, conquered as many strongholds as their means allowed and then established a summary plan of campaign: the next aim was to increase the possessions already acquired by seizing the coastal cities and the lands immediately bordering on Palestine and the states of Antioch and Edessa. They must not venture too far because it was necessary to live in peace with their stronger neighbors, or at least not to have them as enemies all the time.

This state of constant warfare was not too much of a strain for the Frankish knights. They were doing their job and they simply had more opportunity of exercising their trade in the East than in Europe, where even so, private wars had long since become a public scourge. Here they could fight with a clear conscience because the Church, far from condemning their wars as fratricidal, proclaimed them agreeable to God. They also got comparatively more profit out of their wars, since in non-Christian lands the rights of pillages were more loosely applied. They very quickly established a *modus vivendi* which reduced the profits gained from the holy war to the same proportions as those of any other war, but there were always a few fortresses left to conquer on the borders—or at least, so men might hope.

The Chivalry

As long as the Frankish kingdom endured, these wars, whether great or small, were extremely murderous. Moreover—something which was not the case in Europe—they were very nearly as lethal to the cavalry as to the infantry.

The Frankish warriors in the East had not given up their heavy armor: experience had shown that it was their best asset. To men less tough it might have seemed an instrument of torture when they had to fight in the heat of summer. Worn in a heat that was almost unendurable even for men very lightly clad, a shirt of mail, steel helmet, and iron greaves—all of which were naturally padded inside for protection against blows—must have been a test which only men of exceptional strength and trained to the wearing of armor from their earliest youth could have borne for long. Their helmets were protected by plumes of feathers, their hauberks by tunics of fine cloth, but even so this costume was a good deal warmer than that worn by Eastern warriors, of whom even the wealthy wore only a light coat of mail beneath their white woolen cloaks. The Frankish knight's shield and lance were much bigger and heavier than those of the enemy. Their battle chargers, protected by leather caparisons padded with horsehair and reinforced with metal plates, carried a hundred pounds of metal on their backs, as well as the weight of a man.

A knight, said al-Imad—who even after ninety years of Frankish presence in the East was still astonished by the fact—was practically invulnerable. Arrows, javelins, and sword cuts were all powerless against him. There was therefore good reason for the assertion that one single Frankish knight was worth ten Moslem horsemen: he could take ten times as many blows and still stand firm when others would have been killed outright. However, as al-Imad noted, there was another side to the coin. Once the knight was off his horse he was helpless, because he could not move fast enough to escape swiftly: "The horse must be wounded or killed before the rider can be unseated." (The Moslems' spears were not strong enough to knock a man off his horse, whereas this happened frequently in Western battles or tourneys.) It was easier to kill a horse than a man, but it must be said that the combatants were reluctant to kill horses and only did so in the last extremity. Horses were the most valuable of all booty, and especially a horse capable of carrying the weight of a knight and enduring the strain, noise, and terror of a battle. But if in the end the horse fell, then the knight was half-disarmed and easily captured. Indeed, it is even somewhat unfair to blame some of these invulnerable cavaliers for not fighting to the death. Arrows and swords slid harmlessly off their armor and it took an exceptional ferocity to get killed if the enemy was determined to take one alive. It was easier to beat the knights down and then tie them up than it was to kill them.

Many were killed in battle. Massacres of prisoners were fairly infrequent—there was an impressive one after the battle of the *Ager Sanguinis,* and occasional others after the storming of castles, but never in any systematic fashion. Saladin's policy toward the warrior monks from 1187 onward was an exception to the rule, and before that date neither Templars nor Hospitalers had been executed. If a knight had money, he was usually able to obtain his release from captivity on payment of a ransom (except during the reign of Nur ed-Din, who was not keen on restoring enemy combatants to freedom). The same was true of eminent Moslem prisoners. Poor prisoners of war became slaves, but they were not compelled to abjure their faith, or only in cases where it was judged the equivalent of capital punishment, and then in most cases the Frankish prisoners preferred death. Those who died rather than surrender were many. A man might live through thirty battles only to fall at last in the thirty-first, and even generals rarely died in their beds.

Not one of the kings of Jerusalem was killed in battle: the King's person was regarded as sacred and was the object of special protection, even in the thick of the fight, while the enemy had more to gain from taking the King alive than from killing him. Only Baldwin I died as a result of wounds, and these he got during a raid against the Bedouin, who cared little for his royal rank. Baldwin II was twice taken prisoner but was never seriously wounded. He lived to a respectable age. Fulk I, it will be remembered, died while still at the height of his powers, as a result of a hunting accident, and his two sons, Baldwin III and Amalric I, died young, of illness. Baldwin IV was already doomed by his leprosy to a short life, and was probably finished off by a fever which shortened his agony. All of them, however, were excellent soldiers.

Of the princes of Antioch, only Tancred died of illness. Roger of Salerno was killed at the *Ager Sanguinis* and Bohemond II in Cilicia, Raymond of Poitiers perished at Fons Murez, and all three fell with the greater part of their knights, when it would probably have been possible for them to ransom themselves later if they had surrendered, since the value of their heads was common knowledge. Only two counts ruled over Edessa. Joscelin I died as a result of an accident which occurred while he was supervising mining operations, and Joscelin II died as a prisoner of Nur ed-Din. Of the rulers of the county of Tripoli, only Bertrand of Toulouse died a natural death, after he had been in the Holy Land for three years. Raymond of Saint-Gilles died—when he was over sixty—of the aftereffects of injuries received in a fire; William-Jordan of Cerdagne was killed by an arrow, possibly on Bertrand's orders; Pons, Bertrand's son, was killed when fleeing across country after a defeat, and his son, Raymond II, was killed by the Assassins. Raymond III, the last of the line, died after the fall of Jerusalem, of grief more than sickness. This, in the circumstances, amounts to a natural death, but one even sadder than that of Roger of Salerno or Raymond of Poitiers.

There were leaders, like the two last-named princes, who died in despair at having led their armies to disaster, an emotion not unlike the despair of the old Roman generals who flung themselves on their swords rather than face dishonor. Baldwin I, who escaped alone after his defeat at Ramleh in 1102 to build up a fresh army, may have shown a greater courage because his passionate love for his kingdom was stronger than any other feeling. The Franks' courage was proverbial and generally admired, because the knights had the cult of honor and in the Holy Land this cult had grown to remarkable proportions because of the stimulant provided by the presence of the infidel.

The Mystique of War

Usama compared the courage and ferocity of the Franks to that of wild beasts, and this was also the way in which Europeans once tried to explain the fearlessness of the "savage" African and Indian warriors. In fact, it is well known that nothing could be less animal than the courage of primitive peoples. It is a courage built up painfully in the course of prolonged initiation trials in which the future warriors are conditioned from childhood to endure what are sometimes real tortures, and also a careful psychological training aimed at overcoming fear in all its forms and exalting the ability to resist pain. The training of a medieval warrior was certainly more rudimentary, with less of ritual and "magic" about it, since Christianity had proscribed as impious anything which might have survived of pagan practices of this kind among the Germans and Scandinavians, but the training still existed. It was hard, and to the adolescent of noble birth the idea of sanctity was inseparable from that of courage itself and of physical endurance for its own sake. It is an undeniable fact that the impulse of the Crusades provided a most valuable stimulant for this, so to speak, natural warrior mystique, a fact which has already been noted earlier in this book. Much has been said about chivalric piety and the piety of the Crusaders, a piety which often found its supreme expression in courage. It is worth noting that knights in the Holy Land were probably no more pious than those in Europe, but they were in general braver.

It can be assumed that they were less reluctant to shed "pagan" blood than Christian, but the history of wars in Europe teaches us that no one was afraid of shedding Christian blood and that the rough warriors of the eleventh and twelfth centuries were not unduly fearful of incurring damnation by splitting their countrymen's skulls. The Crusades brought to war an atmosphere of poetry and greatness, and even of purity and sacrifice, which was lacking elsewhere.

It is a fact that the ambitions of the Crusading leaders and their vassals were quite bluntly terrestrial, and even the pious Fulcher of Chartres does not hesitate to present the Crusade as a profitable undertaking primarily on a material level. It would be idle to assume that in this army of volunteers, the leaders were all ambitious vulgarians while the bulk of the knights—who, rich or poor, belonged to the same social class as their leaders—were made up of pure soldiers of Christ. There were good and bad in the army, men like Emich of Leisingen as well as those like Hugh of Payens, and the testimony of historians and of the *chansons de geste* seems to indicate that when it came to fighting, all of them allowed themselves to be carried away by a warlike frenzy which transformed them into heroes of the faith and candidates for martyrdom. It is not easy for us to imagine how much this civilization, which was based on the love of war, had in it of serious and deeply human exaltation. The Moslems of the period were amazed, even though they had their own traditional warrior mystique, perhaps because they had thought they were dealing with ignorant savages.

But the strength of the Franks did not lie only in their armor and their strategy. They did belong to a genuine civilization, suddenly and deeply aware of its own existence, and confronting the East with its own particular weapons because it had no others. It was a civilization which already possessed a rich past of traditions, moral values, myths, and dreams.

The *chanson de geste*—which was not intended for an educated elite—exalts suffering and death above victory. Any people or social class whose vision of the world is essentially tragic has already reached a high degree of moral maturity. The *Song of Roland,* which was written (or at least written down) at the time of the Crusades, without being the story of a Crusade properly speaking, tells us a great deal more about chivalry than the historians do. The hero, formidable to his enemies but gentle and humble with his friends, is "clear of face, broad of shoulder and narrow of hips"; he is prodigiously strong and possesses a horse of exceptional worth, glittering armor, and a miraculous sword studded with relics. He is the saint of a new kind of paradise. Saint Maurice, and to an even greater extent Saint George, with his shining armor and his white horse, are this knight's brothers in arms. Yet these heroes are not loved for their strength but for their weakness.

Roland has certainly slain a hundred, four hundred of the enemy; with the single blow of his fist he can shatter steel helmets, make the eyes start from men's heads and their brains spill. All this is necessary to sustain his reputation. But what matters is that he is ultimately vanquished. He can do no more; he drags himself along, bleeding, with his brains dripping over his ears, until he faints from weakness. Dying, he seeks out the bodies of his comrades, weeps and laments and prays for their souls, overcome with tenderness and pity. He dies, holding his glove up to God and remembering all the lands he has conquered. And if the angels do come at last to find his soul and carry it to paradise, there is nothing joyous in this ending. His friends, including Charlemagne himself, come and bow down over his corpse, but they have come too late. They sob and tear their hair, mourning for the youth and strength of those who are no more: nothing can ever repair such a loss. Vengeance comes, but it is a poor and useless thing; the beauty of the tale lies in its being the story of a great misfortune.

They are stories of passionate love, but for what? Is it for war? Yes, insofar as war is the symbol of the ultimate test, the greatest grief. The funeral passages of the *chansons de geste* have the value of an exorcism. No one wanted to share the lot of Roland and his twelve peers, whose heroic death was lived again in imagination by generations of warriors and released superfluous reserves of emotion. The death of Roland was the moral justification for all war and gave the rudest soldier a sense of the spiritual grandeur of his calling. One could kill, plunder, rape, and burn villages: the lofty figure of Roland was there to remind men that the warrior—especially when he was a soldier of Christ—carried within him a power of redemption through suffering and a mystical purity.

This note of passionate feeling recurs in all warlike civilizations, and is further strengthened among Christian warriors by a dangerous equivocation. The dying hero is unconsciously imitating the Passion of Christ, and struck down, wounded and bleeding, reduced to a glorious wreck of a human being, he comes closer in his agony to the crucified God. The hero's prestige benefitted from the intensity of feeling which surrounded a God "who suffered for our sins," and it was not for nothing that of all the companions of Charlemagne the most popular was Roland, of whom nothing is known except that he was defeated and killed at Roncevaux. Yet Charlemagne's armies had infinitely more victories than defeats.

Thus armed with a pathetic and purifying concept of heroism, the knights of the twelfth century always had good reasons for fighting.

Faith was one form of a warrior's honor. In the *Chanson d'Antioch,* we find Bohemond's brother Guy exclaiming when he hears the news —false, but he does not know that—of the destruction of the Crusading army: "God, if You have permitted this, no one will serve You any more, for there would be no more honor in Your service!" God had a duty to be a faithful suzerain and protect His vassals. His soldiers had to fight for Him because, all-powerful though He was, He could not reconquer a land He wished to possess by His own means; the land had to be given to Him. The Crusaders' piety also contained a deep need for loyalty and submission, a need which had long been unsatisfied and which, in imagination, fell back on the person of Charlemagne, the great Charles, the good, the wise, the strong, the very incarnation of God the Father and the God of Battles.

In Germany, the dream of the great empire and the sovereign emperor sought for its incarnation in the German emperors, whose power often remained hypothetical and bitterly disputed. In France there was, not the shadow of an emperor, but a king who was much too weak to challenge the memory of Charlemagne, however faintly. God was the undisputed Emperor (and God is generally given the title of Emperor in all the *chansons de geste*) and more remote even than Charlemagne, but living and powerful to all eternity. He was the perfect *seigneur* in whose service was glory.

In practice, it was not easy to serve Him, because He was not there to be seen riding at the head of His army and giving orders. The authority of the real leaders of the Crusade was precarious and constantly open to question. But God's soldiers felt that they were raised to a dignity which placed them above other soldiers, while the cross sewn on their garments as a sign of their divine protection and calling was loved because through it a man belonged to God, as the slave belonged to his master. They believed that its purifying virtues could sometimes absolve them from the worst of crimes. The only crime it would never absolve was cowardice.

A real and obsessional horror of cowardice can be discerned in all the texts of the period, whether they are the work of clerics or laymen. Courage is the great virtue with which all others have to fall into line, and it is clear that medieval man, and the medieval knight in particular, lived under a moral law of a highly individual kind. It was not altogether Christian, although it contained elements of Christianity, but was based on a stoicism, even an asceticism, that was altogether warlike and on the cult of honor. The old Germanic paganism, which had apparently been defeated and forgotten, was exacting its revenge.

The audiences who listened to the *chansons de geste* found Roland's pride in refusing to sound his horn to call for help perfectly natural, although culpable. Roland was afraid of seeming a coward and so bringing dishonor on his whole family. Similar motives prevented even the least brave from retreating so much as an inch in battle. Rather than draw back they would be killed where they stood. Frankish defeats in Syria were more often followed by massacres of the chivalry than by flight or rout (although the Franks were not bent on suicide and on occasion they did flee or surrender). In general, their endurance seemed to the Moslems something miraculous, as also did their fury in battle.

Once they were taken prisoner, they were quite docile, like people who know the game is lost. They were not like the warriors of antiquity who would fall back, in the last resort, on putting an end to their own lives rather than face dishonor, because their religion forbade suicide. Al-Fadil did, however, witness the suicide of a Templar in command of the castle of Beit al-Ahzan. Seeing that his castle had been stormed and set on fire, "when the flames reached his side . . . he flung himself into the fiery abyss, fearless of the burning heat, and from this fire he immediately entered another [that of hell]."[6] One rash or ill-considered word could send a whole body of fighting men to certain death. ("Do you then love your blond head so much . . . ?" In 1187, when the kingdom was in deadly peril, the deliberate waste of a hundred and fifty Templars was a criminal act, but a knight who had been challenged to go and get himself killed was beyond the help of reason.)

Admittedly, this kind of knightly pride was more suitable for knights of the Temple or the Hospital than it was for laymen, because the soldier monks had nothing to lose. They had already bound themselves by the most terrible of oaths never to draw back or calculate the number of the enemy. An utter disregard for death had been elevated to a point of dogma with them, and these men, far from being the most Christian of fighters, were the most abandoned to a completely pagan exultation in combat. The doubts that their religion was later to arouse have been seen. When they were accused of heresy, at a time when after the evacuation of the last Frankish ports in Syria the military orders had lost the reason for their existence, the Templars did not actually make any precise admissions. Their ritual and their rule were such as to forge men of steel, hardened against all fear, even that of hell (this could have been the meaning of the mysterious abjuration of Christ imposed upon the postulant). A knight might have to fight in a state of mortal sin, and no consideration should make him draw back from death. Such heretical doctrines as there may have been in the teachings of the Temple came from a logical twisting of the warrior mystique which was already to be seen in the *chansons de geste*. Ismailian influences provided a new element in this mystique: the brothers of the sect of the Ismailians were also dedicated to death as to a bride, and whether or not they were raised to their state of mystical exaltation by the use of hashish they were ready to die—and to die on the orders of their leader—as if this were a supreme beatitude and an end in itself. So strong was the cult of ritual death in the fulfillment of duty (in this case murder) that mothers were seen celebrating the heroic death of their sons as a triumph, and putting on mourning when they learned that their sons had escaped from the enemy instead of standing still and waiting for death. The Templars, who were after all Christians, were somewhat less fanatical and did not share this cult of murder and longing for death. But they too systematically cultivated a spirit of extravagance and indifference to danger which made them at once useful and dangerous to the kingdom.

By a fairly natural coincidence, the Frankish knights of Syria found themselves in very much the same situation as Roland and his peers —with this difference: that there was no treachery involved and no invincible Emperor to come to their rescue at the mere sound of a horn. Always there were the countless hordes of the enemy, the pagans who came from beyond the mountains in their tens of thousands, and always the same anxiety: ". . . and we were only a small company." According to the situation, they had to refuse battle and stand on the defensive, close together like a wall, or charge headlong forward. The famous charges of the Franks were prodigies of calculated risk, and to train men to this state of discipline took all the moral and physical strength of the knights. Like professional sportsmen they were obliged to keep constantly in training. They were men who spent their whole lives, between the ages of fifteen and sixty, in fighting or in practicing for future fights, and their relaxations seldom lasted long.

War in this country did not stop for the winter, because the winters were not very severe and all months were good for war. Given the frequency of battles, every knight might reasonably expect to be killed in the end, and those who were taken prisoner were not always certain of their release. The wealthiest ransomed themselves sooner or later. Many ended their days as slaves or shut up in dungeons. After Hattin a certain number of the combatants were released on payment of a ransom, but the majority—more than ten thousand of them

—were never able to ransom themselves. There were poor knights among them, squires and sergeants, and soldiers of the citizen militia. Al-Imad describes the melancholy processions of tens and hundreds of men roped together in columns being led to Damascus at the same time as the "heads of Christians as numerous as watermelons," and sold in the market very cheap because there were so many of them that no one knew what to do with them. Abu Shama writes: "One of the fakirs accompanying the army had as his share of the booty a prisoner whom he exchanged for a pair of sandals which he needed. And when someone remarked on such a bargain with astonishment, he replied, 'I wanted people to remark on it and to say: these Christian slaves were so numerous and so cheap that one of them was sold for a pair of sandals. Praise be to God!' "[7]

The Slaves

How many of these Christian prisoners were there, between 1096 and 1192? In Asia Minor in 1101 there were a very great many, and these were largely women and children, the men having been killed on the spot. Women who were still young, adolescents, small children—anyone who could be useful was taken. The old and the sick were generally not worth the trouble. The victors divided their spoils, keeping pretty women and attractive children for their own pleasure, while the remainder were scattered around the markets and bought like cattle for domestic purposes.

Children were not worth much: a tenth of the price of a man and a fifth of that of a woman; they were long-term goods which had to be fed and trained, and there was a risk that they might die before they could be useful. Children were of course converted automatically to Islam. The Moslems believed they could do no less than save their souls. Many probably became excellent Moslems and excellent servants, forgetting their mother tongue and distinguished from their fellows only by their lighter hair and eyes. If they lived, children were better value than adults because they had no regrets for their lost liberty or their native land. Even children still at the breast were bought. (In 1191 Saladin bought back a baby of three months and returned it to its Frankish mother who, in her delight, put it to her breast at once. The purchaser would have been obliged to procure a nurse for his little slave.)

Women were generally employed in domestic work, or were put to work in textile workshops or at spinning and other skills if they were young enough to learn a trade. If they were still in their teens, or very pretty, they might be bought for a rich man's harem, becoming the slaves of their master's wives, and there was even a chance that they might become favorites themselves. Several thousand Frankish women were sold in 1101, and captives were obviously taken in the various campaigns throughout the century. Many were captured from Conrad III's army in 1147, and the men of this army were also taken and sold. There were also the defeated of Hattin and the fifteen thousand poor Franks from Jerusalem.

Slavery, for adults, was a living death. Families were broken up, unless a wealthy and kindhearted purchaser thought of buying a whole family. Usually they were divided beforehand by the slave merchant, who had nothing to gain from keeping the small family units in his caravan. It was more practical to group people according to their price and the purpose for which they would be used.

The slaves were evaluated according to their abilities, their trade, or their physical strength. One legend has it that a Christian bishop who was a talented sculptor suffered martyrdom for refusing to carve an "idol," when he would have been able to earn a great deal of money if he had shown himself a docile workman. In fact Moslems had no use for carved idols, but slaves who had any skill in a particular art were expected to use it, and frequently were well rewarded for doing so. Young, strong men were used in building work (the same was true of Moslem prisoners of war in Frankish Syria), and their lot was no harder than that of any other laborers, because workmen were always very poorly paid. Slaves were fed and housed, and in theory their masters were not entitled to inflict serious bodily harm on them. But in practice a slave was dead to society; he had no appeal against his master and was severely punished if he ran away.

Slavery as an institution was so deeply rooted in custom that no one thought of finding it unfair. In the West it had practically died out, but the Franks became accustomed to it very quickly in the East. There were slave markets in every Frankish city, and the King of Jerusalem's armies captured and sold into slavery the inhabitants of conquered strongholds. Moreover, the Franks themselves practiced slavery to a certain extent. The great lords had slaves among their servants, and prisoners of war were sometimes sent to forced labor, though for a limited time. The institution never became an accepted habit with Frankish society. The slave trade was a business like any other, and professionals in the traffic were not interfered with in the exercise of their trade. (Moreover, slavery was too powerful an institution for the government to attempt to suppress it.) But it may be said that the Franks regarded it as simply a local custom to be respected but not necessarily adopted.

The reason the Franks had such a bad reputation as slaves—and they were notorious for adapting to slavery very badly—was that they came from a land where people were not sold in the marketplaces. (This is not to say that any of the other peoples were easily resigned to it; the few details mentioned, almost in passing, by Arab chroniclers do however suggest that the Franks, who were perhaps more demonstrative than the Orientals, showed their misery in a more obvious fashion, and the cases already quoted, which are reported by Usama, show that this revulsion from slavery was not unduly frequent.)

The fact was that no idea of degradation was necessarily attached to the word "slave" in the East. Relations between master and slave, even including the actual buying and selling, were a part of normal human relations and too thoroughly accepted in everyday life to arouse any rebellion.

A slave who was chosen as a concubine might well be honored and treated with respect even though she remained a slave, and an able and conscientious slave could become a friend of his master. To have been sold as a result of some misfortune or a defeat in battle was not necessarily shaming, and strictly speaking the purchaser was not acquiring the persons themselves but only a right to their labor.

The only form of slavery officially practiced in our own day is the use of prisoners of war for forced labor, which is a custom as old as the world. Systems of concentration camps and other forms of slavery rest on the principle of disciplinary sanctions against individuals guilty of some infringement of the law (even when this infringement is imaginary and simply intended to justify the practice of forced labor). In the Middle Ages, this aspect of slavery also existed: people who were unable to pay their debts and insolvent criminals who had been sentenced to a fine could be sold as slaves. It can even be said that the conditions of factory workers, miners, and even of workers on the land in our own era is sometimes not very far removed from slavery, because there can be no real freedom for a badly paid man who is completely dependent on his employer and condemned for life to a basically servile condition. Slaves who had lived on one estate for generations had their own families, their own living accommodation, and work assured, and could feel perfectly free so long as they did not want to move away. It was different for a man who had once been free: his was then primarily a social fall.

To foreigners, slavery meant a total and hopeless uprooting and the cruelest mental torment for families who were separated. Consequently slavery, which was generally accepted by law and approximated in time of peace to a system of ensuring cheap labor, became in time of war the most terrible of all misfortunes.

Ever since the Turkish invasions, the East had been permanently at war. In the eleventh and twelfth centuries, the number of Armenians, Greeks, Arabs, Syrians, and Franks who were sold into slavery as a result of the various armies' campaigns was immense, the equivalent of an entire nation of "displaced persons." To these unfortunates were added the travelers captured by pirates and robbers on the great highways, who were nearly as numerous as the war victims. These, since they were bound by no rules of war but simply by the whims of professionals in the traffic, were even more irremediably lost than the rest. A general in war could be held responsible for his prisoners and they could be ransomed from him (it will be remembered that Manuel Comnenus succeeded in negotiating with Nur ed-Din for the release of six thousand Christian prisoners of war, the majority of whom had been slaves for more than ten years). No one could get back the victims of a pirate, whose trade was in any case illegal and whose victims had long been sold to slave traders who were half pirates themselves. This was merchandise of whose origins everyone preferred to claim ignorance.

It is hard to imagine the condition of these vast numbers of Western pilgrims, travelers, and Crusaders being moved in a series of forced marches across the country, examined, bought, and taken to mines, farmyards, harems, or middle-class homes in a country whose language they did not understand and whose climate and customs were completely strange to them. There was a reasonable chance that they might sometimes come across a fellow countryman, but they were frequently cut off from all contact with their past lives. Those who were not young or clever, and learned only the rudiments of Arabic, lost even their language and were doomed to a gradual process of debasement.

Their ethnic type and their ignorance of the language made escape almost impossible for them, and in any case, there was little chance of escape when there were hundreds of miles to be traveled on foot. Christian slaves were sent into provinces as far as possible from the Frankish states or into big cities with a well-organized police force. The women spent the rest of their days carrying jars of water from the well to the house or scrubbing floors—like pack animals, mute and anonymous, waiting for their ration of food and rest at night on the bare ground in some outhouse. For the younger and prettier, if they were lucky enough to escape the brutality of the soldiery on the actual battlefield, the attentions of their master became a happiness which, at whatever cost, at least saved them from a slow process of decay. A woman chosen as a concubine, even an inferior one, was treated with honor, and she rose even higher in the hierarchy of the harem if she had children.

(It is a curious thought that popular legend made the Margravine Ida of Austria the mother of Zengi. This great lady, who was as pious as she was gallant, would probably have preferred a place among the ranks of the martyrs for the faith. She disappeared without trace and was probably slain or trampled to death in the battle, and her mutilated body, robbed of its rich clothes, left a prey to the vultures and jackals somewhere among the great heap of bodies of men and horses. The poor woman might well have turned in what, for want of a better word, might be called her grave with indignation to hear herself—one of the first ladies of Germany—transformed by posterity into a Moslem's concubine. It is not easy to imagine the Moslems bestowing such a dubious honor on the memory of a great Arab princess. It is a fact that the Franks showed little jealousy of the honor of their women. But the legend of the Margravine was an unconscious popular comfort: the fathers, husbands, and brothers of each of these vanished women could console themselves with the hope, the only one that remained to them, that she had escaped the worst and that she was living somewhere rich, honored, and happy and the mother of fine children, even if they were pagans . . . and that it was Frankish women who were giving the enemy their bravest warriors.)

Slaves judged beautiful enough to deserve a happy life were rare; girls and young women were sold to brothels, luxury class or otherwise, and there they did not live long. Perhaps the fate of those vigorous matrons who were capable of hard work was not so unenviable after all. Young boys, if they were pretty, were also destined for their masters' pleasure. Neither the Turks nor the Arabs had any prejudice against homosexuality (frowned on by pious men but sanctioned by custom and widely practiced). Great chieftains—Zengi in particular—surrounded themselves with pages and minions, and caliphs and sultans had their male as well as their female favorites. There was a strong chance of a child slave finding a master with a fondness for boys. If he was intelligent, or had a good voice, or was gentle and considered suitable to serve in the harem, he was also a likely candidate for castration.

Frankish children of all ages—and there were many in the Crusading armies of 1101 and among the civilian captives during the hundred years of the war—mingled gradually with the great mass of slaves from all countries. Even today there are probably Turks and Arabs who are among their descendants, and totally unaware of the tiny drop of Western blood in their veins. For adults, especially men over thirty, there was no hope, because unless they were highly qualified craftsmen they were condemned to a life of hard work, treated little better than animals, with nothing to do but dream regretfully of their native land, so far away and so very different. A few slaves did obtain their freedom, but they were a small minority. When the Emperor Manuel preferred to ransom six thousand Christians instead of capturing Aleppo, it cannot have been the liberated prisoners who thought of accusing him of treason to Christendom.

Reynald of Châtillon remained a prisoner for sixteen years: a record for an important person. As Prince of Antioch he did not live in a dungeon underground, or work in the mines, but was able to lead a fairly comfortable existence. Even so, for a man devoured by his insatiable passion for action, those sixteen years must have been years of torture. Baldwin II spent six years of his life in captivity; Raymond III of Tripoli, eight years; Joscelin II, nine years—until his death. There is no way of knowing how many knights died in captivity, but they were many, especially among the military orders, which did not pay ransoms. Moreover, some Turkish chieftains like Nur ed-Din did not let their prisoners go even on payment of a ransom. If there had been no news of a man for seven years, he was regarded as dead and his wife was allowed to remarry, but some of these living dead did come back. The knight Gauthier already mentioned was captured by the Egyptians in 1103 and came back after thirty-four years, having been released without a ransom (who would have paid it? Everyone thought he was dead) because he was old and there seemed to be no point in keeping him any longer. Ordinary soldiers who either managed to escape or were released by kindly masters also came back like this from time to time and, if they were not too old, went back to the army or took ship for Europe.

There is no record of these thousands of adventures, fantastic, tragic, or merely ordinary because they were so frequent, or even sometimes improbably lucky, which happened in the course of a century of Crusades to tens of thousands of pilgrims. Those lucky enough to make their way back to their countrymen told their adventures, and their family and friends remembered them. But people in the East had heard it all before, and in Europe there were so many tall stories going about that it was not easy to tell truth from lies. Most of these lost men—and lost women—had no one to tell their stories to and ended their days on farms and in workshops, dead to their families long before their actual deaths.

Conclusion

In considering the Crusades from the point of view of their influence on the course of European history, one important initial fact must be borne in mind. This is the conflict, latent at first and finally open, between the Latin West and Byzantium and the ultimate destruction of the Byzantine Empire. The Crusades were not solely responsible for this catastrophe, which undoubtedly was a great loss to European civilization: the old Empire had had too many enemies waiting to pounce for too long. It is for this reason that I have not attempted in the present work to describe what is usually called the Fourth Crusade and is one of the most shameful pages in the history of Western Christendom.

The real reason for the deflection of the new Crusade in 1203, which was originally conceived as an attempt to reconquer the Holy Land, was the ambition and also the understandable rancor of Venice.* Pope Innocent III protested sincerely, though without much effect, against this scandalous transformation of a holy war into an excuse for plunder. The Crusader barons had their hands forced by the Venetians, in whose debt they found themselves. A glance at Villehardouin's chronicle is enough to show that they accepted all the Venetian propaganda very gullibly and, despite the Pope's remonstrances, succeeded in squaring things with their consciences. The hatred and contempt for Byzantium which had been building up during more than a century of wars in the East appeared to justify them

* See page 441.

in launching their armies against a Christian country while keeping the cross sewn on their garments and their flags.

I have endeavored to trace the course of this slow deterioration in relations between the Greeks and Latins. It must be admitted that the Crusades were a major factor in this because it was the Crusades which brought the old antagonism between the two Christian civilizations out into the open.

As early as 1097, Alexius Comnenus had been afraid that the Latin barbarians would seize his capital. Manuel Comnenus, in 1146, feared the Germans and French more than he feared the Turks, and in 1190, the blundering inadequacy of Isaac Angelus almost hastened the fall of the Empire by fourteen years. But however much he hated the Greeks, the great Hohenstaufen was too well aware that he had taken the cross to liberate Jerusalem and not to capture Constantinople. By 1204, however, Western feelings at the loss of the Holy Land had grown blunted: the great Crusading army was busy building a new Latin empire at Constantinople, plundering convents, churches, and palaces, and raping Greek women by the thousands. This was no longer an army with its mind on setting out again on the road to Jerusalem. In this Crusade the Holy Land had been forgotten.

Byzantium, abruptly reduced to its provinces in Asia Minor, which were still threatened by the Turks, did not disarm and the Greek army and nobility finally recaptured Constantinople in 1261, fifty-seven years after the creation of the Latin Empire. But the Byzantine Empire had in fact received its deathblow, and it was never again to become a great power in the political field. In spite of desperate efforts to survive, including attempts to conciliate the West by making motions in the direction of an ultimate recognition of Roman supremacy, Byzantium always remained suspect in the West, which could not forgive the Empire for its own feelings of guilt and failure. The weakened Empire survived for a further two hundred years before it was finally wiped out by the Turks. In 1453, when the Eastern provinces of Europe fell into Moslem hands, the Latin West scarcely felt the event as a loss to Christendom. The Christian nations were too wrapped up in their own troubles and mutual rivalries, and had long excluded the Eastern question from their considerations.

The Crusade of 1204 had been closely followed by another Crusade (quite apart from the Crusades in Spain, which were the earliest and the most enduring because they were waged by the Spaniards themselves). This was the one known as the Albigensian Crusade and was directed not against the Moslems but against Christian dissidents, the Albigensian heretics of the south of France. It was a genuine Crusade in that, although it was directed against Catholic princes and a largely Catholic population, the volunteers who responded to Innocent III's appeal in 1209 were inspired by religious motives, at least as much as the leaders of the first Crusades. This Crusade naturally degenerated into an affair of individual gain and then into the annexation of Languedoc by the Capet line, but it showed that the idea of the Crusade still answered to a need deeply rooted in the Western mind. It was, however, unique of its kind: as an undertaking instigated expressly by the papacy, it remained a matter for the Church and did not win the support of the mass of the people. The Church never repeated this attempt, and only wars against the infidel continued to bear the name of holy wars and bestow on those who took part in them the right to wear the cross.*

In the thirteenth century came the two Crusades of Saint Louis; the political Crusade of Frederick II, which was preceded by the Crusade preached by Pope Honorius III after the Lateran Council. Although there was now a Latin, Catholic "Empire" in Constantinople, the traditional route of the Crusades was closed more firmly than ever, and the Greeks of Asia Minor could not be expected to make the conquest of Jerusalem by Westerners any easier. In future, the Crusaders' efforts were directed against Egypt, but without success, despite the existence of Frankish bases such as the island of Cyprus and the few ports on the coast of Palestine which were still in Frankish hands. To break the power of the Turks, Saint Louis even went to the lengths of seeking an alliance with the Mongol invaders, some of whom were Christians (Nestorians). In fact, the Franks had well and truly lost the game in 1192. The Latin kingdom which had been grafted onto Syrian soil some ninety years before was dead, and there was no real point in trying to reconquer it.

A number of the European nobility, especially in France, continued to put in some service in the coastal ports of Palestine, in Acre or Jaffa, or possibly Constantinople or Cyprus, and knights were eager to enter the still powerful military orders. The popes had not given up hope of recovering the Holy Land. They still preached wars of reconquest and excommunicated monarchs who tried to wriggle out of this sacred duty. The most pious monarch of all made this duty the

---

* In eastern Germany, during the thirteenth and fourteenth centuries, the German knights, and in particular the Hanseatic League and the Order of the Teutonic Knights, carried on periodical wars of conquest which were with some justification regarded as Crusades owing to the fact that their adversaries, Lithuanians, Letts, or Slavs, were still pagans. These people were converted, usually by force, by the Germans and Scandinavians.

great task of his life, consecrated to it large amounts of his country's revenues, and twice embarked on costly and murderous wars and ultimately died in the task. Saint Louis was not an exception; he was merely the most outstanding representative of a certain pious section of the nobility, conscious of his duty to God and believing that to please God it was necessary to endeavor to recover His "inheritance." Men still dreamed of Jerusalem. Two years before the birth of Saint Louis, hosts of peasant children left their homes at the summons of a young shepherd who saw visions and made their way down the Rhône valley, hoping that their poverty and their innocence would obtain what wealth and strength had been unable to win. The tragedy of the Childrens' Crusade is a well-known story, but the Jerusalem they were seeking had very little to do with the ancient city in Palestine occupied by the Turks.

If the Crusades of the thirteenth century all ended in failure, this was not entirely because Islam had actually become stronger and Christendom weaker—in consequence of the ruin of Byzantium. In the West itself, after the failure of 1192 and the change of direction of the Crusade in 1203, much of the former enthusiasm for the Holy Land had been lost. It had become a pious dream and not a necessity, and the days when Jerusalem had been a Frankish city were slipping further and further into the past. Christianity did not sing songs of triumph when Frederick II obtained Jerusalem through a treaty which placed the city actually under the rule of a Christian monarch. Admittedly, Frederick was under sentence of excommunication at that moment, precisely because of his delay in fulfilling his vow to go on the Crusade, and his diplomatic triumph did nothing to diminish the power of Islam. In fact, the Latin West, once it had destroyed with its own hands the Christian power which had really had something to gain by standing up against the Turks, had resigned itself, with understandable political realism, to leaving Islam in control of the East.

Particular stress has been laid on the history of the Christian kingdom of Jerusalem because this kingdom, short-lived though it was, stands for the positive side of the Crusading movement. It was a state whose political importance was small but not negligible, a state whose existence was somewhat artificial but not hallucinatory, whose chances of enduring were slender but not nonexistent. This little kingdom with the outsize name had only begun to win its real right to exist when it was demolished. The tens of thousands of Franks who were scattered far and wide throughout the slave markets and harems and the great roads of East and West after Hattin were not yet altogether a nation; they had already lost their country at the same time as their freedom and security. It is hard to say what this contact, on a footing of comparative equality, between people of East and West would have achieved. As soon as a glimmer of mutual understanding began to appear, it was very quickly rendered impossible. The same experiment was never to be repeated.

The existence of the Frankish kingdom was actually independent of the various Crusading movements which in the course of the twelfth century created an intense and lasting contact between East and West, but it was to some extent parallel to them. The initial object of the promoters of the First Crusade had not been to turn Palestine into a small feudal state. Their goal was simultaneously more modest—to drive the Seljuks out of Asia Minor—and more vast—to eliminate Islam from the Near East once and for all.

It has been said that by summoning Christians to the aid of the Holy Land the Church, in the person of Urban II, had been trying to relieve the Western nations of some of the superfluous soldiers, unemployed workers, and ruined peasants who constituted useless citizens and even a threat to public order. This is certainly true as far as the soldiers were concerned: the knights, who were getting poorer and poorer and consequently more and more aggressive, were becoming a real scourge for what already deserved to be called nations, and for the Church in particular. Urban II laid particular emphasis on this fact in his sermon: Christendom was being ruined by impious and fratricidal wars, and the warriors had a duty to atone for their crimes by turning their weapons against God's enemies. Moreover, they would acquire greater wealth and lands in the process than any they could find in their own countries.

As far as the "poor" were concerned, this appeal naturally attracted people bound as serfs to a particular lord, who, by taking the cross, became freemen, serfs only of God, as well as anyone in want who could escape from their troubles hoping to find better things elsewhere.

But it is a fact that the majority of the nobles who took the cross were obliged hastily to liquidate their personal possessions—and often at a very bad price—in order to equip themselves. It was usually the Church that benefitted, because it was abbeys and bishoprics who advanced the money. The second to benefit were the bourgeois communes, which frequently did well out of the trade that was also encouraged by the Crusades. The nobles certainly plundered a great deal, especially at the outset, but they gained little from it and what money they made was spent principally on war. Whether the gains they were seeking were material or spiritual, the noble Crusaders, unless they were great barons, had first to ruin themselves to do it. It was the same for the middle-class people who possessed some property and even for the poor who were not absolute beggars. Most of the Crusaders who succeeded in settling in Syria did actually make money, sometimes in a spectacular fashion, but these were only a very small minority, even of the knights. It can hardly be said of the poor that their pilgrimage had a happy ending.

Urban II had certainly not meant to send hosts of Christians to their deaths. He had not foreseen the mass departure of poor people, and the Church did make some efforts—though these were tentative in the extreme—to put a brake on the movement. Ultimately, the effect was as if society had found a new and drastic way of getting rid of a great many useless mouths. Even the sketchiest historical handbooks make a point of observing that the Crusades were a stabilizing factor for the European nations because they decimated and impoverished the nobility and also contributed to the concentration of power in the hands of the Church and of the heads of state. The disappearance of several hundred thousands of the poor—possibly over a million in all if we include all the pilgrim bands—does not seem to have affected the life of the countries from which these people had set out. On the other hand, the Crusades did bring the Latin West a revival of prosperity through the increase of trade, but this was not, or was only indirectly, due to the Crusaders themselves. Despite initial successes, the Crusades were a failure on a military level, responsible for an appalling waste of human life, even counting the lives of Crusaders alone; and however profitable they were in the long run, the benefit belonged chiefly to the commercial republics.

Based as they were on murder and expropriation, the Crusades can hardly be called a very Christian undertaking, but they were long renowned as a glorious adventure. Glorious it undoubtedly was, insofar as Jerusalem could be regarded as something more than an earthly city; but heavenly cities are not to be taken by storm and their inhabitants murdered. The dubious nature of the initial Crusading impulse was never to be completely resolved. Western people gained from it the myth of Jerusalem reconquered and Jerusalem lost.

The important thing is that the Crusade (or the idea of the Crusade) provided the young nations of the West with a common ideal and an apparently concrete and precise means of realizing this ideal. This was only apparent because, consciously or unconsciously, it was always the celestial Jerusalem which lay at the root of all the Crusaders' sermons, speeches, and ambitions. This kind of surge of mystical feeling in politics, in which material aspirations were overlaid with a veneer of mysticism, cannot be said to be unique in history, but rarely have the two motives been so perfectly fused. Indirectly, but quite clearly, the Crusades acted as a catalyst on the national pride of the Western peoples, and united in a fight for the same cause, these peoples learned to know one another better and also to hate one another. They learned even more to hate their great ally and rival, the Empire of Byzantium. Any deep sense of national pride finds a need to seek something more than glory and prosperity for its native land, and to go beyond the idea of the nation itself. In this light, the Crusading impulse was one factor in the creation of Western nationalism.

If, as we have seen, the life of people in the West does not seem to have been deeply affected by the tragedy of the Crusades (except perhaps, briefly, in 1190), the feeling of Latin superiority, of the inalienable and implicit right of Catholic peoples to rule the world, was working its way secretly into their minds by means of these distant and apparently gratuitous wars which gave Latin chivalry possession of the Holy Sepulcher for almost a century.

Clearly, the second and only too easily foreseeable stage in this adventure was the conquest of Constantinople, which at the time was also regarded as a glory for the West. Here, nationalism took over from whatever religious motives might have been left in the Crusading movement. It should not be forgotten that in 1203 some of the Crusader knights were honest enough to admit that this deflection from the original object of the Crusade was a scandal (as even Innocent III himself agreed). Simon of Montfort and his companions left the Crusading army and went directly to the Holy Land, but the majority of the chivalry, far from following their example, blamed them severely, and the accounts of Villehardouin and Robert of Clary amply demonstrate that the whole idea of the holy war had given way at the time to a crude and selfish nationalism. The result was that while the Crusaders of 1204 remained God's soldiers and continued to wear the cross on their garments, they cheerfully transferred their holy detestation of the infidel to other Christians, who had a reputation for perfidy and were at any rate schismatics. A not very different state of things occurred in Languedoc.

Later, when there had been no talk of Crusades for a long time, Western wars of conquest were still to be dominated by this same spirit of dishonesty. It was enough that the enemy could be, in one way or another, regarded as an enemy of religion or of some other of

the higher moral values. Even when he was not, it was easy enough
to claim that this was so, and any war could therefore be regarded
as holy.

The Crusades in Western Literature in the Twelfth and Thirteenth Centuries

This attitude seems to have been encouraged by defeat more than
by the early victories. If we consider the growth of the Crusading
idea in the public mind of the Middle Ages, it seems (as far as it is
possible to judge from the written evidence) that the ideal of the
Crusader knight, of whom Saint Louis remains the best example, did
not actually develop until the thirteenth century, when the Crusading
movement was already on the wane.

Most of the polemical writings and propaganda glorifying the Crusades date from the end of the twelfth or the thirteenth century. The
songs of Conon of Bethune or the Castellan of Coucy celebrate the
glory of serving God and of serving their lady through God's service.
In fact, they are referring either to the Crusade of 1190 or to that of
1204. Ecclesiastical literature in the thirteenth century is full of eloquent appeals to Western chivalry, inviting it to place itself at the
service of its only real suzerain, Jesus Christ. Before the fall of Jerusalem, the Crusade seems to have been regarded much more as a
means of salvation than a source of glory. The twelfth century has left
numerous *chansons de geste,* but only one (or only one cycle, at
least) deals directly with the Crusades. This is the work usually referred to as the *Chanson d'Antioch* because the siege of Antioch
forms its principal subject. Possibly the work of an eyewitness, and
probably of a *trouvère* in Bohemond's entourage, this *chanson* is
an alliterative verse account of actual events. It is not an imaginative
work, but it is nonetheless a *chanson de geste,* of popular inspiration
and intended for a wide public. The same is true of the poem of
Ambroise, but the Norman *jongleur,* who cannot be said to have
possessed an epic talent, was content to versify his own conscientious
and detailed account of the events of which he was a witness.

In general, contemporaries of the Crusades who embarked on literary works seem to have been very little inspired by events which were
too close and consequently too commonplace. One can only dream of
the *chansons de geste* which might have been made about the brilliant
and dramatic battles of Baldwin I, about the tragedy of the *Ager
Sanguinis,* or about Reynald of Châtillon or Joscelin of Courtenay.

The deeds and actions of the barons of the East, God's soldiers though they clearly were, did little to tempt European poets, who were more interested in celebrating heroes whose names were already legend. The *Chanson d'Antioch,* however, did have a real success in the twelfth century and was still highly thought of at the beginning of the thirteenth, for the author of the *Canzon de la Crozada* (the *chanson* of the Albigensian Crusade) refers to it as his model. The example of this same *Canzon* shows that contemporary events were not always considered unsuitable inspiration for an epic poem. It seems that events in Syria quite simply did not interest the Western public very much.

Of the countless epic poems of the twelfth century, those belonging to the cycle of Charlemagne and the cycle of William of Orange often take the struggle against the Saracens as their subject and one can sometimes sense a breath of the Crusades in them. But Charlemagne was a great conqueror and could not be insulted by comparison with the petty kinglets of Syria, while William was defending Christian lands, French lands, against Saracen invasion. Only one poem deals with the relations of the West with Byzantium. This is the *Pèlerinage de Charlemagne à Jérusalem.* (It is a fact that the great Emperor never visited the Holy Places, but a persistent legend asserts that he did, although this was only supposed to have been in order to establish friendly relations with the Caliph Harun al-Rashid.)

At all events, the inspiration of the poem is more popular than classical, and it throws a curious light on medieval Western feelings toward the East. Probably composed somewhere around the beginning of the century, it scarcely mentions the Crusades, although it would seem natural for the author to think of making some reference to them. There is no suggestion either of hatred for the infidel or of pride in the very recent conquests of the Franks. Charlemagne, who has conquered all the kings of the earth, does not have to fight in order to reach Jerusalem. He undertakes the great journey, crosses the whole of Europe with eighty thousand men and the twelve peers, and succeeds in reaching Jerusalem without trouble. There he enters a church, where he finds a great throne with twelve other smaller ones beside it. Charlemagne and the twelve peers sit down on these seats, which have been so conveniently provided, and a Jew who unexpectedly enters the church believes he has seen *God and his twelve Apostles* and is instantly converted. But this adventure, which appears to equate Charlemagne with God's representative on earth, is only a beginning: Charles had not undertaken his pilgrimage solely for reasons of piety. The excuse for the pilgrimage is as follows: the

Empress, Charlemagne's wife, had told her husband that somewhere there was a sovereign who was wealthier and more powerful than himself. This was Hugh the Strong, Emperor of Constantinople. This is a disturbing challenge to Charlemagne, and having first slapped his wife's face, he decides to find out for himself just how powerful this Emperor (or rather King, since the author is reluctant to grant a Greek the imperial title) might actually be. He sets off, with his twelve peers, toward Constantinople by way of Jerusalem.

Here the poet gives free rein to his imagination, and his history is based largely on pamphlets and on popular stories. Hugh the Strong is a curious character who—not being a proper king in the Frankish fashion—tills his own fields, but with a golden plow. This servile occupation puts him at a disadvantage compared to Charles from the beginning, and in addition, his flustered behavior shows that he regards a visit from his Western colleague as a sign of honor. However, Charlemagne and his twelve peers cannot help being amazed at the marvels of a purely technical kind which they behold in Constantinople. These include palaces that revolve and statues that move and speak, marvels which did in fact actually exist in Byzantium and of which the description, however highly imaginative, is based on travelers' tales. The Franks are also struck by the extreme wealth of the country, which is symbolized by the golden plow. The Emperor's daughter, a beautiful golden-haired maiden, also comes in for some praise and excites the interest of the bold Oliver.

Although they are welcomed with the greatest honors, the visitors from the West nevertheless fall, somewhat through their own fault, into a kind of trap. Hugh the Strong mischievously hides in a hollow pillar in the middle of the chamber where his guests are lodged, and listens to their boastful talk. The gist of it is that Charlemagne's knights are not altogether taken in by the splendors of Constantinople and the Greeks' technical refinements, and they consider themselves capable of destroying all these marvels by the strength of their own hands alone. The next day, Hugh expresses his anger and challenges them to put their boasts into practice. Of course, the twelve peers then prove that nothing can resist them, and the poor Emperor, seeing his palace half wrecked and his daughter raped, begs his visitors to stop their demonstration of strength and leave his country.

The author of the poem is clearly not embarrassed by any considerations of historical truth or even of political allusions. He reverts to the traditional theme of the hero who, hearing that there is someone stronger than himself, feels that he must go and measure his strength against that of his distant rival. But the feelings by which the poem is inspired do seem to reflect, almost unconsciously, the attitude of Western man toward Byzantium, and in its comic-heroic extravagance the poem has a vaguely threatening and even prophetic undertone. Under all the pretexts of pilgrimage, the unacknowledged aim of the "barbarians" was really the capture of Constantinople, not, as might have been thought, from a desire for plunder, but from a wish to assert the superiority of the Latins by sacking and humiliating the too wealthy old Empire whose incomprehensible civilization appeared to Western eyes only in the form of useless and frivolous marvels. (The Crusades did, however, give the Latins a chance to appreciate the Greeks' technical ingenuity on a military level, and they used it to improve their own fortifications and siege engines.) At the time when this poem about Charlemagne's pilgrimage was written, Alexius Comnenus certainly did not strike the Western barons as having anything in common with the inoffensive Hugh the Strong. Whether they considered him kindly or treacherous, in the eyes of Latin historians Alexius was still the most powerful of all Christian monarchs. The popular imagination, which cared little for history, even for contemporary history, made up for this by invoking the prodigious figure of Charlemagne, who was so far beyond all earthly monarchs that only Christ surrounded by all his Apostles was a worthy comparison.

The heroes of the First Crusade—with the possible exception of Bohemond—could not bear comparison with the twelve peers, with William of Orange or Aimery of Narbonne, and when one poet tried to glorify Godfrey of Bouillon, he had to devote two-thirds of his story to the legend of the mysterious birth of his hero's progenitors and to variations on the story of the "Knight of the Swan," a distant echo of the legend of Cupid and Psyche, which was later to inspire Wagner's *Lohengrin*. The real merits of Godfrey and his brothers were of secondary importance—and the "immortal glory" which Baldwin I promised his companions cannot have survived across the sea. Baldwin was more esteemed by the Moslems than by Frenchmen at home in France.

Thanks partly to the Crusades, the East did sometimes provide an inspiration for the French romancers who pioneered romantic literature in the West. Medieval literature owes a great many of its themes to Oriental folklore, but literary works whose action is set partly in the East are rare. Although late twelfth-century romances like *L'Escoufle*, or *Cligès* by Chrétien de Troyes, feature in their plots a somewhat vague "Emperor of Constantinople," this is solely in order to raise the prestige of the hero by the introduction of a character at once fabulous and endowed with a semblance of reality. The charming Oriental touches in *Floire et Blancheflor,* for instance, are entirely fantastic and based on secondhand accounts. Admittedly, romancers of the period were not very much interested in realism except in matters of feeling, but even so the author of *Floire* seems to make a genuine attempt to describe the harem of a great Moslem lord, and even to have based his account on some actual observations. But he is ill-informed about the idea of polygamy and imagines—taking his cue from the legend of Sheherazade—that the emir marries a fresh virgin every year and has her executed at the end of it. Despite this sinister detail, Western pictures of the East seem in general to convey a rather pleasant idea of harems which are simultaneously prisons and delightful places where young girls lead a leisurely and luxurious existence. The poem of the *Chétifs,* which forms part of the Antioch cycle, on the other hand traces the miserable existence of prisoners of war with details which seem to have been inspired by the authentic memories of captives. But with these two exceptions, Western countries' curiosity about the East is hardly reflected in the literature of the period, at least insofar as we are able to judge from the literary works which have come down to us.

Very little is known about the oral tradition, and it is not easy to estimate its importance. This was certainly greater in the tenth and eleventh centuries than in the twelfth, since it is in the twelfth that the *chansons,* epic poems, and romances began to be widely circulated in writing. A literature learned by heart and transmitted by word of mouth was becoming obviously inadequate, and although the majority of the public were still illiterate, respect for the written word had grown. Most of the manuscripts existing at the time have naturally been lost, but what remains—with the diverse variants and copies of the texts which were probably most popular—is still considerable. Apart from the *Chanson d'Antioch* and the poems based on it, and an adaptation of Raymond of Aguiler's account in the Provençal tongue, there are no works of literature of the twelfth century dealing with the Crusades. There are a fair number of chronicles written in Latin, the work of both French and German authors, but these were destined for a literate and cultivated public at the time—the clergy and a few great lords who understood Latin. It was not until the thirteenth century, after the kingdom of Jerusalem was destroyed, that anyone felt the need to translate William of Tyre's *Estoire d'Éracles* into French, and at the same time, Geoffrey of Villehardouin and Robert of Clary were writing down their chronicles directly in the vernacular. The number of people really able to read had increased considerably, and interest in contemporary history and in events in the East seems to have grown keener.

To judge from the echoes left in written works, the oral tradition was not particularly influenced by the events of the Crusades. Twelfth-century lyric poetry was also very little affected by them. We find one or two songs in which a woman complains that her lover is away on a Crusade and exposed to the perils of a long sea voyage (at a time when battles were commonplace, the sea was more terrifying than the Moslem swords). A *sirventès* of Marcabru contains a clear though guarded allusion to the failure of the Crusade of 1147 and laments the death of Raymond of Poitiers, a prince who spoke the *langue d'oc,* a friend to poets, and the son of the first great troubadour. But William IX scarcely refers in his songs to his own somewhat inglorious adventure in 1101, except to mourn for the misfortunes of the Crusaders, misfortunes in which he himself had shared. Subjects of this kind do not, at the period, seem to have been the province of courtly literature.

The fall of Jerusalem at the end of the century inspired poets like the Castellan of Coucy and Conon of Bethune to write songs proclaiming their desire to go and defend God's heritage. These songs are also chiefly remarkable for a somewhat banal conformity. By about 1190, all Western chivalry felt bound to display its zeal for the cause of the Holy Places, but neither Conon of Bethune nor the Castellan of Coucy seems inspired by a real burning passion for Jerusalem. The first indignantly denounces persons who put the funds collected for the holy war to improper use, and further stresses the shame which is the lot of those who refuse to take the cross, rather than the misfortunes of the Holy Land itself;* the Castellan of Coucy seems chiefly distressed at parting from his beloved.

It can be said that lyric poetry was not taken very seriously, especially in France, and was regarded—even when it dealt in passing with serious events—as a worldly diversion, or simply one way of winning the ladies' hearts. However, genuine sincerity is to be found even in poems which were not about love, such as Bertran de Born's lament over the death of the young Henry of England, or his description of the joys of battle. It is also present in Richard Coeur-de-Lion's complaint at his captivity and in the thirteenth-century *sirventès* of

---

* Conon of Bethune is, however, known to have been anything but a fervent defender of the "heritage of Jesus Christ." He was one of the architects of the sack of Constantinople, and he remained in Greece until his death, which occurred fifteen years after the Crusade of 1204.

Bernard de la Barthe, B. Sicart de Marvejols, or Guilhem Figueyras, passionate laments for the miseries of their country and attacks on the injustice of Rome. Poetry was already a mode of expression which could be adapted to a wide range of feelings. But no troubadour, no *trouvère*, weeps for the loss of Jerusalem except in the form of a conventional pious obligation. German poets are more ardent and also lay more stress on the Crusades as a mystical rather than a worldly adventure.

As for the Frankish poets of Syria, if there were any, neither their works nor even their names have been preserved. The greatest of all medieval poets, writing a hundred years after the event, placed Saladin in the paradise reserved for the just who were not Christians, but never thought of mentioning the great Sultan's unfortunate adversaries.

For the vast majority of Europeans in the twelfth century, the Holy Land remained a half-legendary country to which a pilgrimage was something to be simultaneously longed for and dreaded. Because Languedoc, through the Provençal county of Tripoli, retained closer ties than any existing between France and the rest of Frankish Syria, a princess of Tripoli is honored with a place in the poetic legend of the *Lives* of the troubadours. This story gives the young Princess Melisende her revenge for the insult put on her by the Emperor Manuel Comnenus. The poet Jaufré Rudel is supposed to have conceived a great love for the princess although he has never seen her. He goes to Tripoli where, dying, he recovers consciousness for a moment in the arms of Melisende, his *"amor de lonh."* After one kiss he dies, and the princess retires to a convent. Her retreat is therefore imputed to the effects, not of injured pride, but of a mysterious passion for Jaufré Rudel.

In the thirteenth century, largely as a result of the Crusades of Saint Louis, poets were still arguing about the necessity, or lack of necessity, for the holy war (see Rutebeuf, *"Dit du croisé et du decroisé,"* Tibald of Champagne, etc.), and romancers seem to have regarded the Holy Land chiefly as a place to which to send undesirable characters who were compelled to become Templars or Hospitalers in order to expiate their sins (such as the Duke of Burgundy in the *Châtelaine de Vergi,* who exacts vengeance on his wife, or the seneschal in the *Roman de la Rose,* who slanders the Emperor's betrothed).* People were still taking the cross: in 1235, Tibald of

* Furthermore, the obligation to take the cross became to some extent a punitive measure, generally applied to soldiers guilty of some dereliction not deserving the penalty of death or imprisonment, or even replacing these penal-

Champagne announces loudly: "All the wicked who love neither God, nor honor nor glory, will remain. . . . From now on valiant knights who love God and honor in this world will set out." This is a singularly abstract summons since it is clear that although Christ says to the Crusaders in the same poem, "You shall help me to carry my Cross," Christians no longer really saw how a war in the East could actively further the cause of Christ.

The strange thing is that for more than a century a section of Western Christendom had genuinely believed in this myth and had, in some inexplicable way, confused Christ and the place where Christ lived on earth to such an extent that they saw him banished, driven out of his birthplace, or a prisoner, tortured by his enemies in his own lands. This was an extremely strong and precise feeling and one which emerged more than once in the course of the century, after the fall of Jerusalem in particular. For the majority of Crusaders, it was an excuse for a mystical adventure on a personal level before it developed into a real common bond. The idea in itself was too farfetched to exercise any real influence over Western thought and opinion.

---

ties. After the setting up of the Inquisition in 1233 in particular, we find a great many Southern knights suspected of tolerating heresy setting out for the Holy Land in this way.

Genealogical Tables
Chronology
Notes
Bibliography
Index

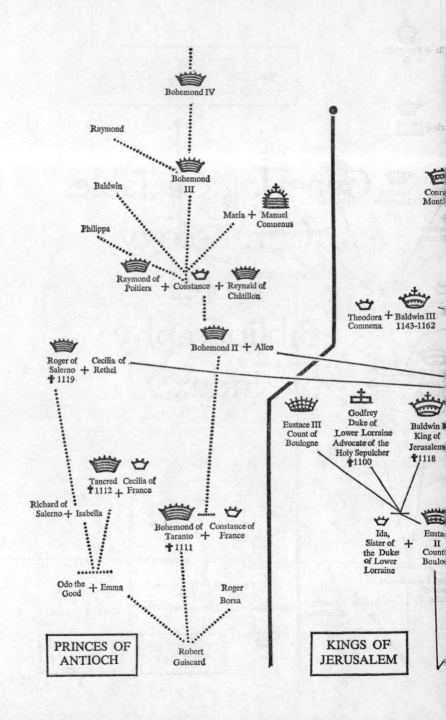

Bohemond IV

Raymond

Bohemond
III

Maria + Manuel
Comnenus

Baldwin

Philippa

Raymond of
Poitiers + Constance + Reynald of
Châtillon

Theodora + Baldwin III
Comnena   1143-1162

Bohemond II + Alice

Roger of
Salerno + Cecilia of
Rethel
†1119

Eustace III
Count of
Boulogne

Godfrey
Duke of
Lower Lorraine
Advocate of the
Holy Sepulcher
†1100

Baldwin I
King of
Jerusalem
†1118

Tancred   Cecilia of
†1112 + France

Richard of
Salerno + Isabella

Bohemond of   Constance of
Taranto + France
†1111

Ida,
Sister of +
the Duke
of Lower
Lorraine

Eusta
II
Count
Boulo

Odo the + Emma
Good

Roger
Borsa

PRINCES OF
ANTIOCH

KINGS OF
JERUSALEM

Robert
Guiscard

Conra
Mont

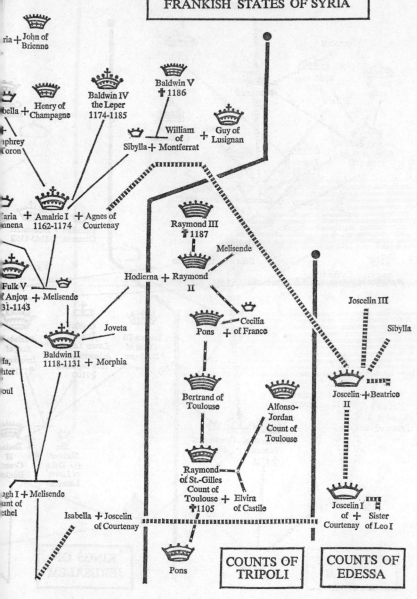

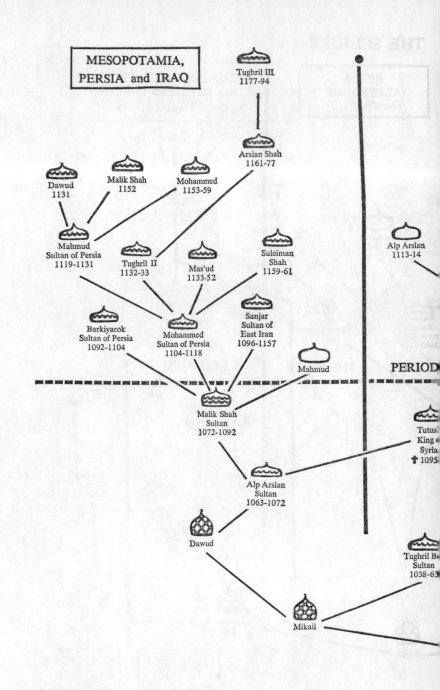

MESOPOTAMIA, PERSIA and IRAQ

Tughril III
1177-94

Arslan Shah
1161-77

Dawud
1131

Malik Shah
1152

Mohammed
1153-59

Mahmud
Sultan of Persia
1119-1131

Tughril II
1132-33

Mas'ud
1133-52

Suleiman
Shah
1159-61

Alp Arslan
1113-14

Barkiyarok
Sultan of Persia
1092-1104

Mohammed
Sultan of Persia
1104-1118

Sanjar
Sultan of
East Iran
1096-1157

Mahmud

PERIOD

Malik Shah
Sultan
1072-1092

Tutus'
King
Syria
✝ 1095

Alp Arslan
Sultan
1063-1072

Dawud

Tughril B
Sultan
1038-63

Mikail

THE SELJUKS

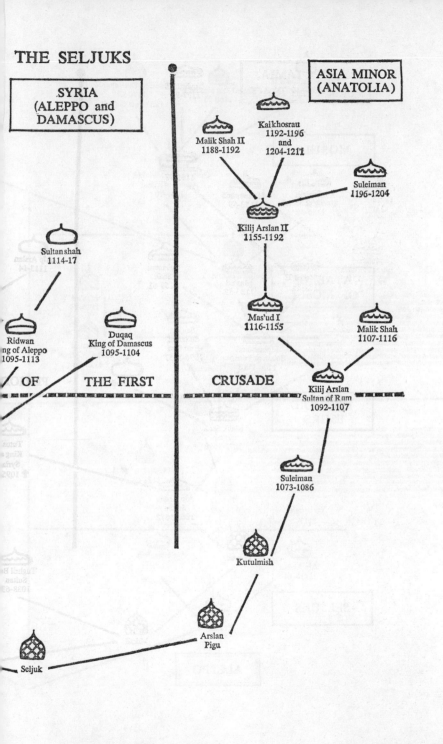

SYRIA
(ALEPPO and
DAMASCUS)

ASIA MINOR
(ANATOLIA)

Malik Shah II
1188-1192

Kaikhosrau
1192-1196
and
1204-1211

Suleiman
1196-1204

Kilij Arslan II
1155-1192

Sultan shah
1114-17

Ridwan
King of Aleppo
1095-1113

Duqaq
King of Damascus
1095-1104

Mas'ud I
1116-1155

Malik Shah
1107-1116

OF   THE FIRST   CRUSADE

Kilij Arslan
Sultan of Rum
1092-1107

Suleiman
1073-1086

Kutulmish

Arslan
Pigu

Seljuk

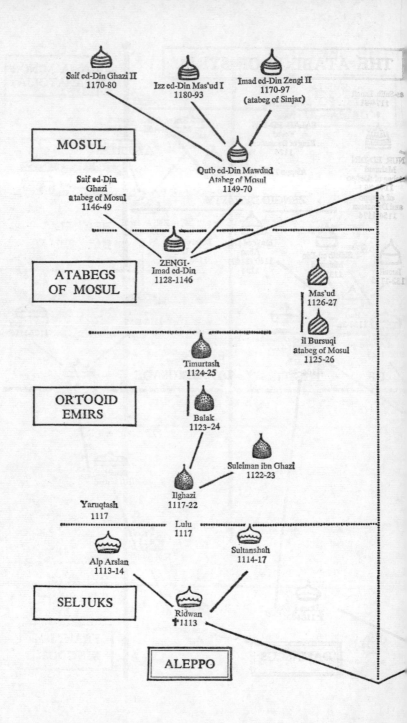

Saif ed-Din Ghazi II
1170-80

Izz ed-Din Mas'ud I
1180-93

Imad ed-Din Zengi II
1170-97
(atabeg of Sinjar)

MOSUL

Saif ed-Din
Ghazi
atabeg of Mosul
1146-49

Qutb ed-Din Mawdud
Atabeg of Mosul
1149-70

ATABEGS
OF MOSUL

ZENGI-
Imad ed-Din
1128-1146

Mas'ud
1126-27

il Bursuqi
atabeg of Mosul
1125-26

ORTOQID
EMIRS

Timurtash
1124-25

Balak
1123-24

Suleiman ibn Ghazi
1122-23

Ilghazi
1117-22

Yaruqtash
1117

Lulu
1117

Sultanshah
1114-17

Alp Arslan
1113-14

SELJUKS

Ridwan
✝1113

ALEPPO

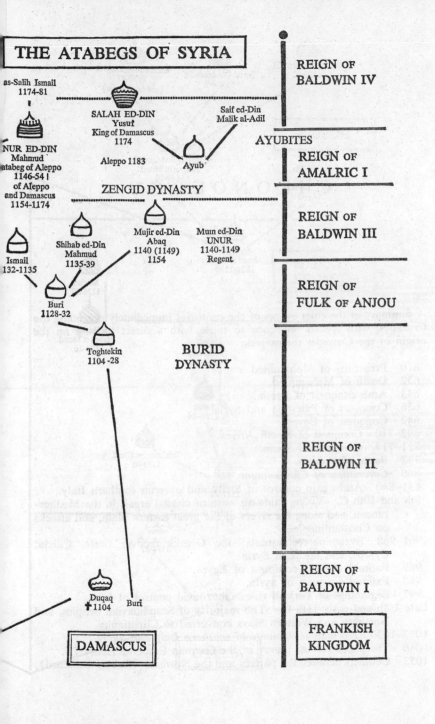

THE ATABEGS OF SYRIA

REIGN OF
BALDWIN IV

as-Salih Ismail
1174-81

SALAH ED-DIN
Yusuf
King of Damascus
1174

Saif ed-Din
Malik al-Adil

AYUBITES

NUR ED-DIN
Mahmud
atabeg of Aleppo
1146-54 I
of Aleppo
and Damascus
1154-1174

Aleppo 1183

Ayub

REIGN OF
AMALRIC I

ZENGID DYNASTY

Mujir ed-Din
Abaq
1140 (1149)
1154

Muin ed-Din
UNUR
1140-1149
Regent

REIGN OF
BALDWIN III

Shihab ed-Din
Mahmud
1135-39

Ismail
132-1135

REIGN OF
FULK OF ANJOU

Buri
1128-32

Toghtekin
1104 -28

BURID
DYNASTY

REIGN OF
BALDWIN II

REIGN OF
BALDWIN I

Duqaq
†1104   Buri

FRANKISH
KINGDOM

DAMASCUS

CHRONOLOGY

A summary of the chief events of the centuries immediately preceding the Crusades, with special reference to those with a direct bearing on the origin of the Crusades themselves.

610   Preaching of Mohammed.

632   Death of Mohammed.

633   Arab conquest of Persia.

636   Conquest of Palestine and Syria.

642   Conquest of Egypt.

692–710   Conquest of North Africa.

711–717   Conquest of Spain.

732   Battle of Poitiers.

800   *Coronation of Charlemagne.*

831–840   Arabs gain control of Sicily and overrun southern Italy.

9th and 10th C.   Viking raids on western coastal areas, in the Mediterranean, and along the rivers of the great eastern plain, and attacks on Constantinople.

961–968   Byzantine reconquests: the Greeks recover Crete, Cilicia, Cyprus, and northern Syria.

969   Fatimid (Shiite) conquest of Egypt.

988   Fatimid conquest of Syria.

997   Beginnings of Turkish rule: Ghaznavid control of Iran.

Late 10th and early 11th C.   The majority of Scandinavian peoples, and Northern and Western Slavs converted to Christianity.

1012–1030   *Norman settlements in southern Italy and Sicily.*

1046   The papacy at the mercy of the German Emperor Henry III.

1053   Conflicts between the papacy and the Normans (Robert Guiscard).

1054   *Official proclamation of the Great Eastern Schism (the break between the Greek and Roman Churches).*

1055   Abbasid caliphs under official domination of Turkish sultans.

1066   Norman conquest of England. King William the Conqueror.

1071   *Turkish invasions of Asia Minor. Defeat of Byzantium at Manzikert.* Capture of Bari by Robert Guiscard. Normans eliminate the Greeks in Italy.

1038–1092   *Seljuk Turks control Persia, Mesopotamia, Syria, and Asia Minor.*

1071   The Turk Atsiz captures Jerusalem from the Fatimids.

1076   The War of Investitures.

1077   Humiliation of the German Emperor Henry IV at Canossa.
        Second capture of Jerusalem by Atsiz. Massacre of the Moslems.

1078   *Seljuk control of Damascus and the whole hinterland of Palestine.*

1081   *Accession of Alexius Comnenus.*

1084   Alexius Comnenus grants trading privileges to the Venetians.

1077–1092   Struggle between the Holy Roman Empire and the papacy. The Pope forms an alliance with the Normans (Robert Guiscard).

1085   Death of Gregory VII in exile at Salerno. Pontificate of the Antipope Clement III.

1086   The Almoravides in Spain.

1089   Pope Urban II returns to Rome.

1090   Urban II driven out of Rome by the Emperor.

1093   Urban II returns to Rome after the defeat of Henry IV at Canossa, with the help of the Normans.

1095   Alexius Comnenus appeals to the Pope for help against the Turks. *Council of Piacenza. Council of Clermont and preaching of the Crusade against the Turks.*

CHIEF EVENTS OF THE CRUSADES	CHIEF CONTEMPORARY EVENTS
1096 Preaching of Peter the Hermit. Spring: departure of People's Crusades from France and Germany. Massacres of Jews in Germany. *September–October: Peter the Hermit's force wiped out near Nicaea.* Autumn: departure of barons' Crusade. December: Godfrey of Bouillon's army reaches Constantinople.	1094 Spain: the Cid in Valencia.
1097 April: Bohemond reaches Constantinople. Late April: Raymond of Saint-Gilles at Constantinople. June 19: capture of Nicaea by Greeks and Crusaders.	1097 France: wars of Louis the Fat in the Vexin.

*July 1: Crusaders' victory at Dory-
laeum.*

October: Crusaders outside Antioch.

1098   February: Baldwin of Boulogne at   1098   Foundation of
Edessa.   the Abbey of
June 3: capture of Antioch by the Cru-   Cîteaux.
saders.   1087–1100 England:
June 5–28: siege of Antioch by Ker-   reign of William
bogha.   Rufus.
August: Fatimids recapture Jerusalem
(al-Afdal).

1099   January: Crusading army marches on
Palestine.
Genoese fleets reach coast of Palestine:
capture of Jaffa.
July 15: capture of Jerusalem by the
Crusaders.
Godfrey of Bouillon appointed Advo-
cate of the Holy Sepulcher.
July 29: death of Urban II.   1099   Death of Urban
August 12: Egyptian army defeated by   II and pontifi-
the Crusaders at Ascalon.   cate of Paschal
Autumn: Crusading armies return to Eu-   II (1099–1118).
rope.
December: Pisan fleets off the Syrian   Spain: death of
coast. Daimbert, Archbishop of Pisa,   the Cid.
elected Patriarch of Jerusalem.

1100   July 18: death of Godfrey of Bouillon.   1100   France: the fu-
August: Bohemond taken prisoner by the   ture Louis VI
Danishmends.   heir to the
September: Baldwin of Boulogne King   throne.
of Jerusalem.   England: Henry
March: Tancred regent of Antioch.   Beauclerk King
                                                      of England.
1100–1101 Departure of Crusaders from Lom-   Spain: the Al-
bardy, Nevers, Bavaria, and Aquitaine.   moravid Sultan
1101   Fatimid counter-Crusade. Victory of   Yusuf master of
Baldwin I at Ramleh.   Moslem Spain.
August: defeat of the Lombard Crusade   1101   Italy: death of
at Mersivan.   Roger I, Nor-
Late August: defeat of the Nivernais   man King of
Crusade near Heraclea.   Sicily.
Early September: defeat of the Crusade
from Bavaria and Aquitaine.

CHIEF EVENTS OF THE CRUSADES	CHIEF CONTEMPORARY EVENTS
1102 Conquest of Tortosa by Raymond of Saint-Gilles. Defeat of Baldwin I at Ramleh (May) and massacre of Frankish chivalry. Baldwin's victory over the Egyptians at Jaffa (end May).	1102 France: Abelard teaches (1102–1141). Spain: Almoravides masters of Valencia.
1103 Release of Bohemond.	
1103–1105 Raymond of Saint-Gilles lays siege to Tripoli.	
1104 *Conquest of Acre by Baldwin I.* Death of Duqaq, King of Damascus. Rise to power of Toghtekin (start of dynasty of Burid atabegs). *Battle of Harran, defeat of the Franks,* and captivity of Baldwin of Le Bourg and Joscelin of Courtenay. Departure of Bohemond for Europe.	1104 France: absolution of Philip I. German Empire: rebellion of Henry, second son of Henry IV.
1105 February: death of Raymond of Saint-Gilles.	
	1106 Empire: death of Henry IV.
1108 Siege of Durazzo by Bohemond and his submission to Alexius Comnenus. Release of Baldwin of Le Bourg and wars between Baldwin of Le Bourg and Tancred. Arrival of Bertrand of Toulouse in Palestine, with Genoese fleet.	1108 France: death of Philip I, accession of Louis VI the Fat.
1109 *July 12: Capture of Tripoli by the Franks. Foundation of the county of Tripoli:* William-Jordan and Bertrand. Death (or assassination) of William-Jordan.	1107–1111 Norway: pilgrimage of King Sigurd to Jerusalem.
1110 *Counter-Crusade by Mawdud, atabeg of Mosul. Massacres in Armenia.*	
	1111 Italy: death of Roger Borsa, Bohemond's brother, Prince of Apulia and Calabria. Roger II of Sicily is heir.
1112 Death of Tancred. Death of Bertrand of Toulouse. Patriarchate of Arnulf Malecorne.	

CHIEF EVENTS OF THE CRUSADES

1113	Defeat of Frankish armies at Sennabra. *Assassination of Mawdud in Damascus. Toghtekin allies with Franks.* Death of Ridwan, King of Aleppo. Marriage of Baldwin I and Adelaide of Sicily.	1114	France: Treaty of Gisors. Henry Beauclerk becomes lord of Maine and Brittany.
1113–1115	Baldwin of Le Bourg conquers eastern Cilicia from the Armenian princes.		
1115	*Roger of Salerno, Prince of Antioch, defeats the army of Bursuq, atabeg of Hamadan, at Tel-Danith.*	1115	St. Bernard founds Abbey of Clairvaux.
1117	Baldwin I repudiates Adelaide. Quarrel with Normans of Sicily.		
1118	Baldwin I leads expedition against Egypt. *April 2: death of Baldwin I. Accession of Baldwin of Le Bourg (Baldwin II).* Joscelin of Courtenay Count of Edessa. *Foundation of the Order of the Temple.*	1118	Spain: Alfonso the Warlike takes Saragossa.
		1118–1119	Death of Paschal II. Pontificate of Gelasius II.
1119	*June 28: Roger of Salerno defeated by the Ortoqid Ilghazi near al-Balat (Ager Sanguinis). Massacre of Norman chivalry.* Baldwin II regent of Antioch (July). August 14: Baldwin II repels Ilghazi and Toghtekin at Tel-Danith.	1119	Calixtus II, Pope.
1119–1120	Ilghazi ravages the counties of Edessa and Antioch. Ortoqids rule over Aleppo.		
		1122	France: Suger Abbot of St. Denis. Empire: Concordat of Worms, end of the War of Investitures.
1123	Baldwin II taken prisoner by Balak. Regency of the constable Eustace Garnier (April).		

May: Venetian Crusade. The Venetian fleet (under the Doge Domenico Michiel) defeats Egyptian fleet at Ascalon (May 30).

May 29: Frankish victory over the Egyptians at Ibelin.

Balak (Ortoqid emir of Diarbekir) master of Aleppo.

1124 February 15: siege of Tyre by Franks and Venetians.

Death of Balak.

July 7: Franks capture Tyre.

Release of Baldwin II.

Franco-Moslem coalition against Aleppo (Baldwin II and Dubais). Siege of Aleppo.

1125 *Il-Bursuqi, atabeg of Mosul, master of Aleppo.*

1126 January 25: Victory of Frankish coalition over Toghtekin at Tel es-Saqhab.

Majority of Bohemond II. Arrival in Syria and marriage with Alice of Jerusalem (end 1126).

Assassination of il-Bursuqi by the Ismailians.

1127 Caliph of Baghdad declares war on the Sultan Mahmud. Defeat of Caliph's troops by Zengi.

Zengi atabeg of Mosul.

1128 Death of Toghtekin. *Zengi master of Aleppo.*

1129 Marriage of Melisende, heiress to the throne, with Fulk of Anjou. Combined expedition against Damascus by Baldwin II and Fulk of Anjou.

1124 Death of Calixtus II. Honorius II, Pope. France: Emperor Henry V invades Champagne. Defeat at Reims.

1125 Empire: Death of Henry V.

1126 Spain: Alfonso VII King of Castile.

1127 France: death of William IX, Duke of Aquitaine. France: assassination of Charles the Good, Count of Flanders. Italy: death of Roger Borsa's son William. Roger II defeats Pope.

1128 Italy: Roger II of Sicily Duke of Apulia.

1130   Death of Bohemond II. Rebellion of   1130   Italy: Roger II
        Alice. Baldwin II regent of Antioch.   crowned King
                                                       of Sicily.
                                                       Death of Hono-
                                                       rius II. Pontifi-
                                                       cate of Innocent
                                                       II. Antipope An-
                                                       acletus.

1131   *Death of Baldwin II (21 Aug.). Acces-* 1131   Innocent II in
        sion of Fulk of Anjou.   France. The fu-
                                                        ture Louis VII
                                                        anointed by the
                                                        Pope. Suger in
                                                        power.

1131–1132 Love affair between Hugh of Pui-
        set and Melisende. Scandal and death of
        Hugh.

                                                1134   Spain: defeat
                                                        and death of Al-
                                                        fonso the War-
1136   Marriage of Raymond of Poitiers and   like, King of
        Constance of Antioch.   Aragon.
1137   March: death of Pons, Count of Tripoli. 1137   John Comnenus
        Siege of Antioch by John Comnenus.   reconquers
        Fulk besieged in Montferrand by Zengi.   Cilicia.
                                                        France: death
                                                        of William X of
                                                        Aquitaine. Suc-
                                                        ceeded by his
                                                        daughter Elea-
                                                        nor. Marriage
                                                        of Eleanor with
1137–1138 Franco-Byzantine   agreement.   Louis VII.
        Siege of Shaizar. Break with John Com-   Death of Louis
        nenus.   VI.
                                                1138   Empire: acces-
                                                        sion of Conrad
                                                        III of Hohen-
                                                        staufen.
1138   *Franco-Damascene alliance (Fulk and*   Death of the
        Muin al-Din Unur, regent of Da-   Antipope Ana-
        mascus).   cletus.
                                                1139   Victory of
                                                        Roger II over

CHIEF EVENTS OF THE CRUSADES	CHIEF CONTEMPORARY EVENTS
	the Pope. Treaty of Mignano.
	1140 Spain: creation of the kingdom of Portugal.
	1141 France: Louis VII excommunicated.
1142 John Comnenus returns to Antioch. Quarrel with Raymond of Poitiers.	1142 France: war with Tibald of Champagne.
1143 *April 8: death of John Comnenus. November 10: death of Fulk of Anjou.* Regency of Melisende.	1143 Rome rebels against the Pope, founds commune. Death of Innocent II.
	1143–1144 Pontificate of Celestine II.
1144 *Capture of Edessa by Zengi.*	
1145 Preaching of the Crusade in the West.	1145 Eugenius III, Pope. Arnold of Brescia becomes leader of Roman commune. The Pope appeals to the Emperor.
1146 *September 15: death of Zengi. His son Nur ed-Din inherits Aleppo.* Revolt of Edessa. Capture of Edessa by Nur ed-Din and destruction of the city (November). Quarrel between kingdom of Jerusalem and Damascus. *March 31: preaching of St. Bernard at Vézelay. Louis VII takes the cross. December 25: preaching of St. Bernard at Speyer. Emperor Conrad III takes the cross.*	1146 Italy: Roger II takes Tripoli (in Africa), Gabès, Barca, and Kairouan.
1147 Manuel Comnenus declares war on Anatolian Turks (Sultan Mas'ud). September: Conrad III reaches Constantinople. Manuel makes peace with Mas'ud. October: German Crusade wiped out. French Crusade encounters difficulties	1147 Crusade of German princes against the Wends.

in Asia Minor. Conrad III in Constantinople.

1148	March: Louis VII at Antioch. Projected campaign against Aleppo. Quarrel between Louis VII and Eleanor and break with Raymond of Poitiers. April: Death of Alfonso-Jordan, Count of Toulouse. Crusaders quarrel with Count of Tripoli. May–June: Louis VII marches to Jerusalem. Crusader princes gather at Jerusalem. *July 24–28: siege of Damascus by Franks and Crusaders. Retreat.* September: departure of Conrad III for Europe.	1148	Italy: conflict between Normans and Byzantines. Roger II occupies the Abruzzi, plunders Corfu and Greece.
1149	Early summer: departure of Louis VII for Europe. Nur ed-Din makes war on Antioch. *June 29: defeat and death of Raymond of Poitiers at Fons Murez.*	1149	Normans lay siege to Constantinople.
1150	May: Joscelin II of Edessa a prisoner. August: remnants of the county of Edessa sold to the Greeks (Turbessel).		
1151	Nur ed-Din master of Turbessel.	1151	England: death of Geoffrey Plantagenet.
1152	End of Melisende's regency. Accession of Baldwin III. War between Melisende and her son. Assassination of Raymond II, Count of Tripoli.	1152	France: Louis VII and Eleanor of Aquitaine divorced. Henry Plantagenet marries Eleanor. Frederick I of Hohenstaufen (Barbarossa) King of Germany.
1153	Constance of Antioch marries Reynald of Châtillon. *August 19: Baldwin III takes Ascalon from the Fatimids.*		
1154	*Nur ed-Din master of Damascus.*	1154	Italy: Normans capture Bône. England: Accession of Henry II Plantagenet.

CHIEF EVENTS OF THE CRUSADES	CHIEF CONTEMPORARY EVENTS
	1153–1154 Anastasius IV, Pope.
	1154–1159 Adrian IV, Pope.
	1155 Rome: victory of the papacy. Torture and execution of Arnold of Brescia. Coronation of Frederick I as Emperor and his expulsion and revolt from Rome.
1156 *Reynald of Châtillon ravages Cyprus.*	
1157 Baldwin III raids the herds at Banyas. War with Nur ed-Din. Defeat of the Franks. August: Earthquake in northern Syria. Destruction of Shaizar. October: Illness of Nur ed-Din. Crusade of Thierry of Flanders. Siege and abandonment of Shaizar.	1157 Break between the Emperor and the Pope. Spain: Almohades recapture Almería.
1158 *Alliance between King of Jerusalem and Manuel Comnenus.* Baldwin III marries Theodora Comnena (September). Manuel Comnenus marches on Antioch. Humiliation of Reynald of Châtillon (October).	1158 France: Treaty with England. Frederick I in Italy. Peace between William I of Sicily and Manuel Comnenus.
1159 April: Solemn entry of Manuel into Antioch. Coalition between Franks, Armenians, and Byzantines. Manuel refuses to march on Aleppo.	1159 Alexander III Pope. Victor IV imperial Antipope.
1160 Reynald of Châtillon taken prisoner by Nur ed-Din. Baldwin III regent of Antioch (during minority of Bohemond III).	1160 Excommunication of Frederick I.
1161 Manuel Comnenus breaks off engagement with Melisende of Tripoli. Betrothal to Maria of Antioch. Wedding takes place in Constantinople December 25.	

1162   February 10: death of Baldwin III.
       February 18: accession of Amalric I.
       Kilij Arslan II at Constantinople. Sel-
       juks of Anatolia vassals of Byzantium.
       Asia Minor and Frankish Syria become
       Byzantine protectorate.

1162   Frederick Bar-
       barossa destroys
       Milan. Pope
       Alexander III
       flees to France.

1163   Decadence of Fatimid caliphate. Revo-
       lutions in Cairo. Intervention of Nur ed-
       Din and Amalric I, in Egyptian affairs.
       (First clash between Amalric and Shir-
       kuh.) Frankish victory over Nur ed-Din
       at Buqaia.

1163   Moslem Spain
       under domina-
       tion of Almo-
       hades of North
       Africa.

1164   *August 10: Combined Frankish armies*
       defeated by Nur ed-Din at Harenc. Ray-
       mond III, Bohemond III, and Joscelin
       III taken prisoner.
       Amalric's second Egyptian expedition.
       Retreat of Shirkuh.

1165   Bohemond III released. Greek patriarch
       in Antioch. Armenian counterattacks in
       Cilicia. Thoros II halts progress of Nur
       ed-Din in the west.

1165   France: birth of
       the future Philip
       Augustus.
       Germany: can-
       onization of
       Charlemagne.

1166   Italy: death of
       William I of
       Sicily. Minority
       of William II.
       Revolts at Mes-
       sina and Pa-
       lermo.

1167   Shirkuh attacks Egypt (January). Vizier
       Shawar appeals to the Franks. Egypt be-
       comes Frankish protectorate (pact be-
       tween Amalric and the Caliph). Amalric
       seeks Byzantine alliance and marries
       Maria Comnena (August 29).

1167   Frederick I
       temporary mas-
       ter of Rome.

1166–1173 Cam-
       paigns of Louis
       VII against
       feudal lords.

1168   Projected Franco-Byzantine expedition
       against Egypt. William of Tyre ambas-
       sador.

October: Amalric launches surprise attack on Egypt. Capture of Bilbeis. Cairo holds out. Shawar appeals to Nur ed-Din.

1169 January 2: Frankish armies withdraw from Egypt.

January 8: Shirkuh and Saladin in Egypt. Assassination of Shawar. Triumph of Shirkuh.

March 23: death of Shirkuh. Saladin master of Egypt.

August: revolt and massacre of the Fatimid Caliph's black guard.

October–December: abortive siege of Damietta by the Franks and the Byzantine fleet.

1170 Great earthquake in northern Syria. Truce between Franks and Moslems.

1170 England: assassination of Thomas Becket.

1171 January: Nur ed-Din master of Mosul. Spring: Amalric in Constantinople. New plans for Franco-Byzantine alliance.

September 10: Egypt officially returned to Sunnite orthodoxy. Extinction of Fatimid caliphate.

1171 Manuel Comnenus grants trading privileges to Genoa and Pisa, to the detriment of Venice.

1173 Break between Nur ed-Din and Saladin.

1173 Victory of Florence and Pisa at Castelfiorentino.

1174 *May 15: death of Nur ed-Din.*

July 11: death of Amalric I. Accession of Baldwin IV, the leper King (aged 13). Regency of Miles of Plancy, and his assassination (end 1174). Regency of Raymond III, Count of Tripoli. Saladin master of Damascus. Frankish alliance with the kingdom of Aleppo (the boy al-Salih, son of Nur ed-Din).

1174 Siege of Alessandria by Frederick I. France and England: treaty of Montlouis between Henry II and his sons; division of Plantagenet domains.

1176 Marriage between Sibylla of Jerusalem and William of Montferrat.

Release of Reynald of Châtillon and marriage to Stephanie of Milly, lady of Kerak of Moab.

1176 Frederick I defeated by Italians at Legnano.

	CHIEF EVENTS OF THE CRUSADES		CHIEF CONTEMPORARY EVENTS
	Defeat of Manuel Comnenus at Myrio-cephalum. End of Byzantine hegemony in Asia Minor.		
1177	Death of William of Montferrat (June). Crusade of Philip of Flanders. Abortive siege of Harenc (November). *November 25: Frankish victory at Mont-gisard near Ascalon (Baldwin IV against Saladin).*	1177	Peace of Venice between Frederick and Pope Alexander III.
		1178	Break between Henry II and the King of France.
1179	Defeat of Franks at Banyas. Death of the constable Humphrey of Toron.	1179	Coronation of future Philip II of France.
1180	Truce with Saladin. Easter: Marriage of Sibylla to Guy of Lusignan. Heraclius elected Patriarch of Jerusalem. *September 24: death of Manuel Comnenus.*	1180	Death of Louis VII. Accession of Philip II (Augustus). Alliance between England and Champagne against Philip II. The English land in France. Treaty of Gisors. Rome: end of schism. Antipope Innocent III deposed.
		1181	Lucius III, Pope.
1182	Regency of Andronicus Comnenus.		
1183	Reynald of Châtillon raids Red Sea area in direction of Arabia. Breach of truce. *June 12: Saladin master of Aleppo.* November: marriage of Isabella of Jerusalem and Humphrey IV of Toron. Saladin lays siege to Kerak of Moab. Baldwin IV saves Kerak.	1183	Peace of Constance between the Emperor and the Italian communes.
1184	Disgrace of Guy of Lusignan. Second regency of Raymond III of Tripoli.		
1185	*March: death of Baldwin IV.* Accession of boy King Baldwin V. Regency of Raymond III.	1185	Normans capture Durazzo and Salonica.

Revolution in Constantinople. Death of Andronicus Comnenus. Accession of Isaac Angelus. Normans of Sicily invade the Empire and Macedonia. Summer: Raymond III concludes four-year truce with Saladin. Saladin attempts to take Mosul.	Urban III, Pope. France: Treaty of Amiens. Philip Augustus gains possession of Amiens and Vermandois.

1186 *Death of the infant King Baldwin V. Expulsion of Raymond III and coronation of Sibylla and Guy of Lusignan (September?).*
Pact of alliance between Raymond III and Saladin.
End of year: Reynald of Châtillon captures caravan belonging to Damascus. Declaration of war.

1187 May: defeat of the Templars near Sephoria. Reconciliation between Guy of Lusignan and Raymond III.
July 4: Battle of Hattin. Frankish army annihilated. Execution of Reynald of Châtillon and the Templars and Hospitalers.
July 5: Saladin takes Tiberias.
July 10: fall of Acre.
July 14: Conrad of Montferrat reaches Tyre.
July: capture of Jaffa, Haifa, Caesarea, Toron (Tibnin), and Sidon by Saladin.
August 6: capture of Beirut.
September 4: capture of Ascalon.
September 20–October 2: siege and capture of Jerusalem. Exodus of Frankish population.
End of year: death of Raymond III of Tripoli.
August–December: preaching of the Crusade in the West.

1187 Philip Augustus gains possession of Tournai.
Break with Henry II.
1187–1188 Philip Augustus takes Berry and enters Touraine.

1188 January 21: Meeting of Henry II of England and Philip II of France (Philip Augustus) with a view to reconciliation in order to take the cross.

1188 Asia: Genghis Khan unifies Mongolia.
France: War

CHIEF EVENTS OF THE CRUSADES

1188–1189 Last castles of kingdom of Jeru-   with England.
salem hold out: Beaufort, Kerak of   Philip Augustus
Moab, Krak of Montreal, Krak des   in Touraine. Re-
Chevaliers. Resistance of Tyre under   volt of sons of
Conrad of Montferrat. Arrival at Tyre   Henry II, with
of Crusader contingents.   support of
Philip.
Clement III rec-
ognizes the com-
mune of Rome.

1189   May: Departure of Frederick Barba-   1189   Italy: death of
rossa and the German Crusade.   William II of
August: Guy of Lusignan lays siege to   Sicily.
Acre.   England: death
August: Frederick Barbarossa at Con-   of Henry II. Ac-
stantinople.   cession of Rich-
ard Coeur-de-
Lion.
1187–1191 Pontifi-
cate of Clement
III.

1190   May: Frederick Barbarossa at Konya;   1190   Italy: Crusaders
agreement with Kilij Arslan II.   plunder Mes-
June 10: death of Frederick Barbarossa   sina.
in Cilicia. His army disbanded.
July: Philip Augustus and Richard
Coeur-de-Lion set out for the Crusade.
July: siege of Acre. Rebellion of the
sergeants and their massacre by the
Turks.
July: siege of Acre. Arrival of Crusade
led by Henry of Champagne.
October–March 1191: Philip Augustus
and Richard Coeur-de-Lion in Sicily.
1190–1191 Winter: siege of Acre. Famine.
Death of Sibylla of Jerusalem (October)
and marriage of Isabella with Conrad of
Montferrat (November).
1191   *April 20: arrival of Philip Augustus at*   1191   Germany: coro-
Acre with Hugh of Burgundy and Philip   nation of the
of Flanders.   Emperor Henry
May: Richard Coeur-de-Lion conquers   VI, son of Fred-
Cyprus.   erick. German
June 7: Richard's arrival at Acre.   invasion of Italy.

July 12: surrender of Acre.

August 3: Philip Augustus returns to Europe.

August 20: massacre of the garrison of Acre.

August 22: Crusading army marches south.

September 7: Crusaders' victory at Arsuf.

Summer-autumn: Crusaders reconquer coastal area. First march on Jerusalem.

1192 January: Crusaders abandon siege of Jerusalem. Negotiations with Saladin.

April: Conrad of Montferrat elected King of Jerusalem.

April 28: assassination of Conrad of Montferrat.

May 5: remarriage of Isabella with Henry of Champagne.

June: Richard's second march on Jerusalem.

July 4: Crusaders withdraw to Jaffa, then to Acre.

August 1: Richard reconquers Jaffa.

August: Peace talks with Saladin.

September 2: Peace with Saladin.

October 9: Richard and the Crusading army embark for Europe.

1193 *March 3: death of Saladin.*

1193–1201 Struggles for Saladin's succession and triumph of Saladin's brother Malik al-Adil.

1197 Death of Henry of Champagne. German Emperor Henry VI prepares a fresh Crusade. German Crusaders recapture Beirut. Death of Henry VI.

1198 January: Isabella marries Amalric of Lusignan, King of Cyprus, uniting the crowns of Jerusalem and Cyprus.

Innocent III, Pope.

Henry IV halted outside Naples.

1191–1198 Pontificate of Celestine III.

1192 Richard Coeur-de-Lion taken prisoner in Germany.

1193 France: Philip Augustus marries and then repudiates Ingeborg of Denmark.

1194 Henry VI inherits the kingdom of Sicily at the death of Tancred of Lecce. Richard released; recaptures English fiefs in France.

CHIEF EVENTS OF THE CRUSADES	CHIEF CONTEMPORARY EVENTS
1199 Preaching of new Crusade to reconquer Jerusalem.	1199 Death of Richard Coeur-de-Lion. Accession of John Lackland.
1201 Crusaders sign treaty with Venetians. Death of Bohemond III of Antioch. His son, Bohemond IV, reigns over Antioch and Tripoli.	
	1202–1205 War between France and England. The English lose Normandy, Poitou, Maine, Touraine, and Anjou.
1203 Venice and the Crusaders decide to attack Constantinople.	
1204 *Capture of Constantinople by the Crusaders.* Baldwin of Flanders Emperor of Constantinople. The Franks recapture Sidon.	
1208 Preaching of the Crusade against the Albigensians.	
1209 *Albigensian Crusade.* Sack of Béziers. Simon of Montfort viscount of Béziers and Carcassonne.	
1212 The Children's Crusade.	1212 Spain: battle of Las Navas de Tolosa. Peter II of Aragon defeats the Almohades.
	1213 Battle of Muret: death of Peter II.
	1214 Battle of Bouvines.
	1215 Fourth Lateran Ecumenical Council. Magna Carta.
1216 Pope Honorius preaches Fifth Crusade. *Fifth Crusade, led by Cardinal Pelagius, papal legate, and John of Brienne.*	1216 Death of Innocent III. Pontificate of Honorius III.

England: death of King John. Accession of Henry III.

1218 Death of Simon of Montfort and end of the Albigensian Crusade.
1219 Crusaders capture Damietta.
1221 Disaster of Mansourah. Damietta abandoned. End of the Fifth Crusade.

1222 Eastern Europe: Mongol invasion. Battle of Kalka.
1223 Death of Philip Augustus.
1226 Louis IX (St. Louis) King of France. Regency of Blanche of Castile. Italy: death of St. Francis of Assisi. Formation of the Lombard League: Guelfs and Ghibellines.

1227 Excommunication of Frederick II.

1227 Death of Genghis Khan.

1228 Frederick II lands in Syria.
1229 *Treaty between Frederick II and the Sultan of Egypt: Jerusalem ceded to the Emperor.*
Treaty of Paris (Meaux). End of the Albigensian wars. Capet dynasty seizes Languedoc.

1231 Setting up of Dominican Inquisition.
1236 Spaniards capture Cordoba.
1239 Frederick II invades Papal States.
1241 Death of Pope Gregory IX.

NOTES

(Note: The abbreviations *R.H.C.Occ.*, etc.,
refer to volumes of the *Recueil des Historiens
des Croisades*. See Bibliography.)

Chapter I: MEDIEVAL MAN

1. Fulcher of Chartres, *R.H.C.Occ.*, III, p. 323; Robert of Reims, *R.H.C.Occ.*, III, p. 727; Guibert of Nogent, *R.H.C.Occ.*, IV, p. 137; Chalandon, *Essai sur le règne d'Alexis Comnène*, pp. 325–26.

Chapter II: THE LATIN WEST AND BYZANTIUM

1. Guibert of Nogent, *R.H.C.Occ.*, IV, pp. 132–33.
2. William of Tyre, *R.H.C.Occ.*, I, p. 254.
3. Anna Comnena, *Alexiad*, X, ch. 10.

Chapter III: THE FIRST CRUSADE (1096–1099)

1. Anna Comnena, *Alexiad,* X, ch. 5, par. 4.
2. *Anonymi Gesta Francorum* (ed. Bréhier), p. 47.
3. William of Tyre, *R.H.C.Occ.*, I, ch. 17; *Anonymi Gesta Francorum,* p. 65.
4. William of Tyre, *R.H.C.Occ.*, I, p. 401.
5. *Ibid.*, p. 402.
6. *Ibid.*, p. 143.
7. *Ibid.*, p. 254.
8. *Ibid.*, p. 190.
9. Albert of Aix, *R.H.C.Occ.*, IV, pp. 346–47.
10. Matthew of Edessa, *R.H.C.Arm.*, I, pp. 37–38.
11. Raymond of Aguilers, *R.H.C.Occ.*, III, p. 271.
12. *Ibid.*, pp. 279–85.

13. William of Tyre, *R.H.C.Occ.*, I, p. 341.
14. *Anonymi Gesta Francorum,* p. 203.
15. William of Tyre, *R.H.C.Occ.*, I, p. 354.
16. *Ibid.*, p. 356.
17. *Ibid.*, pp. 356–57.

Chapter IV: THE PIONEERS OF FRANKISH SYRIA (1099–1102)

1. Ibn al-Athir, *Kamil at-Tawarikh, R.H.C.Or.*, I, p. 202.
2. William of Tyre, *R.H.C.Occ.*, I, pp. 395–96.
3. *Ibid.*, pp. 364–66.
4. *Gesta Francorum Iherusalem expugnantium, R.H.C.Occ.*, III, p. 519.
5. William of Tyre, *R.H.C.Occ.*, I, p. 406.
6. *Ibid.*, p. 450.
7. Anna Comnena, *Alexiad,* XI, ch. 6, par. 3.
8. William of Tyre, *R.H.C.Occ.*, I, p. 452.

Chapter V: THE FORMATION OF THE
FRANKISH STATES OF SYRIA (1102–1112)

1. Matthew of Edessa, *R.H.C.Arm.*, I, pp. 80–81.
2. Radulph of Caen, *R.H.C.Occ.*, III, pp. 712–13.
3. Al-Modhafer, *R.H.C.Or.*, I, ch. 1.
4. Fulcher of Chartres, *R.H.C.Occ.*, III, p. 468.
5. William of Tyre, *R.H.C.Occ.*, I, pp. 469–72.
6. Michael the Syrian, *Chronicle* (ed. Chabot), III, p. 186.
7. Matthew of Edessa, *R.H.C.Arm.*, I, p. 19.
8. Albert of Aix, *R.H.C.Occ.*, IV, p. 564.
9. Matthew of Edessa, *R.H.C.Arm.*, I, pp. 93–94.

Chapter VI: THE KINGDOM AND ITS NEIGHBORS (1112–1131)

1. Ibn al-Athir, *Kamil at-Tawarikh, R.H.C.Or.*, I, p. 290.
2. *Ibid.*, p. 270.
3. William of Tyre, *R.H.C.Occ.*, I, p. 493.
4. *Ibid.*, p. 508.
5. Fulcher of Chartres, *R.H.C.Occ.*, III, p. 442; William of Tyre, *R.H.C.Occ.*, I, p. 526.
6. Al-Adhimi, quoted by Ibn al-Athir, *R.H.C.Or.*, I, p. 325.
7. Derenbourg, *Ousâma,* I, p. 117.
8. Ibn al-Athir, *Kamil at-Tawarikh, R.H.C.Or.*, I, pp. 332–33.
9. Usama, *Autobiography,* pp. 445–46.
10. Kemal ad-Din, *R.H.C.Or.*, III, p. 642.
11. William of Tyre, *R.H.C.Occ.*, I, pp. 575–76.
12. Kemal ad-Din, *R.H.C.Or.*, III, p. 647.
13. Ibn al-Athir, *Kamil at-Tawarikh, R.H.C.Or.*, I, pp. 34–35.
14. Ibn al-Athir, *Atabegs, R.H.C.Or.*, II, p. 69.

15. William of Tyre, *R.H.C.Occ.*, I, p. 589.
16. Derenbourg, *Ousâma*, I, pp. 137–39.
17. Michael the Syrian, *Chronicle*, III, p. 227.
18. William of Tyre, *R.H.C.Occ.*, I, pp. 599–601.
19. Matthew of Edessa, *R.H.C.Arm.*, I, pp. 105–6.
20. *Ibid.*, p. 36.
21. William of Tyre, *R.H.C.Occ.*, I, pp. 601–2.
22. *Ibid.*, pp. 514 ff.
23. *Ibid.*, p. 541.
24. William of Tyre, *R.H.C.Occ.*, I, pp. 609–11.
25. *De laude novae militiae*, in *Patrologia Latina*, CLXXXII, 923–26.
26. William of Tyre, *R.H.C.Occ.*, I, p. 821.
27. William of Tyre, *Continuation, R.H.C.Occ.*, II, pp. 51–52.

Chapter VII: THE FRANKS BETWEEN
BYZANTIUM AND ISLAM (1131–1174)

1. William of Tyre, *R.H.C.Occ.*, I, p. 633.
2. *Ibid.*
3. Ibn al-Athir, *Kamil at-Tawarikh*, *R.H.C.Or.*, I, p. 419.
4. William of Tyre, *R.H.C.Occ.*, I, p. 460.
5. Anna Comnena, *Alexiad*, XIV, ch. 2, par. 4.
6. *Ibid.*, par. 6.
7. Michael the Syrian, *Chronicle*, III, p. 262.
8. Ibn al-Qalanisi, (ed. H. F. Amedroz, Leyden, 1908), pp. 284–85.
9. Michael the Syrian, *Chronicle*, III, p. 272.
10. William of Tyre, *R.H.C.Occ.*, I, p. 753.
11. Michael the Syrian, *Chronicle*, III, p. 276.
12. Ibn al-Athir, *Kamil at-Tawarikh*, *R.H.C.Or.*, I, pp. 469–70.
13. William of Tyre, *R.H.C.Occ.*, I, p. 773.
14. Ibn al-Qalanisi, quoted by Abu Shama, *R.H.C.Or.*, IV, p. 62.
15. William of Tyre, *R.H.C.Occ.*, I, p. 787.
16. *Ibid.*, pp. 782–83.
17. *Ibid.*, p. 803.
18. Ibn al-Qalanisi, p. 309.
19. Ibn al-Athir, *Atabegs*, *R.H.C.Or.*, II, p. 234.
20. Ibn al-Athir, *Kamil at-Tawarikh*, *R.H.C.Or.*, I, p. 542.
21. William of Tyre, *R.H.C.Occ.*, I, p. 837.
22. Ibn al-Qalanisi, p. 341.
23. *Ibid.*, quoted by Abu Shama, *R.H.C.Or.*, IV, p. 90.
24. William of Tyre, *R.H.C.Occ.*, I, p. 842.
25. Cf. Derenbourg, *Ousâma*, II, pp. 241–48; Ibn al-Athir, *Kamil at-Tawarikh*, *R.H.C.Or.*, I, pp. 492–93, 520–21; Abu Shama, *R.H.C.Or.*, IV, p. 107; William of Tyre, *R.H.C.Occ.*, I, pp. 833–34.
26. William of Tyre, *R.H.C.Occ.*, I, p. 857.

27. Chalandon, *Les Comnènes*, p. 444.
28. Choniates, quoted by Diehl, *Figures byzantines*, II, p. 89.
29. Kemal ad-Din, *R.H.C.Or.*, III, p. 549; William of Tyre, *R.H.C.Occ.*, I, p. 837.
30. Ibn al-Athir, *Atabegs*, *R.H.C.Or.*, II, p. 224.
31. William of Tyre, *R.H.C.Occ.*, I, pp. 910–11.
32. Ibn al-Athir, quoted by Abu Shama, *R.H.C.Or.*, IV, p. 112–13.
33. Abu Shama, *R.H.C.Or.*, IV, p. 136.
34. *Ibid.*, p. 114.
35. *Ibid.*, p. 117.
36. William of Tyre, *R.H.C.Occ.*, I, pp. 1004–5.
37. Ibn al-Athir, *Atabegs*, *R.H.C.Or.*, II, p. 211; Kemal ad-Din, *R.H.C.Or.*, III, p. 535.
38. Abu Shama, *R.H.C.Or.*, IV, p. 20.
39. Ibn al-Athir, *Atabegs*, *R.H.C.Or.*, II, p. 152.
40. *Ibid.*, p. 220.
41. Beha ed-Din, *R.H.C.Or.*, III, p. 23.
42. Ibn al-Athir, *Atabegs*, *R.H.C.Or.*, II, pp. 254–55.
43. *Ibid.*, pp. 282–83.
44. Ibn al-Athir, *Kamil at-Tawarikh*, *R.H.C.Or.*, I, pp. 581–82.
45. *Ibid.*, p. 608.

Chapter VIII: THE FALL OF THE
FRANKISH KINGDOM (1174–1188)

1. William of Tyre, *R.H.C.Occ.*, I, p. 1009.
2. Abu Shama, *R.H.C.Or.*, IV, p. 168.
3. *Ibid.*, p. 185.
4. Ibn al-Athir, *Kamil at-Tawarikh*, *R.H.C.Or.*, I, p. 628.
5. *Ibid.*, p. 635.
6. *Itinerarium Peregrinorum et Gesta Regis Ricardi* (ed. Stubbs), Rolls Series. (London, 1864), p. 120.
7. Ernoul, *Chronique* (ed. Mas Latrie), p. 83.
8. *Ibid.*, p. 55.
9. Quoted by Abu Shama, *R.H.C.Or.*, IV, p. 233.
10. *Ibid.*, p. 258.
11. Ernoul, p. 136.
12. Ibn al-Athir, *Kamil at-Tawarikh*, *R.H.C.Or.*, I, p. 674; Abu Shama, *R.H.C.Or.*, IV, pp. 257–58.
13. *Estoire d'Éracles*, *R.H.C.Occ.*, II, p. 34.
14. *Ibid.*, p. 40.
15. Ibn al-Athir, *Kamil at-Tawarikh*, *R.H.C.Or.*, I, p. 678.
16. Abu Shama, *R.H.C.Or.*, IV, p. 263.
17. Ernoul, p. 159.
18. *Ibid.*, p. 100.

19. Abu Shama, *R.H.C.Or.*, IV, p. 265; Ibn al-Athir, *Kamil at Tawarikh*, *R.H.C.Or.*, I, p. 683.
20. Quoted by Abu Shama, *R.H.C.Or.*, IV, p. 270.
21. *Ibid.*, p. 275.
22. *Ibid.*
23. Beha ed-Din, *R.H.C.Or.*, III, p. 39.
24. Ibn al-Athir, *Kamil at-Tawarikh*, *R.H.C.Or.*, I, p. 687.
25. Abu Shama, *R.H.C.Or.*, IV, p. 271.
26. Al-Fadil, on the battle of Kawkab, *R.H.C.Or.*, IV, p. 222.
27. Abu Shama, *R.H.C.Or.*, IV, p. 247.
28. Quoted by Abu Shama, *R.H.C.Or.*, IV, p. 266.
29. *Ibid.*
30. *Ibid.*, p. 268.
31. Ibn al-Athir, *Kamil at-Tawarikh*, *R.H.C.Or.*, I, p. 686.
32. Imad ed-Din, quoted by Abu Shama, *R.H.C.Or.*, IV, pp. 272–73.
33. *Ibid.*, p. 274.
34. *Ibid.*, p. 290.
35. *Ibid.*, p. 277.
36. *Ibid.*, p. 278.
37. Quoted by Abu Shama, *R.H.C.Or.*, IV, p. 288.
38. *Ibid.*, p. 260.
39. Ibn al-Athir, *Kamil at-Tawarikh*, *R.H.C.Or.*, I, p. 696.
40. Quoted by Abu Shama, *R.H.C.Or.*, IV, pp. 321–23.
41. *Ibid.*, pp. 319–20, 324.
42. *Ibid.*, p. 325.
43. *Ibid.*, p. 326.
44. Ibn al-Athir, *Kamil at-Tawarikh*, *R.H.C.Or.*, I, pp. 700–1.
45. *Estoire d'Éracles*, *R.H.C.Occ.*, II, p. 91.
46. Imad ed-Din, quoted by Abu Shama, *R.H.C.Or.*, IV, p. 330.
47. Ernoul, pp. 229, 234; *Estoire d'Éracles*, *R.H.C.Occ.*, II, pp. 100–3.

Chapter IX: THE CRUSADE OF THE KINGS (1188–1192)

1. Ibn al-Athir, *Kamil at-Tawarikh*, *R.H.C.Or.*, I, p. 706.
2. *Ibid.*, II, p. 5.
3. *Ibid.*, p. 3.
4. *Ibid.*, p. 5.
5. Ambroise, *Estoire de la Guerre Sainte*, vv. 616–18.
6. Beha ed-Din, *R.H.C.Or.*, III, p. 231; Ibn al-Athir, *R.H.C.Or.*, II, p. 13.
7. Ibn al-Athir, *Kamil at-Tawarikh*, *R.H.C.Or.*, I, pp. 50–51.
8. Ambroise, *op. cit.*, vv. 7044–46.
9. *Ibid.*, vv. 9500–5.
10. Beha ed-Din, *R.H.C.Or.*, III, pp. 312–13.
11. *Ibid.*, p. 318.
12. *Ibid.*, p. 350.

Chapter X: FRANKISH SYRIA, A DOOMED KINGDOM

1. Beha ed-Din, *R.H.C.Or.*, III, p. 8.
2. Ibn al-Athir, quoted by Abu Shama, *R.H.C.Or.*, IV, p. 182.
3. Beha ed-Din, *R.H.C.Or.*, III, p. 11.
4. Michael the Syrian, *Chronicle*, III, p. 228.
5. Ibn Jubayr, *R.H.C.Or.*, III, p. 448.
6. *Ibid.*, pp. 450–51.
7. Usama, *Autobiography*, p. 359.
8. *Ibid.*, p. 465.

Chapter XI: FRANKISH SYRIA AS AN EASTERN PROVINCE

1. Abu Shama, *R.H.C.Or.*, V, p. 169.
2. Usama, *Autobiography*, p. 356.
3. *Ibid.*, p. 97.
4. Derenbourg, *Ousâma*, I, p. 45; Usama, *Autobiography*, p. 460.
5. Quoted by Abu Shama, *R.H.C.Or.*, IV, p. 274.
6. *Ibid.*, pp. 321–22.
7. *Ibid.*, pp. 361–63.
8. Röhricht, *Beiträge*, I, p. 200.
9. Abu Shama, *R.H.C.Or.*, IV, p. 179.
10. Caesarius of Heisterbach, *Dialogus Miraculorum*, IV, ch. 15.
11. *Estoire d'Éracles*, *R.H.C.Occ.*, II, p. 953.
12. Quoted by Abu Shama, *R.H.C.Or.*, IV, p. 372.
13. *Ibid.*, p. 400.
14. *Estoire d'Éracles*, *R.H.C.Occ.*, II, p. 111.
15. Usama, *Autobiography*, p. 39.
16. Imad ed-Din, *Kharidat al-Kasr, Nouveaux Mélanges Orientaux*, pub. École des langues orientaux (Paris, 1886), p. 121.
17. William of Tyre, *R.H.C.Occ.*, I, pp. 886–88.
18. Derenbourg, *Ousâma*, I, p. 189.

Chapter XII: EASTERN CHRISTENDOM

1. Abu Shama, *R.H.C.Or.*, IV, p. 178.
2. Michael the Syrian, *Chronicle*, III, p. 339.
3. Ibn al-Athir, *Kamil at-Tawarikh*, *R.H.C.Or.*, I, p. 445.
4. Michael the Syrian, *Chronicle*, III, p. 262–63.
5. *Ibid.*, p. 295.
6. *Ibid.*, p. 304.
7. *Ibid.*, p. 339.
8. Raymond of Aguilers, *R.H.C.Occ.*, III, p. 302.

Chapter XIII: THE RECKONING

1. Anna Comnena, *Alexiad*, IV, ch. 6.
2. *Anonymi Gesta Francorum* (ed. Bréhier), p. 53.
3. *Ibid.*, p. 94.
4. William of Tyre, *R.H.C.Occ.*, I, p. 254.
5. *Anonymi Gesta Francorum*, p. 203.
6. Quoted by Abu Shama, *R.H.C.Or.*, IV, p. 208.
7. Imad ed-Din, quoted by Abu Shama, *R.H.C.Or.*, IV, p. 289.

BIBLIOGRAPHY

Author's note: There is such an abundance of literature devoted to the Crusades that I have had to restrict myself to a brief bibliography providing a general outline of sources and documents by authors contemporary with the events, and of the principal later works on the subject.

1. LATIN HISTORIANS

FULCHER OF CHARTRES was present at the Council of Clermont, accompanied Count Stephen of Blois to the Holy Land, and later became chaplain to Baldwin of Boulogne. He remained in the Holy Land until his death. His *Gesta Francorum Iherusalem Peregrinantium* was written between 1101 and 1106, and continued in about 1124.

RAYMOND OF AGUILERS (or d'Agiles) was a Provençal in the army of Raymond, Count of Toulouse, whose chaplain he was. In his *Historia Francorum qui ceperunt Jerusalem* he described the siege of Antioch, the campaign in Judaea, and the capture of Jerusalem in 1099.

The *Anonymi Gesta Francorum et Aliorum Hierosolimitorum,* an anonymous chronicle written by a soldier who was one of Bohemond's followers, ends with the battle of Ascalon in 1099. It was first published in 1100 or 1101.

The account given in the *Anonymi* was used by EKKEHARD OF AURA and by TUDEBOD, and it was also rewritten in 1109 by GUIBERT OF NOGENT, who added material borrowed from Fulcher of Chartres. This narrative was also adapted by BAUDRI OF BOURGUEIL (*c.* 1110) and by ROBERT OF REIMS (*c.* 1122).

EKKEHARD, Abbot of Aura, came to Palestine in 1101 and wrote his chronicle, *Hierosolymita,* in about 1115.

RADULPH OF CAEN came to Syria in about 1108. He wrote the story of Tancred: *Gesta Tancredi Siciliae Regis in Expeditione Hierosolymitana.*

ALBERT OF AIX was a German monk who wrote about 1130. He never visited Syria but evidently bases himself on the evidence of eyewitnesses. He wrote a complete history of the first Crusades: *Liber Christianae Expeditionis pro Ereptione, Emundatione et Restitutione Sanctae Hierosolymitanae Ecclesiae.*

WILLIAM OF TYRE was born in Jerusalem in about 1130. He was a statesman who became Archbishop of Tyre, tutor to Baldwin IV, and historian and historiographer of the Frankish kingdom of Jerusalem. William of Tyre began his history in about 1169, and when he died suddenly in 1186 he was still engaged in describing the events of the year 1184. His book, *Historia Rerum in Partibus Transmarinis Gestarum,* is based, in its account of the first half of the twelfth century, on the work of earlier historians, but from 1160 onward the author is describing events in which he himself took part.

William of Tyre's history was translated into French at the beginning of the thirteenth century, under the title of *L'Estoire d'Éracles,* and the translator, a Frenchman from Europe, added a number of personal comments to his translation.

The history was continued by an anonymous Frankish Syrian author, writing about 1194.

ERNOUL, a Syrian Frank attached to the household of Ibelin, also wrote a continuation of William of Tyre's history, in French, toward the end of the twelfth century.

ODO OF DEUIL is the author of a history of Louis VII's Crusade: *De Ludovici VII profectione in Orientum.*

OTTO OF FREISINGEN, a German bishop, wrote the *Gesta Frederici,* a history of the German Crusade of 1147.

ORDERIC VITALIS was a Norman chronicler. In his *Historia ecclesiastica,* he deals with events in Syria prior to 1138, and in particular with those concerning the principality of Antioch.

AMBROISE, a Norman troubadour-chronicler, wrote *L'Estoire de la Guerre Sainte,* a fairly detailed verse history of the Third Crusade, of which he was himself an eyewitness.

2. GREEK HISTORIANS

ANNA COMNENA is the only Greek historian who mentions the Crusades. She deals with the Crusades in books X and XI of the *Alexiad,* her biography of her father, Alexius Comnenus, but she describes only events which took place before her father's death in 1118, and is particularly informative on the subject of relations between the Greeks and the Crusaders.

3. ORIENTAL HISTORIANS

No contemporary documents relating to the earliest Crusades have survived.

Arabic

IBN AL-QALANISI was a native of Damascus, writing between 1140 and 1160. His work, entitled *Continuation of the Chronicle of Damascus*, deals chiefly with events concerning Damascus.

KEMAL AD-DIN, author of an unfinished *Chronicle of Aleppo*, was writing in the second half of the thirteenth century, but used older sources which have not survived.

IBN AL-ATHIR of Mosul (1160–1233), the great historian of the early thirteenth century, wrote a general history of the Islamic world, *Kamil at-Tawarikh*, and also a *History of the Atabegs of Mosul*.

IMAD ED-DIN (al-Imad) was an official at the court of Iraq and later secretary to Nur ed-Din and Saladin. He wrote a history of the Seljuks and the history of the wars of Saladin.

BEHA ED-DIN, a member of Saladin's suite from 1188, wrote a life of Saladin: *Life of Yusuf*.

ABU SHAMA was born in Damascus in 1203. In about 1251, he wrote a history of the reigns of Nur ed-Din and Saladin: *Book of the Two Gardens*, in which he quoted extensively from the works of Ibn al-Qalanisi, Ibn al-Athir, Beha ed-Din, al-Fadil, and Imad ed-Din.

ABU'L FEDA, a prince of Hama in the early fourteenth century, is the author of a compendium of earlier historians.

IBN JUBAYR, a Spanish Moslem traveler, wrote an account, entitled *Travels*, about his journey in the Holy Land in 1181.

USAMA IBN MUNQIDH (1095–1187) was an emir of Shaizar. A diplomat and adventurer, he visited many Eastern courts, especially those of Damascus and Egypt, and in his old age wrote an *Autobiography*.

Eastern Christian

MATTHEW OF EDESSA was an Armenian cleric who wrote before 1140. His *Chronicle* describes events between 952 and 1136.

MICHAEL THE SYRIAN was the Jacobite Patriarch of Antioch from 1166 to 1199. His *Chronicle* is a general history of Syria and the Syriac Church.

GREGORY THE PRIEST, an Armenian from Kaisun, wrote a *Chronicle* dealing chiefly with the affairs of Cilicia and northern Syria (1162).

NERSES SHNORHAL I, Catholicus from 1166 to 1172, was the author of a long poem, *Elegy on the Fall of Edessa*.

Jewish

BENJAMIN OF TUDELA, a Spanish Jew, wrote an account of his travels, *Voyage*, which contains descriptions of the life of Jewish colonies in Frankish Syria in 1166–1170.

4. COLLECTIONS AND EDITIONS OF ORIGINAL SOURCES

Editions of the works of most of the forementioned historians were published in France in the nineteenth century by the Académie des Inscriptions et Belles Lettres, under the general title *Recueil des Historiens des Croisades*. This collection includes Latin, Old French, Arabic, Armenian, and Greek texts, with French translations of the Arabic, Armenian, and Greek writers. Divisions of this collection are as follows:

Historiens occidentaux. 5 vols. Paris 1844–1895 [*R.H.C.Occ.*]
Historiens grecs. 2 vols. Paris 1875–1881 [*R.H.C.G.*]
Historiens orientaux. 5 vols. Paris 1872–1906 [*R.H.C.Or.*]
Documents arméniens. 2 vols. Paris 1869–1906 [*R.H.C.Arm.*]

A sixteenth volume is devoted to the *Assises du royaume de Jérusalem*, a collection of laws and official acts dating from the thirteenth century.

The *Anonymi Gesta Francorum* has been edited by L. BRÉHIER as *Histoire anonyme de la Première Croisade* (Paris, 1924).

Ousâma ibn Mounkidh: un Émir syrien au premier siècle des Croisades, an edition of Usama's autobiography by H. DERENBOURG, was published in Paris, 1886–1893, in two parts: the Arabic text, and a volume of glossaries and commentaries. A one-volume edition was published by the same author in 1895 (cited in notes as Usama, *Autobiography*).

A four-volume translation of the *Chronicle* of Michael the Syrian, by J. B. CHABOT, was published in Paris 1899–1910.

An edition of Ernoul's history, entitled *Chronique d'Ernoul et de Bernard le Trésorier*, by L. DE MAS LATRIE, was published by the Société de l'histoire de France (Paris, 1871).

La Revue de l'Orient latin has published a great many documents, in particular *Lettres de chrétiens en Terre Sainte* by H. DELABORDE (Le Puy, 1894), and *Itinéraires de Jérusalem et descriptions de la Terre Sainte* by H. MICHELANT and G. RAYNAUD (Geneva, 1882).

Other collections of documents pertinent to the Crusades include:

HAGENMEYER, H. *Die Kreuzzugsbriefe aus den Jahren 1088–1100*. Innsbruck, 1902.
RÖHRICHT, R. *Regesta Regni Hierosolymitani*. 2 vols. Innsbruck, 1893–1904.
TOBLER, T., and MOLINIER, A. *Itineraria Hierosolymitana et Descriptiones Terrae Sanctae*. 2 vols. Geneva, 1879.

5. MODERN WORKS

ALPHANDÉRY, P. *La Chrétienté et l'idée de croisade*. Paris, 1954.
BLOCH, M. *La Sociéte féodale*. Paris, 1939–1940.
BRÉHIER, L. *Les Croisades*. Paris, 1907.

CAHEN, C. *La Syrie du Nord à l'époque des Croisades et la Principauté franque d'Antioche.* Paris, 1940.

CHALANDON, F. *Essai sur le règne d'Alexis Comnène.* Paris, 1907.

————. *Les Comnènes: Jean et Manuel.* Paris, 1912.

————. *Histoire de la première croisade.* Paris, 1925.

COHN, N. *Les Fanatiques de l'Apocalypse.* Paris, 1962.

DIEHL, C. *Figures byzantines.* Paris, 1948.

————. *Les Grandes Problèmes de l'histoire byzantine.* Paris, 1943.

DODU, E. (Abbé). *Essai sur la formation de l'idée de croisade.* Toulouse, 1941–1944.

Encyclopédie de la Pléiade, Histoire universelle, Vol. I: *De l'Islam à la Réforme.* Paris, 1957.

GROUSSET, R. *Histoire des Croisades et du royaume franc de Jérusalem.* 3 vols. Paris, 1934–1936.

HAGENMEYER, H. *Chronologie de la Première Croisade.* Paris, 1902.

————. *Chronologie du Royaume de Jérusalem.* Paris, 1902.

Histoire des civilisations, Vol. III: *Le Moyen Age.* Paris, Presses Universitaires Françaises, n.d.

A History of the Crusades. Kenneth M. Setton, ed. 2 vols. (3 in preparation). Philadelphia, University of Pennsylvania Press, 1957–1961.

LA MONTE, J. L. *Feudal Monarchy in the Latin Kingdom of Jerusalem.* Cambridge, Mass., 1932.

LONGNON, J. *Les Français d'outre-mer au moyen-âge.* Paris, 1929.

LOT, F. *L'Art militaire et les armées du Moyen Age.* Paris, 1946.

MUNRO, D. C. *The Kingdom of the Crusaders.* New York, 1936.

OLLIVIER, A. *Les Templiers.* Series "Le Temps qui court." Paris, n.d.

PERNOUD, R. *Les Croisés.* Paris, 1959.

————. *Lumière du Moyen Age.* Paris, 1946.

REY, E. G. *Les Colonies franques en Syrie aux XIIe et XIIIe siècles.* Paris, 1883.

RICHARD, J. *Le Royaume Latin de Jérusalem.* Paris, 1953.

RÖHRICHT, R. *Beiträge zur Geschichte der Kreuzzüge.* 2 vols. Berlin, 1874–1878.

————. *Geschichte des ersten Kreuzzuges.* Innsbruck, 1901.

————. *Geschichte des Königreichs Jerusalem.* Innsbruck, 1898.

ROUSSET, P. *Histoire des Croisades.* Paris, 1957.

RUNCIMAN, S. *A History of the Crusades.* 3 vols. Cambridge, 1951.

————. *Byzantine Civilization.* New York, 1952.

SCHLUMBERGER, G. *Byzance et les Croisades.* Paris, 1927.

————. *La Fin de la domination franque en Syrie.* Paris, 1914.

WAAS, A. *Geschichte der Kreuzzüge* (Freiburg, 1956).

INDEX OF NAMES OF
PERSONS

AUTHOR'S NOTE: The names included in this index are only those that have a direct bearing on the history of the Crusades; I have therefore omitted references to France, England, Italy, Byzantium, and so forth, as well as the names of the various nationalities such as French, German, Italian, and Greek. This index is confined to names of people and places.

INDEX OF PLACE NAMES